TIME, WORK,

& CULTURE IN THE

MIDDLE AGES

TIME, WORK, & CULTURE IN THE MIDDLE AGES

JACQUES LE GOFF

Translated by Arthur Goldhammer

THE UNIVERSITY OF CHICAGO PRESS
CHICAGO   LONDON

THE UNIVERSITY OF CHICAGO PRESS, CHICAGO 60637
THE UNIVERSITY OF CHICAGO PRESS, LTD., LONDON

© 1980 by The University of Chicago
All rights reserved. Published 1980
Paperback edition 1982
Printed in the United States of America
03 02 01 00 99 98 97 96 95   6 7 8 9 10

Library of Congress Cataloging in Publication Data

Le Goff, Jacques.
  Time, work & culture in the Middle Ages.

Translation of Pour un autre Moyen Age: temps,
travail et culture en Occident.
  Includes index.
  1. Social history—Medieval, 500–1500.   2. Civilization, Medieval.   I. Title.
HN11.L4413   940.1   79-25400
ISBN: 0-226-47081-4 (paper)

This book is printed on acid-free paper.

CONTENTS

PREFACE

To me, the articles collected here appear to possess a unity which may, however, be no more than a retrospective illusion.

This unity stems, in the first place, from the era I chose, some quarter of a century ago, as a field for reflection and investigation, without then being clearly aware of my motives for turning in this direction. Today, I would say that I was attracted to the Middle Ages for two reasons. First, there were professional considerations. I was determined to become a professional historian. Most sciences are incontestably the affair of professionals, or specialists. Historical science is not so exclusive. While I believe the problem to be one of major importance for our times, in which the media bring the possibility of writing or narrating history in images or words within everyone's reach, I will not consider the question of the quality of historical production here. I claim no monopoly for scientific historians. Dilettantes and vulgarizers of history are agreeable enough and useful in their way, and their success is indicative of a need among our contemporaries to participate in some form of collective memory. I wish history, even as it becomes more scientific, to remain an art. To supply the needs of man's memory requires as much taste, style, and passion as it does rigor and method.

History is made with documents and ideas, with sources and imagination. The ancient historian seemed to me condemned (needless to say, I was mistaken, if only by exaggeration) to a discouraging choice between two alternatives: either he could limit himself to what meager spoils were provided by the legacy of a past ill-equipped to perpetuate itself, and consequently succumb to the emasculating attractions of pure erudition, or else he could yield to the charms of an always risky reconstruction. The history of recent eras (and, here again, my views were overstated, if not false) worried me for opposite reasons. Either an overwhelming mass of documentation would force the historian to take a statistical and quantitative approach, which would nevertheless remain reductionist (for, while one must count what can be counted in the source material, history must be made out of that which escapes enumeration, which is frequently what is important). Or else he would have to be willing to forego the possibility of achieving an overall vision. History was condemned to be either specialized or plagued with lacunae. The humanists may have seen the Middle Ages merely as a mediocre interlude, an intermission in the great pageant of history, a trough in the wave of time, rather than as a transition or passage. To me, however, the Middle Ages, standing between ancient and modern times, appeared the field of choice for effecting a needed alliance between erudition (was not scientific history born between the mid-seventeenth and mid-nineteenth centuries from the study of medieval charters and scripts?) and a kind of imagination based on solid foundations to legitimate its flight without clipping its wings. Was not my model of a historian, then as now, Michelet? It has become commonplace to say that he was a man of imagination, capable of working a resurrection. Yet it is often forgotten that he was also a man of the archives who resuscitated not phantoms or fantasies but real beings interred in the documents, like the truths petrified in cathedrals. Did I not choose to follow in the footsteps of Michelet, who, though he believed he could breathe only after the dawn of the Reformation and Renaissance, never showed greater sympathy with the past than when he spoke of the Middle Ages?

Michelet, moreover, was a model in another sense, in that he was conscious of being a historian who was the product of his times, a partisan of a society struggling against injustice and the shades of obscurantism and reaction, as well as against illusions of progress. An embattled historian in his work and his teaching, a historian perhaps anguished, as Roland Barthes has said,[1] to find himself the bard of an impossible lyric—the people's—Michelet nevertheless knew better than to try to escape his anguish by confusing the historian's discourse with popular discourse in treating the people's historical struggles. We know only too well that such a confusion is likely to lead to the utter ideological subjection of both history and the people to whom the historian is claiming to give voice.

1. Roland Barthes, *Michelet par lui-même* (Paris, 1954), p. 161. "He was perhaps the first modern author who could only sing an impossible lyric." Barthes alludes to Michelet's confession: "I was born a man of the people, the people were in my heart.... But their language, their language was inaccessible to me. I couldn't make them speak."

I was soon drawn to the Middle Ages for a more profound reason, which did not discourage my continued interest in both earlier and later periods. I belong to a generation of historians marked by the problematic of the long period (*longue durée*). This is due to the threefold influence of a Marxism both modernized and rooted in its original sources, of Fernand Braudel,[2] and of ethnology. Among the disciplines which, in French, are so awkwardly referred to as *sciences humaines* (why not simply call them social sciences?), ethnology is the one with which history has established (despite certain misunderstandings and obstinacies on both sides) the most natural and fruitful dialogue. For my generation, Marcel Mauss belatedly became the leaven that Durkheim had been fifty years earlier (and even then, belatedly) for the best historians of the period between the First and Second World Wars.[3] In an essay which is but a first step along a path of reflection and research I hope to explore further,[4] I have tried to set down the relations which existed between history and ethnology in the past and which are in the process of being reestablished today. I am a follower of those scholars and researchers who prefer an anthropology applicable to all cultures, now that an older ethnology, too intimately connected with the era and dominion of European colonialism, has run its course. Consequently, I would rather speak of historical anthropology than of ethnohistory. I must point out, however, that although certain historians have been attracted by ethnology because it advances the notion of difference, ethnologists have, in the meantime, been turning toward a unified conception of human societies and even toward the concept of "man," which history, now as in the past, neglects. This interchange of positions is both interesting and worrisome. If the historian were to allow the temptations of historical anthropology—i.e., of a history other than that of the white ruling classes, a history which moves more slowly and deeply than the history of events—to lead him to the discovery of a supposedly universal and static history, then I would advise him to pick up his marbles now and go home. For the moment, however, I

2. Fernand Braudel, "Histoire et sciences sociales: la longue durée," *Annales E.S.C.*, 1958, pp. 725–53; reprinted in *Ecrits sur l'histoire* (Paris, 1969), pp. 41–83.

3. For example, Marcel Mauss's important article "Les techniques du corps," *Journal de Psychologie* 32 (1936), reprinted in *Sociologie et Anthropologie* (Paris, 1950; 5th ed., 1973), pp. 363–86, seems long to have been without influence. In a somewhat different spirit, historians and anthropologists have recently studied *Langages et images du corps* in a special issue of *Ethnologie française* 6, nos. 3/4 (1976). This piece by Marcel Mauss is the basis for the seminar at the Ecole des Hautes Etudes en Sciences Sociales in which Jean-Claude Schmitt and I have been studying, since 1975, systems of gestures in the medieval West.

4. Reprinted in *Mélanges en l'honneur de Fernand Braudel*, vol. 2: *Méthodologie de l'histoire et des sciences humaines* (Toulouse, 1972), pp. 233–43, and in the present volume, pp. 225–36.

think that a history which concentrates on the long period is far from played out. The field of folklore, moreover, while too cut off from history, offers the historian of European societies who is eager to make use of anthropology a treasure trove of documents, methods, and monographs which he would do well to examine before turning to extra-European anthropology. Unjustly scorned as the "poor man's anthropology," folklore is nevertheless an important source for historical anthropology of our so-called "historical" societies to tap. The long period relevant to our history—for us both as professionals and as men living in the flux of history—seems to me to be the long stretch of the Middle Ages beginning in the second or third century and perishing slowly under the blows of the Industrial Revolution—Revolutions—from the nineteenth century to the present day. The history of this period is the history of pre-industrial society. Prior to these extended Middle Ages, we face a different kind of history; subsequent to them, we confront history—contemporary history—which is yet to be written, whose methods have yet to be invented. For me, this lengthy medieval period is the opposite of the hiatus it was taken to be by the Renaissance humanists and, but for rare exceptions, by the men of the Enlightenment. It was the moment when modern society was created out of a civilization whose traditional peasant forms were moribund but which continued to live by virtue of what it had created which was to become the essential substance of our social and mental structures. Its creations include the city, the nation, the state, the university, the mill and the machine, the hour and the watch, the book, the fork, underclothing, the individual, the conscience, and finally, revolution. It was a period which, for Western societies, at least, was neither a trough in the wave nor a bridge between the neolithic era and the industrial and political revolutions of the last two centuries, but was, rather, a time of great creative growth, punctuated by crises, and differentiated according to the region, social category, or sector of activity in its evolutionary chronology and processes.

We need waste no time indulging in the silly pastime of substituting a new legend of a gilded Middle Ages for the legend of the Dark Ages favored in centuries past. This is not what we mean by "another Middle Ages."[5] Our new view must be a total one, which the historian will construct with the aid of archeological, artistic, and

5. I have elsewhere stated why I, as one who aspires to be the historian of another Middle Ages, a Middle Ages of the depths, as it were, would not subscribe to either the traditional myth of a dark age or the myth of a gilded age which some people today would like to substitute for it. Jacques Le Goff, *La Civilisation de l'Occident médiéval* (Paris: Arthaud, 1965), Introduction, pp. 13–24. ["Another Middle Ages" refers to the French title of the present work, *Pour un autre Moyen Age.*—Trans.]

juridical sources in addition to the kinds of documents which traditionally were the sole sources allowed to "pure" medievalists. It bears repeating that the Middle Ages I have in mind are a long period, which should be regarded as having the structure of a system that begins to function, in all important respects, in the late Roman Empire and continues in operation until the Industrial Revolution of the eighteenth and nineteenth centuries. I have in mind a Middle Ages of the depths, which can be studied with the aid of ethnological methods giving access to its daily habits,[6] beliefs, behavior, and mentalities. It is through study of this period that we are best able to understand our roots in, as well as our breaks with, the past; our troubled modernity; and our need to understand change, the stock-in-trade of history, both as a science and as we experience it. It is the time of our grandparents, as it were, at such a distance from us that we can observe our collective memory taking shape. I believe that mastery of the past such as only the professional historian is capable of achieving is as essential to contemporary man as the mastery over matter offered by the physicist, or the mastery of the processes of life offered by the biologist. I would be the last to wish to pluck the Middle Ages out of the continuous stream of historical time in which they are immersed. They must be understood in terms of the long period, which does not, however, imply a belief in any sort of evolutionism. Yet I believe it is true, nonetheless, that the Middle Ages are the primordial past in which our collective identity, the quarry of that anguished search in which contemporary societies are engaged, acquired certain of its essential characteristics.

Guided by Charles-Edmond Perrin, a rigorous and liberal teacher and a great figure in a university which scarcely exists any longer, I had started out to write a rather traditional history of ideas. Even at that early stage, however, these ideas interested me only as they were embodied in institutions and men and as they functioned within societies. Among the creations of the Middle Ages were universities and academics. It seemed to me that the novelty of a form of social and intellectual advancement based on a technique previously unknown in Western societies, the examination, had not been adequately recognized at that time. The exam had won a modest

6. I borrow this expression from Emile Souvestre, who writes, in the introduction to his collection *Le Foyer breton* (1844), as a precursor of ethnohistory: "If history is the complete revelation of a people's existence, how can it be written without knowledge of what is most characteristic of that existence? You show me the people in their official life; but who will tell me of their home life? After I become acquainted with their public acts, which are always the work of a small number of men, where can I learn the daily habits, the predilections, the fantasies which belong to all? Don't you see that these indices of a nation's innermost life are to be found primarily in the popular traditions?" (new ed., [Verviers: Marabout, 1975], p. 10).

place for itself, alongside the drawing of lots (which, within rather narrow limits, had been used by the Greek democracies) and quality of birth. I soon realized that academics issuing from the urban movement raised problems comparable to those of their contemporaries, the merchants. In the eyes of traditionalists, both sold goods which belonged exclusively to God—knowledge (*science*) in the one case, time in the other. "Word vendors" was a revealing epithet. Thus Saint Bernard flagellated the new intellectuals, whom he exhorted to attend the only school worthy of a monk, the cloister school. For twelfth- and thirteenth-century clerics, the academic, like the merchant, could please God and win his salvation only with difficulty. Confessor's manuals began to multiply in the wake of the Fourth Lateran Council in 1215, a major date in medieval history, for by making auricular confession at least once a year mandatory for everyone the council opened up a new path for every Christian—the examination of the conscience.[7] When I studied these manuals, a source then little exploited, I noticed that the academic, like the merchant, was justified by reference to the labor he accomplished. The novelty of the academics thus ultimately appeared to lie in their role as *intellectual workers*. My attention was therefore drawn to two notions whose ideological avatars I attempted to trace through the concrete social conditions in which they developed. These notions were labor and time. Under these two heads I maintain two open files, from which some of the articles collected here are drawn. I am still persuaded that attitudes toward work and time are essential aspects of social structure and function, and that the study of such attitudes offers a useful tool for the historian who wishes to examine the societies in which they develop.

To simplify a complex affair, let me say merely that I observed an evolution from the penitential labor of the Bible and the early Middle Ages toward a rehabilitation of labor, which in the end became a means of salvation. This advance—which was brought about and justified by monastic laborers belonging to the new orders of the twelfth century, urban workers in the cities of the era, and intellectual workers in the universities—led, in dialectical fashion, to other new developments: from the thirteenth century on, the gap between manual labor, held in greater contempt than ever, and intellectual labor (the merchant's as well as the academics') grew more pronounced, and the new valuation of labor, by subjecting the worker to a still greater degree of exploitation, led to his increased alienation.

As for *time*, I investigated in particular the question of who became

7. The importance of this date did not escape the notice of Michel Foucault. Cf. *Histoire de la sexualité*, vol. 1: *La Volonté de savoir* (Paris, 1976), p. 78.

master of the new forms it took in changing Western medieval society (and how they achieved this mastery). I believe that control of time and power over time are essential components in the functioning of societies.[8] I was not the first—Yves Renouard, among others, had written some brilliant pages on time as conceived by Italian businessmen—to take an interest in what, for the sake of abbreviation, might be called *bourgeois time*. I tried to relate to the theological and intellectual movement the new forms of appropriation of time made manifest by clocks, by the division of the day into twenty-four hours, and, before long, in its individualized form, by the watch. At the heart of the "crisis" of the fourteenth century, I again encountered these two factors, labor and time, in intimate relationship. Labor time turned out to have been a major stake in the important struggle of men and social groups over units of measure—the subject of a great work by Witold Kula.[9]

I continued in the meantime to be interested in what I was subsequently inclined to call the history of culture rather than of ideas. I had been attending Maurice Lombard's lectures at the Sixth Section of the Ecole Pratique des Hautes Etudes. He is one of the greatest historians I have known, and meeting him was the major scientific and intellectual encounter of my professional life. I am indebted to Maurice Lombard on several counts. Not only did he introduce me to, and inspire my taste for, civilization's vast reaches (and hence the idea not to separate space and time, to treat the broad vistas and the long period together), but he also taught me that the Western medievalist must constantly keep one eye peeled toward the East, the purveyor of trade goods, myths, and dreams (even if the persistent necessity of specialization made it prudent to keep to one's own territory). He further insisted that history must be total history, in which material civilization and culture must interpenetrate one another within a socioeconomic analysis. I sensed the crudeness and inadequacy of a vulgar-Marxist problematic of infrastructure and superstructure. Although I acknowledged the importance of theory in the social sciences and in history, in particular (the historian, out of disdain for theory, is all too often the unconscious tool of implicit and simplistic theories), I did not embark on a theoretical quest for which I feel I have no gift, and I fear getting myself involved in what

8. Georges Dumézil, a great awakener of ideas, whose work is increasingly being drawn upon by medievalists, has written: "Repository of events, site of enduring forces and actions, locale of mystical occurrences, the time-frame (*temps-cadre*) takes on a special interest for anyone—god, hero, or chief—who would triumph, reign, or be a founder: whatever he may be, he must try to appropriate time for the same reason that he appropriates space." ("Temps et Mythes," *Recherches Philosophiques* 5, 1935–36).

9. W. Kula, *Miary i ludzie* (Measures and Men) (Warsaw, 1970).

I, in company with many other historians, believe to be history's worst enemy, the philosophy of History. The history of mentalities treats a concept which has become fashionable. Fashion has positive aspects, but it is also risky. I have tried, therefore, to show the interest of a notion which makes history a dynamic subject, while at the same time pointing out the ambiguities of a vague concept, which is fruitful precisely because it is vague and therefore neglectful of certain obstacles, but which is also dangerous because it makes it easy to slip into pseudo science.

What was needed was a central theme in this quest for cultural history, a tool for analysis and investigation. I hit upon the opposition between the high culture of the scholars and the erudite, and popular culture. Its use is not without difficulties. High culture is not as easy to define as one may think, and popular culture partakes of the ambiguity of that dangerous epithet "popular." I associate myself with Carlo Ginzburg's recent pertinent remarks.[10] If one takes the precaution of identifying what documents are used, and if one states carefully what is being included under each of the two heads, then I see no reason why this should not be a useful and effective tool.

A whole range of phenomena can be subsumed under this opposition between high and popular culture. We can make out the great dialogue between the written and the oral. That most important absentee from the history of the historians, speech, can be heard, at least in the form of echo, rumor, or murmur. The conflict of social categories makes its appearance in the area of culture. At the same time, the complexity of borrowings and exchanges necessitates a more sophisticated analysis of cultural structures and conflicts. I have therefore set out to discover historical folklore through scholarly texts, the only ones I am presently capable, to any degree, of reading. In taking the direction of tales and dreams, I have not abandoned labor and time. To understand how a society functions and, as a historian by definition must do, how it changes and is transformed, one needs to keep an eye to the imaginary.

The more ambitious tasks, of which the articles presented here give only some preliminary idea, remain. In this regard, I would like to make a contribution to establishing a historical anthropology of the preindustrial West. I would hope to contribute a few solid pieces to the study of the medieval imagination. Having done this, I should like to turn my experience and training as a medievalist to the problem of laying down new methods of scholarship adapted to our new historical objects and reflecting the twofold nature of history in general and medieval history in particular, namely, that it is a study

10. C. Ginzburg, *Il formaggio e i vermi* (Turin, 1976), pp. xii–xv. Cf. also J.-Cl. Schmitt, "Religion populaire et culture folklorique," *Annales E.S.C.*, 1976, pp. 941–53.

requiring both rigor and imagination. Such new methods of scholarship would include a critical apparatus suited to a new idea of the document, the concept of the monument-document.[11] The new methods will lay the foundations of a new chronological science which no longer rests on a linear conception of time. One aim of this new science will be to determine the scientific conditions under which comparative study would be legitimate, so that two objects or time periods could not be compared without critical justification.

Let me conclude with a line of Rimbaud's, not, as so many intellectuals do, and as so many medieval intellectuals did before them, in order to contrast manual with intellectual labor, but rather to join the two together in the context of the solidarity of all workers: "La main à plume vaut la main à charrue" ("The hand that holds the pen is worth as much as the hand that guides the plow").

NOTE

In the original versions of the essays collected here, most of the citations were given in the original language, primarily Latin. For the reader's convenience, these citations have been translated [into English from the author's French translations—Trans.] Latin has been kept, however, in the notes which are not indispensable to comprehension of the text.

The essays were first published as follows:

"Les Moyen Age de Michelet." In Michelet, *Œuvres complètes*, edited by P. Viallaneix, I, IV, *Histoire de France* I (Paris, 1974), 45–63.

"Au Moyen Age: Temps de l'Eglise et temps du marchand." *Annales: Economies. Sociétés. Civilisations*, 1960, 417–33.

"Le temps du travail dans la 'crise' du XIVe siècle: du temps médiéval au temps moderne." *Le Moyen Age* 69 (1963), 597–613.

"Note sur société tripartie, idéologie monarchique et renouveau économique dans la chrétienté du IXe au XIIe siècle." In *L'Europe aux IXe–XIe siècles*, edited by T. Manteuffel and A. Gieysztor (Warsaw, 1968), 63–72.

"Métiers licites et métiers illicites dans l'Occident médiéval." *Etudes historiques. Annales de l'Ecole des Hautes Etudes de Gand* 5, 41–57.

"Travail, techniques et artisans dans les systèmes de valeur du haut Moyen Age (Ve–Xe siècle)." In *Artigianato e Tecnica nella società dell'alto Medioevo occidentale*, Settimane di studio del Centro italiano di studi sull'alto medioevo XVIII (Spoleto, 1971), 239–66.

"Les paysans et le monde rural dans la littérature du haut Moyen

11. Pierre Toubert and I have recently taken up this problem in a contribution to the 100th Congress of the Sociétés savantes (Paris, 1975): "Une histoire totale du Moyen Age est-elle possible?" in *Actes du 100e Congrès National des Sociétés Savantes*, vol. 1, *Tendances, Perspectives et Méthodes de l'Histoire Médiévale* (Paris, 1977), pp. 31–44.

Age." In *L'agricoltura e il mondo rurale nell'alto medioevo*, Settimane . . . XIII (Spoleto, 1966), 723–41.

"Dépenses universitaires à Padoue au XVe siècle." *Mélanges d'Archéologie de l'Histoire*, published by the Ecole française de Rome (1956), 377–99.

"Métier et profession d'après les manuels de confesseurs du Moyen Age." In *Miscellanea Mediaevalia*, vol. 3, *Beiträge zum Berufsbewusstsein des mittelalterlichen Menschen* (Berlin, 1964), 44–60.

"Quelle conscience l'Université médiévale a-t-elle eue d'elle-même?" In ibid., 15–29.

"Les Universités et les Pouvoirs publics au Moyen Age et à la Renaissance." In *XIIe Congrès international des Sciences Historiques* (Vienne, 1965), *Rapports III; Commissions*, 189–206.

"Culture cléricale et traditions folkloriques dans la civilisation merovingienne." *Annales: Economies. Sociétés. Civilisations*, 1967, 780–91.

"Culture ecclésiastique et culture folklorique au Moyen Age: saint Marcel de Paris et le Dragon." In *Ricerche storiche ed economiche in memoria di Corrado Barbagallo*, edited by L. De Rosa (Naples, 1970), 2, 51–90.

"L'Occident médiéval et l'océan Indien: un horizon onirique." In *Mediterraneo e Oceano Indiano*, Atti del VI Collequio Internazionale di Storia Marittima (Florence, 1970), 243–63.

"Les rêves dans la culture et la psychologie collective de l'Occident médiéval." *Scolies* 1 (1971), 123–30.

"Mélusine maternelle et défricheuse." *Annales: Economies. Sociétés. Civilisations*, 1971, 587–603.

"L'historien et l'homme quotidien." In *Mélanges en l'honneur de Fernand Braudel*, vol. 2, *Méthodologie de l'Histoire et des Sciences Humaines* (Toulouse, 1972), 233–43.

"Le rituel symbolique de la vassalité." In *Simboli e Simbologie nell' alto Medioevo*, Settimane . . . XXIII (Spoleto, 1976), 679–788.

I

TIME AND LABOR

THE SEVERAL MIDDLE AGES
OF JULES MICHELET

Michelet does not presently enjoy a good press among medievalists. His *Moyen Age* seems the most dated part of the *Histoire de France*—especially in relation to the evolution of historical science. Despite the Pirennes, the Huizingas, the Marc Blochs, and those of their successors who opened the Middle Ages as a field for the history of mentalities and depths, for total history, the Middle Ages remain the period of history most marked by nineteenth-century erudition (from the Ecole Nationale des Chartes to the *Monumenta Germaniae Historica*) and by the positivist school of the turn of the century. One has only to read the still unsurpassed volumes of Lavisse's *Histoire de France* devoted to the Middle Ages to become aware of how remote Michelet is. Michelet's Middle Ages are apparently part of his most literary and least "scientific" side. This is where romanticism is supposed to have been able to wreak the greatest havoc. Michelet as medievalist seems scarcely more serious than the Victor Hugo of *Notre-Dame de Paris* or *La Légende des siècles*. Both are "medieval-esque" (the connotation is pejorative).

The Middle Ages became and have remained the citadel of erudition. Michelet's position with respect to erudition is ambiguous. A devourer of history, he displayed, of course, an enormous appetite, an insatiable hunger for documents. He searched the archives with passion, as he reminds us constantly, working in the Archives Nationales in Paris. In his 1869 *Préface* he emphasized that one of the novelties of his work was its documentary foundation. "Before 1830 (or even 1836), no noteworthy historian of this era had yet thought it necessary to seek the facts outside of printed books, in the original sources, most of which were then unpublished, in the manuscripts in our libraries, in the documents in our archives." He goes on to point out: "No historian, as far as I know, prior to my third volume

3

(as can be easily checked), made use of original, unpublished material ... this is the first time history has had so solid a foundation (1837)." Yet documents, and, in particular, archival documents, were merely springboards for Michelet's imagination, triggers for his vision. His celebrated pages on the Archives Nationales testify to this role of the document as poetic stimulus, which begins even before the document is read, thanks to the creative force with which the sacred space of the archives is imbued. The historian succumbs to the power of the atmosphere. Here, in these vast cemeteries of history, where the past is buried, it is also resurrected. The fame of these pages may have diminished their power. Yet they are the product of something deeper in Michelet than a literary gift for evocation of place. Michelet is a necrophile: "I loved death ... " Yet he combs the necropolises of the past and the walks of Père-Lachaise in order to wrest the dead from their tombs, to "waken" them, to make them "live again." The Middle Ages, whose frescoes and tympana have conveyed down to the present day the rousing call of the trumpets of the Last Judgment, found in Michelet the person best able to make those trumpets sound: "In the deserted galleries of the Archives, where, for twenty years, I wandered in profound silence, I nevertheless heard a murmuring in my ears." And in the lengthy remarks which close the second volume of the *Histoire de France*, we read: "This volume has been drawn largely from the Archives Nationales. It was not long before I perceived that, in the apparent silence of its galleries, there was a movement, a murmuring, which was not death's ... A host were alive and speaking ... As I blew the dust from these volumes, I saw them arise. From the sepulcher they took now a hand, now a head, as in Michelangelo's *Last Judgment* or in the *Dance of Death*." Of course, Michelet is much more than a necromancer; according to his own fine neologism, which no one since has dared use, he is a "resuscitator."[1]

Michelet was a conscientious archivist, passionate about his craft. His present-day successors know this and can prove it by pointing to the traces of his labors. He enriched his *Histoire de France* and, in particular, his Middle Ages, with notes and supporting documents which testify to his attachment to erudition. He belongs to those generations of romantics (as did Victor Hugo) who knew how to combine erudition with poetry. Prosper Mérimée, first inspector general of historic monuments, was another writer of this kind, although he separated his trade from his life's work to an even greater degree. It was in Michelet's time that the Société Celtique became the Société Nationale des Antiquaires de France, and it was also the time of the Ecole Nationale des Chartes, of the then abortive Inventory of Monuments of France, today renascent, and of Viollet-le-Duc's erudite architecture. For Michelet, however, erudition was merely part of an initial phase of preparation. History began afterward, with the writing. Erudition was thus no longer a mere scaffolding, which the artist, the historian, had to remove when the work was completed. It was a consequence of the imperfect state of science and of the need for popularization. The time would come when erudition would cease to be the visible prop of historical science and would be incorporated into the historical work itself, where the reader trained to work with this inner knowledge would recognize it. Michelet expresses this conception with an image from cathedral construction in his 1861 *Préface:* "The supporting documents, shores and buttresses of the historical edifice, may disappear to the extent that the education of the public keeps pace with the progress of criticism and science." To develop in and around himself an instinct for history as infallible as the instinct of the animals he was to study at the end of his life was Michelet's grand design as a historian.

Would any present-day medievalist find it easy to give up the ostentation of footnotes, annexes, and appendixes? Let us imagine a debate—which might go a long way toward clarifying the social processes by which history is produced—between two arguments that initially seem equally convincing. The first argument continues Michelet's attitude on an ideological and political plane by rejecting the use of an erudition whose consequence, if not its aim, is to perpetuate the domination of a sacrosanct caste of authorities. Proponents of the second argument might also claim Michelet as a forebear. They assert that there can be no science without verifiable proof and that the golden age of a history without erudite documentation is still merely a utopian dream. It would be pointless to carry this imaginary debate too far. The facts are there. A present-day medievalist can only shrink back or hesitate upon confronting Michelet's conception of erudition. The Middle Ages are still the concern of clerics. The time has not yet come, it seems, for the medievalist to renounce the liturgy of erudite epiphany and drop his Latin. Even if one takes the point of view that Michelet as medievalist was, on this important point, more prophetic than outmoded, it must still be conceded that his Middle Ages are not those of today's medieval science.

Even relative to Michelet himself, his Middle Ages seem outmoded. Whether we read him as a man of his own time, the seething nineteenth century, or from the point of view of our own convulsive era, Michelet seems quite remote from the Middle Ages he is writing about. This impression is only strengthened if we do as he asked and decipher his historical work as though it were an autobiography— "the biography of history written like the biography of a man, of myself." Here we find the unchanging Middle Ages in contrast with the twentieth century of revolutions, the obedient Middle Ages in contrast with the twentieth century of protest. Michelet's Middle Ages? Gloomy, obscurantist, petrified, sterile. Michelet, by contrast, the man of festival, light, life, exuberance. If he lingered so long over the Middle Ages, from 1833 until 1844, this could only have been to mourn a while at its graveside. It is as if the winged Michelet could not free himself from the suffocating darkness of a long tunnel. His beating wings struck against the wall of a cathedral shrouded in shadow. He begins to breathe, to come to life, to blossom—our bird-flower—only with the coming of the Renaissance and the Reformation. At last, Luther came.

And yet...

Within what is called the Annales school, it may have been the "modern" historians, yesterday a Lucien Febvre, today a Fernand Braudel, who were the first to see Michelet as the father of the new history, of the total history whose mission is to understand the past in all its density, from material culture to mentalities. But isn't it now primarily the medievalists who are turning to Michelet for enlightenment in their quest—advocated by him in his 1869 *Préface*—for a history at once more "material" and more "spiritual"? Doesn't the modernity of which Roland Barthes has shown Michelet to have been one of the earliest representatives first become evident in his view of the age that may be regarded as the childhood of our society, the Middle Ages?

In order to shed some light on this apparent contradiction, let us try examining Michelet's Middle Ages in a way which satisfies the dual demands of modern science and of Michelet himself. In other words, let us conduct our investigation in such a way as to pay heed to the way Michelet's view of the Middle Ages evolved during the course of his life. From 1833 until 1862, this view was not static. It underwent transformations. To understand the Middle Ages as they existed for Michelet, and as they exist for modern medievalists and their contemporary public, it is essential to study the period's various avatars in Michelet's work. As Michelet himself (with or without Vico) was fond of doing, and as contemporary historical science likes to do, let us periodize Michelet's Middle Ages, even at the cost of oversimplifying somewhat. The process of a life—like that of history—consists more of overlapping periods than of clear successions. Still, though they may be interwoven, the various avatars occurring in the course of this evolution assume distinct successive configurations.

I believe that three or perhaps four of these can be distinguished in Michelet's Middle Ages. The key to understanding this evolution is to observe that Michelet, more than anyone else, read and wrote the history of the past in the light of the present. Michelet's "historical" relation to the Middle Ages changes according to his relation to contemporary history. This unfolds between two important milestones in Michelet's evolution, 1830 and 1871, which frame the historian's adult life (he was born in 1798 and died in 1874). Between the July Revolution and the twilight of France's defeat by Prussia, the struggle against clericalism, the disappointments that followed the abortive revolution of 1848, disgust with the business orientation of the Second Empire, the disillusionment born of the materialism and injustice of nascent industrial society all changed Michelet's image of the Middle Ages.

From 1833 to 1844, the period during which the six volumes of the *Histoire de France* devoted to the Middle Ages were published, Michelet's Middle Ages have a positive cast. They deteriorate slowly between 1845 and 1855, keeping pace with the appearance of each new edition, into an inverted and negative Middle Ages. Finally, the curtain is lowered in the *Préface* to volumes 7 and 8 of the *Histoire de France* (1855), devoted to the Renaissance and Reformation. After the great interlude provided by the *Histoire de la Révolution*, a new Middle Ages emerges, which I call the Middle Ages of 1862, the year *La Sorcière* appeared. These Middle Ages are dominated by the witch; a strange dialectical movement has brought a Satanic Middle Ages forth from the depths of despair. Being Satanic, these Middle Ages are Luciferian, that is, bearing light and hope. It may, futhermore, be possible to include a fourth Middle Ages. In antithesis to the contemporary world of the "great Industrial Revolution" to which the little-known last part of the *Histoire de France* is devoted, Michelet here rediscovers the fascination of a lost childhood. It is no more possible to return to this collective childhood than it is to return, from the threshold of a death which always haunted him, to the warm haven of the womb.

THE GOOD MIDDLE AGES OF 1833–44

As Robert Casanova has established in painstaking detail, the portion of Michelet's *Histoire de France* which concerns the Middle Ages went through three editions with variants: the first edition (called A), six volumes of which appeared between 1833 and 1844 (the first and second in 1833, the third in 1837, the fourth in 1840, the fifth in 1841, and the sixth in 1844); the Hachette edition of 1852 (B); and the definitive edition of 1861 (C). In the meantime, partial reissues appeared, for volumes 1 and 2 in 1835 and volume 3 in 1845 (A'), and for certain parts of volumes 5 and 6 in 1853, 1856, and 1860 (*Jeanne d'Arc* from volume 5, and *Louis XI et Charles le Téméraire* from volume 6, published in Hachette's "Chemin de Fer" series). Edition A' of the first three volumes is not very different from edition A. The major change occurs between A-A' and B, especially for volumes 1 and 2, while volumes 5 and 6 of B reproduce those of A. C merely reinforces, roughly speaking, the tendencies present in B, though it is true that this reinforcement is considerable.

Between 1833 and 1844 Michelet was captivated by the charm of the Middle Ages, which, even in its misfortunes and horrors, he saw in a positive light. What then constituted the primary attraction of the Middle Ages was that this was an era of which he could render a total history of the sort he was subsequently to glorify in the 1869 *Préface*. The Middle Ages lent themselves to such total history because they were amenable to the sort of historical writing of which Michelet dreamed, at once more material and more spiritual than other history, and because there was available in archives and monuments, in texts of parchment and stone, a documentation adequate to nourish the historian's imagination so that he could make a total resuscitation of the era.

From the material Middle Ages he drew a number of "physical and physiological" factors, such as the "soil," the "climate," the "diet." One could think of medieval France as a physical object because this was the era when French nationhood made its appearance along with the French language; but it was also the time when provincial France was brought into being by feudal parcelization (for Michelet, *feudal* France and *provincial* France were the same thing). This provincial France was "shaped by its physical and natural division." From this he took the brilliant idea of placing the *Tableau de la France,* that marvelous descriptive meditation on French geography, not at the beginning of the *Histoire de France* in the banal guise of a table of "physical factors" which had somehow conditioned history for all time, but around the year 1000, when history was to make of this Eurasian peninsula both a political unity, the kingdom of Hugh Capet, and a mosaic of territorial principalities. France was newborn. With the infant still in its cradle, Michelet could predict the fate of the various provinces and bestow upon each its due portion.

We encounter the history of climate, food, and physiology. All these factors are in evidence in the calamities of the year 1000: "The order of the seasons seemed to have been reversed, the elements appeared to obey new laws. A terrible plague devastated Aquitaine; the flesh of its victims seemed as though eaten away by fire, falling away from their bones, rotting."

These Middle Ages are built out of matter, out of products that are exchanged, out of physical and mental disorders. All this is evoked anew in the 1869 *Préface:* "The important thing is the way England and Flanders were married by wool and cloth, the way England drank Flanders in, became impregnated with her, and lured away the weavers forced out by the brutality of the House of Burgundy by paying whatever price was necessary." He continues: "The black plague, Saint Vitus' dance, flagellants, and those carnivals of despair, the witches' sabbaths, drove the people, abandoned and leaderless, to act for themselves . . . The disease reached its full paroxysm in Charles VI's raging madness." Yet these Middle Ages were also spiritual, and first of all in the sense Michelet then gave the term: this was the period during which "the great progressive inward movement of the national soul" was accomplished.

In two churches in the heart of Charles VI's Paris, Michelet even managed to find the incarnation of the two poles, materiality and spirituality, between which he believed the new history must oscillate: "Saint-Jacques-de-la-Boucherie was the parish of butchers and Lombards, of money and meat. Fittingly surrounded by skinners, tanners, and houses of ill fame, this rich, dirty parish extended from the rue Trousse-Vache to the Quai des Peaux ou Pelletier . . . In contrast to the materiality of Saint-Jacques, the spirituality of Saint-Jean loomed just a few steps away. Two tragic events had transformed this chapel into a great church at the center of an enormous parish: the miracle of the Rue des Billettes, where 'God was boiled by a Jew,' and the destruction of the Temple, which extended the parish of Saint-Jean over the vast and silent quarter."

These Middle Ages also abound in specimens on which the historian can exercise his erudition and imagination, exercises in which, the "document as voice," in Roland Barthes's phrase, can make itself heard: "Entering the centuries rich in authentic records and documents, history reaches its majority." The "murmurs" in the Archives begin to make themselves heard, and royal edicts live and speak, as does even mute stone. Where it had been material and inert, the historian makes it spiritualized and alive. The hymn to living stone is the central portion of the famous passage on "passion as artistic principle in the Middle Ages." "Ancient art, worshiper of matter, was characterized by the material support of the temple, the column . . . Modern art, child of the soul and spirit, has as its principle not form but the face and the eye, not the column but the arch, not solidity but the void." He goes on: "Stone is animated and spiritualized by the artist's severe but ardent hand. The artist brings forth the life within."

"I have defined history as *Resurrection*. If ever this was so, it has to be in the fourth volume (*Charles VI*)" (Michelet's emphasis). The same medieval archives which enable the historian to bring the dead back to life also made it possible for Michelet to bring back those who touched him most, the little people, the weak and the unimportant who were even more dead than the rest and whose recall to life made Michelet the great resuscitator that he was. "History! Reckon with us! Your creditors summon you! We have chosen death in exchange for a line from you." Michelet was now able to "plunge into the populace. While Olivier de la Marche and Chastellain lolled about the Toison d'Or over their meals, I took soundings in the cellars in which Flanders fermented, those masses of brave and mystical workers."

For Michelet, the Middle Ages of 1833 were the era of marvelous apparitions. These jump from the documents before his very eyes, wide with amazement. The first ghost to awaken was the Barbarian, who was childhood, youth, nature, life. No one has surpassed Michelet in expressing the romantic myth of the noble Barbarian: "The word pleases me . . . I accept it, Barbarians. It means full of a new sap, alive and rejuvenating . . . We Barbarians have a natural advantage; if the upper classes have culture, we have a good deal more of life's warmth." Other marvelous children were to pass through his Middle Ages at a later date, such as the one hailed in the 1869 *Préface*: "Saint Francis, a child who knew not what he was saying, and so only said it better." And of course there is Joan of Arc: "It was a divine spectacle when the child, alone and abandoned on the scaffold in the midst of the flames, maintained her own inner Church against the priest-king and the murderous so-called Church, and, uttering the words 'My voices!' took wing." The whole of the Middle Ages was, in a sense, a child: "Melancholy child, ripped from the very entrails of Christianity, born in tears, grown up in prayer and reverie and in heartrending anguish, dead without achieving anything; but it has left behind so poignant a memory that all the joys and all the grandeurs of the modern age are not enough to console us." It was around the year 1000 that the well beloved woman France, the physical, biological France, rose from the earth, the forests, the rivers, and seacoasts: "When the wind had dissipated that worthless and featureless mist with which the German Empire had covered and beclouded everything, the country appeared." And the famous sentence, "France is a person." It is sometimes forgotten that this was followed by: "The only way to make myself clearer is to reproduce the language of an ingenious physiology." This did not escape Roland Barthes's notice: "The *tableau de la France,* . . . which is ordinarily treated as the ancestor of our geographies, is in fact the report of a chemical experiment: the enumeration of the provinces it contains is less a description than a methodological tabulation of the materials and substances necessary to synthesize, in an altogether chemical manner, the French generality."

Once France has come into being, her people can come to her side.

Their first rising results in the Crusades. This gives Michelet a ready-made opportunity to set the common man's generosity, spontaneity, and spirit off against the calculation and equivocation of the great: "The people set out at once, without waiting for anything, leaving the princes to deliberate, arm themselves, count their number; men of meager faith! The plain people worried about none of this: they were sure of a miracle." It should be noted that, in this case, Michelet's Middle Ages, which seemed such a far cry from the "scientific" Middle Ages of twentieth-century medievalists, actually foreshadow what today's most innovative historians are uncovering bit by bit, with improved documentary support for their contentions. To verify this assertion, one has only to look at that great book which, along with three or four others, ushered in the history of collective mentalities: *La Chrétienté et l'idée de croisade*, by Paul Alphandéry and Alphonse Dupront (1954). In this book it is shown that there were, in fact, two contrasting kinds of crusades, the crusade of the knights and the crusade of the people. One chapter is even entitled *La croisade populaire*. Pope Urban II had preached to the wealthy at Clermont. But it was the poor who departed—or, at least, departed first. "The nobles took the time to sell off their possessions, and the first troop, a numerous throng, was made up of peasants and relatively impoverished nobles. But another difference, a much more fundamental difference in mental outlook was soon to separate the poor from the lords. The latter set out to use the leisure time afforded them by the Truce of God against the infidel; for them, it was a question of a limited expedition, a sort of *tempus militiae*. By contrast, among the people there was an idea of remaining in the Holy Land. ... The poor, who had everything to gain in the adventure, were the really spiritual Crusaders for the accomplishment of prophecies." And if Michelet had known of the recent research into the children's crusade of 1212, think what he could have written. In another chapter (*Les croisades d'enfants*), Alphandéry and Dupront showed that, through the term "children," "the deep, inner meaning of the very idea of crusade is revealed with an intensity in which the miraculous gleams," and Pierre Toubert later proved that this term denoted the poor and humble, such as the Shepherds of 1251 ("the poorest inhabitants of the countryside, the shepherds especially...," wrote Michelet). Here, childhood and the common people are inextricably intertwined, as Michelet would have liked.

Michelet was most deeply taken by the second appearance of the people in the Middle Ages. He was more a reader of chronicles and archives than of literary texts. He seems not to have known of the monstrous, bestial villains in the literature from around the year 1200, such as *Aucassin et Nicolette*, or *Ivain* by Chrétien de Troyes.

11

The people had arisen as a crowd, collectively, with the Crusades. Quite suddenly, in documents from the fourteenth century, one sees the people embodied in a single personage, "Jacques." A Parisian, son of a craftsman and man of the bourgeois era, Michelet had previously seen only the people of the cities and communes. "The countryside? Who knows anything about it before the fourteenth century? (This, of course, makes the present-day medievalist smile, armed as he is with so many studies and a few great books, like Georges Duby's, devoted to the peasants of the time before the plague and the jacquerie.) It is as though day has broken over this immense world of shadows with its numberless masses. In the third volume (particularly erudite), I was not alert and expected nothing when the figure of "Jacques" standing in his furrow blocked my path; a monstrous and terrible figure." It is the revolt of Caliban, foreseeable as early as the time of Aucassin's encounter with the young peasant, "big,monstrously ugly and horrible, clad in a huge sackcloth blacker than coal, with more than two hands' width between his eyes, immense cheeks, a gigantic flat nose, enormous wide nostrils, fat lips redder than a beefsteak, and frightful long yellow teeth. He wore leather shoes and leggings tied about his legs up to the knee with cords of linden bark. His cloak was unlined, and he held himself erect with a long club. Aucassin hurried toward him. Imagine his fear when he saw this creature up close!" (From the 1973 French translation by Jean Dufournet).

The people appear a third time in the Middle Ages with Joan of Arc. Immediately, Michelet points out her essential trait: she belongs to the people. "The originality of the Maid of Orleans, which accounts for her success, was not so much her valor or her visions as her common sense. Her enthusiasm revealed to this child of the people what the question was and how to settle it." Yet Joan was more than a popular emanation. She was the end product of the whole Middle Ages, the poetic synthesis of all the miraculous apparitions that Michelet saw in the period. She was a child, she was the people, she was France, she was the Virgin: "Let the romantic spirit reach this far, if it dares; poetry will never do it. And what could poetry add? . . . The idea it had pursued throughout the Middle Ages from legend to legend turned out in the end to be a person; the dream could be touched. The Virgin whose aid knights in battle begged and awaited from on high was actually here below. Who was she? This was the miracle. She was one of the contemptible mass, one of the humble, a child, a simple country girl, one of France's poor . . . For there was a people, there was a France . . . This last figure of the past was also the first of the time which was just beginning. In her could be seen both the Virgin and . . ., already, the fatherland." More than she was either people or nation, however, Joan was first of all woman. "There is yet something else we must see in her and that is the Passion of the Virgin, the martyr of purity . . . France's savior had to be a woman. France was herself a woman . . ." Another of Michelet's obsessions found sustenance here. Nevertheless, Joan marks the end of the Middle Ages. Meanwhile, another marvelous apparition had occurred: the nation, the fatherland. This represents the grandeur of the fourteenth century, and for Michelet, the fourteenth was the great century of the Middle Ages, the one he deemed worthy of a separate publication. In the *Préface* to volume 3 in 1837, he spoke of his amazement at this century, which saw the achievement of France. The child became a woman, passing from physical to moral personhood; she at last became herself: "France's national era is the fourteenth century. The Estates General, the Parlement, all our great institutions either began or achieved stable form at this time. The bourgeois makes his appearance in Marcel's revolution, the peasant in the Jacquerie, and France herself in the war with the English. The saying 'a good Frenchman' dates from the fourteenth century. Until then, France was less France than Christendom."

Besides the cherished personages of the child-Barbarian, the woman-France, the nation, and the people, two other forces came into view which called for Michelet's enthusiasm: religion and life. As Jean-Louis Cornuz has skillfully shown, Michelet at this time held that Christianity was a positive force in history. In an admirable piece which remained unknown for a century until discovered recently by Paul Viallaneix, and entitled by him *L'Héroïsme de l'esprit,* Michelet explains: "Why have I devoted such care to the treatment of this period, which all our effort is tending to wipe from the face of the earth? Must I say it? One of the principal reasons is that surprising state of abandonment in which the friends of the Middle Ages have left it. Its partisans display an incredible inability to make either visible or attractive a history which they profess to love so much . . . Who knows what Christianity was?" For Michelet in this period, Christianity was subversion of the hierarchy, a means of advancement for the humble: the last shall be first. It was a place where freedom was fermenting, although already, in a material sense, it was partly powerless. It was primarily the champion of the most oppressed and unfortunate, the slaves. Even if it was unsuccessful in its desire, it wanted to free the slave. In Gaul in the late third century, the oppressed rebelled. "All the serfs in Gaul then took up arms under the name *Bagaudes* . . . It would not be surprising if this claim of the natural rights of man was in part inspired by the Christian doctrine of equality."

At a time when, by his own admission, he was more a "writer and artist" than a historian, Michelet saw in Christianity a marvelous inspiration for art. He wrote the sublime text of *La Passion comme principe d'art au Moyen Age,* which would appear, in a corrected version, in the 1852 edition and be relegated to the *Eclaircissements* [Clarifications] of the 1861 edition: "In this abyss lies the thought of the Middle Ages. The entire period is contained in Christianity, and Christianity in the Passion... This is the whole mystery of the Middle Ages, the secret of its inexhaustible tears and its profound genius. What precious tears they were, flowing in limpid legends, in marvelous poems, and piling up toward heaven, crystallizing in gigantic cathedrals which aspired to climb all the way to the Lord. From beside this great poetic river which runs through the Middle Ages, I can make out two separate sources to account for the color of its waters... Two poetries, two literatures: one chivalrous, military, amorous; from early on, this was aristocratic; the other religious and popular." In a moment of intuition he added: "The first, too, was popular at its inception." Of course, he believed that our high medieval literature had been influenced by "poems of Celtic origin," at a time when his friend Edgar Quinet was writing the admirable and neglected *Merlin l'Enchanteur.* Today, he would be excited by research which has brought to light not only the Celtic oral literature but also the important current of popular folklore in the background of the gests and courtly romances. It was this amalgam of religion with the people which charmed Michelet in the Middle Ages: "The Church was then the home of the people... Worship was a tender dialogue between God, the Church, and the people, expressing a single thought."

Finally, the Middle Ages were life. Michelet had no feel for antiquity, which he considered spiritless. We have seen how he set "ancient art, worshiper of matter," against "modern art," that is, medieval art, "child of soul and spirit." For him, as for the other great romantics, this deep vitality of the Middle Ages culminated in the Gothic. In Gothic art he was fond not only of the beginnings, such as that day in the twelfth century when the "ogival eye" opened, or the period in the twelfth and thirteenth centuries when "the vault sunk in the depths of the walls... began to meditate and dream," but also of the exuberance and folly of the finish, the flamboyant: "The fourteenth century was barely over when these rose windows changed into flamboyant figures; were they flames, hearts, or tears?"

The vital impulses characteristic of the Middle Ages culminate in the medieval festival. The ideal of the festival which Michelet so skillfully exalted, especially in *L'Etudiant,* was one which he found no other era to have succeeded as well as the Middle Ages in achieving.

It was "the long festival of the Middle Ages"; the Middle Ages were a festival. This was a foreshadowing of the role—today clarified by sociology and ethnology—played by the festival in a society and civilization of the type that existed in the Middle Ages.

In the great 1833 piece, *La Passion comme principe d'art au Moyen Age,* Michelet at last reaches the deepest, most visceral reasons for his fascination with the Middle Ages. He sees the period as a return to the origins, to the maternal womb. Claude Mettra (*L'Arc,* no. 52) has given an inspired commentary on a February 1845 text in which Michelet, having completed his history of medieval France, compares himself to the "fertile womb," the "mother," "the pregnant woman who does everything with an eye to her eventual fruit." The obsession with the Womb, with its image and its realm, is fed on the Middle Ages, out of which we were born, from which we have emerged. "The old world must pass away, the traces of the Middle Ages must completely disappear, and we must watch the dying of all that we loved, all that suckled us as infants, that was mother and father to us and sang so tenderly to us in our cradles." This sentence is even more topical today in 1974. Traditional civilization, created during the Middle Ages, struck with an initial blow by the Industrial Revolution in Michelet's time, is now disappearing forever in the wake of a series of transformations which have rocked and buried "the world we have lost" (Peter Laslett).

The Dark Middle Ages of 1855

The good Middle Ages of 1833 deteriorated rapidly. Between 1835 and 1845, in new editions of the first three volumes, Michelet began to take his distance from the Middle Ages. The turn in his thought is clear in the edition of 1852. The break was finally consummated in 1855 in the prefaces and introductions to volumes 7 and 8 of the *Histoire de France.* The Renaissance and the Reformation had relegated the Middle Ages to the shadows. "The bizarre, monstrous, amazingly artificial state which was that of the Middle Ages . . . "

The break came with Luther. More than the now shadow-shrouded apparitions of the Middle Ages, Luther was the real epiphany: "Here I stand!" "It was most salutary for me to live with this great-hearted man who said *no* to the Middle Ages."

Somewhat embarrassed by having loved the Middle Ages too much, Michelet sought to take his distance from the period—from his *own* Middle Ages. "This beginning to my history pleased the public more than myself." He tried to make corrections without repudiating what he had written. He claimed that he had revealed the Middle Ages. He had believed what the Middle Ages wanted him to believe and had not seen the reality, which was somber. "Our candor will not permit us to erase what is written . . . What we wrote then is true as the ideal which the Middle Ages set themselves. What we give here is the reality, as it stands accused by its own testimony."

It was, of course, the perverse seductiveness of art, during that time when, as he said of himself, he was more an artist and a writer than a historian, which had inspired in him his unpardonable indulgence for this era: "Then (in 1833), when enthusiasm for the art of the Middle Ages made me less severe toward its system in general . . ." Now even this art was to be disparaged. It was "Gothic disorder," visible in the clownishness of romantic neo-Gothic art. Three guilty individuals were named. Chateaubriand: "M. de Chateaubriand early on chanced a very grotesque imitation . . ." Victor Hugo: "In 1830, Victor Hugo took it up again with the vigor of genius, and gave it wing, taking off, however, from the fantastic, strange, and monstrous, or, in other words, the adventitious . . ." Finally, Michelet arraigned himself: "In 1833, . . . I tried to give the vital law of this vegetation . . . My blind enthusiasm can be explained in a word: we were divining, and we suffered from the fever of divination . . ." Even where the Middle Ages seem to be great, the period itself failed to recognize it. It did not recognize Joan of Arc: "It saw Joan of Arc come and said: 'What is this girl?'" Would the fourteenth century continue in its exalted status? It might, but only after "the denigration of the thirteenth century": "The darkest, most sinister date in all history is for me the year 1200, the '93 of the Church." The fourteenth and fifteenth centuries were carried away in a Dance of Death, the spectacle of a Middle Ages which would not be done with dying: "It ended in the fourteenth century, when a layman set his hands upon the three worlds, enclosed them in his *Comedy*, humanized them, transfigured them, and closed the entire realm off from view." Subsequently, Michelet could only be amazed at "his naïveté, his benevolent ingenuousness in remaking the Middle Ages," as he put it, "century by century". Once adored, now ignominiously burned, the period became "my enemy, the Middle Ages (I, son of the Revolution, revolutionary to the bottom of my heart) . . ."

As subsequent editions appeared, Michelet retouched, corrected, and darkened his portrait of the good Middle Ages of 1833. What do we learn from his repentances? The specialists in Michelet will tell us what caused this estrangement from his earlier self, this quasi-reversal of his previous position. He himself presents it as stemming from the revelation of his encounter with the Renaissance and the Reformation. After discovering Luther, Michelet had to cast the Middle Ages into the shadows, as his hero had done before him. It is fair to assume, however, that Michelet's evolution with respect to the

16

Church and Christianity played an important part in this turnabout. It is important to keep his simultaneous interpretation of past and contemporary history constantly in mind. Michelet's anticlericalism grew more confirmed throughout the July monarchy. This undermined what had been the central inspiration of his earlier version of the Middle Ages.

Michelet pointed out that he had had the advantage of approaching Christianity without the prejudice of a religious training which would either have filled him with uncontrolled admiration or forced him to a rebellious act of intemperate and unexamined rejection. It was rather the "deceivers" of his own time who revealed to him the harm done by their ancestors: "My perfect solitude and isolation in the midst of the men of the time, so hard to believe and yet so true, prevented me from sensing sufficiently how much these ghosts of the past were still to be feared in the deceivers who claim to be their natural heirs."

From correction to correction and variant to variant, one can make out the critical points around which Michelet's revised view of the Middle Ages crystallized. In the first volume, whatever had glorified or excused the Church and the Christian religion was eliminated or toned down. Western monasticism had been praised to the detriment of "Asiatic cenobites." Michelet suppressed this favorable comparison: "Freedom was destroyed in the East in the quietude of mysticism; in the West, it was disciplined. For the sake of redemption, it submitted to the rule, the law, obedience, and labor." What may have been excessive in the Barbarians had been civilized by Christianity, whose poetic force had been stressed in the early versions. "To civilize and tame this raging barbarism was not too much to ask of the religious and poetic strength of Christianity. The Roman world sensed instinctively that it would soon need the religion's ample bosom for its refuge." This passage, too, disappeared. The conversion of the Franks had been hailed as a recognition of this poetic power of Christianity, contrasted with rationalism, which was said to be unsuited to the impulsiveness of childhood. Letting stand that "they (the Franks) alone received Christianity through the Latin Church," Michelet then deleted the conclusion: "that is to say, in its complete form, in its high poetry. Rationalism may follow after civilization, but it only desiccates barbarism, dries up its sap, drains away its power." Christianity had been presented as the refuge of all social classes. This was changed by the elimination of the following sentence: "The small and the great met in Jesus Christ." The younger Michelet had been full of understanding and indulgence for the Church's complacent participation in the spirit of the age, its compromises of conscience with power and wealth: "It had to be so. As

17

an asylum and school, the Church needed to be rich. The bishops had to treat as equals with the great and powerful in order to be listened to. The Church had to become materialist and barbarous in order to raise the barbarians to its level, had to make itself flesh in order to win over men of flesh. Like the prophet who lay down on the child in order to revive him, the Church made itself small to incubate the young world." None of this remained. Sometimes a slight retouching gives the best evidence of Michelet's cooling toward the Middle Ages. Pascase Radbert had been "the first to teach explicitly the marvelous poetry of a God contained in a piece of bread." "Marvelous" poetry is downgraded to "prodigious" poetry in later editions.

The revision of the second volume in 1861 is even more extensive. Numerous cuts were made, some long citations were relegated to the appendix, and whole passages relocated to the *Eclaircissements,* as we have already seen in the case of the digression on *La Passion comme principe d'art au Moyen Age.* It is true that in 1845, Ludovic Vivet, in his *Monographie de l'Eglise de Noyon,* had contended that Gothic architecture was the work of laymen, an idea which Michelet had found attractive. Religion and the Church are invariably the major victims of these excisions and cuts. A eulogy to the "good Irish priests" disappeared, for instance, together with another to ecclesiastical celibacy, which Michelet had at first called "that virginal wedlock of priest and Church." The Church ceases to be associated with the ideas of freedom, the people, and poetry. In commenting on the story of Thomas à Becket, Michelet had exclaimed: "The freedoms of the Church then belonged to all." Henceforth it was out of the question to speak of such freedoms.

A bold comparison between Saint Bernard and Byron was cut. Of the knight, Michelet had said: "The knight became a man, a common man, and gave himself to the Church." This was because it was the Church alone that then possessed man's intelligence, his true life, and his repose; the Church watched over the infant people. The Church was of the people." All this was relegated to the *Eclaircissements.*

The Crusades were spared, though (the Crusaders "sought Jerusalem and found freedom"), and there were other unexpected rehabilitations. In the first edition, Michelet had frequently criticized the Church's adversaries, since the Church was a progressive force. Now that the Church had been depreciated, its enemies could rise again. Two important beneficiaries were Abelard and the Albigensians. Abelard's doctrine on intention had been qualified as "slippery...dangerous" and prefiguring the Jesuits! Now a precursor of the Renaissance, Abelard no longer incurs such opprobrium. The Albigensians had not been spared in early editions. Their culture had been vilified and Occitanian literature characterized as a "sterile perfume, an ephemeral flower which had grown on rock and faded away of its own accord." Far from representing progress, the Albigensians had been exemplars of backwardness, of the same family as those Eastern mystics whom Western Christiantiy had been quite right to reject; they were no better than their persecutors: "It is still believed that during the Middle Ages only heretics were persecuted. This is an error. Both sides believed that violence was a legitimate means to conduct one's neighbor to the true faith . . . The martyrs of the Middle Ages were rarely as meek as those of the first centuries, who knew nothing but how to die." Everything that tarnished the reputation of the Albigensians was now deleted.

The reader will have gathered by now that the Middle Ages had come to inspire horror in Michelet. Subsequently, he came to regard them as a sort of anti-nature. Instead of stimulating those marvelous apparitions that had so astonished him, the period would hereafter inspire only what Roland Barthes has called "malefic themes." The Middle Ages thus entered that "bizarre, monstrous, amazingly artificial state" of the 1855 *Préface:* "Proscribed nature was succeeded by anti-nature, from which the monster was spontaneously born, with two faces, one of false knowledge, the other of perverse ignorance."

These Middle Ages condemned all that Michelet regarded as spontaneous, good, fruitful, generous—childhood, the family, the school: "The Middle Ages are as impotent for the family and education as for science." As it was anti-nature, so, too, was the period *counter-family* and *counter-education.* The era never witnessed what might have been "the very touching and beautiful festival of the Middle Ages, condemned by the Church, the festival of simplicity and simple people," which never came to pass because religion forbade it.

From the medieval Pandora's box, three miasmas now escaped, which Roland Barthes has categorized under the headings of the dry, the empty and swollen, and the ambiguous. The dry included the aridity of the scholastics: "Everything comes to an end in the twelfth century; the book is closed; that bountiful efflorescence, seemingly inexhaustible, suddenly dried up." Scholasticism "ended in the *thinking machine.*" Nothing remained but imitation and repetition ad nauseam; "the Middle Ages became a civilization of copyists" (Barthes). After a brief moment of life, Gothic art declined, and stone once again became inert; the Middle Ages returned to the mineral state. Worse still, as personified by their most symbolic and venerable king, Saint Louis, the Middle Ages did not know how to weep, could not shed a tear. The "gift of tears" was denied them. This causes the historian to repent of his earlier interpretation and issue a new judgment: "I traversed ten centuries of the Middle Ages, blinded by legends, made stupid by scholasticism, sometimes weak in my juvenile admiration for the sterility of this world in which the human spirit fasted so much that it grew thin." From the category of the empty and swollen, we have the following example: "From the forbidden philosophy was born the infinite legion of quibblers, locked in relentless and serious dispute over emptiness and nothingness . . . an immense army of sons of the School, born of wind and inflated with words." And, of course, these Middle Ages are also the disquieting and despicable era of ambiguity. On the subject of the serf, that "equivocal, bastard being," Michelet generalized thus: "Everything is doubtful and nothing is clear." The Middle Ages were sick with a vague malady, an instability of the blood. Sickness marks the thirteenth century in the form of leprosy. It eats away the fourteenth as the plague.

The Middle Ages have become a long tunnel of fasting, sadness, boredom. Roland Barthes, once again, says it well: "The Middle Ages were yawning, suspended in a state midway between wakefulness and sleep." But did the Middle Ages actually exist? "That is the darkest part of all the obscurity." Yet in the depths of this obscurity and in spite of the Church, a light is lit, Satan's, and a woman, the witch, holds the flame in her hand.

Toward Another Middle Ages: The Luciferian Witch

From the depths of despair, a new light appears, the light of Satan and the witch. A new Middle Ages emerges, which I have been calling the Middle Ages of 1862, the year Michelet, between January and October, wrote La Sorcière. These Middle Ages are positive. They are once again a healthy era but, by virtue of a strange detour, constitute a surprising reversal. Indeed, the Middle Ages are saved by what the period had itself condemned, silenced, and martyred. These inverted Middle Ages ("the great revolution of the witches, the most important step inverse to the spirit of the Middle Ages") may not have flowed from Michelet's pen until 1862, but he believed they had always been in his mind. Whether as revelation or reconstruction, he believed he had recognized them as early as his first essays in history. In L'Héroïsme de l'esprit he traced his conception of the antagonistic pair, Middle Ages–Satan, back to the Introduction à l'histoire universelle of 1831: "My critical beginnings and independence of mind are marked in the Introduction à l'histoire universelle, in which I charge the Middle Ages with having prosecuted under the name of Satan the idea of freedom, which the modern age at last calls by its right name." He points to the virtues of Satan and his creature, the witch. They are beneficent virtues. They introduced freedom and fecundity into the very heart of the Middle Ages. Satan is the "peculiar name of the still young idea of freedom, at first militant, negative, and creative, and later ever more productive." The witch is "hot and fertile reality."

Surprisingly, Michelet thought the witch productive primarily because she gave birth to modern science. While the clergy and the schoolmen were mired in the world of imitation, bloatedness, sterility, and anti-nature, the witch was rediscovering nature, the body, mind, medicine, and the natural sciences: "Look again at the Middle Ages," Michelet wrote in *La Femme* (1859), "a closed era if ever there was one. It was Woman, alias Witch, who kept alive the great current of beneficial natural science."

The Middle Ages of 1862 finally and fully satisfy not only Michelet's existential obsessions but also his historical theories. In these Middle Ages the body finds its place, for better or for worse. These are the times of disease and epidemic, of love, of going back to life. Jeanne Favret has seen and expressed it well: "To speak of Satan was perhaps a way to speak of a discomfort located 'elsewhere' than in the conscience or in society, and, in particular, in the body. Michelet had a presentiment of this—a good deal more strongly than his successors, whether historians, ethnographers, or folklorists— when he asserted that the witch's three functions were concerned with the body: 'to heal, to bring love, and to bring back the dead'" (*Critique*, April 1971). The witches' great revolution, in fact, "is what might be called the rehabilitation of the stomach and digestive functions. They belatedly taught that there was nothing impure and nothing unclean. From then on the study of matter was unlimited and unfettered. Medicine was possible." The witch's master, Satan, was, of course, the "Prince of the world." Paul Viallaneix has rightly said of Michelet that "Satan became the Prometheus of his old age." The exceptional, revelatory character of the fourteenth century is again evident. Instead of announcing the coming of the nation, the people, and Jacques, however, it is a century which reveals Satan, the witches' sabbath, and the plague: "this happened only in the fourteenth century ... "

In the morbid trilogy of the last three centuries of the Middle Ages, the fourteenth marks the apogee of the physical despair which, together with spiritual despair, gave rise to the witch: "Three terrible blows in three centuries. In the first came the shocking metamorphosis of the body's exterior, in the form of skin diseases and leprosy. In the second, the internal ailment, strange stimulation of the nerves, epileptic dances. Then everything quieted down, but the blood was changing, the ulcer was paving the way for syphilis, the scourge of the fifteenth century." And he goes on: "The fourteenth century went from one to another of three scourges—epileptic fits, plague, and ulcerations." This was the great divide, the historical nexus in which Michelet saw his conception of history embodied, material and spiritual together, physical and social body joined in a single movement, a common impulse. "The record of a trial in Toulouse in 1353 in which the dance of the sabbath is mentioned for the first time put my finger on the precise date. What could be more natural? The black plague had scourged the earth and 'killed a third of the world.' The pope was debased. Defeated lords taken prisoner extracted their ransoms from the serf, taking the shirt from his back. The epidemic of epilepsy was getting under way with the war of the serfs, the Jacquerie . . . People were so crazed that they danced."

Bewitched by the spectacle of Satanism, the fourteenth century's most modern accomplishment, Michelet detached Satanized Christendom from its historical and geographic roots. He no longer regarded it as a continuation of Antiquity. The witch was neither "the aged Magician nor the Celtic or Germanic Seer." The bacchanalia, "small rural orgies," were not "the black masses of the fourteenth century, solemn challenges to Jesus." When Michelet comes to the Luciferian dawn, moreover, he seems to believe he is no longer in the Middle Ages. As the great epidemics are about to be loosed, he turns back toward the slack morbidity of earlier centuries and identifies them with the Middle Ages: "The diseases of the Middle Ages were . . . less specific: primarily hunger, languor, and poor blood."

We note a similar detachment from other worlds, including the Arab, and the East in general. The witches' sabbath is an invention of the Christian West: "Saracen superstitions originating in Spain or in the Orient had only a secondary influence, along with the old Roman cult of Hecate or Dianon. The great cry of fury which is the real meaning of the Sabbath reveals something of quite another order."

Concerning despair and the West, Michelet proposes what we, with our jargon, would call a new periodization: before and after the plague. Of course, present-day medievalists would characterize differently the two periods of history defined by this catastrophic event. Before the plague, the world was not a place of barrenness and stagnation; it was something more in the nature of a universe in movement, where man leaped forward with an expansion of the area under cultivation, a proliferation of cities, an explosion of monuments, an effervescence of ideas during the Middle Ages' remarkable growth phase. After the plague, a long period of depressed equilibrium begins: the population is smaller, conquests are fewer, and the spirit is less bold, if the expansion outside of Europe is neglected. Yet even if one prefers to change the signs from positive to negative, the definitive break in the middle of the fourteenth century does increasingly seem to be established as the line of demarcation separating a world still rooted in its ancient origins, bound to the Eurasian and even African continents, from a universe which by way of upheavals had begun to progress toward a modernity that began in the age of the witch, illuminated by the bonfires of a great physical and moral crisis.

RETURN TO A MIDDLE AGES OF CHILDHOOD

The view of the Middle Ages that Michelet seems to have achieved in 1862 was the bottom of the abyss, the ultimate "depth of moral suffering" that was reached "around the time of Saint Louis and Philip the Fair." Yet, when we think of Michelet in his old age—the Michelet that Paul Viallaneix has shown to be less a declining old man dominated by his second wife and his senile obsessions than a man delving ever more deeply into the philosophy of love, harmony, and unity which had always occupied his mind—may we not suspect that this ultimate Michelet was ready to "salvage" the Middle Ages?

In his 1869 *Préface*, which shows no tenderness toward the Middle Ages, Michelet nevertheless recalls an anecdote from the time subsequent to the July revolution, which shows him as a man ready to defend the Middle Ages against certain of its detractors, the Saint-Simonians, whom he detested even more vigorously: "Quinet and I, at a solemn meeting to which we had been invited, looked with admiration upon this bankers' religion, in which we saw a peculiar return of what was supposed to have been abolished. We saw a clergy and a pope...The old religion they were supposed to be fighting had been restored in all its worst forms; neither confession nor supervision of consciences nor any of the rest was lacking. The Capuchins had come back as bankers, industrialists...They wanted the Middle Ages abolished immediately, because they were stealing it blind. I thought this was quite something. Upon my return, in an unthinking impulse of generosity, I wrote a few warm words for this terminal case whose final agony was being disturbed by these thieves." In fact, Michelet was increasingly turning away from the world he saw developing before his eyes. In the victory of the revolution of industry, "new queen of the world," he came more and more to see a tidal wave of materialism which, rather than merging with the spirit, demolished it and "subjugated human energy." When the present edition of the *Œuvres complètes* [to volume 4 of which this essay is an introduction.—Trans.] reaches the *Histoire du XIXᵉ siècle* (1870–73), the reader will be in a better position to appreciate how far Michelet—although he tried to remain, as in the epilogue to *La Sorcière*, a man of the dawn, of progress, of hope,

23

constantly anticipating miracles and transformations—was distressed by the mechanized universe which was tending to engulf everything. "I was born in the midst of the great territorial revolution and I will have seen the sprouting of the great industrial revolution." The latter was the real Terror.

Rather than flee into the future, Michelet may have been tempted to turn back to the Middle Ages of his youth, which in 1833 he had depicted virtually as the maternal womb to which he dreamed of returning. It was a childhood world to be recaptured later, when mankind, in a new Satanic leap, would come to require an accounting from an industrialism with which it had become disenchanted and to revolt against the oppression of growth.

This was the man who had previously written in *La Femme* (1859): "I cannot do without God. The temporary eclipse of the high central Idea has plunged this marvelous modern world of science and discovery into darkness"; and it was the man of whom Paul Viallaneix has said: "The farther he went, the less he could do without God." How could such a man do without the Middle Ages?

MICHELET'S MIDDLE AGES: MIDDLE AGES FOR TODAY AND FOR TOMORROW?

I have frequently allowed Michelet to speak for himself in the preceding pages. When he speaks, how can one improve on what he says?

I began by noting the indifference or estrangement felt by most medievalists today with regard to Michelet's Middle Ages, and then I tried to show his view or, rather, his views of the period. In doing so, I tried to indicate how a contemporary medievalist might respond to the various aspects of these views. I deliberately intended to raise the possibility, moreover, that the disdain of medievalists for Michelet's work may well be due to ignorance of what he wrote, to a positivist bias, and to antiliterary prejudice. I do not believe that the time has come—quite the contrary—when ignorance of historiography and scorn for imagination and style are the qualities which make good historians.

This is not to deny that historical discourse has changed, or that Clio, a century after Michelet's death, makes legitimate demands which he could not have satisfied. The historian, the medievalist in particular, must work on a new level of technique; Michelet, regardless of how extraordinary his passion for the document may have been in his own time, can no longer serve as a model. From an intellectual and scientific point of view, however, it seems to me that Michelet's Middle Ages accord astonishingly well with—I won't say our modes, which would be ridiculous, but rather with our best-established tendencies, with the historian's, and particularly the medievalist's, deepest needs. His lesson in method also serves as an antidote to certain fashions and as a precursor and guide, not in yesterday's pathways, but for today and tomorrow.

The Middle Ages which remain for us to "invent," that is, to discover, after him and in his manner, are a total Middle Ages based on all available documents, on law and on art, on charters and on poems, on the soil and on libraries. We must make full use of the combined arsenal of the human sciences—which Michelet lacked, but which his method called for—in trying to overcome the still troublesome specialization of medievalists (in areas such as law, art, literature, and even what is called plain history, all too plain). We must resuscitate not phantoms but men of flesh and spirit. And we must not refuse what the sociologist, the ethnologist, the economist, the political scientist, and the semiologist can add to our mental and scientific equipment. Let Michelet speak for himself, that he may urge us to restore to the Middle Ages their "flesh and blood, costume and ornament . . . adorning them with the beauty they had" and even "with the beauty they had not but acquired with time and perspective." In this romantic formulation we may glimpse that new dimension of history, the history of history, or the art of placing one's subject in historiographic perspective.

History today is, and must be, concerned to an ever greater degree with figures, calculation, and measurement. The Middle Ages are relatively refractory to quantitative attack. For a long while the period was ignorant of calculation and regarded number as merely a symbol or a taboo. It is fortunate that statistics, curves, and graphs are growing more numerous in the works of medievalists and that the monster computer, like the Leviathan of Gothic tympana, is succeeding in its search for an adequate diet made up of a Middle Ages reduced to punched cards and programs; unlike the other Leviathan, this one will make restitution for what it consumes by providing medievalists with more solid foundations for a truer picture of the Middle Ages. Still, the medievalist should be aware that when the computer has done its work, he will still have only a corpse on his hands. A "resuscitator" will always be needed. The medievalist will still need the qualities of a Michelet, who pointed out that the quantitative was not everything and that, necessary as figures might be, quantitative accounting still falls short of history. While it is fine to apply the latest scientific refinements to the study of the past, medievalists should know how to dismantle the quantitative scaffolding in order to get at the Middle Ages "as they were in themselves," approximate and crude, afraid to offend God by too much computation, imputing to Cain the diabolical invention of weights and measures.

The history of an era is never limited to the documentation on which it is based. Since Herodotus and, in particular, since Michelet, progress has been made in increasing the documentary base, refining critical techniques, and in a growing insistence on the scrupulous use of documentation. We must, however, resign ourselves to the impossibility of ever knowing the Middle Ages completely. It would be dangerous to wish to fill the gaps and give voice to the mute without method. Still, between antiquity, whose silences leave perhaps too much to conjecture, and modern times, overwhelmed by a mountain of documents, the Middle Ages may have been the time when the balance was proper to permit a fruitful interplay between a judicious use of documentation and a well-grounded imagination. That the historian, and the medievalist, in particular, has a right to use his imagination is a lesson still best taught by Michelet. How else can we explain and revive an era whose imagination enabled it to raise so great a dream civilization above its inadequacies and shortcomings? The Crusades were launched, after all, by the call of an imaginary Jerusalem. How can such an event be understood without the aid of imagination to transcend the texts and monuments? Medieval man, even when he had no mystical bent, was a pilgrim, a wanderer, *homo viator*. How can bureaucrats of erudition, pencil pushers of "medieval studies," catch up with men who were always on the road?

Since Michelet's time, social analysis has become more methodical. Whether we follow Marx, in seeking out the classes and the mechanisms of their struggle, or modern sociologists, in studying the structure and interaction of socioprofessional categories, or certain historians, in looking at a system of orders and estates, we make a more subtle analysis than Michelet, who was content to use the collective singular—the noble, the cleric, the serf, Jacques—and combine his characters, always under the influence of his overall vision, in such phenomena as the Crusades, the commune, or the witches' sabbath. He especially liked to incorporate them all in "the people," a vague word, not liked by historians, even those least tainted by sociology. Nevertheless, we are today rediscovering the historic reality and weight of social actors whose precise outlines are poorly defined: the young, the masses, public opinion, the people. In this, Michelet was a child of his century, a "child of the people": the term was actually more precise in the nineteenth century. *Populus* meant the mass of the faithful, God's people, or simply the people. Of course, we must not reject the finer analysis of a more modern, more "scientific" sociological model, but neither should we forget that it is also important to understand how societies of the past appeared when seen through their own spectacles. In this respect, Michelet, for whom the people were of primary importance, was at ease with the Middle Ages and can help us to uncover, if not the social reality, at least the contemporary image of that reality. Michelet goes farther, however, in taking the measure of the *popular*, approaching the world of popular culture, of the Other, to which modern ethnologists have taught us to be attentive even in so-called "historical" societies. As he put it: "The Middle Ages, with their scribes, all ecclesiastics, were not interested in admitting what deep, silent changes were taking place in the popular mind." From the perspective of our "hot" societies, what era is better suited than the Middle Ages to instruct us as to the nature of the varied dialogue carried on by high and popular culture over ten centuries, consisting of pressures and repressions, borrowings and rejections, and full of confrontations between saints and dragons, Jesus and Merlin, Joan of Arc and Melusina? If Keith Thomas is right, medieval Christianity's great triumph was the partial but successful integration of the popular faith with that of the clergy. When the symbiosis broke down, witches and the Inquisition were the result. As mass phenomena, these came later than the fourteenth century, as Michelet had thought. But the documented hypothesis is substantially the same.

It is not merely his famous declaration of failure that makes Michelet a man and scholar of the present day: "I was born among the people, the people were in my heart . . . But their language was inaccessible to me. I could not give them voice." According to Barthes, this confession makes Michelet "the first among modern authors only capable of singing an impossible lyric." But it also warns us that discourse on the people is not necessarily the discourse of the people. Thus we are invited to begin a patient search, taking our inspiration from the ethnologists' study of the Other, for a method which will enable us to give voice to the silences and the silent people of history. Michelet was the first historian of these silences. His failure was prophetic and illuminating.

In approaching these silences, Michelet discovered a marginal, peripheral, eccentric Middle Ages which can and should still inspire the present-day medievalist. "The Middle Ages always confronted the very high with the very low," he exclaimed. He went on to confront—and to explain coherently, even if we don't accept his explanations—God and Satan, the witch and the saint, the rib vault and the leper. Like Michel de Certeau, who used the theory of deviations [*théorie des écarts*] to penetrate to the heart of a society by looking at what it excluded, Michelet found himself at the center of the Middle Ages. We say this while bearing in mind that, for him, the situation was inverted in 1862, when what was lowest turned out to be more fruitful than what was highest. An inverted view is, after all, a fruitful way of approaching an age which invented the wheel of fortune and Never-Never Land, and preached, even if it did not practice, that "whatever goes up must come down and vice versa"! And what a trail he blazed, above all, for that growing number of medievalists who have chosen to approach the reality of the age by way of the interesting detours through heresy and the leper colony.

One final aspect of the relation between Michelet and the Middle Ages makes him comparable not only with contemporary medievalists but also with many people in our "developed" societies. Michelet was attracted to the Middle Ages because he recaptured his childhood in the period, returning, as it were, to the womb, while preserving his sense of difference and distance (and, for a time, hostility). The current interest in history and ethnology, which frequently crystallizes in a taste or passion for the Middle Ages, seems to me related to this twofold attraction of the "same" and the "different." In view of what it has become commonplace to call the accelerated pace of history, our contemporaries are aware of losing contact with their origins, of becoming orphans of the past. What attracts them to this past, however, is as much the melancholy familiarity of a known but disappearing world as it is the exotic strangeness of a rapidly receding universe that represents a primitive childhood. The charm of the Middle Ages, for us as for Michelet, is that the period is both reminiscent of "our own childhood" and "different" at the same time. Michelet, in a celebrated passage, made the *Histoire de France* his own autobiography: "Inward method: simplify, write the biography of history as of a man, as of myself. Tacitus saw nothing but himself in Rome, and it really was Rome." Like Flaubert asserting "Madame Bovary, c'est moi," Michelet might have said *"L'Histoire de France,* c'est moi." Through both love and hatred, the part of that long history in which Michelet himself is best reflected is the Middle Ages, with which he lived and struggled all his life. This autobiography became our collective biography. He was the Middle Ages, as we are.

MERCHANT'S TIME AND CHURCH'S TIME IN
THE MIDDLE AGES

The merchant in the Middle Ages was not held in contempt as commonly as he is said to have been, particularly in the wake of certain remarks of Henri Pirenne, who placed too much confidence on this point in theoretical texts.[1] Nevertheless, while the Church very early gave protection and encouragement to the merchant, it long allowed serious suspicions to persist as to the legitimacy of essential aspects of his activity. Some of these aspects enter profoundly into the world view of medieval man. Or rather, in order not to yield to the myth of an abstract collective individual, one should say that these factors entered profoundly into the world view of those men in the West between the twelfth and fifteenth centuries who were in possession of sufficient cultural and mental equipment to reflect on professional problems and their social, moral, and religious consequences.

Among the principal criticisms leveled against the merchants was the charge that their profit implied a mortgage on time, which was supposed to belong to God alone. For example, we have the following remarks of a lector-general of the Franciscan order in the fourteenth century concerning a disputed question: "Question: is a merchant entitled, in a given type of business transaction, to demand a greater payment from one who cannot settle his account immediately than from one who can? The answer argued for is no, because *in doing so he would be selling time* and would be committing usury *by selling what does not belong to him.*"[2]

Before isolating the conception of time hidden behind this argument, we should point out the problem's importance. The whole of economic life at the dawn of commercial capitalism is here called into question. To reject the notion of earnings on time and to identify the practice with the basic vice of usury is not merely to attack the principle of interest but to destroy the very possibility of credit. For the merchant, time is a prime opportunity for profit, since whoever has money counts on being able to profit from the expectation of reimbursement by someone who has none immediately available, inasmuch as the merchant's activity is based on assumptions of which time is the very foundation—storage in anticipation of famine, purchase for resale when the time is ripe, as determined by knowledge of economic conjunctures and the constants of the market in commodities and money—knowledge that implies the existence of an information network and the employment of couriers.[3] Against the merchant's time, the Church sets up its own time, which is supposed to belong to God alone and which cannot be an object of lucre.

In fact, this is the same problem which, at this crucial point in the history of the West, took an acute form in the matter of teaching: could knowledge be sold, since, as Saint Bernard had pointed out in his usual forceful manner, it, too, belonged only to God?[4] What is at stake here is the whole process of secularization of the basis and context of human activity: labor time, and the conditions of intellectual and economic production.

The Church no doubt tried to lighten ship when conditions changed. In the first place, it accepted and soon came to encourage the historic evolution of economic and professional structures. But the theoretical elaboration of this adaptation at the canonical and theological level proceeded slowly and with great difficulty.

The conflict, then, between the Church's time and the merchant's time takes its place as one of the major events in the mental history of these centuries at the heart of the Middle Ages, when the ideology of the modern world was being formed under pressure from deteriorating economic structures and practices. We would like now to explain the major points at issue in this conflict.

I

Christianity is frequently judged to have fundamentally transformed the problem of time and history. Sustained by Holy Scripture and used to basing all their thinking on the Bible, medieval clerics regarded time in the light of biblical texts and, beyond the Good Book, in the light of the tradition passed down through primitive Christianity from the Fathers and the exegetes of the early Middle Ages.

For the Bible and primitive Christianity, time is primarily theological time. It "begins with God" and is "dominated by Him." Consequently, divine action in its totality is so naturally connected with time that time cannot pose a problem; it is rather the necessary and natural condition of every "divine" act. We are following Oscar Cullmann, who is no doubt correct in maintaining against Gerhard Delling that primitive Christianity is close to Judaism in this respect and did not bring about an "irruption of eternity into time, which would thus have been vanquished."[5] For the early Christians, eternity was not opposed to time, nor was it—as it was, for example, for Plato—"the absence of time." Their eternity was merely the extension of time to infinity, "the infinite succession of eons," to use a term from the New Testament, these being both "precisely delimited expanses of time" and unlimited and incalculable durations.[6] We will return to this notion of time when it becomes necessary to oppose it to the tradition inherited from Hellenism. For our present purposes we need only say that, from this point of view, there is a quantitative rather than a qualitative difference between time and eternity.

As compared with Judaic thought, the New Testament introduces, or, rather, makes explicit, one new condition. The appearance of Christ, the fulfillment of the promise, the Incarnation give time a historic dimension or, better still, a center. Subsequently, "the whole history of the past, from the Creation until Christ, as told in the Old Testament, becomes part of the history of salvation."[7]

This is an ambiguous development, however. For Christians as for Jews, time had an end, a *telos*. In this respect, the Incarnation was a crucial event. "The future is no longer, as it is for Judaism, the *telos* giving a sense to the whole of history."[8] Eschatology takes its place in a new perspective, becoming, in a sense, secondary. It, too, belongs to the past, since Christ has somehow abolished it by bringing certainty of salvation. The problem becomes one of how to achieve what Christ has begun once and for all. The Second Coming was not merely prefigured on the day of Pentecost; it has already begun, although its completion depends on the cooperation of the Church, clergy and laymen, apostles, saints, and sinners. The "Church's missionary duty and the preaching of the Gospel give meaning to the time between the Resurrection and the Second Coming."[9] Christ brought the certainty of eventual salvation with him, but collective and individual history must still accomplish it for all, as well as for each individual. Hence the Christian must simultaneously renounce the world, which is only his transitory resting place, and opt for the world, accept it, and transform it, since it is the workplace of the present history of salvation. In this connection, Oscar Cullmann gives a very convincing interpretation of a difficult passage in Saint Paul (1 Cor. 7:30 ff.).[10]

We should point out, before we encounter the problem of time in a concrete medieval context, that this problem was to arise as one of the essential aspects of the notion of time during the crucial period in the eleventh and twelfth centuries that also witnessed a rebirth of eschatological heresies in certain social groups, including merchants.

In this growth of millenarianism, unconscious class reactions, along with individual destiny, played a part. There is a history to be written which will explain Joachimism as well as many other revolutionary movements involving both the soul and economic status. In this era the Apocalypse was not an enthusiasm of fringe groups or misfits, but the hope and sustenance of oppressed groups and hungry people. Saint John's horsemen of the Apocalypse number four, of course: three of them represent the "wounds," or earthly calamities—famine, epidemic, war—but the first sets out as a conqueror in search of victory. For Saint John he was the Missionary of the Word; for the medieval masses, however, he was the guide who would lead them in a dual victory, here below and in the hereafter.[11]

Once relieved of the explosive charge of millenarianism, biblical time was left to the orthodox, around the beginning of the twelfth century. It became a part of eternity. It has been said that "for the Christian in the Middle Ages . . . to feel his existence was to feel his being, and to feel his being was to feel himself not changing, not succeeding himself in time, but subsisting . . . His tendency to nothingness (*habitudo ad nihil*) was compensated by an opposite tendency toward the first cause (*habitudo ad causam primam*)." This time, moreover, was linear and had a sense or direction, tending toward God. "Time ultimately carried the Christian toward God."[12]

This is not the place to describe in its full complexity and welter of interrelations that "major break in the twelfth century, one of the most fundamental in the development of European society."[13] The accelerating economic pace, of great importance, will be indicated when we return to the subject of the merchant. For now, it is enough to notice how the disturbance of mental structures opened fissures in the traditional forms of thought; through the openings thus provided, spiritual needs connected with new economic and social conditions entered, leading to a variety of repercussions.

There can be no doubt that the disappearance of the Roman Empire, the barbarization of the West, and, to a lesser degree, the imperial restorations wrought first by Charlemagne and later by Otto gave rise to thought about history; Christianity took its place in a historical evolution which, though dominated, for its adepts, by Providence and directed toward salvation, had to appeal to secondary causes, both structural and contingent, in fashioning its explanations. Unfortunately for historical thought, Augustine's interpretations were weakened and distorted during the late Middle Ages. With Saint Augustine, in Henri Marrou's felicitous terminology, historical time kept a certain "ambivalence" so that, within the framework of eternity and subordinated to Providential action, men had some control over their own and mankind's destiny.[14] As Bernheim and Monsignor Arquillière have shown,[15] however, the great ideas in *De civitate Dei,* in which historical analyses echo theological developments, are emptied of historicity by political Augustinism, from Gelasius to Gregory the Great and Hincmar. The feudal society in which the Church becomes mired between the ninth and eleventh centuries congeals historical thought and seems to stop historical time or at least assimilate it to the history of the Church. In the twelfth century, Otto of Freising, uncle of Frederick Barbarossa, wrote: "From that time (of Constantine) on, since not only all men but even emperors, with few exceptions, were Catholics, it seems to me that I have written the history not of two cities but, so to speak, of only one, which I call the Church." The epic and gest were also negations of history by feudal society, which used historical items only to strip them of historicity in the context of an atemporal ideal.[16]

Father Chenu has recently shown brilliantly how, during the course of the twelfth century, the traditional framework of Christian thought on time was seriously shaken.[17]

In this, the urban schools probably played only a secondary role, and Father Chenu notes "that the scholastic masters made virtually no use of the great historical texts of *De civitate Dei,* which were rather meditated upon by monastic writers."

Without doubt, the Old Testament still held sway over men's minds. Against a more flexible conception of time it set up the dual impediment of the Judaic view of a petrified eternity and a symbolism which, as systematized in an explanatory and exploratory methodology, and through Old–New Testament parallelism, completely did away with the concrete reality of historical time.[18]

History got a new start, albeit on a modest basis, with Hugh of Saint-Victor, who devoted a large part of his *Didascalicon* to "historia." His definition, "historia est rerum gestarum narratio," simply echoes the one that Isidore of Seville borrowed from the Latin grammarians who commented on Vergil. Being expressed in the form of a *series narrationis,* however, it is "a succession, and an organized succession, an articulated continuity, whose interconnections have a meaning which is precisely the object of historical intelligibility; not Platonic ideas, but rather God's initiatives in human time, events in salvation."[19]

This history borrowed from the ancients—and from the Bible—the theory of ages, periods which for most clerical historians reproduced the six days of the Creation—that other event that weighed heavily in the thought of twelfth-century theologians, but which we cannot here examine without going too far afield. The sixth age, which saw the advent of mankind, raised certain implicit problems, however: according to the typical parallelism drawn with the six ages of human life, this was the time of old age. In the twelfth century, though, many men and many of the clergy felt themselves to be "modern."

"How could modern developments, which did not seem to be nearing their end, be integrated into this scheme?"[20] This view of history, useful as a classificatory scheme and a tool for ordering and articulating the past, was also cause for concern and a stimulus to research.

Similarly, the idea that history consisted of transferences made its appearance. The history of civilizations was no more than a sequence of *translationes*. Two aspects of the notion of *translatio* are well known. First, in the intellectual sphere, there was the theory according to which knowledge was handed from Athens to Rome, then to France, and finally to Paris, where the most famous university was to grow out of the urban schools: *translatio studii*, which Alcuin had already noted in the Carolingian era.[21] More generally, historians believed they were observing a movement of civilization from East to West. Emergent nationalisms were to arrest this progress in a particular chosen country: Otto of Freising in the German Empire, Ordericus Vitalis among the Normans, and, in the fourteenth century, Richard de Bury in Great Britain.[22] All these pseudo-explanations (of which our own century has seen others, from Spengler to Toynbee) are significant. In any case they assure a connection between the sense of time and the sense of space, an innovation more revolutionary than is initially apparent, and of great importance for the merchant.

An outline of a positive political economy appears with the *Polycraticus* of John of Salisbury: "It prefigures the evolution which . . . would proclaim the autonomy of natural forms, methods of thought, and laws of society . . . It went beyond the moralism of the 'mirrors of princes' in order to begin a science of power, in a State conceived as an objective body, in an administration based on function rather than feudal homage."[23] It is significant that, in his organicist conception, the feet of the State, which had to support the entire body and enable it to move, represented rural workers and tradesmen.[24]

II

And what of the merchant? He had become a man involved in complex and far-flung operations, spanning the Hanseatic region or, better, the Mediterranean, which was dominated by the Italian merchant. His techniques had grown increasingly specialized, and his tentacles stretched all the way from China, visited by Marco Polo, to Bruges and London, where he had established himself or installed his brokers.[25]

Like the peasant, the merchant was at first subjected by his professional activity to the dominion of meteorological time, to the cycle of seasons and the unpredictability of storms and natural cataclysms. He long had no choice but to submit to the natural order and no means to act other than prayer and superstitious practice. Once commercial networks were organized, however, time became an object of measurement. The duration of a sea voyage or of a journey by land from one place to another, the problem of prices which rose or fell in the course of a commercial transaction (the more so as the circuit became increasingly complex, affecting profits), the duration of the labor of craftsmen and workers (since the merchant was almost always an employer of labor), all made increasing claims on his attention and became the object of ever more explicit regulation. Coinage of gold was resumed, and new monetary instruments were introduced. Exchange transactions became more complex, due not only to bimetalism and the newly created fluctuations in the commercial price of silver but also to the first "monetary disturbances," that is, to the first inflationary and, more rarely, deflationary measures. All this enlargement of the monetary sphere required a more adequate measurement of time.[26] At a time when the new aristocracy of money changers was supplanting that of the coiners of the early Middle Ages, the sphere of money exchange prefigures the future stock market, where minutes and seconds would make and unmake fortunes.

The statuses of corporations, together with such commercial documents as account sheets, travel diaries, manuals of commercial practice,[27] and the letters of exchange[28] then coming into common use in the fairs of Champagne (which in the twelfth and thirteenth centuries became the "clearinghouse" of international commerce),[29] all show how important the exact measurement of time was becoming to the orderly conduct of business.

For the merchant, the technological environment superimposed a new and measurable time, in other words, an oriented and predictable time, on that of the natural environment, which was a time both eternally renewed and perpetually unpredictable.

We will cite one illuminating text, chosen from among many.[30] In 1355, the royal governor of Artois authorized the people of Aire-sur-la-Lys to build a belfry whose bells would chime the hours of commercial transactions and the working hours of textile workers. The use for professional purposes of a new technique for measuring time is plainly evident. It is the instrument of a class, "since this particular city is governed by the textile trade," which shows to what extent the evolving mental structures and their material expression were deeply implicated in the mechanism of the class struggle. The communal clock was an instrument of economic, social, and political domination wielded by the merchants who ran the commune. They required a strict measurement of time, because in the textile business "it is fitting that most of the day workers—the proletariat of the textile trade—begin and end work at *fixed* hours." This was the beginning of the organization of work, a distant precursor of Taylorism, which Georges Friedmann has shown was also an instrument of class.[31] Already, the "infernal rhythms" can be felt.

The same process responsible for the rationalization of time was responsible also for its secularization. More for reasons of practical necessity than because of the underlying theology, the concrete time of the Church, as adapted from antiquity, was the time of the clerics, given its characteristic rhythm by the religious offices and the bells which announced them. This time was determined, as required, by imprecise and variable sundials or, on occasion, measured by crude water clocks. Merchants and artisans began replacing this Church time with a more accurately measured time useful for profane and secular tasks, clock time. The clocks which, everywhere, were erected opposite church bell towers, represent the great revolution of the communal movement in the time domain. Urban time was more complex and refined than the simple time of the countryside measured by "rustic bells," for which John of Garland, at the beginning of the thirteenth century, gave this fantastic but revealing etymology: "Campane dicuntur a rusticis qui habitant in campo, qui nesciant judicare horas nisi per campanas."[32]

Another important change was due to the merchant's discovery of the price of time in the course of his exploration of space. For him, the important duration was the length of a trip. In the Christian tradition, time was neither "a sort of lining or backing of space nor a formal condition of thought." We will find later that Christian theologians faced this same difficulty when the introduction of Aristotelian thought at this precise juncture, the twelfth and thirteenth centuries, confronted them with the relation between time and space.

The medieval merchant's simultaneous conquest of time and space deserves greater attention from historians and sociologists of art. In a now classic book, Pierre Francastel has shown how painting and society are connected and what technical, economic, and social pressures can destroy a "plastic space."[33] Along with perspective, medieval painting discovered pictorial time. Previous centuries had represented the various elements on a single plane, in conformity with the view derived from the constraints on both time and space, which excluded both depth and temporal progression. Differences of size expressed only the hierarchy of social ranks and religious dignities. Disregarding temporal hiatuses, successive episodes were juxtaposed, thus constituting a history abstracted from the caprices of time, determined from the beginning in all its phases by God's will. Subsequently, perspective, even if it was only a new schematization which did not reflect a "natural" view but rather corresponded to what could be seen by a hypothetical abstract eye, was a visual statement of the results of a scientific experiment and expressed a practical knowledge of space, in which men and objects are reached in successive, quantitatively measurable steps by methods within the reach of human capacities. In a similar way, the painter confined his picture or fresco to the temporal unity of an isolated moment and focused on the instantaneous (which, ultimately, photography would take for its domain), while time, one might say narrative time, was to be found restored in mural cycles. It was in this very area, in fact, that Florentine painting, under the patronage of the merchant aristocracy, displayed its most startling progress. The portrait was triumphant; it was no longer the abstract image of a personage represented by symbols or signs materializing the place and rank assigned him by God, but rather the rendering of an individual captured in time, in a concrete spatial and temporal setting. Art's new function and goal, in fact, was not to capture the eternal essence but rather to immortalize this ephemeral being of the individual in a particular space and time. Thus at a relatively late date, we can still observe a large number of trials, hesitations, and compromises, as well as such delectable fantasies as Paolo Uccello's *Miracle of the Host* at Urbino, where the original treatment of space in the predella also gives the painter the opportunity to dissect the narrative time of the tale into separate episodes, while preserving both the continuity of the story and the unity of the episodes.[34]

Although the merchant's time was measurable, and even mechanized, it was nevertheless also discontinuous, punctuated by halts and periods of inactivity, subject to quickenings and slowings of its pace. These were frequently connected with technical backwardness and the inertia of natural factors: rain and drought, calm and stormy weather had great influence on prices. Debts came inexorably to term, and yet time was pliable, and it was in this pliability that profit and loss resided. This was where the merchant's intelligence, skill, experience, and cunning counted.

III

What about the Church's time? For the Christian merchant, this was essentially a second horizon of his existence. The time in which he worked professionally was not the time in which he lived religiously. Where salvation was concerned, he was content to accept the Church's teaching and directives. Contact between these two horizons was merely exterior. From his profits, the merchant withheld God's portion, which went toward good works. Existing in a time which bore him toward God, he was aware that eternity, too, was susceptible to halts, stumblings, and quickenings of its pace. There was a time of sin and a time of grace. There was a time of death to the world before the resurrection. Occasionally, he would hasten it by making a final retreat into a monastery. More frequently, he would accumulate restitutions, good works, and pious gifts against the hour of the frightening passage into the hereafter.[35]

Natural time, professional time, and supernatural time were, therefore, both essentially distinct and, at particular points, contingently similar. The Flood became a subject for reasoned speculation, while ill-gotten gains opened the gates of heaven. It is important to eliminate the suspicion that the psychology of the medieval merchant was hypocritical. In different ways, the ends pursued in the distinct spheres of profit and salvation were equally legitimate for him. It was this very distinctness which made it possible to pray to God for success in business. Thus in the sixteenth and later centuries, the Protestant merchant brought up on the Bible and particularly attentive to the lessons of the Old Testament would readily continue to confuse, albeit in a world where it had become customary to distinguish them, the designs of Providence with his own prosperity and fortune.[36]

In some incisive pages, Maurice Halbwachs has asserted that there were as many collective notions of time in a society as there were separate groups, and has denied that a unifying time could be imposed on all groups simultaneously.[37] He reduces the individual notion of time to no more than the internalized point of contact of the several collective notions. It is to be hoped that an exhaustive investigation will someday be made with the intention of showing in a particular historical society the interaction between objective structures and mental frameworks, between collective adventures and individual destinies, and between the various times within Time. This would help to shed light on the very substance of history, and to replace man, the historian's quarry, in the complex fabric of his existence.[38] Here, we must settle for sketching the behavior of the medieval merchant within this multifarious interplay.

The merchant was accustomed to acting in the context "of durations, so to speak, piled one on top of the other."[39] Neither rationalization of his behavior and thought nor introspective analysis had yet habituated him to the harmonization of his various activities or to the feeling, or the wish, of wholeness. It was actually the Church that opened the way to a unification of conscience through the development of the confession. The Church also contributed to the coherence of behavior by elaborating a body of canon law and a theologico-moral theory of usury.

This decisive change in Western man's mental structures began in the twelfth century. In a highly developed form, it was Abelard who shifted the focus of penitence from external sanction to internal contrition. Through the analysis of intentions, he inaugurated the field of modern psychology. It was in the thirteenth century, however, that this movement acquired an irresistible force. At the same time, the mendicant orders were discovering a theater for missionary activity in Africa and Asia—precisely where the merchant had previously found scope for the expansion of his activity—and were pioneering a new frontier in human consciousness. In place of the penitentials of the early Middle Ages, which were guides to extroverted pastoral action based on schedules of sanctions, they introduced confessors' manuals, introverted apostolic instruments oriented toward the discovery of internal dispositions to sin and redemption, dispositions rooted in concrete social and professional situations. For them, the demon took the form not so much of the seven deadly sins as of the countless offenses against God that a trade or group might foster in a variety of ways. They closed the merchant's loophole; the time of salvation and the time of business were reunited in the unity of individual and collective life.

It is not within our competence to examine the contribution made by Hellenic thought at this period to the development of a new approach to the problem of time. This came after a long and hazardous journey in which Arab manuscripts played an important intermediary role.[40]

In a magisterial analysis, Father Chenu reveals how Greek theology, particularly in the work of John of Damascus, beginning in the twelfth century and alongside the various Platonisms and, even this early, Aristotelianisms, gave a serious jolt to Western theology.[41]

Traditionally, it will be recalled, the Hellenic conception of time has been contrasted with the Christian. In Oscar Cullmann's terms, "since the Greeks did not conceive of time as a straight line, the field of action of Providence could not be history as a whole, but only the destiny of individuals. History was not subject to a *telos*. To satisfy his needs for revelation and deliverance, man had no alternative but to have recourse to a mystical conception for which time did not exist, expressed with the help of spatial concepts."[42] We know that the Renaissance and, as a modern thinker influenced by Hellenism, Nietzsche rediscovered the Hellenic sense of cyclic time and eternal recurrence. Heraclitean and even Platonistic time, the "time of pure mobility," would also be rediscovered. The reader will recall Aristotle's definition of time: "Time is the number of motion." This was adopted by Saint Thomas, according to some authorities with a very different sense, in so far as "to pass from the potentiality to the act was necessarily in no way temporal." It seems to us that this opposition has to be attenuated. No doubt, as Etienne Gilson has clearly shown, "into Aristotle's eternal world, which has its duration outside God and without God, Christian philosophy introduced the distinction between essence and existence."[43] But no more than Bergson was correct in accusing Aristotle of having "reified" motion, and no more than Descartes was right in mocking the Aristotelian definition of motion, which he judged only on the basis of the caricatural statement in late scholasticism, it is not certain that Saint Thomas was unfaithful to Aristotle in seeing motion as "a certain mode of being," thereby restoring to time both its contingent, yet measurable plasticity and its fundamental essentiality.

In any case, this was the theoretical basis, in theology, metaphysics, and science combined, of a contact between the Church's time and the time of men acting in the world, in history, and, most important, in their occupations.

Even without giving theoretical reasons, a Franciscan like the author of the text cited at the beginning of this essay (see note 2) understood that the traditional opinion that "time cannot be sold" was unacceptable. The whole practice of the confessional and its canonical elaboration in the thirteenth century sought to give the true justification of the merchant's activity, while circumscribing it within a system of regulations in which religion all too often deteriorated into casuistic moralism. The aim was to keep the merchant's activity within the framework of a tradition for which respect was compulsory. Thus the immutable time of the Old Testament and Judaic thought disintegrated in minor questions and problems of conscience. Condemnations for all the offenses which went by the name of usury,[44] a word with obvious temporal implications, became more flexible—"consideranda sunt dampna quibus mercatores se exponunt et que frequenter occurunt ex hoc quod vendunt ad tempus," says our magister, in a current but revealing expression—and the length of time required in fast, abstinence, and Sunday rest was no longer strictly prescribed but rather, in view of occupational necessities, given in the form of recommendations to be interpreted according to the spirit rather than the letter.[45]

Nevertheless, in the fourteenth and fifteenth centuries, the bankruptcy of the traditional conception of time in Christian theology was to undermine the new equilibrium which had begun to develop in the thirteenth century as a result of the work of theologians, canon lawyers, and moralists under the influence of the mendicant orders. This occurred within the more general context of a reconsideration of *homo faber* imposed by the new socioeconomic factors in the techniques of production—a problem beyond the scope of this essay.

With the Scotists and Ockhamists, time was relegated to the sphere of unpredictable decisions of an omnipotent God. The mystics Meister Eckhart and Johannes Tauler[46] believed that every duration was mixed indistinctly with every other in a general movement in which each creature was "deprived of the capacity to obtain the duration which is properly his."

It is useful at this point to follow Gordon Leff[47] in observing how fourteenth-century scholasticism encouraged the explosion that was to be the Renaissance of the following two centuries, which was both an unleashing of pent energies and a liberation. Freedman or tyrant, the Renaissance man who was sufficiently powerful economically, politically, or intellectually could, by using the capacities determined by his *virtù* as Fortune willed, go where he pleased. He was master of his time as of the rest of his existence. Death alone lay down a limit. But the living attempted to imagine death before it snatched them away, which led to a new point of view. The end became the point of departure for a reflection in which the decomposition of the body instigated a sense of duration, as Alberto Tenenti has recently shown through new analyses of the *artes moriendi* and the thought of French and Italian humanists.[48]

Later, when quantitative growth had pushed back the merchant's horizons and expanded the arena of his action without fundamentally changing economic structures, the merchant was able to use and abuse time. If he remained Christian, he could not avoid rude confrontations and contradictions between time as he used it in his business and time in his religion without paying the price of mental conflict and practical trickery, for the Church was caught in the old regulations even when it capitulated on the essential issues to nascent capitalism and went so far as to make a place for itself in the new order.

IV

This essay has no other purpose than to stimulate a more intensive study of a history which raises numerous problems. Among these problems, one which seems to us of the utmost importance is that of examining the possible impact of the works of the scientific masters of the turn of the fourteenth century on the evolution of ideas about time. The English school, with the Mertonians in the front ranks, has yet to give up its secrets, nor have the Parisian masters of arts, of whom we can make out no more than the inertial mass bulking behind Nicholas d'Autrecourt, Jean de Mirecourt, Jean Buridan, Nicole Oresme, and Jean de Ripa (recently uncovered[49] by Abbot Combes), who are themselves poorly known. The critique of Aristotelian metaphysics in these circles, together with mathematical speculation and concrete scientific research, must have given rise to new views concerning time and space. It is fairly well known that kinematics, through the study of uniformly accelerated motion, was transformed by this critique.[50] This should be enough to arouse the suspicion that time as well as motion was understood in a new way. Earlier, complementary research in science and philosophy among the Arabs had taken a new approach to the key notions of discontinuity inherited from the atomists of antiquity, which led to a new view of time.[51]

Perhaps the connection is closer than has been thought, and certainly closer than the parties involved believed, between the lectures given by the masters of Oxford and Paris and the enterprises of the merchants of Genoa, Venice, and Lübeck in the waning Middle Ages. Their joint efforts may have been responsible for fracturing time and for freeing the time of the merchants from biblical time, which the Church was not capable of maintaining in its fundamentally ambivalent form.

LABOR TIME IN THE "CRISIS" OF THE FOURTEENTH CENTURY: FROM MEDIEVAL TIME TO MODERN TIME

> *Fiorenza, dentro della cerchia antica,*
> *ond'ella toglie ancora e terza e nona,*
> *si stava in pace, sobria e pudica.*
>
> Dante, *Divina Commedia,*
> *Paradiso,* XV, 97–99

There has been a surfeit of commentaries on two passages of the *Divina Commedia,* the point of which was to try to show that they contained a description of a mechanical clock.[1] The effort seems to have been in vain. Less attention has been paid, however, to the verses of canto XV of the *Paradiso,* in which the measurement of time is portrayed in its true historical context, the context of society as a whole rather than of technique.[2]

Speaking through the mouth of Cacciaguida, Dante, that *laudator temporis acti,*[3] makes the antique bell of the Badia above the *mura vecchie* of the eleventh to thirteenth centuries the symbol and expression of an era and a society, in its economic, social, and mental structures. These were the bells that rang Terce and None and marked the beginning and end of the working day in Florence.[4]

After 1284, however, Florence was changing, expanding within the new circle of the *mura nuove,* and the old bell, voice of a dying world, had to give way to a new voice—the clock of 1354. What changes were marked by this change of bells?

Seventy years ago in a pioneering work, Gustav Bilfinger observed that technical history by itself cannot account for the transition from medieval to modern times: "In addition to technical history, social and cultural history must be taken into consideration. For the transition is not merely a passage from the ancient to the modern hour, but also from an ecclesiastical division of time to a secular division."[5]

What segment of secular society was it that stood in need of this change, a fundamental one because it was the whole society which was changing, shedding its old temporal framework and transforming its rhythms?

Gustav Bilfinger has already given his answer: urban society. My aim is merely to make a few remarks and point out certain facts and documents, in order to draw attention to one of the major needs of fourteenth-century urban society that brought about a change in the measurement of time, which was indeed a change in time itself. The need I have in mind was that of adjusting to economic development and, more precisely, to the conditions of urban labor.

The unit of labor time in the medieval West was the day. At first, this meant the rural working day, which one finds reflected also in metrological terminology, for example, the *journal* (a French dialect word for the amount of land that can be plowed in one day, or *jour*.— Trans.). Analagously, the urban working day was defined with reference to variable natural time, from sunrise until sunset, which was marked off in an approximate way by religious time, the *horae canonicae,* borrowed from Roman antiquity.[6]

Within this basic framework, few conflicts arose over the time of work with the exception of one particular point, night labor. In this natural and rural context, night labor was a sort of urban heresy, generally prohibited and subject to fines. Despite the complexity of the problem, it was also an aspect of the Malthusian system of corporations, as Gunnar Mickwitz has clearly seen.[7]

On the whole, labor time was still the time of an economy dominated by agrarian rhythms, free of haste, careless of exactitude, unconcerned by productivity—and of a society created in the image of that economy, *sober and modest,* without enormous appetites, undemanding, and incapable of quantitative efforts.

One isolated development has perhaps been neglected. It has been observed that between the tenth and the end of the thirteenth centuries, one component of diurnal chronology underwent evolution: None, at first set at the hour corresponding to our two o'clock in the afternoon, advanced slowly and became established around noon.[8] This change has been blamed on a sort of sleight of hand, it being said that, in monastic circles, the long wait for mealtime and rest during a day which began before dawn gave rise to increasing impatience. Thus the insidious advance of None is supposed to be indicative of monastic decadence. I do not see that this explanation is confirmed by the documents, and it seems to me gratuitous. I think that another hypothesis is more plausible, although, to my knowledge, the documents are no more helpful in confirming it. None was also the hour when the urban worker, under the jurisdiction of the clerical time rung by the church bells, took his pause.[9] In this connection, one can imagine a more likely form of pressure for a change in the hour of None, which led to an important subdivision of labor time: the half-day. This was to become established, moreover, during the fourteenth century.[10]

From the end of the thirteenth century, this system of labor time found itself under challenge and entered upon a crisis: an emphasis on night work and, most important, harshness in the definition, measurement, and use of the working day, as well as social conflicts over the duration of work—such was the form taken by the general crisis of the fourteenth century in this particular domain. Here as elsewhere, general progress went hand in hand with serious difficulties of adaptation.[11] Labor time was transformed along with most other social conditions; it was made more precise and efficient, but the change was not a painless one.

Curiously, it was at first the workers themselves who asked that the working day be lengthened. In fact, this was a way of increasing wages, what we would today call a demand for overtime.

An ordinance from Arras of January 1315 illustrates this case quite well. The fullers' assistants had demanded longer working days and higher wages, and their demands were satisfied by a commission composed of delegates of the masters of the cloth trade and representatives of the assistants.[12]

In this case, of course, a technical reason was given for the demand, namely, the increase in the weight and size of the fabrics. Still, it is legitimate to assume that it was the first expedient adopted by the workers to mitigate the effects of the wage crisis, which was no doubt connected with the increase in prices and the deterioration of real wages due to the first monetary mutations. Thus we see Philip the Fair authorizing night work and his ordinance subsequently invoked and reaffirmed by Gilles Haquin, provost of Paris, on 19 January 1322.[13]

Before long, however, a contrary sort of demand arose. In response to the crisis, employers sought to regulate the working day more closely and to combat workers' cheating in this area. It was at this time that the proliferation of work bells noted by Bilfinger occurred.[14] It may perhaps be useful to point out a few examples of these *Werkglocken*.

In Ghent, in 1324, the abbot of Saint-Pierre authorized the fullers "to install a bell in the workhouse newly founded by them near the Hoipoorte, in the parish of Saint John."[15]

At Amiens, on 24 April 1335, Philip VI granted the request of the mayor and aldermen "that they might be permitted to issue an ordinance concerning the time when the workers of the said city and its suburbs should go each morning to work, when they should eat and when return to work after eating; and also, in the evening, when they should quit work for the day; and that by the issuance of said ordinance, they might ring a bell which has been installed in the Belfry of the said city, which differs from the other bells."[16]

At the end of this same year of 1335, the bailiff of Amiens satisfied the aldermen's desire that "the sound of a new bell" should serve as the new means of regulating the "three crafts of the cloth trade"—as then existed in Douai, Saint-Omer, Montreuil, and Abbeville, as a study has shown—given that the old ordinances concerning working hours were "corrupt."[17]

In Aire-sur-la-Lys, on 15 August 1335, Jean de Picquigny, governor of the county of Artois, granted to the "mayor, aldermen, and community of the city" the right to construct a belfry with a special bell because of the "cloth trade and other trades which require several workers each day to go and come to work at certain hours."[18]

Our investigation has by no means been exhaustive, but it is sufficient to indicate that the problem of the duration of the working day was especially acute in the textile sector, where the crisis was most noticeable and where wages played a considerable part in production costs and employers' profits. Thus the vulnerability of this advanced sector of the medieval economy to the crisis[19] made it the prime area for progress in the organization of labor.

This is made clear in the Aire text, which explains that the new bell is necessary "because the said city is governed by the cloth trade." We also have negative evidence: where cloth does not occupy a dominant position, we do not observe the appearance of the *Werkglocke*. Fagniez has rightly noted this fact in the case of Paris.[20]

Thus, at least in the cloth manufacturing cities, the town was burdened with a new time, the time of the cloth makers. This time indicated the dominance of a social category. It was the time of the new masters.[21] It was a time which belonged to a group hard hit by the crisis but in a period of progress for society as a whole.

The new time soon became a stake in bitter social conflicts. Worker uprisings were subsequently aimed at silencing the *Werkglocke*.

In Ghent on 6 December 1349, the aldermen issued a proclamation ordering the weavers to return to the city within a week, but thereafter allowed them to start and stop work at the hours of their choosing.[22]

At Thérouanne on 16 March 1367, the dean and chapter had to promise the "workers, fullers, and other mechanics" to silence "forever the workers' bell in order that no scandal or conflict be born in city and church as a result of the ringing of a bell of this type."[23]

In view of these revolts, the cloth-manufacturing bourgeoisie took more or less draconian measures to protect the work bell. Fines were tried first. In Ghent between 1358 and 1362, shearers not obeying the injunctions of the *Werkglocken* were fined.[24] In Commines in 1361, "every weaver who appears after the sounding of the morning bell will pay a fine of five Parisian *solz*." Another set of penalties makes clear the stake represented by the bell. If the workers seized the bell in order to use it as a signal of revolt, they incurred the heaviest fines: sixty Parisian pounds for anyone who should ring the bell for a popular assembly and for anyone who should come armed (with *baston*, the people's weapon, and *armeures*); and the death penalty for anyone who should ring the bell to call for revolt against the king, the aldermen, or the officer in charge of the bell.[25]

It is clear that in the late fourteenth and early fifteenth centuries, the duration of the working day rather than the salary itself was the stake in the workers' struggles.

From a celebrated set of documents, we learn about the struggles of a particularly combative category of workers,[26] the vineyard day laborers. This was a time when vineyards were found in urban and suburban settings. The documents tell us how these workers waged the battle against their noble, ecclesiastic, and bourgeois employers for a reduction of the working day, a battle which led to a trial before the Parlement of Paris.[27]

Archival documents[28] show us that real conflicts did in fact take place, predictable with the aid of the ordinance of the provost of Paris of 12 May 1395: "Whereas . . . several men of crafts such as weavers of linen or cotton, fullers, washers, masons, carpenters, and several other kinds of workers in Paris have wanted and do want to start and stop work at certain hours while they are being paid by the day as though they were on the job the whole day long," the provost reminds them that "the working day is fixed from the hour of sunrise until the hour of sunset, with meals to be taken at reasonable times."[29]

Documents from Auxerre and Sens, moreover, even when we allow for the fact that they concern a special category, enable us to understand the workers' goals in the struggle for mastery of their own labor time: at bottom, no doubt, was the desire for protection against the tyranny of employers in this respect, but there was also the more specific need that leisure time[30] be set aside along with working hours; and, in addition to regulation wage labor, they wanted time allotted for personal work or for a second job.[31]

It should be noted, however, that the influence of the agitation related to labor time in bringing about a general metamorphosis of social time was limited by certain further considerations.

In the first place, the question was a more general one of urban time, which served needs broader than those concerning the organization of labor. Economic needs were no doubt of great importance among urban concerns; a market bell appears here, a mill bell there, and so forth.[32] Defense of the city was of prime concern: witness the curfew (*ignitegium*) and watch bells. In the 1355 Aire text it is stated that the *clocquier* [bell tower] built by order of the aldermen, in which they asked that the work bell be placed, had been built in the first place "so the gate of said city could be raised at the stroke of daybreak and at vespers and to warn of any danger or difficulty which might arise as a result of evildoing or otherwise."

There were also the *campana bannalis, campana communitatis,* and *bancloche,* which were used to call the bourgeois to the defense or administration of their city, and sometimes the oath bell (Durlach's *Eidglocke*) or council bell (*Ratsglocke*).[33]

What was clearly new, however, in the contribution of the work bell or the city bell used for purposes of work was that instead of a time linked to *events,* which made itself felt only episodically and sporadically, there arose a regular, normal time. Rather than the *uncertain* clerical hours of the church bells, there were the *certain* hours spoken of by the bourgeois of Aire. Time was no longer associated with cataclysms or festivals but rather with daily life, a sort of chronological net in which urban life was caught.

In a century when quantitative elements were timidly making their way into administrative and mental structures,[34] the requirement that a better measure of labor be found was an important factor in the secularization process, of which the end of the monopoly of church bells in the measurement of time is an important index. Once again, however, in spite of the importance of the change, we should be careful not to make too bald a distinction between secular and religious time. At times, the two sorts of bells coexisted without confrontation or hostility. In York, for instance, between 1352 and 1370, at the work site of the cathedral itself, a work bell was installed, relieving the church bells of this function.[35] Nor should it be forgotten that, even in this sphere, the Church took initiatives. Monks, especially, as we shall see subsequently, were masters in the use of *schedules.* Cities, in imposing fines on councillors or aldermen who were late in answering the call of the city bell, were merely imitating the monastic communities' punishment of the tardy monk. The severe Columban punished tardiness at prayer with the singing of fifty psalms or with fifty lashes. The more indulgent Saint Benedict was content to have the guilty monk stand in the corner.[36]

Rung by ropes, that is, by hand, the work bell was no technical innovation. Decisive progress toward "certain hours" clearly came only with the invention and spread of mechanical clocks and the escapement system, which at last made it possible for the hour to achieve its mathematical sense, the twenty-fourth part of the day. It was undoubtedly in the fourteenth century that this essential step was taken. The principle of the invention was known by the end of the thirteenth century, and the second quarter of the fourteenth saw its application in urban clocks distributed throughout the major urbanized areas: northern Italy, Catalonia, northern France, southern England, Flanders, and Germany. With a more intensive study, it might be possible to determine whether the location of the crisis-ridden textile industry coincided more or less with the region where mechanical clocks were to be found.[37] From Normandy to Lombardy, the sixty-minute hour was firmly established; at the dawn of the preindustrial era, it replaced the day as the fundamental unit of labor time.[38]

Again, it is important to avoid exaggeration. For a long while to come, a time associated with natural rhythms, agrarian activity, and religious practice remained the primary temporal framework. Whatever they may have said about it, men of the Renaissance continued to live with an uncertain time.[39] It was a nonunified time, still urban rather than national, and unsynchronized with the state structures then being established: a time of *urban monads*. An indication of this may be found in the diversity of the zero hours of the new clocks: sometimes noon, sometimes midnight, which is not a very serious difference, but more frequently sunrise or sunset—such was the difficulty of freeing preindustrial time from natural time. In his *Voyage en Italie*, Montaigne, like many other travelers before him in the fifteenth and sixteenth centuries, noted what confusion and disorder were caused by the changing origin of time from one city to the next.[40]

Down to the time of Huygens, moreover, the new mechanical clocks were fragile, capricious, and irregular. There were numerous breakdowns of the new time, and the city clock was frequently out of order.[41] More than just a tool of daily life, the clock was still a marvel,[42] an ornament, a plaything of which the city was proud. It was a part of the municipal adornment, more a prestige item than a utilitarian device.

Furthermore, although the new time owed its inception primarily to the needs of a bourgeoisie of employers whose concern, in view of the crisis, was to improve the measurement of labor time—the source of their profits[43]—it was quickly taken over by higher authorities. An instrument of domination, it was also an object of amusement as well as a symbol of power for lords and princes.[44] It might become even more. In a capital city, for instance, it could become an effective symbol of government. In 1370, Charles V ordered that all the bells of

Paris be regulated by the clock at the Palais-Royal, which tolled the hours and the quarter-hours. The new time thus became the time of the state. The royal reader of Aristotle had domesticated rationalized time.

Though the change was imperfect and limited in certain respects, the disturbance of the chronological framework in the fourteenth century was also a mental and spiritual disturbance.

Perhaps the place to look for the appearance of a new concept of time is in science itself, namely, in scientific scholasticism. Here, time as an essence was supplanted by time as a conceptual form and mental tool; the mind could make use of time according to its needs, and might divide or measure it. It was a discontinuous time. To the question "does time exist outside the mind?" Pierre Auriol responded that time was nothing but "a being in the mind (i.e., a concept)" and, furthermore, that "the parts of time, which are perceived at the same time, have no rational basis but in the mind, which perceives all the parts which are involved in the act simultaneously and in them conceives succession, priority, and posteriority." Using the Aristotelian definition not exploited by Saint Thomas, according to which "time is the number of motion," Ockham stressed that this was not a "definition according to the thing" but rather a "definition according to the name."[45] As mechanics was being revolutionized by investigations of *impetus* and modern perspective was beginning to turn the visual world upside down, a new time was taking shape in scholasticism. The century of the clock was also the century of the cannon and of depth of field. For both scholar and merchant, time and space underwent joint transformation.

Perhaps the time of the mystics, especially the great Rhenish mystics, was also the fruit of a new approach or intuition which gave a fresh temporal dimension to the life of the soul.[46] The *devotio moderna* was developed in the rhythm of Suso's *Horologium Sapientiae*.

Where a more accessible, more typical piety is concerned, the disturbance can be plainly seen. The ancient, eternal theme of time's flight was present in Christianity, where it was at once exacerbated and assuaged by transformation into fear of eternal death[47] and stimulus to prepare for salvation. "Nothing is more precious than time," Saint Bernard is supposed to have said, stating a theme which was, in any case, taken up and propagated by his disciples.[48]

From the first half of the fourteenth century on, the theme became more specific and dramatic. Wasting one's time became a serious sin, a spiritual scandal. On the model of money and of the merchant who, in Italy, at least, became an accountant of time, there arose a calculating morality and miserly piety. One of the most significant exponents of the new spirituality was a preacher fashionable at the beginning of the fourteenth century, the Dominican Domenico Calva of Pisa, who died in 1342. He devoted two chapters of his *Disciplina degli Spirituali* to the "waste of time" and to the duty to "save and take account of time."[49] Beginning with traditional considerations of idleness and using a merchant's vocabulary (wasted time was for him the lost talent of the Gospel[50]—time was already money), he developed a whole spirituality of the calculated use of time. The idler who wastes his time and does not measure it was like an animal and not worthy of being considered a man: "egli si pone in tale stato che è piu vile che quello delle bestie." In this way, a humanism based on a nice computation of time was born.

The man representative of the new time was, indeed, the *humanist*, specifically the Italian humanist of the first generation of around 1400, himself a merchant or close to business circles. He introduced his business organization into everyday life and regulated his conduct according to a schedule, a significant secularization of the monastic manner of regulating the use of time. Yves Lefèvre has found one of these schedules, so characteristic of the behavior and mentality of the good Christian bourgeois humanist, at the end of a manuscript of the *Elucidarium* altered at the beginning of the fifteenth century.[51] Only the morning was reserved for work—"and all this must be done in the morning." The bourgeois businessman, by contrast with the common *laborator*, worked only half a day. "After eating" came the time of rest ("rest one hour"—one new hour!), diversion, and visiting, the leisure time and social life of men of substance.

Thus the first virtue of the humanist is a sense of time and its proper use. Gianozzi Manetti's biographer, for instance, extols his sensitivity to time.[52]

A more precisely measured time, the time of the hour and the clock, became one of man's primary tools: a Florentine humanist in the second half of the fourteenth century thought every study should have a clock in it.[53]

"Time is a gift of God and therefore cannot be sold." The taboo of time with which the Middle Ages had confronted the merchant was lifted at the dawn of the Renaissance. The time which used to belong to God alone was thereafter the property of man. The famous text of Leon Battista Alberti is worth rereading:

> GIANOZZO: There are three things which man may say properly belong to him: his fortune, his body—
> LIONARDO: And what might the third be?
> GIANOZZO: Ah! a very precious thing indeed! Even these hands and these eyes are not so much my own.
> LIONARDO: Incredible! What is it?
> GIANOZZO: Time, my dear Lionardo, time, my children.[54]

What counts hereafter is the hour—the new measure of life: "never waste a single hour of time."[55]

The cardinal virtue of the humanist was temperance, which, in the new iconography[56] as early as the fourteenth century was given the clock as attribute. Henceforth, the clock was to be the measure of all things.

A NOTE ON TRIPARTITE SOCIETY, MONARCHICAL IDEOLOGY, AND ECONOMIC RENEWAL IN NINTH- TO TWELFTH-CENTURY CHRISTENDOM

A description of society dividing it into three categories or orders appeared as a theme in medieval literature at the end of the ninth century, flourished during the eleventh, and by the twelfth had become a commonplace. According to Adalbero of Laon's classic formulation at the beginning of the eleventh century, the three components of this tripartite society were *oratores, bellatores,* and *laboratores,* or clergy, warriors, and workers.

The origins of the schema need not concern us here. Whether it was a traditional representation common to the Indo-European peoples generally,[1] or more particularly to the Celts or Germans, or, on the other hand, a schema which appears in every society at a particular stage of development,[2] whether it was the resurgence of an old theme from previous civilizations or an original creation of medieval Christian thought, the important point for our purposes lies elsewhere.

Hitherto absent from Christian literature, this theme appeared between the ninth and eleventh centuries because it corresponded to a new need. It was a conceptual image which corresponded to new social and political structures. Like every conceptual tool, it did not aim merely to define, describe, and explain a new situation. It was also a new instrument of social action. In the first place, on the most obvious level of action, it was an instrument of propaganda.

It seems clear to me that the elaboration and dissemination of the theme of tripartite society should be related to the progress of monarchical ideology and to the formation of national monarchies in post-Carolingian Christendom.

To support this hypothesis, I will consider three examples.

The first medieval text in which the theme of tripartite society is encountered in an explicit form is a passage from King Alfred the

Great's Anglo-Saxon translation of Boethius' *De consolatione philosophiae*, which dates from the last quarter of the ninth century.[3] It is significant that this passage was added by Alfred to Boethius' text. It treats, moreover, a passage devoted to the portrait of the ideal king. Having defined the three orders of society, Alfred describes them as "tools and materials" necessary to the accomplishment of the work of the monarchy and to the exercise of power "with virtue and efficiency." Finally, it is possible to relate this text to Alfred's actual efforts to establish a solid and prosperous state under the royal aegis.[4]

The second example relates to the beginnings of the Capetian monarchy in France. While the famous passage by Adalbero of Laon, which probably dates from the years 1025–27,[5] explicitly lists the three orders of the tripartite schema, there is a less explicit but earlier text from around 995 by Abbo of Fleury, which may be considered an approximate version of the tripartite theme and, more precisely, an index of the transition from a bipartite to a tripartite schema.[6] Abbo takes the two orders which, according to a commonplace of Christian literature, constitute society, viz., clergy and laymen, and subdivides the latter into two suborders, the farmers (*agricolae*) and the warriors (*agonistae*). Of course, both Abbo of Fleury's *Apologeticus adversus Arnulphum Episcopum Aurelianensem ad Hugonem et Robertum reges Francorum* and Adalbero of Laon's *Carmen ad Robertum regem* were occasional works intended to support the role of the regular clergy, in the first case, and the secular clergy in the second; but both works, in seeking royal support for a particular party, are naturally led to define and strengthen the monarchical ideology.[7] Moreover, by virtue of their geographic location at the northern and southern extremities of the Capetian realm, both the monastery of Fleury and the episcopal church of Laon played spiritual and political roles of the first order in the establishment of the Capetian dynasty and the development of the monarchical ideology in *Francia occidentalis*.[8]

The third example takes us to the eastern frontiers of Latin Christendom in the early twelfth century, to the Poland of Boleslav the Wry-mouthed. In his celebrated *Cronica et Gesta Ducum sive Principum Polonorum*, written in the years 1113–16, the anonymous chronicler known as Gallus Anonymus gives a description of the elements of Polish strength in his Prologue, in which he divides the population into *milites bellicosi* and *rustici laboriosi*. With the clerical order left aside, as in Abbo of Fleury's text, these two terms refer to the two lay orders and should be regarded as an expression of the tripartite schema of society.[9] The differences of vocabulary between this text and Abbo's, and the analogies between these terms and Adalbero's *bellicose soldiers* and *laborious peasants*, underscore better than would identical terminology the ideological convergence of these three passages and Alfred the Great's text. Even more than the earlier texts, that of Gallus Anonymus was closely connected with monarchical propaganda. The entourage of Boleslav the Wry-mouthed that inspired the chronicler had in fact wanted the work to be a eulogy of the Polish state under Boleslav the Bold (992–1025) and a propaganda instrument for the restoration of the power and dignity of the monarchy in Poland.[10]

Whether or not their efforts were crowned with success, these three texts show that, from the end of the ninth until the beginning of the twelfth century, throughout Latin Christendom, the tripartite schema can be related to the efforts of certain secular and ecclesiastical circles to lay the ideological foundations for the consolidation of national monarchies.

To understand how this theme could have served as a monarchical and national ideal, we must first make explicit what social and mental realities corresponded to the three orders of the schema—especially to the third order, which, in my view, is the one that gives the whole model its most original and significant aspect.

There are no great difficulties in characterizing the first two orders, although it is not without interest to take note of certain special features in the definition of each, or in the nature of their relations with the king as implied by the schema.

The clerical order was characterized by prayer. This was perhaps indicative of a certain primacy accorded to the monastic ideal or, rather, to a certain form of monasticism;[11] but it was especially related to the essential nature of clerical power, which came from its specialized capacity to obtain divine aid by means of its professional activity, prayer. As king of the *oratores*, the monarch in a sense shared the ecclesiastical and religious nature of the clergy, as well as their privilege.[12] He maintained, moreover, an ambivalent relationship with the clerical order, being both protector and protected with regard to the Church, a relationship worked out by the Carolingian clergy in the ninth century.[13]

The military order, too, was perhaps a little more complex than is at first apparent. No doubt it was less unified and coherent in reality than was the clerical order. The term *milites*, which, from the twelfth century on, became the usual designation of the military order within the tripartite schema, no doubt came to correspond to the emerging class of knights within the lay aristocracy, but it brought more confusion than clarity into the relations between the social reality and the ideological themes that claimed to express it. In any case, the appearance, between the ninth and twelfth centuries, of *bellatores* in the tripartite schema corresponded to the formation of a new nobility[14] and, during a time when military technique was undergoing profound transformation, to the preponderance of the warrior function in this new aristocracy. As for the king of the *bellatores,* he was primarily a military chief and had the same ambivalent relation to the warrior order as the "feudal" king, being head of this military aristocracy and at the same time placed outside and above it.

Although it is easy to see what these first two terms in the tripartite schema of society designated, it is not so with the third term. Who were the *laboratores*?[15] While it is clear, as the equivalent terms *agricolae* and *rustici* (encountered previously) attest, that we are speaking of rural people during the period under consideration and in the regions where these texts were written,[16] it is more difficult to determine what social group is being designated here. Generally, the term is taken to embrace all the rest of society, the whole working population, in other words, essentially the peasant mass. This interpretation is lent credence by the phenomenon of increasing uniformity in peasant conditions, observable throughout large areas of Christendom between the tenth and twelfth centuries.[17] From the twelfth century on, no doubt under the dual influence of economic and social evolution of both cities and countryside, the third order generally included the totality of manual labor, or what we would call the primary sector. As early as the period we are considering, certain authors tended to use the word *laboratores* in this broad sense.[18]

For the authors and first users and proponents of the schema, however, I believe the term had a narrower and more precise meaning, which can be explained by certain economic and social innovations. Such an interpretation, I think, appreciably alters the significance of the tripartite schema of society as an instrument of national monarchical ideology between the ninth and twelfth centuries.

From the end of the eighth century or even earlier, words belonging to the family of *labor* tended to designate forms of rural labor involving an idea of development, improvement, and quantitative or qualitative progress in agriculture. *Labor* and *labores* were the results, fruits, and profits of labor rather than the labor itself. Beginning in the ninth century, there was appreciable agricultural progress in many regions, and it was around this family of words that the vocabulary designating such progress seems to have crystallized, whether it concerned extension of the cultivated area by land-clearing (and *labores* could be synonymous with *novalia,* the tithe exacted from newly cleared land)[19] or increased yields due to technical improvement (expanded tillage, improvement of "methods," the use of fertilizer, perfection of the iron tool—while awaiting the diffusion of the asymmetrical plow and the use of the horse).[20]

Thus *laboratores* came more particularly to designate those agricultural workers who were the principal artisans and beneficiaries of economic progress, an elite, a group of peasant *improvers*, or, as nicely defined in a tenth-century text, "those, the best, who are *laboratores*."[21]

The third order of the tripartite schema, then, consisted of an economic elite which was in the front rank of the agricultural expansion of Christendom between the ninth and twelfth centuries. Giving expression to a consecrated, sublimated image of society, this schema did not include all social categories but only those worthy of representing fundamental social values, which were religious, military, and, for the first time in medieval Christendom, economic. Even in the area of labor, medieval society remained, culturally and ideologically, an aristocratic society.

The king of the *laboratores* was the head and guarantor of the economic order and material prosperity. This was largely because he maintained the peace indispensable to economic progress.[22] The ideological purpose of the tripartite schema was to express the harmony, interdependence, and solidarity of classes and orders. The three orders constituted the social structure of the state, which would collapse if the equilibrium among the three groups, each of which stood in need of the two others, were not respected. The equilibrium could only be guaranteed by a chief, an arbiter. This arbiter was, of course, the king. The monarchy only became more necessary when economic function made its appearance as an ideological value. This marked the end of the duality of pope and emperor, which corresponded more to the distinction between clerics and laymen than to the difficult and unrealizable distinction between the spiritual and the temporal.

The kings were to become the real lieutenants of God on Earth. The gods of the ancient mythologies were combined in triads which grouped together the three fundamental functions.[23] In a society which had become monotheistic, the monarch concentrated in his person all three functions[24] and expressed the unity of a trinitarian national society.

Medieval kingship was thus the beneficiary of the tripartite schema, but there was also a danger that it would fall victim to it if the irrepressible class struggle should turn all three orders against the arbiter-king. This is the meaning of the nightmare of King Henry I of England, who dreamed in 1130 that first the *laboratores*, then the *bellatores*, and finally the *oratores* attacked him, the first with their tools, the second with their weapons, and the third with the emblems of their office.[25] After that, the *laboratores* appeared no longer as a collaborating elite but rather as a hostile mass, a dangerous class.

LICIT AND ILLICIT TRADES IN THE
MEDIEVAL WEST

Every society has its social hierarchy, which is revealing of its structures and mentality. It is not my intention here to outline the sociological schema of medieval Christendom and the metamorphoses it underwent.[1] In one way or another, the trades found their place in it, a broad or a narrow place according to the era. My intention is to study the hierarchy of trades in the medieval West. Noble and ignoble, licit and illicit trades—such categories overlay economic and social realities and, to an even greater degree, mentalities. In the present essay I am particularly interested in the latter, with the understanding, of course, that the relations between concrete situations and mental images not be neglected. Mentality is what changes most slowly in societies and civilizations; yet it is imperative that mentality follow and adapt to infrastructural transformations in spite of resistances, delays, and different temporal rhythms of development. The portrait we present, therefore, will not be a static one but rather a portrait of an evolution, of which we will try to identify the stimuli, agents, and modalities. What was held in contempt in the year 1000 will occupy a proud position at the dawn of the Renaissance. We shall here attempt to follow the wheel of Fortune as it determines the movement of the status of the medieval trades.

Certain of these trades, such as usury and prostitution, were unreservedly condemned, while others incurred condemnation only in certain cases.[2] This depended on the circumstances (for example, all "servile occupations," or *opera servilia*, were banned on Sundays), on the motives (commercial trade was proscribed when conducted with an eye to profit—*lucri causa*—but authorized when for the purpose of serving one's neighbor or the common good), and, above all, on the sort of person involved, which generally meant that certain activities were forbidden to clerics.[3] It is clear, however, that even in these latter cases the trades thus prohibited from time to time were in fact held in contempt, whether because they had been placed on the black list due to their having been traditional objects of contempt or, on the other hand, because, proscribed for reasons long since forgotten, their presence on the list in itself aroused such contempt. When a profession was forbidden to a cleric in a religious and "clerical" society like that of the medieval West, this was clearly no recommendation; the profession so marked earned an opprobrium which reflected on its lay practitioners. This was felt by surgeons and notaries, among others.

No doubt there were both practical and juridical distinctions between forbidden trades, or *negotia illicita,* and occupations which were merely dishonorable or ignoble, *inhonesta mercimonia, artes indecorae, vilia officia.*[4] Both classes, however, were included in the category of contemptible professions in which we are interested here as a component of mentality. It is significant, moreover, that if we were to give an exhaustive list of these professions, it would be necessary to include virtually all medieval professions,[5] for they vary according to the document, region, or era, and sometimes grow inordinately in number. It will suffice to cite those which occur most frequently: innkeepers, butchers, jongleurs, mountebanks, magicians, alchemists, doctors, surgeons, soldiers,[6] pimps, prostitutes, notaries, merchants,[7] among the first ranks. But also fullers, weavers, saddlers, dyers, pastry makers, cobblers;[8] gardeners, painters, fishermen, barbers;[9] bailiffs, game wardens, customs officers, exchange brokers, tailors, perfumers, tripe sellers, millers, etc.,[10] figured on the index.[11]

Behind such prohibitions, we find survivals of primitive mentalities enduring in the medieval mind: the old taboos of primitive societies.

In the first place, there is the blood taboo. Primarily affecting butchers and executioners, it also bore on surgeons and barbers, and apothecaries who engaged in the practice of bleeding—all of whom were more harshly treated than physicians; in addition, soldiers were affected. The sanguinary medieval West seems to have oscillated between relish and horror of the blood it spilled.

Next comes the taboo of impurity, of the unclean, which struck fullers, dyers, and cooks. Textile workers, the "blue thumbs" of the fourteenth-century riots, were held in contempt. At the beginning of the thirteenth century, John of Garland shows them exposed to the hostility of their peers, especially women, who found them repugnant.[12] Cooks and laundrymen, too, were regarded as contemptible, as we find naïvely expressed around the year 1000 by the bishop Adalbero of Laon, who, in praising clerics exempt from servile labors, declares: "They are neither butchers nor inn-keepers...and know nothing of the searing heat of a greasy pot...they are not laundrymen and stoop not to boil linen."[13] It is with some astonishment that one notices this same aversion in Saint Thomas Aquinas, who, in the midst of a philosophical and theological argument, pauses to place dishwashers, curiously enough, at the bottom of the scale of professions, owing to their contact with the unclean![14]

The taboo on money played an important role in the struggle of societies living within the framework of a natural economy against the invasion of a monetary economy. This panicky flight before the precious metal coin incited medieval theologians like Saint Bernard to pronounce curses on money and aroused hostility against merchants—who were attacked, in particular, as usurers and ex-change agents—and, more generally, against all handlers of money,[15] as well as all wage earners, who were grouped together under the name "mercenaries"; the texts are particularly hard on those champions who faced ordeals for a fee in place of the person concerned, and on prostitutes, an extreme case of *turpe lucrum*, ill-gotten gains.

To these atavisms, Christianity added its own condemnations. First, it should be noted that it often cloaked primitive taboos in its new ideological guise. Soldiers, for example, were condemned, as in question 1 of case 23 of the Decretum of Gratian, not directly as spillers of blood, but indirectly, for contravening the commandment "Thou shalt not kill" and in view of the judgment of Saint Matthew (26:52): "All they that take the sword shall perish with the sword."

It should also be noted that, in this regard, Christianity was often influenced by its twin heritage of culture and mentality, Jewish and Greco-Roman, and was ideologically dominated by the idea that the original activities of the ancestors were morally superior. Thus nonagricultural trades were accepted only with great difficulty by these descendants of farmers and shepherds, and the Church often repeated the anathemas of a Plato or a Cicero,[16] spokesmen for the landed aristocracies of antiquity.

Most important, however, Christianity lengthened the list of for-bidden professions in the light of its own particular view. Thus trades in which it was difficult to engage without committing one of the deadly sins were condemned. Lust, for example, was the basis for condemnation of innkeepers and bathkeepers, whose premises were frequently notorious, as well as jongleurs, who incited lascivious and obscene dances (as the comparison with Salome's impious dance makes clear), tavern keepers, who lived on the sale of the triply damned pleasure of wine, gambling, and dance, and even women in the textile trade, who were accused of supplying large contingents to prostitution,[17] which must have been at least partly true, in view of the miserable wages they received. Avarice, or greed, was in a sense the professional sin of both merchants and men of the law—lawyers, notaries, judges. The condemnation of gluttony naturally led to the condemnation of cooks. Pride and avarice no doubt added to the condemnation of soldiers already established on grounds of their blood spilling. Albertus Magnus enumerated the three principal dangers of the military profession as follows: "murder of the innocents," "the lure of greater gains," and "the vain display of strength." Even sloth could be used to justify the presence on the index of the beggar's profession, or, more precisely, the able-bodied beggar who "does not want to work out of sloth."[18]

In a more profound sense, trades which were opposed to certain of Christianity's most important tendencies or dogmas were condemned. Lucrative professions were attacked in the name of *contemptus mundi,* the contempt for this world which every Christian ought to exhibit. Jurists, too, were condemned, the Church stressing the opposition between legitimate canon law and pernicious civil law.[19] More generally, Christianity tended to condemn all forms of *negotium,* all secular activity; on the other hand, it encouraged a certain *otium,* an idleness which displayed confidence in Providence.

Men were children of God and hence participated in his divinity. The body was a living temple, and whatever soiled it was sinful. Thus the trades related to lust, or supposed to be, were especially stigmatized.

The brotherhood of man—of Christians, at least—was the basis for the condemnation of usurers, who ignored Christ's precept: "Lend, hoping for nothing again—*nihil inde sperantes*" (Luke 6:35).

On an even more profound level, man's work was supposed to be in the image of God's.[20] God's work, of course, was Creation. Any profession, therefore, which did not create was bad or inferior. It was imperative to create, as the peasant, for example, created the harvest, or, at least, to transform raw material, like the artisan, into an object. If there was no creation, then there should be transformation (*mutare*), modification (*emendare*), or improvement (*meliorare*).[21] The merchant, who created nothing, was thus condemned. This was an essential mental structure of Christian society, sustained by a theology and morality developed during a precapitalist regime. Medieval ideology was materialistic in the strict sense. Only production of matter had value. The abstract value defined by capitalist economy eluded its grasp, disgusted it, and was condemned by it.

The portrait we have sketched thus far is valid particularly for the early Middle Ages. Essentially rural during this period, Western society held in contempt any activity not directly linked to the land, practically without exception. Humble peasant labor derived its humility from the interdiction of *opera servilia*, or servile jobs, on Sundays, and from the fact that the dominant classes, the military and landed aristocracies, held themselves aloof from all manual labor. A few artisans or, rather, artists were no doubt haloed with a special prestige which gave positive satisfaction to the magical mentality. Among these were goldsmiths, ironsmiths, and, especially, sword makers. Numerically, they have little importance. To the historian of mentalities, they are more sorcerers than practitioners of a trade. Their prestige attached to the techniques which produced luxury and the means of power in a primitive society . . .

Between the ninth and the thirteenth centuries, however, the context changed. An economic and social revolution took place in the Christian West, of which urban expansion was the most striking symptom and the division of labor the most important characteristic. New trades came into being or developed, new professional categories made their appearance or grew more substantial, and new socioprofessional groups, strong in numbers and by virtue of their roles, demanded and won esteem and even a prestige appropriate to their strength. They wanted consideration, and they got it. The time was over when they could be held in contempt.

There was a revision of attitudes with regard to trades. The number of forbidden or disgraceful professions decreased, and there were many new grounds for excusing the practice of any of the previously condemned trades.

The major intellectual instrument of this revision was scholasticism. A method of distinctions, it overthrew the crude, Manichaean, and obscure classification of the prescholastic mentality. As a casuistry, which, in the twelfth and thirteenth centuries was its great merit before becoming its great defect, it distinguished occupations illicit in themselves, by nature (*ex natura*), from those condemnable according to the case (*ex occasione*).

What was important was that the list of trades condemned without remission, *ex natura*, was greatly and continually reduced.

Usury, for instance, which in the middle of the twelfth century was still damned without recourse in the Decretum of Gratian, would be differentiated by imperceptible degrees into a variety of practices, increasing numbers of which gradually gained toleration.[22]

Before long, only jongleurs and prostitutes were banned from Christian society. They enjoyed a de facto toleration, however, which was even accompanied by theoretical accommodations and attempts at justification.

In the thirteenth century, Berthold of Regensburg rejected only the rabble of vagabonds and vagrants, the *vagi,* from Christian society. They made up the *familia diaboli,* the devil's family, in contrast to all other trades or "estates" henceforth admitted into Christ's family, the *familia Christi.*[23]

Condemnations placed increasingly strict and exceptional conditions on the prohibition of a given occupation, which was consequently rehabilitated and legitimated thereafter in the form in which it was regularly practiced. Thus, for instance, on grounds of bad intentions, only merchants who acted out of greed, *ex cupiditate,* or love of profit, *lucri causa,* had to be condemned. This left a large field open to "good" intentions, that is, to all sorts of camouflage. Judgments of intention were a first step in the direction of tolerance.

Besides these condemnations *ex causa* and *ex intentione,* there were prohibitions on individual grounds, or for reasons of time and place.

One sign of the change of mentalities was that prohibitions incurred by clerics *ex persona* came to appear less as marks of the eminent dignity of the minor orders than as vexations limiting their empire. The fields of medicine and civil law were abandoned to laymen (Pope Alexander III, in 1163, forbade the regular clergy to leave their convents *ad physicam legesve mundanas legendas,* to teach medicine or civil law), as well as the field of commerce. This did not come without protest. The protests attest to the fact that both the profits and the prestige of the clergy were diminished by such interdictions.

Certain prohibitions were related to time. The prohibition of night work, for example, ultimately protected the trades and countered unfair practices.

Finally, some condemnations attached to particular places. Thus professional activities might be proscribed in dubious locales (*ex loci vilitate*) or, by contrast, in churches (*ex loci eminentia*). This led to the development of "professional locales" and specialized shops, just as the restrictions placed on clerics assured monopolies to lay specialists and technicians.

Significantly, the reasons for granting excuses and the means by which they were justified indicate a radical evolution. The traditional excuse of "necessity" was now extended to a greater number of cases, including the indigent cleric who was obliged to engage in a trade (with a few exceptions), and the peasant who had to bring in his harvest on a Sunday for fear of rain.

There was also the excuse of good intentions, *recta intentio,* which could justify the arms manufacturer interested only in equipping the combatants in a licit cause, *ad usum licitum,* as well as the manufacturers and sellers of leisure games, which could be a remedy for sadness and black thoughts, *ad recreationem vel remedium tristitiae vel noxiarum cogitationum.* Thus, with the subjectivization of psychological life, an appreciation of inner dispositions replaced consideration of external behavior alone. Professional taboos receded with the assertion of the individual conscience.

Two further justifications were established at the end of the twelfth century. The first was concern for the common good, a notion which achieved the highest status with the growth of public, urban, and princely administration, and which was canonized by Aristotelian philosophy. In this way, "mechanical trades, such as textiles, clothing, and the like, which are necessary to man's needs,"[24] were legitimated. This was also the way the merchant was justified, as his efforts were responsible for products unavailable in one country being brought there from abroad, a special case of serving the common welfare, which was, of course, related to the resumption of "international" trade over long distances and to the beginnings of a *Weltwirtschaft*, a "world economy."

The second new justification was labor. No longer grounds for contempt and a mark of inferiority, labor became meritorious. The pains taken justified not only the practice of a trade but the profit it earned. Thus professors and masters in the new urban schools, which proliferated in the twelfth century and became universities in the thirteenth, gained acceptance. In contrast with the practice among the monks of the monastic schools, these new teachers were paid for their instruction in the form of salaries from the public authorities, special ecclesiastical prebends, or, most frequently, monies paid by the students themselves. These intellectual wage earners, who swelled the ranks of the traditionally contemptible category of "mercenaries," encountered a strong opposition, which condemned the sale of knowledge, "God's gift which cannot be sold."[25] Soon, however, the academic's remuneration came to be justified by the labor he expended in the service of his students— wages for his toil rather than price of his knowledge.

By observation of three exemplary trades, we can follow the development of the new attitude toward professional activity. These three cases were particularly delicate, involving trades which continued to be regarded as especially "dangerous," quite difficult to practice without committing sins.

We will first examine the jongleurs.[26] In the early thirteenth century, we can identify three types of jongleurs: acrobats, who contorted their bodies shamelessly, undressed without modesty, and wore frightening disguises; jesters, those parasites of the courts and noble entourages, who hurled insulting remarks around and were useless vagrants good for nothing but injury and slander; and musicians, whose aim was to charm their listeners. The first two categories were condemned; in the third, another distinction was made between those who frequented public balls and revels and encouraged wild abandon and those who sang gests and lives of saints and brought consolation to the sad and troubled. Only the latter group engaged in legitimate activity, but this approval was an open door through which jongleurs of all kinds were to make a place for themselves in the continually expanding world of allowable professions.

We can see how the newcomers were integrated into "proper" society, not in a merely theoretical but in a practical sense. One way was by means of anecdotes, taken as *exemplum*, which we find in stereotypical form in sermons and edifying works. Thus the story is told of the jongleur who questions Pope Alexander III as to the possibility of his being saved. The pontiff asks if he knows any other trade and, the response being negative, assures him that he need not live in fear because of his trade, provided he avoids doubtful and obscene behavior.[27]

The case of the merchant is the best known and the most highly charged with consequences. Decried for so long, his trade became the object of an increasing number of excuses, justifications, and even expressions of respect. Having become classics in scholastic exposés, certain of these are well known. They are related to the risks taken by the merchants: damages actually sustained (*damnum emergens*), tying up of cash in long-term undertakings (*lucrum cessans*), hazards of trade (*periculum sortis*). The uncertainties of commercial activity (*ratio incertitudinis*) justified the merchant's profit, even the interest he obtained from the money involved in certain transactions and thus, to an ever greater extent, "usury," hitherto damned.

Above all, the merchant was justified by his labor and by his service to the common good, his social utility. Theologians, canon lawyers, and poets were all in agreement.[28]

In his manual of confession from the early thirteenth century, Thomas of Chobham wrote: "There would be great poverty in many countries if merchants did not bring what abounds in one place to another where these same things are lacking. They can therefore justly receive the price of their labor."

Saint Thomas Aquinas: "If a person engages in trade with an eye to the public utility and wants things necessary to existence not to lack in the country, then money, rather than being the end of the activity, is only claimed as remuneration for labor."

And at the beginning of the fourteenth century, Gilles le Muisit, canon of Tournai, in his *Dit des Marchands:*

Nul pays ne se poet de li seus gouvrener;
Pour chou vont marchéant travillier et pener
Chou qui faut ès pays, en tous règnes mener;
Se ne les doit-on mie sans raison fourmener.

Chou que marchéant vont delà mer, dechà mer
Pour pourvir les pays, che les font entr'amer;
Pour riens ne se feroient boin marchéant blasmer
Mais ils se font amer, loyal et bon clamer.

Carités et amours par les pays nouriscent;
Pour chou doit on moult goïr s'il enrikiscent.
C'est pités, quant en tière boin marchéant povriscent
Or en ait Dieus les âmes quant dou siècle partiscent!

For itself no country can provide; / For that merchants travel far and wide; / Their work and toil feeds the nation / So refrain from baseless fulmination. Merchants cross the seas and back / To bring each nation what it lacks / No good merchant would reap blame / But love, honor, and a just good name. They contribute to the love of nations / Thus their wealth is cause for jubilations / A good trader's ruin is cause for pity / May their souls see the light of the Heavenly City.

In one astonishing text, we even see the outline of a justification of prostitution. The problem raised by the legitimacy of earnings from prostitution—the most infamous classification in the mercenary category—a problem traditionally resolved in a negative way, found a practical application in the case of the receivability of alms and gifts offered by the "mad women." This case caused quite a stir in Paris in the late twelfth century. When Notre Dame was being constructed, we are told, a group of prostitutes asked the bishop for permission to offer a window in honor of the Virgin, a very special instance of a guild window, which, of course, had to exclude any representation of the activities of this particular trade. Embarrassed, the bishop made consultations and finally refused. Today we possess the opinion offered by the author of one of the first manuals of confession, Thomas of Chobham. The learned canon's argument is curious.

Prostitutes must be counted among the mercenaries. They hire out their bodies and supply labor... Whence this principle of secular justice: she does evil in being a prostitute, but she does not do evil in receiving the price of her labor, it being admitted that she is a prostitute. Whence the fact that it is possible to repent of practicing prostitution while keeping the profits of prostitution for the purpose of giving alms. If, however, prostitution is engaged in for pleasure, and the body is hired out so that it may experience ecstasy, then one's labor is not being hired and the profit is as shameful as the act. Similarly, if the prostitute perfumes and adorns herself so as to attract with false allures and give the impression of a beauty and seductiveness which she does not possess, the client buying what he sees, which, in this case, is deceptive, the prostitute then commits a sin, and she should not keep the profit it brings her. If the client saw her as she really is, he would give her only a pittance, but as she appears beautiful and brilliant to him, he gives a handsome sum. In this case, she should keep only the pittance and return the rest to the client she has deceived, or to the Church, or to the poor.

So great has the prestige of justification by labor become by the end of the twelfth century that our author lets himself become involved in outlining a morality of the profession of prostitution. Thomas of Chobham does finally get hold of himself, and, seeming suddenly to recall that there are overwhelming reasons for condemning prostitution "in itself," *ex natura*, he nullifies the potential impact of his earlier argument. The example shows, nevertheless, in an extreme case, virtually a reductio ad absurdum, how a contemptible trade could be legitimated.

The world was subsequently conceived as a vast workplace on the analogy of the urban workplace in which various trades collaborated. Each profession had its material role to play, and its own spiritual value. No trade was an obstacle to salvation, each had its Christian vocation, and all belonged to the *familia Christi*, which bound all good workers together. Sociological models to integrate and structure old and new professions proliferated. The traditional framework of the liberal arts opened up at this time to accept the new intellectual and scholarly specializations. Even more noteworthy, the previously scorned mechanical arts were admitted.[29] Taking up the old anthropomorphic image of the state as a republic in which each trade, including peasants and artisans, represents a part of the body, John of Salisbury emphasized the complementarity and harmony of all professional activities.[30] Honorius Augustodunensis made science man's fatherland and traced his intellectual and spiritual itinerary from city to city, each symbolizing an area of knowledge and a set of trades.[31]

It is at this point that we feel very clearly the need to undertake a more extensive search for the deeper causes of this fundamental evolutionary development in mentalities and behavior relative to trade.

The efficacy of the economic transformations we have seen occurring at various times and places and enforcing fairly rapid and radical changes in attitudes was due primarily to the social evolution, which explains the historical evolution of licit and illicit trades, of professions which were esteemed and others which were held in contempt.

Initially, the society was rural and military, closed on itself, and dominated by two classes, the military and landed aristocracy, and the clergy, which also possessed extensive holdings in land.

There were, then, two reasons why most trades were held in contempt. The first was applicable to the activity of the serf, who was, in this respect, the slave's heir. We recall the long list of "servile works" which went with rural toil (which, in spite of everything, benefited from the halo surrounding the agrarian world in general) and humbled the servile crafts and trades.

The second reason for contempt was applicable to mercenaries, an incongruous category which bore a twofold curse, one attaching to those who alienated their freedom (at a time when freedom and nobility were one and the same thing) and the other to those who worked for money.

Finally, the whole class of *laboratores*, or workers, the mob of lower orders, was an object of contempt—in contrast to the upper strata of *oratores et bellatores*, who prayed and did battle, clergy and knighthood.

The two dominant classes were not, however, on an equal footing. In this hierarchic world, the clergy made the lay aristocracy aware of the distance which separated them. Only the clergy was untainted. It felt a certain contempt for the lay lords and their military trade, which caused blood to be spilled. The clergy was not a stranger to a certain antimilitarism. Cloaked in purity and ingenuousness, it denounced the men with blood-stained hands, who were both allies and competitors.

With the economic renewal of the ninth through thirteenth centuries, however, and the reawakening of long-distance trade and urban expansion, the social landscape changed. New social strata, such as artisans, merchants, and technicians, appeared in connection with new activities. Soon indispensable in a material sense, they wanted their importance confirmed by social consideration. To accomplish this, they had to overcome economic prejudices against labor, the essence of their activity and fundamental feature of their condition. Among the means used to promote their rise, we will single out only religion, which was a necessary instrument in any material and spiritual advance in the medieval world. Each trade, for instance, had its patron saint, sometimes several. The guilds magnified their occupations by having their saintly protectors portrayed in the practice of a given profession with its tools and other symbols of the trade, and so put an end to a contempt which became unseemly with regard to an activity which could boast such powerful and venerable representatives.

These developments were not identical in all respects throughout Christendom. In Italy particularly, the triumph of the new strata was such that the old aristocracy quickly adopted some aspects of the newcomers' way of life. To work or engage in trade was not an occupation unworthy of a noble Italian. The aristocracy there had been urbanized quite early. Bishop Otto of Freising accompanied his nephew, the emperor Frederick Barbarossa, into Italy in the middle of the twelfth century and was astonished to observe that artisans and merchants there enjoyed considerable respect.[32] What must have been the reaction of this thoroughly feudal personage upon seeing Italian lords lower themselves to plebeian occupations? We can imagine his indignation when we read the words of that free spirit, Michel de Montaigne, who was likewise surprised by the Italian business nobility.[33] Elsewhere, in France particularly, the nobility's hostility to labor had hardened and become institutionalized in the social and mental phenomenon known as derogation.[34] Louis XI could do nothing about it. Two sorts of contempt subsequently confronted one another, that of the aristocrats for the toilers, and that of the workers for the idle.

If the world of labor was ever unified in opposition to the world of prayer and war, it was a unity which did not last long. There was unification against the old ruling classes, with the lower strata of artisans infiltrating the citadel of social respect through the breach opened by the upper strata of urban society, and the wealthy bourgeois using the weight and strength of the working masses against Church and nobility. But these social categories were soon differentiated on both spiritual and material levels. A split occurred, separating the upper stratum of urban society, which, for the sake of convenience, we shall call the bourgeoisie, from the lower strata: on one side were large merchants, exchange agents, and the wealthy; on the other, small artisans, journeymen, and the poor. In Italy, in Florence, for instance, the contrast was established even within the institutions; "major arts" were opposed to "minor arts," whose practitioners were excluded from municipal functions.

A new frontier of contempt arose right in the midst of the new classes and even within professions. Discrimination was aided by the extreme fragmentation of trades. In Paris in 1292 there were 130 regulated trades: 18 in foodstuffs, 22 in metalworking, 22 in textiles and leather, 36 in clothing, etc. This fragmentation was horizontal to a degree but vertical to an even greater degree. Weavers were placed near the bottom of the scale in textiles, but above fullers and dyers; cobblers below bootmakers, surgeons and barber-apothecaries below medical doctors, who became increasingly bookish and were willing to leave practice, which was contemptible, to base practitioners.

The Florentine Giovanni Villani, a typical representative of the upper business bourgeoisie in Italy, had nothing but contempt for the Flemish rabble of inferior tradesmen.[35]

Work in itself no longer constituted the distinction between respectable and contemptible categories; instead, it was manual labor that had come to be the key factor in the frontier between respect and contempt. With academics in the universities leading the way, intellectuals hastened to place themselves on the right side of the line. "I don't work with my hands," exclaimed "poor" Rutebeuf. Across from the *manouvriers* and *brassiers*, who worked with hands and arms, was the patrician world, the new aristocracy, consisting of all those who did no manual labor: employers and rentiers. Similarly, in the country, the lords became rentiers of the soil and crushed the peasant lower than ever under the weight of feudal rights and seigneurial contempt.

The new contempt carried with it both survivals of ancestral taboos and feudal prejudices. A striking instance was the case of the butchers, some of whom were among the most well-to-do citizens of the towns. Their wealth was not enough, however, to overcome the barrier of contempt.[36] They were thus a leading element in numerous popular revolts in the fourteenth and fifteenth centuries, supplying the "common" people with cash to incite their uprising and goading them with their grudges. Caboche is typical of these rebels.

Faced with this evolution, the Church followed suit. At first caught up in the feudal world and sanctioning its contempt for trades, it came to accept the rise of the new strata and often encouraged them in their climb, was an early protecter of merchants, and provided new socioprofessional groups with theoretical and spiritual justification of their condition and their social and psychological advance. But it also condoned the noble and bourgeois reaction. In fact, trade did not figure on its horizon. Although it came to admit during the course of the Middle Ages that there were no contemptible trades, the Church was too close to the ruling classes to have a decisive influence on attitudes toward trades, any more than it had been decisive at the end of antiquity with regard to slavery. The Reformation would not change much in this respect. Even if it is true, though not yet proved, that labor was more highly valued in the Protestant than in the Catholic world,[37] this was only in order to permit the Protestant aristocracy and bourgeoisie to subjugate even more effectively masses ruled even more harshly by the law of labor. In this respect, religions and ideologies appear more effects than causes. Ultimately, the history of attitudes toward trades, which is a chapter in the history of mentalities, is primarily a chapter of social history.

LABOR, TECHNIQUES, AND CRAFTSMEN IN THE VALUE SYSTEMS OF THE EARLY MIDDLE AGES (FIFTH TO TENTH CENTURIES)

PRELIMINARY REMARKS

1. Difficulties of a History of Mentalities in the Early Middle Ages

In dealing with any type of society, when we attempt to reach down beneath the exalted—and consequently superficial—level of ideas into the realm of mentalities (rife with distortions, psychic automatisms, survivals and rejects, and obscure, incoherent thoughts erected into pseudo-logical systems), the difficulties we must face are enormous. In large part this is due to the fact that such research has only recently been undertaken and is still without an adequate methodology or theoretical basis. These difficulties are particularly serious in the case of Western society in the early Middle Ages.

Consider the problem, for instance, from the point of view of documentation. The history of mentalities is based on (*a*) a certain type of interpretation, or reading, which can be made of any document, and (*b*) special types of documents which provide fairly direct access to collective psychologies, such as certain literary genres, figurative art, documents which reveal daily behavior, etc. In the case of the early medieval West, however, documents are rare and resist interpretation aimed at grasping the common mental universe. The culture is stunted, abstract, and aristocratic. Scarcely any but the upper strata of society are encountered in the documents, and the Church's very strict control over cultural production further contributes to masking the realities. While Christianity welcomed different value

This essay is merely the outline of a projected study, "Les images du travail au Moyen Age." A bibliography may be found below, pp. 303–6.

systems within its own, or allowed them to subsist, none was consciously elaborated and systematically exposed outside the framework of Christian doctrine. Such value systems must be largely implicit, reconstructed by the historian. The particular value which is the subject of this essay, moreover, as well as the men who embodied it, namely, labor and laborers, did not interest the masters and producers of culture. Labor was not a "value," nor was there even a word to designate it. If the history of mentalities is still a history that stammers, the history of the silences, lacunae, and gaps of the past, which will be an essential part of tomorrow's history, is mute.

2. Justification of the Research.

It is already a significant feature of a mentality that the documents from the early Middle Ages are silent as to labor and laborers. Since there were men during this period who worked, in the sense in which the word is commonly understood today, they, and those of their contemporaries who did not "work," necessarily had attitudes toward labor, techniques, and craftsmen which implied value judgments. It is therefore legitimate to try to uncover their traces with the aid of the documents we possess, even if we must, so to speak, "induce labor" if we hope to deliver the expected knowledge. It would be an abdication of the historian's responsibilities if he were to allow a fetishistic respect for his subject to lead to a submersion in the mentality of the era he was studying, such that he refused to apply to it other concepts than those current at the time. It is as legitimate to attempt to compare our own estimate of the value of labor with that of Charlemagne and his contemporaries as it is to apply to the economy of the Carolingian era the Fisher formula, of which it was ignorant.

3. Analytical Eclecticism and the Method of Successive Soundings

A variety of approaches have been used (philology, analysis of literary and legal texts, archeological and iconographic documents, etc.), not only because of the necessity to make use of whatever materials happen to be available but also because a multifaceted attack has proved fruitful in the area of mentalities. Mentalities are, after all, related to the whole range of historical data but may be better revealed by one type of document rather than another, depending on the region and period. This sort of history must therefore be done by means of a series of successive soundings. This technique offers the additional advantages of providing a periodization and of drawing attention to the areas in which the phenomena under study take the form of *problems*.

Between the fifth and eighth centuries, for example, attitudes toward labor are best understood through examination of monastic rules and the hagiographic literature, for the only area in which labor was at that time a psychological and theoretical problem was the ecclesiastical and properly monastic sphere, where the question was whether a monk could, or should, work with his hands. Between the eighth and tenth centuries, priority must certainly be given to legal, literary, and iconographic texts, for it was in the context of the cultural ferment which has been called the Carolingian renaissance that labor made a certain advance. Beginning in the eleventh century, the *terminus ad quem* of this sketch, attitudes toward labor were supported by a more or less conscious ideology which was best expressed in genuine value systems, such as the ideology of the tripartite society composed of *oratores, bellatores,* and *laboratores;* iconoraphic series (the labors of the months or illustrated technical encyclopedias); scientific classifications (*artes liberales* and *artes mechanicae*); and concrete systems of social hierarchy based on socioprofessional *status* more than juridico-sacred *ordo.*

If such a method makes it possible to observe modifications in mentalities and attitudes, it is also useful for disclosing continuities, for determining the respective portions of tradition and innovation and their interrelations. Individually and collectively, men are in the first place determined by their heritages and by the attitudes they adopt toward them. This is even more true of mentalities, since mentalities, as we have said, are what changes most slowly in history. Research into heritages is all the more imperative in the present case because the men of the early Middle Ages, and first of all the intellectuals whom we know from the works of the period, felt the need to invoke the support of the *auctoritates* of the past. In every area, they exerted themselves not in developing or creating, but in saving and preserving.

I The Ambiguity of the Legacies

Early medieval man inherited a variety of mental traditions, in which the attitude toward labor ranged from contempt to respect. This fact should not, however, lead to a skeptical attitude toward the historical approach undertaken here. Even if the pair labor and nonlabor is linked to the eternal dilemma of the human condition, oscillation between the two terms depends on history and requires a historical type of explanation. The fact that a single cultural heritage contained two opposite attitudes with regard to labor did not prevent these legacies from influencing early medieval mentalities according to the nature of their content: the fact that Roman praise of *otium* was linked, for instance, to a social conception (the *otium cum dignitate* of the aristocracy), or that for pagan barbarians the opposition labor-nonlabor referred to the opposition warrior–manual laborer, or, furthermore, that the main Christian reference in favor of labor was Pauline, all had undeniable importance for the definition and evolution of early medieval man's attitudes toward labor.

Furthermore, these ambiguities—or ambivalences—were influential not only as a result of conjunctural conditions (even outside a problematic of infrastructure-superstructure, the historian should be aware that a given historical situation either favors respect for labor or the contrary) but also because of structural situations. Two elements of the mental structure of early medieval man allowed the ambiguity in these heritages a greater influence: (1) because the overall mentality of the era was one which had broken with the past rather than maintained a continuity, these heritages were more an inert treasure to be drawn from at will than a living tradition to be respected (this is evident for the Roman tradition despite the scruples of a few clerics, and true as well for the various barbarian heritages, which were relegated to a time gone by as a result of both Christianization and profound changes in modes of life; and, finally, it is also valid for the Judeo-Christian heritage, which was quite composite and very different in its post-Constantinian form from what it had been in paleo-Christian times); (2) early medieval man did not conceive of the cultural legacies of the past as wholes whose internal contradictions had to be, if not resolved, at least explained; for him, these legacies were mere juxtapositions of texts without a context, of words without discourse, of gestures without action. To give one example, they made separate use, without confronting the two, of the gospel texts which recommended imitating the idleness of the lilies of the fields and the birds of the sky and, on the other hand, of the Pauline texts which enjoined man to work; their choice depended on their needs and desires.

Finally, a distinction should be made, in analyzing how a society used its heritage historically, between the influence of the heritage in everyday experience on the one hand, and as a conscious mental tradition on the other. For example, the tradition of idleness among warriors handed down from the barbarians was continued in practice by the early medieval aristocracy without being accompanied by conscious justification—or at least without leaving explicit written traces of such—while the monk's manual labor was supported by scriptural references or by an explicit Christian ethic (idleness is the enemy of the soul and an invitation to the devil).

a) The Greco-Roman Legacy

First, in the Greek city, the situation of *techne* was one falling "between labor and technical know-how," a victim of the "disparity between the technical level and the appraisal of labor" (J.-P. Vernant). The scope and limitations of the Prometheus myth were an index of this. There is also the ambiguity of the Stoic *ponos*, "which applies to all activities requiring a painful effort, not only to tasks productive of socially useful values" (J.-P. Vernant). And there was also the ambiguous position of the Greek philosophers with regard to "machinism" (A. Koyré).

Another element was the equivocation between *ars* and *artes*, indicating on the one hand technical skill and on the other creative genius. There was the pair *manus-ingenium* (medieval avatars of the symbolism of the hand: symbol of command or of labor? How can we know the mental reactions of the unlearned to the sight of the hand of God, which appeared with increasing frequency in iconography?) And there was oscillation between *negotium* and *otium* (from which derived the problems of *otium monasticum* and the definition in the twelfth century of an *otium negotiosum* for monks).

Under the late Empire, there was an ambivalence in the estimation of the value of labor, due to a mixture of an artisanal mentality, a corporative yoke, and the existence of forced labor. Vergil's energeticism was more closely related to rural life than it was artisanal.

Early medieval man faced the problem of understanding certain distichs of the *Disticha Catonis*, which very early became a reading primer (for example, I, 39: Above all, save what you have earned by your labor / When labor is considered baneful, deadly poverty grows apace).

There was an ambiguity in the inherited vocabulary: *labor* with its psychological and moral overtones (pessimistic connotations of pain, fatigue, toil . . .), *opus* oriented more toward the result of labor than the laborer . . .

Above all, there was the weight of the association of labor with slavery. This gave rise to the notion of *opus servile* and the antithesis of labor and freedom. During the various medieval "renaissances," from Charlemagne to the Renaissance, and including both the legal revival connected with the renaissance of Roman law and the Aristotelian fashion which culminated in Thomism, the mere use of the ancient vocabulary (e.g., *opera servilia*) encouraged a contempt for labor which was frequently in contradiction with the social evolution.

b) Barbarian Legacies

A rough distinction may be made between poorly Romanized old traditions (Italic, Iberic, Celtic) and the traditions of the invaders, mainly Germanic.

In the first case, what was likely to have become established after the removal of the Roman veneer were traditions of artisanal techniques associated with particular socioprofessional groups and surrounded with an aura of religious belief. With the Gauls, for instance, craftsmen occupied an important position, attested to by artistic works and sanctioned by the religious pantheon (the primacy of the god Lug, the "Gallic Mercury," god of techniques and crafts).

In the second, we find once again the ambiguity in the opposed values of labor and nonlabor. On the one hand, there was the warrior's contempt for economic activity and manual labor (see the famous example in Tacitus, *Germania* XIV–XV: "It was not as easy to persuade them to till the soil and await the harvest as to challenge the enemy and earn wounds as a reward. They held it lazy and spiritless to earn by the sweat of their brow what they could obtain for blood. When they were not making war, they gave themselves over to hunting and mainly to idleness, spending their time sleeping and eating, and the bravest and most warlike did nothing"). On the other hand, there was technical and artistic virtuosity, the social prestige of metal workers and sacred craftsmen (such as the ironsmith and goldsmith in Germanic mythology).

c) The Judeo-Christian Legacy

Here we encounter the same ambivalence and ambiguity in more systematic form, at times embodied in symbolic antitheses, both at the level of principles and written texts and in social and cultural practice.

In the book of Genesis, there are contradictory bases for a theology of labor: on the one hand, the active, "worker" God ("tired" after the six days of the Creation, who created man for a sort of labor (*operatio* in the Vulgate) in the prelapsarian Paradise (Genesis 2:15: "And the Lord God took the man, and put him into the garden of Eden to dress it and to keep it"), and, on the other hand, man condemned by the original sin to labor as punishment and penitence (Genesis 3:19: "In the sweat of thy face shalt thou eat bread"). The ambiguity reaches its peak in Genesis 3:23, which is a terrestrial echo of the paradisiacal labor of 2:15: "Therefore the Lord God sent him forth from the garden of Eden, to till the ground from whence he was taken."

The Old Testament is full of contradictions with regard to technical civilization: there is a sketch of a Providential history of arts, crafts, and techniques (in the person of Tubal-Cain), but there is also a condemnation of urban technological and economic life (Cain is the founder of the first city and the inventor of weights and measures). This latter theme opens another front of Christian controversy in the battle over labor: the opposition of rural and urban labor on the model of Abel and Cain.

There is also the basic opposition of the active life and the contemplative life: Martha and Mary in the New Testament (with an echo, according to the typological symbolism which was to be developed in the Middle Ages, in the opposition of Rachel and Leah in the Old Testament).

There is the difficult problem of evaluating the social recruitment of primitive Christianity and the impact of such recruitment on the socioreligious interpretation of Christianity: the importance of strata of urban craftsmen in paleo-Christianity does not necessarily imply the validity of the notion that Christianity was a religion of labor and laborers.

Primitive Christian symbols are ambiguous. They are often taken from the sphere of labor, but with essentially symbolic and spiritual connotations (the vine, wine-press, plow, sickle, axe, fish, trowel; cf. the works of J. Daniélou). Can any conclusion be drawn from the fact that in one of the oldest extant Christian paintings (frescoes in a sanctuary at Dura Europos from the third century), the episode of man's condemnation to labor is absent from the cycle of the Fall, whereas this was to be one of the favorite iconographic themes of the Middle Ages?

Like the other legacies, the Judeo-Christian was to offer medieval man an ideological arsenal containing weapons for the defense of every position, in favor both of labor and nonlabor. The richest and most important of these arsenals was the Bible, and particularly the New Testament. Medieval man would not make equal use of all the weapons provided him by these relevant texts. The defense of the two extreme positions was polarized around the Gospel texts which proposed submission to Providence on the example of the lilies of the fields and birds of the sky (Matthew 6:25–34 and Luke 12:27) on one side, and the Pauline texts in which the apostle offers himself as an example of a laborer, indeed a manual laborer (the essential text being 2 Thess. 3:10: "if any would not work, neither should he eat"), on the other. In close rapport with the economic and social conjuncture, the ideological conjuncture underwent an oscillation of attitudes toward labor, techniques, and craftsmen, ranging from an atmosphere of contempt and condemnation to a tendency to respectful evaluation. The time lag between mentalities and material evolution and the specificity of the mechanisms of ideological justification make this research ideal for investigating the relations between the history of ideas and mentalities and that of economic and social life.

II THE DISAPPEARANCE OF LABOR AND LABORERS FROM THE SOCIETY,
MENTALITY, AND IDEOLOGY OF THE EARLY MIDDLE AGES
(FIFTH TO EIGHTH CENTURIES)

A. The technical, economic, and social bases of the disappearance.

a) Technical regression, the near disappearance of *specialized* labor.

b) Reduction of the notion of labor to that of manual labor, and of the latter to rural labor. For example, between the sixth and eight centuries, the verb *laborare* became restricted to the specialized sense of agricultural labor, either as a transitive verb (*laborare campum, terram*, etc.) or in an absolute usage (*laborare* = to plow) (cf. G. Keel). Most craftsmen were rural, at first slaves and later domanial serfs. From the point of view of mentalities, it is impossible to speak of attitudes toward any form of labor without calling to mind *manual* labor, meaning, in the Middle Ages, agricultural labor and, in industrial societies, the labor of a simple worker.

c) The social evolution was unfavorable to laborers: craftsmen and free peasants disappeared progressively (from which came the consolidation of the notion of *opus servile*), and the "idle," the warriors and clerics, were preeminent.

B. Manifestations of the disappearance: silence and contempt of the sources.

a) The virtual silence of the hagiographic sources, except for the manual labor of certain saints. This, however, was presented (cf. infra) as a penitence.

b) Praise for the contemplative life. For example: the success of Julius Pomerius' *De vita contemplativa* (cf. Laistner); Gregory the Great complained in his letters of having been uprooted from the contemplative life and cast into the active, and of having had to abandon Rachel for Leah and Mary for Martha (Epist. I, 5; VII, 25); one of the rare figurative sculptures from this era, the Ruthwell cross in Dumfriesshire (last quarter of the seventh century) represents Mary Magdalene at the feet of Christ and is interpreted by specialists as a symbol of the contemplative life, probably influenced by the asceticism of one of the principal religious currents in the Christianity of the early Middle Ages, Irish asceticism. That this ideal of idle piety had adherents in the early Middle Ages is borne out by a sermon of Caesarius of Arles (sermon XLV, published by G. Morin, 2d ed., p. 205).

c) Labor, techniques, and laborers in barbarian legislation. With only a few exceptions (cf. infra), the *wergeld* system of quantitative evaluation, which made it possible to set up a scale of social values and their ideological foundations, placed workers at the bottom of the scale. For example, in the law of the Burgundii (late sixth to mid-seventh century), plowmen (*aratores*), swineherds (*porcarii*), shepherds (*birbicarii*), and "other slaves" (*alii servi*) were at the lowest level of thirty sous (to be paid to their masters in the event they were killed), while carpenters (*carpentarii*) rose to forty sous, and ironsmiths (*fabri ferrarii*) to fifty, with only the goldsmiths reaching a higher level (150 sous for the *aurifices* and 100 sous for the *argentarii*).

d) The silence of the artistic and archeological materials. The difficulties of interpreting such sources for the purposes of the history of mentalities should not be forgotten. Works of art and archeological monuments are a different sort of repository; their connections with general history and even with ideological history are delicate to define and interpret. Moreover, during the period in question, figurative art had almost entirely disappeared, along with epigraphical inscriptions; and interpretation of the archeological material, in particular of funerary furnishings, for use by the history of mentalities is a particularly delicate task; what relations existed between beliefs and funerary rites on the one hand, and the system of socioprofessional values on the other? Joachim Werner has observed, for example, that while objects from everyday life, such as craftsmen's tools and products, are quite rare in tombs in the eastern part of the Merovingian realm, this may be due as much to their not preserving well as to the possibility that they were not among the funerary gifts. Furthermore, the same archeologist notes that there are no weapons in the tombs of the Goths, who were no less warlike than the Alemanni, the Franks, the Bavarians, the Thuringians, the Lombards, the Anglo-Saxons, and the Scandinavians, whose funerary furnishings generally included weapons. On the other hand, the presence of tools in the funerary furnishings of the tombs of goldsmiths, the only craftsmen honored during the era, precludes ignoring the evidence contained in tombs as to labor's place in the value systems of early medieval societies.

e) Finally, it is clear that the absence of labor and laborers from the cultural products of the early Middle Ages is only one instance of the consequences of the era's taste for abstract symbolism in art and literature, already a fundamental feature of the *tardo antico*. It seems probable, however, that the ideological and social insignificance of workers during this period contributed greatly to the success of this aesthetic tendency.

III PRESERVED SECTORS AND STRUCTURES RECEPTIVE TO A REVALUATION OF LABOR

During the period in question, the values of labor and technique were generally eclipsed in social value systems. There were, nevertheless, isolated instances where labor was more highly valued. These played an important role in subsequent forms and processes through which such values gained wider applicability.

a) Clerical Labor, Especially by Monks

It is on this subject that we are best informed. Indeed, contemporary records are most complete on the problem of whether clerics could—or, indeed, should—devote themselves to manual labor, the very lowest form of an activity widely held in contempt. We have, furthermore, a remarkable study by Etienne Delaruelle of one of the two principal sources which bear on this question, the monastic rules (the other being the hagiographic literature). This is supplemented by a brilliant note of Marc Bloch's.

Manual labor was recommended to bishops (witness the records of councils, particularly the Council of Orleans in 511) and priests (as evidenced by the *Statuta Ecclesiae Antiqua*), and required of monks by the various rules current in the West (witness Cassian, Cassiodorus, and the rules of the Master and Saint Benedict). The hagiographic literature confirms that monks actually did engage in manual labor (cf. the testimony of Gregory of Tours concerning Saint Romanus and Saint Lupicinus at Saint-Oyand-de-Joux and Saint-Claude, Saint Nicetius, bishop of Lyons, Saint Friardus, cloistered on a Breton island, Saint Ursus at Loches, etc.; Saint Hilary of Arles and Gennade concerning the monks of Lérins; Gregory the Great concerning the monks and hermits of Italy in the *Dialogi*; Jonas of Bobbio concerning Saint Columban, etc.)

There should be no mistaking the motives which led the monks to work with their hands and even to construct "machines" (mills: a famous example is Saint Ursus at Loches, according to Gregory of Tours, *Liber vitae patrum*, XVIII). As Marc Bloch has pointed out, recourse to "machinism" was only a means for the monks to make themselves available for the more important, the essential thing—the *opus Dei*, prayer and the contemplative life. Far from being commonplace, mills were rarities and curiosities, and their construction by monks was taken by contemporaries more as proof of the monks' almost supernatural, virtually thaumaturgic knowledge than as an instance of their technical skill. The *Vitae* report these episodes as *mirabilia*. Philippe Wolff has pointed out that "in the middle of the tenth century, the construction of a water mill near Saint-Omer by the Abbey of Saint-Bertin was still 'an admirable spectacle for our time' in the eyes of the chronicler of the monastery."

The meaning of this monastic labor was above all penitential. Because manual labor was connected with the Fall, the divine curse, and penitence, the monks, as professional penitents, penitents by vocation, penitents par excellence, had to set an example of mortification by their labor.

Whatever the motives, the simple fact that the highest type of Christian perfection, the monk, engaged in labor caused a part of the social and spiritual prestige of the practitioner to reflect on the activity of work. The spectacle of the monk at labor impressed his contemporaries in its favor. The monk's self-humiliation in labor raised labor in general esteem.

We offer two further observations concerning monastic labor. First, in the *scriptoria* of the monasteries, *scribere*, to copy manuscripts, was regarded as manual labor and consequently as a form of penitence, which is the origin of the copyists' formulas at the ends of the manuscripts. The Irish showed a particular interest in this form of penitence, at Luxeuil, for example. Second, monastic labor raised problems of diet and dress, since the usual ascetic diet and penitential clothing did not lend themselves to efficient manual labor. The upshot was that the rule was modified in these areas in favor of the monastic "laborers." This was the beginning of a casuistry which condoned the progressive retreat of sacred values in the face of a developing practice and ethics of labor (see the remarkable study by A. de Vogüé on "labor and diet in the Rules of Saint Benedict and the Master" in *Revue Bénédictine*, 1964, pp. 242–51, which shows the influence on the two rules "of a constraining economic conjuncture: *necessitas loci aut paupertas"* and the evolution from the Master, who was opposed to the agricultural labors of the monks and favored work in crafts and horticulture, to Saint Benedict, who adjusted to a more ruralized world in which the area of crafts and gardening was restricted).

b) Sacred and Prestigious Craftsmen

Both the ecclesiastical and the lay hierarchies contributed to the establishment and propagation of the tradition of the sacred ironsmith and goldsmith. The craftsmen who forged the weapons for aristocratic warriors (swords were personalized and sanctified according to the tradition represented by the *Chanson de Roland* and the gests); and the goldsmiths who decorated these weapons and created jewels for the women of these warriors, as well as the gleaming adornment of the churches, which barbarian taste covered with gold, silver, and precious stones—these craftsmen were important personages who upheld the prestige of technical skill. Hagiography bears out the existence of such much sought-after craftsmen (for example, the *plures artifices* whom Ausbert, Bishop of Rouen, invited from various regions to work on the shrine of Saint Ouen). We have already seen how barbarian legislation reflected the prestige of these artist-craftsmen in the form of a higher *wergeld*. Archaeology reveals the survival of pagan beliefs (Wieland the ironsmith) and the charisma of metallurgy (figures on the chest of Aryon). The most striking case is offered by the career of Saint Eligius, a royal goldsmith who became a high court dignitary and then a bishop (according to the *Vita Eligii*, particularly I, 5).

To these virtuosos of metalwork, the early Middle Ages added another category, coin minters (*monetarii*), treated by R. S. Lopez in an excellent study. But the very title of his work (*An Aristocracy of Money*) shows how poorly representative these lords of coinage were of the world of crafts and the universe of techniques in general. They were the beneficiaries of the increasing scarcity of precious metals, of the fragmentation of monetary circulation, of the disappearance of technical, economic, and political controls (cf. Gregory the Great's distressed text regarding counterfeiters!), and of the possible appearance of a prestige coinage without direct connection to any economic activity.

c) Attention to Tools and Machinery

The disappearance or increasing scarcity of raw materials for crafts, of technological apparatus, and of a specialized labor force made tools, particularly the iron parts of tools, rare, hence precious, objects. What remained or was newly built in the way of machinery was regarded as miraculous, as we saw in the case of the mills. An attentiveness to the tool came about, which would become one of the foundations of the technical mentality of future centuries. Barbarian legislation extended protection to precious tools: Salic law (XXI, 12) punished the theft of a coulter by a fine of fifteen gold sous (from the tenth century on, the dukes of Normandy would "nationalize" the coulters on their domains, in a gesture reminiscent of the pharaoh's ownership of the trees in deforested ancient Egypt). The most significant evidence is that of Saint Benedict, transmitted through his Rule and through the miracles attributed to him by Gregory the Great in the second book of the *Dialogi*, which was destined to be popularized throughout the Middle Ages. The Rule assimilated the *ferramenta* (iron tools or parts) belonging to the monastery to the sacred vessels and furnishings (XXXI–XXXII). To lose or damage them was sacrilege. In the miracles, Saint Benedict is depicted exercising his thaumaturgic power over objects connected with crafts (the broken kneading machine); and, particularly in the incident of the iron spade that rises miraculously from the bottom of the monastery lake, the tool is offered as an object of veneration. It should be noted that this Benedictine miracle belongs to a long, deep tradition. The Old Testament attributes a similar feat to Elisha (2 Kings 6:1 ff.). The *Roman de Perceforest* in the fourteenth century speaks of a Shepherds' Fountain, to which shepherds came to immerse their broken tools.

Finally, it should be noted that the hand, whose plurivalent symbolism has already been indicated, also receives juridical protection in barbarian legislation. Variations of the *Wergeld* according to the finger severed refer implicitly to the free man's role as warrior (the value of the finger depends on its function in wielding arms), whereas with craftsmen and slaves the implicit reference is to labor (the tool here replaced the weapon and was, on a lower level, its equivalent).

IV THE CAROLINGIAN RENAISSANCE OF LABOR

The Carolingian renaissance included a genuine ideology of productive effort, an energeticism which can be detected on the economic, political, and cultural planes. This seems to have been the concern of an aristocracy or, rather, of a governmental "elite." It resulted, however, in certain material and mental habits, which gave rise to cultural and ideological themes which were to be developed in the future.

Energeticism found its fundamental expression in a rural context, in the form of an initial wave of land clearing. The progress was marked less by an improvement in techniques than by an extension of the area under cultivation, but these extensive aspects were supplemented by others of an intensive and qualitative nature. The number of plowings and "dressings" was increased, and there was a renaissance in market gardening along with related innovations and refinements, and experiments aimed at increasing yields. Improvements in the organization and management of labor were particularly important. The cultural and documentary expression of this awakening of labor values—at least, of certain aspects of such values—was diverse and abundant.

a) Legal Evidence

Essentially, this takes the form of contracts for the use of land (increasingly common from the end of the eighth century on), which link improvement in the social station and legal rights of individuals on the land to the efficiency of their labor. These included, for example, contracts "ad meliorandem," so-called *complant* contracts (providing for joint planting of different crops on a given piece of land), long-term leases, and forms of precarium which tied land tenure to expansion and improvement of the area under cultivation (such as *laborare, elaborare, acquirere, exquirere, augmentare, meliorare, emeliorare, possidere* in a series of precaria in the cartulary of the Abbey of Fulda for the years 775–95). This may be related to a tradition traceable to the Roman Empire (*lex Hadriana de rudibus agris*), taken up in particular by the Visigoths (whose notion of *melioratio* gave ownership to the pioneer *pro labore suo*), but the phenomenon did not become significant until the Carolingian era. Cf. P. Grossi, *Prob-*

lematica strutturale dei contratti agrari nella esperienza giuridica dell'alto Medioevo italiano. XIII Settimana di Spoleto, 1965.

b) Regulation of Labor

Regulations applicable to labor are found in secular as well as ecclesiastical documents. These indicate a certain renewal of activity in the crafts, especially in the domanial setting. Greater attention was paid to problems raised by work.

In the first case, the primary sources are the capitularies (particularly the capitularies *de villis*). Two concerns of the capitularies are worthy of notice: (1) the regulation of the *Sunday rest,* now more explicit than before, which is not only a sign of the primacy of religious taboos but also an indication of the desire to organize labor's breathing cycles (while at the same time codifying the *opera servilia*)—cf. the studies by W. Rordorf and J. Imbert; (2) the condemnation of the idle and of able-bodied beggars, taken over from the Justinian code and prefiguring certain opinions of the thirteenth century (Guillaume de Saint-Amour, Jean de Meung) and, especially of the end of the Middle Ages and the Reformation (capitulary of 806 to the *missi* at Nimègue).

In the second case, we witness the disappearance of the problem of monks' labor. First, this is no longer the primary ground of the controversy over labor. Second, but for a few exceptions, labor is no longer a problem for the monastic world: the triumph of Benoît d'Aniane's reformed Benedictinism reduced manual labor to a symbolic practice in the face of the encroachments of the *opus Dei.* Along with records of monastic customary law, which enable us to follow the evolution of regulation (*Corpus consuetudinum monasticarum . . .*), abbey statutes, like Adalhard's famous statutes for Corbic in the ninth century, show the progress of craft activity and regulation on monastic estates, as well as the fact that the monks were falling back on particular tasks considered more honorable and less fatiguing (baking, gardening, brewing, etc.), while an increasing manual labor force of serfs and wage earners was taking over the heavier labor.

c) Literary and Artistic Evidence

Iconographers, particularly A. Riegl, followed by J. C. Webster, have shown that around 800 there was a discernible break in the iconography of the seasons and months. A new series, called the "labors of the months," which was to enjoy a singular fortune in the Middle Ages, made its appearance. H. Stern has shed some light on this turning point by making the ideological content of the break between the antique calendar and the Carolingian and medieval iconography of the months explicit and by comparing the iconographic miniatures with contemporary poetic texts.

From the antique calendar, which generally represented genre scenes with several characters of a passive, allegorical, and religious kind, we shift to the representation of a single character actively engaged in a single labor of some sort, generally agricultural, with the scene being treated in a realistic manner (miniatures from two Salzburg manuscripts of the first third of the ninth century and from a manuscript of the Martyrology of Wandalbert of Prüm from the end of the ninth century). To throw into greater relief the realistic theme of the labors of the months, it should be noted, as Stern has observed, that the Byzantine world continues the antique iconography. Thus we have a prime example of a cultural turning point associated with an economic and social turning point. We also find the new ideology of labor in certain contemporary poetic works treating the theme of the labors of the months, particularly in the poem *De duodecim mensium nominibus, signis, aerisque qualitatibus* (848) by Wandalbert of Prüm, which has been studied by K. T. von Inama-Sternegg for the information it yielded concerning progress in rural techniques observed by the poet (additional spring plowing in February–March). The testimony of Einhard, according to whom Charlemagne gave new names to the months related to rural activity, joins these documents in bringing to light a Carolingian ideology of labor, which supported the economic and governmental effort.

d) Scientific and Intellectual Advances of Labor and Technique

Carolingian ideology had highlighted agricultural labor, which it held to be the basis of everything else. For the first time since antiquity, however, the crafts were accorded scientific status by the Carolingian renaissance.

Technical treatises from antiquity (Vegetius) were more common, and, even more important, the first technical treatises of the Middle Ages appeared (cf. the work of B. Bischoff).

For the first time in cultural history, moreover, the notion and the expression *artes mechanicae* appeared, in the commentary by Johannes Scotus Erigena (c. 859) on the *De nuptiis philologiae et mercurii* by Martianus Capella. Technical and artisanal activities attained an equal footing with the *artes liberales* ("The liberal arts derive naturally from the intelligence. The mechanical arts, however, are not naturally innate but are derived *from man's reflection*. Cf. the work of P. Sternagel).

The new iconography of labor joins the new literature treating of technical concerns in 1023 in a manuscript from Monte Cassino in which the Carolingian encyclopedia of Rabanus Maurus is decorated with miniatures that show artisanal activities for the first time in a coherent and realistic fashion.

CONCLUSION

A category of "laborers" has emerged: the *laboratores*.

At the end of the ninth century, in the commentary to King Alfred's Anglo-Saxon translation of Boethius' *Consolations of Philosophy*, and steadily thereafter from the end of the tenth century on, a new schema of society appeared in medieval Western literature. It was a resurgence of the traditional Indo-European schema identified by Georges Dumézil as that of trifunctional or tripartite society, which consisted of men of prayer, men of war, and men of labor: *oratores, bellatores,* and *laboratores.* Whether the *laboratores* are seen as an elite group of land-clearing pioneers (e.g., Jacques Le Goff, based on tenth century records: *illi meliores qui sunt laboratores,* from the cartulary of Saint Vincent of Mâcon brought to light by Georges Duby [and cf. "A Note on Tripartite Society . . .," p. 53 above]), or, by contrast, as laborers as a whole, then primarily rural, and later encompassing the world of urban craftsmen (e.g., M. David, based on ninth-century literary texts), the new schema did, in any case, consecrate the ideological breakthrough of laborers, who had already become established in the economy and society. The semantic aspect of this ideological breakthrough brings a certain process to light: after the eighth century, *labor* and its derivatives and compounds (especially *conlaboratus*) developed a new meaning, centered on the idea of acquisition, profit, and conquest, primarily in a rural context, where the word was connected with pioneering. This semantic evolution reveals another conquest, an advance in the ideological and mental status of labor and laborers. This new valuation was still ambiguous, because labor was exalted mainly in order to increase the productivity and docility of the laborers. There can be no doubt, however, that this valuation was also the result of worker pressure on medieval ideology and mentalities.

PEASANTS AND THE RURAL WORLD IN THE LITERATURE OF THE EARLY MIDDLE AGES (FIFTH AND SIXTH CENTURIES)

Three preliminary remarks are necessary to define the limits of this sketch.

1. Its chronological limits are narrow. The period of the early Middle Ages treated by the lectures of the Spoleto conferences covers a long time span, roughly from the fifth to the eleventh centuries and sometimes beyond. I am well aware that the insufficiency of the documentation, in itself indicative that the historical equipment needed to perpetuate a culture was lacking and that the rate of evolution of the period's structures was slow, forces us to adopt a more drawn-out style and precludes our employing for these centuries the sort of fine chronology we have followed in later ones. I must therefore apologize for limiting my study to two centuries, the fifth and sixth, with a few incursions into the seventh, even though such a time span would appear quite ambitious for other periods. It should be borne in mind, however, that the time we are studying was one in which individual life was brief, but collective life was slow.

The reasons for my choice are the following. First, I am a little less ignorant of the literature of this era than of the centuries following. Second, on the level of mentalities and sensibilities, it was the time when the major themes of what we call the Middle Ages were established. E. K. Rand applied to a few eminent figures of the era a term which may be generalized by stating that it was the time of foundings and foundations,[1] the intellectual and spiritual incubation of the Middle Ages. I have chosen to focus primarily on a few key works: the basic reflections on society coming out of the great invasions which are contained in the *De gubernatione Dei* by Salvianus from the mid-fifth century;[2] the two masterpieces of sixth-century homiletic literature, the sermons of Caesarius of Arles[3] from the beginning of the century, and the *De correctione rusticorum* by Martin of Braga[4] from the end; again from the late sixth century, the one contemporary chronicle, Gregory of Tours's *Historia Francorum;* some specimens of hagiography of the first rank, with Gregory of Tours represented once again by his *Miracula,* the *Liber de gloria confessorum,* and *Vitae patrum,*[5] and Gregory the Great's *Dialogues,* particularly the second book devoted to Saint Benedict;[6] and, finally, representing poetry, Fortunatus.[7]

2. My purpose is not to describe peasants as they appear in the literature of the fifth and sixth centuries. If it were, this essay would have to be very brief, for reasons which will appear shortly. Instead, I would like to use my chosen subject to pose the problem of the relation of literature to society. This relation is not a simple one. The image of society that appears in literature (or iconography, sometimes in kindred forms, sometimes in different ones, as literature and the figurative arts frequently have their own thematic specificity) is related in a complex way to the global society from which it stems, to the ruling classes that dominate it, to the specific groups that sharpen the literary image, and to the writers who actually produce it. For the sake of simplicity, and in order not to linger too long over theoretical generalities, we may say that this image is at once an expression, a reflection, and a sublimation or camouflage of the real society. If it is permissible to define literature, with a certain rhetorical flourish, as a mirror of society, it is nevertheless a more or less distorting mirror depending on the conscious or unconscious desires of the collective soul which is examining itself—depending, more particularly, on the interests, prejudices, sensibilities, and neuroses of the social groups responsible for making the mirror and holding it up to society, or at least to that part of society capable of seeing, that is, of reading. Fortunately, the mirror is also tendered to us as members of a posterity better equipped to observe and interpret the interplay of illusions. To the historian of societies and civilizations, literature offers *imagos* rather than images and thus forces him to attempt to become the psychoanalyst of the collective past.[8] Sometimes the mirror of literature proves to be an unsilvered one from which the image has vanished or has been conjured away by the mirror cutter. This is the case with peasantry and the rural world in the literature of the early Middle Ages.

3. In a sense, my subject does not exist. It is scarcely doing violence to reality to admit that there is no peasantry or rural world in the literature of the fifth and sixth centuries, so that my thesis must first attempt to explain this absence.

It is an absence which, frankly, is surprising and paradoxical. All the papers we have heard this week demonstrate that the most basic fact of the history of the early medieval West was the ruralization of the economy and society. Land became the primary source of subsistence, wealth, and power. The prime movers in this basic development do not appear in the literature of the time. What is still more surprising is that they depart from literature after having played, if not the leading roles, then at least important parts in Greek and Latin literary works. This holds true not only for the mass of peasants. The *dominus,* too, whether an ecclesiastic or layman, who has become basically a landowner from the fifth century on, practically never appears as such in the literature of the era. The first point of this essay will be to attempt to explain this disappearance of rural society and, more particularly, of peasant society, from the literature of the fifth and sixth centuries. I will then try to rediscover, under his various guises, the peasant who disappeared from early medieval literature.

The peasant (*agricola*) was an important character in ancient Latin literature. Indeed, Latin has been described as a language of peasants.[9] The peasant appeared in both the economico-rural treatises of the republican period (Varro's *De re rustica,* Cato's *De agricultura*) and, in an idealized form, in bucolic poetry (especially in Vergil and his followers). Yet he disappeared from the literature of the early Middle Ages.[10] His features were already indistinct in the treatises on rural economy from the imperial era, those of Columella, for example, and, to a greater degree, Palladius. Bucolic poetry (I will not take time here to discuss the distinction, which may be worthy of reflection, between peasant and shepherd) rapidly declined in the Christian environment, as E. R. Curtius has remarked.[11]

In the fourth century, however, two poets tried their hand at it: Pomponius and, more significantly, Endelechius (Severus Sanctus), who gave us a scene between two rather symbolic peasants, a pagan and a Christian, in a moral eclogue devoted to the bovine "plague," an epizootic disease which occurred around 395.[12] After this date, there is nothing further until the Carolingian renaissance. The success of the Eclogue of Theodulf in the tenth century,[13] which is attested by the presence of the work in Conrad of Heisau's catalogue from the early twelfth century and by Rabelais's character Théodelet, seems ascribable mainly to a bookish tradition among erudite humanists. In the poetry of Fortunatus, which, to tell the truth, is marred by a number of decadent commonplaces, we find a countryside of the *tardo antico,* devoid of peasants and of men in general. The fruits he sends Radegonde seem to have been produced by God and nature and particularly by the author's literary reminiscences, without any human intervention. It was not merely that rural images have become purely symbolic and stereotyped (the bishop, for instance, takes over the metaphor of the *pastor gregis*). So common in the Bible, and still frequent in Caesarius of Arles, such images became sparse in literature during the course of the sixth century. What caused the peasant and the rural world to disappear from literature at the threshold of the Middle Ages?

Most likely, the economic, social, and mental underpinnings of the agricultural laborer's important role in the literature of the preceding period had crumbled.

1. The ideology of the early Middle Ages was not favorable to labor, particularly not the humble form of labor involved in providing ordinary subsistence, a description applicable to most human labor at this hour of dawn from which medieval society was emerging slowly and with difficulty. Poverty itself no doubt led to the attribution of a certain value to the improvements produced by labor,[14] but a threefold legacy from the past weighed unfavorably on mental attitudes toward labor: a Greco-Roman legacy shaped by a class which lived on slave labor and prided itself on its *otium;* a barbarian legacy originating with warrior groups used to deriving a considerable portion of their resources from war booty and, in any case, to favoring a militaristic way of life; and, of greater consequence in this Christianized society, a Judeo-Christian legacy which emphasized the primacy of the contemplative life[15] and considered it a sin and a sign of lack of confidence in God not to await Providence for the satisfaction of material needs. This reached such a point that Caesarius of Arles[16] had to refute the objection of those who recalled the necessity for man to provide for his own nourishment, clothing, and lodging and invoked Pauline texts, particularly the phrase from 2 Thessalonians which, from the eleventh century on, was to serve as basic reference for proponents of a revaluation of labor: "If any would not work, neither should he eat."

It is true that Saint Benedict, in the Rule that bears his name, does require the practice of manual labor, but this is a form of penitence and obedience to the law of expiation imposed on man as a result of original sin.

2. While free peasants and small landowners did survive in various places, perhaps more extensively than is generally acknowledged,[17] their economic and social influence had become virtually negligible. The social and juridical condition of the peasant was that of the *servi, mancipia,* and *coloni,* whose condemnation by society and ideology was well described by Salvianus on the threshold of the Middle Ages. It is true that, for Salvianus, just as the barbarian's sin is more excusable than the Christian's, the employer's or master's

mistake is judged more severely than that of the *colonus* or *servus*.[18] But he recognizes the slaves' collective guilt ("It is quite certain that slaves are bad and detestable") and makes no exceptions in the guilt of this class, while, in the higher classes, he does admit exceptions.[19] He has already accepted and begun propounding that un-differentiated image of a class of peasants of hideous visage which was eventually to be taken up by the medieval West.

3. Nevertheless, the disappearance of the peasant from early medieval literature was not due simply to the characteristics of his social class. A general regression of realism, particularly social and human realism, in literature and art affected the peasant. One has only to think of the virtually complete disappearance of figurative art and especially of the human figure in art.

Realism is not "natural" or primary, nor is it the product of a virgin vision, but rather it is the result of a visual, mental, and cultural conquest. Primitive art—and the early Middle Ages were marked by the invasion of a variety of primitivisms—is abstract. The Church replaced pagan realism with a universe of symbols and signs. It denied man's importance in favor of God and the hereafter, and established new patterns for the representation of society. In some cases, this took the form of an elementary dualism: clerics and laymen, or the powerful and the humble (and this latter distinction is indeed fraught with a social content, to which we shall return). These were religious schemata in the full sense, which destructured the traditional images of society organized according to social functions and remodeled them along the lines of vocations subordinated to religious needs. Consider, for example, the case of the city of Rome, an urban society, of course, but one from which the economic and professional categories had been evacuated. Pope Gregory arrayed the Roman population, then decimated by an epidemic of the black plague, in seven expiatory and propitiatory processions: secular clergy, male regular clergy, cloistered nuns, children, lay males, widows, married women.[20] In other instances, the society might be assimilated or reduced to groups of sins: Cassianus' eight deadly sins, Gregory the Great's seven, or the twelve abuses of the Pseudo-Cypriot in the middle of the seventh century.[21] At the risk of anti-cipating what follows, we should point out that in this last list we find our peasants, in the guise of the poor, represented by a major sin: the desire to rise above their humble place, a social ambition which would become the great sin in a society congealed in orders.

This general nonfigurative tendency affected the peasant above all. As with Salvianus, the *servi* as a whole were an anonymous crowd of sinners which admitted no exceptions, no individuals susceptible of salvation. The author of a recent study of the Merovingian warrior was able to write that only clerics and warriors could be understood as human types by the Merovingians.[22] Whether free or not, the peasant of the early Middle Ages was held in deep contempt. The *servus* could not receive holy orders,[23] but even the free peasant, if only because of his lack of culture, had little opportunity to enter the Church, including the still lax and somewhat anarchic monastic order, where the recruitment of peasants seems to have been minimal.[24] František Graus, in his admirable book on Merovingian society,[25] points out that we must wait until the thirteenth century for the Church to canonize a peasant. Before that time, there are no peasant saints.

Although the peasantry seems to be missing from early medieval literature, a close and attentive reading enables us to make out the presence of the peasant in a variety of guises.

1. First, peasants reappear as *pagani*, pagans, during a period marked primarily by the evangelization of the countryside.[26]

The precise meaning and historical limits of the word *paganus* are open to discussion. It is possible to agree with Michel Roblin[27] that the term has the same meaning as the Latin *gentilis*, the Greek *ethnikos*, and the Hebrew *goy*, and "that paganism is not identical with being of rural character and that the use of the term may simply be attributed to the Hebrew origins of the Christian vocabulary." Nevertheless, for Christian authors from the fifth century on, the *pagani* were essentially peasants and vice versa. Cassiodorus and Isidore of Seville testify to a mental reality with their scientifically worthless etymological speculations. "Everyone knows that the *pagani* (pagan peasants) take their name from the *villa* (domain), since what is called *villa* in Latin is known as *pagos* in Greek," writes Cassidorus in the *Expositio in canticum canticorum*; Isidore of Seville says in the *Etymologiae* (VIII, 10) that "the *pagani* (pagan peasants) take their name from the *pagi* of the Athenians, where they first appeared. In rural areas and *pagi* they estabished the pagan holy places and idols." Throughout the *Vita Martini*, Sulpicius Severus identifies the *rustici* with the *gentiles* and *pagani*. Fortunatus does likewise in his life of the same saint. In one place he writes that "the mob of peasants prevented the destruction of the profane temples," and in another that "though he wanted to destroy the temple of Eduens, the rude farmers of the countryside prevented him from doing so."[28]

Furthermore, this *rusticus paganus* was associated with old peasant superstitions as much as with the organized and institutionalized paganism of Roman religion. Caesarius of Arles and Martin of Braga attest to the fact.[29] Ethnographic studies have shown that the peasant superstitions denounced in the *De correctione rusticorum* persist to this day in peasant societies in the northwestern part of the Iberian peninsula.[30]

Thus, our manner of proceeding raises the whole problem of folklore and hence of peasant culture in the literature of the early Middle Ages. What we have here, rather than a sort of involuntary revenge of the peasant against the cleric, appears to be a case of simple appropriation for evangelical purposes of folkloric elements removed from their peasant cultural context.[31]

Beyond this, however, we encounter the problem of the ruralization of the West in the early Middle Ages. During this period there was a resurgence of what we shall call primitive or pre-Roman techniques, social structures, and mentalities. Underlying traditional peasant structures emerged and displayed great resistance to change.[32]

When he reappears in literature, the early medieval peasant is a barely human monster, and subsequent literary production was to continue to present him in this guise to youths and knights lost in the forest, where the peasant-lumberjack was in his own dark and wild element. They were great, ugly, huge-headed beasts with wide eyes fixed in an animal stare as they appeared to Aucassin or Lancelot.[33]

Thus, even after he had become a Christian, the peasant was a sinner of the first order. We need hardly to point to the *servus,* who personified man's servitude to sin,[34] *servus peccati.* All *rustici* were sinners par excellence; they were vicious by birth and nature. Caesarius of Arles did not usually put personalities in his sermons and gave his sinners neither individuality nor social specificity, but he made an exception for three specially selected categories: *clerics,* whose sins were most serious because of their status, but it was only a minority of unworthy clerics who were involved; *merchants,* who constituted a very limited group in southern Gaul at the beginning of the sixth century; and, finally, the *peasants,* who were predestined to certain sins and vices.

The *rustici,* for instance, were preeminent lechers and drunkards.[35] And this was not all. A mentality was forming at this time according to which the venereal diseases were the sign and sanction of sin. Peasants, more than others subject to undernourishment, poor hygiene, and physical defects thus exhibited their fundamentally flawed nature. Leprosy in a child was a sign of lewdness in the parents, and, according to Caesarius, lepers were mainly peasants, because peasants procreated in lust.[36]

2. The peasant was also the *pauper* and, more frequently, one of a crowd of paupers less and less differentiated. It is at times difficult to

distinguish the city poor from the country poor in the *pauperes* of the texts.[37] This is the case with Gregory of Tours, in whose writings Gaul still appears to be highly urbanized; yet virtually no distinction is ever made between urban and rural populations. A sign? Although he was observing the peasant society before his own eyes in writing the *De correctione rusticorum*, Martin of Braga may have had, besides the sermons of Caesarius of Arles, another model in the *De catechizandis rudibus* by Saint Augustine.[38] Saint Augustine, however, distinguished between categories of the faithful to be indoctrinated: "the few or the many, the learned or the ignorant, the city-dwellers or the peasants." Of course, one later encounters *urbanus* and *rusticus* in the figurative sense of civilized and ignorant which they respectively came to take on, but the distinction, and the reference to the opposition of city and country, which are still clear in Augustine, are no longer apparent in Martin of Braga.

There are, however, unambiguous texts which make it possible to identify the pauper with the peasant. It should be noted that, of the four peasants who, to our knowledge, are the only ones to appear in a concrete form in the literature of the very early Middle Ages, none has a name. In each case, the hero of the story is actually a saint, the peasant being merely an anonymous object in the hagiographic tale. On the other hand, although they are characterized simply as "poor," the poverty of these peasants seems relative. In one case it is stressed that the unfortunate fellow has no animals to help him, whereas the other three possess oxen. Apart from the use of the term *pauper*, the social condition or, in any case, the juridical condition is not made explicit in any of the four cases.

The first three of these texts are from Gregory of Tours.

In the first of these, an itinerant priest asks a peasant of Limagne to provide him hospitality for the night, "ad hospitiolium cuiusdam pauperis Limanici mansionem expetit." The peasant rises before dawn to go cut wood in the forest, and, following the habit of the peasants, which establishes the identity *pauper* = *rusticus*, he asks his wife for bread for his breakfast. He asks the priest to bless the bread and to make several hosts from it which he might carry with him to enable him to resist the assaults of the devil, who tries to throw him into the water when he crosses a bridge with his cart and oxen.[39]

In the second text, a *poor man*, who has lost the oxen who worked with him ("quos ad exercendam culturam habebat"), dreams that Saint Genesius shows him the place on the forest trail where he will find his oxen, which he will then use to transport an enormous marble slab miraculously to the site of the saint's sepulcher, which will become a place of miracles.[40]

The third text again shows us a peasant characterized as poor, whose total possessions consist of two oxen ("erat enim quidam pauper habens duos boves ad exercendam culturam suam, nec ei erat alia possessio"). A thief steals them, and he recovers his possessions by going in pilgrimage to the tomb of Saint Felix.[41]

The finest text, the fourth, is actually a Carolingian recasting of a Merovingian hagiography. It shows us an ordinary man, a poor peasant without oxen whom Saint Sigiran meets while the peasant is pulling a wagonload of manure by himself ("accidit . . . ut quendam homunculum es ruricolis unum videlicet plaustrum fimo honustum sine cuiuspiam animalis auxilio cum vi nimia trahentem conspiceret"). The saint, movèd by pity, speaks to the peasant: "Oh, unfortunate pauper, you have no oxen to help you." He harnesses himself to the wagon alongside the peasant and, when the labor is done, gives him three pieces of gold to buy an ox. This is a text abounding in information of an economic order, even if such information is difficult to organize and interpret, and one which offers the most concrete and human of the rare peasant figures in early medieval literature.[42]

The pauper who figures in these texts as an object of solicitude for the saints of Merovingian hagiography, the brother of Gregory the Great's peasant who takes refuge with Saint Benedict from a Goth who wants to torture him into revealing the hiding place of his fortune,[43] was in reality regarded by the upper strata of society as an object and a danger.

In the first place, he serves merely to set off the qualities of the wealthy man or saint in these tales. His only reason for existing is to furnish them an instrument or opportunity for salvation. In a society in which spiritual salvation was the essential aim, and in which the dominant classes conferred priority upon themselves in this respect, the pauper made it possible for the rich man or saint who gave him alms to save his own soul. Reified by the charity of his betters, the peasant was a *Gegenstand* in the full sense of the German word, an object, who would only later and with difficulty achieve the dignity of a social status, a *Stand*.[44] Caesarius of Arles gave a good definition of the peasant, who existed only in relation to the rich: "God has allowed the poor into this world so that every man might have the means to redeem his sins."[45]

The peasant was also a danger. In the early Middle Ages the peasant class was the dangerous class. As early as the end of antiquity, this was illustrated by the Circumcellions and the Bagaudes.[46] We encounter these half savage peasants in the life of Saint Wandrille, abbot of Fontenelle: "Upon coming into a place in the midst of very wicked peasants, who did not fear God and revered no man, a conflict arose."[47]

Most important, it was in the peasant masses that the *pseudo-*

prophetae, the popular religious leaders, originated and recruited their followers. These Antichrists arose in the peasant world, and their activities were shaped during a time when a variety of calamities and a worsening of life's basic conditions nourished an apocalyptic and millenarist tide. Gregory the Great, particularly, evokes these peasant agitators in the midst of the catastrophic atmosphere of the Great Plague of the sixth century;[48] their presence even in the cities worried the bishops and the wealthy.

In the year 590, for example, while plague and famine were ravaging Gaul, a peasant of Berry was driven mad by a swarm of flies[49] while cutting wood in the forest. He became an itinerant preacher, cloaked in animal hides and accompanied by a woman he called Mary, while he represented himself as Christ. He predicted the future and healed the sick. A crowd of peasants and paupers followed him, and there were even priests among them. His activities quickly took on a revolutionary aspect. As he traveled about preaching, he took from the rich and distributed their goods to the poor ("non habentibus"). He acquired thousands of followers. His coming was announced by nude dancing messengers ("homines nudo corpore saltantes atque ludentes"), reminiscent of characters from peasant folklore and the Adamite heresies. The bishop of Puy had him killed and tortured Mary to extract the desired confessions from her. The followers of the defunct leader did not, however, return to the fold ("homines illi quos ad se credendum diabolica circumventione turbaverat, nunquam ad sensum integrum sunt reversi"). Antichrists appeared all over Gaul and in similar demonstrations stirred up popular mobs and aroused the peasant world.[50]

3. Finally, the peasant reappeared as *rusticus*, which had become a synonym for ignorance and illiteracy, personifying the totally uncultured masses in the eyes of the educated clerical elite. The clerics, of course, did resign themselves, for pastoral reasons, to use *sermo rusticus*.[51] This was a time when technology, too, was monopolized by an elite (including craftsmen like ironsmiths and goldsmiths, warriors in the military, minters of coinage in the economic realm and clerics in the intellectual). These techniques, along with landed wealth and brute force, were the basis of social consideration. The peasant was a loser on this plane as well. He was no more than a bumpkin.

Isidore of Seville does, it is true, distinguish the rural moral character from the social and professional character of rural life, *rusticitas* from *rusticatio*.[52] In practice, however, the peasant, or *rusticus*, partook of both. In a word, he was a country bumpkin.

In the Life of Saint Patrocleus,[53] Gregory of Tours has the brother of the saint who has symbolically chosen to become *rusticus, pastor,* say: "Go on, peasant. Your occupation is to graze the sheep, mine is to become civilized through the study of literature. My ministry thus ennobles me, while your service makes you base."

The peasant, then, has become an anonymous, nonindividualized creature who serves merely to set off the character of the military and cultivated elite, the main burden of the Church.

When he reappears in literature with the economic revival, the peasant, now a villein (and the semantic evolution[54] of the word is in itself significant), retains the pejorative traits which originated in the early Middle Ages. Vicious, dangerous, and illiterate, he remains more animal than man. Although he did become a part of medieval humanism through art, where iconographic themes such as the Nativity or the monthly cycle of labors served as intermediaries, he was for the most part excluded from literature or relegated to teratological bestiaries. Literature, when it became realistic, would then endow him with the characteristics abstractly defined during the early Middle Ages: in Coulton's phrase, those of a medieval Caliban.

II

LABOR AND VALUE SYSTEMS

ACADEMIC EXPENSES AT PADUA IN THE FIFTEENTH CENTURY

Historians and scholars who have tried to give an approximate idea of the "budget" of a teacher or student in a medieval university have tended to neglect an element of undeniable importance and interest: the gifts in money or in kind required of students at the time of examinations.

Distinct from the banquets traditionally staged by successful doctoral candidates after obtaining the "licentia docendi",[1] these gifts were required expenses whose amount and type were soon fixed in statute.[2]

We reproduce in appendix I (p. 309) the account of such expenses kept by a law student at the University of Padua in the early part of the fifteenth century on a cover page of the manuscript *Vaticanus latinus* 11503, which contains a course of canon law.[3]

These expenses, indicated in detail both for the examination itself (*examen, examen privatum*)[4] and for the ceremony of investiture (*conventus, conventus publicus, doctoratus*),[5] were both "university dues"—fees intended either to fill the coffers of the University[6] and colleges or to pay the costs of courses[7]—and presents for the examiners, the scholastic and ecclesiastical authorities,[8] and the employees of the university.[9]

To gain a proper appreciation for the relative magnitude of these gifts, it should be recalled that the material needs of teachers in the Middle Ages were only very imperfectly provided for.[10] While academic employees made progress from the thirteenth century on, it came slowly and with great difficulty, and no gain was permanently assured. This was because their remuneration necessitated solutions to serious problems. First, teachers belonged to the class of paid workers, which the Middle Ages, like antiquity, held in contempt.[11]

Second, clerics had to be regarded as merchants, albeit of knowl-edge;[12] and teaching, which was both an inherent duty[13] for certain ecclesiastics and a noble activity,[14] was seen as a kind of commerce, albeit one which dealt in spiritual commodities.[15] Finally, even if these theological and psychological obstacles could be overcome, it had still to be determined who would pay the teachers and how they would be paid. The University of Padua, insofar as the secular au-thorities increasingly encroached upon its power over the course of the Middle Ages,[16] and insofar as there occured a relative secularization of instruction in terms of recruitment, methods, spirit, and sub-sequent career opportunities,[17] represents a particularly useful case for study. For more than two centuries, its activity was closely con-nected with its rivalry with Bologna. The university depended on migration from Bologna for the size of its membership and the extent of its instruction. It was very early encouraged by the commune of Padua, which saw it as a source of glory and profit; for a university was a market,[18] a center of attraction for foreigners, and, con-sequently, a factor in the development of contacts at a time when the urban cells of which economic and political life was made up de-pended on increasing relations with an expanding world in which trade was on the rise. Thus, beginning in 1260, the commune of Padua provided the teachers at its *studium* with a salary.[19]

This salary, however, did not prevent the doctors from claiming the traditional university gifts. Beginning in the fourteenth century, probably under the influence of the economic crisis and its re-percussions on the value of money and the cost of living, teachers' demands became increasingly urgent and the implementation of "examination dues" more scrupulous.[20]

In the first place, the distribution of the gifts among teachers and other academic personnel was set out in detail. The 1382 statutes of the college of jurists of Padua have been published,[21] along with short extracts from the additions and modifications subsequently made to them. A study of these corrections carried out in the archives of the University of Padua[22] has made it possible for us to trace this evolution.

The pecuniary advantages that the masters derived from these examinations seem to have been sufficiently important that, in order to combat doctors' absenteeism from these sessions, they were en-ticed by attendance fees paid by the students.

While the 1382 statutes had approved a 1355 decision[23] in virtue of which the alternates (*surnumerarii*) would receive no money unless actually called to replace one of the twelve regular masters, a decree of 25 July 1453 reserves a portion of the funds collected during the examination for the alternates; previously, all this had gone to the bishop.[24]

Elsewhere, sanctions to be imposed on students in default in settling their accounts are set out. On 18 November 1441, measures were decreed against students who had been content merely to pay a deposit (*brevia*).[25]

This urgent desire for profit helps to explain the progressive diminution of the number of students exempt from payment of the dues. The Church's traditional protection had assured poor students a place in the universities. Then, too, particularly in the thirteenth century, the movement of the population toward the cities had filled the faculties with crowds of young people with no resources, who were noteworthy as a cause of the ferment in the faculty of arts.[26] With the subsequent demographic ebb, the number of such students decreased, and the masters took advantage of the opportunity to encourage the decline by eliminating exemptions from dues as far as they were able; between 1405 and 1409, a modification in the statutes reduced their number to two for the whole of the school of law, one in canon law and one in civil law.[27] Thereafter, the principle was reduced to virtually symbolic form. The time of the poor at Padua was over. Democratic recruitment was permanently ended. Yet another regulation of 25 February 1428 would require the two remaining "privileged" students to submit to an extra preadmission examination and to supply conclusive proof of their poverty.[28]

Simultaneously, however, an inverse process was opening the doors of the university free of charge to a whole category of youth: the children of academics.

In 1394, an initial decision granted free entry into the college of jurists to any new doctor belonging to the male lineage of a doctor, even if one of the intervening descendants was not himself a doctor.[29] On 17 August 1409 it was specified that the son of a living or deceased doctor had to be examined free of charge, and sanctions were declared against anyone contravening this decision.[30]

Besides an academic ancestry, another condition was required of these new doctors: Paduan citizenship. A statute of 13 January 1418 even specified that this condition was an absolute necessity and limited the scope of earlier decrees; an exception was made in favor of a famous teacher commonly regarded as Paduan by adoption.[31] A statute of 11 November 1440 excluded alien doctors from the examining jury and denied them the right to receive the ducat paid to the twelve regular and alternate examiners.[32]

These texts enable us to describe the three convergent evolutionary processes affecting the University of Padua in the late fourteenth and first half of the fifteenth centuries. The main tendencies were the elimination of poor students; the formation of a caste of academic families; and nationalization, or a tendency to restrict recruitment—at least as far as masters were concerned—to the local population. In just two centuries, higher education had come a long way since the days when the nascent universities were welcoming students of every social origin from all over Europe, and the most famous schools were attracting students who came to acquire the *right to teach anywhere* (i.e., in any university).

Still, the student who recorded on a cover leaf of his law book the expenditures that had to be made—and no doubt that he himself had to make—at Padua in order to be examined was a student who came from the other end of Italy.

Folios 7–8, 9–41 verso, 42 verso –447 of the *Codex Vaticanus latinus* 11503 were written by the same hand that signed the last folio (447): "scripsit Matthaeus de Grandis Siracusanus," dated 1427.

We are familiar with this Sicilian. On 24 September 1424 he attended the ceremonies conferring a doctorate in theology on Fra Giovanni de Borometis.[33] We know that in 1426 he received a scholarship from the municipality of Syracuse to enable him to continue his studies at Padua.[34] When he returned to Sicily, he was first archdeacon of Syracuse and then elected vicar general, *sede vacante,* in 1443.[35] In 1462 we meet him again as a member of the college of doctors of the University of Catania, and subsequently, until 1466, he was vicar general of the bishop of Catania and vice-chancellor of the university.[36]

His was an exemplary career. Lacking in their own university,[37] young Sicilians of the early quattrocento eager to obtain a reasonably rigorous education and titles went to seek them on the continent. At which university, Bologna or Padua? The question as to which of the two was preferred is controversial.[38] It is probable, however, that with the decline of Bologna and the concurrent beginning of Padua's most eminent phase,[39] the latter would have attracted a greater share of the young islanders.

Like many of his compatriots, Matthew of Grandis enjoyed a scholarship to Padua provided by his native city.[40] The city, however, exercised a certain control over the students it subsidized[41] and the uses to which they put the money allotted to them. Do we owe our manuscript text to this control, in view of which our student may have been keeping a statement of expenses in order to render his accounts to the municipality of Syracuse? In any case, Syracuse's reason for helping to defray young Matthew of Grandis's educational expenses was to reap the eventual profit from what he had learned. Like most of the other scholarship holders, therefore, we find him returning to Sicily once he has his doctorate to take up various posts in the ecclesiastical administration of the island. The final phase of his career comes in 1444 when Alfonso the Magnanimous and Pope Eugenius IV approve the foundation of a university at Catania. Matthew was one of the Padua graduates who quite naturally assumed the leadership roles in the new institution.[42]

At Padua, Matthew de Grandis was no more than a scholarship student representing his nation. Unfortunately we have no way of learning any further details about his social origin, but his career is one of a well-defined type: destined to play a role in the administration of the Church, he was a student of the most traditional sort. For him, surely, the problem of providing for his needs at Padua was solved. Why, then, did he record his expenses? We have suggested that he had to account to his sponsors. Wouldn't it have been sufficient to have referred to the university statutes? In fact, he does note at the bottom of his statement that what he has just tabulated is in conformity with these statutes. But which statutes was he referring to? The fees and gifts in kind or in money which he indicates are not always equivalent to the amounts prescribed in the statutes of 1382, and another list of expenditures on examinations at Padua, probably dating from the middle of the fifteenth century, provides us with still different data.[43] Was there a modification of the statutes during the first half of the fifteenth century? Examination of the previously cited manuscript in the archives of the University of Padua discloses among the additions to the 1382 statutes a particularly interesting text dated 12 May 1400.[44]

This decree, indeed, established a genuine sliding scale for university dues. Such automatic modification of the amounts paid by students to their masters at a time of monetary deterioration stands in strange contrast with the fixed amounts of scholarships granted during the same period to the Sicilian students at Padua, for example. Here, what we began to observe above becomes more evident, namely, that an academic oligarchy was forming, an oligarchy which sought increasingly to profit from its educational activities. Its avidity in the pursuit of profit derived both from a desire to strengthen its prestige relative to the students and from a concern to acquire insulation from economic fluctuations. In short, its motives were pride and self-interest.[45]

On the subject of economic instability, the text of 12 May 1400 in which variations in exchange rates are explicitly mentioned is an invaluable piece of evidence. It makes Matthew de Grandis's list of expenditures all the more valuable, for it, and others like it which may yet be discovered, give us the means to evaluate variations in the value of money, changes in prices, and economic tendencies in general. The information relates to Padua, of course, but through Padua to Venice as well. Reflecting the monetary instability that Venice, along with most of the rest of Italy, experienced in the first half of the quattrocento,[46] the decision of 12 May 1400 also shows that, as of this date, Paduan money, whose value had been tied to that of Verona during the trecento,[47] had entered the Venetian monetary orbit. The 1405 annexation was only the culmination of an evolution long since evident in the economy.

Related to this is one last feature of the history of the University of Padua. While the university, as we have seen, was tending to limit its student base to the immediate locality, it was becoming the University of Venice. The regionalization of universities actually strengthened Padua and may have been responsible for its development and renewal. Venice, in fact, subsequently forbade its subjects to study anywhere else and required training at Padua for certain of its own public offices. Of even greater consequence was the fact that Venice, as a bastion of religious tolerance, made Padua a broad-based institution open to students of all religious persuasions during the period of the Reformation and Counterreformation. As a result, Padua became the center of ideological coexistence in fifteenth- and sixteenth-century Europe.[48]

In appendix II (p. 310), the statement of expenditures for maintenance and upkeep of the furnishings of the college of jurists at Padua for 1454 may be found. Discovered on a flyleaf inserted in the manuscript of the statutes, this text is illustrative of a whole series of decisions found in these same statutes. Certain decrees of 1365 and 1382 concern the acquisition of furniture for use during examinations, its maintenance to be financed by assessment of the candidates[49]—which is confirmed by the particulars of the expenses noted by Matthew de Grandis. This particular list was preserved because in 1454 the prior Franciscus of Alvarotis had advanced the required sum and so had the amount totaled up in order to obtain partial reimbursement from the college. He even took the precaution of mentioning it in an addition to the college's book of statutes.[50]

This text will be of interest to anyone studying the history of wages and prices in the fifteenth century.[51] It contains information concerning such items as the importance of waterways for transport of building materials. Specialists will even find it a valuable resource for adding to our knowledge of the technical vocabulary of the trades.[52]

TRADES AND PROFESSIONS AS REPRESENTED IN MEDIEVAL CONFESSORS' MANUALS

To study such concrete realities as trades and professions, even if one acknowledges their important connection to mental attitudes, through the medium of confessors' manuals requires justification or, at least, explanation.

How can we expect the clerics who wrote such manuals, outsiders to the world of the active life, to have been trustworthy observers of the problems of that life?

This question is, in fact, part of a larger one bearing on the whole history of the medieval West. Virtually all the works by which the period is represented to us are religious in nature. Since our own world is one in which, at every level, the religious sphere is distinguished from the secular, a question arises as to what value should be accorded to evidence which, at first sight, seems to distort the facts under consideration.

It is therefore important to examine briefly the significance of the medieval religious document.

First, it should be pointed out that, throughout the Middle Ages, education was the privilege of clerics. The equations *clericus = litteratus, laicus = illiteratus* are significant. *Litteratus*, of course, meant one who knew (more or less) Latin. For a long while, however, Latin was the essential medium of culture in the Middle Ages.[1] By this we do not wish to deny the importance of a certain secular culture then coming into being. Nor do we wish to argue for the precedence formerly accorded to written records, now displaced to a certain extent, as they ought to be, by nonwritten evidence such as the archaeological and folkloric data which are disclosing a broader and deeper culture than that of the *litterati*.[2] In the Middle Ages, however, the expression of thought and feeling by the majority, even of laymen, was influenced by religion and directed toward religious ends. In addition, all mental equipment, such as vocabulary, thought patterns, aesthetic and moral norms, etc., was religious in nature. In this area, "progress"—but that is another problem—would indeed take the form of secularization of the cultural instruments.

What do we know about the material reality of the Middle Ages? It is this very material reality that is important in the workers' awareness of their own daily activity. Such awareness begins with the tool, with the job, with everyday life. To what extent did religion's hold over the medieval mind put a screen between *homo faber* and ourselves, or, conversely, how far can we legitimately consider the religious representation to offer a valid intermediary between concrete reality and our historical enterprise?

My feeling is that literary sources can play a role of great importance in the work of the historian studying mentalities that were connected with material life and work. I am speaking not only of clerical literature but even of religious documents, of which confessors' manuals are a primary instance.

In the first place, it is possible for the historian to rediscover the material substratum behind its religious translations. The plow, the mill, and the press, to name a few basic pieces of technical and economic equipment, do, of course, appear as symbols in medieval literature and iconography.[3] Even at this very basic level of descriptive inventory, however, there is an extraordinary wealth of detail and material content in religious works. Medieval hagiography, for example, has supplied a mine of information on material life, particularly for the early Middle Ages: the beginning of coal mining in Dauphiné, the transportation of salt on the Moselle from Metz to Trèves in the seventh century, the presence of a plane or a wheelbarrow on a capital or in a miniature, and so forth.[4] During the Middle Ages technical progress was perceived as a miracle, as a domination of nature which could have no origin other than divine grace.[5] In such a context, however, the material detail is already a feature of a mentality and has consequences beyond the descriptive or anecdotal.

On this level, the use of written religious sources for the history of techniques and of the technical mentality presupposes an analysis in depth of religious themes and their relation to the global historical conjuncture. Thus the evolution of the theme of the active versus the contemplative life—Martha and Mary, Rachel and Leah—is explained by the growth of artisanal and commercial activity beginning in the eleventh century; representations of cities in seals, windows, miniatures, and frescoes are connected with urban development, but historical changes have been taken into account: the Urbs is no longer Rome, the city that obsessed the ancient imagination, but rather Jerusalem, and not merely the real, earthly Jerusalem, which was invested with all the signs of the prestige of the celestial Jerusalem for which it stood, but Jerusalem as a concrete symbol for all cities, for the essential city ...

Such relations between the religious universe and the material world remain external. On a more profound level, that of spirituality, it should be noted that nothing could become an object of conscious reflection in the Middle Ages except by way of religion. It would almost be possible to define a medieval mentality by its inability to express itself apart from religious references. As Lucien Febvre has brilliantly demonstrated, this remains the case as late as the sixteenth century. Craft guilds represented themselves to the world by taking the tools of their trade and making them the attributes of a saint, integrated in a hagiographic legend, in works they commissioned. This was quite natural, since the members of such guilds formed their conceptions of their work through the mediation of religion. Consciousness of an individual or collective situation, including a professional situation, is a form of participation; in the Middle Ages this could only have been participation in a religious universe—more precisely, the universe offered or imposed by the Church. But the problem is precisely here: wasn't the Church's universe one that excluded the trades?

First, it should be noted that in the medieval West, at least until the fifteenth century, a revolt against the Church and its mental and spiritual universe almost always took on a somewhat hyperreligious character—a form of mystical religiosity, one of whose principal characteristics was to exclude material, and consequently professional, life from integration into the religious universe. Almost all such revolts expressed themselves as heresies, usually of Manichaean, dualist character. Material life was classified as a part of the universe of evil. Labor, as performed, and consequently conceived, by the heretics, served the Church-supported established order and was therefore condemned as a form of servitude to, or even complicity with, a reviled state of affairs. It seems to me certain that medieval heresies had a social basis and, still more, a social origin, although the composition and social structure of heretical movements is complex. Certain social groups rushed headlong into heresy because of discontentment with their social and economic situation—for example, nobles envious of ecclesiastical property; merchants irked that they did not occupy a place in the social hierarchy commensurate with their economic strength; and workers, whether serfs or wage laborers in the countryside or weavers and fullers in the city, who rose against a system to which the Church seemed to give its support. But on the level of consciousness, all forms of labor were irrevocably condemned. Among the Cathari, for example, labor was tolerated for those believers who continued to lead a worldly existence tainted with evil, but it was forbidden to the *perfecti*, or the pure. It is likely that the inability of medieval heresies between the eleventh and fourteenth centuries to define a spiritual and ethical system appropriate to labor was an important cause of their failure. Conversely, a reason for the present success of the various forms of socialism, primarily of Marxism, might be that they did succeed in defining such a system.[6]

By contrast, the medieval Church was able to fashion ideological structures suited to the spiritual needs arising out of professional activity. It is this fact that makes it legitimate to approach questions of professional consciousness through the orthodox penitential literature of the Middle Ages.

For the Church to have succeeded as it did, it of course had to evolve. From its inception, Christianity did offer a spiritual approach to labor, a veritable theology of work.[7] Its bases are to be found in the Bible, notably in Paul's writings (2 Thess. 3:10: "If any would not work, neither should he eat"), as well as in the works of the Fathers, particularly the Greek Fathers such as Saint Basil and Saint John Chrysostomos. Between the fourth and twelfth centuries, however, this aspect of Christianity remained merely a latent and undeveloped possibility, perhaps overwhelmed by other aspects. The economic and social condition of the early Middle Ages found its expression in the well-known tripartite schema of society, which was a resurgence of a concept common to all Indo-European societies, as Georges Dumézil, among others, has shown.[8] This schema, which divides society into the three classes of *oratores, bellatores,* and *laboratores,* is a hierarchical one. If the *oratores*—the clerics—ultimately came to accept the *bellatores* at their side in a position of eminence, both these groups were in accord in regarding the inferior order of workers, *laboratores,* with the utmost contempt. Labor was thus discredited by association with the baseness of the class that monopolized toil. The Church explained the serf's lowly condition as that of society's scapegoat, invoking man's servitude to sin. Labor's disgrace was the result of original sin, on which the text provides all the necessary commentary. In this connection, there should be no mistaking the position of Saint Benedict and Benedictine spirituality with regard to labor.[9] The Benedictine Rule imposes labor on monks in two forms, manual and intellectual, and both are penitences, in conformity with the ideology of the time. In the Benedictine mind during the early Middle Ages, both labor's spirituality, which was merely a penitential instrument, and its theology, according to which labor was a consequence of original sin, had only negative value, as it were.[10] Scarcely more positive was the accompanying conception of labor as a remedy for idleness, which stood in the way of the temptations of the devil.

If the Church had persisted in this attitude, professional consciousness would no doubt have been quite different from what it was. The Church's opposition to this consciousness came not only in the form of a perceptual screen but also in the shape of a physical obstacle. There were two principal ways in which the Church manifested its hostility.

First, it was directed at the guilds. Hostility to the guilds was not merely reserved for the occasions when they spearheaded the fight against the temporal power of the lord-bishops of cities in the name of urban, primarily economic freedom. As an enemy of monopoly and supporter of the *justum pretium*, or free-market price,[11] the Church was in a more profound sense opposed to the fundamental aim of the guilds, which was to eliminate competition in the urban marketplace.[12] The Church was suspicious of the guild as such, moreover, because it recognized as legitimate only those groups which it held to derive from the divine will and human nature; it regarded the tripartite schema as being at once natural and supernatural, and it accepted classifications based on proper religious or ecclesiastical criteria, such as Christian–non-Christian, clerical–lay, etc. Organization of the trades was accepted only to the extent that it also had the character of religious organization: the brotherhoods (*confréries*). This meant that professional consciousness was formed under very special conditions, involving a sort of dialectic between the corporative spirit and the confraternal spirit which it is important to take into account, despite the great difficulty of doing so as long as our understanding of the history of the brotherhoods remains poor.[13]

Second, the Church's hostility to trade was reflected in its suspicion toward many professional activities. The whole gamut of illicit trades was implicated in this suspicion; their history is particularly illuminating.[14] How often the Middle Ages must have witnessed the inner drama of men anxiously wondering whether they were really hastening toward damnation because they were engaging in a trade suspect in the eyes of the Church. The merchant comes naturally to mind. Such dramas must ultimately have played a leading role in the formation of professional consciousness. In the end, the Church had to capitulate to the pressures exerted by the trades. Only then could the seed of a positive theology of labor contained in Christian doctrine at last germinate, which ultimately led to a conquest of spiritual dignity by groups that had first risen to material power.

The world of religion is thus an ideal area for adding to our knowledge of mental representations of the technological and professional domain in the medieval West, provided that the historian does not lose sight of the situation of the latter domain within the encompassing religious world. There is a triple aspect to this situation; explicitly, the former is contained in the latter in (1) a state of *transformation*, (2) a state of *expression*, and (3) a state of *pressure*.

In this connection, we shall use confessors' manuals to help answer the following question: how did the Church change the tripartite schema into one that was more flexible and open to the diversified working world of trades and professions, and what new mental representations resulted from this change?

Confessors' manuals are valuable as evidence in dealing with professional consciousness because they reflect the pressure brought to bear on the Church by men engaged in given types of work. Conversely, they were one of the principal tools in the formation of professional consciousness in medieval men from the thirteenth century on.

The doctrine embodied in such manuals was not merely dispensed in the confessional. They had a more direct and lasting influence on men who obtained and read them for themselves. In contrast with today's practice, these manuals were not restricted to confessors but were available to penitents as well. Significantly, the first confessors' manuals to be translated into vulgar tongues *ad usum laicorum* were those which devoted the greatest amount of space to the problems of professional conscience, such as the *Summa* of John of Freiburg translated into German by the Dominican Berthold Hunlen as early as the end of the thirteenth century. Evidently they were acquired principally by merchants who had the money and education to purchase and read them, and whose professional activities raised the thorniest questions of conscience.[15] After the end of the fifteenth century, printing further extended, at least for a while, the influence of the most important of these manuals.

It is worthwhile pausing to give some additional details concerning the kind of evidence these manuals offer as to the ideological pressure exerted by various professional milieus.

The origins of the evolving professional consciousness which culminated in the confessors' manuals can be traced back to the twelfth century,[16] where a threefold evolutionary process may be observed: (1) a subjectivization of the spiritual life, accessible primarily through the development of the confession; (2) the emergence of a spirituality and theology of labor; (3) the transformation of the tripartite schema of society into models better adapted to the increasing differentiation of social and economic structures, due to the increasing division of labor.

1. The barbarized world of which the early medieval Church was a part was an extrovert world, oriented toward exterior tasks and material ends or rewards, such as conquest, food, power, and salvation in the hereafter. It was a world we may call primitive, defined by attitudes, conduct, and gestures. Men could be judged only according to their acts, not according to their feelings. This may be seen in barbarian law as well as in any of the codes of the early Middle Ages. The *Wergeld,* for example, does consider men as well as their acts, according not to their intentions but rather to their objective situation, using a very rudimentary classification (free and nonfree, membership in such and such a national community). This was also the practice of the Church, whose only access to souls was through bodily gestures. Its codes were the penitentials, tables of spiritual penalties, which were more concerned with the sin than with the sinner.[17] At best, two classes of sinners were singled out, clerics and laymen, sanctions against clerics being heavier than those against laymen. The sins themselves existed not because of the sinner but rather because of a vice that was independent of him, to which he fell prey when it entered him as an alien being, a materialization of the devil. Throughout the early Middle Ages, spiritual life was conceived as a combat modeled on Prudentius' *Psychomachia.* According to the most widespread codification, the vices in question were the deadly sins.[18] Should one succumb to the enemies pride, gluttony, avarice, lust, sloth, envy, or vainglory, one was required to pay, and the amount of the penalty was almost automatically specified by the penitentials. In a world ruled by external forces of good and evil, it is not surprising that judgment should be left to chance, characterized as Providence: the ordeal was the form of God's judgment.[19] There was no room for individuals in this world, unless they were truly extraordinary beings such as saints or heroes, the former excelling among the *oratores,* the latter among the *bellatores.* In fact, there were only two literary genres in the early medieval West, the gests and hagiography. Other individuals existed only through participation in the being of the hero or saint: the biographer who wrote or the minstrel who sang his praise, the ironsmith who forged his sword, the goldsmith who fashioned the outward signs of his wealth and power. During this era family names did not exist, and the anonymous masses derived their meager portion of individuality from the first name of their patron saint, which conferred on whoever bore it a little of the exalted being of the spiritual father.

In the twelfth century a considerable change came about. The history of the confession and penitence has been written.[20] The role played by such great minds as Saint Anselm and Abelard in this development is known. Yet they only gave expression and polish to what was a broad trend. Roman law, particularly through its influence on canon law, acted as a stimulus and a source of methods and formulas. Subsequently, the sin was to be considered less than the sinner, the offense became less important than the intention, and contrition was sought rather than penitence. This was a phenomenon of subjectivization and internalization of the spiritual life, from which introspection and hence the whole of modern Western psychology originated. It is no accident that all the important spiritual doctrines of the twelfth century may be defined as Christian Socraticisms, whether intellectualist as in Abelard; mystical as in Hugh of Saint-Victor, Hildegard of Bingen, or Saint Bernard; or even the grammatical and scientific humanism of Chartres.

The West had hitherto been closed in on itself and even colonized by the more advanced civilizations of Byzantium and Islam, but now, just as it was embarking on foreign conquests from Scandinavia to the Holy Land, another pioneer frontier was being opened within Western man himself, the frontier of conscience. We find ourselves at the threshold of the inner world of conscience.

It will not be possible here to follow this major development in all its detail. We should, however, mention the essential role of the technical and economic evolution which began around the year 1000 and became solidly established in both quantitative and qualitative senses during the twelfth century. The resumption of trade and the growth of cities made possible by agricultural and demographic advances, and the resultant specialization of labor by trades, brought about a new social mobility which led to mental and spiritual transformation. Man emerged from the indistinct mass in which he had languished. The time of the individual had not yet come, however. The individual was a creation of the modern world, of the Renaissance. What has been called the twelfth-century renaissance was only an intermediate, though important, step. Each man's new consciousness of himself came to him only through the *estate* to which he belonged, the professional group of which he was a part, or the trade in which he engaged. The process of personalization took place within a larger process of socialization. Since this consciousness could only be religious, it offered itself in the form of a *vocation*.

2. This self-consciousness became possible, however, only because of a change in attitude with regard to labor. The change begins to be evident at the beginning of the twelfth century. The confrontation between the active and contemplative lives was revived in the debate between canons and monks, fed by a number of burning issues of the day. On the theoretical plane, there was a rehabilitation of Martha, and in practice, manual labor was restored to a place of honor with the Carthusians and particularly the Cistercians and Premonstratensians. Of course, the influence of tradition continued,

and strong resistance to change appeared. Still, the founding of new orders makes clear that something had changed, that a mutation had occurred in the Benedictine spirit, for why else would such new rules be necessary? It is, of course, possible to point to a Rupert of Deutz, who was irritated by the vogue for manual labor, or to a Peter the Venerable somewhat stunned by the attacks of Saint Bernard, both of whom point out that, according to Saint Benedict, manual labor, advisable but not obligatory, was merely a means and not an end of spiritual life. But there is abundant evidence from every quarter that the spiritual attitude toward labor was undergoing a crucial development through practice. A genuine debate was begun around Prémontré over the issue of peasant monks, and, with the Umiliati, the question of worker-monks arose soon thereafter.[21] Meanwhile, theoretical consideration of the value of labor was in a state of agitation, exemplified by the *Liber de diversis ordinibus*.[22] The concept of penitential labor was supplanted by the idea of labor as a positive means to salvation.[23] Behind the growing importance of this new monastic world, it is impossible not to notice the pressure being exerted by new professional categories, such as merchants, craftsmen, and workers, concerned with finding religious justification for their activity and vocation, anxious to assert their dignity and obtain assurance of their salvation, not in spite of, but rather because of, their profession. Once again, the image of such aspirations as projected in hagiography is instructive. With the beginning of the thirteenth century, the working saint was losing ground, giving way to the saintly worker.[24]

This new spiritual attitude towards labor tended, naturally, to strike deep roots with a theology of labor. For the outlines of this theology, we must look to the commentaries on Genesis, which attempted to demonstrate that labor had its positive roots in God because (1) the Creator's work (here, the development of the theme of the *summus artifex* or *summus opifex* should be traced) was genuine labor—sublime labor, to be sure, a creation, but one which entailed the usual painful consequences, as seen in the fact that the creation was a *labor* from which God had to rest on the seventh day. God was the first worker. (2) Man, Adam, had been given a certain labor as his vocation before the Fall, a labor which was to be understood as a kind of maintenance, since God had placed him in the Garden "to dress it and to keep it" (Genesis 2:15). Thus before penitential labor, which was a consequence of sin and the Fall, there had been joyful labor, blessed by God, and earthly labor had kept about it something of the quality of the paradisiacal labor from before the fall.

3. It is hardly surprising that, in such a conjuncture, the tripartite schema of society should no longer correspond well to social and

mental realities. What is interesting, however, is that in primitive Indo-European societies the appearance of a self-assertive economic class brought about only a limited reworking of the tripartite schema, involving either the addition of a fourth class or the absorption of the new category into one of the already existing classes, whereas in medieval Western society the old schema fell apart completely. The tripartite schema did, of course, persist (although not without transformation, it survived, for instance, until 1789 in the France of the Three Estates), but it receded before more elaborate categorizations, which took hold thanks to a growing awareness and sanctioning of the diversification and division of labor.

It is true that there was continuity and even reinforcement of the unitary conception of Christian society, and this fact even played a role in assuring the new socioprofessional categories the right to a vocation. But the Christian *corpus* acquired a new structure, based on function, trade, and profession. The *corpus* was no longer composed of *orders*, as it had been in the sacred society of the early Middle Ages, but rather of estates, which could, and actually did, coexist within a hierarchy. It was a horizontal rather than a vertical hierarchy, however. Literature and art developed and canonized the theme of the *worldly estates* (*états du monde*), of which the ultimate and terrible expression in the waning Middle Ages was the dance of death. In certain respects, the confessors' manuals, or at least some of them, were related to this new literary genre, in imitation of the *ad status* sermons.

Regardless of the influences or vocabularies involved, we encounter this tendency in nearly all thought and doctrine of the twelfth century.

In John of Salisbury, it was integrated with the old organic conception of humanity. Mankind was held to resemble a human organism, each part of which corresponded to a profession or trade guild—peasants, craftsmen, and workers were the feet of the *respublica*.[25]

Using what may have been a Stoic vocabulary, Geroch of Reichersberg evoked "the great factory of the universe, a sort of universal workshop." However theologically inclined twelfth-century man was, what overtones of the concrete reality of the material world he must have felt behind words like *fabrica* and *officina*. In his book with the already significant title of *Liber de aedificio Dei*, Geroch goes on to assert that every human condition has a Christian value and that every profession is a valid means to salvation.[26]

For Honorius Augustodunensis, ignorance was exile for man; man's true home lay in the wisdom achieved through study of the liberal arts. He compared their study to passage through as many different cities (note, in passing, the urban reference). Ten such arts were listed: the seven traditional ones, to which Honorius added physics, mechanics, and economics. His was a universe of doing and making as well as knowing.[27]

As the new world was conceptualized, a role of great importance was played by the idea of the *common good.* It became the touchstone of the utility and legitimacy of every profession.

It should be noted that along with the collapse of the tripartite schema came the end of the traditional framework of the seven liberal arts and the division between the mechanical and the liberal arts. While Otto of Freising had been surprised to find that in Italy "even the craftsmen of the mechanical arts" were held in high esteem, Hugh of Saint-Victor in the *Didascalicon* put the mechanical arts alongside the liberal arts in a new classification of the sciences, which we later encounter in Robert Grosseteste and Saint Thomas Aquinas in the thirteenth century.[28]

By the beginning of the thirteenth century the spiritual guides had been affected by the evolution of public opinion, in whose consideration the virtuous hero had been supplanted by the skillful technician. The Guiot Bible declared that henceforth knights had to give precedence to crossbowmen, miners, stonecutters, and engineers. The evolution of military technique compromised the professional supremacy of the feudal knight. The developments were comprehensive. Guiot de Provins exaggerates, anticipates, but he does reveal one tendency of public opinion.

Thus, on the threshold of the thirteenth century, the ideological conditions and mental structures needed for the consecration of the various professions were present. In the accomplishment of this consecration, the transformation of penitential practices as guided by the confessors' manuals played a leading role.

We have been observing a threefold evolutionary process: the evolution of confession, of the conception of labor, and of the schema of social structure. At this point, two developments of major importance made it possible for this evolutionary process to produce its full effect.

The first of these was canon 21 of the Fourth Lateran Council of 1215, which made annual confession obligatory for all Christians, in other words, for virtually all people in the Western world. Thereafter, confessors were regularly besieged with questions, many of which were embarrassing because (1) many confessors were inadequately informed and knew nothing of recent developments in canon law, particularly since the Decretum of Gratian; and (2) most of them had been trained in a traditional spirit and atmosphere and were incapable of resolving (and at times even of comprehending) the problems put to them by their penitents, in particular the problems represented by *cases of conscience* (a new and revealing term, often called *De casibus conscientiae* in the confessors' manuals) arising in the course of professional activity: was such and such an operation legitimate? Should the necessities of the job take precedence over prescriptions of the Church concerning fasting, Sunday rest, etc.? The confessors needed guides and manuals, and for these, capable authors were required.

This brings us to the second of the two developments mentioned above. These authors appeared in the form of certain members of the new mendicant orders. They derived their competence from the fact that they were educated, for in addition to their own *studia* they were quick to attend the new universities, and from the fact that, in contrast to the twelfth-century orders and to a large portion of the Benedictines, they did not live in solitude or in rural surroundings but rather in the cities, in the heart of the urban enrivonment with its diverse forms of labor and professional activity and new forms of spiritual curiosity, among the sort of men who raised problems and asked questions of themselves and their confessors.

Confessors' manuals are in two respects an accurate reflection of the growing self-consciousness of the professionals and of the pressure they brought to bear on the Church to take them into consideration. First, they contain the actual concrete questions raised by men in the trades. When we read questions such as "Is it legitimate to sell on credit?" or "Is it legitimate to work in fields or sell at fairs on Sundays?" we can be sure that we are looking at the Latin translation of a question a penitent has put to his confessor and not at a theme of abstract scholastic discussion. Second, the authors of the manuals were specialists in matters of professional conscience, well acquainted with the world to which they offered guidance. At the end of the thirteenth century, Pierre Dubois wrote: "The Franciscan and Dominican friars, who know better than anyone else the actual state of society ... , who know how everyone behaves ... "

Three themes relevant to our subject emerge from these manuals,[29] in particular from the most important and widely used of them, from the *Summa* of Raymond de Peñafort (between 1222 and 1230) to the *Summa pisanella* completed by Bartholomew on 7 December 1338 at Sancto Concordio, along with the intervening Franciscan *Summa molindina* and *Astesana* and another by the Dominican John of Freiburg. These themes are the following: (1) Every Christian is essentially defined in relation to his profession: vocation and salvation. (2) All labor deserves compensation: vocation and money. (3) Every profession based on labor is justified: vocation and labor.

1. Previously, sinners had been classified according to the list of deadly sins. This traditional classification was continued in the

confessors' manuals. Another scheme of classification tended to supplant it, however, one which considered categories of sinners rather than sins, such sinners being grouped by profession: clerical sins, academic sins, judges' sins, peasants' sins, mechanics' sins, etc. In both confession and preaching (and the thirteenth century was a great one for preaching, with the mendicant and particularly the Dominican friars, known as the Preachers), we thus have a new genre, the teaching of religion *ad status*. Alan of Lille in the *Summa de arte praedicatoria*, Humbert of Romans in the second book of the *De eruditione praedicatorium*, and James of Vitry, among others, have left *sermones ad status*. The new penitential texts lay stress on questions to be put *secundum officia*.[30]

The twenty-first canon of the Fourth Lateran Council specifies "that the priest be capable of discernment and prudence, so that he may pour wine and oil on the wounds of the victim in the manner of a competent physician, after conducting a careful inquiry into the circumstances surrounding the sinner as well as the sin."

The *Summa Astesana* of ca. 1317 is still more explicit (lib. V, cap. XVII, "Questions to ask during confession"): "Sins typical of men of the penitent's station must be inquired about. A knight must not be questioned about the sins of a monk, or vice versa... To gain a better understanding of whom you must question about what, observe that princes are to be questioned about justice, knights about plunder, merchants, officials, craftsmen, and workers about perjury, fraud, lying, theft, etc.... bourgeois and/ city dwellers generally about usury and chattel mortgage, peasants about covetousness and theft, especially in regard to the tithe, etc."

This principle of confession according to professionally categorized sins was clearly the inspiration for the plan of a manual in widespread use at the end of the thirteenth century, the handbook "for less educated and less competent confessors" taken by John of Freiburg from his *Summa confessorum* and commonly entitled *Confessionale*. The first section of this handbook, devoted to sins found generally in all sinners, is followed by a second section which treats the sins of the various socioprofessional categories: (1) bishops and other prelates; (2) clerics and holders of benefices; (3) curates and their vicars and confessors; (4) friars and monks; (5) judges; (6) attorneys and solicitors; (7) physicians; (8) professors and academics; (9) princes and other nobles; (10) married laymen; (11) merchants and bourgeois; (12) craftsmen and workers; (13) peasants and farmers; (14) manual laborers.[31]

All the professional categories are treated by this catalogue, which has here been reduced to its table of contents, although a detailed commentary could be developed. This was possible because the number of illicit and proscribed trades had been reduced to the point of excluding only a very small number of fringe groups and individuals.[32] The distinction made between illicit trades *de sui natura*, which were consequently condemned absolutely, and other trades only occasionally discredited *ex causa, ex tempore,* or *ex personna* contributed to the reduction of the domain of the excluded and damned to quite small proportions. For instance, the merchant, a pariah of the preceding period, was no longer banished from society unless he engaged in certain activities which were becoming ever less common.[33] For him and others, casuistry brought justification and liberation.

Formerly tabooed areas gained acceptance.

2. Primary among them was the world of money.

In the barbarian West before the thirteenth century, all remunerated activity incurred the opprobrium reserved for so-called mercenary categories. Whatever could be bought and paid for was considered odious. Honor and duty were defined in terms of services involving reciprocal obligations. Money, marginal in an economic sense, was no better off morally. This belief on the part of Christian society in the early Middle Ages was reinforced by the sight of a monetary sector "infested" with Jews. The continuous progress of commercialization and the wage-earning sector revolutionized these values.

Two categories or trades were leaders in this movement. First were the teachers. Science and culture before the twelfth century were limited to clerics, who acquired and dispensed learning parsimoniously without money changing hands. Monastic and episcopal schools trained disciples for the *opus Dei*, which could not be converted to cash.

The material, social, and spiritual status of knowledge was fundamentally transformed when the urban schools of the twelfth century were caught up in the growth of the cities. These schools were run by masters, who, like their students, had to provide for the needs of their families.[34] This situation explains the point of the debate which began in the middle of the twelfth century over the slogan "Knowledge is a gift from God and therefore cannot be sold." It is not important to examine here in detail what possibilities of remuneration were offered the new masters or which solutions would carry the day, whether public salary, payment by the clients, i.e., students, or ecclesiastical benefices. The crucial matter was the question: "Can the masters legitimately receive money from students?" to which the confessors' manuals, echoing actual practice and public opinion, replied in the affirmative.[35]

An analogous question arose in connection with credit for merchants when the expanding monetary economy relegated Jews, confined to making loans of limited scope, to the second rank. Subsequently, the problem of Christian *usury* had to be faced. Interest, without which precapitalist monetary economy could not develop, involved an activity previously damned, in scholastic terms: the sale of time. In precise symmetry with the problem of trade in knowledge, a problem of trade in time arose and was opposed by the same tradition and slogan: "Time is a gift from God and therefore cannot be sold." Once again, though coupled, to be sure, with certain precautions and a restrictive casuistry, the answer found in the confessors' manuals was favorable to the new practices.[36]

3. In both cases, the same justification was offered, significantly changing the interpretation of the Gospel text. Where Matthew had said "the workman is worthy of his meat" (Matthew 10:10), exegetes now said the workman was worthy of his wages, evidence of transition from a natural to a money economy. The important point was that for a salary to be merited, labor had to be performed. Labor was still an ambiguous concept, marked by the essentially medieval confusion between trouble, fatigue, and the performance of an economic task in the modern sense. Labor was toil.

The necessary and sufficient condition for legitimization of a trade and for payment of a wage was the requirement of labor.

Here again, the intellectual and the merchant found similar justification for their new socioprofessional status. If the *magister* or the merchant were to receive a legitimate wage without fear of damnation, the remuneration or benefice (the late Middle Ages maintained no clear distinction between the two) had to be compensation for their toil. It was necessary and sufficient that they work. The confessors' manuals were confirmed by the guild statutes: a wage or benefice was legitimate when it was accepted *pro labore*.[37] Labor became the standard reference value.

This outline should be complemented with a history of the postfourteenth-century avatars of labor value in Western society. In spite of its absolution by the Middle Ages, labor remained a fragile value, threatened and arraigned continually by social and economic evolution. Before as well as after the Industrial Revolution, social classes which had risen owing to labor hastened to deny their working roots. Labor has really never ceased to be a sort of mark of servility. As early as the thirteenth century, a new social cleavage came into being. Although idleness had no future as a social and ethical value, labor was arraigned at its most basic level, that of manual labor. "I do not work with my hands," proclaimed the poor man Rutebeuf. John of Freiburg's *Confessionale* reserved the lowest position for the simple workers, *laboratores*. Hardly had *feudal* values been vanquished when workers divided against themselves. History was not over.

HOW DID THE MEDIEVAL UNIVERSITY
CONCEIVE OF ITSELF?

We beg the reader to excuse the rapid and fragmentary character of the following remarks, intended as a modest contribution to the statement and discussion of the problem of the medieval universities' awareness of their own specificity.

We have gathered a series of notes relating to a limited number of works and individuals associated with a single academic center, Paris. Our investigation rests primarily on Abelard's *Historia calamitatum* and Philip of Harvengt's *De institutione clericorum* (glossed with some extracts from his correspondence) for the twelfth century, a few documents relating to the important doctrinal and corporative conflicts of the thirteenth century (with special attention paid to Sigerian circles and the condemned propositions of 1277), and, finally, a few of Gerson's writings representing the early fifteenth century. We have, then, three clearly characterized periods in the history of the university: the genesis, the crisis of maturity, and the torpor of the waning Middle Ages.

These choices bring with them certain obvious limitations. The evidence is tainted by the often powerful, if not blinding, personalities of the protagonists and by the distortion caused by the transient circumstances of a polemical quarrel. We must also be wary of the narrowing of our field of view caused by reliance on a few elements chosen from a much vaster range of thought and from very full lives: neither Abelard nor Siger of Brabant nor Gerson is contained in the tiny portion of their work that we are considering.

The notes we have gathered give only a hasty impression, in part because such chronological cross-sections involve the risk that the underlying, continuous life of the university will escape our notice, and in part because we cannot examine here in any depth the complex of economic, social, political, institutional, intellectual, and spiritual problems from which the moments in time studied here have been isolated.[1] Where, for instance, would the great debates of the thirteenth century have led us? Then, too, our impression is a hasty one particularly because we have resigned ourselves to do no more than shed a little light on certain aspects of the larger theoretical problem, which is still somewhat undefined.

In the question of how consciousness is formed, we face one of the central—and most difficult—problems of history. The investigation should be designed to proceed along several convergent paths. The central areas of observation, and even experimentation, have to be defined, and tools and methods chosen. Finally (perhaps?) we need to adopt a basic criterion for identifying the essential phenomenon, the decisive moment at which the infrastructures are perceived, in which the group recognizes and affirms itself and comes into being for a second time through a conscious awareness of its own originality.

Its very difficulties, then, make this an excellent theme, of heightened interest by reason of its connection with the theme of the 1960 Mediävistentagung, vocation, which it extends and develops.

In this essay, we have chosen one of several possible avenues of approach, adopting the point of view of the intellectual formulation of the university's role relative to other groups and classes of the society. In looking particularly for difference and, at times, opposition, we shall attempt to locate some of the key stages in the formation by academics of a consciousness of their status and its changing fortunes within medieval Western society.

In the days of Abelard and Philip of Harvengt, of course, there were as yet no academics. In the urban schools, however, of which Abelard was the first brilliant representative, and whose existence, novelty, and utility Philip of Harvengt was one of the first to recognize, a new trade and a new kind of artisan were coming into existence. Academics would emerge from the hierarchical milieu of the scholarly trade, and its *scolares* and *magistri*.[2]

In the *Historia calamitatum*, which adopts the point of view of the individual temperament, though a temperament that is professional at the same time, Abelard[3] defines himself in relation to the petty nobility from which he sprang. He imparts the invaluable information that in his circles it was the rule to couple a certain intellectual culture with military skill, *litterae et arma*.[4] For him, a choice between the two became necessary and dramatic. A latterday Esau, he had to renounce his birthright when he sacrificed the "pompa militaris gloriae" to the "studium letterarum." Thus the choice of what was to become a profession was a radical one which forced him to quit his

123

social group and renounce a way of life, a mentality, an ideal, a family and social structure. Instead, he was faced with a total commitment: "Tu eris magister in aeternum."

It is interesting, however, to observe that Abelard expresses himself on the subject of his career with the aid of a military vocabulary, and this choice is surely no mere rhetorical artifice. He regards dialectic as an arsenal, arguments as weapons, *disputationes* as battles. The Minerva for whose sake he abandons Mars is an armed and warlike goddess.[5] Like a young knight, he attacked his old masters,[6] and his scholastic apprenticeship was that of a conscript—*tirocinium*.[7] Intellectual struggles he regarded as tournaments.[8] Thus the son of a minor nobleman of Pallet preserved the imprint of his origin, just as his century had retained the mark of its origins in the style of life and vocabulary of the dominant class. This was the century of Saint Bernard, in which the *athletae Domini* made up the *militia Christi*.[9]

Having found his identity in freeing himself from the world of knights, Abelard was less successful in differentiating himself from another milieu, that of the monks. This difficulty was due not only to the vicissitudes of his existence but also, in a more profound sense, to the condition of the clergy in his time. In the monasteries in which he was forced to closet himself, it was less the baseness of the manners, the coarseness of the rural way of life, and the hostility that made his exile unbearable than it was the impossibility of leading a life devoted to intellectual research and teaching, activities that had become incompatible with monastic life.[10]

Transplanted to the monastery as to a foreign soil, he wasted away and turned sterile: "In tears, I considered the futility and wretchedness of the life I was going to lead; and the sterility, for my own sake as well as others, of my existence; and the fact that, after being of great use to the clerics, now, forced to abandon them because of the monks, I would be of no use either to them or to the monks, and the fruit of my research and striving would be wasted."[11]

We notice a hostility not only to the monastic tradition but also to the new monasticism, already beginning to run out of steam in the twelfth century. This was the monasticism of the hermits, the itinerant preachers, the regular canons, and all the reformers of monastic life, to whom Abelard refers disdainfully as *novi apostoli*.[12]

By contrast, his was the urban world: "ad urbem . . . rediens"[13] was the direction in which he, his disciples, and his imitators were constantly pushed. At the time of the "eremitical" episode at Paraclet—"they looked more like hermits than students"[14]—the students' enthusiasm was rapidly transformed into nostalgia for the city. The future academics' self-consciousness was only one aspect of the self-awareness of the new urban society.

Besides differentiating itself from the monastic world, this new social group of scholars more generally asserted that to live in any way other than by its special profession and its own type of labor was impossible and repellent: "At that time, an intolerable poverty forced me more than ever in the direction of a school, since I was incapable of working the land and ashamed to beg. Returning, therefore, to the only trade I knew, I was forced to turn away from manual labor in order to make use of my tongue."[15] This is an important passage, the refusal of manual labor and beggary foreshadowing the great conflicts and choices of the thirteenth century: "I do not work with my hands," Rutebeuf would say.

For the "new students and scholars," the object of the quest was thus *pecunia et laus:*[16] a wage, in one form or another,[17] and glory. Here we touch on two further elements of the group's consciousness, its economic base and its professional morality.

This morality was in the first place a morale, a state of mind. Still enmeshed in the moral conceptions of the day and the traditional list of sins,[18] Abelard made no secret of the fact that the new group's *dignity*[19] could easily be turned into glory—*dedecus, gloria*[20]—and ultimately, pride, that *superbia* "which came to me particularly from science and letters."[21] The sin was merely a distortion of the professional consciousness. By way of an Aristotelian theoretical treatment, it would become, particularly in Sigerian circles in the thirteenth century, the *magnanimity* of the *philosopher.*

This last term, moreover, is indicative of the height of Abelard's awareness of the specificity of the new group to which he belonged. For a new group or type, consecration came in the form of a label.

The term philosopher also conveys the limitations, in several senses of the word, of the medieval academic. It was the name by which he preferred to be known—in itself worthy of a detailed analysis which we must beg indulgence for not attempting here. We shall confine ourselves to calling attention to the reference to the ancients, to pagans or *gentiles,* and to the intellectual and metaphysical implications of the word. Along with the assertion of the primacy of philosophy, the primacy of reason over authority was also being proclaimed. In the word philosopher, Abelardian attitudes are crystallized—"Outraged, I answered that it was not my habit to proceed by routine but rather by intelligence",[22] expressing opposition to the old dialectic and the old philosophy.[23]

Even when all due precautions are taken not to endow twelfth-century vocabulary with an anachronistic sense and scope, we are obliged to recognize the innovative, bold, and far-reaching character of what has taken place here. When we look at Sigerian circles, we will again find that the idea of the "philosopher" has made progress; when it becomes appropriate, we will point out the word's overtones and its influences on subsequent history. "Philosopher" is a name which connotes not only self-consciousness but also commitment.[24]

In turning to Philip of Harvengt, we scarcely advance in time, but we are compensated by the invaluable example of a personality different in every respect from Abelard's, which only makes his case more valuable as a complement to and confirmation of what we have learned from looking at the Parisian master.

Philip of Harvengt[25] was a moderate and in many respects a traditionalist. His enlistment in the new scholastic movement was all the more significant because the abbot of Good Hope was a member of one of those orders more given to populating and praising the wilderness than to frequenting the cities, where pre-university life was centered. We may therefore take it as a sign of the times that this Premonstratensian recognized the necessity of clerical participation in the movement, a sign which prefigured the founding in the thirteenth century of monastic academic colleges, following in the footsteps of the mendicants.

True, Philip does condemn *vagabond* students[26] as well as those hungry for pure science, knowledge for knowledge's sake—which, incidentally, is an interesting indication of the existence of this *scientistic* current, or, to put it another way, of a group interested solely in trading on its knowledge.[27]

True, he believed that the crowning science was the science of Scripture—which, moreover, accorded with the primacy that the university curriculum would grant to theology.[28]

Nevertheless, he was not only fully aware, as many others were, of the necessity for clerics to study, but he also knew and accepted the new conditions under which knowledge was acquired.

In the first place, students had to travel to one of the scholastic cities; Paris, according to him, was among the foremost of these. His praise for Paris in his letter to Heroaldus is famous.[29] As a place of learning and culture, however, Paris receives his approval in other places as well, in his letter to Engelbert, for instance: "The honor lies not simply in having been to Paris but in having acquired an honorable knowledge there."[30]

He knows that the scholarly life is a trade, *negotia scholaria*,[31] having its own economic and technical requirements. To become a scholar, one has to spend money, or rather face poverty, and not the *paupertas voluntaria* of the mendicants but the inevitable poverty of the penniless student.[32] The apprentice has need of the tools of his trade; while instruction was still mainly oral,[33] the book had already become an indispensable item: "Fortunate city," he says of Paris, "where the sacred scrolls of manuscript are examined with such zeal",[34] and further, "I doubt that there is anything better suited to a cleric than to lose himself in the study of *belles-lettres*, to sit with book in hand."[35]

Above all, he is conscious that the cleric must choose between intellectual and manual labor, although his solution, as usual, is one of moderate compromise. The passage in which he treats this problem is of special importance.[36] In the great debate over manual labor which raged in the monastic world in the twelfth and thirteenth centuries, he in effect adopted the attitude of the old monasticism. Despite the concessions that had been made to manual labor, a fashionable slogan in the twelfth century, this was in fact a hostile attitude, but in a clearly different perspective from that of a Rupert of Deutz or a Peter the Venerable, who were mainly concerned with defending the post-Benedictine and Cluniac tradition of a monastic life devoted to the *opus Dei*, as opposed to the new monasticism. We will see this modern perspective become established in the thirteenth century with the mendicants. The scholarly cleric's consciousness of specialization sharply limited the part of manual labor in his existence. Less trenchant, as always, than Abelard, Philip of Harvengt nevertheless agrees with him in this case that manual labor is no longer the business (*negotium*) of the *clericus scolaris*.

Finally, even in working out in his own fashion a reconciliation and a sort of hierarchical relationship between the monastery and the school, the cloister and the study, Philip of Harvengt carefully distinguished one from the other in yet another passage of far-reaching consequence: "For clerics, the monastic cloister must be given primary importance... Second place, however, should be given to attending schools, love of which should lead the enlightened cleric to reject secular things, so as not to embark insufficiently laden on the cloister-vessel, in order not to be shipwrecked but rather to be in a position to catch hold of the nearby bark or raft."[37]

Thus the antagonism between Saint Bernard and Philip of Harvengt went far deeper than the miscellany which brought them into conflict.[38] The soldier-monk who came to Paris to try to entice the students away, who held that the monastery was the only *schola Christi*, who hurled anathema at Paris-Babylon,[39] was opposed to the enlightened abbot who, besides trying to reconcile cloister and school, recognized the usefulness, the necessity, and the specificity of the latter and hailed the holy city of science—"merito dici possit civitas litterarum"[40]—Paris-Jerusalem.

The serious conflict between the mendicants and the secular clergy in the thirteenth century reveals just how sharply conscious of their existence as a body the Parisian academics had become.[41] Although the debate was camouflaged with a cover of doctrinal questions, and problems unrelated to corporate matters played a leading role, there is no doubt that the secular party attacked the mendicant academics because it was convinced that it was incompatible to belong both to a monastic order and to a university corporation.

We shall single out only two points of particular interest in the present context.

The first of these, of considerable importance, was the effort of certain individuals, particularly Siger of Brabant and his allies, to lay the theoretical foundations of their professional consciousness. Second, it is sometimes forgotten that the mendicants' entry into the universities caused them a number of problems, particularly in the case of the Franciscans, and that these problems shed some light on the growth of self-consciousness in the academic estate.

We shall confine ourselves to examining this inner conflict in one exemplary case, which is illuminating beyond the boundaries of the monastic world.

Although the question of learning did not involve the Franciscans in internal quarrels as bitter or as central for the order as the question of poverty, it was one of the order's key problems after the death of Saint Francis. Learning was in fact often equated with attendance at the universities, and this equivalence is revealing of the intellectual situation in the thirteenth century.

The saint's position is known. While he accepted the pursuit of a deeper knowledge of Scripture, he condemned learning in general for the Franciscans. His attitude was based on the conviction that learning was incompatible with poverty. To begin with, this incompatibility was derived from Saint Francis' traditional view of knowledge. He was imbued with the early medieval conception of knowledge as hoarding, and so regarded learning as a possession, a form of property, a treasure. This idea was reinforced by the novel aspects of learning in his own time: to attend university and possess books ran counter to the practice of poverty.

Justification of knowledge occupies a primary place in the dramatic effort of certain among the most important and illustrious of Saint Francis's disciples to adapt to the practical conditions of existence in the thirteenth century without denying the spirit of their founder.

The most important text in this connection is the *Expositio IV magistrorum super regulam*.[42] The following sentence from the rule is the object of its commentary: "From the wages of their labor, they shall accept for themselves and their brothers only what is necessary for the body, exclusive of money."

The masters comment thus: "Concerning this point, the question is to know whether the brothers, just as they receive books and other things which they may use, may receive the raw material of their trade and by their labor make something of it with which they might then acquire what they need in the way of bodily necessities, such as parchment for making books, leather for making shoes, etc. Could they, moreover, receive gold and silver and metals with which they might fashion coins and other precious things, with which they might buy what they need? Some hold that no raw material may be received as property, but labor may be lent to others who possess the raw material only in order to obtain what is necessary for the lender. This is because possession of the raw material received with an eye to selling it constitutes possession of property. Others say that distinctions must be made among various raw materials. There are in point of fact some raw materials which have no value, all value stemming from the labor involved, such as, for example, curtains and matting made from cane or similar material; such a raw material is not part of anyone's fortune, and those holding this view say that brothers may receive such raw material."

The argument is a traditional one in the monastic world, placing the accent on the *ars*, or labor, and the craft. Once the material book had been accepted, there was then a still stronger reason for accepting its contents and the intellectual labor that it inevitably supported.

Saint Bonaventura, in the *Epistola de tribus quaestionibus*, was not satisfied merely to legitimate the use of books and the pursuit of learning. At the cost, at times, of surprising contradictions with the letter of the Testament of Saint Francis itself, he limits the obligation concerning active labor as much as possible, with the evident intention of safeguarding all the necessary time and attention for intellectual work.[43]

Similarly, both the essential activity of begging and intellectual labor were absolved of the objection to manual labor. This was the culmination of an important debate in which the earlier texts of Abelard and Philip of Harvengt figured. Saint Thomas Aquinas, in the face of attacks by William of Saint-Amour and his allies and disciples, brought the controversy to a striking conclusion in his *Contra impugnantes*.[44]

With Saint Thomas, the necessity of specialization for the intellectual worker was asserted in a plain and straightforward manner. The academic had his trade. The job of working with one's hands was to be left to others—it, too, had spiritual value—but the intellectual worker was not to waste time in what was not his affair. In this way, the division of labor was legitimated on the theoretical plane and became the basis of academic specificity.

The attempt to give academic self-consciousness its most uncompromising formulation, however, was the work of secular masters and proponents of "integral Aristotelianism" or Averroism.

This formulation may be found in the first place in the *Quaestiones morales* of Siger of Brabant[45] and in the *De summo bono* of Boethius of Dacia.[46] As Father Gauthier has observed,[47] the battle raged around humility and its ethical antithesis, *magnanimity*. The problem was one of giving a theoretical basis for the *dignitas* and *gloria* of the academic already put forward by Abelard; Aristotle's *Nicomachean Ethics* proved ideally suited to the task. It was the "pagan aristocraticism of Aristotelian morality" that provided an answer. The academic's conscious self-awareness culminated in the definition of a specific virtue that was placed at the summit of the ethical hierarchy and served as a basis for proclaiming the superior status of the academic, who characteristically possessed this major virtue.[48]

Thus we have Siger's *quaestio* 1a: "First question: Is humility a virtue?" to which he responds: "It is demonstrated that it is not. For humility is the opposite of the virtue magnanimity, which is the pursuit of great things. Humility, on the other hand, drives great things away."[49] He naturally goes on to exalt the intellectual virtues connected with academic status, as in *quaestio* 4a, for instance: "Another question: Is it better for a philosopher to be celibate or married? The answer has to be that the philosopher's aim is knowledge of the truth... The moral virtues have their purpose in the intellectual virtues. Knowledge of the truth is therefore man's final cause."[50]

Now we begin to perceive the route that led to some of the propositions condemned in 1277. Proposition 40: "There is no condition better than that of the philosopher."[51] Proposition 104: "Humanity is not the form of a thing but rather of reason"[52]—which points beyond scholasticism to the possible beginnings of an academic, intellectual, and "rationalistic" "humanism." Proposition 144: "All the good accessible to man resides in the intellectual virtues."[53] Proposition 154: "The only sages of the world are the philosophers."[54] Proposition 211: "Our intellect can, by means of its natural gifts, achieve knowledge of the first cause."[55]

This is an extreme position, particularly as it appears, in what may be a distorted and caricatural version, in the Syllabus of 1277. Yet it was a position sufficiently widespread among Parisian academics in the second half of the thirteenth century to be found in scarcely mitigated form in "a moderate and well-informed contemporary" like James of Douai.[56]

The key label, the defining or signal term, as the reader will have noticed, was the word *philosopher* previously used by Abelard. This term was not insignificant. For the Sigerians, it no doubt referred primarily to antique paganism. For us, though, it evokes a whole lineage. In the various forms which time was to impose, mutatis mutandis, we may legitimately recognize in this thirteenth-century philosopher the abortive ancestor of the sixteenth century philosopher—that religious skeptic who would be the ideal of a Charron, for example—or of the eighteenth-century *philosophe*. As individual types and as a professional and intellectual group, the *viri philosophici* of the MS Paris BN Lat. 14698 are effectively precursors of the philosophes of the Aufklärung.

The philosophers were, of course, opposed in the first place to the theologians (and this was also the rivalry of the "artist," the pure academic, with the theologian);[57] they were distinguished as well from the *homines profundi*—pseudo-learned obscurantists attacked in proposition 91 of 1277: "The philosopher's reason, when it demonstrates that the motion of the heavens is eternal, is not guilty of sophistry; it is surprising that some *homines profundi* do not see this."[58]

The philosophers were, of course, confident of their reason, or, rather, of their intellectual virtues, which raised their *estate* above others, but they were also aware that their *dignity* perhaps lay in limiting themselves to certain demonstrable truths, and that their vocation was to be satisfied to explain and not to preach. In "the famous dialectical duel" between Saint Thomas Aquinas and Siger of Brabant of which Father Gauthier speaks,[59] do we not perceive an awareness on Siger's part of that *scholarly neutrality* that is so difficult to achieve even today?

To conclude, we propose to make an epilogue of a description of the academic self-image in the early fifteenth century. To do so, we shall inquire of the chancellor Jean Gerson what this image was.[60] Once again, we are no doubt being presumptuous in trying to define the Gersonian academic and determine his self-consciousness without first having sought to clarify his relation to the fundamental new phenomena of *docta ignorantia* and *devotio moderna*.

Without seeking to analyze either the positive content of these intellectual and spiritual phenomena or the underlying causes of such repudiations and mutations among academics in the waning Middle Ages, it should be noted simply that the foundations of academic specificity and dignity, as defined from Abelard to Siger of Brabant, had either crumbled or been undermined.

Gerson does, of course, point out the basically intellectual and scientific virtues of the University of Paris. It was the "mother of studies, mistress of learning, instructress of truth." Repeatedly (with an emphasis which must be understood in light of the mad king and his entourage to whom these words were addressed), Gerson stresses the superiority of medicine over charlatanry. He praises physicians in contrast to "sorcerers, magicians, charmers, and such madmen",[61] and he ranks above all false healers the "masters in medicine who have devoted all their time to the study of the books of those who discovered and set forth medicine."

But what was the truth that the university taught? What light did it spread, as the "beautiful, bright sun of France and all Christendom,[62] the beautiful, bright illumination of every holy Church and of Christianity?"[63]

There were *three ways of life:* (a) the corporeal, carnal, personal life; (b) the civil, political, or universal life; (c) the life of grace, divine or spiritual. Of these three ways, however, "the first is ephemeral, the second durable, the third eternal."[64] The university, of course, ministered to all three, in other words, to everything: corporeal life was instructed by the faculty of medicine, political life by the faculties of arts and decrees, and divine life by the faculty of theology. In virtue of the hierarchy between the levels, however, a special value was conferred on the second and third.

The intellectual role of the university, therefore, gave way to its political and spiritual role. The political role, moreover, was defined so as to be subordinated to basically spiritual ends. The university "is conducive to freedom and independence for the people of France and to the restoration, not of the material temple, but of the spiritual and mystical temple which is the entire Holy Church."[65]

The aim was, in fact, *order* and *peace.* Beyond the momentary goals of national reconciliation of the faction-ridden French people and the overall reconciliation of Christendom with the end of the Great Schism, however, a more fundamental objective is evident, the preservation of the existing order. Gerson put it quite well to the graduates in civil law.[66] When he came, with a certain hesitancy, to mention *tyrants,* his purpose, in the final analysis, was to congratulate them for enforcing respect for property and order.[67]

The academics of the twelfth and thirteenth centuries consciously took their vocation to be that of discoverers, but their successors in the fifteenth were satisfied to be conservatives. This accounts for a persistent denigration of the intellectual and material aspects of the academic profession, a far cry from the earlier notion of magnanimity. Curiously, Gerson, when he appeared before the future jurists, reduced the contribution of their discipline to the common good to a purely negative utility, which existed only as a consequence of sin; law and justice were only inevitable effects of evil: "In a primitive state of nature, the Lord would have no need of jurists or canon lawyers, just as He will have no need of them in the state of nature glorified."[68] In conclusion, he adds that theology is superior to law.

The brief text in which he states his desire to resign his office of chancellor[69] is at first sight a mere formality. But Gerson was sincere. He held all the *technical* aspects of the academic profession in contempt. He would rather be saying mass, praying, or meditating than be doing *administrative work.*

Finally, he gave the students of the college of Navarre a singular charter for conservatism. His praise of the "beaten path"[70] is surprising, even after one has become well versed in the writings of this grandiloquent and mediocre conservative. Rereading his praise of the physicians, we notice that his respect for them is merited only by their bookish knowledge of the ancients. O Hippocrates! O Galen!

What was the university in his eyes? It had become a part of the pageant of divine right, a *daughter of the King* and particularly of Adam, come from the Earthly Paradise by way of the Hebrews, Abraham's Egypt, Athens, and Rome. The *translatio studii* was transformed into a law of succession *by the grace of God.* The craft guild became a prince of the blood.[71]

This accounts for the arrogance with which he treated those boorish voices which had been brash enough to point out that the university had a professional function: "And if someone says: What does it [the university] want to get involved or mixed up in? To look at books and study them is not very well advised, what good is knowledge without action?"[72]

The Gersonian academic, then, had become aware of a new vocation, on the whole political, but in a broader sense national and international. The professional consciousness of the medieval academic was changing, on the threshold of the modern world, into a moral consciousness. What was the place of the academic in the nation and in universal society? What values was he to assert, promote, and defend?

The product of a profound upheaval, had this new consciousness fully penetrated the minds of academics of the period?

We can say, in any case, that by repudiating his professional consciousness, the Gersonian academic deprived himself of the means to exercise these new prerogatives. The university was reduced to a mere caste. No doubt it was still open to new arrivals; Gerson insists on the fact that the university of Paris, as a result of its recruitment policies, was open to all classes and effectively represented the whole society. It was nevertheless a caste by virtue of its mentality and function. The corporation of book users had changed into a group of repetitious theologians bent on setting themselves up as mental and moral policemen, as book burners. They went so far as to burn Joan of Arc—in spite of Gerson.

Apart from a few commendable efforts, they left it to the

humanists, most of whom were strangers to their caste, to assume the burden of advancing knowledge, and thus renounced the spiritual role whose only legitimate basis lay in performance of their professional function. Their perverted corporate consciousness prevented them from achieving a full consciousness of their public role.

THE UNIVERSITIES AND THE PUBLIC
AUTHORITIES IN THE MIDDLE AGES AND
THE RENAISSANCE

I GENERAL CONSIDERATIONS

The difficulty of studying the relations between the universities and the public authorities from the twelfth to the seventeenth centuries lies not only in the gaps in the documentary record, particularly for the most remote period, nor in the relative paucity of monographic studies, nor in the lack of numerical data and statistically based works. It originates in the subject itself. There are, indeed, several inherent difficulties:

1. The diversity of the universities themselves and their internal contradictions.

Even if we do not regard the universities in the original sense of the term as *corporations* (*universitas* in general *magistrorum* and *scolarium*) but rather as *centers of higher education* (i.e., *studium generale*, without embarking on any discussion of the precise meaning of this expression or of the exact level of the education provided by medieval universities), we still confront a complex and ambiguous variety of institutions:

a) The *professional organization* (generally in the hands of the masters grouped in colleges of doctors) did not always coincide with the *corporate or fiscal organization,* in which masters and students did not play the same role in all universities (compare, for the twelfth to fourteenth centuries, at least, the Bolognese model with student preponderance and the Parisian model with master preponderance).

b) The universities varied from the standpoint of learning, with respect both to the *disciplines* taught and to the institutional organization in *faculties*. It was rare for a university to include all the faculties, and rarer still for them to have equal importance (from the point

A bibliography for this essay may be found below, p. 321.

135

of view of relations with the public authorities, for instance, it was of great moment whether the dominant faculty was that of theology or of some other discipline oriented toward "lucrative" or "utilitarian" careers—law or medicine—and, even more important, whether the university did or did not include a faculty of *civil law*, i.e., Roman law; cf. the case of Paris and the bull of Honorius III of 1219).

c) The legal status of academics was poorly defined. It is true that the privileges they acquired tended to define a special academic status (*status studentium* or *ordo scholasticus*), comparable to ecclesiastical status, but it was applicable to persons of varying *social conditions* and was for many reasons ambiguous, neither wholly ecclesiastical nor wholly secular. Indeed, the evolution of the meaning of the term *clericus*, which acquired the particular meaning of learned or lettered and, in certain languages, even took on the sense of administrative official (English *clerk* or French *clerc*), is indicative of the process by which the vocabulary adapted to academic reality. "Academic jurisdiction" remained difficult to define and was a source of continual conflict as long as the status of academics fluctuated between secular and ecclesiastical extremes.

d) Academics were not the only members of society in the Middle Ages and the Renaissance whose status was defined both from an economic point of view, as professionals, technicians, practitioners of a trade, and from a social point of view, as a privileged group. This was the case with all guild members. In the learned world, however, this ambiguity was allowed to deepen to the point where there were two fundamentally contrasted types of academic, depending on whether the individual received a *salary* or a *prebend*. These two types were radically different insofar as their economic and legal dependence on the public authorities was concerned; yet not only could both be found within a given university, but a given academic might frequently be living on a mixture of the two forms of remuneration. Finally, particularly for the students, the character of a university changed a good deal depending on the proportion of poor to rich in its makeup. This proportion could vary considerably from one university to the next (depending especially on the sociological character of its urban base: Paris and Cambridge were virtually polar opposites in this respect).

e) Just as they accepted members from *every social origin*, which confronted the public authorities with virtually unique groups in the stratified society of the Middle Ages and the Renaissance, the universities were also open to all nationalities. Not only did this cause a fundamental tension between the local or national authorities and this *international group*, but the organization of the academic body into "nations," whose number and kind varied from university to university and which never conformed to strictly national or geographic criteria, further complicated the structure and character of the universities in the eyes of the public powers.

2. Confronting this protean partner, *the public authorities themselves appeared in a wide variety of forms.*

a) Even when the university was confronted with only a single public authority, this might take one of several forms. It may have been a *city* (and it is important to distinguish between the relations of the university with the political body governing the city, whether urban council, commune, board of aldermen, Podesta, etc., with the social group dominating the city, and, further, with the overall urban society). Or it may have been a *seigneurial, princely, or royal power*, or *the imperial power* (in this latter case, the problem of the specific local form of the imperial power arises: for example, the relations of the University of Bologna with Frederick Barbarossa or Frederick II, or of the University of Prague—was it a Bohemian or an imperial university?).

b) The case of imperial power introduces the point that the universities were usually involved not with a single public power but with several, among which there might exist either a hierarchy, frequently difficult to define or respect, or else fairly clear conflicts of interest and policy (the case of Bologna between the Commune and Empire). This was a situation characteristic of the Middle Ages, reminiscent, mutatis mutandis, of cases of multiple vassalage.

3. Between the twelfth and the seventeenth centuries, not only did the two partners, universities and public powers, change, but the nature of their relationship changed as well. We are therefore faced with an *evolution in several variables.*

a) One difference was due to distinct *origins,* with the major contrast being between universities *created* by the public authorities and "spontaneously born" universities. The opposition is not as clear, however, as it might appear at first sight. In fact, the "spontaneously born" universities arose out of situations in which the attitudes and needs of the public authorities and the forces they represented always played a fairly large role. Furthermore, these universities were established either with the aid of the public powers or in the face of their rather considerable hostility.

b) Whether created or born spontaneously, universities differed as to the definition and orientation of their relations with the public authorities, depending on *when they were founded.* Although the general trend was toward a uniformization of the relations between university and public authorities, the nature of these relations depended, in general, on whether the university had come into being in the twelfth, thirteenth, fourteenth, fifteenth, or sixteenth century.

4. The relations of both partners to the *Church* added a considerable complexity to their relations with one another, not only because of the leading role played by the Church and religion (with the Reformation further complicating the situation in the sixteenth century), but also because of the Church's ambiguous position as both a temporal and a spiritual power and because of the largely "clerical" character of the universities. As far as it is possible to make the distinction, only the temporal aspect of the relations between the Church and the universities will be taken into account here in the cases where the ecclesiastical power appears in the guise of a public authority.

5. Finally, it is important to point out a difficulty inherent in much of the documentary record relevant to our problem. This is often composed of statutes, grants of privilege, constitutions, etc.—that is, legislative, administrative, and theoretical documents. The real, concrete relations between universities and public authorities must frequently have been rather far removed from these statements of principle. The difficulty of gaining access to such concrete relations makes our subject still more delicate.

In view of these difficulties, we have resigned ourselves to the following choices:

a) What we have done was more to make an inventory of problems and lay out the framework for treating them than to give solutions.

b) We have excluded three possible avenues of approach: (1) an approach by *type of university;* while a *typology of universities* would be of great use to the historian of the university, and while we would hope that the discussion of this paper might contribute something to the elaboration of one, it did not seem to us that there could be an operational criterion for classifying universities relative to our subject; (2) an approach by type of *public authority,* which seemed to us no more than a path of least resistance, rather unsuitable for clarifying the aspects of our subject most important for establishing the place of academic history within general history and historical methodology; (3) a *chronological* approach, which would run the risk of losing the essential points in a welter of events, the essential being to point out the structures and problems. We have, however, identified one *major chronological break;* this falls in the *middle of the fifteenth century* and, regardless of the diversity of local, national, or regional cases, separates a medieval period from a period of renaissance. We believe that this break is fundamentally valid both for our problem and, equally, for the general history in which we are trying to situate it.

We have therefore chosen an approach determined by the *characteristics and functions* of the universities. We will not try to disguise the fact that this approach leads us to make rather abstract analytic distinctions. Nevertheless, it seemed to us the best way to shed light on the essential point, the *nature and role of the academic world* in relation to the larger society of which it was a part, whether urban, seigneurial, or national.

c) We have particularly endeavored to explicate these relations through *tensions and conflicts,* which are particularly revealing of the nature of the social groups and institutions in which they occur. We do continue to bear in mind, however, that the relations between universities and public authorities were not characterized solely by antagonism, nor can they be reduced to a series of crises and struggles. Instead, both partners mutually supported and sustained each other, and their relations were marked by reciprocal *services* and mutual *respect* which often triumphed over fundamental and circumstantial divergences.

II Universities and Public Authorities in the Middle Ages (Twelfth to Mid-Fifteenth Centuries)

1. Universities as *Corporations*

a) As corporations or guilds, medieval universities sought to obtain a *scholastic monopoly,* primarily in the form of a monopoly on the granting of degrees, as a result of which they came into conflict, particularly in their early history, with ecclesiastical authority but not with the public powers.

b) They subsequently sought legal autonomy, which they obtained relatively easily from the public authorities. The latter generally followed the tradition inaugurated by Frederick Barbarossa in 1158 in the case of Bologna (authentic *Habita,* "source of all academic freedoms"). In Paris, for example, the university's legal autonomy was recognized by Philip Augustus as early as 1200, before it was recognized by the papacy (which happened either in 1215 or possibly as late as 1231).

c) To the extent that the university, like any other corporation, aimed at *controlling* the scholastic trade, the public authorities could only regard it as advantageous that there should be such an organization of the *professional order* fitted into the general public order.

d) With this view of things, the public authorities saw no disadvantage in granting special privileges to the academic corporation as they did to other corporations. These included exemption from watch duty and military service, which accorded, moreover, with the "clerical" character of academics.

e) Just as municipal, seigneurial, or royal officials supervised other corporations on the corporation's own behalf and in the interest of its leaders (e.g., quality control, supervision of working conditions, of weights and measures, fairs and markets, enforcement of statutes, etc.), there seem to have been no major difficulties caused by the control over the universities exercised by certain communal officials, particularly in Italy, although the activities of these magistrates (*reformatores, gubernatores, tractatores studii*) have not been sufficiently studied.

f) One particular characteristic of the academic corporation might have led to conflict with the public authorities. In most other guilds, the members, or in any case the masters, were economically independent of the public authorities, since they lived on the earnings of their trade. Academic masters, on the other hand, although they won the right to be paid for their *work* by the students, did not succeed in living on these *collectae* or on what other material payment they managed to extract from the students (such as the fees and gifts for examinations, despite the fact that the award of the *licentia docendi* was in theory free). The bulk of their remuneration, apart from ecclesiastical benefices, came, therefore, from the salaries and grants afforded them by cities, princes, or sovereigns. In return, the public powers claimed the right—which went with patronage—to sponsor candidates for university positions. As a result, the academic corporation did not fully enjoy one of the basic privileges of all other guilds, the right of *self-recruitment*. Yet the academics seem to have accepted this limitation on their independence quite easily in exchange for the material benefits represented by the endowment of chairs by the public authorities (cases arising from this problem, moreover, generally appear rather late, such as the consultation on this matter between the University of Cologne and the University of Louvain, and the events of 1443–69 regarding the magistrate of Louvain's interpretation of the 1443 bull of Eugenius IV which established nomination procedures for professors with prebends).

g) Cause for conflict remained, however, and on occasion broke out in real disputes, in the frequent violation of the academic preserve by communal or royal officials: students and masters were imprisoned in defiance of statutes and removed from the university's jurisdiction (a frequent occurrence at Oxford, Cambridge, and particularly Paris, where the provost was usually the academics' bête noire). Usually, however, it was a matter of abuse of power by an official, disavowed fairly rapidly and voluntarily by higher public authorities. Such cases rarely went beyond jurisdictional conflicts in police matters. If, at times, they became bitter, it was because of other characteristics of the academic environment (see sections 4 and 5 below).

2. Universities as *Centers of Professional Training*

a) Academics were motivated either by a straightforward desire for knowledge, or by an interest in pursuing a career which would bring them honor or money, or by all of these at once. Nothing in this implied necessary conflict with the public authorities, but rather the opposite. In fact, the time of the founding and growth of the universities was a period of growth, specialization, and increasing technical requirements in public offices. The faculties of medicine were just one instance of a response to the increased efforts of the authorities in the field of public health and sanitation following on the growth of cities. After the Black Plague, the battle against epidemic came to be considered an essential part of the role and obligation of the public authorities. The academics' search for *career opportunities* was met by an increased demand on the part of the public powers.

b) The highly theoretical and bookish character of professional training in the academy did not prevent it from responding to the needs of the public authorities. The degree of specialization required by public offices was in fact quite limited: the ability to read and write, knowledge of Latin, and familiarity with legal principles or the capacity to argue from certain texts were essential, along with some elementary accounting principles and some still more rudimentary economics (see *De moneta* by Nicole Oresme). Furthermore, a taste for political theory on the part of princes and sovereigns, and even a taste for "scientific" government, i.e., government inspired by scholastic principles (cf. the role of Aristotelianism at the court of Charles V of France, and at the Polish court, and the role of Aristotelianism and Platonism or an amalgam of the two in the government of the Italian oligarchies and seigneuries), coincided with the intellectual tendencies of the academics.

c) Apart from the *utilitarian* aspect of academic work, its disinterested aspect was far from displeasing to the public authorities and indeed seemed an essential part of their glory. Thus a considerable place was allowed *intellectual prestige* alongside the other forms of prestige which were vital to regimes half-utilitarian and half-magical in character (see section 5 below).

d) The fact that the careers pursued by academics were still for the most part ecclesiastical was also not regarded unfavorably by the public authorities. In the first place this was because a large proportion of public servants were still ecclesiastics: ecclesiastic and civil officials were often indistinguishable. Second, the authorities were also Christian, and religion and men of the cloth seemed useful and necessary in themselves. Furthermore, it was rare that what was useful to the Church was not in some way useful to the state: for example, preachers or theologians trained by the universities to fight heresy or paganism (e.g., Toulouse and the struggle against Catharism, Krakow and the evangelization of Lithuania) could also be employed in furthering political designs (the kings of France and the penetration of Languedoc, the Lithuanian policy of Ladislas Jagellon).

e) When there was conflict between the academy and the public authorities, it was usually limited to certain local questions in which the university was only indirectly involved; it was not generally the primary target (e.g., the hostility of the people of Toulouse toward the Dominican inquisitors trained by the university). Many of the conflicts were basically internal and moved outside the university only when the public authorities took the side of an academic faction (in Paris, Saint Louis's support of the masters belonging to the mendicant orders; at the time of the Great Schism, the departure of academics in connection with obedience to one pope or another; in Prague in 1409, the Bohemian king's support of the Czech "nation" against the Germans of the other "nations," etc.)

3. Universities as an *Economic Group of Consumers*

Within a medieval city, the university represented a *group of nonproducers*, a *consumer market* whose size should not be underestimated (according to the 1380–81 poll tax at Oxford, there were probably around 1,500 academics, i.e., persons enjoying the privileges of the university, out of a total population of 5,000 to 5,500, or one academic out of every three or four Oxonians).

a) Normally, such a clientele must have pleased city authorities to the extent that it "promoted trade."

b) In what was still largely a subsistence economy, however, such a large group of nonproducers must have increased the difficulties city authorities faced in provisioning the population and in dealing with the imbalance of the economy in university cities.

c) Furthermore, the academic population included a large number (whose relative size depended on the era) of poor students (in 1244, Henry III provided meals at Oxford for a thousand *pauperes scolares* on the birthday of "his late sister, Eleanor"), which raises the question of the *purchasing power* of the academic group.

d) Above all, academics enjoyed *economic privileges* of great importance: exemption from taxes, levies, tolls, etc. They further benefited from special controlled prices for lodging and food (and what is more, in certain academic cities like Oxford, owing to the scarcity of academic accommodations, once lodging had been rented to academics at controlled prices, it could not subsequently be rented to nonacademic tenants at uncontrolled prices). Finally, they had the right to survey and enforce throughout the city such price controls as they had obtained or contributed to obtaining (*assises*); consequently, it has been said that all the inhabitants of academic cities in the Middle Ages enjoyed a lower cost of living than residents of other cities. It was in connection with an economic conflict, moreover, that the townspeople of Oxford saw fit to assert in a petition to the king of England that there were "two communities in Oxford, one of townspeople and the other of the university, and it is the latter which is stronger." In fact, this was the issue over which differences between city authorities and academics were sharpest, giving rise to numerous violent conflicts. The academic community's economic privileges and the hostility they aroused in the dominant bourgeois circles within the cities are in contradiction with the notion of "economic justice" that has often been held to have characterized medieval cities, which shows that the law of supply and demand was regarded as the rule in such cities, regardless of all the regulation. In this connection we may even wonder whether scholastic theories of the *just price* (insofar as they did not merely sanction the free play of market forces) did not correspond to the economic interests of the academic community in the urban marketplace.

e) There was one sector, however, in which the academic group was both producer and consumer: the *manuscript market* (cf. the importance of this market in the overall urban economy of Bologna). In any case, an evaluation of the *influence of the academic market on prices over time* (including rents, food, and other primary necessities, luxury and semiluxury goods) would be an important contribution to historiography.

4. Universities as a *Sociodemographic Group*

Finally, academics constituted a *group of males, largely young bachelors,* in the midst of the urban population. The clerical character of this group was sufficiently loose that a good many did not feel constrained by certain ecclesiastical rules of conduct, such as continence, sobriety, and nonviolence. Instead, encouraged by legal privileges which granted them, if not immunity, at least milder punishment, a great many academics (including masters as well as students, although obviously to a lesser degree) took part in the sort of violent acts to which they were driven by their age, their uprootedness, and the fact that a majority of them belonged to the two social classes most given to violence, the nobility and the peasantry: this was "the wilder side of University life" (Rashdall). It is, furthermore, quite clear that the provocations and excesses of police repression accentuate what in any event appears to us basically as an aspect, no doubt marginal but nevertheless real, of social conflict if not class struggle. Such an interpretation is reinforced by the fact that the bourgeois (even though they are seen taking violent measures against academics on certain occasions, and although academics of bourgeois origin were sometimes implicated in violent acts) sought to establish a peaceful orderliness in daily conduct, whereas the academics, by contrast, belonged to the world of medieval violence.

If we think of the extent to which academics took part in brawls, nocturnal disturbances, gambling, prostitution, and other moral offenses, as well as the life of the taverns (it has been observed that some of the most serious conflicts between "town and gown" originated in taverns, e.g., at Paris in 1229, Oxford in 1355), we become aware of the extent to which the "way of life" of a considerable part of the academic population was incompatible with the social morality of the dominant strata of urban society.

Finally, although violent or "scandalous" behavior of this kind was rather widespread in the academic population (although we should take care not to accept literally such undue generalizations as those of the morose and peevish moralist James of Vitry), it was particularly characteristic of one segment of the student body, the *vagabond clerics,* descendants of the Goliards, a special category of gyrovagues, the ancestors of student bohemianism. It would be quite interesting to know the history of this group, which did not coincide with the *pauperes scolares* (many of whom, including the recipients of collegiate scholarships, for instance, were rather well integrated in the "better-behaved" portion of the academic community). Its size, social composition, and behavior varied over the course of time. Study of the marginal components of social groups, especially when such components are as important as this one was, is always enlightening.

5. Universities as *Prestigious Bodies*

Important aspects of the relations between universities and the public authorities are explicable in terms of the *prestige* attaching to universities.

a) First of all, learning itself had prestige. It is true that the universities introduced new methods and a new state of mind which contributed importantly to changing the character of learning, ending its magical and accumulative orientation and diverting it toward rational, practical know-how which could be transmitted by technical training rather than sacred initiation. Nevertheless, the learning embodied in the university very quickly acquired the character of a *power* or *order*. The university was the *Studium*, alongside the *Sacerdotium* and the *Regnum*. Academics consequently sought to define themselves as an *intellectual aristocracy*, endowed with its own

144

specific morality and code of values. This attempt went farthest in some Aristotelian and Averroist circles, where an effort was made to establish and legitimate in theory a caste of *philosophi* (academic sages) whose essential virtue was supposed to be *magnanimity* (cf. Sigerian circles at the University of Paris in the thirteenth century).

b) During the Middle Ages, the Sacerdotium and Regnum were more at odds than they were mutually supporting. The same was not true of the relations between Regnum and Studium. In the main, the public authorities regarded their academics as "adornment and part of the common wealth" on account of the prestige of learning which they seemingly monopolized. From the time of the *Authentica habita* ("because the world will be ruled and illuminated by its learning"), we find the radiance of academic learning celebrated in the texts by which the public authorities granted privileges to the universities, in formulations which are no mere commonplaces or empty clichés but reveal an underlying motivation.

c) Concomitant with this intellectual prestige, universities sought to acquire an outward prestige which could serve as the sign of their eminent dignity in the form of costumes, ceremonies, etc. *Academic pomp* became one of the outward signs of the wealth and dignity of cities and states. Thus *conflicts of precedence* in matters of protocol and slights between academics and certain public officials gave rise to some of the sharpest disputes between the universities and the public authorities (e.g., the public repentance of the collector-general of taxes in front of the University of Paris on the Place de Grève in 1372, the conflict of precedence on the occasion of Charles V's funeral procession in 1380, the "Savoisy affair" in 1404).

d) The public authorities recognized this representative and illustrative function of the universities by bestowing prestigious gifts (game from the royal forests, wine offered by the commune, etc.) either individually (*inceptio* of the new masters) or collectively (corporate banquet of the *dies Aristotelis*).

e) Although the universities profited from such prestige in fulfilling their public role, they rarely participated in genuinely *political* activity which could have brought them into conflict with the public powers (unless it was a question of religious politics, as at the time of the Great Schism, which accorded well with their "clerical" and, to a certain extent, their international character). For instance, if Simon de Montfort seems to have enjoyed the sympathy of Oxford, it seems to have been largely individual sympathy; even at Paris, the most politicized of the universities, the attitude toward the English and the Burgundians after the treaty of Troyes was not, properly speaking, political, and the title "eldest daughter of the King" then assumed by the university was more a dignity than recognition of a political role; even the University of Prague was not called upon after the decree of Kutna Hora to play an official political role in the Bohemian kingdom; and so forth.

f) In conflicts with the public powers, universities used the prestige element in conjunction with their most effective pressure tactic and major weapon, the threat or the actuality of a *strike* or a *secession*. This accounts for the bitterness surrounding the efforts of young universities to win recognition of this right with the help of the papacy, which was readily granted because the pope's interests were in general not directly at stake.

6. Universities as *Social Milieu*

Ultimately, the basis of the relations between medieval universities and the public authorities should be sought in the fact that the medieval universities were a new kind of social milieu: *a medieval intelligentsia*. The characteristics of this milieu, however, remain to be determined by detailed studies.

a) Recruitment took place in every social category, but it is of great importance to determine, as far as the documentation will allow, what percentage of each university's membership in a given period of its history was drawn from the various social categories, and what careers were pursued by the members as a function of their social origins. It is equally important to find out how the various categories within the academic community were structured: poor and non-poor, masters and students, members of the various faculties, etc. Only then will it be possible to make a comparative study of the social structure of the academic community with that of the surrounding society, which will enable us to understand their relations in sociological terms.

b) The academic milieu was a *temporary* social group; except for a small minority, academics eventually left the university. A series of statistical studies of the careers pursued by graduates is needed: How many actually took degrees, how many remained in the university, what became of those who left? Only then will it be possible to evaluate the return on capital invested by the public authorities in financial, legal, and moral aid to the universities.

c) It was also an *international* milieu; here again, we must know how the nationalities were distributed initially (upon recruitment) and ultimately (in the various careers of the graduates) in order to clarify the relations between the universities and political organs.

d) Finally, we should like to be able to evaluate the cohesiveness and homogeneity of this medieval intelligentsia and define its essential characteristics, in order to determine what it contributed to political institutions: competence, prestige, opposition? Was the academic "estate," which offered most of its members a means to a higher social status, a threat or a reinforcement to the stability of medieval societies? Did it contribute to order, catalyze progress, support tradition, or destroy old structures?

III GENERAL LINES OF EVOLUTION IN THE RELATIONS BETWEEN THE UNIVERSITIES AND THE PUBLIC POWERS IN THE RENAISSANCE (MID-FIFTEENTH TO SIXTEENTH CENTURIES)

a) If the evolution of the relations between the universities and the public authorities was largely due to changes taking place on each side individually, the greater change seems to have been in the public authorities. Or, to put it another way, the public authorities were the driving force, and the universities a braking influence. In the Middle Ages, the universities seemed to have overtaken the public authorities (originally, in any case, "spontaneously born" universities had imposed themselves on public authorities more than the latter had instigated universities; instead, the powers sought to manage and control the schools). Subsequently, however, the universities trailed behind the public powers.

b) Universities did, however, evolve during the Middle Ages. The tendency, though, was toward degeneration of the academic community into a caste; there was a relative restriction of the social base (a decrease in the number of poor students, nepotism), an acrimonious defense of privileges as distinctive marks of caste, increasing emphasis on a privileged way of life, etc. Along with this social sclerosis went a certain intellectual sclerosis (*Spätscholastik*), so that by the end of the Middle Ages the university environment was less open and offered relatively fewer possibilities than during the preceding period from the point of view of the public authorities.

c) As the powers of the public authorities increased, the universities lost a considerable portion of their basic *freedoms*, particularly where the power of the monarch or prince advanced at the expense of local powers (in France especially): there was *loss of legal autonomy* (the University of Paris came under the jurisdiction of the Parlement in 1446) and of the *right of secession* (the last attempt in Paris was in 1499, and in 1564 at Louvain the German nation threatened to leave the city).

d) Once legally subjugated, the universities became economically dependent as well. Although a variety of means were employed by the public authorities in financing universities (salaries and prebends, of course, but also endowments linked to income derived from the expansion of trade, from tools in Heidelberg or taxes on salt at Krakow, for instance, or, in Reformed states, from secularized monastic properties, as at Tübingen, Wittenberg, Leipzig, Heidelberg), the increasing proportion of the budgets of academics and their institutions subsidized by the public further reduced their independence.

e) The international character of the universities also diminished. In the first place, the doors of the university were closed, either by statute or in practice, to students from cities or countries at war with the political authorities on which it depended; the national character of wars thus affected the academic community. Furthermore, after the Reformation and the triumph of the principle of *cuius regio eius religio*, universities were divided between Catholic and Protestant denomination, and the religious division tended to accentuate the nationalization or, at least, the regionalization of the university. Even where foreign attendance remained considerable (and a rather broad internationalism did continue in universities during the Renaissance), foreigners were increasingly barred from holding offices or leadership positions within the university.

f) Certainly the prestige of academics and their institutions remained great, and it was largely for reasons of prestige that growing numbers of princes and cities in the second half of the fifteenth and throughout the sixteenth centuries established universities (particularly in Central Europe, which, despite an initial wave of foundings beginning in 1347, fell behind in academic matters for reasons not yet well explained). *Utilitarian* aims, however, increasingly took precedence over disinterested motives; universities were primarily intended to produce officials, administrators, magistrates, diplomats, and other public servants. The fact that humanism developed in part outside the universities, which thus lost their monopoly on culture and learning, encouraged conversion of these institutions into training grounds for practical careers and also facilitated their increasing secularization. During the Middle Ages, the general policy of the public authorities had been to give only secondary consideration to *pro commodo suo*, with the clear exception of Naples, the one medieval example of a state university, and perhaps the Iberian universities as well. In the subsequent period, however, this concern became preeminent.

g) From the spiritual point of view, as well, the universities tended more and more to play a utilitarian role. They became the keepers and guardians of orthodoxy and fulfilled the function of *ideological police* in the service of the political powers. Actually, there was a whole spectrum of shadings of strictness in exercising this function, ranging from Paris, where the Sorbonne distinguished itself in witch-hunting, to Venice (i.e., Padua, where a good deal of ideological freedom seems to have prevailed).

h) In becoming professional training centers in the service of states rather than centers of disinterested scientific and intellectual work, the universities changed their role and social character. Rather than crucibles in which a new intelligentsia was produced, they became centers of social education, which trained the future members of the group that formed the administrative and social backbone of the modern state and, before long, of absolute monarchy. Although it is not easy to determine what was cause and what effect of the changing role of the university, the social origin of the academic class, or, in any case, of the student body, seems to have changed considerably during the Renaissance ("seems," because although the documentation for the Renaissance is much richer than for the Middle Ages, detailed studies are lacking to an even greater degree for the later period, so great is the historian's fascination with periods marked by beginnings. The proportion of academics of bourgeois and particularly of noble origin greatly increased, which again shows *the involvement of the universities with the ruling social groups* of the age of monarchy.

i) Thus the Renaissance witnessed a *domestication* of the universities by the public authorities, which significantly reduced the number of potential causes of conflict. Subsequent disputes were limited to minor issues relating particularly to questions of material interest and corporate prerogative on the local level and to religious problems and matters of intellectual administration on the national level.

Conclusion

Although the nature of the relations between universities and public authorities underwent a major metamorphosis from the Middle Ages to the Renaissance, due primarily to the submission of the schools to the authorities, it may be said that in both periods the conflicts involved minor matters, and *Regnum* and *Studium* mutually supported and respected one another. Not until the upheavals of the Industrial Revolution would the universities come to harbor a new intelligentsia, even while continuing in certain respects to be the keepers and defenders of certain traditions and a certain idea of order. This new intelligentsia was a revolutionary one which more directly challenged the public authorities and obeyed their command only insofar as these powers themselves were the servants of ideals and principles transcending mere raison d'état and ruling-class interest.

III

HIGH CULTURE AND
POPULAR CULTURE

CLERICAL CULTURE AND FOLKLORE TRADITIONS IN MEROVINGIAN CIVILIZATION

The influence of popular images on the religion of the learned is a phenomenon well known to all historians of medieval Christianity. Its earliest manifestations probably belong to a much earlier time. Is it legitimate to formulate the problem of the "decadence" of ancient intellectual civilization without asking whether this "culture," born in the particular societies of a few Hellenic cities and subsequently adapted by the Roman oligarchy, was not predestined to be distorted in peculiar ways as soon as what was still, of course, limited to an elite, though an elite that was now spread throughout an immense world, inevitably came into contact with masses steeped in quite different mental traditions?

Marc Bloch, *Annales d'Histoire sociale*,
1939, p. 186.

The desire to establish an association between social groups or communities and cultural levels at the time of the transition from antiquity to the Middle Ages is not new. We need go back no farther than Ferdinand Lot's famous article, "A quelle époque a-t-on cessé de parler latin",[1] later echoed by Dag Norberg.[2] I am quite incapable of following these two learned authors onto the philological ground where they have taken up their positions. Although I greatly admire the relevant remarks with which their articles abound and am grateful that they chose to root their linguistic studies in the broader analysis of social conditions, I believe that the essential point for our purposes lies elsewhere.

No doubt linguistic apparatus is a fundamental part of intellectual and mental equipment and is therefore embodied in the social context which profoundly colors that equipment. From the central standpoint of cultural communication between social milieus, however, at least so far as the fifth and sixth centuries are concerned, I believe Dag Norberg is right and Ferdinand Lot wrong: "From a social point of view, during this period there were not two languages but several forms of a single language related to the different groups within society."[3]

Linguistically speaking, then, the people and the aristocracy understood one another—except where Latin was spoken, an important reservation. Although the clergy spoke Latin everywhere, laymen frequently continued to speak "barbarian" tongues, whether these were the vulgar languages of peoples long since included within the Roman cultural and political sphere, or the languages of Barbarians in the strict sense, spoken by the immigrants or invaders recently established within the limits of the Roman Empire. In the first case, it was primarily the peasants who kept their traditional languages—Coptic, Syrian, Thracian, Celtic, Berber—as A. H. M. Jones has pointed out in a remarkable study.[4] To confine our attention to the West, the persistence of Celtic tongues is attested by various sources, particularly Saint Jerome[5] and Sulpicius Severus.[6] Among new arrivals, Germanic dialects continued to be encountered from the top to the bottom of society. There was some Romanization of the Barbarians, of course, but it remained quite limited.[7]

Thus we note two important phenomena: the emergence of the peasant masses as a cultural pressure group,[8] and the growing lack of cultural differentiation—but for a few individual or local exceptions—of all lay social strata as against the clergy, which monopolized all advanced and particularly written forms of culture. The weight of the peasant mass and the clerical monopoly are the two basic factors that influence the association between social groups and cultural levels in the early Middle Ages. I think these relations may best be explored not through language but rather by investigating the broader and more fundamental area of mental and intellectual equipment.

To obtain a better understanding of the role of the social bases of culture in the early Middle Ages, it is essential to note the infrastructural evolution which suddenly brought Christianity to the front of the historical scene in the fourth century. A. H. M. Jones[9] has shown that Christianity's diffusion in the Roman world of the fourth century was not a purely political or spiritual phenomenon which followed from the conversion of Constantine and the missionary zeal of the Christians with the subsequent support of the public authorities. In the early fourth century, Christianity was mainly lodged in the "middle and lower urban classes," while the peasant masses and the aristocracy had hardly been touched by it. Economic contraction and bureaucratic expansion brought about the rise of those urban classes in which Christianity was already strong. Their rise led to the Christian breakthrough. When Christianity's triumph took shape, however, the classes that had carried it forward were declining. Christianity survived the collapse of the fragile superstructures of the Late Empire, but only by separating itself from the classes that had assured its success, which were destined to disappear with the movement of history. Their social role was taken over by the aristocracy, and then by the peasant masses, which gave roots to Christianity, but at the price of a good deal of distortion, particularly noticeable in the cultural area. Christianity was caught between a clergy increasingly colonized by an aristocracy formed on Greco-Roman *paideia*[10] and a mainly rural lay population, which was rendered increasingly vulnerable to the advance of a renascent primitive culture by the decline of official paganism. Established by moribund urban social categories, would the Christian religion succeed in defining itself within a common culture through a subtle interplay of internal acculturations?[11]

I   The basic characteristics of the history of Western culture from the fifth to the eighth centuries may be outlined as follows:

a) A thinning of the middle classes in the cultural sphere, as the gap widened between the uncultured masses and a cultivated elite.

b) The cultural split did not, however, coincide with social stratification, because intellectual culture became the monopoly of the Church. Although there were great differences in degree in the culture of the clerics, it was a culture of a single kind, and the important division was between clerics and laymen.

c) Regardless of the individual or collective responses of the clerics to the problem of what attitude to adopt toward profane pagan culture, ecclesiastical culture made use of intellectual equipment perfected between the third and fifth centuries by didactic authors who systematized, on a simplified, mediocre level, the methodological and scientific legacy of Greco-Roman culture.[12] The most important part of this intellectual equipment was probably the framework of the "liberal arts," and the most important author Martianus Capella (*De nuptiis Philologiae et Mercurii* from the first half of the fifth century).[13] It would be useful to have a good overall knowledge of this first stratum of "founders of the Middle Ages," often still pagans like Macrobius.[14]

d) The ecclesiastical leadership was all the more receptive to such intellectual influences because it was drawn, particularly in the fifth and sixth centuries, largely from the indigeno-Roman aristocracies. Barbarian prelates and abbots who were able to advance in their careers, however, were also disposed to acquire this sort of culture precisely because it was one of the best ways of achieving assimilation and of climbing socially. The hagiographic stereotype of the bishop-saint generally included "illustrious" origins and almost always, either before or after conversion, training in the liberal arts (such as Paulinus of Milan in the *Vita Ambrosii*, c. 422; Constantius of Lyons in the *Vita Germani*, c. 470–80, etc.).

e) Despite the tendency toward regionalization, this ecclesiastical culture was almost everywhere identical in structure and quality (cf. two examples as remote as possible from one another: Isidore of Seville and Visigothic culture of the early seventh century; and Irish monastic culture at Ynis Pyr in the time of Iltud, in the first half of the sixth century, according to the *Vita Samsonis*).[15]

f) By contrast with ecclesiastical culture, lay culture shows a much more drastic regression from as early as the second century, reinforced by the material and mental chaos which became catastrophic with the invasions and with the fusion of Barbarian elements with indigeno-Roman societies. Cultural regression primarily took the form of a resurgence of "traditional" techniques, mentalities, and beliefs. Ecclesiastical culture confronted, not so much a single pagan culture with a uniform organization—quickly vanquished despite the final stirrings of the early fifth century—as a "primitive" culture with a bellicose tinge among the Barbarians (particularly in the upper strata; cf. funerary furnishings),[16] and a peasant tinge throughout the rural lower strata.

II   Leaving archaeological evidence aside, we may attempt to define the relations between the two levels of culture by way of the relations between clerical culture and folklore.

The fact that this sketch is based on documents belonging to the written ecclesiastical culture (in particular, lives of saints and pastoral works such as the *Sermons* of Caesarius of Arles, the *De correctione rusticorum* of Martin of Braga, the *Dialogi* of Gregory the Great, texts of synods and councils, and Irish penitentials) involves a risk of distorting the perspective of the inquiry if not its objectivity. We are not, however, attempting to study the resistance of folkloric culture in its various forms (passive resistance, contamination of ecclesiastical culture, alliance with political, social, and religious movements, such as the Bagaudes, Arianism, Priscillianism, Pelagianism, etc.). We shall be satisfied to define the attitude of ecclesiastical culture towards folkloric culture.[17]

Clerical culture did undoubtedly accept folklore to some degree:

a) Its acceptance was encouraged by certain mental structures common to both cultures, in particular the confusion between terrestrial and supernatural, and material and spiritual spheres (e.g., attitudes toward miracles, cults of relics, use of phylacteries, etc.).

b) Such acceptance was a practical and tactical necessity for evangelical purposes. Evangelization demanded that the clerics make some effort to adapt culturally: language (*sermo rusticus*), use of oral forms (sermons, chants), certain kinds of ceremony (liturgical culture, processions—the Rogation days[18] and processions instituted by Gregory the Great),[19] and satisfaction of "client" requests (miracles "to order").

Ecclesiastical culture frequently had to take its place within the framework of folkloric culture: the location of churches and chapels, pagan functions bequeathed to Christian saints, etc.

The essential point, however, is that folkloric culture was *refused* by ecclesiastical culture:

a) *By destruction*. The many destructions of temples and idols were mirrored in literature by a proscription of distinctively folkloric themes, of which there is no more than a scanty harvest even in hagiographic literature, which a priori one would expect to enjoy a special position in this respect. The yield is even smaller if folkloric themes from the Bible are eliminated (it is important in this connection to distinguish between the Old Testament tradition, rich in folkloric motifs, and the New Testament tradition, in which they are rare). Furthermore, we must be careful to identify the various chronological layers in hagiographic tales due to a series of revisions. Certain writers (such as P. Saintyves, *En marge de la Légende dorée*, or H. Günther, *Psychologie de la légende*) have not gone far enough in distinguishing these strata and have therefore tended to trace certain elements of folklore back to the very early Middle Ages, when in fact they were introduced in Carolingian times or during the great wave of folklore of the twelfth and thirteenth centuries, which crests in Jacobus da Varagine's *Golden Legend*.

b) *By obliteration*. The superimposition of Christian themes, practices, monuments, and characters on pagan predecessors was not a "continuation" but an abolition. Clerical culture covered over, hid, and blotted out folkloric culture.

c) *By adulteration*. This was probably the most important tactic in the battle against folkloric culture: the themes of folklore radically changed their meaning in their new Christian form (consider the dragon, e.g., in Fortunatus' *Vita Marcelli*;[20] or the phantoms in Constantius of Lyons's *Vita Germani*, in comparison with the Greco-Roman model in Pliny the Younger and the theme from folklore of the unburied dead).[21] Even the essential nature of a theme might be altered (e.g., saints became mere auxiliaries in miracle-working, as only God could perform miracles).[22]

The real cultural gap was between the fundamental ambiguity and equivocation of folklore (belief in forces which were both good and bad *at the same time* and, in general, a basic *ambivalence* in the cultural apparatus) and the "rationalism" of ecclesiastical culture, heir of Greco-Roman aristocratic culture:[23] separation of good and evil, true and false, black and white magic, with Manichaeanism as such being avoided only by dint of God's omnipotence.

The two cultures were effective in different ways on different levels. Clerical culture opposed folklore not only out of conscious and deliberate hostility but equally out of incomprehension. The gap between rural masses and the ecclesiastical elite was one of ignorance. The elite's intellectual training, social origins, and geographical situation (urban setting, monastic isolation) made it impervious to the culture of folklore (cf. Constantius of Lyons's uncomprehending astonishment at the miracle worked by Saint Germain on the mute roosters at the request of the peasants).[24]

What we see in the early Middle Ages in the West is a *blockage* of the "lower" by the "higher" culture, a relatively hermetic stratification on two cultural levels, more than a hierarchization incorporating means of transmission between levels for the purpose of facilitating unilateral or bilateral influence. While this cultural stratification may have resulted in the formation of a clerical aristocratic culture,[25] it did not, however, coincide with the social stratification. Beginning in the Carolingian era, the "folkloric reaction" would involve all lay strata. It would burst upon Western culture beginning in the eleventh century, alongside the great heretical movements.[26]

ECCLESIASTICAL CULTURE AND FOLKLORE IN THE MIDDLE AGES: SAINT MARCELLUS OF PARIS AND THE DRAGON

Saint Marcellus, bishop of Paris in the fifth century, after having accomplished his destiny, seems to have fallen back into the obscurity in which his humble origins ought to have kept him. At a time when episcopal recruitment was limited essentially to the aristocracy—to such a degree, in fact, that illustrious birth was counted among the hagiographic commonplaces repeated by the authors of the *Vitae* without much risk of being mistaken, even when they were poorly informed as to their hero's genealogy—Marcellus was an exception.[1] Venantius Fortunatus[2] was asked by Saint Germain, bishop of Paris, to write a biography of his predecessor, Marcellus,[3] who probably died in 436. This Fortunatus did during Saint Germain's lifetime, hence prior to 28 May 576. In the course of gathering such rare data as he could by word of mouth, he learned of Marcellus' humble origins and was thus forced to reconstruct the saint's career with the aid of miracles. Each stage in Marcellus' ecclesiastical career follows a miracle, and these miracles are arranged in a qualitative progression as well, each being superior to the one before. The text is thus invaluable for gaining access to the psychology of the miracle in Merovingian times. Marcellus is elevated to a subdeaconship (*Vita* V) by dint of the first miracle, which belongs to everyday life and asceticism: challenged by an ironsmith to say how much a red-hot piece of iron weighs, he takes it in his hand and gives a very accurate measurement of its weight. The second miracle has a certain Christological character about it; it is reminiscent of one of Christ's early miracles, prior to the decisive apostolate of the later years, the miracle of the marriage at Cana. It occurs when Marcellus is drawing water from the Seine so that his

For the illustrations referred to in the text, see the original version of this essay in *Ricerche storiche ed economiche in memoria di Corrado Barbagallo*, ed. L. De Rosa (Naples, 1970), 2, 51–90.

159

bishop can wash his hands. The water turns to wine and swells in volume to the point where the bishop is able to give communion to all present; the author of the miracle is made a deacon. In the third miracle, which does not represent a qualitative advance ("miraculum secundum ordine non honore," *Vita* VII), Marcellus is surrounded by a sacerdotal scent. As part of his liturgical duties, he once again offers water to his bishop, and this time it begins to give off a fragrance like holy chrism, as a result of which Marcellus becomes a priest. No doubt because the bishop has shown some unwillingness to recognize Marcellus' miracles, he himself has to be the beneficiary of the next one in order to put an end to his hostility and hesitancy. Having fallen mute, he regains the power of speech through his priest's miraculous powers. The priest is at last judged worthy—in spite of his obscure birth—to succeed as bishop (*Vita* VIII). As bishop, Marcellus accomplishes the great deeds the era demanded of its ecclesiastical chiefs, who had become protectors of their flocks in virtually every area: he goes on to bring about a twofold miraculous liberation by causing the chains to fall from a prisoner, liberating him physically, and by delivering the bound man, who is possessed as well, from sin, thus liberating him spiritually (*Vita* IX).

Finally we come to the crowning achievement of Saint Marcellus' career—worldly and spiritual, social and religious, ecclesiastic and miraculous in one (*Vita* X): "We come to that triumphant miracle (mystery) which, though it is the last in time, is the first in value." A monster—a serpent-dragon—that has been terrorizing the populace in the environs of Paris is driven away by the holy bishop, who, in a dramatic confrontation with the beast before the eyes of his people, subjects it to his supernatural powers and causes it to disappear.

The hagiography tells us that this last great deed has survived in the collective memory. And in a collection of miracles made slightly after Fortunatus' account and about a century and a half after the death of Marcellus, Gregory of Tours reports this one miracle of a saint to whom he pays no further attention.[4]

The cult of Saint Marcellus would seem, then, to have had a promising future in store. Yet from the outset this cult was limited to a local area. One obstacle to its spread was the veneration of other saints of the same name, among them the saintly Pope Marcellus (probably martyred under Maxentius in 309) and Saint Marcellus of Chalon, whose cult competed with that of Marcellus of Paris in the Parisian region itself.[5]

As a Parisian saint, Marcellus appeared to be successful. Although the history of his cult—even apart from its traditional dragon, the object of this study—is full of obscurities and legends, we know that the site of his last miracle was the location of his tomb and of a suburban church dedicated to him. According to tradition, this was "the first church" of Paris; even today, it gives its name to one of the most active districts in the history of Paris, in both the economic and the political sense: the *faubourg* Saint-Marcel.[6] At a date not easy to determine between the tenth and twelfth centuries, his relics were transported, perhaps in connection with an epidemic of Saint Anthony's fire, to the cathedral of Notre-Dame,[7] where they subsequently played a leading role in Parisian worship. Together with the relics of Saint Genevieve, with which they were always exhibited in tandem, they remained until the Revolution the most popular of Paris's protectors. Even the important relics for which Saint Louis built the Sainte-Chapelle were unable to supplant them in the sentiments of pious Parisians.[8] Along with Saint Genevieve and Saint Denis, Marcellus became a patron saint of Paris; he was consequently attributed a legendary house, naturally located on the Ile de la Cité.[9] As late as the seventeenth century, Le Nain de Tillemont could admire Saint Marcellus' historical success: "Neither the great length of time," he wrote, "nor the fame of his successors has been able to prevent the (Parisian) Church's reverence for him from surpassing its reverence for all others, and it considers him its first patron and protector after Saint Denis."[10]

It was not long thereafter, however, before Marcellus returned to virtually total obscurity. His cult began to wane in the eighteenth century, and after the Revolution he fell victim to the progressive purification of the religion, which in Paris saw a decline of local piety; after many centuries, Saint Marcellus was finally eclipsed by Saint Denis and Saint Genevieve. His dragon, as we shall see, was one of the first victims of his disgrace, and since the nineteenth century it has rarely been cited among the dragons of hagiography and folklore whose fortunes it long shared.

In that case, what is the point of bringing it back to life in this scholarly essay? Quite simply, it is a case which, though apparently quite banal if judged by a quick glance at Fortunatus' text and its medieval posterity, turns out on closer examination to be complex, instructive, and perhaps exemplary.

At first sight, there is nothing very original about the two forms in which Saint Marcellus' dragon appears in medieval history. In its sixth-century literary form in Fortunatus' text, it seems to be no more than one of those dragons which served as attributes for a good many saints, particularly evangelical bishop-saints, symbolizing the devil and paganism. After a certain date, probably not before the twelfth century and in any case between the twelfth and fifteenth centuries, it becomes merely one of the processional dragons paraded almost everywhere in the liturgy of the Rogation days.

Nevertheless, an investigation of this dragon may be not without interest. In undertaking it, we shall ask several questions designed to shed some light on the history of worship, culture, and sensibility in the medieval West and, more particularly, in one of the great centers of its civilization, Paris.

Was Saint Marcellus' Merovingian dragon merely a symbol of the devil—a symbol the Church had created by transforming a monster that had formerly carried one of the most complex symbolisms in the history of culture?[11]

Was Saint Marcellus' dragon of the classical Middle Ages the same as its ancient precursor? Or did the variety of meanings that had somehow been unified come apart at that time, revealing sociocultural tensions, differences, and conflicts?

Is it not possible to identify two poles in such tensions? The first pole was the learned tradition developed by the clerics, which cast the dragon in the role of a symbol embodying the forces of evil. The second was a popular tradition which invested the same symbol with an ambiguous value as a result of a long series of contaminations and metamorphoses. If this turns out to be correct, if we succeed in outlining a plausible affirmative answer to the question, we may also shed a good deal of light on the structure and contour of medieval culture.

We begin with Fortunatus' abundant text, neglecting those elements irrelevant to our subject or schematically considering only the relation of a particular aspect of them to dragon symbolism.

First, we shall separate the two themes found intertwined here: one relates to the serpent that devours the corpse of an adulterous woman, the other to the dragon resoundingly defeated by the saint. The former is not without interest. It persisted throughout the Middle Ages and became the iconographic symbol of lust.[12] Here, however, it is more or less artificially linked (whether by tradition or literary skill is unimportant) to the theme of the dragon-slaying saint. Beyond noting the serpent-dragon identity that emerges from the two anecdotes, we shall not concern ourselves with it.

We shall also omit from our detailed study any discussion of the often obscure "Parisian antiquities" on which this text might shed some light. The traditions of suburban culture and extramural tombs elsewhere attested to by the archaeological and written record are beyond the scope of this essay. The marshes of the lower Bièvre valley, the geographical setting of the combat in question, and the local character of the adventure will, however, contribute useful material to the interpretation of the tale.

It might also be useful to study the composition and mise en scène of the tale. The skillful use of terrain, public, and gestures make this tale of combat a bravura piece which must have delighted the Ravenna-trained author, as well as readers still nostalgic for circus games and antique triumphs and quite willing to substitute a Christian arena. From this Christian gladiatorial combat, we shall single out only the type of relationship it defined between saint and monster.

Finally, we should point out in passing the comparison Fortunatus makes between Pope Sylvester's taming of a dragon in Rome[13] and the Parisian episode he is recounting. A historian of nationalist sentiment might see the comparison as one of the earliest medieval expressions of a Christian Gallic patriotism. We are interested in this analogy only insofar as it shows that the author was to some extent aware that the story he was telling was typical of a genre and not an isolated case.

Before analyzing the episode in terms of the question that interests us—viz., what does the dragon signify in this text?—we should take care to rule out one hypothesis which, if true, would make our study useless: the historical reality of the episode in the narrative. If the dragon of which Saint Marcellus rid the Parisians really existed, this essay is pointless. By dragon, of course, we mean a serpent, a real animal, but one of such extraordinary size that, in the imagination of the native populace and of posterity, it has the character of a monster which only a person endowed with supernatural powers could subdue, by miraculous means.

We know that such a hypothesis has been put forward to cover all cases of this sort; and in Paris itself, Saint Marcellus' dragon was concretely interpreted, by the clergy anyway, in this manner. Indeed, on the eve of the Revolution, a stuffed animal—a giant serpent, crocodile, or lizard—was suspended from the vaults of Saint Marcellus' Church in the Paris *faubourg* of the same name,[14] having been donated, perhaps, by a traveler originally from the parish and evidently intended to embody Saint Marcellus' dragon in a realistic and scientific fashion. It should be noted that the clergy of the Ancien Régime favored such *scientistic* interpretation, which was to be continued by the rationalist mythologists and folklorists of the nineteenth and twentieth centuries. Such explanations were applied to Saint Marcellus' dragon, among others, by Eusèbe Salverte. An article by Salverte, originally entitled "Légendes du Moyen Age—serpents monstrueux,"[15] and revised under the title "Des dragons et des serpents monstrueux qui figurent dans un grand nombre de récits fabuleux ou historiques,"[16] was incorporated in his work *Des sciences occultes ou Essai sur la magie, les prodiges et les miracles.* The third edition, in 1856, bore an Introduction by Emile Littré, the mere mention of whose name is enough to disclose the *positivist* spirit of the work.[17] Louis Dumont, among others,[18] has refuted this scientistic, pseudo-scientific theory, which he calls *naturalistic* and is applicable only to a very limited number of legendary occurrences.[19] Monstrous animals, particularly dragons, are real legendary phenomena. It is impossible to explain them scientifically in the framework of a purely positivist scientism. Phenomena of civilization are involved, which history can attempt to explain only with the aid of folklore, ethnography, and the history of religion. Such beasts are facts ascribable to a collective mentality,[20] which does not mean that they stand outside time and history. Their actuality, however, lies in the depths of the psyche; the pace of their chronological development is not identical with the pace of traditional history.

The first thing one notices in Fortunatus' text is a total absence of symbolic interpretation by the author. The saint's victory over the dragon is material, psychological, and social in nature, not religious. It is a triumph that comforts the terrorized populace ("perterriti homines," "hinc comfortatus populus"). The dragon-slaying bishop here appears in his worldly role as chief of an urban community rather than in his spiritual role as pastor. He is the bulwark of the nation (*propugnaculum patriae*), vanquisher of the public enemy (*inimicus publicus*). Mention is made of his religious character only in order to bring in a theme dear to Christian hagiography since the late fourth century: with public institutions in disarray, the *vir sanctus* is able to mitigate their deficiencies with his spiritual weapons, private rather than public but placed at the disposal of the civil community. The *arma privata* serve to protect the *cives*; the insignificant bishop's crook turns out to be a potent weapon, owing to the material transformation brought about by the saint's miraculous power—"In his light staff the weight of miraculous power was displayed"; Marcellus' frail fingers became as solid as chains: "cuius molles digiti fuerunt catenae serpentis."

Thus it is in his civic rather than in his religious role that Marcellus is shown triumphing over the dragon. As for the beast, its nature is as vague as the *episcopus* Marcellus' is precise. Three times it is referred to as *bestia*, which evokes the combat of the *bestiarius*, the gladiator; once it is called *belua*, alluding to the extraordinary size and ferocity of the monster; four times the term used is *serpens* and once *coluber*, its poetic equivalent; it is called *draco* on only three occasions. By contrast, certain of the monster's physical peculiarities are emphasized: its bulk ("serpens immanissimus," "ingentem beluam," "vasta mole"); and the three parts of its body, the sinuous curves ("sinuosis anfractibus") connecting two clearly individualized extremities, head and tail, at first held erect and threatening, later lowered in defeat ("cauda flagellante," "capite suplici," "blandiente cauda"). One particular point on the body is stressed by the narrator: the nape of the neck is the point at which the beast will be miraculously subdued. The saintly tamer, having struck the beast's head three times with his staff, subdues it by putting his stole around the nape ("missa in cervice serpentis orario"). These are crucial details, because they establish the symbolism of the creature, the heraldic stylization of its body, and at the same time a ceremonial and ritual of subjection. We shall return to this point.[21]

There is one further sentence in the story that forces us to go beyond the symbolism of the beast and its taming in search of a meaning hidden behind a piece of descriptive detail: "Thus, it came to pass that in this spiritual circus, with the people as spectators, he single-handedly fought the dragon." The spectacle described is merely the double of another, truer spectacle. We must now leave the material circus and place ourselves in its spiritual counterpart.

Between the time of Marcellus' death and the writing of his *Vita* by Fortunatus, what possible meanings could this arena and combat have had? We shall neglect for the moment the problem of whether there was a change of interpretation from the mid-fifth to the late sixth century, and, similarly, in passing from oral legend to literary biography.

Since Venantius Fortunatus' work belongs to a well-defined literary genre of the era, hagiography,[22] it is important that we first investigate what significance combat with dragons had in Christian and particularly hagiographic literature at the end of the sixth century. Then we may proceed to consider how this hagiographic cliché could have been applied to a story Fortunatus was supposed to have heard at the time of his inquiries in Paris.

Since the Bible is the prime source of all Christian literature, it is there that we should first look for dragons or serpents likely to be taken for dragons.[23] There are a good many in the Old Testament. Three of them stand out: the serpent-tempter of Genesis (3);[24] and Behemoth and Leviathan, more harshly treated by Isaiah (27:1), who identifies them as serpents, than in Job (40–41), where no animal name is given them.[25] More individualized dragons are found thrashing about in the psalms.[26] Finally, although the Gospels neglect the dragon, the Book of Revelation gives it a decisive lift. This text was to provide the medieval imagination with the most extraordinary arsenal of symbols,[27] and it was here that the dragon was given the interpretation which would hold sway over medieval Christendom. This dragon is the serpent of Genesis, man's old enemy, the devil, Satan: "the great dragon . . . that old serpent, called the Devil, and Satan" (12:9). It was destined to become the dragon of ecclesiastical literature. It would relegate the other dragons, whose existence the Book of Revelation does not deny, to the shadows and become the great dragon, the dragon par excellence, leader of the rest and incarnation of all the world's evil: Satan.

Had the Book of Revelation's version of the dragon become the usual one among Christian authors by the end of the sixth century?[28] We shall inquire of two authorities: Saint Augustine and, though he follows Fortunatus by about half a century, Isidore of Seville, the first encyclopedist of the Middle Ages. We hope the reader will allow us to extend this rapid survey as far as Bede, the last of the "founders" of the Middle Ages, to use E. K. Rand's term, because the cultural world of the clerics did not change before the middle of the eighth century. Saint Augustine paid little attention to the dragon. As an exegete, he was obliged only to explain the word's meaning as it occurred in the Bible. It is primarily in his *Commentary on the Psalms* (*Enarratio in Psalmos*) that he treats the dragon. He was aware of its identification with Satan and used it to explain Ps. 91:13, "the young lion and the dragon shalt thou trample under feet," and Ps. 104:26, "There is that leviathan whom thou hast made to play therein." Augustine saw "our ancient enemy" in the dragon.[29] The interpretation of the dragons in Psalm 148 proved more embarrassing. In this text, the Psalmist exhorts all creation to sing the Lord's praise and invites the dragons to join the choir: "Praise the Lord from the earth[30] ye dragons and all deeps" (148:7). Aware of the contradiction in having God praised by creatures whose evil and rebellious nature is known from other passages, Augustine overcame the difficulty by explaining that here the Psalmist is referring to dragons only as the largest living creatures on Earth ("majora non sunt super terram"). Filled with admiration for the powers of a God capable of creating such immense beings, it is man himself who associates dragons with the hymn that the world, by its mere existence, offers the Lord.[31] The dragon thus figures here in a basically realistic, scientific, form: it is the largest animal.

The early medieval commentators on the Book of Revelation were led quite naturally to identify the dragon with the devil. For example, Cassiodorus,[32] Primasius, bishop of Hadrumetum (d. 586),[33] and Bede all identify the devil with the serpent of Genesis as well as with the dragon of the Book of Revelation.[34]

Isidore of Seville, however, treats the dragon in an essentially scientific rather than symbolic manner. He is "the largest of all the animals": "the dragon is the largest of the serpents and land animals."[35] Two important details of its behavior are noted: it is an animal at home both underground and in the air, which likes to leave its hiding places in caves to fly through the air; and its strength lies not in its mouth and teeth but in its tail.[36] Two scientific problems of

166

the dragon concern Isidore. First, what distinguishes the dragon from similar animals, primarily the serpent? The answer seems clear. Using mainly Vergil, Isidore establishes the difference between *anguis, serpens,* and *draco: anguis* lives in the sea, the serpent on earth, the dragon in the air.[37] This brings him to the second problem: what is the dragon's habitat? He cannot ignore the variety of elements in which the dragon lives and moves about, in particular its connections with water, which do not appear in either of the two definitions above. This leads him to identify a special type of dragon: the sea dragon, *draco marinus.*[38]

On the other hand, the dragon carries no moral or religious symbolism in Isidore. In a passage from the *Sententiae* (III, v, 28; *PL* LXXXIII, 665) he lists the animal forms taken on by the devil when he embodies one of the deadly sins: animal, not further specified, when he takes the form of lust (*luxuria*), serpent (*serpens*) when he changes into greed or malice (cupiditas ac nocendi malitia), or bird (*avis*) when he is pride (*superbiae ruina*). The dragon is not among these forms. Nevertheless, Isidore, the compleat scholar, was aware of other aspects of the dragon which we do not think very useful for understanding Fortunatus' text yet are invaluable additions to the dossier on the dragon we are assembling here. He knows of three other dragons: the guardian dragon that watches over the golden apples in the garden of the Hesperides;[39] the banner-dragon of military emblems, used by the Greeks and Romans, as Isidore recalls, claiming that its origin dates from the ceremony commemorating Apollo's victory over the serpent Python;[40] and the ring-shaped dragon which, because it is biting its own tail, can represent the year-round or circular time, the time of eternal recurrence, which Isidore says was invented by old civilizations, specifically Egypt.[41]

Finally, Isidore knows of a battle between a bishop and a dragon. He cites the case of Donatus, bishop of Epirus at the time of the emperors Arcadus and Honorius. Donatus was said to have killed an enormous dragon whose breath made the air stink, and whose weight caused a great deal of trouble for the eight teams of oxen which dragged the body to the pyre where it was burned.[42] Isidore does not interpret this great deed symbolically.

It is very difficult to compile a chronological catalogue of the battles waged by saints, and more particularly by bishops, against dragons. Existing works are both imprecise and untrustworthy.[43] The historian of traditional civilization who wishes to take such deeds into account has to make his way uneasily between the positivists, who neglect this sort of phenomenon or subject it to inadequate methods, and the parahistorians, who, out of contempt, naïveté, myopic erudition, and muddle-headed curiosity, forget chronology altogether. The history of mentalities, sensibilities, and beliefs unfolds over long periods of time but is nevertheless subject to diachronic rhythms of its own. For the purposes of this outline, we shall look at just a few important landmarks.

The motif of a dragon's defeat by a saint (and, we reiterate, particularly a bishop-saint) goes back to the sources of Christian hagiography. We find it, in fact, in the first hagiography, the life of Saint Anthony by Saint Athanasius, which, together with the *Vita* of Saint Ambrose by Paulinus of Milan and the subsequent biography of Saint Martin by Sulpicius Severus, would serve as models for the whole genre.[44] In Athanasius, the dragon is interpreted diabolically. This episode, among others, seems not to have enjoyed widespread success in the West nor to have influenced the story of Saint Caesarius and the dragon very directly, however, either because the hermetic atmosphere of Athanasius' *Historia monarchorum* disconcerted Western Christendom or because the dwindling knowledge of Greek in the Latin Church limited, for a while at least, the influence of the life of Anthony. The one episode of a dragon-slaying saint that seems to have caused much of a stir in the early Middle Ages was that of the dragon and the pope, Saint Sylvester, which Fortunatus compares to the story of Saint Marcellus, to the advantage of the latter.

Unfortunately, this legend from the life of Sylvester has attracted the attention of historians mainly in connection with the saint's historical role and its particular juncture.[45] Because he was pope when Constantine converted, historians have tended to interpret his pontificate politically. In this context, the battle with the dragon naturally became the symbol of the victory over paganism. Nevertheless, another interpretation, more Roman than ecumenical, which seems to have been favored over the Catholic interpretation in Rome itself during the Middle Ages,[46] puts the miracle into another context. According to this view, Sylvester's dragon should be identified with a giant serpent that washed ashore when the Tiber flooded and was supposed to symbolize the role of the pope-bishop in the fight against natural disasters in Rome.[47] Thus the episode takes its place in the Roman tradition of prodigious deeds connected with natural disasters[48] and prefigures an incident in the career of Gregory the Great: according to the account given by Gregory of Tours, a monster was cast ashore by the Tiber during a flood, at the time when Gregory (the Great) was just assuming his post as Bishop of Rome. Having already attracted notice in his public role, particularly in provisioning the city, Gregory inaugurated his pontificate by protecting the Roman populace from natural disasters (flood and plague) and their consequences.[49]

The Christian symbolism of the dragon and the battle between the saint-bishop and a dragon was not, therefore, firmly established by the end of the eleventh century. There was a tendency to identify the dragon-serpent, in the manner of the Book of Revelation, with the devil and to give the saint's victory the meaning of a triumph over evil. During this phase of Christianization of the West, such identification would have made the combat a symbol of a decisive episode in the victory of Christianity over paganism in a given region, particularly a *civitas*. Other traditions in which the dragon's meaning is different may still be detected in these legends, however. Christianity itself was heir to these other traditions. As handed down they are generally colored by certain developments and contaminations which make analysis difficult. Nevertheless, one can try to distinguish the contributions of several cultures, as we have seen Isidore of Seville attempting to do: there are Greco-Roman, Germano-Asiatic, and autochthonous legacies.

What we extract from this immense and complex heritage is, of course, the result of selection and choice. We nevertheless hope we are not distorting the significance of the various traditions.

Three aspects of the dragon and of the heroic combat against it in the Greco-Roman tradition seem essential to us.[50] The first emerges in rituals, beliefs, and legends connected with incubation. We know how important this practice was during the Hellenistic period. The major figure was Asclepius of Epidaurus, and the practice was subsequently continued in the Roman world, particularly in its eastern part.[51] In a sacred place, a distressed or ailing person would await a vision or dream in answer to a question they had put to the god. This was an extension of a tradition of supernatural sexual relations between a woman and a god, which were supposed to produce a hero. The traditional form of the fertile god was the serpent-dragon. The most celebrated child of such nuptials was Alexander. Suetonius recounts, however, that Apollo, in the form of a dragon, slept with Atia, who had come to practice incubation in his temple, and so produced Augustus.[52] The legend of the dragon of Cos grew up around Asclepius in the form of a dragon, together with the Hippocratic tradition.[53] Here we are concerned with the connection between the dragon and the nocturnal and oneiric world, and the mixture of desire and fear, hope and fright which suffused its apparitions and actions. Much later psychoanalysis was to grapple with these problems. We shall return to them.[54]

The second of the three aspects noted above has to do with the significance of the conection, in the Greco-Roman myth, between a dragon-slaying god or hero and the liberation of a particular site. Although Apollo's installation at Delphi after the victory over the serpent Python transcends the local setting,[55] and Perseus' battle with the dragon that is holding Andromeda prisoner is not directly connected with the founding of Mycenae, yet we have in the myth of Cadmus, for example, a useful means of determining what the precise significance of the victory over the dragon was. In the first place, the triumph made it possible to establish a community at a certain location and was the symbol of this fact. It was a ritual connected with the foundation of a city and the development of agriculture in a certain area. Here the dragon symbolized the natural forces which had to be tamed. Its death may have been necessary not merely to remove an obstacle but rather as a contribution to the fertility of the undertaking. Cadmus planted the teeth of the immolated dragon in the soil of the future Thebes.

Behind the Greco-Roman legacy we can make out the contribution of the oriental cultures which nourished it. A fundamental study by G. Elliot Smith[56] traces the evolution of dragon symbolism in Babylonia, Asia Minor, and Egypt. In the area covered by Asiatico-Egyptian culture, the dragon was originally the personification of the forces of water, at once fertilizing and destructive. The dragon's most important power was its ability to control water: when benevolent, it brought rain and fertilization thanks to the river's overflow; when hostile, it unleashed deluges and devastating floods. In the beginning, the positive role dominated, and dragons were primarily benevolent creatures, personifications and symbols of fertility gods and of civilizing heroes or kings; this was the case with the dragon incarnating Tiamat, one of the forms of the Great Mother, and with the sea dragon connected with Aphrodite's birth, Aphrodite being another form of the Great Mother. Thereafter, the dragon's status declined until it came ultimately to symbolize evil. In Egypt it was identified with Seth, Osiris' murderer and victim of Osiris' son Horus. Thus the Egyptian *rationalization* preceded the Christian. In Egypt, moreover, we can observe the transition from Horus to Christ, on the one hand, and from Seth to Satan on the other. What concerns us here, however, is that despite its kinship with the serpent, the chthonic animal par excellence, the dragon was fundamentally connected with the powers of water.

The Far East was another breeding ground of dragon symbolism. It seems to have influenced the West only rather late, not until the thirteenth century according to Jurgis Baltrusaitis.[57] In China, the dragon seems to have been linked mainly with the celestial world and the solar myth; it is winged. Along the routes through the steppes, however, this celestial dragon merged, more or less, with a chthonic serpent and with another chthonic dragon which was a guardian of treasures related to the griffin, whose avatars in syncretic symbolism were also endowed with wings.[58] The important point is that the progress of these Far Eastern dragons along the routes of the steppes brought them to the West during the Merovingian era. Developing an idea of Forrer,[59] Edouard Salin has analyzed Merovingian art forms to show the arrival in the West of the Asiatic dragon. He has laid stress on two important characteristics of its symbolism: polyvalence and ambiguity. "The Merovingian dragon takes diverse forms; its symbolism is no less diverse; very likely it represented equally diverse beliefs, just as it reproduced quite different divinities."[60] He continues: "Usually solar in character when they are akin to the griffin and chthonic when they derive from the serpent, the representations of the variously benevolent or malevolent dragons ultimately appear to be the legacy of beliefs almost as old as the world, from the Orient through Eurasia to the West."[61]

In this complex of traditions and beliefs we should attempt to isolate the part due to indigenous traditions, separating it from the Greco-Roman legacy and the Asiatico-Barbarian contribution. If we take the Celtic world as a whole, certain areas were swarming with dragons;[62] in Ireland, for instance, saints had to devote themselves especially to combating them.[63] Gallic beliefs and symbols, however, do not seem to have been rich in dragons, although the chthonic serpent was accepted as an attribute of gods and goddesses[64] and was killed by the Gallic Hercules, Smertrios, the "Provider."[65]

Underlying all these traditions, do we not find the quasi-universal serpent-dragon common to all primitive beliefs and myths? Was not the Merovingian dragon above all a monster of folklore[66] which had resurfaced during an interregnum between two beliefs, when pagan culture was fading before the Christian cultural system had really taken root?[67] It may indeed have been the Christian, ecclesiastical interpretation of Saint Marcellus' dragon that Fortunatus was sketching, but did not this creature have a different significance in the oral tradition from which he drew? Should we not try to find out what this significance was by looking into the depths of a renascent folklore, laden with bits of earlier cultures that had been turned into folklore and brought up to date under the impact of new historical conditions? Underlying the legend reported by Fortunatus is the image of a miracle worker who has tamed an awesome power. This power is related to nature. There is ambiguity in the tale between a chthonic animal (serpent) and a more or less aquatic one (dragon), inasmuch as the saint orders it to disappear either into the desert or into the sea. Of course, given the Parisian geographic setting, the "sea" was no doubt taken from a hagiographic model copied by Fortunatus with no serious effort at adaptation. Still, should we not explain this borrowing by the fact that it was relatively appropriate in a similar context, indeed an aquatic one, which G. Elliott Smith has shown to be of fundamental importance to dragon symbolism?

If we now shift our attention from the setting to the hero, does not the saint here appear in the role of the dragon-slaying liberator and civilizing hero? He is described with a vocabulary more typical of the civic than the religious hero.[68] As for the dragon, if the danger it represents is eliminated, is it not nevertheless significant that it is not killed but only driven away? "The monster was quickly driven off and no further trace of him was found." The battle recounted by Fortunatus was not a duel to the death, but a taming. For a brief moment, the bishop-tamer and the subdued monster establish a relationship reminiscent of the friendship between hermits or saints and animals, particularly wild animals—from Saint Jerome's lion to Saint Francis' wolf:[69] "and the monster, with bowed head, came to ask for pardon, its tail trailing." The dragon was a creature to be neutralized rather than killed. Here, then, we have a scene in which a hero tames natural forces; the hagiographer is neither willing nor able to make this an explicit episode of evangelization. What could conceivably lie behind it?

An episode in material civilization. The topographical setting for such a scene is easy to guess. It was the site on which the Middle Ages would build the town or *faubourg* which would come to bear the name of Saint Marcellus, hence the lower Bièvre valley, whose marshy character can still be glimpsed in the low-lying areas of the present-day Jardin des Plantes.[70] The leading authority on Parisian topography during the early Middle Ages, Michel Roblin points out that "the old Christian *faubourg* of Saint-Marcel"[71] was a center of Parisian Christianization and notes that "its origins have not been explained clearly." He mentions the presence of stone quarries, which may have facilitated the construction of catacombs as at Rome, and considers the possible uses of the waters of the Bièvre, which, centuries later, would attract dyers and tanners to the *faubourg* Saint-Marcel. In the final analysis, he believes that Saint-Marcel "was more likely just a way station on the road to Sens." "Then it would be normal," he continues, "that Christianity, imported from Italy by way of Lyons and Sens, should first have settled in Saint-Marcel, the first district of Lutetia one encounters when arriving by the road along the left bank." Our text may shed some light on the origin of the *faubourg* Saint-Marcel. Is it not a foundation myth, Christian or otherwise? Marcellus' victory over the dragon is a taming of the *genius loci*, the preparation of a natural site between the *deserta* and the forest (*silva*), the lair of the chthonic serpent on the one hand, and the marshland at the confluence of the Seine and the Bièvre (*mare*) on the other; in defeat, the dragon is invited to quit the locale and lose himself in one of these wastes.[72] May we not look upon this text as evidence of an early example of medieval construction, after a hesitant clearing of land and installation of rudimentary drainage, under the aegis of a bishop-entrepreneur who was also a spiritual pastor and political leader?[73] It is also the creation of an early medieval community, instituted by the preparation of urban and suburban sites to be inhabited by a body of citizen-faithful (*cives*) near a road of some importance.[74]

This is not the only text in which Fortunatus narrates the story of a saint who performs a miracle that rids a region of monsters and turns it to productive use.

In the life of Saint Hilary,[75] Fortunatus tells how the saint comes to pass close by the Isle of Gallinaria, opposite Albenga on the Ligurian coast, and is warned by coastal dwellers that it is impossible to settle on the island because of the enormous serpents infesting it ("ingentia serpentium volumina sine numero pervagari"). Like Marcellus, Hillary goes forth bravely to do battle with the wild beasts ("vir dei sentiens sibi de bestiali pugna venire victoriam"). The serpents flee at the sight of him, and he uses his bishop's crook as a marker to divide the island into two parts: one that the serpents are forbidden to enter, the other where they may remain free. More clearly than in the case of Saint Marcellus, we have here a dangerous monster, symbol of hostile nature, being contained and tamed rather than annihilated.[76] Here, too, the serpents are told that if they do not wish to respect the division established by the saint, they always have the sea, which in this case really is at hand.

As in the life of Saint Marcellus, the author's discussion turns the interpretation toward a diabolical symbolism. Fortunatus points out that Christ, the second Adam, is greatly superior to the first, because rather than obey the serpent he has servants, like the saint, capable of giving it orders.[77] Once again the allusion is not further explained. By contrast, the conclusion is purely materialist and incontestably makes Hilary a "civilizing hero": "He increased the territory available to man, for on the animal's land man came to settle."

Even if our hypothesis concerning the symbolism and significance of Saint Marcellus' battle with the dragon is rejected, it is nonetheless true that ecclesiastical writers in sixth-century Gaul did not succeed in completely masking a symbolism quite different from the Christian when they attempted to Christianize the legends of the dragon-slaying saints by identifying the vanquished serpent or dragon with the devil. Besides the contributions of various pre-Christian cultures, this complex symbolism seems to reveal a traditional fund of folklore. It appears in relation to a system of mental responses and physical observances which show great respect for powerful and equivocal natural forces. In a sense, once the dragon is tamed, a compact is drawn up with him.

Six centuries later, Saint Marcellus and his dragon reappear. At the end of the twelfth century, a sculpture clearly inspired by Fortunatus' text and depicting the scene we have just analyzed was in evidence at the cathedral of Notre-Dame. We have good reason to believe, furthermore, that from this time forward Saint Marcellus and his dragon figured in the Rogation Day processions which took place in the vicinity of Notre-Dame. What had become of our heroes—and what was the dragon's new meaning?

It will be useful first to sketch out the major developments in dragon symbolism between the sixth and twelfth centuries.

In one of the principal works bequeathed to the Romanesque faith by the early Middle Ages, the *Moralia in Job* by Gregory the Great, the Old Testament's Leviathan is identified with Satan.[78] In the ninth century Rabanus Maurus gave Christian encyclopedism its polished form. We know that he drew heavily on Isidore of Seville. The differences between them are only more significant as a result. The abbot of Fulda treats the dragon in his chapter on serpents.[79] The first portion is scientific: the dragon is the largest of all the serpents, indeed of all the beasts. It frequently emerges from its cave to fly through the air. It has a crest on its head and breathes and darts its tongue from its tiny mouth. Its strength lies not in its teeth but in its tail. It is untrue that its poison is to be feared. The article quickly moves on to another level—mystical significance.[80] Here, the interpretation is clear: the dragon is the devil or his ministers or the wicked persecutors of the Church. Scripture is cited in support of this interpretaiton: the Psalms, Job, the Revelation of Saint John. The occurrence of both singular and plural forms in these texts leads to the explanation that the dragon may signify evil spirits as well as the devil: "a dragon" is Satan, "the dragons" are his henchmen.

In Romanesque iconography, it is this diabolical dragon, dedicated to evil, that holds sway.[81] The naturalistic current stemming from Isidore and reinforced by the increasing influence of the *Physiologus*[82] on the bestiaries allowed the sculptor or miniaturist some freedom in depicting the crest, scales, and tail. The dragon nevertheless continued to serve as a malefic symbol and came to merge with the tradition of Satan-Leviathan which started with Gregory the Great and became established in the best-known commentaries on the Book of Job, such as Odo of Cluny's or Bruno of Asti's. Ultimately, it was Honorius Augustodunensis who synthesized the mystico-allegorical current and the pseudo-scientific current.[83] Even where it was not the seven-headed dragon of Revelations,[84] the Romanesque dragon was evil.

There were two reasons for the dragon's success in Romanesque art, which may be identified with the twin roots of all such art, aesthetics and symbolism. Making use of the legacy of Irish art and the art of the steppes, Romanesque forms took advantage of the dragon's flexible body. It was the perfect theme for a Romanesque artist bent on satisfying the canon laid down by Henri Focillon: "the law of the greatest number of contacts with the frame."[85] Furthermore, since evil was omnipresent in the Romanesque world, dragons abound on every page of manuscript, every block of sculpted stone,[86] every piece of forged metal.

The Romanesque, however, was the world of psychomachy, the battle of virtue and vice, good and evil, righteousness and wickedness. Individuals and classes rose up as champions of God against Satan and his accomplices, the dragons. In Carolingian times, the supreme dragon fighter, Saint Michael, had attacked the beast in a new Christian mythology of salvation;[87] now the knights came to join the clergy in fighting the monster. Beginning in the eleventh century, Saint George, who arrived from the Orient before the Crusades to lend a hand, ideologically speaking, to the military aristocracy in its social ascent, won an unending series of victories over one dragon after another, in the name of all knights. More than once, though, a real but anonymous knight, armored from head to toe, would attack the monster, sometimes even dismounting to fight it on foot, like the knight who is finishing his battle in stone, at the Musée de Gadagne in Lyons.[88] Among these fearless warriors, bishops occupy a distinguished place, just as in the heroic period of evangelization, but now openly symbolic. It is a rare bishop's crook that does not hold captive in its curved head a defeated dragon, offering its twisted body to the goldsmith's triumphant skill and the prelate's symbolic power.

The advance of funerary art in the Romanesque and Gothic periods offered the vanquished dragon a new career. It was allowed to sleep at the feet of its vanquishers, whose victory was thus immortalized in stone. Bishops like Hugh of Fouilloy at Chartres[89] and even lay lords like Haymo, count of Corbeil,[90] thus used the dragon as a symbolic cushion. Apart from the diabolical symbolism here, may we not read this as another instance of the symbolic victory of the civilizing hero, the cathedral builder or land clearer, organizer of the feudal order?

Dragons were not always so docile in the Romanesque world. They forced their way into the dreams of heroes, haunting their nights with terrifying apparitions. The frightened Charlemagne of the

Chanson de Roland sees them descend on his armies in a nightmarish pack.[91] The dragon is the oneiric beast par excellence in the Romanesque universe. In dreams the ambiguity of its origins[92] was extended, and the collective obsessions of the feudal class and its civilization were exhibited.[93]

Finally, certain other, emancipated dragons seem to have almost fully succeeded in shedding both the confusion of their origins and the rationalizing explanations of diabolical symbolism. These were the standard-dragons. Isidore of Seville has let us glimpse their antique origins. As Christianity was enjoying its political victory in the early fourth century, the military dragon was taken over by the new converted masters: on the *labarum* of Constantinian currency, the sacred emblem's staff crushes the dragon.[94] But the standard-dragons of the eleventh and twelfth centuries were undoubtedly the descendants of Asiatic standards which reached the West through the Anglo-Saxons and Vikings in the north and the Arabs in the south. In the second half of the fifteenth century, they appear on the Bayeux tapestry,[95] and in the *Chanson de Roland* they seem limited to the standards of the Saracens; it is true that the *Chanson* has come down to us in the form of a rather well clericalized text, in which diabolical symbolism is employed for purposes of politico-religious propaganda.[96] Over the course of the twelfth century, however, the standard-dragon developed a symbolism of its own, the upshot of which was to make the dragon the emblem first of a military community, then of a nation. The *draco normannicus*, or Norman dragon, which lent its name to the title of a poem by Etienne de Rouen, was merely a metaphor for the people of Normandy, the Normans, in the usage popularized by Geoffrey of Monmouth.[97] By the author's own admission, the two dragons discovered by Merlin are actually symbols of the Breton and Saxon people.[98] Behind them, however, as Jean-Charles Payen has observed,[99] we can make out the confused outlines of a whole folklore repressed by the early medieval Church, a folklore which suddenly resurged in Romanesque times alongside the perfected system of ecclesiastical symbolism.[100]

Saint Marcellus and his dragon appear twice among the sculptures of Notre-Dame: on the facade, on the pier of the Saint Anne portal; and on the north side, in the archway of the canons' portal.[101]

The two sculptures are not contemporaneous. The history of the Saint Anne portal is the more complicated of the two: most of the sculptures date from the beginning of construction work on the church, around 1165, and were reused later, around 1230, when the entrances in the facade were complete. The tympanum and the center portion of the upper band of the lintel are from the twelfth century, but the two scenes at the end of the upper lintel and the lower lintel are from the thirteenth century. In all probability, the pier belongs to the "archaic" period.[102]

Regardless of such details, the Saint Marcellus of the Saint Anne portal clearly fits into the program of the facade.[103] In this sculpted triptych, the central panel is dedicated to Christ and represents man's destiny, progressing toward the Last Judgment by way of the struggle between vice and virtue and the mediation of the New Testament, embodied by the apostles. The two flanking panels are dedicated to the Virgin Mary. On the left, however, the crowned Virgin plays the role of patroness of the liturgical cycle. It is the triumph of Maria Ecclesia, gathering together the occupations of the months, and, according to Adolph Katzenellenbogen's formulation, a series of characters drawn from throughout ecclesiastical history. Thus we find Saint Michael laying the dragon low, along with important personages in the history of the Church and traditional Parisian piety: Constantine with a figure that is probably Saint Sylvester; Saint Stephen, protomartyr and patron of the First Parisian cathedral; and Saint Denis and Saint Genevieve.

The Saint Anne portal contains a more chronological and narrative history, placed under the patronage of the Virgin Mother enthroned together with the holy infant. On the lintel the Virgin's life is told, from the story of her parents Anne and Joachim to the final episode of the birth: the visit of the three magi. On the archways and piers are biblical characters: kings and queens, prophets, the elders of the Book of Revelation (4:4), up to the consolidation of the Church with Saint Peter and Saint Paul; this is a portal of *precursors*. But this is also where the cathedral's individuality appears. On the tympanum are its founders, Bishop Maurice of Sully on the left, King Louis VII on the right. Finally, on the pier, we find Saint Marcellus, the Parisian patron who, in the fullest sense, belongs to the cathedral, since his relics are preserved within. Thus Marcellus, more than Saint Denis or Saint Genevieve, represents the Parisian church at Notre-Dame, the Parisian episcopal see, and the Parisian Christian community. Head of his flock, the bishop whose character was drawn and justified in Fortunatus' *Vita* here achieves the natural culmination of his triumph and local significance.

It is clear that at the behest of his commissioners the sculptor who carved Saint Marcellus on the Saint Anne portal has followed Fortunatus' text. The lower part of the group, in fact, contains a representation of the sarcophagus containing the body of the adulterous woman, with the dragon escaping from it.[104] The battle between saint and monster is reduced to the moment of triumph. No doubt technical requirements outweighed iconographic significance: the lines of the lintel made it necessary to have a vertical scene in which the only possibility was for the saint to dominate the dragon, rather than a horizontal battle in which the taming of the beast could have taken a less bloody form more in line with Fortunatus' text. Still, the textual fidelity that transforms the monster's flight into its execution, with the bishop's crook plunged into the animal's throat, thus killing it, expresses the clerical interpretation of the dragon as symbol of evil. In laying out the sculptor's program, the canons of Notre-Dame adapted Fortunatus' text to the evolution of the symbolism of the dragon; the pier of the portal was the ideal setting for this meaningful aesthetic.

The same iconography is used in the scene from Saint Marcellus' life depicting the bishop's triumph over the dragon—a scene that appears in the archway of the canon's portal (also known as the "red portal," from the color of its doors). The saint is seen sinking his crook into the monster's throat. This sculpture dates from around 1270.

The sculptures of Notre-Dame are consistent with the dragon symbolism of Gothic orthodoxy. Undoubtedly this symbolism was somewhat weakened by the Gothic stress on the anecdotal and moralizing aspects of the scene rather than on its theological implications. As in the episodes involving dragon-slaying saints and bishops in Vincent of Beauvais and in Jacobus da Varagine's *Golden Legend,* the dragon was the symbol more of sin than of evil.[105] Still, its intrinsically evil character is confirmed. In the Gothic age, the various dragons of the Old Testament and Revelation converge towards a materialization of hell. This was symbolized by the dragon's throat in the innumerable hells of Last Judgments.[106]

Probably around the same time, a quite different dragon—also associated with Saint Marcellus—haunted the vicinity of Notre-Dame. During the Rogation Day processions, a great wicker dragon was paraded about, to the great delight of the Parisians, who threw fruits and cakes into its gaping jaws. This was certainly Saint Marcellus' dragon, yet quite different from the dragon the clergy had had depicted on the Saint Anne portal and the red portal, and different from the one described by Fortunatus as well. This was one of many well-documented processional dragons which we know were used in the Rogations.[107] It is worth pausing to name a few of the best known: in western France, the Grande Gueule of Poitiers, the crocodile dragon of Niort, the Gargouille of Rouen; in Flanders-Hainault, the dragons of Douai and Mons; in Champagne, the dragon called Chair-Salée of Troyes, the dragon of Provins, and the Kraulla or Grand Bailla of Reims; in Lorraine, the dragons of Toul, Verdun, and particularly Metz, with its famous Grawly or Graouilly, which did not escape the notice of that great consumer of folklore and lover of giants, Rabelais.[108] The South was no less rich in dragons, although excepting the crocodile of Nîmes, the only one of these which is still well known is the Tarasque of Tarascon. This, however, provides us with an exemplary case, both because tradition—continued, or rather revived in the nineteenth and twentieth centuries—makes a concrete study possible, and because this study has been carried out in a magisterial book by Louis Dumont.[109] A more minute inventory would reveal dragons in nearly every city (or celebrated site)—at Sainte-Baume, Arles, Marseilles, Aix, Graguignan, Cavaillon, the fountain of Vaucluse, Avignon, and on the Isle of Lérins.[110]

These dragons had two sources. Some came from hagiographic legends and were connected with saints, frequently bishops (or abbots), often dating from the early Middle Ages. Such was the case with Graouilly of Metz, taken from the legend of the bishop Saint Clement; with the Provins dragon, from Saint Quiriatus; the Marseilles dragon, attributed to Saint Victor; and the Graguignan dragon, attributed to Saint Armentarius. And, of course, there is our dragon and Saint Marcellus in Paris. But many of these processional dragons owed their existence solely to the Rogation processions in which they had an official place, as we shall see shortly. It seems that the most famous of these dragons were those traditionally connected with the legend of a local saint, whereby they could be introduced into the Rogation processions under the saint's patronage and with a pronounced individuality, sometimes emphasized by a proper name or nickname. This was clearly the case with Saint Marcellus' dragon, although it seems not to have achieved celebrity.

There can be no doubt, moreover, that these processional dragons were integrated into folkloric rituals. Either for themselves or for the benefit of the organizers or actors of the procession (curates, sacristans, members of the procession), they attracted offerings in kind which were propitiatory rites connected with ceremonies intended, from earliest antiquity, to win the favor of the fertility deities.[111] Young Roman girls used to go in springtime to leave cakes in the grottoes inhabited by the serpents (dragons) of Juno of Lanuvium, an agrarian goddess, in the hope that she would provide a good harvest.[112] Plato set such offerings of fruits and cakes in the context of perpetual fertility of the golden age (*Laws* VI, 782 c-e).

The problem is to make the chronology of the appearance of these processional dragons precise, as an aid to understanding their significance for the medieval men and women who were actors or spectators at these processions.

As an initial hypothesis, one might guess that beliefs and rites connected with dragons exhibit a continuity from antiquity and even prehistory through the late Middle Ages. Frazer sought to establish this filiation by associating the processional images with the giants of Druidic sacrificial rites.[113] Such a hypothesis would seem to take it for granted that the Rogation Day processions incorporated earlier ceremonies. This has scarcely been established. We know that the Rogation processions were begun by Saint Mamertus, bishop of Vienne (d. 470), and underwent rapid diffusion, according to the testimony of Saint Avitus, also bishop of Vienne between 494 and somewhere around 518.[114] Some have held that these Christian festivals were intended to replace the Gallo-Roman *ambarvalia* and borrowed many rituals from them, including the use of animal disguises. The relatively scarce bits of information to be found in early medieval texts, which do not concern Rogations, indicate how carefully the Church proscribed such disguises. According to one text, in the mid-seventh century under the reign of Grimoald, Lombards worshiped the image of a serpent. Yet, Caesarius of Arles, in one of his sermons, bans the custom of going from house to house disguised as a deer, cow, or any other prodigious animal, and in 578 the Council of Auxerre issued a similar ban.[115] Besides, these two texts are concerned with folklorico-pagan customs of the calends of January—"diabolical New Year's gifts," as the fathers of Auxerre put it. All indications are that the early medieval Church was particularly intent on proscribing pagan and, especially, folkloric rites, either by obliterating or adulterating them, or else, where possible—and at that time, a great deal was possible for the Church—by repressing and destroying them.[116] We know nothing of how the Rogations developed in the early Middle Ages. We think it rather unlikely that they incorporated processional monsters, especially dragons. It is more probable, we believe, that there was either a resurgence or a rebirth of such rites rather late in the course of the Middle Ages. Can we set a date to it?

Arnold van Gennep has put forward several hypotheses concerning the origin of the processional giants of Flanders and Hainault, including dragons.[117] According to him, though dragons were integrated into the processional cortèges which in Flemish were called *renzentrein* (procession of giants) and, in Wallon, *ménageries*, they were originally alien to these ceremonies. The first creatures to appear in the menageries were the dragon, the elephant, the camel, the lion, and the whale, "in other words, the animals spoken of in the Bible or Apocalypse, familiar from illustrations in manuscripts and the first printed books. Later, a whole variety of other foreign creatures also appeared, including ostriches, crocodiles, pelicans, etc." Thus van Gennep is of the opinion that these menageries were organized in the fifteenth century, rather near the end, that they were unrelated to the cycle of Lent and the carnival, and that their origin "was more literary and semischolarly than popular." On the other hand, he believes that monstrous dragons appeared earlier in processions, and that the ensuing vogue of gigantism subsequently came to apply to other animals and, still later, to human figures. He points to such dragons in Antwerp in 1394, Cierre in 1417, Alost in 1418, Furnes in 1429, Audenarde in 1433, Malines in 1436. The dates in this chronology can be pushed back somewhat. As early as 1361, the ledgers of Saint Aimé of Douai record that year's expenditures "for making a new tail of bright red *cendal* (a silk fabric) for the dragon carried in the procession."[118] The source for these processional dragons was clearly the Rogation processions. But when did these first incorporate dragons?

To our knowledge, Flanders offers no individualized dragon before the Douai dragon of 1361. Is it possible to use our knowledge of the Parisian dragon of Saint Marcellus to make this chronology more precise and to extend it farther back in time?

Louis Réau states: "In the Rogation processions, the clergy of Notre-Dame had a great wicker dragon carried about in commemoration of the miracle it symbolized, and fruits and cakes were thrown into its gaping jaws by the populace."[119] He does not specify the era he is speaking of, and it is clear that he has reproduced without reference a passage from Alfred de Nore's *Coutumes, mythes, et traditions des Provinces de France* (Paris, 1846), or from this author's model, the early nineteenth-century historian of Paris, J. A. Dulaure.[120]

We have been unable to discover in any medieval record or chronicle or in any ancient or modern history of Paris any reference to a processional dragon of Saint Marcellus. This dragon's existence was asserted only when it was about to disappear in the eighteenth century. J. A. Dulaure, and de Nore after him, claimed that the processional dragon of Saint Marcellus fell into disuse around 1730. Nevertheless, in the second edition (1733) of his *Histoire et recherches des antiquités de la ville de Paris* (2, 620), Henry Sauval, clearly an enthusiast of the Enlightenment, states with undisguised contempt that "every year in the processions staged by Notre-Dame and her four daughters for the Rogation Days, we continue to see a large dragon behave as stupidly as that great devil," i.e., the devil that fought with Saint Michael as the dragon had done with Saint Marcellus.

Must we give up the possibility of setting a date to the appearance of the processional dragon of Saint Marcellus and resign ourselves to calling it, with Dulaure, "a custom from earliest antiquity," without, however, adding the hypothesis which we have already found too bold: "which could well date from pagan times?" A note to the second edition of Dulaure's *Histoire de Paris* shows that the only source which can support the assertion of the ancient existence of the Parisian processional dragon is a well-known text of a general character. "All the churches in Gaul in the thirteenth century," Dulaure writes,[121] "had their dragon. Durand, in his *Rational,* speaks of them as being in general use. These dragons, in his view, signified the *devil.*" In fact, Guillaume Durand, in his *Rationale divinorum officiorum* from the late thirteenth century,[122] merely copies a text of the Parisian liturgist Jean Beleth from around 1180,[123] and James of Vitry had dealt with the Rogation Day processions in a sermon at the beginning of the thirteenth century.[124] We learn from these texts that in certain places processions were held over a period of three days at the time of Rogations and that a dragon figured in them. On the first two days, the dragon took the head of the procession, preceding cross and banners, with its long tail erect and inflated—"cum cauda longa erecta et inflata." On the third day, it followed at the rear, its tail deflated and lowered—"cauda vacua aeque depressa." The dragon represents the devil ("draco iste significat diabolum"), and the three days signify the three eras of history—*ante legem, sub lege,* and *tempore gratiae.* During the first two eras the devil reigned and, full of pride, deceived mankind. Christ had won over the devil, however, and, as told in the Apocalypse, the dragon had fallen from heaven— "draco de caelo cadens"—and henceforth could do no more than try humbly to tempt man.

The symbolism is clear. Louis Dumont, who was familiar with these texts, has given an admirable explanation of the tail symbolism in connection with the ritual of the Tarasque.[125] We believe we have shown that this symbolism is very ancient, rooted in the pseudo-scientific symbolism of antiquity and folklore.[126] We have also pointed out that it occurs in Fortunatus' text too.

Are we then using this detail, important as it is, as a basis for reiterating the hypothetical continuity of the dragon of folklore?

Louis Dumont has made an authoritative analysis of the most ancient of the texts in which the Tarasque appears—the *Life of Saint Martha,* allegedly written by Marcella, Martha's serving girl, composed between 1187 and 1212, and utilized by Gervase of Tilbury, Vincent of Beauvais, and Jacobus da Varagine.[127] Dumont demonstrates that, despite the bookish influence of the bestiaries, the monster described in this text presupposes the existence of a "ritual effigy."[128] Similarly, his iconographic inquiry leads him to believe that the ritual Tarasque appeared at the turn of the thirteenth century, no doubt as the culmination of a long prehistory.[129]

We are inclined to believe that the history of Saint Marcellus' processional dragon must have been virtually the same. We have been

no more successful than was Louis Dumont in the case of the Tarasque in establishing an "iconographic index"[130] for Saint Marcellus'
dragon, and we are less fortunate than he in having no image of the
processional dragon. We have only the ecclesiastical dragon of
Notre-Dame to work with. Dragon iconography does, however,
seem to have acquired some ritual effigies in the early thirteenth
century; like the Tarasque, these can only have been inspired by real
models. We believe we have an example of one in an early thirteenth-century fountain top from northern France, now in the
Dahlem Museum in Berlin. I do not think the devil astride a dragon
was created either by the genius of traditional Romanesque forms or
by the pure imagination of a gifted artist. It seems to me to be a
processional mask, related to carnival masks.[131]

What is the significance of this new type of dragon, directly inspired by folklore? Is Jean Beleth's text, together with the example of
the Tarasque and possible iconographic analogies, sufficient to confirm the hypothesis that Saint Marcellus' processional dragon was
probably introduced in the late twelfth or early thirteenth century?

At the conclusion of his study, in a review of the major characteristics of the Tarasque rite analyzed in the course of his "ethnographic snapshot," Louis Dumont states that "the sociological factor is
fundamental: the Tarasque is above all the eponymous animal, the
palladium of the community."[132] The latter phrase is strikingly reminiscent of an expression in Fortunatus' text concerning Saint Marcellus' victory over the dragon: "propugnaculum patriae." Is it possible that what in the fifth and sixth centuries may have symbolized
the constitution of the Chirstian community and the organization of
the urban and suburban terrain for human use had taken on, locally
and generally, a new meaning, but one of similar import, by the end
of the twelfth century? This was the time, at the end of Louis VII's
reign and during that of Philip Augustus, when Paris became the
capital and grew in size within the limits of its new walls, and when
its flourishing and concerted urban functions brought Parisians to a
new local self-awareness and stimulated a search for a new civic
emblem. In the fourteenth century, of course, Etienne Marcel and a
whole group of wealthy bourgeois behind him would impose a
political emblem on Paris which was borrowed from the great merchants: the Seine ship, the half blue and half red hood. But was not
Saint Marcellus' dragon an earlier version of a Parisian emblem?
Simultaneous with the clergy's use of Marcellus as a visible and
immortal patron of the city in the Saint Anne portal, were not the
people introducing a different kind of dragon into the Rogations,
drawn from different sources, but a creature in which local patriotic
feeling crystallized?

Though the absence of documentation in the case of Paris precludes our making this idea more than a hypothesis, a glance outside Paris and Tarascon proves that the hypothesis is not absurd. In fact, in the second half of the twelfth and throughout the thirteenth century, the Christian West witnessed the development of the dragon as an urban emblem. A student of municipal monuments in the north of France and Belgium, M. Battard,[133] has described what was generally a movable sort of animal or monster, pivoting on an iron rod, which became the "city's protective emblem." He points out that this emblematic creature was usually a dragon. This was the case in Tournai, Ypres, Bethune, Brussels (where the dragon was felled by Saint Michael), and Ghent (where the restored Draak is now in the belfry museum). The Draak measures 3.55 meters and weighs 98 kilograms; according to legend, it was brought from Constantinople to Bruges by the Crusaders, which would place its arrival at the beginning of the thirteenth century, and taken by Ghent in 1382. This urban dragon is an example of what became of the old treasure-guarding dragon when taken over by city dwellers. From the top of the belfry, it watched over the communal archives and treasury.

Friedrich Wild's study of epic literature, particularly Beowulf, has also disclosed such standard-dragons serving as emblems for families, communities, and guilds.[134]

There has even been an attempt to explain the episcopal dragon as having originated as a banner-dragon in the Rogation processions. Concerning the Graouilly of Metz, R. De Westphalen has written that "some time around the twelfth century, the mayors and judges of Woippy, a village dependent on the cathedral chapter of Metz, were required to carry three red banners, one of them topped by a dragon head, in the processions of Saint Mark and the Rogations. A century later, this *vexillum draconarium* had been supplanted by the Grolli, which was supposed to represent the dragon defeated by the apostle of Metz, its first bishop, Saint Clement." This is a skillful job of rational and chronological organization of themes whose convergence around the twelfth century is obscure. It has only one flaw: it is not based on any document.[135]

Whether we are confronted with a case in which one Parisian ecclesiastical dragon encounters another Parisian dragon which has sprung from folklore, or with different emblematic interpretations of a single traditional animal, presumably the dragon of Saint Marcellus, bishop of Paris in the fifth century, the question remains: is the phenomenon indicative of a convergence of clerical and popular culture, the former having materialized its meaning in stone, the latter in wicker?

It should be noted that, for the clerics, the emblem was the bishop in his role as dragon killer, while for the people it seems to have been the dragon itself, as its relations with the prelate follow its changing fortunes. Furthermore, while the ecclesiastical dragon is unequivocally designated a symbol of evil, which must be suppressed, the popular dragon is the object of more mixed feelings: the people first try to cajole it with offerings to satisfy its demands; later, they ridicule its defeat, but without wishing for its death. Of course, the processional dragon was integrated in a Christian ceremony, and the liturgists had given the orthodox theological interpretation of its behavior, as well as that of the spectators, in the course of the processional triduum. By the same token, we cannot rule out the hypothesis that the processional dragon had a learned, ecclesiastical origin, which popular tradition may have distorted. Arnold van Gennep has spoken of "folklorized liturgical festivals," and numerous instances are known of the degradation of saints of erudite origin into cult folklore.[136] Nevertheless, even if there was a mutual contamination of the clerical idea and the popular belief—popular in that period being virtually equivalent to lay—we are still faced with the difference and even the opposition between two mentalities and two sensibilities. On the one hand we have clerical culture, sufficiently secure to claim the triumph of good over evil and to impose clear distinctions. On the other, we have the traditional culture of folklore. Faced with forces not yet stripped of their ambiguity, this traditional culture is prudent to the point of preferring primitive, yet also equivocal and shrewd approaches, which are intended, through flattery and gifts, to render the natural forces symbolized by the dragon not only inoffensive but even beneficial.

From the sixth to the thirteenth centuries, we have seen a striking evolution. In Fortunatus, the Christian Manichaean interpretation is not yet fully formulated, but its outlines are clear enough to repress the ambiguities of popular interpretations. In the heart of the Middle Ages, the ecclesiastical interpretation has achieved its definitive expression, but it has to coexist with a neutral folkloric interpretation that has powerfully reasserted itself.

We believe it likely that this resurgence dates from the twelfth century and expresses the growth of a lay popular culture, rushing into the breach opened during the eleventh and twelfth centuries by a lay aristocratic culture[137] thoroughly imbued with the one available culture system distinct from the clergy's, namely, the tradition of folklore. If this is the case, the Parisian example is then a perfected model: the clerical dragon in stone and the folkloric dragon in wicker are contemporaries. One revolves around the other as if defying it, but no attempt is made to force the doors of the sanctuary guarded by the latter.

The total absence of explicit documentation in the case of Saint Marcellus' dragon prevents us from rejecting the hypothesis that the processional dragon of Marcellus came into existence in the second great wave of folklore during the fifteenth century, which in any case belongs more to the Renaissance than to the Middle Ages. We should point out, moreover, that it disappeared before the Revolution, so that the traditional explanation in terms of events is once again faulty. While we cannot confirm the approximate date of 1730 put forward by Dulaure, it appears credible. For the dragon no longer existed at the time of the Revolution, and it was in 1728 that an analogous dragon named Chair-Salée in Saint-Loup de Troyes disappeared, with the biship adducing rather serious reasons for his decision to forbid this "indecent figure," on 25 April 1728, "in order to put an end in the future to the disorders so inimical to the sanctity of our religion."[138] The enlightened mentality of the eighteenth century, which affected a portion of the high clergy, made it possible for ecclesiastical culture to win a victory over popular culture, thanks to the *lumières,* a victory that medieval obscurantism had put out of reach. Such is the complexity of the great movements of collective sensibility.

In the course of this study, we may, of course, have succumbed to the demon of folklore[139] in trying to establish, on the one hand, a clerical interpretation (which may be forced, but which is roughly true insofar as the Church imposed a coherent interpretation of the dragon onto a situation that actually involves the whole Christian theology of good and evil), and, on the other hand, a folkloric interpretation which, one might suppose, must surely be mistaken. We have not forgotten what André Varagnac has called "the plurifunctional character of traditions,"[140] nor has it been our intention, in Louis Dumont's terms, to substitute "clarity for obscurity, rationality for irrationality" at the risk of reducing "the popular reality to something other than itself."[141] Research on folklore can contribute substantially to the human sciences only if the specificity of its object is respected, which means respecting the phenomena of contamination which in folklore are fundamental. Here, our hope has been simply to show the complexity of a theme which may have seemed simple to a naïve reader of Fortunatus or an ingenuous viewer of the sculptures of Notre-Dame. As historians, our procedure has merely been to take account of the absence or presence of documentary records and to try to provide a chronological account of certain rather broad rhythms, with the intention of establishing a significant context in which to set the phenomena of sensibility and mentality studied here. We hope that we have not made too weighty the ludic but ambiguous grace of this devilishness: the dragon of Saint Marcellus of Paris.

Saint Marcellus of Paris and the Dragon

We now come to that triumphal miracle *(mysterium)* which, though chronologically the last, was first in supernatural importance *(in virtute)*. Noble by origin but base by reputation, a matron, having sullied the brightness of her birth by a low crime, lived out the days of her life in blindness and went to her tomb, followed by a vain cortege. She had been in the ground but a few moments after the funeral rites when there came to pass an event the tale of which filled me with horror. A double lamentation rose from the dead woman's body. A gigantic serpent set assiduously about consuming her corpse. To put it more clearly, the dragon itself became the sepulcher of this woman, her limbs being devoured by the monster. Thus the unhappy burial had a serpent for a gravedigger, and the corpse could not rest in peace after death, for although she might have expected a place to lie down from life's end, her punishment required her always to be on the move. Oh, execrable and awful fate! The woman, who had not respected the integrity of the marriage bed in this world, did not deserve to lie in her tomb, for the serpent who during her lifetime had enticed her to the crime continued to torment her corpse after death. The members of her family who were still nearby heard this noise and rushed to the grave, where they saw an immense monster leave the tomb, uncoiling itself, and, crawling with all its huge mass, whip the air with its tail. Terrified by the sight of it, they abandoned the place. When informed of the event, Saint Marcellus understood that he had to defeat the bloody enemy. He gathered the people of the city and marched at their head. Then, after ordering the citizens to stop, but still in view of all the people, he went forward by himself, with Christ for his guide, toward the place of combat. When the serpent came out of the forest on its way to the tomb, they moved toward each other. Saint Marcellus began to pray, and the monster, with bowed head, came to ask for pardon, its tail trailing. Then Saint Marcellus struck its head three times with his crook, put his stole around its neck, and showed his victory to the citizens. Thus it came to pass that in this spiritual circus, with the people as spectators, he single-handedly fought the dragon. The reassured people ran toward their bishop to see his captured enemy. Then, with the bishop leading a throng of nearly three thousand, all followed the monster while giving thanks to God and celebrating the funeral rites of their enemy. Then Saint Marcellus reprimanded the monster and said to it, "Hereafter thou must either stay in the desert or hide beneath the waters." The monster quickly disappeared, and no further trace of it was ever found. The protector of the fatherland was thus a lone priest who, with his fragile crook, tamed the enemy more surely than if he had pierced it with arrows, for, even if it had been struck with arrows, it might have thrown them back, if the miracle had not vanquished it. Oh, most holy man, who, with the power of his frail crook, showed where the strength lay, and whose delicate fingers were the serpent's chains! So private arms vanquished a public enemy and a single victim aroused the applause of a general victory. If the saints' merits are compared according to their exploits, Gaul must admire Marcellus as Rome does Sylvester, and the former's exploit is the greater, since, where the latter could only set his seal on the dragon's mouth, the former made him disappear.

Venantius Fortunatus, *Vita Sancti Marcelli*, cap. X, (*MGH, Scriptores Rerum Merovingicarum*, IV/2, ed. B. Krusch (1885 [2]), pp. 53–54

THE MEDIEVAL WEST
AND THE INDIAN OCEAN:
AN ONEIRIC HORIZON

The medieval West knew nothing of the real Indian Ocean. As late as the mid-fifteenth century, the Catalonian mappemonde in the Biblioteca Estense in Modena shows utter ignorance of the Indian Ocean.[1] On the planisphere of Fra Mauro of Murano (1460), the east coast of the Persian Gulf "no longer has the form of land."[2] Despite his use of Marco Polo, Martin Behaim's globe of 1492 shows no knowledge of India. South Africa, Madagascar, and Zanzibar are depicted on it in extravagant and fantastic form. We must await the first Portuguese discoveries before geographical—or, rather, coastal—knowledge of the Indian Ocean begins to take shape. The most important date is 1488, the year of Diaz's return to Lisbon. There is still a good deal of fantasy in Doctor Hamy's *Carta navigatoria auctor incerti* (1501–2), but its map of eastern Africa is very good. The portolano-mappemonde of Caneiro Januensis (1503) is much more precise.[3] On the whole, knowledge of the Indian Ocean begins with Africa—and the Portuguese—in contrast with medieval dreams, which turned primarily toward Persia, India, and the islands.

Nevertheless, there had been some progress in the fifteenth century.[4] This was due primarily to the rediscovery of Ptolemy, who, unlike the ignorant Roman geographers who were the main source for medieval cartographers, knew the Indian Ocean fairly well. Ptolemy's rediscovery dates from 1406 but bore fruit only with the introduction of printing. The earliest printed editions I have been able to locate in the Bibliothèque Nationale in Paris are from Vicenza (1475), Rome (1478 and 1490), Bologna (1482), and Ulm (1482 and 1486). The work was not always put immediately to good use, however, as Martin Behaim's globe indicates, although he did in fact use the Ulm editions.

Ultimately, the most important advance in the fifteenth century was that certain scholars abandoned the Ptolemaic view—for Ptolemy entombs a certain precision of detail in a monumental overall error—of a *closed* Indian Ocean, actually considered as a river, the circular river-ocean. Some writers have pointed out the famous passages on this subject—without practical consequences, however—by Pierre d'Ailly in his *Imago Mundi* and by Pius II in his *Cosmographia*.[5] The first medieval map to show an *open* Indian Ocean was that of Antonin de Virga (1415).[6] Not until Martellus Germanus' mappemonde (1489)[7] was the notion—accepted by Martin Behaim, for example—of an open Indian Ocean adopted, however.

The opening of the Indian Ocean not only marked the end of a long period of ignorance but also destroyed the very basis for the myth of the Indian Ocean in the medieval mentality. The portolano had come close to making a breach in the closed world dreamed of by the medieval West in its oneiric Indian Ocean. Jurgis Baltrusaitis has given a good description of the mental revolution caused by the portolano, which "upset the bases" of cartography and, in the same stroke, the whole view of the world. "Instead of spaces enclosed within a narrow circle, endless vistas came into view . . . Instead of the regular, stable boundaries of continents which the imagination could stock at will with cities and countries of uncertain location, the outlines of coasts began to develop around fixed points . . . The whole aspect of the earth suddenly changed."[8] As we have seen, however, the portolanos long neglected the Indian Ocean and had scarcely shaken its mythical completeness.

The fecundity of the myth lay in the belief in a *mare clausum*, which made the Indian Ocean a repository of dreams, myths, and legends for the medieval mentality. This sea was the medieval West's closed world of oneiric exoticism, the *hortus conclusus* of an Eden in which raptures and nightmares were mixed. Once its wall had been pierced, the dream evaporated.

Before we sketch the views of the closed oneiric horizon, it is important to raise a few questions concerning this medieval ignorance, without presuming to answer them. The medieval West did have contacts with the Indian Ocean. Merchants, travelers, and missionaries reached its shores.[9] Some, including Marco Polo, had written about it. Why did the West so stubbornly refuse to take notice of what it really was?

First of all, despite such excursions, which were more the work of individuals than collective undertakings, the Indian Ocean was effectively closed to Christians. Arabs, Persians, Indians, and Chinese, to name only the most important groups, had made it a private preserve.

The few Westerners who reached it almost always approached from the north by land routes, not to mention those who missed it, as it were, passing to the north on the Mongolian road, the sometimes-cut umbilical cord of East-West relations during the Middle Ages.

Psychological taboos must have played a role for some missionaries and merchants: the fear of revealing what might be considered a commercial secret in a trade that was full of such secrets, and lack of interest in geographical facts which were negligible in comparison with spiritual truths. Even someone as exceptional in culture and "scientific spirit" as John of Monte Corvino is disappointing. In contrast to men of the Renaissance, medieval men did not know how to look but were always ready to listen and believe all they were told. In the course of their travels, they soaked up any number of marvelous tales and believed that they had seen what they learned, on location no doubt, but nonetheless by hearsay. Already stuffed with legends taken for true before their departure, they carried their mirages with them, and credulous imagination materialized their dreams in surroundings disorienting enough to make them even more natural daydreamers than they were at home.[10]

Finally, we may ask ourselves what those who seemed to know the Indian Ocean best, like Marco Polo, really knew about it. When he reaches India "major," in the area of Madras on the east coast, his narrative ceases to have the character of a genuine travel diary and becomes a systematic, traditional, bookish description. Westerners were suspicious of the strange types of boat they found, particularly the sewn boats, which seemed fragile to them, and so were deterred from hazarding a feared sea.[11]

To go even farther, we might ask ourselves what the Arab geographers knew of the Indian Ocean. Western writers and merchants sometimes turned to them for information. Their descriptions, too, are frequently full of fables and demonstrate ignorance of the facts. It is quite possible that the Indian Ocean was a forbidden and unknown world for the Arabs as well, at least for their scholars. Thus it may be that this potential source of information only reinforced the illusions of Westerners.[12]

Where did the medieval West get its idea of the Indian Ocean? Its sources were mediocre Hellenistic-Latin ones and legendary writings.

Antiquity experienced a brief "critical" period with regard to legends about the Indian world, what Rudolf Wittkower calls "an enlightened interlude." This incredulous line of thought is represented principally by Strabo, who did not hesitate to call those who had written on India before him liars.[13] Aulus Gellius was later to proclaim his disgust with fables, which he thought offered nothing of aesthetic or moral value.[14] Ptolemy himself, despite the more scientific character of his geographical method and a better knowledge of cartographic detail, had been unable to counterbalance the pseudo-science which derived largely from Indian epic poetry. This poetry held that myths were the essence of reality and knowledge. In the degenerate form of the merely picturesque or gimcrack, such mythical scientific poetry would saturate the imagination of the medieval West.[15] Here we must hasten to point out that two great Christian spirits belong, more or less, among this small group of skeptics, in order to make clear how little their "skepticism" met with response in the Middle Ages. Saint Augustine, concerned with the problem of justifying an anthropology based on Genesis, was troubled by the possibility that in India monstrous men existed whose place in the posterity of Adam and Noah was difficult to account for, but he does not rule out the possibility that in them God created models of the same sort of freaks that we see among ourselves, which we are tempted to attribute to a shortcoming in His wisdom. Eight centuries later, Albertus Magnus hesitates to comment on deeds and creatures whose existence he has not seen for himself.[16]

In his *Historia Naturalia,* on the other hand, Pliny the Elder had accepted all the fables concerning India and for centuries provided the sanction of "scientific authority" for belief in India as a world abounding in marvels.[17] Even more than Pliny, Gaius Julius Solinus, author of one of those digests which, in the late Empire, inaugurated medieval culture, was to serve as inspiration for medieval ramblings about the Indian Ocean and its surroundings with his mediocre *Collectanea rerum memorabilium,* written during that wreck of a third century from which the first debris of Greco-Roman culture emerged.[18] Its authority was reinforced when it was used by one of the leading Christian rhetoricians of the early fifth century, Martianus Capella, who was until the twelfth century the great master of the "liberal arts" in the medieval West.[19]

In addition, there were the fantastic writings attributed to some great name, whose authorship medieval credulity was willing to accept with neither examination nor doubt. These fueled the Indian sector of a pseudo-science which displayed a predilection for drawing on apocryphal literary sources. For example, there is the letter of a certain Fermes to the emperor Hadrian "on the marvels of Asia," which probably dates from the fourth century, based on a lost Greek original, and which purports to recount a trip in the Orient.[20] Between the seventh and tenth centuries, three treatises of a similar sort, including an *Epistola Premonis regis ad Traianum Imperatorum* lent credence in the West to the theme of the *mirabilia Indiae.*[21] The apocryphal correspondence concerning India and its miracles also drew upon the *Letter from Alexander to Aristotle* which was in circulation around 800 and the correspondence between Alexander and Dindymus.[22] Lastly, the Indian myth acquired a new character in the twelfth century in the person of Prester John, who was supposed to have sent a letter to the Byzantine emperor Manuel Comnenus in 1164.[23]

In all this fictional literature, we must set aside a special place for a romantic set of adventures which endowed the theme of Indian marvels with extraordinary prestige. One of the adventure cycles most admired 'by the Western public was devoted to the medieval Alexander, a legendary hero, who, by a slight alteration of history, appropriated the whole vast area of miraculous India. The Indian myth took a romantic turn with the adventures and exploits imputed to the explorer king with the insatiable curiosity who sounded the depths of the earth, the forests, the seas, and the skies. He turned medieval science fiction from geographic marvels and picturesque teratology to adventure in the sense of a quest for marvels and monsters.[24] He also led the medieval West to rediscover the original Greek sources for the India of fable. It was not so much the *Indica*, composed in the early fourth century B.C. by Ctesias of Cnidus, who had been the physician to the king Artaxerxes Mnemon in Persia,[25] as the treatise written by Megasthenes around 300 B.C. that was at the bottom of all the ancient and medieval fables concerning India's marvels. Sent as ambassador to Sandracottus (Chandragupta) at his court in Pataliputra (Patna) on the Ganges by Seleucus Nicator, Alexander's heir in Asia, Megasthenes there learned of and embellished the mythical tales and fables which for eighteen centuries would make India the marvelous world of Western dreams.[26]

Medieval writers in the West made no hard-and-fast distinctions between scientific or didactic literature and fiction. All these genres incorporated Indian marvels. Throughout the Middle Ages, these marvels would contribute a standard chapter to the encyclopedias in which a whole line of scholars sought to hoard up the West's treasure in knowledge. After Martianus Capella, first among them was, of course, Isidore of Seville, who devoted a paragraph to India and its miracles in each relevant article of his *Etymologiae*.[27] Rabanus Maurus' great Carolingian encyclopedia *De universo* borrows from Isidore's text and adds allegorical interpretations as well as the amazing miniatures of manuscript 132, illuminated around 1023 at Monte Cassino. These illustrate the monsters of India alongside realistic scenes in which some authors claim to see one of the earliest representations of technical equipment in the medieval West.[28] In the *Imago Mundi* attributed to Honorius Augustodunensis, there is one chapter *De India*, not counting the Indian references in the chapters *Paradisus*, *De Monstris*, and *De Bestiis*.[29] James of Vitry drew on these sources for his *Historia Orientalis*, which shows that Christian scholars of the Holy Land continued to rely on the Western storehouse of knowledge, in this case the *Epistola Alexandri*, rather than use written or oral Eastern sources.[30] All the thirteenth-century encyclopedists used Indian myth: Walter of Metz, in his *Imago Mundi*, which was translated into English, French, and Italian until the end of the Middle Ages;[31] Gervase of Tilbury, who borrowed heavily from the *Letter from Fermes to Hadrian*[32] for his *Otia Imperialia*, written around 1211 for Otto IV; Bartholomew the Englishman, who relied on Solinus, whose *De proprietatibus rerum* would enjoy success until the beginning of the seventeenth century;[33] Thomas of Cantimpre, whose *De natura rerum* was translated into Flemish at the end of the thirteenth century by Jacob Maerlant and into German in the mid-fourteenth century by Conrad von Megenberg;[34] Brunetto Latini, in his *Treasury*, from which Dante may have taken his references to India;[35] Vincent of Beauvais, who treats the subject on three occasions, once in the *Speculum naturale* and twice in the *Speculum historiale*.[36] The late Middle Ages would perpetuate and supplement the Indian myth. In his imaginary trip around the world, Mandeville introduced a new "Indienfahrer," Ogier the Dane, whose exploits rival Alexander's.[37] The *Gesta Romanorum*, a collection of fables and moralizing stories used as a source by preachers, extended Indian fantasy to those who listened to sermons,[38] and Pierre d'Ailly, in his *Imago Mundi* of 1410, assembles in one chapter all that is known about the *Mirabilia Indiae*.[39]

The success of this literature was increased by the illustrations in many of the manuscripts, which sometimes spilled over into sculpture, as shown by numerous works of art, of which the most famous and impressive is the tympanum at Vézelay.[40] This is not the place for a digression into an iconography that would take me far from my subject and competence, but it will be useful to make a few remarks about these images. First, their abundance shows how much the marvels of India inspired Western imagination; the sculptors and miniaturists, better than their written sources, depicted the whole range of fantasy and dream which the Middle Ages lavished on these marvels. An imaginary world, it was to be a favorite theme for the exuberant medieval imagination.

Iconographic studies are also useful for showing the complexity of the various artistic and literary traditions that combined in a myriad of ways to produce the Indian inspiration of the medieval Western mind, an effect that went far beyond the few major influences and central lines.[41] Perhaps it would be revealing to single out, from among the confused mass of contaminations, two distinct inspirations, two divergent interpretations of Indian marvels in medieval ideology and aesthetics. First, we have the tendency that Rudolf Wittkower calls "geographical-ethnological," and which seems to me to refer to a universe of myth and folklore, to a conception of India as *anti-nature* and of its marvels as "counter-natural" phenomena.[42] Stamped with the seal of Greco-Roman paganism, this conception belongs, I think, primarily to a primitive, savage store of material. It may be connected with that medieval anti-humanism which inspired the most impressive artistic creations of the western Middle Ages. Opposed to this notorious interpretation, a more "rational" tendency sought to domesticate the Indian marvels. This tendency had come down from the naturalistic interpretations of Saint Augustine and Isidore of Seville, for whom the marvels were merely special, extreme cases of natural phenomena and hence a part of the natural and divine order; this led to an allegorization and particularly a moralization of the marvels. Under the influence of the *Physiologus,* the bestiaries, particularly from the twelfth century on, thus gave a *meaning* to Indian extravagances, which tended to strip them of their scandalous power. The pygmies were symbols of humility, giants of pride, dog-headed men of quarrelsome people, and so on, thus reducing such freaks to representatives of the ordinary run of mankind. The process of domestication continued by way of an evolution which transformed mystical allegories into moral allegories and ultimately degraded them to the level of social satire. In a fifteenth-century manuscript from the *Liber de monstruosis hominibus* by Thomas of Cantimpre (*Bruges Cod.* 411), we find the fabulous Indian races dressed as Flemish burghers.[43]

From both points of view, the Indian Ocean was a mental horizon, the exotic fantasy of the medieval West, the place where its dreams freed themselves from repression. To explore this ocean, then, is to recognize an important dimension of the period's mentality and sensibility, visible in many aspects of its art and one of the principal storehouses of its imagination.[44]

Before we go on to sketch the oneiric map of India as seen from the medieval West, we still have to ask ourselves what land it was whose shores were washed and whose marvels were protected by the Indian Ocean. Along this coastline, which, for Westerners, seems to have run without major irregularities from Africa all the way to China, three sectors, three Indias, were usually singled out. India Major, which includes the largest part of our India, was flanked by an India Minor extending from the north of the Coromandel Coast and including the southeast Asian peninsulas on the one hand, and by a Meridional India including Ethiopia and the southwest Asian coastal areas on the other.[45] The interesting connection—or confusion—is the one which linked Ethiopia and India and made a single marvelous world of East Africa and southern Asia, as though the Queen of Sheba had given her hand to Alexander rather than to Solomon. This may be seen clearly in the legend of Prester John. At first he was supposed to be located in what is properly called India, but he was nowhere to be found in Asia and was finally transferred during the fourteenth and fifteenth centuries to Ethiopia. In 1177, Pope Alexander III had sent his physician Philip to the Orient carrying, in vain, a letter addressed to *Johanni illustri et magnifico Indorum regi*.[46] Despite such hesitancy, however, Westerners were certain of one thing: the world of marvels lay to the east, in the Orient. Only Adam of Bremen would attempt to transplant the *mirabilia Indiae* to the northern world.[47]

In the first place, the medieval West dreamed of a world of riches in India. Impoverished Western Christendom—*latinitas penuriosa*, Alan of Lille called it—thought the Indian Ocean abounded in riches, was swamped in a flood of luxury. This dream settled mainly on the islands, the innumerable "fortunate isles" which were supposed to be the pride of the Indian Ocean, a sea dotted with a myriad of islands. "In this India sea," Marco Polo had written, "there are twelve thousand seven hundred islands... No man alive can tell the true story of all the isles of the Indies... They are the best, the flower of India."[48] Christian symbolism surrounded these islands with a mystical aura by using them as an image for saintliness, keeping the treasure of their virtues intact despite the battering waves of temptation on all sides.[49] The islands were said to produce luxury goods: precious metals and stones, fine woods, spices. These were so abundant that, according to Marco Polo, from May to July in the kingdom of Coilum (the Indian coast southwest of Malabar), pepper was harvested continually: "they load it loose onto vessels as we do wheat."[50] The kingdom of Malabar was blessed with such "enormous quantities" of pearls fished from the sea that its king went naked, covered from head to toe with nothing but pearls, "a hundred and four of the largest and most beautiful" on his neck alone.[51] Some islands were made of solid gold or silver, such as the isles of Chryse and Argyre. The "best" of all these islands, meaning the largest and richest, was Taprobane, or Ceylon. Thus the oneiric horizon reflects the psychological repercussions of the very structure of medieval trade; for the West was an importer of precious products from far-off places, which it thought of in part as real, in part fantastic, in part commercial.

With this dream of riches was connected another, of fantastic exuberance. The lands of the Indian Ocean were believed to be populated by fantastic men and animals, a world full of monsters of both kinds. As Honorius Augustodunensis put it, "There are monsters there, some of which belong to the human species, others to the several animal species."[52] These dream creatures enabled the western imagination to free itself from the mediocrity of the fauna actually to be found in its own world and to discover the inexhaustible creativity of Nature and God. There were men whose feet were turned around; dog-headed men who barked, lived well beyond the normal life span, and whose skin turned black in old age rather than white; monopodes who shaded themselves with their raised foot; cyclops; headless men with eyes on their shoulders and two holes in their chest for nose and mouth; men who lived on the scent of a single kind of fruit and died if they could not smell it.[53] It was a surrealistic anthropology, comparable to something from Max Ernst. Besides these monstrous men, fantastic beasts pullulated. Some were constructed of bits and pieces, like the *bestia leucocroca,* which had the body of an ass, the hindquarters of a deer, the breast and thighs of a lion, the hooves of a horse, a large forked horn, a broad mouth which went from ear to ear and emitted an almost human voice; others had human faces, like the *mantichora,* with three rows of teeth, a lion's body, scorpion's tail, blue eyes, a blood-red cast, a whistling voice like a serpent's, faster on the ground than a bird in flight, and anthropophagous to boot.[54] A poor and limited world formed for itself an extravagant combinatoric dream of disquieting juxtapositions and concatenations. The irony was that these monsters often served as screens between man and the riches he glimpsed, dreamed of, and desired: the dragons of India guarded treasures of gold and silver and kept men from coming near.

The dream expanded to a vision of a world where a different kind of life was lived, where taboos were eliminated or exchanged for others. The weirdness of this world produced an impression of liberation and freedom. The strict morality imposed by the Church was contrasted with the discomfiting attractiveness of a world of bizarre tastes, which practiced coprophagy and cannibalism;[55] of bodily innocence, where man, freed of the modesty of clothing, rediscovered nudism[56] and sexual freedom; and where, once rid of restrictive monogamy and family barriers, he could give himself over to polygamy, incest, and eroticism.[57]

Going farther still, medieval man dreamed of the unknown and the infinite, of cosmic fear. The Indian Ocean became the *mare infinitum,* the entry to the world of storms, to Dante's *terra senza gente.* Here, however, Western imagination ran up against the limits of what was ultimately a closed world, its dreams going around in circles within it. On the one hand it encountered the walls that confined, for the time being, the Antichrist and the damned races of the earth, Gog and Magog; it came upon its own apocalyptic destruction. On the other hand, it discovered a mirror image of itself, an upside-down world; it was turned back in on itself by the anti-world of which it dreamed, the oneiric and mythic archetype of the *antipodes*.[58]

There remained no choice but to be satisfied with tranquil, virtuous, reassuring dreams. Thus we have the Catholic dream of the Indian Ocean. Its tempests could not prevent the apostles from carrying the gospel to the Orient. Saint Matthew was supposed to have converted meridional India, Saint Bartholomew upper India, and Saint Thomas, especially, lower India, where medieval Christians pursued one more mirage in searching for his tomb. A lost Christian was said to be awaiting his Western brothers on the shores of the Indian Ocean. This dream gave rise to Prester John, who was to be given a semblance of reality by the discovery of the Nestorian communities. From Gregory of Tours to William of Malmesbury, Henry of Moringen, and Caesarius of Heisterbach, apostolic India would haunt Christian imaginations. It was Far Western Christendom that made one of the earliest attempts to open friendly relations with Far Eastern Christendom: in 883, King Alfred of England sent Bishop Sigelmus on a voyage toward Christian India.[59] The shores of the Indian Ocean were the favorite object of missionary dreams. Even the more realistic Marco Polo carefully noted down which peoples were pagan, Moslem, Buddhist, or Nestorian, as so much useful information for the great undertaking.

This Christian dream had a still more prestigious goal: to find the way into the Earthly Paradise. For it was indeed on the borders of India that medieval Christendom thought this Eden was located. From it flowed the four rivers of paradise which Christians identified with the Tigris, the Euphrates, the Ganges (under the name Pison), and the Nile (under the name Gihon). Most medieval cartographers, beginning with the monk Beatus on his famous map from the second half of the eighth century, carefully noted the location of Paradise on India's borders.[60]

Here, too, however, a more pagan dream frequently supplanted the Christian one. The Earthly Paradise of India then took the form of a primitive world enjoying its Golden Age, the dream of a happy and innocent humanity prior to original sin and Christianity. Perhaps the most curious aspect of the Indian myth in the medieval West was that of a world of noble savages. From the *Commonitorium palladii* in the late fourth century to Roger Bacon's *Opus majus* and Petrarch's *De vita solitaria*, the theme of the virtuous peoples of the Indian Ocean underwent continual development. The Alexander cycle dwells indulgently on "virtuous Ethiopians" and "pious Brahmins." Although their piety might bear some resemblance to a certain Christian evangelism, it was distinguished by the absence of all reference to original sin and by the rejection of all social and ecclesiastical organization. Thus the Indian dream culminated in a humanism hostile to all civilization and to all religion other than natural religion.[61]

We have reached the end of our rapid excursion through the oneiric universe projected by medieval Western man onto the world of the Indian Ocean. Ultimately, this sea was conceived as an anti-Mediterranean, a place contrasted with the familiar world of civilization and rationalization. At this point we may ask ourselves whether the contradictions we have noted in the Indian dream are merely those inherent in any oneiric universe. To return to a distinction suggested above, I would be tempted to see two opposing systems of thought, two opposing mentalities and sensibilities, frequently found, moreover, in combination. On the one hand we have a tendency toward the domestication and exorcism of marvels, which were brought within reach of the Western mind by being associated with a familiar universe. This tendency Christianity reinforced through the influence of its allegorical explanations. Tailored for instructional use, the India thus moralized might still inspire desire or fear, but it was primarily sad and saddening. The lovely substances are now mere allegorical baubles, and the poor monsters, created for edification, as well as the unfortunate race of wicked men with large lower lips who rank just above the monsters in the scheme of things, all seem to repeat the verse in Psalm 140 that they personify: "malitia labiorum eorum obruat eos."[62] *Tristes tropiques* . . .

On the other hand, we have not left the ambiguous world of marvels which captivate and frighten at the same time. The psychic complexes of primitive mentalities have been transferred onto the plane of geography and civilization.[63] Barbarism both attracts and repels. India is the world of men with an incomprehensible language, men denied articulate and intelligent speech, and even the possibility of utterance. This is the meaning of the "mouthless" Indians which some have foolishly sought to identify with one or another Himalayan tribe.[64] During the Middle Ages, moreover, the West and India held each other in contempt. Since the time of Greek antiquity, monoculism had been the symbol of barbarousness in the West, and for medieval Christians India was populated with Cyclops. We can imagine the surprise of the fifteenth-century traveler Niccolò de Conti when he heard Indians say they were quite superior to Westerners because those men from the West had only one eye, unlike themselves, two-eyed and hence wise.[65] When Westerners dreamed of motley Indians, half men and half beasts, were they not merely projecting their own complexes onto these fascinating and disquieting monsters? *Homodubii* . . . [66]

NOTE

The Celtic world was another oneiric horizon for the medieval West. Clerical culture colored it strongly, however, with Eastern influences. Indian myths invaded the Arthurian legend. Cf. *Arthurian Literature in the Middle Ages*, edited by R. S. Loomis (Oxford, 1959), pp. 68–69, 130–31.

I have not treated the problem of possible Indian influences on the fabliaux, which was raised by Gaston Paris on 9 December 1874 in his inaugural lecture at the Collège de France, "Oriental tales in French literature of the Middle Ages" (in *La Poésie du Moyen Age*, 2ᵉ série [Paris, 1895]), based on the works of the great nineteenth-century German orientalists (particularly T. Benfey, *Pantschatantra: Fünf Bücher indischer Fabeln, Märchen und Erzählungen aus dem Sanskrit übersetzt* [Leipzig, 1859]). On this debate, cf. Per Nykrog, *Les Fabliaux* (Copenhagen, 1957).

DREAMS IN THE CULTURE AND
COLLECTIVE PSYCHOLOGY OF
THE MEDIEVAL WEST

This theme was chosen as a topic for extended investigation during an introductory course for young historians at the Ecole Normale Supérieure. The object of the endeavor was to show the structures, continuities, and turning points in the history of medieval culture and mentalities—starting from a few basic obsessions.

Such a study must inevitably touch on psychoanalysis, but owing to the insufficient competence of the leader in this area and the unresolved problems[1] connected with making the transition from individuals to groups in psychoanalysis, we had to be content with occasionally approaching the psychoanalytic extensions of the investigation, without really pursuing them. Thus a study of Saint Jerome's dream[2] made it possible to close in on the Christian intellectual's feeling of guilt, which can be made out throughout medieval cultural history, and an analysis of Charlemagne's five dreams in the *Chanson de Roland*[3] led to recognition of a possible "feudal libido." We also tried to exploit and develop Freud's beginnings[4] of a social psychoanalysis rooted in professional or class consciousness. In this regard, the royal dream of Henry I of England[5]—structured, incidentally, by Dumézil's tripartite schema of society—was taken as a point of departure.

Throughout this preparatory work for a psychoanalytic approach, we attempted to determine how the literary packaging of dream stories parallelled, as it were, and increased the distortion of the manifest content in relation to the latent content of the dream. In this respect, the often strict obedience of medieval literature to well-established rules of genre, to the weight of constraining authority, and to the influence of clichés and obsessive images and symbols, while it may have impoverished the manifest content of the dreams, was perhaps better suited to the purposes of an investigator seeking to reach the latent content. Finally, it appeared promising to consider culture in the light of its obsessions and repressions, examining both individual and collective mechanisms of censorship.

The investigation followed two lines, depending on the kind of documentation available on the one hand, and following the chronology of developments on the other.

For the time being, we confined ourselves to written texts, postponing until later the less familiar approach through iconographic studies of art, which promises to be a fruitful source of decisive information.

We distinguished the theoretical texts, which offer frameworks for interpretation (dream typologies or keys), from the specific examples of dreams.

From the diachronic point of view, we have thus far limited ourselves to exploring two chronological cross-sections: the inaugural phase of medieval culture and mentality, from the end of the fourth century to the beginning of the seventh; and the great upheaval of the twelfth century, in which, within the continuity of the resistant deep structures, we witness a cultural and mental "take-off."

For the first period we subjected the following texts from the theoretical group to close analysis: the dream typologies of Macrobius,[6] Gregory the Great,[7] and Isidore of Seville.[8] And in the category of dream records: Saint Jerome's dream,[9] Saint Martin's dreams in the *Vita Martini* by Sulpicius Severus,[10] and two dreams taken from Gregory of Tour's hagiographic researches.[11]

For the twelfth century, in the first group, we studied John of Salisbury's dream typology,[12] Hildegard of Bingen's analysis of the causes of dreams,[13] the classification in the *Pseudo-Augustinus*[14]— texts supplemented by a thirteenth-century dream key in old French.[15] In the second group, we interpreted the dreams of Charlemagne, the nightmare[16] of Henry I, and three dreams relating to the Virgin Mary: two taken from John of Worcester's Chronicle[17] and the third from the *Roman de Sapience* of Herman of Valencia.[18]

In explaining the limits of this research, we have called attention to its possible psychoanalytic orientation, but this should not mask the contributions of the history of ideas, literary history, the history of medicine and science, mentality and sensibility, and folklore. The study of the dream yields invaluable information concerning the place of the body and phenomena associated with the internal functions (techniques of the body in the Maussian sense,[19] nutrition, physiology)[20] in the medieval world view. Furthermore, we have here an approach to the phenomena of "tradition" which goes beyond the narrow methods of "traditional" cultural history. Finally, we may evaluate from this point of view the extent to which a comparison between medieval society (or societies) and so-called "primitive" societies might be valid and informative.[21]

First of all, our research called attention to the fact that it was characteristic of medieval culture and mentality to elaborate what it had inherited from the past. From the oneiric science of Greco-Latin antiquity, medieval clerics selected mainly those texts open to an interpretation compatible with Christianity and relatively accessible—at the cost of distortions and misinterpretations, usually unconscious—to less sophisticated minds. In Macrobius, the great master of medieval oneiric science, Pythagoreanism and Stoicism, through Cicero, join neo-Platonic influences already mixed in Artemidorus' eclectic crucible.[22] A Vergilian text[23] offers the notion of true and false visions,[24] important for crude medieval Manichaeanism. This withering of the oneiric diversity and richness of antiquity was augmented by the mistrust of the dream deriving from the biblical legacy: prudence in the Old Testament,[25] silence in the New.[26] Oneiromantic practices derived from pagan tradition (Celtic, Germanic, etc.)[27] further increased hesitancy with regard to dreams and even caused them to be shunned quite routinely in the early Middle Ages. Already questionable in Saint Jerome and Saint Augustine,[28] the dream had swung over to the side of the devil for Gregory the Great and, with nuances, for Isidore of Seville... Nevertheless, a sort of typecast "good" dream remained, inspired by God through the new agency of angels and particularly of saints. The dream came to be associated with hagiography. It served to authenticate the important milestones of Martin's progress towards sainthood. As we learn from Gregory of Tours, the old practices of incubation were reclaimed on behalf of the sanctuaries of saints (Saint Martin of Tours, Saint Julian of Brioude).[29] In general, however, dreams were relegated to the hell of things dubious, and the ordinary Christian had carefully to refrain from placing his faith in them. Only a new elite of the dream measured up to the task of interpretation: the saints. Whether their dreams came from God (Saint Martin) or from Satan (Saint Anthony—and, in this case, resistance to visions and oneiric heroism became one of the battles of sainthood, which could no longer be conquered by martyrdom), saints replaced the ancient elites of the dream: kings (Pharaoh, Nebuchadnezzar) and chieftains or heroes (Scipio, Aeneas).

The twelfth century may be considered the age of the reconquest of the dream by medieval culture and mentality. To put it briefly and crudely, the devil gave way before God, and there was a notable expansion of the domain of the "neutral" dream, or *somnium*, more closely connected with man's physiology. This relationship between the dream and the body, this shift from oneiromancy to medicine and psychology, came about in the thirteenth century with Albertus Magnus and, after him, Arnaud de Villeneuve.[30] As it lost its sacred character, the dream was also democratized. Simple clerics—preceding common laymen—were favored with significant dreams. With Hildegard of Bingen, the dream, together with the nightmare, took its place as a normal phenomenon in the *"healthy*-spirited man."

The dream's role in culture and politics widened. It played a part in the rehabilitation of ancient culture: the dreams of the Sibyl foreshadowed Christianity, and there were the dreams of the great intellectual precursors of the Christian religion, Socrates, Plato, and Vergil. This was the oneiric source of a new history of civilizations and salvation. A certain political literature also tapped the oneiric vein—even if the dream was reduced therein to a literary device. Henry I's dream marks a stage on the way to the *Songe du Verger.*

Even with its diminished, accessory role, the dream continued to serve as an escape from repression, as an instrument for overcoming censorship and inhibition. In the late twelfth century, Herman of Valencia's dream is striking evidence of the dream's effectiveness in a new battle in the process of cultural evolution: the replacement of Latin by the vulgar tongues. Only an authentic dream—and a Marian dream, a sign of the times—could legitimate the traumatic audacity of recounting the Bible in a vulgar tongue.[31] Finally, with John of Salisbury, the dream took its place in a veritable semiology of knowledge.[32]

MELUSINA: MOTHER AND PIONEER

Popular creativity did not supply all the mathematically possible forms. Nowadays there are no new creations. It is certain, however, that there were exceptionally fertile and creative eras. Aarne thinks that the Middle Ages in Europe were such a time. When we realize that the centuries during which the folktale enjoyed its most intense existence are lost forever to science, we can comprehend that the present absence of a certain form is not enough to invalidate the general theory. Just as we infer the existence of stars we do not see on the basis of general astronomical laws, so we may infer the existence of tales that have not been collected.

V. Propp, *Morphology of the Folktale*, translated from the French edition cited by Le Goff (Gallimard, Paris, 1970), pp. 188–90.*

In chapter 9 of the fourth part of *De nugis curialium*, written between 1181 and 1193 by Walter Map, a cleric living at the English royal court, we may read the story of the marriage of a young man, evidently a young lord, "Large-toothed Henno" (*Henno cum dentibus*), "so-called because of the size of his teeth," to a strange creature.[1] At noon one day in a forest near the beaches of Normandy, Henno meets a very beautiful young girl dressed in royal garb. She is weeping. She confides to him that she is a survivor of the wreck of a

Independently, Jacques Le Goff and Emmanuel Le Roy Ladurie each encountered Melusina in the course of explicating texts for their respective seminars at the Sixth Section of the Ecole Pratique des Hautes Etudes. They subsequently compared the two texts and their ideas concerning them. This joint study was the result. Le Goff was responsible for the medieval portion—the only part reproduced here—and Ladurie for the modern portion. A joint bibliography may be found in *Annales E.S.C.*, 1971.

*A slightly different text may be found in the standard English translation by L. Scott (Indiana University Research Center in Anthropology, Folklore, and Linguistics, 1958), pp. 103–4.—Trans.

ship that was taking her to the king of France, whom she was supposed to marry. Henno falls in love with the beautiful stranger, marries her, and gives her handsome offspring *(pulcherrimam prolem)*. But Henno's mother notices that the young woman, who feigns piety, avoids the beginning and the end of mass and does not participate in the sprinkling of holy water or communion. Curious, she cuts a hole in the wall of her daughter-in-law's bedroom and surprises her in the midst of bathing in the form of a dragon *(draco)*, after which she resumes her human form, but not before cutting a new cloak into tiny pieces with her teeth. Informed by his mother, Henno, helped by a priest, sprinkles holy water on his wife, who, accompanied by her maid, jumps across the roof and disappears into thin air, emitting a terrible scream. In Walter Map's time, many offspring *(multa progenies)* of Henno and his wife are still alive.

The creature is not named, and the historical era is not specified; but "large-toothed Henno" may perhaps be identical with the Henno (without epithet) who appears in another passage of *De nugis curialium* (chapter 15 of the fourth part) among half-legendary, half-historical characters and events which can be assigned to the mid-ninth century.

Some critics have compared the story of "large-toothed Henno" with that of the "Lady of Esperver Castle" recounted in the *Otia Imperialia* (part 3, chapter 57), written between 1209 and 1214 by another old protégé of Henry II of England, who subsequently moved to the service of the kings of Sicily and then to Emperor Otto IV of Brunswick. He was Otto's marshal for the kingdom of Arles when the *Otia Imperialia* was written.[2] Esperver Castle is located in this kingdom, in the diocese of Valence (Drôme department of France). The lady of Esperver also came late to mass and could not participate in the sacrament of the host. One day, her husband and his servants having forcibly restrained her in the church, she took flight upon hearing the words of the communion ceremony, destroying part of the chapel and disappearing forever. A ruined tower adjacent to the chapel remained in Gervase's day as a memento of the event, which also is assigned no date.[3]

While there is an evident similarity between this story and the story of large-toothed Henno's wife, in that, although the lady of Esperver is not identified as a dragon, she is nevertheless a diabolical spirit driven away by Christian rites (holy water, consecrated host), Gervase of Tilbury's text is quite poor in comparison with Walter Map's. On the other hand, few have thought of comparing the story of large-toothed Henno with another recounted by Gervase of Tilbury, the story of Raymond (or Roger) of Château-Rousset.[4]

Not far from Aix-en-Provence, the lord of the castle of Rousset, in the valley of Trets, encounters near the river Arc a magnificently dressed beauty who calls him by name and ultimately consents to marry him on the condition that he never look at her naked. If he does, he will lose whatever material prosperity she should bring him. Raymond promises, and the couple prosper, with health, wealth, power, and many fine children. One day, however, the foolhardy Raymond pulls back the curtain behind which his wife is bathing in her room. The beautiful wife turns into a serpent and disappears forever into the bathwater. Only the governess hears her when she returns at night, invisible, to see her children.

Once again, the woman-serpent has no name, and the story is not dated; but the knight Raymond, despite the loss of much of his fortune and happiness, has had a daughter by his ephemeral spouse (Gervase no longer speaks of the other children) who is also very beautiful and who has married a Provençal nobleman. Her descendants are still living in Gervase's time.

There are two women-serpents (one winged and one aquatic) in the *Otia Imperialia*, and, similarly, there are two in *De nugis curialium*. In addition to the story of large-toothed Henno, we find that of Edric the Savage ("Eric the Savage, meaning 'who lives in the woods,' so called because of his physical agility and his gifts of speech and action"), the lord of North Ledbury, which is told in chapter 12 of the second part.[5] One night, after the hunt, Edric loses his way in the forest. In the middle of the night, he comes to a large house[6] in which very beautiful and very large noble ladies are dancing. One of them inspires him with such overpowering passion that he carries her off at once and spends three days and nights of love with her. On the fourth day she promises him health, happiness, and prosperity if he will never question her about her sisters nor about the place and the woods from which he abducted her. He gives his word and marries her. But several years later, he is annoyed not to find her when he returns at night from the hunt. When she finally arrives, he asks her angrily, "Why did your sisters keep you so long?" She disappears. He dies of sorrow. But they leave a son of great intelligence who is soon afflicted with paralysis and with a shaking of his head and body. A pilgrimage to the relics of Saint Ethelbert of Hereford cures him. He leaves the saint his land at Ledbury and a yearly income of thirty pounds.

At approximately the same time that Map and Gervase of Tilbury were writing, around the year 1200, the Cistercian Helinand of Froimont recounted the story of the marriage of a noble with a woman-serpent. This tale is lost, but it was collected in the form of a dry summary about a half century later by the Dominican Vincent of Beauvais in his *Speculum naturale* (2,127). "In the province of

Langres,[7] a noble in the densest of forests encountered a beautiful woman richly dressed, whom he fell in love with and married. She liked to bathe frequently and was one day seen by a servant slithering in her bath in the form of a serpent. Accused by her husband and surprised in the bath, she disappeared forever, and her descendants are still living."[8]

At this point, the erudite literature on Melusina jumps nearly two centuries and produces in close succession two works: one in prose, the other in verse. The first was composed by Jean d'Arras for the duke Jean de Berry and his sister Marie, duchess of Bar from 1387 to 1394; its title in the oldest manuscripts is "The Noble History of Lusignan," or "The Book of Melusina in Prose," or "The Romance of Melusina in Prose." The second, completed by the Parisian bookseller Couldrette between 1401 and 1405 is called "The Romance of Lusignan or of Parthenay," or "Mellusine."

Three characteristics of these two works are important for our subject. They are much longer, the little story having grown to novel-sized proportions. The woman-serpent is named Melusina (or, more precisely, Melusigne in Jean d'Arras, with variants Mesluzine, Messurine, Meslusigne; Mellusine or Mellusigne in Couldrette). Finally, her husband is a member of the Lusignan family, a line of important nobles in Poitou, whose eldest branch died out in 1308 (its lands passing into royal hands, and then into the apanage of Berry). A younger branch had borne the imperial title "de Jerusalem" since 1186 and the royal title "de Chypre" since 1192.

The tales told by Jean d'Arras and Couldrette are quite similar and, as far as the most important features touching on Melusina are concerned, identical. For our purposes, it is of little importance to know whether Couldrette, as most commentators think, condensed and put into verse Jean d'Arras's prose romance or whether Leo Hoffrichter is correct in thinking that both texts are more likely based on the same lost model, a French verse tale from around 1375. On certain points Couldrette's poem retains elements neglected or misunderstood by Jean d'Arras, such as the agrarian curses Melusina makes as she is disappearing.

Here is what we believe to be the essential content of the "Romance of Melusina" of the late fourteenth century, following Jean d'Arras.

Elinas, king of Albania (= Scotland), while hunting in the forest, encounters a remarkably beautiful woman singing with a marvelous voice, Presine. He declares his love and proposes marriage. She accepts on the condition that, if they have children, he not be present at their birth. His son by a former marriage incites Elinas to have a look at Presine, who has just given birth to three daughters: Melusina,

Melior, and Palestine. Presine disappears with her three daughters and takes them to Avalon, the Lost Isle. When the daughters are fifteen, they learn of their father's betrayal, and, to punish him, imprison him inside a mountain. Presine, who still loves Elinas, is furious and punishes them. Melior is locked in the castle of Epervier in Armenia; Palestine is sequestered on Mount Canigou; Melusina, the eldest and guiltiest, is turned into a serpent every Saturday. If a man marries her, she will become mortal (and die naturally, thus escaping her eternal punishment), but her torment will begin anew if her husband sees her in the form she assumes on Saturdays.

Raimondin, son of the Count of Forez and nephew of the Count of Poitiers, inadvertently kills his uncle during a boar hunt. At the Fountain (Fountain of Thirst or Fairy Fountain), Raimondin meets three beautiful women, one of whom is Melusina, who comforts him and promises to make him a powerful lord if he marries her, which he agrees to do. She makes him swear never to try to see her on Saturday.

Prosperity overwhelms the couple. Melusina takes an active part in bringing this about, clearing land as a pioneer and building cities and fortified castles, starting with the Castle of Lusignan. They also have many children: ten sons, several of whom become kings through marriage, such as Urian, king of Cyprus, Guion, king of Armenia, and Renaud, king of Bohemia. Each one has a physical blemish on his face, however; Geoffroy, the sixth, has a large tooth, for example.

Jean d'Arras comments lengthily on the exploits of these sons, particularly on the battles they wage against the Saracens. During a stay at La Rochelle, however, Raimondin is visited by his brother, the Count of Forez, who tells him of the rumors about Melusina that are going around. She hides herself on Saturdays either because she is spending the day with her lover or because she is a fairy and must do penitence on Saturday. Raimondin, "stricken with rage and jealousy," makes a hole in the cellar where Melusina is bathing and sees her in the shape of a mermaid. But he tells no one, and Melusina pretends to know nothing, as if nothing had happened.

The exploits of the sons are not always praiseworthy. Geoffroy burns the monastery (and the monks) at Maillezais. Raimondin is furious with him, and Melusina tries to calm him. But in his rage her husband says, "Oh, most false of serpents, by God and His great deeds, you are nothing but a phantom, and no heir born of you will be saved." Melusina flies out the window in the form of a winged serpent. She returns (but only the nurses see her) to Lusignan at night to take care of her two youngest children, Remonnet and Thierry, making herself known by a mournful howl, "the fairy's cries." Raimondin goes in despair to become a hermit at Montserrat. Geoffroy goes to confess to the pope in Rome and rebuilds Maillezais.[9]

We have included the story of Edric the Savage (of Walter Map) and that of the lady of Esperver (from Gervase of Tilbury) because there are obvious connections between them and the stories of large-toothed Henno and Raymond of Château-Rousset. The woman-fairy in the latter differs from Melusina, however, in that she is not represented as a serpent.[10]

Our basic group, then, consists of three texts from around 1200, Walter Map, Gervase of Tilbury, and Helinand of Froimont (by way of Vincent of Beauvais), and two romances from around 1400, one in prose by Jean d'Arras, the other in verse by Couldrette.

How may the historian read—or begin to read—this group of texts?

HYPOTHESES AND PROBLEMS OF INTERPRETATION

What are the "sources" for our texts? Couldrette mentions two Latin books found "in the tower of Mabregon" and translated into French, and another work supposed to have been procured for him by the "Count of Salz and of Berry" (the Count of Salisbury is also cited as an informant by Jean d'Arras). Whether this is the truth or a ruse of the author, whose real source was Jean d'Arras's romance or an earlier text, it remains true that the bookseller Couldrette was familiar with Melusina through his reading in erudite literature.

Jean d'Arras also mentions books as sources, "the true chronicles" procured for him both by the Duke of Berry and the Count of Salisbury and "several books which have been found." He cites Gervase of Tilbury (Gervaise) by name.[11] He adds, however, that he has been able to supplement the true chronicles with what he has "heard our elders tell and recount" and with what he has "heard has been seen in the vicinity of Poitou and elsewhere." Hence he has used oral traditions transmitted through aged persons: the value of Jean d'Arras for our study lies here. Despite the author's literary talents, his attention to oral culture prevents him from subjecting tradition to too great a distortion, and, consequently, he notes and includes elements which had been misunderstood or neglected by the clerics of the late twelfth century and rediscovers the previously effaced meaning of the marvelous.[12] The *Melusina* of Jean d'Arras is fair game for the folklorist, although, forty years ago, Louis Stouff could do no better than decipher it clumsily, though usefully, using the methods of traditional literary history.

Jean d'Arras was receptive to folklore in another, indirect way: by his use of the traditional material already collected and partially integrated into high culture by the clerics of the year 1200.

We cannot say much about Helinand of Froimont on the basis of Vincent of Beauvais's brief summary. We do know, though, that the Cistercian was interested in the marvelous of a more or less folkloric sort. He was part of a small group of clerics who, again around the year 1200, took pleasure in the *mirabilia* that concerned Naples and Vergil the magician.[13] Even if it is true, as has been suggested,[14] that he is alluding not to Langres but to the vicinity of Linges, which could be Saintonge, hence, roughly speaking, the region of Lusignan, this is still evidence of the presence of Melusina (even before she was Melusina) in the West, as in Normandy and Provence, around the year 1200.

Walter Map drew abundantly on the libraries to which he had access. Alongside the Church Fathers and Latin classics, however, are numerous tales taken from oral tradition. The editor of the *De nugis curialium* speaks of "the unidentified romances and sagas from which many of his longer stories are supposed to be derived."[15] Map often refers to the *fabulae* from which his information was taken. While he gives no source for the story of large-toothed Henno, for Edric the Savage he refers to the Welsh, "Wallenses," whom he calls elsewhere "compatriote nostri Walenses." This is evidence for the importance of oral, if not popular, tradition.[16]

With Gervase of Tilbury, matters are clearer. Apart from his bookish baggage, the Englishman, in the course of a career which took him from England to Bologna and Naples to Arles, gathered a full harvest of oral traditions. At the beginning of the chapter in which he relates the story of Raymond of Chateau-Rousset, he cites his source: "The common people tell it."[17]

No matter how contaminated she may have been, then, by the readings of the writers who gave her voice, chances are good that we shall find the medieval Melusina—who, as we shall see, has relatives (or even ancestors) in ancient societies—by looking in the direction of folklore. Melusina—and, more particularly, the Melusina of our texts—can easily be located in the reference works on folklore and the folktale.[18]

Arnold van Gennep devoted seventeen entries to Melusina in the bibliography of his *Manuel de folklore français contemporain;*[19] but, although he cites Jean d'Arras, he explicitly stops at the threshold of the Middle Ages.

Stith Thompson, in his *Motif-Index of Folklore*, classifies Melusina under several headings. First, from the angle of taboo (C.30, *Tabu:* "offending supernatural relative," and more specifically, C.31.1.2, *Tabu:* "looking at supernatural wife on certain occasion"). Then, concerning *animals,* and particular men- (or women-) serpents (B.29.1, *Lamia:* "Face of woman, body of serpent," with reference to F.562.1, *Serpent damsel,* B.29.2, *Echidna:* "Half-woman, half-serpent," and

B29.2.1: "Serpent with human head"), and men- (or women-) fish (B812: "Mermaid marries man"). Then, in the chapter on marvelous creatures (*Marvels*, F.302.2: "Man marries fairy and takes her to his home"). Finally, among witches (G. Ogres [*Witches*], G.245. "Witch transforms herself into snake when she bathes"). If we bring actual medieval conditions into these categories, we encounter the following problems:

1. What is the importance of the *transgressing* of the taboo? It is essential because it is the crux of the story, and, in the Christian atmosphere of the medieval tale, a further question arises: is not the husband's failure to keep his promise less culpable because of his wife's "diabolic" character? The era's "culture" alters the terms of the problem.

2. In "pagan" religions, a god may perfectly well assume the form of an animal, and union between a mortal and a supernatural animal may be glorious. But for Christianity, which holds that man is the unique, incarnate image of God, is not union between a man and a half-beast automatically considered degrading? The question arises in connection with Nebuchadnezzar and the werewolves in Gervase of Tilbury (*Otia Imperialia* III, 120).

3. As regards "marvelous" women, how can white magic be distinguished from black, and fairies from witches? Does Christianity offer Melusina hope of salvation or consign her to inevitable damnation?

In their classification of the *Types of the Folktale*,[20] Antti Aarne and Stith Thompson do not finally settle the question of Melusina but place her among types T400–459 = "Supernatural or enchanted Husband (Wife) or other relatives," more particularly among numbers 400–424 (*wife*) and, better still, T411: *The King and the Lamia* (the snake-wife), which brings up the problem of the vocabulary and frame of reference used by the work's authors: while *Lamia* explicitly refers to the Bible, to Greco-Latin writers of antiquity, to Saint Jerome, and to our medieval authors (Gervase of Tilbury, particularly *Otia Imperialia* III, 85), the reference given for the tale is Indian!

Melusina has a still smaller place in the catalogue of Paul Delarue and Marie-Louis Tenèze. T.411 is not illustrated in this work by any examples; on the other hand, T449 offers the case of "the man who has married a woman-vampire," and T425 goes into great detail regarding the "search for a husband who has disappeared," which includes the story of Melusina with sexes reversed (31, the daughter who marries a serpent).

It is therefore legitimate to raise some of the basic problems involved in studying folklore in connection with the medieval versions of Melusina, particularly the problem of folktales and, still more precisely, of marvelous tales.[21]

In the first place, are we really dealing with a *tale?* Is it not rather a matter of a *legend,* in the sense of the German word *Sage?* German uses two words, *Sage* and *Legende,* where French uses one, *légende* [and English *legend,* although *saga,* apart from its specialized sense, may also be used to mean "a historical legend" (O.E.D.).—Transl.] In German, *Legende* is reserved in literary typology for the *religious legend,* in the sense of the medieval Latin *legenda,* equivalent to *Vita (alicujus sancti).*[22] The difference between tale and legend was carefully noted by the brothers Grimm, authors, as everyone knows, of a famous collection of *Märchen* and a no less important collection of *Deutsche Sagen: "the tale is more poetic, the legend more historical."* Is it not true that the medieval stories of Melusina correspond exactly to their definition: "The legend, whose colors are less iridescent, is also peculiar in that it establishes a connection with something consciously familiar, such as a place or a genuine name from history."[23]

Instead of regarding the tale and the legend as two parallel genres, as the Grimms did, it may be that the legend should often be considered a possible avatar of the tale, though not necessarily so. When a tale falls into the sphere of the upper social strata and high cultural circles and passes into a new spatial and temporal setting with a more definite geographic location (a certain province, city, castle, or forest) and a quicker tempo, when it is snapped up by the more hurried history of "hot" social classes and societies, it becomes legend.

This is exactly what seems to have happened with our story. In the late twelfth century, the tale of the man married to a woman serpent was common in a number of regions: Normandy, Provence, and the vicinity of Langres or Saintonge. Under certain conditions, as to which we shall offer certain hypotheses below, men such as large-toothed Henno, Raimondin of Château-Rousset, the nobleman spoken of by Helinand of Froimont, or their descendants, rather, tried to take possession of the tale and make it their legend. The Lusignans were successful at this. When, how, why? It is difficult to know. Aficionados—many of them and often quite ingenious—of the disappointing little historicist game of pin-the-tail on the myth have tried to discover which Lusignan was Jean d'Arras's Raimondin and which countess of Lusignan was Melusina. The only probable link with a real historical character in the affair is in connection with "Geoffroy with the large tooth," sixth son of Melusina. In the fourteenth century, at least, he seems to have been identified with Geoffroy de Lusignan, Viscount of Chatellerault, who, though he did not burn either the abbey or the monks, did lay waste the domain of the abbey of Maillezais (and had to go the following year to Rome to obtain the pope's pardon). His motto was supposed to have ben *non est Deus* ("there is no God"), and he died childless before 1250. This

Geoffroy, reminiscent of "large-toothed Henno," who was the husband (and not the son) of the woman-serpent of Walter Map, unknown to Gervase of Tilbury but taken up by Jean d'Arras, nevertheless seems to have been the hero of a story different from Melusina's. In any case, it is nonsense to make the historical Geoffroy's mother the Melusina of the legend. Nor does it appear to have been possible to determine precisely when Melusina became part of the Lusignan coat of arms.[24] The connection with the Lusignans of Cyprus, suggested by Heisig, with the old sea-serpent of oriental influence and Indian tales in the background, does not stand up well under scrutiny. The story of "large-toothed Henno," set in Normandy, is prior to the story of Raymond of Château-Rousset, for which there is no demonstrable link with the Lusignans of Cyprus. The dates make it difficult to accept the possibilty of such a course of diffusion, and the text of Gervase of Tilbury evokes rural and wooded Provence, culturally quite distant from Marseilles.[25]

What is likely is that the name Melusina was connected with the success of the Lusignans. It is difficult, however, to determine whether the name Melusina led to Lusignan, or whether the Lusignans, having taken the fairy for their own, gave her their name to cement the connection. In any case, the etymological route seems disappointing to us. It cannot answer the important question: why was there an interest in the various "Melusinas," from the end of the twelfth century on, on the part of certain persons and groups (knights, clerics, "people")?[26]

Let us attempt to make clear what the limits of "diffusionism" are. Where did the legend of Melusina come from? In our earliest texts we notice that several similar forms of an identical legend were in existence in several regions, with no detectable common basis among them. Subsequently, the house of Lusignan and, later, the houses of Berry and Bar (according to Jean d'Arras, it was Marie, Duchess of Bar, sister of Jean de Berry, who asked her brother to have the legend of Melusina put in writing) promoted a diffusion of the legend usually linked to members of the Lusignan family: in the Agenais, Cyprus, Sassenage in the Dauphiné, Luxembourg. One route of diffusion can be traced more precisely. At the outset, we find Jean d'Arras's *Roman de Mélusine* in the library of the dukes of Burgundy in the early fifteenth century, soon flanked by Couldrette's verse romance. From there it penetrated Flanders in one direction, Germany in another. A manuscript in Bruges dates from about 1467. It was printed in a Flemish tanslation in 1491. In the other direction, the Margrave of Hochberg, the confidential adviser to Philip the Good and Charles the Bold, introduced it to Switzerland. Thuring of Renggeltingen, bailiff of Berne, translated Couldrette's *Melusine* in

1456, and his translation was printed around 1477 (in Strasbourg?), and in 1491 at Heidelberg. Another translation appeared in Augsburg in 1474.[27] A German version was translated into Polish in 1569 by Siennik. The success of this translation is evident in the many Melusinas to be found in both high and folk art and in the seventeenth-century folklore of Poland and the Ukraine.[28]

If we turn now not to the posterity of the medieval Melusinas but rather toward precursors and counterparts in other cultures, the whole vast field of myth opens up to us. The comparative study begun by Felix Liebrecht,[29] editor of the anthology of folklore from the *Otia Imperialia* of Gervase of Tilbury, yielded three first-rate studies at the end of the last century: *Der Ursprung der Melusinensage: Eine ethnologische Untersuchung*, by J. Kohler (1895), most suggestive of the three and most "modern" in its problematics; Marie Nowack's dissertation, *Die Melusinensage: Ihr mythischer Hintergrund, ihre Verwandschaft mit anderen Sagenkreisen und ihre Stellung in der deutschen Literatur* (1886), oriented toward the study of German literary works; and, finally, Jean Karlowicz's article, *La belle Mélusine et la reine Vanda* (1877), focused on Slavic Melusinas.

In these studies, the Melusina legend is compared with: (1) the Greek myths of Eros and Psyche and Zeus and Semele, and the Roman legend of Numa and Egeria, from European antiquity; (2) with several myths from ancient India, that of Urvashti being the oldest Aryan version; (3) with a whole series of myths and legends from a variety of cultures, from the Celts to the Amerindians.

Kohler defined the characteristic feature of all these myths as follows: "A being of another kind marries a man and, after leading an ordinary human life for a time, disappears when a certain even occurs." The variable is the type of event that causes the disappearance. This event is usually a revelation of the nature of the magical being. The principal type in this category, according to Kohler, is the "Melusina type," in which the magical being disappears when its earthly partner has seen it in its original form.

This analysis has the great merit of having started mythology down the path of structural analysis, but it gives a poor account of the real structure of the legend (or myth). The framework of the tale (or legend) is neither a major theme nor a motif but rather its structure, what von Sydow calls *composition*, Max Luthi *form (Gestalt)*, and Vladimir Propp *morphology*.[30]

If we had the competence and the desire, we could undoubtedly give a structural analysis of the various versions of the Melusina legend according to Propp's schemas. For instance:[31]

1. *A member of the family leaves the house* (Propp): the hero goes hunting.

2. *A ban is imposed on the hero* (Propp): Melusina will marry the hero only on the condition that he respect a taboo (childbirth or pregnancy, nudity, Saturday).

3. *The ban is violated.* "Now there appears a new character in the tale, who may be called the antagonist. His role is to disturb the peace of the happy family, to provoke some misfortune" (Propp): The mother-in-law in Walter Map, the brother-in-law in Jean d'Arras.

4. *The antagonist attempts to obtain information* (Propp): In Walter Map, this is the mother-in-law, but usually the curious hero, Raymond himself. Etc.

It would be equally possible, I think, to find examples of inversions, a phenomenon which plays an important role in the mechanism of transformation of tales, from Propp to Claude Lévi-Strauss, another virtuoso in this domain. Kohler had already spoken of *Umkehrung* in connection with Melusina. E. Le Roy Ladurie notes further examples in the German versions of Melusina. In the second version of the myth of Urvashti, the magical woman *(aspara)* disappears when she sees the mortal man naked.

Even if we had been capable of carrying structural analysis further, we would undoubtedly have drawn only modest, commonsensical conclusions which, for that very reason, would have been useful for demonstrating the importance of structuralist interpretation of his sources to the historian, as well as the limits of such methods.

The first conclusion is that the tale is not open to just any sort of transformation, and that, in the battle between structure and conjuncture, the resistance of structure ensures that the assaults of the conjuncture will for a long while be doomed to failure. Yet there will come a moment when the system will come undone, just as it was put together long before. In this respect, *Melusina* is both medieval and modern. We note that when she appears around 1200, she is the written, high-cultural manifestation of a popular oral phenomenon whose origins are difficult to identify. By the same token, we know that Melusina, who detaches herself from the multisecular structure along with Romanticism, continues to be a part of an undying folklore tradition.[32]

Still, over the long period of structural constancy, it is the transformations of content rather than structure that are of major importance to the historian. These transformations are not mere products of some internal mechanism. They are the tale's answers to history's entreaties. Before we turn to the study of the content of the Melusina story in an attempt to determine its historical significance, a few further remarks on form are in order. These will prepare the way for the hypotheses we shall offer subsequently.

The tale, especially the marvelous tale of which *Melusina* is incontestably an example, is centered on a *hero*.[33] Who is the hero of *Melusina?* The fairy's husband, no doubt. According to the logic of the tale, reinforced by contemporary ideology in the sight of which she is a devil (Christian symbolism of serpent and dragon), Melusina should be wicked; Walter Map qualifies her as *pestilentia,* and Jean d'Arras calls her "most false serpent" (in the words of the enraged Raimondin). And yet, by the end of the tale, she appears to be the victim of her husband's betrayal. She becomes a pretender to the place of the hero. Marc Soriano discovered in La Fontaine a wolf that is a pitiful victim, alongside the detestable aggressor wolf; by the same token, Melusina arouses pity as victim-serpent. The affecting representation of this pseudo-heroine is given a psychological dimension by the final touch which has her come invisible and wailing by night to the side of her young children. What accounts for this tenderness toward a demonic woman?

One of the characteristics of the marvelous tale is the happy ending. *Melusina* turns out sadly. No doubt this story was near to being a legend, and the marvelous tale had begun to evolve toward the heroic poem, with its often tragic tone. Why was there this trend toward a genre which implied the failure or death of the hero?

Finally, there is the "psychologization" of the tale (Raimondin's inner states play an important role at several places in the narrative: passion, curiosity, rage, sadness, or despair; and we have just pointed out the development of Melusina's character in this sense), along with a tendency toward coherent rationalization of the narrative, in which we can undoubtedly see the standard (but not obligatory) development from myth to tale or epic and then to the romance in the ordinary sense (a literary genre) or in Dumézil's sense (an evolutionary form and phase).[34]

Turning now to problems of interpretation, we should first observe that medieval authors explained very clearly what Melusina represented for them. All of them took her for a demonic succubus, a fairy identified with a fallen angel. She was half-human, half-beast; when she mated with a mortal, exceptional children were produced, physically fortunate (beautiful daughters, strong sons) but blemished or unhappy.[35] Some also explain why these marriages took place. Condemned for an error to suffer eternally in the body of a serpent, the serpent-woman seeks to wed a man, her only chance to escape eternal misery and regain the right to a natural death and to the subsequent enjoyment of a happy life.

This Christian dress is not surprising if one recalls that the whole cultural life of the Middle Ages was bound up with Christianity. By the late twelfth century, moreover, Christianity had begun to elaborate rational explanations, even if the reasons given were applied to perfectly irrational data. It should be pointed out in passing that while the legend is in fact circumscribed by a Christian explanation (before or after), there are few Christian elements in the legend itself. Although we find, in the story of "large-toothed Henno" and in the legend of the lady of Esperver, that the woman arouses suspicion by her bad conduct as a Christian (not attending the whole mass) and is unmasked by Christian exorcisms (holy water, oblation of the host), yet in the adventure of Raymond of Château-Rousset there is no Christian element. While in one sense Jean d'Arras's romance is permeated by a Christian climate, in another sense we may say that no Christian element plays an important role in the story's unfolding. At most, one can cite the fact that Raimondin's fatal rage is set off by the burning of a monastery. Melusina comes from sources more remote than Christianity. The habits and customs of demonic succubuses may have sufficed to explain Melusina's nature and fate to the medieval clergy, but we cannot settle for so little.

Around what sort of stakes does the story revolve, then? Whether the initiative comes from Melusina herself, whose eagerness to escape her fate drives her to make advances to her future spouse, or from Raymond (fired by passion), Melusina's dowry represents prosperity for Raymond. After Melusina is betrayed, Raymond finds himself in more or less the same straits as before. The horn of plenty has run dry.

Thus Melusina's *nature* emerges through her *function* in the legend. She brings prosperity. Whether she has some concrete historical connection (we shall probably never know) with a Celtic or autochthonous fertility goddess or spirit, or a culture-heroine of Indian (or more likely Indo-European) origin, whether she is of chthonic, aquatic, or celestial origin (she is at one time or another, or all at the same time, a serpent, mermaid, and dragon, and from this point of view it is perhaps true that, in Jean d'Arras, the *fountain* has a rather clear Celtic savor, while in Walter Map the sea, and in Gervase of Tilbury a river—and in both, a "bath"—merely refer to the fairy's aquatic nature), in all those cases she appears as the medieval avatar of a mother-goddess, as a fertility fairy.

What kind of fertility? She assures her husband health and strength. But she gratifies him—unequally—in three areas.

First, she brings prosperity in a rural setting. The rural reference may be allusive in Walter Map and Gervase of Tilbury (although the setting of the encounter in a forest is highly symbolic of an association with the forest which, as we can see more clearly elsewhere, probably has to do with land clearing). But in Jean d'Arras, Melusina's *pioneering* work is considerable. Clearings open up under her feet, and forests are transformed into fields. One region, Forez (perhaps in Brittany), is indebted to her for its transition from nature to cultivation.

In Jean d'Arras, however, another creative activity has taken the fore: construction. As much as she is a pioneer, Melusina is even more a builder. In the course of her many travels, she leaves behind fortified castles and cities, often built with her own hands as the head of a work crew.

No matter how wary one may be of historicism, it would require a real will to let the truth slip through one's fingers to refuse to see the connection between Melusina's historical aspect and an economic conjuncture: land clearing and construction. Melusina is the fairy of medieval economic growth.

There is, however, yet another area in which Melusina's fertility is even more astonishing—demography. What Melusina gives Raymond is, above all, children. Even when there are not ten of them, as in Jean d'Arras, they are the survivors after the fairy-mother has disappeared and the father has been plunged into ruin. Edric *"left his inheritance to his son."* After Henno and his *pestilentia*, *"many of their descendants are still alive today."* Raymond of Château-Rousset has kept from his adventure and misfortune a daughter *"whose descendants are among us."*

Melusina disappears when she has accomplished her essential function as mother and nurse. Driven from the light of day, she remains a parent by night.

Who could resist bringing in at this point the feudal family and lineage, the basic cell of feudal society? Melusina is the womb that gave birth to a noble line.

This structuralism (and comparative history) not only helps us to do away with the fallacious historicism of an "event-ridden" history of tales and legends (which sought the explanation and, worse still, the origin of a tale or legend in a historical event or character). It also makes it possible, if we pay attention not only to form but also to changing content, to comprehend the historical function of both, in relation not to an event but rather to social and ideological structures themselves.

At this point, we cannot evade two major problems.

One of them we shall merely name: totemism. Kohler has developed this theme at length in connection with Melusina. Are we not obliged to restate the problem of totemism by this woman-beast who is the origin and emblem of a bloodline?[36]

The second problem relates to the connections between literature and society. Who produced these tales or legends, and why?

Were they produced by the writers who left us the erudite versions on which this study is based? Yes and no. Three sorts of constraints were imposed on those writers, by their patrons, by the (folk?) sources from which they drew their material, and by the literary forms they chose, all of which considerably limited their freedom of initiative. We do sense, in Walter Map, for instance, his attraction to the marvelous; in Gervase of Tilbury his desire to make a scientific work by integrating the *mirabilia* into reality and knowledge; and in Jean d'Arras the formal aesthetic pleasure of dealing with a pleasant subject. We see, nevertheless, that they were basically allowing others to express themselves through their work. Who were these others?

We are struck by the fact that all the heroes belong to the same high social class. Why should this surprise us? Are we not aware that the king's son is the principal hero of the folktale? But this is just the point: we are not dealing here with the king's son. We are looking instead at the world of the small to middling aristocracy, the *knights* or *milites*, sometimes designated as *nobles*. Henno, Edric, the lord of Espervier, Raymond of Château-Rousset, Raimondin de Lusignan are all *milites*. Indeed they are ambitious *milites*, eager to push back the boundaries of their little seigneuries. The fairy is the instrument of their ambition. Melusina brings the knightly class land, castles, cities, progeny. She is the symbolic and magical incarnation of their social ambition.

The knights who have turned this storehouse of marvelous literature to their own use are not, however, its makers. Here we encounter Erich Köhler's ideas[37] on the small and middle aristocracy. In the twelfth century this group was the instigator of a culture of its own, which soon came to be couched in the vulgar tongue. The knights' cultural arsenal was supplemented by a whole world of folk marvels. This consisted of the treasures of folklore which the knights heard from their peasants (to whom they were still close in the twelfth century) or which they had their writers listen to once they had taken their distance, together with an admixture of folklorized ancient myths, recently "popularized" clerical stories, and tales thought up by peasant storytellers. We should add that this class felt a certain distance from, and perhaps even a hostility toward the Church, if not Christianity itself. It refused to accept the Church's cultural models, preferring fairies to saints, entering into compacts with hell, toying with a suspect totemism.[38] This temptation should not be exaggerated. Melusina's husbands managed to reconcile their profession of Christian faith with a sometimes rather offhand practice of it. Marc Bloch has shown that in actuality their class took some liberties with the Christian doctrine of marriage and the family.

We will content ourselves with these hypotheses, which to a certain extent bring us onto common ground with the ideas of Jan de Vries concerning folktales. More generally, we are pleased to have attempted to apply Georges Dumézil's simple, yet profound, remark: "Myths cannot be understood in isolation from the lives of the men who tell them. Although they are eventually called to a proper literary career, they are not gratuitous dramatic or lyrical inventions unrelated to social or political organization, to ritual, law, or custom; their role is rather to justify all of this, to express in images the great ideas that organize and sustain this system."[39] Should we be satisfied with this much?

That "the fairy tale is linked to a definite cultural period," as Jan de Vries would have it, and that, in the West, particularly in France, this period should have been the second half of the twelfth century, does not appear to me sufficient to account for the extent of the influence of a legend like Melusina.

The tale is a whole. If it is legitimate to isolate its central motif—the idea of prosperity gained and lost in certain conditions—in order to point out a social class's appeal to a mother-goddess, then the "moral" of the tale must be sought in its conclusion above all.

It has been noted that Melusina comes to an unfortunate end. Jan de Vries, referring to the "aristocratic circles which elaborated" (elaborated—I don't think so; monopolized, yes, but the elaboration was the work of specialists, both among the people and the clerics, tellers of folktales and erudite writer-storytellers) the epic and the fairy tale, remarks: "Behind the apparent optimism may lurk the feeling that failure is inevitable."[40]

It is beyond the scope of this essay to determine how and why the search for prosperity, particularly family prosperity, ended in partial or total failure. We simply observe the fact. Compare this with what has been said about the pessimism—at the end of a literary evolution—of the nineteenth- and early twentieth-century novel. For many novelists of this period, the subject was the rise and crisis of a family. In different social settings, with various intellectual and artistic resources, and in a variety of ideological climates, from the Rougon-Macquarts to the Buddenbrooks, a family flourishes and disintegrates.

So it was with the Melusinian lineage. Yet just as Roger Martin du Gard, at the end of *Les Thibault*, leaves a child as a tiny hope, Melusina's medieval storytellers stopped the fairy in mid-flight on her way to hell—the soul's journey, which for Propp was ultimately the unique theme of the tale[41]—long enough to take from her the small children through whom everything continues; or, if not everything, then the essential thing, which is continuity itself. *Adhuc extat progenies.*[42]

221

POSTSCRIPT

We had completed this article when we learned, thanks to the kindness of Mme Marie-Louise Tenèze, of the two-volume work by Lutz Röhrich, *Erzählungen des späten Mittelalters und ihr Weiterleben in Literatur und Volksdichtung bis zur Gegenwart: Sagen, Märchen, Exempel und Schwänke* (Berne and Munich: Francke Verlag, 1962–67). Röhrich includes (vol. 1, pp. 27–61) and comments on (pp. 243–53) eleven texts, at intervals from the fourteenth to the twentieth century, concerning a Melusina of Baden connected with the legend of the knight Peter von Staufenberg *(Die gestörte Mahrtenehe)*. In his commentary, Röhrich compares the legend with that of the knight Raymond of Château-Rousset in Gervase of Tilbury and of the Lusignans in Jean d'Arras. His interpretation resembles ours in that it makes the Baden fairy a "totemic" character (the word is not used) taken up by a line of knights: "The Staufenberg type belongs to that group of tales which try to trace the origin of a medieval noble line back to a marriage with a supernatural being, so as to give the family claims to legitimacy a higher, more metaphysical foundation. This is the case with the genealogical legend of the noble family settled in the Staufenberg castle in the Orenau (Mortenouwe) in the central part of the Baden region" (p. 244). The oldest version of the legend is from around 1310 but undoubtedly has roots in the thirteenth century.

IV

TOWARD A HISTORICAL ANTHROPOLOGY

THE HISTORIAN AND THE ORDINARY MAN

History and ethnology became distinct disciplines only in the mid-nineteenth century, when evolutionism, triumphant even before Darwin, caused the study of developed societies to part company with the investigation of so-called primitive societies. Previously, history had embraced all societies, but with the emergence of a consciousness of progress, history limited itself to those portions of humanity liable to rapid transformations. The remainder of mankind was given over to minor scientific or literary genres—the *mirabilia*, in which primitive men ranged with monsters; travelogues, in which natives were seen as a variety of the local fauna; or, at best, geography, in which men became a component of the landscape—or else were consigned to oblivion.

Herodotus, the "father of history," is equally the father of ethnography. The second book of the *Histories*, which is placed under the patronage of Euterpe, is devoted to Egypt. Its first half is the work of an ethnologist who is not satisfied merely to describe manners and customs but rather chooses to lay stress on what the Greeks borrowed from the Egyptians, thus contradicting the notion that a gulf separates the Hellenes from the barbaric nations. The second half of the book reflects a historian's concern with the diachronic, following the succession of dynasties even at the risk of frequently reducing history to a collection of anecdotes.

In Tacitus, this ethnographic outlook takes on a different character. In the manner of Rousseau, Tacitus contrasts the corruption of civilization, exemplified by Rome, to the health of "noble savages" like the Bretons and Germans. He points to his father-in-law, Agricola, attempting to lead the Bretons toward civilization: "To accustom these dispersed and ignorant, and consequently warlike, men to the pleasures of a tranquil and stable existence, he privately encouraged and officially helped them to build temples, markets, and dwelling places, bestowing praise on the most energetic and condemning the indolent . . . And he had the children of the important men educated in the liberal arts . . . so that people who a short while before refused even the language of the Romans had come to desire to emulate their eloquence. Thus even our clothing was favored, and the toga fashionable; and, little by little, men drifted towards the pleasures of vice, porticoes, baths, elegant banquets; among the naïve, this was known as civilization: it was nothing but a form of servitude."

Here again, however, the privileged nature of Roman history tends to exclude other peoples from the historical literature of the Late Empire. The Christians inherited this prejudice. Salvian, in the middle of the fifth century, is virtually the only one to utter the thought that simple and decent Barbarians might be worthier than Roman sinners.

Subsequently, only Christians are entitled to history. Pagans are excluded from it. "Pagan" includes not only pagans proper but also "infidels" and, at least in the beginning, peasants. It is true that for a long while the reigning idea would be not progress but, rather, decline. *Mundus senescit.* The world grows old. Mankind has entered the sixth and final epoch of its existence: old age. Yet this reverse progress is itself a unilinear process, giving priority to societies which change their form, albeit in the wrong direction. When, moreover, medieval Christianity comes to rehabilitate pagan antiquity, its purpose is to underscore the exceptional merits of the Roman Empire and to lay down a new line of progress: from Rome to Jerusalem. As Augustin Renaudet has noted, Dante "repeats with pride the prophecy of old Anchises: *Remember, Roman, that you are to reign over the Universe.*" Vergil and the Sibyl presage Christ in a teleological perspective which leaves those who are not Rome's heirs outside the movement toward salvation.

Christianity's universal vocation, however, is structured so as to maintain a place of welcome for ethnology. All history being universal history, all peoples of the world are called to enter into it, even if it remains the case that only those undergoing rapid evolution are worthy of interest.

When the occasion arose, medieval clerics, mixing times and places, history and geography, would practice ethnology without being aware of it. Gervase of Tilbury, for instance, in his *Otia Imperialia*, a collection of *mirabilia* intended for Emperor Otto of Brunswick (c. 1212), after tracing the history of mankind up to the Flood based on the account in Genesis, devoted the second part of his work to a potpourri of geographic, historic, and ethnographic notes on the various peoples of the world, and the final part to a recital of rites, legends, and miracles collected in the various places he had lived in England, the Kingdom of the Two Sicilies, and Provence.

The Middle Ages also furnished all that was necessary to prepare the way for a "noble savage": a millenarianism that awaited a return to a golden age; the conviction that historical progress, if it exists, takes place by way of rebirths, or reversions to a primitive state of innocence. But medieval man lacked a content to give to this myth. Some looked to the East and, with the help of a belief in Prester John, thought up an anthropological model, the "pious brahmin." Yet Marco Polo was not taken seriously. Others baptized "savage man" and changed Merlin into a hermit. The discovery of America suddenly provided Europe with "noble savages."

The Renaissance continues both lines, both attitudes. On the one hand, "official" history is tied to political progress and to the fortunes of princes and cities, the princely bureaucracy and urban bourgeoisie being the two rising forces with an interest in discovering the justification of their promotion in history. On the other hand, the curiosity of scholars extended to explorations in the ethnographic area. In literature, for example, Rabelais's genius and erudition are displayed in an imaginary ethnography—but one which is often not far removed from its peasant bases. As George Huppert wrote, "There are certainly other eras, less fortunate in this respect than antiquity, whose history has not yet been written. The Turks or the Americans, who lack a literary tradition of their own, would certainly present a modern Herodotus with an opportunity."

Herodotus was expected, Livy came. Etienne Pasquier, in his *Recherches,* took on the role of ethnographer of the past and provided science with "origins."

This coexistence of historian and ethnographer was not to last. The rationalism of the classical age and subsequently of the Enlightenment reserved history for peoples caught up by progress. "In the sense that Gibbon or Mommsen were historians, there was no such thing as an historian before the eighteenth century." From this point of view, R. G. Collingwood is right.

II

After a divorce lasting more than two centuries, historians and ethnologists are showing signs of converging once again. The new history, having taken on a sociological guise, is tending to become ethnological. What, then, does the ethnological outlook reveal to the historian in his own domain?

First, ethnology modifies history's chronological perspectives. It leads to a radical abandonment of the singular event, and thus realizes the ideal of a history without events. Or, rather, it proposes a history made up of repeated or expected events, such as festivals on the religious calendar, or events linked to biological or familial history, such as birth, marriage, and death.

Second, ethnology obliges the historian to differentiate a variety of time scales in history, and to pay special attention to the domain of the long period *(longue durée)*, that virtually stationary time defined by Fernand Braudel in his famous article.

Looking at the societies he studies with the eyes of an ethnologist, the historian better understands what may be called the "liturgical" aspect of historical society. Study of the calendar in its secularized and residual forms (strongly marked in industrial societies by Christianity's having continued ancient religious practice, as exemplified by the cycle of Christmas, Easter, the weekly pattern, etc.) or in its new forms (e.g., the calendar of sports competitions—and festivals) reveals the weight of ancestral rites and periodic rhythms on so-called developed societies. Here, more than ever, collaboration between the two attitudes, historical and ethnological, is needed. A "historical" study of festivals could be of decisive importance in understanding the structures and transformations of societies, especially in periods which are rightly called "transitional," such as the Middle Ages, which may in the end turn out to have been well named. It might be possible to trace, for instance, the evolution of the carnival as a festival, as a psychodrama of the urban community, which came into being during the late Middle Ages and declined in the nineteenth and twentieth centuries under the impact of the industrial revolution.

Emmanuel LeRoy Ladurie has given a brilliant analysis of the bloody carnival at Romans-sur-Isère in 1580, "a ballet-tragedy, in which the actors played and danced their rebellion rather than compose manifestoes on the subject." At Romans in that year, however, the annual game changed into a singular occurrence. As a rule, the significance of the festival must be sought in the ritual rather than the act. Thus, in an exemplary study, Louis Dumont has shown in the ceremonies in which the Tarasque appears the magico-religious meaning of the rites by which the Tarascon community sought, between the thirteenth and the eighteenth centuries, to win the good graces of an ambiguous monster which had become its "eponymous animal" or "palladium of the community." "The principal festival, that of Pentecost," Louis Dumont remarks, "associates it [the monster] with the important local review of the craft corporations." This can be seen in London as well, at least since the sixteenth century, in the Lord Mayor's procession, in which the traditional folkloric groups were taken over by the corporations. Thus in urban society, new social groups play the role, in community rituals, played by the class of youths in traditional rural societies. These historical mutations bring us to the majorettes and the huge "hippie" gatherings of the present day. Are liturgy and festival, present in all societies, particularly connected with archaic societies? Evans-Pritchard seems to think so: "An anthropological training, including field work, would be especially valuable in the investigation of earlier periods of history in which institutions and modes of thought resemble in many respects those of the simpler peoples we study." But was medieval Western man (Evans-Pritchard stops at the Carolingian era) archaic? And are we not archaic, in our world of sects, horoscopes, flying saucers, and racing lotteries? Do the terms "liturgical society" or "ludic society" accurately express the nature of medieval society?

As distinct from the historian of societies in flux and of urban dwellers influenced by changing modes, the ethnologist will choose for his object conservative rural societies (which are not so conservative as is sometimes said, as Marc Bloch has reminded us), the connective tissue of history. Thus, owing to the ethnological outlook, there has been a ruralization of history. The reader will allow the medievalist to look once again to his own specialty. After the urban and bourgeois Middle Ages imposed by nineteenth-century historians from Augustin Thierry to Henri Pirenne, we have what seems to us the truer rural Middle Ages of Marc Bloch, Michael Postan, Léopold Génicot, and Georges Duby.

Through this shift in interest toward the life of ordinary men, historical ethnology leads naturally to the study of mentalities, considered as "that which changes least" in historical evolution. Even at the heart of industrial societies, archaism becomes evident as soon as collective psychology and behavior are examined. Mental time being "out of joint" with other historical time scales, the historian is compelled to become an ethnologist. But the mental world he seeks to grasp is not lost in the night of time. Mental systems are historically datable, even if they do carry a heavy freight of debris from archeo-civilizations, dear to André Varagnac.

III

Ethnology also leads the historian to place in relief certain social structures which are more or less effaced in "historical" societies, and to complicate his picture of social dynamics and the class struggle.

Notions such as class, group, category, and stratum should be reconsidered by introducing into the model of social structure and interaction certain concepts and realities which, though fundamental, have been relegated by post-Marxist sociology to the margins of social theory:

a) Family and kinship structures, for example, whose introduction into the historian's problematics may lead to a new periodization of European history based on the evolution of family structures. By such means, Pierre Chaunu and members of the Centre de Recherches d'Histoire Quantitative in Caen identify as "the great immutable factor in the dialectic of men and space from the twelfth or thirteenth century until the end of the eighteenth, throughout the span of traditional peasant civilization over the long period, 'the existence of *communities of inhabitants*' (only 80 percent coincidental with the parishes)." Ethnological, no longer merely juridical, methods, applied to the study of lineage and to the silent community, to the extended as well as the narrow family, should renew the bases of comparative studies between past and present and between Europe and other continents in areas such as feudal society.

b) The sexes, consideration of which should bring about a demasculinization of history. How many paths through the history of the medieval West lead to woman! The history of heresies is, in many respects, a history of woman in society and religion. If there is one innovation in the area of sensibility with which the Middle Ages are generally credited, it has to be courtly love. It is built around an image of woman. In seeking the medieval soul, Michelet, always shrewd in appropriating what is essential in the legacy of the past, finds what he is looking for in the diabolical beauty of the sorceress and in the popular, hence divine, purity of Joan of Arc. Who will unravel the most important phenomenon of the "spiritual" (in Michelet's sense) history of the Middle Ages: the Virgin Mary's stunning breakthrough in the twelfth century?

c) Age classes, a study of which has yet to be made in the case of gerontocracies, but is off to a brilliant start where youth is concerned: Henri Jeammaire and Pierre Vidal-Naquet, for Ancient Greece; Georges Duby and Eric Köhler for the medieval West.

d) Village classes and communities, whose importance was previously recognized by Marc Bloch in the case of medieval Christianity, and which are now being analyzed by the Marxists. If the results avoid the pitfalls of dogmatism, they will help to renew social history. Here, moreover, we may perceive one of the possible paradoxical consequences of the regeneration of historical problematics through the ethnological outlook. Old style history took pleasure in its anecdotal and novelistic manner of evoking events linked with certain classical structures within "historical" societies. To take another medieval example, the history of feudal wars begs to be redone in the context of a comprehensive study of private war and vendetta. The history of factional disputes within families, cities, and dynasties could also be redone from such a perspective: Guelphs and Ghibellines, Montagues and Capulets, Armagnacs and Burgundians, heroes of the Wars of the Roses, once rescued from the anecdotal recitation of events—of which they provided some of the worst examples—may find a new scientific relevance and dignity within the framework of a broadly comparative ethnological history.

IV

To do ethnological history is also to give a historical reevaluation of magical factors and charismas.

For instance, there are dynastic charismas, knowledge of which would make it possible to "rehabilitate" feudal monarchy, long treated as different in kind from all other institutions. Marc Bloch's evocation of thaumaturgic kings and Percy Ernst Schramm's explanation of the emblems of power were forerunners of an approach which aims to attack medieval monarchy's center rather than its survivals or magical signs. An ethnographic outlook should bring about a metamorphosis in the value of the testimony regarding sacred kingship in the medieval West provided by Helgaud's life of Robert the Pious, Giraud le Cambrien's diabolical genealogy of the Plantagenets, and Charles the Bold's attempts to cross that magical barrier.

There are also professional and occupational charismas. To stay with the Middle Ages, think of the prestige, from the fifth century on, of the blacksmith and the goldsmith, whose magical image is recounted in gests and sagas. The recent discovery in Normandy of the extraordinary Tomb 10 in the Merovingian cemetery at Hérouvillette has brought back to life a magician-craftsman of the High Middle Ages who was buried with the arms of an aristocratic warrior and the tool kit of a technician and whose social position can be understood only through the convergence of technological study, sociological analysis, and an ethnological point of view. The evolution of the doctor and the surgeon, heirs of the sorcerer, ought to be traced in our societies. The "intellectuals" of the Middle Ages, the academics, monopolized certain charismatic features that "mandarins" have been adept at manipulating down to our own day: the faculty chair, the gown, the sheepskin, all signs that are more than mere signs. In this way, the most prestigious of their number take their place with the "luminaries" of society, from the gladiator to movie stars and "pop idols." The ablest and grandest of these intellectuals will even manage to enjoy their charismatic power without needing to invoke its signs, as has been the case from Abelard down to Sartre.

Finally, there are individual charismas, which make possible a reconsideration of the "great man's role" in history. Reduction to the sociological level has brought only a limited clarification in this area. To return once more to the Middle Ages, the transition from dynastic charisma to individual charisma is expressed, for example, in the figure of Saint Louis, who ceases to be a sacred king to become a saintly king. Laicization and canonization go together. What was gained in one respect was lost in another. Is it possible not to harbor a suspicion that the historical study of charisma might contribute something to the understanding of a nonanecdotal phenomenon of twentieth-century history, the cult of personality?

In such a perspective, moreover, we may find a place for the eschatological beliefs and millenarianisms that mark the return of the sacred in all parts of societies and civilizations. Far from being limited to archaic or "primitive" societies, such millenarianisms manifest failures of adaptation (or of resignation) in societies caught up in an accelerating pace of technologigal change. Norman Cohn has told what these apocalyptic outbursts were in the Middle Ages and the Renaissance. The success today of religious sects, astrology, and the "hippie" movement is indicative of the permanent character—in precise historical conjunctures—of the adepts of the "gran rifiuto."

V

Unlike François Furet, who has concentrated on the "savage" aspect of history as perceived from the ethnological viewpoint, I will emphasize primarily its everyday aspect.

Ethnology's immediate contribution to history is surely the promotion of material civilization (or culture). This has not come about without hesitations on the part of historians. In Poland, for example, where developments in this area have been prodigious since 1945, fostered by national and "materialist" motivations (and epistemological misunderstandings), rigorous Marxists feared the invasion of social dynamics by material inertia. In the West, Fernand Braudel's great work, *Capitalism and Material Life (1400–1800)*, did not allow the new discipline to occupy the historical field of study without subordinating it to a properly historical phenomenon, capitalism.

From the enormous area newly opened to the historian's curiosity and imagination, I shall single out three aspects.

1) The emphasis on techniques. The most interesting problem seems to me to be the reconsideration of the notions of invention and inventor that ethnology imposes on the historian. Marc Bloch had made a start in this field as far as medieval "inventions" are concerned. Once again, we encounter here, from a Lévi-Straussian point of view, an opposition between *hot* and *cold* societies, or, rather, between *hot* and *cold* milieus within the same society. The discussions involving the construction of the cathedral in Milan in the fourteenth century brought to light the opposition between science and technique in the conflict between architects and masons. "Ars sine

scientia nihil est," said the learned French architects; "Scientia sine arte nihil est," replied the Lombard masons, no less learned, but in another system of knowledge. This interest, in any case, has begun to stimulate a history of building materials and raw materials, not necessarily noble or precious, such as salt and wood.

2) The emergence of the body in history. Michelet had already laid claim to this theme in his 1869 *Préface* to the *History of France*. He there deplored history's lack of interest in *foods*, and in *innumerable physical and physiological circumstances*. His wish is beginning to be fulfilled. This is largely the case, at least, for the history of food, thanks to the impetus provided by journals and centers such as *Annales—Economies, Sociétés, Civilisations* (Fernand Braudel, co-director); *Zeitschrift für Agrageschichte und Agrasoziologie,* around Wilhelm Abel at Göttingen; and the *Afdeling Agrarische Geschiednis,* conducted by Slicher van Bath at the Landbouwehogeschool in Wageningen.

Biological history is getting underway. A special issue of *Annales E.S.C.* set out the prospects. The great book by a biologist turned historian, François Jacob's *La Logique du vivant,* a history of heredity, shows that the encounter between biology and history may be approached from either side.

To move nearer the domain of ethnology proper, it is to be hoped that historians will follow the path laid out by Marcel Mauss in his famous article on the *techniques of the body,* historical knowledge of which should be of decisive importance in the characterization of societies and civilizations.

3) Dwellings and clothing should provide the historian-ethnologist with the opportunity for an interesting dialogue between stability and change. The problems of taste and fashion, essential in dealing with these subjects, can be treated only through interdisciplinary collaboration among students of aesthetics, semiologists, historians of art, historians, and ethnologists. Here again, work such as that of François Piponnier and Jacques Heers illustrates the desire on the part of historians to root their research in the proven fertile soil of economic and social history.

4) Finally, there is the immense problem for which historians and sociologists should join forces to study a phenomenon of capital importance for both, *tradition*. Particularly illuminating among recent work in this area is that of Jean-Michel Guilcher, an ethnologist specializing in popular dance.

VI

I will not insist on the fact that the ethnological outlook offers the historian a new sort of documentation, different from that to which he is accustomed. The ethnologist does not disdain the written document, quite the contrary. But he encounters it so rarely that his methods are designed to enable him to get along without it.

In this connection, then, the historian is called upon to look over the shoulder of the ordinary man who does not—did not—burden himself with a mass of documentary records, and to accompany him through a world without written texts.

He will first encounter archaeology, but not of the traditional sort, oriented toward the monument or object and intimately connected with the history of art, but rather the archaeology of everyday life, of material life. This sort of work is illustrated by the English excavations of Maurice Beresford in the "lost villages," in the digs of Witold Hensel and his collaborators in the *grods* (pre-urban fortified settlements or nuclei) of the ancient Slav area, and in the work of a Franco-Polish group from the Sixth Section of the Ecole Pratique des Hautes Etudes on several medieval French villages.

He will next come upon iconography, but here again not so much that of traditional art history, tied to ideas and aesthetic forms, but rather that of gestures, utilitarian forms, perishable objects unworthy of written record. If an iconography of material culture has begun to be constituted, at the other end of the spectrum a difficult but necessary iconography of mentalities remains in limbo. It should, however, be implicit in the card catalogue of Princeton's Department of Art and Archaeology, for example.

Finally, he will run into oral tradition. Here the problems are formidable. How is the oral to be apprehended in the past? Can the oral be identified with the popular? What were the meanings of the expression *popular culture* in various historical societies? What were the relations between high and popular culture?

VII

I will treat even more briefly certain other important but rather obvious aspects of ethnology's influence on history.

Ethnology accentuates certain of history's present tendencies. It invites, for instance, a generalization of the comparative and the regressive methods. It hastens the abandonment of the Europe-centered point of view.

VIII

I will conclude on a different note, by emphasizing the limits of the collaboration between ethnology and history. I want to point out some problems bearing on their association, as well as certain dangers that a pure and simple substitution of the ethnological for the historical outlook would involve for the study of historical societies.

Special attention ought to be paid to zones and periods where contact took place between societies and cultures traditionally in the domain of history on the one hand and of ethnology on the other. In other words, the study of *acculturations* should make it possible to clarify the relative positions of the ethnological and the historical. In particular, the historian will be interested in knowing to what extent and under what conditions the terminology and problematics of acculturation may be extended to the study of *internal acculturations* within a given society—for example, between popular and learned culture, regional and national culture, the North and the South, etc. How is the problem of the "two cultures," of hierarchization and domination between the two, formulated in such a case?

The terminology must be made more precise. Erroneous comparisons will then perhaps be eliminated. I suspect that the notion of the *diachronic*, which Claude Lévi-Strauss borrowed from Saussure and Jakobson and introduced so felicitously into ethnology, is quite different from the notion of the *historical* with which it is frequently confused in the desire and belief that a tool common to linguistics and to all the human sciences may thus be found. I wonder if the diachronic, forged by Saussure to restore a dynamic dimension to the abstract object he had created, language, is not subject to abstract systems of transformation very different from the evolutionary schemes used by the historian in attempting to apprehend the process of becoming in the concrete societies he studies. I am not trying to restore the old distinction, which seems to me false, between ethnology, the science of directly observing living phenomena, and history, the science of reconstructing dead phenomena. There is no science but abstract science, and the ethnologist, like the historian, finds himself facing the *other*, a being of an alien nature. He, too, must find his way to reunion with this *other*.

From another vantage, is it not possible that, after having favored unduly that which changes and moves quickly, the historian-ethnologist is hastening too rapidly toward making paramount that which moves slowly and changes little or not at all? In trying to draw closer to the ethnologist, does not the historian risk binding himself to the opposition between structure and conjuncture, structure and event, in such a way as to place himself on the side of structure, while the problems of today's history require us to go beyond the false dilemma of structure versus conjuncture and, even more important, structure versus event?

Would the historian not do better to take notice of the increasingly widespread tendency in the human sciences (ethnology included) to adopt a critical view of that which is static? At a time when ethnology is taking on a new burden of historicity and Georges Balandier is showing that there are no societies without history and that the idea of static societies is an illusion, is it prudent for the historian to give himself over to an ethnology that stands outside time? To put it in Lévi-Straussian terms, if there are no hot and cold societies but, rather, as is obvious, societies more or less hot or more or less cold, is it legitimate to treat hot societies like cold ones? And what about "tepid" societies?

While ethnology helps the historian rid himself of illusions of a linear, homogeneous, and continuous progress, problems of evolutionism remain. In relation to history, is the neighboring discipline of prehistory, which is also devoted to societies without writing, really a prehistory, or a different history?

If the historian takes a view of the world too close to that of ethnology, how can he explain *growth*, an essential phenomenon in the societies he studies, a modern, economic, insidious form of progress, which must be demythified (as, for example, Pierre Vilar has done in unmasking the ideological presuppositions in Rostow's takeoff) but which is also a reality to be explained?

Are there not, moreover, several ethnologies that should be distinguished from one another, among which the European will be of a different kind from that of more or less preserved areas such as the Amerindian, African, or Oceanic?

A specialist in change (by saying *transformation*, the historian places himself on potentially common ground with the ethnologist, providing he does not revert to the notion of *diachronic*), the historian should beware of becoming insensitive to change. His problem is not so much to seek a transition from the primitive to the historical or to reduce the historical to the primitive as to explain the coexistence and interaction within the same society of phenomena and groups not located within a single time or a single evolutionary scale. It is a problem of levels and of temporal displacements. As for the way in which the historian might teach the ethnologist how to *recognize*—and respect—the *other*, this is a lesson that should not, unfortunately, be overestimated, for, beyond the often regrettable polemics, ethnology today shows us that the negation or destruction of the *other* is not the privilege of a human science.

THE SYMBOLIC RITUAL OF VASSALAGE

INTRODUCTION: MEDIEVAL SYMBOLISM

Under the quite general heading of symbolic gestures in social life, I would like to approach the problem of symbolism in connection with a basic institution of medieval society: vassalage.

Every society is symbolic to the extent that it employs symbols in its practices and that it may be studied with the aid of a symbolic type of interpretation.

In the case of medieval society, this symbolic aspect common to all societies was reinforced by the application of an ideological system of symbolic interpretation to the majority of its activities.

To my knowledge, however, clerics in the Middle Ages gave at best a far from complete symbolic explanation of the rites regulating the fundamental social institution of vassalage. This is our first problem.

Not entirely satisfying, yet not to be rejected out of hand, is the explanation that the significance of the rites of vassalage was so immediately apparent that no gloss was needed by either participants or witnesses.

It should be noted, in any case, that similar rites were given more or less explicit symbolic interpretations.

One group of such rites was concerned with kingship. Emblems of power, as well as coronation, funeral, and succession ceremonies, gave rise to symbolic elucidations. In the medieval West, the most important symbolic reference system was the Bible, especially the Old Testament and the typological symbolism that established an essential relationship between the Old and New Testaments. It

Appendixes to this essay and a bibliography may be found below, pp. 354–57, 367.

supplied the symbolic image of King David, which, if I am not mistaken, was mobilized for the first time in the service of Charlemagne.[1] Later, in the age of chivalry, it yielded the image of Melchizedek, the priest-king, *rex sacerdos*. Nothing of the kind exists for the lord or vassal.

A better example is offered by rites of dubbing, which were described in symbolic, mystical, and religious terms that depicted the institution as an initiation on which Christianity placed its seal. This was true to the point that dubbing came to take on the aspect of a quasi-sacrament, following the line laid down by Saint Augustine in *De civitate Dei* X, 5, where he holds that the *sacramentum* is a *sacrum signum*, a conception that Hugh of Saint-Victor would develop in the *De sacramentis* at approximately the time that dubbing began to take on its full religious panoply. Nothing of the kind exists in the case of vassalage.

There are, to be sure, a scant few indications that permit us to believe that the men of the Middle Ages or, at least, the clerics who were their ideological guides and interpreters did in fact outline a symbolic interpretation of the rites of vassalage.

The Middle Ages had no words for symbol, symbolism, or symbolic in the sense in which we use the term today and as it has been used, in essential respects, since the sixteenth century. The medieval clergy used the term *symbolum* only in the quite specialized and restricted sense of an article of faith—the most telling example is the Nicene Creed (*symbolum* of Nicaea). The semantic field of "symbol" was mainly occupied by the term *signum*, closest to our "symbol," defined by Saint Augustine in the second book of the *De doctrina christiana*. But there were also *figura, imago, typus, allegoria, parabola, similitudo speculum*, which define a quite special symbolic system.[2]

On occasion we find the term *signum* used in connection with objects delivered at the investiture of a fief. Thus in a charter of 1123 now in the cartulary of Saint-Nicolas d'Angers: "Quirmarhoc and his two sons bestow this benefice (gift) on Gradelon, monk of Saint Nicolas, with a book in the Church of Saint-Pierre of Nantes and give him a kiss to seal this donation by their faith; and this book which they thus bestow on the monk, they do also place symbolically on the alter of Saint Peter."[3]

As Emile Chénon has observed, we also find, though rarely, an explanation of the *osculum*, the kiss of fidelity, as a symbol of oblation. In 1143, for example, according to a text in the cartulary of the monastery of Obazine in Limousin: "This gift was made in the great hall of the castle of Turenne, into the hand of Monseigneur Etienne, prior of Obazine, the viscountess having kissed the hand of the prior as an authentic sign of oblation."[4]

Another symbolic interpretation of the ritual of entry into vassalage dating from the late thirteenth century may be found in one of those rare texts that give symbolic explanations of certain points in the rites of vassalage, the *Speculum juris* of Guillaume Durand (1271, recast in 1287): "because he who does homage, on his knees, places his hands between the hands of the lord and does him homage; he promises on his honor, and the lord, in a reciprocal sign of faith, gives him a kiss," and, further: "immediately afterward, as a sign of reciprocal and perpetual love, the kiss of peace is given."[5]

What interests me here, however, more than identifying symbols in the current sense of the term, i.e., as concretizations of an abstraction, "close to emblematic analogy," is rather the possibility of a symbolic ritual in the whole complex of acts by which vassalage was constituted. In this regard, the traces of a conscious conception of this ritual are still more tenuous. Lambert of Ardres, for instance, does write, in his *Historia comituem guinensium* at the very end of the twelfth century, that "The Flemish did homage to Count Thierry according to the rite,"[6] but can we take the term "rite" in the strong sense, as expressing awareness of an actual rite of homage, or is it merely a worn-out and devalued word, devoid of its initial semantic charge?

If I may temporarily leave aside the problem of the silence of medieval documents with respect to an explicit symbolic interpretation of the rites of vassalage, I would like to offer the hypothesis that such rites were indeed a symbolic ritual and that an ethnological type of approach might be able to shed some light on important aspects of the institution of vassalage.

Not that I am unaware of the risks of applying such methods to the study of vassalage in the medieval West. A society which has traditionally been the object of study by historians does not easily lay itself open to methods used by ethnologists to study other societies. In attempting this approach, I shall try to preserve the meaning of such differences—of a certain basic difference.

I DESCRIPTION

One is struck at once by the fact that the rites of vassalage involve three preeminently symbolic categories: speech, gesture, and objects.

Lord and vassal make certain speeches, perform certain gestures, and give or receive certain objects which, to quote Augustine's definition of the *signum-symbol,* "in addition to the impression they make on our senses, impart something further to our knowledge."

Let us review briefly the three stages of entry into vassalage which were distinguished by men of the Middle Ages and, after them, by historians of medieval institutions, among the first rank of whom is our teacher and colleague, F. L. Ganshof—homage, faith, investiture of the fief.[7]

Before doing so, however, we must make two more preliminary remarks. Not only do medieval documents provide no symbolic interpretation of the rites of vassalage, but they offer few detailed descriptions of such rites. Even so justly famed a text as the one in which Galbert of Bruges relates the homages done in 1127 to the new count William of Flanders is quite miserly with detail. As we shall see shortly, an ethnographic approach to these phenomena involves the very sort of question to which the medieval documents rarely supply the desired answer.

Second, as the reader will have noticed, I frequently rely in this essay on documents more recent than the *alto medio evo,* even understood *lato sensu* as is traditional in these *Settimane.* This is because the older texts are generally even more laconic than those of the ninth to thirteenth centuries, and I believe I am entitled to turn to this period insofar as I am dealing with realities which have not evolved appreciably since the ninth and tenth centuries. When I come to attempt an interpretation of the symbolic ritual of vassalage, moreover, I shall try to restore the chronological perspective, and I shall then use documents from the "genuine early Middle Ages," the eighth to tenth centuries.

Galbert of Bruges distinguishes three phases of the entry into vassalage.

"First, they did homage in the following manner...": this is the *homage.*

"Secondly, he who had done homage engaged his faith...": this is the *faith.*

"Then, with the wand which he held in his hand, the count gave investiture to all...": this is the *investiture of the fief.*[8]

First phase: *hominium,* homage. It normally consisted of two acts. The first was verbal. Usually it took the form of a declaration or engagement by the vassal, stating his willingness to become the *man* of the lord. In the text of Galbert of Bruges, the vassal answers a question from his lord, the count. "The count demanded of the future vassal if he wished without reserve to become his man, and he replied, 'I wish it.' " Only a statistical study of the extant documents would make it possible to answer in a relatively precise way a question of great importance, particularly from an ethnographic point of view: which of the two participants has the initiative, who speaks and who does not? It is hardly necessary to point out that one can expect at best a relative precision from such a study, because the statistical result would depend on chance, which determined what was written down and preserved. It would also depend on the exactitude of the documents and might require a consideration of regional differences and chronological changes.

The speech is symbolic, however, in that it is already the *sign* of a relationship between lord and vassal that goes beyond the words exchanged.

There is an analogous case, although it raises the problem of vassalage between kings to which we shall return. In this instance, according to Ermold the Black, Harold the Dane was even more explicit when he became the vassal of Louis the Pious in 826.

"Receive me, Caesar," he said, "with my kingdom, which is subject to you. Of my own free will, I place myself at your service."[9]

There is a similarity with baptism, during which the new Christian answers God, who has questioned him through the baptizing priest, either speaking himself or through his godfather: "Do you want to become a Christian?—I do." By the same token, the vassal enters into a total, but definite, engagement to his lord at this first stage.

A second act completes the initial phase of entry into vassalage. This is the *immixtio manuum:* the vassal places his joined hands between the hands of his lord, which close over them. Galbert of Bruges is quite precise on this point: "then he (placed) his clasped hands in those of the count, who grasped them."

The oldest documents on rites of vassalage mention this rite of the hands.

In the first half of the seventh century, formula 43 of Marculf states, concerning the antrustion of the king: "He was seen to swear in our hand fidelity *(in manu nostra trustem et fidelitatem)."*[10]

In 757, according to the *Annales regni Francorum,* Tassilo, Duke of Bavaria, comes "recommending himself in vassalage by the hands" to King Pepin.[11]

In the previously cited poem by Ermold the Black, Harold the Dane makes the same gesture to Louis the Pious in 826: "Shortly thereafter, with hands joined, he delivered himself voluntarily to the king."

At this point, a comment is in order. Here we are certain that there was a reciprocity of gestures. The vassal's gesture was not enough by itself. The lord's had to respond to it.[12]

Furthermore, we are here touching on one of the great chapters in medieval and universal symbolism. This symbolism was polysemic, expressing instruction, defense, judgment, but especially, as in this case, protection, or rather the encounter between power and submission. The gesture revived a shopworn image of Roman legal terminology by restoring to *manus* its full scope as one of the expressions of *potestas,* and, in particular, one of the important attributes of the *paterfamilias.*[13] But we must not get ahead of ourselves.

A noteworthy variant of this first stage of the ritual of entry into vassalage should be noted. We have the Spanish case in mind.

As demonstrated by Claudio Sanchez Albornoz, in his *Origines del feudalismo*,[14] and, later, by his pupil Hilda Grassotti, in the first volume of her *Instituciones feudo-vassaliticus en León y Castilla* (both works published by this center),[15] in León and Castille homage was usually done by means of a special rite, the hand kiss. Hilda Grassotti writes: "The vassal stated to the lord that he wished to be his man and kissed his right hand." It should be noted that the declaration accompanied or, rather, preceded the gesture. I am not concerned here with the question of the origin of hand kissing by vassals in Spain, whether Spanish, as Don Claudio Sanchez Albornoz seeks to show, or oriental and, more precisely, Moslem, as Hilda Grassotti is inclined to think. In any event, I do not believe that there is any association between the foot kissing vouched for by the famous document of 775 in connection with the founding of the monastery of Lucis and the hand kissing homage done by vassals in Spain. Nor will I enlarge upon the discussions which have been stimulated by the possibility that the *hominium manuale,* the *commendatio in manibus,* was introduced into Catalonia, Navarre, and Aragon by Carolingian and, later, French influence. For the moment, it is sufficient to point out that the Spanish *osculatio manuum* differs from the *immixtio manuum* at least by the fact that the lord is more clearly superior to the vassal in the former rite, since he does nothing more than refrain from refusing to allow his hand to be kissed, and the vassal's gesture of humility is much more pronounced.[16]

If I may be allowed to return once more to the text of Galbert of Bruges, which I propose to use as a central thread in this essay, it seems to me anomalous in that it includes the *osculum,* the kiss exchanged between lord and vassal, in the first phase, or *hominium,* of the entry into vassalage, whereas this rite is normally considered to belong to the second phase, the *faith* or *oath of fealty.* "Then, his hands clasped in the count's, who grasped them, they became allies with a kiss."

The *osculum* or *osculatio* was more generally related to the *fides.* For example, according to the 1123 charter of Saint-Nicolas d'Angers, "they gave him a kiss to seal this donation by their faith."[17]

Some texts—most of them rather late, usually from the thirteenth century, such as the *Livre de jostice et de plet*—emphasize that the kiss is given "en nom de foy" (in the name of faith).[18]

From our chosen ethnographic point of view, one detail that might otherwise seem trivial assumes considerable importance. We are referring to the nature of the kiss, the manner in which it is given. On the basis of the documents gathered by Chénon, there appears to be no doubt on this point. The *osculum* of the vassal was a kiss on the mouth, *ore ad os,* as the cartulary of Montmorillon puts it in connection with an analogous type of contract. In light of our own customs, one intriguing detail is that women seem to have been exempt from the rite of the *osculum* of vassalage, and a late interpretation, from the fourteenth century, explained this fact by invoking decency, *propter honestatem.*[19] I believe this interpretation is incorrect for reasons I shall try to show later.

In connection with the *osculum,* historians of medieval law have put forward a distinction which, if confirmed by as exhaustive a study of texts as is possible, is not without interest but which, I believe, is inessential. According to these writers, a distinction must be made between what was practiced in countries governed by unwritten law, where the lord gave the *osculum,* and the custom in countries with written law, where the vassal gave the kiss to the lord, "who confined himself to returning it to him."[20] In my view, however, what is important is not who initiated the gesture but rather its reciprocity, which seems to have existed everywhere. The *osculum* was a mutual ritual kiss between lord and vassal. One gave it, the other received.

The second stage of the ritual of vassalage, the fealty, was completed by an oath. Once again we find speech used in this phase, but here its symbolic import is even greater than in the homage, since the oath was usually sworn on the Bible or certain relics.

A text from the *Casus S. Galli* is often presented as one of the oldest documents on the *osculum* of vassalage. It tells how Notker, elected abbot of Saint Gall in 971, became a vassal of Otto I. It clearly connects the rite to that of the oath, in this case on the Gospel. "Now you will be mine," said the emperor, "and after receiving him by the hands, he kissed him. Soon thereafter, a gospel-book having been brought in, the abbot swore fealty."[21]

The text of Galbert of Bruges is certainly invaluable for its precision and analytical presentation, but it should not be taken for *the* model of the ritual of entry into vassalage; in this text, just as the *osculum* is made part of the initial phase of homage, the plan of the fidelity ritual is broken down by the same token into two steps: first a promise, then an oath on the relics. "Secondly, he who had done homage engaged his faith in the following terms: 'I promise by my faith that from this time forward I will be faithful to Count William and will maintain toward him my homage entirely against every man, in good faith and without any deception.' Thirdly, all this was sworn on the relics of the saints."

In 757, according to a famous passage of the *Annales regni Francorum* cited earlier, we know how Tassilo, Duke of Bavaria, behaved toward Pepin the Short. After the *commendatio per manus,* "he swore many and innumerable oaths with his hands placed on the relics of the saints. And he promised fealty to King Pepin and to his aforementioned sons, the lords Charles and Carloman, as by law a vassal must do."[22]

At this stage of the ritual of vassalage, the vassal has become the "man of mouth and hands" of the lord. In 1110, for example, Bernard Atton IV, Viscount of Carcassonne, swore homage and faith in return for a number of fiefs to Leon, abbot of Notre-Dame-de-la-Grasse in the following terms: "In the name of each and every man, I do homage and faith by my hands and mouth to thee, my lord Leon, abbot, and to thy successors."[23]

We see the same frequently-used expression, "man of mouth and hands," in still more explicit form in the *carta donationis* of 1109 of Doña Urraca, in which Alfonso the Battler uses it in addressing his wife: "Let all the vassals (*homines*) who today hold this fief (*honor*) from you, or will hold it in the future, swear fealty to you and become your vassals (*men*) of mouth and hands."[24]

This expression is manifestly important because it shows the essential place occupied by the symbolism of the body in the cultural and mental system of the Middle Ages. The body not only reveals the soul but is the symbolic site where man's fate—in all its forms—is fulfilled. Even in the hereafter, at least until the Last Judgment, it is in corporeal form that the soul meets its fate, for better or worse, or for purgation.

Finally, the ritual of entry into vassalage concludes with the investiture of the fief, which is accomplished by the lord's delivery of a symbolic object to his vassal.

"Then," says Galbert of Bruges, "with the wand which he held in his hand, the count gave investiture to all."

What we have here is, in my view, a relatively minor aspect of the symbolism of the ritual of vassalage, the involvement of symbolic objects rather than speech or gesture. Nevertheless, our approach to the question, which is not without interest, is facilitated by the fact that Du Cange has treated it in the admirable article *Investitura* in his glossary.[25]

This article is admirable in three respects. First, because it collects a range of texts which comprise a veritable *corpus* of objects and symbolic gestures used in the course of investiture: ninety-nine varieties![26]

Second, because it begins with a veritable essay on the symbolism of medieval investiture.

Finally, because it proposes a tentative typology for symbolic objects used in investiture in the Middle Ages. Du Cange points out that investitures were not only made orally or with the aid of a simple document or charter *sed per symbola quaedam*. These symbolic objects had to serve two purposes: to mark the transfer of possession of a thing (*dominium rei*) from one person to another, and to conform to a consecrated custom so as to be perceived by all as an act having legal force.

Du Cange then classifies the various symbolic objects culled from documents of investiture according to two successive typologies.

In the first schema, he distinguishes objects having some relation with the thing transmitted, for example, the branch, the clod of earth, or sod, which signifies investiture of a piece of land. Next, he singles out those which indicate transmission of power, *potestas*, essentially in the form of a stick, *festuca*. Then come objects symbolizing, beyond the transmission of power, the right to do violence to the property (*ius evertendi, disjiciendi, succidendi metendi*, right to uproot, throw out, cut down, or divide): these are primarily knives and swords. Two additional categories of symbolic objects of investiture are related to customs, tradition, and history. Some are connected with ancient traditions, like the ring or standard. Others became symbolic during the Middle Ages, apart from any ancient tradition. These were taken in particular from the realm of weaponry, such as helmets, bows, and arrows, or from daily use, like horns, cups, etc.

In his second typology, Du Cange gives a special place, before listing all other objects in alphabetical order, to three sorts of objects which he says occur most frequently in investitures: (1) objects connected with the earth, and, more particularly, *cespes* or *guazo* (clods or turf); (2) the various staffs of command: particularly *baculum, fustes* (scepter, twig); (3) objects connected with the *ius evertendi* (right to uproot), particularly *cultellus* (knife).

I have no intention of launching into a thorough study of the ninety-eight symbolic objects inventoried by Du Cange (see Appendix I [A]) nor of undertaking to criticize his work in detail—it is, I repeat, remarkable.

I shall merely make three comments.

The first is that, to my mind, another typology would be preferable, which would take account of (a) references of an ethnohistorical kind; (b) the frequency of occurrence in the documents.

As a first approximation, subject to revision, I would distinguish:

1. Socioeconomic symbols—in which the preeminence of what is related to the earth is apparent, with an apparent preference for the natural, uncultivated earth.

For example: *per herbam et terram, per festucam, per lignum, per ramum, per virgam vel virgulam*, etc. (by grass and earth, by the stick, by the wood, by the branch, by the twig or shoot), with occasional borrowings from fishery (*per pisces*, by the fish) or the money economy (*per denarios*, by deniers).

2. Sociocultural symbols (I am taking culture here in the an-

thropological sense, in opposition to nature), with two major sub-groups:

a) bodily gestures: *per digitum, per dextrum pollicem, manu, per capillos, per floccilum capillorum* (by the finger or toe, right thumb, hand, hair, or lock of hair);

b) clothing: *per capellum, per corrigiam, per gantum, per linteum, per manicam, per mappulam, per pannum sericum, per pileum, per zonam* (by the hat, leather belt, glove, shirt, mantlet, handkerchief, silk cloth, Phrygian cap, sash) (with emphasis therefore on the belt and the glove).

3. Socioprofessional symbols, in which symbols of the two leading functional social categories dominate: clergy (*per calicem, per claves ecclesiae, per clocas ecclesiae, per ferulam pastoralem*, etc., by the chalice, the keys to the church, the bells of the church, the pastoral ferula), and knighthood (*per gladium, per hastam*, by the sword or lance), but where, in the case of the clergy, objects relating to books and writing frequently stand out (*per bibliothecam, per chartum, per librum, per notulus, cum penna et calamario, per pergamenum, per psalterium, per regulam, per textum evangelii*, by the library, charter, book, charters, with ink and inkwell, by the parchment, psalter, rule, or Gospel text). Furthermore, objects symbolic of the peasant are observed—often both tool and weapon: (*per cultellum, per cultrum vel cultellum, per forfices, per furcam ligneam, cum veru*, by the knife, coulter or knife, shears, or wooden pitchfork with sharpened pike).

The second comment I wish to make is that the bases of classification should be revised, because they correspond neither to the mental and cultural equipment of the Middle Ages nor to our modern scientific categories. They are based on notions from Roman law, such as *dominium, ius evertendi, potestas*, etc., which do not seem relevant for the essential points in our subject.[27]

Finally, a new look should be taken at the symbolism of objects itself, and our explanations recast on a primary level (the much more complex symbolism of the *festuca* or *cultellus*). We must be careful not to isolate the objects and their significations from the whole of the ritual.

To comprehend this whole, we must add to our description of the rites of entry into vassalage an analysis of the rites connected with the *exit from vassalage*.

At this point, I must cite the only study which, to my knowledge, has tried to pursue the investigation of the ritual of homage in the direction of comparative symbolism and, in a certain sense, legal ethnography. It makes use of the 1900 article of Ernst von Moeller, *Die Rechtssitte des Stabsrechens*, and the "great work" of Karl von Amira of 1909, *Der Stab in der germanischen Rechtssymbolik*.[28] I am thinking of Marc Bloch's remarkable youthful article, which already displays the promise of the future author of *Rois thaumaturges*, entitled "Les formes de la rupture de l'hommage dans l'ancien droit féodal," which appeared in 1912.[29]

To my mind, this study is interesting on three counts. It points out, first of all, that the ritual of vassalage must be studied on what I call its two slopes, entry and exit: the breaking off of homage, to which we must add abandonment. The symbolism of a ritual intended to create a social bond can be completely understood only if we consider both the establishment and the destruction of that bond, even if the latter occurs only rarely.

Second, the study indicates that the ceremonial forms of the institutions of vassalage can be clarified only by comparing them with analogous or closely related rites.

Finally, in an appendix, commenting on a passage of Salic law cited by Ernst von Moeller, Marc Bloch suggests that the rites of vassalage may be studied in relation to a hypothesis concerning the "origins of feudalism." Later, he himself partially rejected this idea (recall his critique of the search for origins in *Apologie pour l'histoire*), but it may perhaps prove useful to us today as a guide for interpreting the symbolic system of vassalage—with the suggestion that we should look in the direction of kinship symbolism.

Marc Bloch has gathered examples of *exfestucatio* generally taken from chronicles or gests of the twelfth and thirteenth centuries, including cases in which an object other than a *festuca* is thrown. In particular, he comments at length on a passage from the late twelfth-century gest *Raoul de Cambrai* in which Bernier, squire to Raoul, breaks off his homage when Raoul tries to do Bernier's family out of its legitimate inheritance. Bernard "took, through the mail of his hauberk, three tufts from his ermine garment and threw them toward Raoul; then he said to him: 'Man! I withdraw my faith from you. Do not say that I betrayed you" (lines 2314–18, ed. P. Meyer and Longnon). He cites another particularly interesting text, an *exemplum* in which the Cistercian Caesarius of Heisterbach, in his *Dialogus miraculorum* (c. 1220), recounts the story of how a young knight broke off his homage to God and gave it to the devil: "He denied his creator by his mouth, broke off his homage by throwing straw with his hand, and did homage to the devil." Here again we find the idea of the man of mouth and hands, and Marc Bloch points out, in connection with *manu*, "that the essential act must be sought in a gesture of the hand." I do not follow Marc Bloch, however, when he assimilates the *exfestucatio* to abandonment. I believe that Chénon is right to reserve this term for a *divestiture*, or abandonment by agreement, between the two parties, lord and vassal, the divorce agreement being sealed, so to speak, with an *osculum*.[30]

Once again, Galbert of Bruges provides us with invaluable information, this time concerning the ritual of *exfestucatio*. After the murder of Charles the Good, Count of Flanders, a difference arises between the new count William Clito and certain of his subjects and vassals. As we have seen, the latter had done homage as vassals at Bruges. Some of them, however, Ivan of Alost among the leaders, felt that the new count had not kept his commitments, and the burgesses of Ghent supported them against the count. The count would have liked to break off the homage Ivan had done him, if he had dared face the revolt of the burgesses ("igitur comes prosiliens exfestucasset Iwanum si ausus esset prae tumultu civium illorum"), but he settles for a symbolic speech and says that he wishes to reject the homage done him in order to lower himself to the level of his former vassal so that he can make war against him ("valo ergo rejecto hominio quod michi fecisti, parem me tibi facere, et sine dilatione bello comprobare in te . . . ").

The count's desire to break off homage was matched by an actual instance the year before, in 1127, when some vassals of the castellan of Bruges, who had taken in the assassins of Charles the Good, broke off homage. In this case, the *exfestucatio* was not only declared; it was executed in the concrete form of a symbolic gesture: "Having taken up the straws, they threw them to break off homage, fealty, and the guarantee of security to the besieged."

Still, it is not only, as Marc Bloch seems to have believed, because the texts are silent that we possess even fewer details on the breaking off of homage than we have concerning the entry into vassalage. For reasons that in part are obvious, rites of breaking off were briefer, disagreement lending itself less well than agreement to a complex ceremony. It is especially important, I think, to note that the two slopes of the ceremony of vassalage are asymmetrical. Not every symbolic element of one has a counterpart in the other. This asymmetry should perhaps be studied more closely.

In this preliminary outline, it will suffice to explain the system constituted by the several phases and gestures just described, to which we now turn.

II System

It must be stressed that the whole body of symbolic rites and gestures of vassalage constitutes not merely a ceremonial or ritual but a system; that is, it functions only if all the essential elements are present and is significant and effective only by virtue of each one of those elements, whose meaning individually can be made clear only by reference to the whole. Homage, fealty, and investiture are necessarily interdependent and constitute a symbolic ritual that remains intact not so much because of the force and, in this case, the almost sacred character of tradition as because of the internal coherence of the system. It seems, moreover, that contemporaries perceived it in this way.

The sequence of acts and gestures, from homage to fealty to investiture, was not merely temporal. It also had the character of a logical, necessary unfolding. One may even wonder whether descriptions of the rites of vassalage were as succinct as they are because of a more or less conscious desire to indicate without unnecessary digression that the essential rite in all its necessary phases had indeed been performed. Quite frequently all three ritual actions are expressed in a single sentence covering homage and fealty. To use the previously cited examples:

a) When William Long Sword became a vassal of Charles the Simple in 927, "he placed himself between the hands of the king to be his man of war and pledged his faith and confirmed it with an oath."[31]

b) According to Thietmar of Merseburg, when Henry II arrived at the eastern border of Germany in 1002, "all who had served the previous emperor crossed their hands with the king's and confirmed with oaths that they would help him faithfully."[32]

The way the symbolic gestures are connected together in time and in the internal necessity of the system is frequently underscored by coordinating conjunctions (*et, ac, que*).

When the narrative is broken down into several episodes and phases, the brevity of the interval between successive episodes is frequently stressed.

a) In Ermold the Black's story of the Danish king Harold's becoming a vassal of Louis the Pious and his investiture in 826:

> *Soon thereafter,* hands joined, he delivered himself of his own free will to the king...
> *And* Caesar himself received his hands in his own honorable hands...
> *Soon* Caesar, following the old custom of the Franks, gave him a horse and weapons...
> *Meanwhile* Caesar made offering to Harold who was *thereafter* his faithful servant.[33]

b) In the story of the entry of Notker, elected abbot of Saint Gall, into the vassalage of Otto I in 971: "'Finally you will be mine,' said the emperor, and after having received him by the hands, he kissed him. *And soon,* a gospel book having been brought in, the abbot swore fealty."[34]

In what is undoubtedly the most detailed account we have of this system, Galbert of Bruges's description of the entry into vassalage and investiture of various Flemish lords on the occasion of the coming of the new count William of Flanders in 1127, the narrator, in view of the relative lengthiness of his account, feels the need to place strong emphasis on the sequence of phases: "*First,* they did homage in the following way . . . *Secondly,* he who had done homage engaged his faith in these terms . . . *Thirdly,* he swore on the holy relics . . . *Then,* with the wand which he held in his hand, the count gave investiture to all . . . " To round out this impression of a solidly integrated whole in which each successive gesture leads ineluctably to the following one so as to constitute a closed system, Galbert concludes by recalling the initial episode in the final phrases " . . . all of them, who, by this pact, had promised him security, done homage, and at the same time sworn an oath."[35]

Only by giving a plausible interpretation of such a system of symbolic gestures can we render its existence probable, even if we cannot prove it. I will attempt to do this on two levels.

The first level of interpretation focuses on each of the phases of the symbolic ritual and defines a relationship between the two participants: lord and vassal.

Anticipating the comparisons offered below between vassalage in the medieval West and other social systems, I will clarify this interpretation by referring to Jacques Maquet's study *Pouvoir et société en Afrique,* which I find well suited to the task of illustrating the significance of the social relations I am studying here.[36] Initially, without bringing in such significant features as an ethnographic type of analysis will be able to reveal below, we can say that what seems important in the first phase, *homage,* is the expression of the more or less marked subordination of the vassal to the lord. Of course, as we have seen, the action may be initiated by the lord, and the *immixtio manuum*—to which I shall return—is a gesture of meeting, a mutual contract. I will not consider the too-obvious case of the Spanish hand kiss, in which the vassal's inferiority is even more marked. In all cases the inequality of conditions and attitudes is evident in gestures as well as speech. In the *immixtio manuum* it is clear that the enveloping pair of hands belongs to a person superior to the one whose hands are enclosed. According to Galbert of Bruges, the vassal of the Count of Flanders, after joining his hands, becomes the acquiescent, passive object of the embrace or envelopment by the hands of the count (the passivity is indicated by the grammatical form): "and, hands clasped, he was grasped by the hands of the count." Of course, the lord's gesture includes a promise of aid and protection, but this very promise implies an ostentatious display of a superior—in every sense of the word—power. The relationship is one of dependence. On the basis of African examples, Jacques Maquet defines it in this way: "Dependency, the need for the aid of others in order to exist fully, is the most important characteristic of certain relationships, which are recognized and even institutionalized in several societies. We will consequently call these relationships of dependence. They are asymmetrical: one aids and supports, the other receives this aid and support and otherwise renders various services to his protector. The relationship cannot be reversed: protection and services are not of the same kind."[37] He adds: "To fulfill his role, the protector must have the necessary means. This implies that, even before the relationship begins, he must be more than his dependent-to-be."[38]

If we look at the gesture from the vassal's point of view, we find, if not humiliation, then at least a sign of deference and inferiority, through the simple gesture "manus alicui dare," "in manus alicuius dare," or through the signification given it: "sese...committit" (William Long Sword before Charles the Simple), "se commendans" (Tassilo with Pepin), "se tradidit" (Harold toward Louis the Pious). If we adopt the lord's viewpoint, we see the superior's acceptance "aliquem per manus accipere." When the expression emphasizes the joining of hands, something in the sentence expresses the lord's superiority. Henry II's eastern vassals "regi manus complicant," but they are already, if not vassals, at least military subordinates of the previous emperor: "who had served the previous emperor."

The same inequality is displayed in the associated words. If the instigation comes from the lord, as in Galbert of Bruges's text, it is couched in terms proving the lord's superior position, virtually a demand: "the count demanded (*requisivit*) (of the future vassal) whether he wished without reserve (*integre*) to become his man," and *integre* requires virtually an "unconditional surrender." When the vassal answers "I wish it" (*volo*), the word expresses the commitment of an inferior, not the will of an equal.[39]

Finally, the terms defining *homage* leave no doubt that what is involved at this stage is the vassal's recognition of his subordinate position, which he comes forward to confirm in ritual: "...if he wished to become (*fieri*) his man," says Galbert, and the English charter cited above puts it still more clearly, "to become (*fore*) his feudal man." Before a superior, homage makes an inferior a subordinate. *Fieri* and *fore* express this transformation or birth of a vassal quite well. As for *homo*, it should not be forgotten that in a society in which the *man* had long been quite insignificant relative to the *dominus*, the earthly lord being image and representative of his heavenly counterpart, the term indicates subordination, with the specialized senses of vassal on one end of the social scale of *homines,* and serf on the other.

Thus the first act of the ritual, the first structure of the system creates an unequal relationship between lord and vassal.

The second act, the act of *faith,* noticeably alters things. Because I think the detail important, I want to recall that it is marked by a symbolic gesture, the *osculum,* which is a kiss on the mouth. I will also recall for the reader my admission that I am not persuaded of the importance—as regards the essential significance of the gesture—of the hypothesis, assuming that it is correct, advanced by some legal historians, according to which in countries with unwritten law it was the lord who gave the osculum, while in countries with written law this initiative belonged to the vassal.[40] I reiterate that, if true, this fact would be of interest for legal history and, in a broader sense, for the history of cultural traditions. Nevertheless, the essential point is that the texts stress mainly the conjunction of attitudes and equality in the physical gesture. Galbert of Bruges, precise and attentive to terminological exactitude like a good attorney, says after stressing the asymmetry of the *interlacing of hands:* "They became allies with a kiss." And Guillaume Durand, who gives the initiative of the kiss to the lord even though he is writing in a country with written law, stresses that the meaning and purpose of the symbolic gesture was to establish a mutual faith: "And the lord, as a sign of mutual fidelity, kisses him (the vassal)."[41]

We cannot be satisfied, however, with merely examing the evidence of the texts. If the joining of hands fits into a very rich but rather clear symbolism of gesture, the kiss involves a symbolism no less rich but considerably less clear, with a large and complex variety of practices and significations. I shall return to the kiss presently.

I shall begin by turning to the ethnologists. Despite the variety of ethnological theories, the kiss *on the mouth* seems definitely to be connected with beliefs which prescribe exchange either of *breath*[42] or *saliva.*[43] The practice is reminiscent of the exchange of blood found in other kinds of solemn contracts or alliances. Of course, I do not think that the lords and vassals of the medieval West were aware of engaging in an exchange of this type, and, despite the "paganism" conveyed by their Christianity, I do not see how they could have been conscious of exhibiting the beliefs underlying these practices. I do think, however, that lords and vassals had preserved some of the essential symbolic significance of the initial rite. The exchange of breath or saliva, like the exchange of blood, apart from other consequences to which I shall return, took place between equals, or, rather, made the participants *equal.*[44]

Finally, investiture is clearly related to the practice of the gift/ counter-gift. After the inequality-equality phase, the system is completed with a genuinely mutual bond, a reciprocal contract. It suffices to look once more at the end of the ritual described by Galbert of Bruges in 1127: "Then with the wand which he held in his hand, the count gave investiture to all those who had done homage to him and promised him their fealty and taken an oath on it."[45] Everything is included here: the definition of the ceremony as the conclusion of a *pact* or contract and the counter-gift of the investiture which corresponds to the gift of homage and faith (oath).

In 787, at the chronological beginning of the process, Tassilo had been confirmed in his duchy of Bavaria in exchange for his oath of fealty ("And Tassilo having renewed his oaths, he was permitted to keep the duchy"),[46] and, in a manner still more closely related to vassalage, Harold, in 826, had received vineyards and fertile lands from Louis the Pious in reply to the homage and oath which made him a faithful servant of the emperor.

"Meanwhile Caesar made offerings to Harold, who was thereafter his faithful servant . . . of vineyards and fertile lands."[47]

Jacques Maquet has observed this aspect of vassalage in an African institution based on the gift/counter-gift, in which a man who has done homage and promised service is invested with a fief consisting of livestock, which calls to mind the probable source, according to etymology, of the medieval fief. The institution in question is that of the Ruandan *ubuhake*. "By *ubuhake*—a word which comes from a verb meaning 'to pay homage by visiting'—one man promises another that he will provide certain allowances in kind and in service and asks that he be given the use of one or more head of livestock." *Ubuhake* creates a reciprocal bond between a lord (*shebuya*) and a vassal (*garagu*).[48]

Thus the system is complete.

No doubt reciprocity is established already in the *homage* and reinforced by the *osculum*, but only investiture of the fief, by offering the material counter-gift in response to the promises made by the vassal in doing homage and swearing fealty, puts a seal on the mutuality of the contract of vassalage. Marc Bloch stressed this reciprocity, which corrected—without eliminating—the inequality between lord and vassal. Comparing—in order to point out the differences—feudal bonds with forms of free dependence found in other civilizations, he wrote: "The very ceremonies perfectly express the contrast. The 'prostration' of the Russian 'men of service' and the kissing of hands practised by the warriors of Castile contrast with the French form of homage which, by the gesture of hands closing upon hands and by the kiss on the mouth, made the lord no mere master with the sole function of receiving whatever was due to him, but a partner in a genuine contract."[49]

Finally, it should be noted that if homage, the oath, and investiture of the fief constitute a single complete system, the significations of the successive symbolic rites do not destroy but rather complement one another. There is no contradiction in the fact that the system of vassalage is a contract between two persons, one of whom, the vassal, while remaining inferior to the other (an inferiority "symbolized" by homage), becomes, as a consequence of a mutual contract (whose "symbol" is the fief), his equal in relation to all who remain outside the system of contracts. In Jacques Maquet's terms, vassalage "is a societal relationship at the origin of a network, identified by a name known to all members of the society at large."[50]

At the second level of interpretation of the system of symbolic gestures of vassalage, we go beyond each of the phases and elements and consider the system as a whole.

In fact, the rites of vassalage that we observe in medieval western society constitute a comprehensive *symbolic system*, and this system is *novel*, as I will try to show in what follows.

Merely because the system is novel in its comprehensiveness, however, we should not infer that it was built up without reference to a general model of some sort.

I believe that social systems can express themselves symbolically by reference either to economic models, to political models, or to familial models.

One may consider an economic model insofar as the investiture of the fief, which we have seen was a necessary complement to homage and the oath, represents a counter-gift with an economic significance both fundamental and obvious, regardless of what form the fief takes. Yet neither of the two principal economic models of reciprocity found in preindustrial societies seems applicable to the feudal system of vassalage.

The potlatch system, on the one hand, cannot be the model for the feudal gift/counter-gift, because it is inappropriate to speak of potlatch in a society where the practice is not economically generalized. Potlatch cannot be limited to a customary practice. In the case of the medieval West, whatever the economic importance of the feudal system of vassalage was, it did not exhaust the whole range of the medieval economy. It shared the field with allodial property and with exchange of a precapitalist variety and so accounted for only a portion of medieval economic practice. Furthermore, although the feudal gift/counter-gift did bring prestige and women into play in the system of exchange, it was a part of an economic and social structure different from the type in which potlatch operates. More generally, and perhaps simplistically, we may say that the potlatch model of reference is not applicable to the feudal system of vassalage because medieval western society and economy, though in certain respects similar to so-called "primitive" societies, are in other respects quite different.

Second, the contract system, as it existed in the Roman world (and in Roman law), offers no more satisfactory a model for the feudal system of vassalage. The Roman system included transfer of property, as, for example, in the contract of *emptio/venditio*, while in the feudal contract of vassalage, the lord did not give up *dominium* to the vassal. It is probably unnecessary to point out that, although medieval society was not as innocent of either the notion or the practical aspects of property as has been said, it is nevertheless true that the contract of vassalage, and the investiture in particular, established a hierarchy of rights and obligations rather than a transfer of property from lord to vassal.

One may next consider a reference system of a political type. Just as the prominence of the gift/counter-gift or contractual aspect of vassalage symbolism suggested an economic reference, some if not all of the symbolic gestures associated with the ceremony of entry might be referred to the sphere of *power*. The *immixtio manuum* might bring to mind the *manus* of Roman law, the incarnation and ultimately the synonym of *potestas*. But in the symbolic ritual of vassalage, the *manus* is not an abstract concept. What is important, significant, and even symbolic is what the hand *does*, not what it is. Similarly, the *osculum* might call to mind the idea of a transmission of vital force, and consequently of strength, a magical transfer of power(s). But even if this was the original meaning of the kiss in these or any other societies, I must reiterate that it is alien to the meaning of the *osculum* in the vassalage ceremony, or at least has disappeared by the time the oath of fealty has become part of a complete system. Even if its significance was closely related to that of the *kiss of peace* of Christian liturgy—a possibility I shall rule out shortly—it would have established a relationship between lord and vassal different from that of a transmission of power. Like the *immixtio manuum*, the mouth-to-mouth kiss places the two participants in a hierarchical relationship, in the one case on a footing of inequality, in the other of equality. Finally, one could—as, indeed, some have actually done—single out among the symbolic objects of investiture the emblems of power (ring, staff, sword, scepter), in particular the frequently found stick, which has been identified with a symbol of command. Where emblems of power are concerned, however, historians and jurists have erroneously confused (as men of the Middle Ages themselves sometimes did—but they had their reasons) ecclesiastical or royal investitures with investitures of vassals, although in my view two clearly different systems are involved. I shall return to this question. As for the stick, I refer the reader to the

critique by von Amira and Marc Bloch of von Moeller's thesis.[51]
Finally, it is worth pointing out once more the well-known fact that
the contract of vassalage created a system of mutual obligations; it
was not the transfer of *potestas* over the fief from the lord to the
vassal.

Finally, we should warn against the temptation to use communal
seigniory as a model, which would lead to applying to the feudal
system of vassalage those forms of power which have rightly been
identified and emphasized in connection with the former institution.
In the first place, banal seigniory was a development of the manorial
regime which does not reflect the essence of the system of vassalage,
and while it is wise to insist on the links between fief and seigniory,
they must be carefully distinguished in other respects.

We have now reached the point where we must state and attempt
to justify the central hypothesis of this essay. The essential reference
model for the symbolic system of vassalage was a familial model, a
kinship system.

The vocabulary itself impels us to look in this direction.

The vassal is defined essentially as a "man of mouth and hands."

We repeat that what is important about the hand is what it *does*. It
plays a part in each phase of the ritual. In the *homage,* it serves to
unite the lord and the vassal in an unequal encounter. In the *oath,* it
is placed on the Bible or relics as a confirmatory gesture accompanying the kiss of equality. In the *investiture,* it either gives or receives,
as the case may be, the object that seals the contract. I have ruled out
the reference to the *manus* of Roman law because, since Roman times,
the word had become an abstract term synonymous with power, but
I cannot overlook the fact that it denoted in particular the power of
the *paterfamilias,*[52] and that in medieval Christianity one particular
hand, if I may say so, was singled out above all others: the hand of
God the Father, everywhere present, as witnessed by iconography
for a start.

As for the *mouth,* i.e., the *kiss,* I find that it played a different role
from the ancient Christian liturgical kiss, which probably dates from
the time of Saint Paul, and from the kiss of peace, although in the
latter case there was probably contamination in the eleventh and
twelfth centuries, during which we often find charters speaking of
the *osculum pacis* and *fidei* in connection with various types of contracts. If the kiss of vassalage is comparable with another ritual kiss, I
should suggest the betrothal kiss, to which Chénon has also devoted
an excellent study.[53] More generally, the kiss marks the entry into a
nonnatural family community, especially marriage. The custom is
pre-Christian. It was in vain that Tertullian condemned it as pagan.[54]

Although these comparisons are useful as leads, they are not

proofs. In my view, more importance should be given to the place occupied by a particular symbolic object in the phase of investiture. I
am thinking of precisely that object singled out by Marc Bloch in the
article cited above. This was the *festuca*, literally "straw," which can
be a twig or small stick.

Word and object both have a long history.

We find evidence of that history (was it the beginning? probably
not) as early as in Roman law. Commenting on the fourth book of
Institutes of Gaius, Edoardo Volterra describes the *sacramentum in
rem*, the second of the acts, after the statement of the laws, which
make up the *legis actio*, as follows: "The first party (*actant*), taking a
small rod (*festuca*) in his hand as a symbol of the military spear,
stated the thing (or part of the thing) and pronounced the solemn
words... In response, the second party (*declarant*) laid the *festuca*
on the thing claimed." He adds: "As Gaius explains, given that
the *festuca* symbolized the military spear, this act, representing
occupation (in the military sense) (*occupatio bellica*), signified legitimate ownership of the thing (*signo quodam iusti dominii*)... If, on the
other hand, the third party (*convenant*) made the same declaration
and also laid his *festuca* on the same object, there were then two
equal declarations of ownership and two symbolic *occupationes
bellicae*."[55]

I will not belabor my conviction that this symbolism is inadequate
to explain the feudal ritual of vassalage. When lord and vassal use the
festuca, there is no question of ownership or of a right acquired by
military occupation.

The *festuca* took on a new appearance in medieval institutions.

We had best proceed here by letting Paul Ourliac and J. de
Malafosse have the floor:

> Among the Franks there existed a strange act, *affatomie* (Salic
> Law XLVI) or *adoptio in herediatate* (Ripuarian Law XLVIII). This
> was a way of transmitting a patrimony which included some
> quite complicated formalities:
>
> a) The alienor had to appear before the tribunal of the *mallus*,
> in front of the *thunginus*, along with a third party from outside
> the family, often called *salmann*.
>
> b) He symbolically delivered the property to the latter by
> throwing the *festuca* (cf. vol. 2, p. 318), indicating the name of the
> actual donee on whom he wished to bestow his inheritance (*illo
> quem heredem appellat similiter nominet*).
>
> c) The intermediary then went to the home of the donor, in-
> stalled himself there, received at least three guests, served them a
> meal, and received their thanks; the purpose of this, the text
> adds, was to ensure that he had at least three witnesses to the fact
> that he had taken possession.

d) Finally, after a lapse of twelve months, the intermediary had to return to the *mallus* to give up all that he had received: he had to "throw the *festuca* at the actual heirs," thus delivering to them "neither more nor less" than he had received.

In Lombard law, there is an analogous institution, the *thinx:* before the armed populace (which calls to mind the Roman testament before the comitia), the *thingans* transferred a lance to the donee as a symbol of power, receiving from him a counter-gift (*launegild, guiderdone*). The idea of adoption is quite clear in this case, since the alienor must not have a male heir (ed. Roth., 157, 158, 170, 172; ed. Liutprand, 65).[56]

Although the use in Lombard law of the lance as symbol may accord with the symbolic interpretation of the *festuca* in Roman law as representing a military lance, it is clear that for our purposes the greatest interest attaches to the texts from Ripuarian and particularly Salic law.

The differences between the Frankish ritual and the feudal ritual of vassalage are obvious: the role of the intermediary, the lapse of time involved in completion of the act, the absence of reciprocity—to consider only the ritual, without taking account of the completely different context: there is neither homage nor oath, and possession rather than rights is transferred, in contrast with the ceremony of vassalage.

Nevertheless, there is still the solemnity of the act, the presence of witnesses, the role of a superior, the same symbolic object (*festuca*), and the necessity of a gesture (a *throw*, of course, rather than the tradition involving hands and the breaking of the stick or straw).

This characteristic alliance of a gift with the establishment of a personal relationship gives the impression, even though we are still a long way from the feudal ritual of vassalage, that a decisive break has occurred with respect to the custom of the *festuca* in the Roman *sacramentum in rem*. The important accent falls on the *adoption,* on the transferral of a *patrimony,* on the entrance into a family. In the *Monumenta Germaniae Historica,* the editor of the volume on Salic law, K. A. Eckhardt, does not hesitate in his index to translate the term denoting the custom of *affatomie, acfatmire,* as *ankinden.*[57] The German word cogently expresses the idea of entry into a *familia.*

If we have singled out the *festuca* among the symbolic objects connected with the ritual of vassalage, this was not merely because Roman law and Frankish law of the early Middle Ages make it possible to trace the prior history of this object. Nor is it because the common translation of *festuca* as "stick" [*bâton* in French] brings us close to those erudite scholars, from Du Cange to von Amira, who were particularly interested in such symbols in the institutions of the past, and the Middle Ages in particular. It is also because, to our knowledge, among symbolic objects of the vassalage ritual only the *festuca* has given rise to a family of words which, we believe, offers proof that it played a fundamental role in the practice as well as the symbolism of vassalage.

Of course, lacking a special study devoted to these terms, we can say only that the derivatives of *festuca* seem to have been primarily employed in speaking of the exit from vassalage and of abandonment. In his pioneering article, which we have already cited several times, Marc Bloch gives numerous examples of the verb *exfestucare* and the noun *exfestucatio*, the action of breaking off homage by throwing the *festuca*.[58] Du Cange, however, vouches for the existence of the verb *festucare*, with the following noteworthy example taken from a charter of count Philip of Flanders dating from 1159, from the chartulary of Saint Bertin: "triginta septem mensuras, quas a me tenebat, in manus meas reddidit et *festucavit*"; and he goes on to cite an *infestucare* with the meaning *in possessionem mittere, adheritare*.[59]

We mentioned the *festuca* among the symbolic objects given by the lord to the vassal at the time of investiture; so it is easy to understand how *festucare* or *infestucare* may have been regarded as synonyms for taking possession and *exfestucare* as a synonym for abandonment. But Marc Bloch, in contrast to J. Flach's interpretation (and before him, in the sixteenth century, Etienne Pasquier) of the throwing of the straw as the "counterpart of investiture," made the following observation: "The texts are unanimous and precise: none says *feodum exfestucare*; almost all say *hominium* or *dominium exfestucare*. The vassal is renouncing homage, i.e., the personal bond which attached to him to the lord, and lordship, i.e., all the rights which made the lord superior to him."[60] Here, I think, we have proof that, since the early Middle Ages, the *festuca* played an essential role in a practice which was less a transfer of goods or rights than an adoption procedure, and hence that the *exfestucatio* relates primarily to the personal bond. Furthermore, this shows that the symbolic system of vassalage was a whole, all of whose parts were essential. I do not, however, follow Marc Bloch when he adds that the vassal who broke off homage in this way was in no way renouncing the fief but rather intended to deprive the denied lord of his rights over the fief, which would then have passed to the new lord to whom the vassal would do homage. It is quite likely that the vassal intended to keep his fief and that he justified his gesture of *exfestucatio* by the unworthiness of the lord, who, by reason of his failure in his duty, should, in the vassal's opinion, have been deprived of the latter's service and of his rights over the fief. I doubt, however, that the vassal's performance of *exfestucatio* allowed him the legal right to keep his fief. Moreover, in the text of Galbert of Bruges discussed by Marc Bloch, it is the lord, the Count of Flanders, who has the idea (which he cannot put into practice owing to the unfavorable balance of power) to *exfestucare* his vassal Ivan of Alost (*exfestucasset* Iwanum). As Marc Bloch clearly observed, once again it is the person who is rejected and the personal bond that is broken, but in breaking off the vassal's homage the lord is also and perhaps primarily thinking of the fief he would like to confiscate. Investiture, together with homage and fealty, form a juridically (and, if I may say, symbolically) indissoluble unity. If the vassal breaks off his homage to the lord by *exfestucare*, then he must at the same time give back the fief. If he does not do so, the resulting situation is one of fact, not of law; legal justification must be obtained in another way, according to another system.[61]

We have just put forward the hypothesis that the reference model for the symbolic system of vassalage was a kinship system. In order to clarify the implications of this hypothesis and to stimulate study of kinship systems as a way of deepening our comprehension of the feudal system,[62] I will close this portion of my essay with a few refinements.

Clearly, the kinship model that we believe to have been the reference for the symbolic system of vassalage is not that of "natural" kinship. Roman law, as well as certain other factors, might incline one to think of a patron-client relationship or an adoption model. The client idea must be set aside. Of the basic differences between the two systems we cite only one, which we think essential. One became a client by a private act, while one became a vassal in a public ceremony. The model of adoption deserves closer scrutiny, if only because of the possible role of *affatomie*. To my knowledge, however, the Middle Ages were only dimly aware of the problem of adoption. Furthermore, although *affatomie* does furnish leads to be followed in interpreting the symbolism of the rites of vassalage, the differences between the two rituals are serious, and this is important in the area of symbolism.

One might also think of a friendship structure. The Middle Ages invested the word friendship with a very powerful content (attested by literature: friendship plays a large role in the gest, with Olivier's for Roland as prototype) as well as a quasi-judicial, institutional character (we need only think of the role of "friends by blood" in the lineal system).[63] This is another lead to follow up, though I do not expect much to turn up in this direction, either.

A good deal of progress is still to be made in the study of kinship structures, familial relations, and interpersonal bonds in medieval society. We may anticipate some far-reaching results. For our purposes, however, it is not likely that future research will add much to what, in our view, are the two most important observations which can be made by way of provisional conclusion to this study of the symbolic *system* of vassalage.

First, I should make it clear that I am not claiming that this system is copied from a kinship system or that the relationship between lord and vassal must be as one between father and adoptive son or between friend (in the medieval sense) and friend. I mean that the system's symbolism, as it appears in the ritual of entry into or exit from vassalage, was perceived (more or less consciously—I shall return to this important point) as a symbolism related to the domain of family symbolism, and structured as such. In my view, a society possesses only a few basic symbolic systems, to which all other systems refer. In the case of the symbolic gestures of vassalage, this referent was the system of gestures associated with kinship symbolism.

Second, the symbolic system of vassalage did not embrace all members of the society. Just as kinship symbolism excludes (what is left outside the family model) more than it integrates, the symbolic gestures of vassalage not only exhibited this exclusion but were also responsible for bringing it about, among their other functions.

The society of kinsmen created by the symbolic ritual of vassalage was masculine and even virile, as well as aristocratic. In other words, women and commoners were excluded. A masculine society: if we return to the case cited by Chénon involving the homage done by a minor child to his lord, the bishop-elect of Carpentras, in 1322[64], we observe that although the child requires the assistance of his governess in doing his homage (the lord takes in his hands the hands of both child and governess), it is the child alone who gives (or receives) the *osculum*, the governess being excluded ("remisso ejusdem dominae tutricis osculo"). I have already stated my skepticism as to the interpretation offered by the author of the charter, who invokes decency ("propter honestatem"). To me, the real reason for the exclusion of women seems to lie in the social hierarchy with which the hierarchy implicit in the symbolic system of vassalage was confronted. Homage was the phase of inequality. Woman was allowed to participate in this part of the ritual. The faith, on the other hand, as symbolized by its component kiss, was the phase of equality between the partners. As a minor from a social and religious point of view, the woman could not receive it. In reality, of course, greater latitude was probably shown at times, but primarily on a more elevated level, where great ladies or, in particular, women in possession of royal authority were involved, such as Doña Urraca, with regard to whom Alfonso the Battler used the expression "your men of mouth and hands."[65]

An apparently stronger objection to this interpretation comes from another quarter, the ritual of courtly love. I will not discuss here the problem of whether or not this love was purely literary in character. It is a fact that, in courtly love, the man is the woman's vassal and that an essential part of its symbolic system is the kiss. It is important to point out, however, that, in principle at least, courtly love in the twelfth century was a scandalous phenomenon of protest and a manifestation of an inverted world.[66] Nevertheless, it is true that the highest expression of the system of courtly love was in the Marian cult, where the contamination of Marian ritual by the ritual of vassalage is striking. It is significant, I think, that the only time that Georges Duby speaks of symbolism in connection with the gestures of social existence in his celebrated thesis on *La Société aux XIe–XIIe siècles dans la région mâconnaise* is in connection with the Virgin. "The rite of dedition," he writes, "which, it seems, was different from the rite of commendam, was not forgotten in the eleventh century: the abbot Odilo of Cluny, who wished to indicate his submission to the Virgin, passed a symbolic cord around his neck and became her *servus*."[67] Although vassalage is not involved and the symbolic gesture of inferiority is not an act of homage, we recognize here an early example of inversion of normal social relations, which the Marian cult would bring to a peak. Christianity, through its practice of humility and asceticism, has always held such scandalous social inversions to be sacred. Although courtly love and the Marian cult do, at their inception, bear witness to a certain improvement in the status of women in medieval society during the growth period of the eleventh and twelfth centuries, their function nevertheless appears to have been to stabilize and coopt the "feminist" movement of the Romanesque era, diverting its energies toward the sentimental, aesthetic, and religious idealization and alienation of the Gothic age. The courtly kiss, therefore, in spite of appearances, is, I think, not relevant to our concerns.

Also excluded from this hierarchy of equals, if I may be permitted such a paradoxical expression, was the commoner or villein. We have only to quote a passage that marvelously illustrates this exclusion. It is from Guillaume de Lorris, in the first part of the *Roman de la Rose:*

> Je vueil pour ton avantage
> Qu'orendroit me fasses hommages
> Et me baises emmi la bouche
> A qui nus villains home ne touche
> A moi touchier ne laisse mie
> Nul home où il ayt villenie
> Je n'i laisse mie touchier

Chascun vilain, chascun porchier;
Mais estre doit courtois et frans
Celui duquel homage prens.[68]

(For your sake from this day / From my person I shall turn
away / Any man low-born or uncouth / Who would do me homage or kiss my mouth. / No man who is base / May have leave to
touch my face. / Neither swineherd nor villein / Will tomorrow
my presence gain. / He to whose homage I agree / Must be one
both courtly and free.)

There can be no doubt that in certain regions, at least, commoners
and even serfs acquired fiefs and did servile homage, an interesting
phenomenon which requires further study. But the enfeoffed commoner would never be a real vassal. The symbolic kiss, the *osculum,*
was refused to him as it was to women.

Clearly, we should find some part of the system wherever servile
homage existed. But neither the commoner nor, for even stronger
reasons, the serf entered fully into the symbolic system. It is therefore impossible to draw any conclusion from Charles-Edmond Perrin's interesting remark that in Lorraine in the early twelfth century,
the granting of a peasant holding to a tenant was expressed in legal
documents by the word *investire.*[69]

The exclusions thus support our interpretation of the symbolic
gestures associated with vassalage as expressive of a relationship
which, through a reciprocal commitment sanctioned by the fief,
makes the lord and vassal equals by virtue of the oath and a hierar-
chized couple by virtue of the homage.

III   RESTORING THE SPATIO-TEMPORAL PERSPECTIVE

In order to improve our understanding of how the system operated
and what its function was, it will be useful to study its geographical
variants and its chronological development.

I will be brief on this subject for two contrasting reasons.

First, a detailed geography and chronology of the rites of vassalage
have yet to be established, although the standard works were concerned about these problems, and a good many monographs do provide invaluable bits of information. Nevertheless neither the map
nor the evolutionary curve has been plotted, a deficiency which
makes it quite hazardous to try to relate our own point of view to this
still incomplete and frequently unreliable context.

Second, there is a consensus as to certain regional or "national"
peculiarities on which it would be pointless for me to expand, since I
have been unable to make any serious effort to verify these accepted
ideas, which, on the whole, appear well founded and correct.

A. The Geographic Perspective

From our point of view, the one important novel element in the symbolic ritual of vassalage is the *hand kiss*, which seems generally to have replaced the *immixtio manuum* in Spanish homage. Generally speaking, this custom reinforces the symbolism of inequality which marks this first phase of the ritual. In a more restricted sense, it strengthens certain features peculiar to feudalism as it existed in medieval Spain: oriental influences (although the Arab influence probably only reinforced the earlier Visigothic and Byzantine influences), and the prominent role of royalty (the ceremony being fundamentally a royal rite).

We mentioned above that Chénon and the traditional historians of medieval law believed that the gesture of *osculum* was different in countries with written as opposed to unwritten law.[70] Although I am not entirely persuaded by this argument, it does point out the importance of the cultural boundary between northern and southern countries, in which the difference in kind of law and the unequal degree of Roman influences are, to my mind, merely supplementary, though certainly quite important, elements in a more far-reaching and profound cultural split. Here again, it would be desirable to have a comparative study treating the whole ritual.[71]

Similarly, it would be useful if we possessed a study of the Italian case from the point of view of symbolic ritual, on the assumption that Italy was a uniform entity in this as in other areas.

Italy very early shows a tendency toward rigidity of ritual in the realm of symbolic gesture, since it was quick to employ writing in connection with these ceremonies, and what is written down is more difficult to change than what is not. A suggestive remark of Gina Fasoli's brings this to mind: "Another Italic tendency was to set down in writing the customary norms that governed feudal relations." In support of this hypothesis, we may cite a Carolingian text addressed to the kingdom of Italy, in answer to a question that had been asked. "If the lord is able to undertake the defense of his vassal after the latter has commended himself by placing his hands in the lord's, and if said defense is not undertaken, the vassal is permitted to withdraw his homage from the lord."[72] The author points out that "this is the first explicit statement of the bilateral character that the relation of vassal to lord had begun to assume."[73] This remark is also useful as a reminder that it is artificial to separate spatial from temporal considerations, as we are doing here for the sake of clarity.

The so-called "imported" feudalisms are also worthy of investigation: those in Spain, to a certain extent (and also Italy, as the passage cited by Gina Fasoli recalls), but primarily in Norman England and in the Latin states in the East. Does the symbolic ritual of vassalage in these cases reveal the same "pure form" of feudalism that some others have been pleased to find in them? This could prove quite illuminating for the definition of the symbolic "system," although I remain somewhat skeptical as to the reality of the concept of "imported feudalism." In the first place, my doubts arise from the arbitrariness of saying of a historical institution that it was "pure" in one instance and not in another. Furthermore, I do not believe that institutional or cultural borrowings are successful, or even that they are actual historical occurrences. To take root, a foreign model must find the ground already prepared and must adapt to new conditions. In this as in other respects, I find the notion of "purity," which accompanies that of "importation," to be antiscientific, and in the present instance, antihistorical.

On the other hand, I do believe that our understanding of a given historical phenomenon could profit from the study of regions where there was acculturation (such as those cited above) or which were boundary zones on the fringes of medieval Christendom and feudalism. These areas are too often forgotten by medievalists. More than the zones of contact with the major competitors or adversaries (Byzantium and Islam), which were mainly areas of conflict and rejection of alien forms, the areas of contact with "paganism"—Ireland, Scotland, Iceland, Scandinavia, the Slavic countries—deserve to be studied on a variety of grounds and according to a different chronology.

B. Chronological Perspectives

In spite of the gaps, the hazards of record keeping and preservation, and the lack of interest that we have noted on the part of medieval clerics in the ritual of vassalage, such documents as we do have allow us to ascribe dates to the evidence.

One point seems certain. The system, in all essential respects, was in place at the end of the eighth century, and this must have been the time of its formation. The silence of earlier texts accords with what we know of early medieval society, which was not yet, in the strict sense, "feudal."

Two further remarks are called for, however.

First, most of the evidence concerns relations between personages of very high rank, frequently of royal rank.

The *Formulae Marculfi* (first half of the seventh century) concern the antrustion of the king. The "first known example of the oaths of vassalage" involves King Pepin and Tassilo, Duke of Bavaria (757). The text of 787 in which we witness the commitment of the vassal by means of a symbolic object, "a stick with a human figure carved at its head" (*cum baculo in cujus capite similitudo hominis erat scultum*), concerns Tassilo III, Duke of Bavaria, and Charlemagne. And one of the earliest texts to describe the whole ritual—homage, oath, and investiture, with gestures, words, and symbolic objects—that of Ermold the Black (826), features the Danish King Harold and Emperor Louis the Pious.[74]

Of course, the writers were particularly interested in ceremonies involving "stars," which seemed more worthy of record; still, the text relating Tassilo's submission to Pepin, for example, stresses that this act was no different from what vassals performed for their lords: "As by law a vassal must do, with a loyal spirit and steadfast devotion, as a vassal must have toward his lords"[75]—which proves that vassalage was widespread in the Frankish aristocracy and that a ritual of vassalage existed.

The selectivity of the documents, however, shows that the important part of the ritual of vassalage at this time was the homage, a sign of recognition of the lord's superiority and of submission to it. There is nothing surprising about this if one bears in mind that what probably assured the success of the institution of vassalage was the use made of it by the Carolingian dynasty with the intention of creating its own network of loyal supporters.

The second observation is of a similar nature. Even if, as I have stated, the system was complete as early as the end of the eighth century, investiture was clearly the weakest and least distinctive feature of the rite. This accords well with what is known of the origin of the fief, which would later become the perfected form of the benefit or honor that the vassal received from the lord in exchange for his homage, oath of fealty, and service.

Apparently the connection had not yet been made (assuming that this was the way things happened—a permissible interpretation of the origin of the symbolic system of entry into vassalage) between a ritual that created a personal bond, and another (the ritual of *affatomie*, for instance), using the *festuca* for a symbol, that was primarily intended to transmit an inheritance, a piece of property, through a personal bond or adoption viewed more as a means of transferring the property than as the end in itself of the institution and ritual.

Nevertheless, there is one point, of the first importance in my view, on which the system was not completed before perhaps the end of the tenth century. This was the *osculum*, or kiss, which sealed the oath and faith. The text in the Saint Gall collection which describes how Notker, abbot-elect of that monastery, became a vassal of Otto I in 971 ("Finally, he kissed him. And soon, a gospel book was brought, and the abbot swore fealty") is given by one of the leading historians of feudalism as "one of the earliest examples" of the kiss of vassalage.[76] It should be noted, moreover, that here the kiss precedes the oath.

That the *osculum* came to complete the system only at the end of the tenth century remains to be proved or to be shown to be a virtual certainty through as complete as possible a study of pre-eleventh-century texts. If true, it would accord with and complement what we know of the general historical trend.

If, in fact, the symbolic *osculum* was the element that established a certain equality between lord and vassal, as well as the most trustful act in the agreement between the two parties, the gesture that went farthest toward engaging their faith, then it can be fitted quite well into a twofold pattern of evolution.

In the first place, there was the appearance of the *peace* movement, which grew inexorably around the year 1000. Although, as I have said, I do not believe that the kiss of vassalage was a transfer of the Christian kiss of peace into the feudal symbolic system, it was nevertheless influenced by the religious atmosphere that was that of the era in general and of the peace movement in particular.[77]

The second phenomenon with which introduction of the *osculum* into the ritual of vassalage would fit in especially well was the growing self-consciousness of the military class around the year 1000. I am bearing in mind, of course, that this was also the class of large property owners, so that even ecclesiastical patrons thus found themselves involved in the feudal institution of vassalage. It was at the end of the tenth and the beginning of the eleventh centuries that the tripartite, trifunctional schema of society was perhaps constituted and in any case diffused; this doctrine was expressed in its most arresting form in 1027 by Adalbero of Laon. In contrast to the *oratores* and *laboratores*, the *bellatores* established themselves not merely by virtue of their military role but also through the accompanying institutions, powers, and symbols, such as the fortified castle and the feudal system of vassalage. The *osculum* was one of these emblems, the mortar that held together this hierarchy of equals and excluded women and commoners from it. This feudal hierarchy also played a major role in the peace movement led by the Church. To a certain extent, this was directed against the *bellatores*, but it was also carried on *with* their cooperation, as the Church wanted to make them the guarantors of order, particularly by using their military capabilities to protect other social categories, which could be done thanks to the strength of the network of vassalage.[78]

Let us turn next to an important characteristic of the feudal system in the medieval West which the use of ethnographic methods and the focus on symbolic expression enables us to bring to light. I am thinking of the system's *novelty*. I have tried to give some indications of this above, by rejecting any possible assimilations of feudal to prior institutions, to Roman institutions in particular, and by arguing against attempts to establish continuities between these and the feudal system. I will endeavor to prove my case below by means of comparisons with closely related systems in both modern societies and non-European societies of the period. Although I have looked to *affatomie* and the *festuca* in Salic and Ripuarian law and Lombard edicts as one of my major themes in this essay, this was only to clear the ground for two hypotheses: that the symbolic ritual of vassalage refers to a kinship system, and that there were barbarian institutions and rites in the early Middle Ages revealing a society with structures that seem ripe to have produced the symbolic system of the vassalage ritual. Nothing more. I do not see in these societies the *origins* of either the system of vassalage or its symbolic ritual. There was, of course, a *genesis* of this system, and I have tried to indicate some of the central points and important moments in this process between the end of the eighth and the end of the tenth centuries. Still, although the system was *original* (in the sense of novel), I believe *it had no origins*. Surely, it did make use of elements from earlier models and elaborated solutions in part closely related to institutions found in other societies in other eras on other continents. Without such selections and "borrowings," without such kinship, there would be no point to history or comparative study. Nevertheless, I think that the search for the origins of vassalage, as of many other things, is rather fruitless.

This, we know, was Marc Bloch's position at the end of his too brief life. It was not entirely his position in his youth, at the time he wrote his article, "Les Formes de la rupture de l'hommage dans l'ancien droit féodal." I hope the reader will allow me to quote at some length from this pioneering text, for the passage in question seems to me to have far-reaching consequences for our work.

> Hitherto, however, I have left unmentioned an example taken by von Moeller from Frankish law. Title LX of Salic law indicates the procedure to be followed by a man who wants to abandon his family, his kin; the essential feature of this procedure is the following: the man takes three or four sticks—the figure varies with the different manuscripts of the law—breaks them above his head and throws the pieces to the four corners of the *mallum*. It would be fascinating to prove a filiation between this rite, which marked abandonment of the family in Frankish law, and the quite analogous rite by which . . . abandonment of the lord was sometimes marked in twelfth-century law. It would be of considerable interest for the problem of the "origins of

feudalism" to establish a filiation between the solemn act by which the family bond, surely one of the strongest social bonds in the old Germanic societies, was broken, and the act by which, six centuries later, the bond of vassalage, the master link of a new society, was broken. I do not think there is much argument that one can bring against such a theory. Neither do I think it possible to base it on any solid proof: perhaps there is no filiation but only similarity between the two rites. The present hypothesis will be accepted or rejected according to what general conception of vassalage one holds.[79]

I will therefore not treat the problem of "origins," which I do not think relevant. Marc Bloch's remarkable flair for history, already supported by a considerable erudition, had led him toward an intuition of great importance. To shed some light not on the origins but on the structure and function of the system of vassalage, and in particular on its symbolic apparatus, it is important to turn our attention to the laws of the Germanic peoples, particularly the Franks, in the early Middle Ages. Combining prudence with bold hypotheses and a sense of differences and novelties with an interest in comparisons and continuities, Bloch's genuine historian's instinct had already taken him far from the much belabored problem of origins. He contrasts the "old Germanic societies" with a "new society"—the feudal. And in comparing rites, he ultimately prefers to envisage "similarity" rather than filiation.

This is our position. We must indeed look to the Germanic societies of the early Middle Ages not for the origin but for the system of representations and symbolic references on which the system of the symbolic gestures of vassalage was built.

Since this is a lecture [as originally conceived—Transl.], I hope I may be permitted to end this part of my argument with three brief methodological remarks on the study of symbolism in history.

Among the many pitfalls to be watched out for in the history of symbols, three are particularly to be feared: false continuities (symbols change their meaning in a disconcerting way), false resemblances (comparative study, always delicate to handle, is even riskier here, just as it is even more necessary), and, finally, the polysemy of symbols, which frequently makes their interpretation uncertain: which of many possible meanings is the correct one? (Often, two diametrically opposite meanings are possible.) In view of these dangers, it is imperative that we consider a symbol in its context or, preferably, in the system to which, in general, it belongs.

There is another serious problem, complicated by the absence of texts: what awareness did participants and spectators have of the symbolism of a symbolic act? The point is, to a certain extent, moot if one accepts the ethnographic method, since this assumes that a symbolic system can be fully effective without explicit awareness.[80]

IV PROBLEMS

The preceding discussion included a certain number of hypotheses and research problems along with some substantial and well-documented propositions. Several important problems remain to be formulated, however, which I shall do as I give some further details concerning the method proposed for attacking them and make a few additional comments.

Although I have mentioned a kinship model as reference for the vassalage ritual, this does not mean that I am assimilating family ceremonies to the ceremonial of vassalage. While it is not without interest to observe the role of the *osculum* in betrothal, I do not think that the symbolic gestures of vassalage and those of betrothal must be considered as belonging to a single, unified whole. In studying the *osculum* in both these rituals, Chénon quite commendably sought to make useful comparisons between them, and he pointed out a very significant phenomenon, the use of the *osculum* in abandonment.[81] As with the *festuca*, the presence of the *osculum* in both the entrance and the exit rites supports our conviction that a system is involved. To broaden the meaning of the *osculum* to a vague guarantee that a contract will be observed, however, seems to me to dilute the symbolism to the point where it no longer signifies very much. One of the temptations—and dangers—connected with the study of symbols is the desire to find a common denominator for practices, functions, and meanings which in reality were different.[82]

Similarly, certain medieval contracts involved a symbolism which I think was different from the symbolism of the feudal system of vassalage. The only commonality is the use of the same symbolic objects. These details—at bottom, they are only details—are not without interest. A society's store of symbols is limited, and in defining a medieval social entity, it is important to compare the collections of symbolic objects used in different domains and to note the recurrence of certain objects in several of them. Du Cange was well aware of the unity of medieval symbolic material. While a mistaken viewpoint rooted in Roman law led him, in the article on Investitura in his glossary, to define the term as "traditio, missio in possessionem" (delivery, transfer of possession), he was nevertheless able through this error to grasp a certain unity of the symbols found in contracts and investitures. This accounts for his interesting view of the function of symbolism: "Deliveries and investitures were accomplished not only by oral agreement or a mere document or charter, but also by various symbols."[83] By the same token, I thought it would be

270

interesting to give the list of "juridical symbols employed in contracts, procedure, etc.," in Merovingian and Carolingian times, as compiled by Thévenin. Comparing this with the list taken from Du Cange for the subsequent period, we first observe the preponderance of identical terms, the general agreement of the two lists. The importance of the *festuca* is striking and significant. The frequency of the monetary symbol (*denarius*) is the sign of an era in which money still had its symbolic, if not economic, value. The single occurrence of *osculum* is relatively insignificant, for it comes in connection with a marriage rite in accordance with the Roman law then still in force.[84] At the risk of repeating ourselves, we may say that though the resemblances between the lists of Thévenin and Du Cange suggest that a social structure and symbolic complex was being established between the seventh and ninth centuries, and that the system of vassalage would look thereto for its references, they do not in any way prove that the feudal bond of vassalage was of the same nature as the bonds determined by a broad variety of other contracts, and are even less convincing as evidence that such contracts were the origin of the system of vassalage.

Betrothals and contracts aside, we encounter the major problem of royal rites. One has only to read Professor Elze's fine essay[85] to see at once that the two rituals and two domains of symbolism are completely different. Though it is possible to draw from the divine rite or "investiture" the impression that the king profited from a symbolic system which made him a vassal of God, a glance at the ceremonials and symbolic objects reveals at once that neither system can be reduced to the other. On the one hand we have a wholly sacred ritual which brings the king into a religious system, on the other a profane ritual (despite the use of Christian marvels) which brings the vassal into a socioeconomic system. There are two systems, one royal, the other "familial" and aristocratic; two symbolisms, one of transmission of cosmic, supernatural power, the other of familial integration.

No doubt the occasional confusion between the two is due to the use made of vassalic property and the feudal system by the Carolingians, the Holy Roman Emperors, and popes (some of them, at least). Yet the two symbolic domains are fundamentally different.

Certain ethnologists specializing in Africa have attempted to introduce the concept of feudalism into the study of African societies, which is commendable, but they made the mistake, I think—and I shall come back to this point—of looking for common features in royal ceremonials and seeking to base their comparisons on political systems and analyses of power structures. The political reference is either totally alien to the feudal system in the medieval West, or strictly secondary.

271

One major problem remains untouched: that of ecclesiastical investitures and their symbolic system of reference. Two facts are beyond question. First, by way of the theory of the two powers, spiritual and temporal, the medieval Church long confused the systems of temporal investiture and of ecclesiastical ordination at all levels. The quarrel between the Priesthood and the Empire known as the "Investiture Conflict" perpetuated and deepened the confusion, and the ambiguity was not really cleared up by the Concordat of Worms (1122), which accorded the pope spiritual investiture by staff and ring and the emperor temporal investiture by the scepter. Furthermore, I think that the ordination ritual and, at the other pole of the system, the ritual of reduction to lay status, aggravated the confusion. Still, a closer examination of symbolic rituals is needed, and such confusion as comes not from modern historians but rather from the men of the Middle Ages themselves should make us prudent about asserting that the symbolic ritual of vassalage was not only novel but also autonomous. There was such a degree of contamination between the ecclesiastical function and the fief that confusion on this point, such as we notice in Du Cange, is not without foundation. In the present state of research, the most that one can tentatively say is that ecclesiastical "investiture" was copied from investiture in vassalage, and that the rites of entry into vassalage were models for the rites of entry into religion.

B. An Attempt at an Ethnographic Type of Interpretation

Thus far I have given no explicit definition of the sort of ethnographic method I am advocating and which I have attempted to apply in the foregoing to the analysis of the symbolic gestures of vassalage. I did mention that this method called for comparisons between the society we are studying and other societies usually studied by the ethnologist rather than the historian. This means that we must temporarily neglect questions of time and place. I have already availed myself of an African example taken from Jacques Maquet. I have also stressed the fact that the method leads to the definition and study of a *ritual*—a ceremonial system traditionally studied by the ethnologist rather than by the historian. Lastly, I have pointed out that in studying a ritual it is imperative not to isolate the elements—the phases and symbolic objects used—but rather to seek their significance within the system in general.

Nevertheless, I have analyzed the ritual of entry into vassalage on the basis of evidence selected by historians and in terms of the phases and components which they drew from the texts according to their own criteria. This analysis took no account of important elements of ritual commonly neglected by historians. The sort of data I have in mind stems more from the context of the description of the ceremony than from the ceremony itself and consists of information which transcends the system of gestures-words-objects implicit in the analysis of the historians.

A more comprehensive ethnographic interpretation of this type is what I shall attempt. What follows is only an outline, since a more intensive collection and interpretation of data than I was able to undertake would be required to carry the study farther.

This analysis will treat the place of the ceremony, the persons present, the respective positions of the participants, and the memorization of the ritual.

a) Entry into vassalage did not take place in just any location, but in a symbolic space, a ritual territory. In a classic study, Jean-François Lemarignier has shown the role of borders as sites for vassalage rituals: this was known as "homage on the march."[86] In the text by Thietmar of Merseburg cited above, it was on the occasion of a trip made by the emperor Henry II to the eastern borders of Germany that acts of homage were done to him.

More generally, we frequently find indications that the participants in vassalage rituals traveled to the site. Sometimes it is the lord who comes to receive the vassal's homage; sometimes it is the vassal who appears before the lord to undertake symbolic acts. In the text of the *Annales regni Francorum,* for example, in connection with the event of 757, we read: "The king Pepin held court at Compiègne with the Franks. *There came Tassilo,* Duke of Bavaria, who commended himself in vassalage by his hands." Similarly, in Galbert of Bruges's text, the new Count of Flanders, William Clito, Duke of Normandy, comes to Flanders to receive the homage of his new vassals; the latter come into his presence, however, in Bruges, where they do homage. It is significant, I think, that the historian Robert Boutruche begins the extract from this text which appears in the documentary section of his book with the beginning of the ceremony of vassalage proper, neglecting the previous phase of traveling, which, to us, appears to be a part of the complete ritual.[87]

Although the lord himself often goes to a particular place for the ritual, the significant journey, from a symbolic point of view, is made by the vassal, who always goes and presents himself to the lord. Such travel has a dual function: it situates the ritual in a symbolic location, and it begins defining the nature of the bond which is to be established between lord and vassal by emphasizing that it is the latter, the inferior, who is showing deference to the lord by coming to him.[88]

In the vast majority of cases, the symbolic space in which the ritual of vassalage is accomplished is either a church or the great hall of the castle (or one of the castles) of the lord.

If it is a church, the symbolic function of the site is that of being itself a sacred space, thus augmenting the solemnity of the ritual accomplished and the contract sealed therein. Frequently, moreover, it is specified that, when possible, gestures are to be executed in the most central, most sacred part of the edifice: the altar, *super altare*. The oath is sworn on the altar, and the symbolic object of investiture placed thereupon.[89]

The other site is of even greater significance, and a detailed investigation might prove it to be the site par excellence of the feudal ritual of vassalage. This is the lord's *aula*.[90] The ceremony takes place on the lord's territory, at its very center, in the place where his role and power are displayed, where he holds audiences and stages luxurious festivals which—in dress, food, and spectacular extravagance—are expressive of his rank and role. The fact that the vassal travels to the lord's terrain (for even in the church, the lord has—by law—an eminent place) is, I think, additional proof of the inadequacy of an interpretation of the ritual of vassalage in terms of adoption. In fact, the opposite occurs: the vassal "chooses" his lord.

b) The symbolic ritual of vassalage does not take place in private. The presence of spectators is required. Normally, there are many of them, and they are a select group. This is not merely to provide a guarantee for the performance of the ritual act in the form of witnesses. It is part of a symbolic system. The presence of spectators creates a symbolic social space in the midst of the symbolic material space.

We find abundant evidence for the existence of this large crowd of onlookers in such expressions as "in the eyes of many," "with the advice of all the spectators," "in the presence of many," etc.[91]

Were these spectators at some distance from the principals in this symbolic space, or did they flank or surround the participants? The evidence provided by iconography is of rather late date and has not, as far as I know, been much studied. One would welcome a monograph furnishing information on the vassalage system comparable to that which P. Walter has obtained in his remarkable study of the iconography of ecumenical councils.[92]

Frequently, especially when the ceremony is described in a document of a juridical nature, like those drawn up by notaries in certain regions from the thirteenth century on, we find that the principal personages present are mentioned by name.[93]

Jacques Maquet has noted the presence of a public of spectators in certain African societies where rites similar to those of vassalage are practiced. This is what distinguishes vassalage from a patron-client relationship. Maquet gives the following explanation for the presence of spectators. "The ceremony makes the feudal bond public. It makes known that a given individual has become the vassal of a given lord."[94]

The spectators did not, I think, play a merely passive role as witnesses but had a more active function as well. Along with the lord, they received the vassal into the masculine and aristocratic society which was "feudal" in the full sense of the word. They were witnesses and guarantors of the mutual commitment of lord and vassal. If the function of the site is to reinforce the hierarchical and inegalitarian aspect of the system of vassalage, then it seems to me that the role of the spectators, by contrast, is to reaffirm the reciprocity of the system.

c) It is also important to take account of the respective positions of the participants during the ceremony. Unfortunately, detailed information on this point is sparse in the documents.

Was the lord seated? On what kind of seat? Was he on a raised platform of some sort?

Was the vassal standing or on his knees?

Did the respective positions of the two participants change during the ceremony?

Do we have the same symbolic significations here that we found in the ritual of vassalage: hierarchy, equality, reciprocity?[95]

Did the positions of the participants refer to the symbolic complex associated with kinship? Although our previous consideration of the two factors of site and spectators may not have confirmed our hypothesis, what we found was certainly compatible with it: church and *aula* were spaces in which marriages took place, and the spectators may have been the same as those who assisted at family ceremonies, but these data are too general and vague to allow us to argue one way or the other.

d) Finally, we must consider elements of the ritual which were intended to insure its perpetuation and memorization.

The witnesses were one of these elements—along with such written documents as were sometimes drawn up, of course, but these represent only a particular case of a broad range of techniques of memorization; writing long had no precedence over other forms.

Another element was the conservation of the symbolic object.

It should be noted first that the object was not always within reach. In this case, Chénon has observed, the *osculum,* curiously enough, could replace the delivery of the object.[96] The texts which show this substitution deserve closer study.

Was the object kept? Who kept it? Where? At the present stage of research, I can only put forward several hypotheses: the object was usually kept; if it was one of the two participants who held it, it was generally the lord; but most frequently the object was kept on neutral and sacred ground, in a church, for instance, even if the ritual did not take place there.[97] On rare occasions, apparently, the object was divided, one part kept by the lord and the other part by the vassal.[98]

Borrowing a distinction traditionally made by Germanic feudalists, F. L. Ganshof stated that when the symbol was one of action, it was either kept by the lord (scepter, rod, gold ring, glove) or broken if of little value (e.g., a knife). When the symbol was an object, the vassal kept it.[99]

I am skeptical of this distinction. In the first place, the difference between *Handlungsymbol* and *Gegenstandsymbol* is not very clear to me. Second, the list includes objects which seem to be parts of the monarchical ritual (scepter, rod, gold ring) rather than the ritual of vassalage. The texts, in any case, need to be reexamined one by one. Finally, I do not think the answers are quite so clearly delineated.

It should not be forgotten, however, that the instruments for perpetuation and memorization of the symbolic ceremony are part of the ritual.

C. References in Other Societies

I will take my examples primarily from non-European societies, particularly African, because I find that they offer the most suitable material for comparison aimed at demonstrating the novelty of the Western medieval system, both because of the types of socioeconomic and cultural structure and because of the type of approach employed by Africanists.

I am not going to discuss the parallel—well known to medievalists—between the medieval West's feudal system of vassalage and Japanese institutions before the Meiji restoration. This particular parallel is useful and enlightening, but the invaluable and detailed works of F. Joüon des Longrais in particular lead, I think, to recognition of important differences between the two systems. Our analysis of the Western system through the medium of the symbolic ritual supports the idea that vassalage and fief were indissolubly linked. Whether the fief was the crowning touch or the foundation of the system, only investiture, as its constituent symbolic gestures make clear, achieved the element of reciprocity essential to the system. No such linkage of vassalage and fief existed in the Japanese system, however.[100]

The subject deserves extensive study. Here, I will confine myself to giving a few references[101] and to stating two or three ideas.

Japan has been the object of so much discussion in comparative work for two reasons. First, Japanese "feudalism" appeared at approximately the same time as our Western variety. Second, the commonly held opinion that Japan had remained "feudal" until 1867 made it easy to find records of its "survival" in the modern period, much richer in documentation. Since there was no question of one "feudalism" having influenced the other, chronological considerations were relatively unimportant.

But why not look to China? The institutions that have been called "feudal" there were established very much earlier than in the medieval West, since the specialists regard the Chou dynasty (c. 1122–256 B.C.) as the "classical" period of Chinese feudalism.

Henri Maspéro prudently chose to ignore a work on which several sinologists had based work on Chinese "feudalism": Li-chi's *Memoirs Concerning Rites,* a collection of Confucian ritualistic pamphlets written between the end of the fourth and the beginning of the first century B.C. He found it difficult to decide whether this book was a description of reality or a work of the imagination.[102] On the other hand, he was quite interested, with good reason, in an inscription from the eighth century B.C. describing the "investiture" of a high royal officer: "In the morning, the king went to the temple of king Mou and took his place ... The officer K'o came in through the door and took his place in the middle of the court, facing north. The king shouted: 'Chief of the Yin family, prepare the tablet prescribing the duties of the officer K'o.' The king spoke thus: 'K'o, formerly I had mandated that you should execute and relay my orders. Now I increase and exalt (?) your duties ... I give you a piece of land at Ye ... ' K'o honored the king by prostrating himself."[103]

I will neglect the problem of what institution we are dealing with here and the fact that, rather than vassalage and enfeoffment, it seems to involve something similar to the fief of function, possibly comparable with the Russian *tchin.* It should be noted that the Chinese, more sensitive than Westerners to the symbolic significance of the ceremonial, carefully describe the time that the ritual takes place (morning), the symbolic site (the temple of king Mou), the situation of the two main actors (the king takes his place, the officer K'o takes his place in the middle of the court, facing north), as well as the fact that both actors have to travel to the ceremony. Furthermore, though the king may have gone to the temple, there is greater stress on the movement of the officer, which is described in detail, including the fact that he enters the symbolic and sacred space through the door. There is at least one spectator, a sort of scribe or notary, the chief of the Yin family, who prepares the tablet. Words are involved in the ceremony, but only the king appears authorized to *speak* in order to pronounce the ritual formulas. On the other hand, the recipient of the honor salutes the king *by prostrating himself,* which evidently represents an *act of respect for a superior,* but I do not know whether it is addressed to the king or to the "lord" who has entrusted to him the office and the land, nor whether it merely expresses gratitude or is *homage* in the sense of "vassalage."

In the valuable collection of essays on comparative feudalism in history edited by R. Coulborn, Derk Bodde gives important details concerning investiture ceremonies during the Chou period.[104]

Here is his description: "The nobles were confirmed in the possession of their territory through a ceremony of investiture which took place in the Chou ancestral temple. There the new vassal, after receiving from the king a solemn admonition to be conscientious in his duties, prostrated himself before him and was given a jade scepter and a written tablet bearing the terms of his enfeoffment. Often these were accompanied by other valuable gifts, such as bronze vessels, clothing, weapons, chariots, and the like."[105] Here again we find the symbolic site (the ancestral temple of the Chou), the royal speech (a solemn exhortation), the silence and prostration of the vassal, and the tablet in evidence of enfeoffment. In addition, there are details concerning the symbolic objects given in the course of the ceremony. Both similarities and differences between this and the feudal ritual of vassalage in the medieval West are apparent. The cultural content is different: writing in the form of a tablet plays a major role in China, unlike the West; the symbolic objects are much more valuable in the Chinese case, and the receipt of a *scepter* (of jade) along with the tablet seems to express transmission of power, which, to my mind, is lacking in the West in the Middle Ages. The vassal's silence and prostration tend to emphasize his subordination to the lord more than the contract binding the two personages. It is true that the lord in this case is the king, which makes this example difficult to compare with the normal Western pair, the latter being situated on a lower symbolic and social level.

Derk Bodde provides further details: "When a new fief was created, the invested noble received from the king a lump of earth taken from the altar of the national Lord of the Soil, which then became the nucleus for the localized altar built by the noble in his own fief."[106]

If we once again neglect the fact that the lord is the king, we can make two comments. The religious character of the institution and ritual is more emphatic than in the previous texts. For the first time, we find not merely a rural symbol but stress on the centrality of the agricultural reference through the role of the Lord of the Soil. Still, we may ask whether the reference has to do with ownership of the land or control of the territory.

Derk Bodde gives us his view of the etymology of the term denoting the institution that apparently corresponds to the Western fief: "The word *feng* means, among other things: a mound, to raise a mound, to earth up (a plant), a boundary, to determine the boundaries of a fief, to enfeoff."[107]

Here, it does look as though the significance of the rite was primarily territorial, without, of course, overlooking the fact that the fief was territory, a piece of land. The Chinese institution thus calls attention to the symbolism of borders—which we have encountered before—and, more particularly, to the material embodiment and symbolism of boundary markers, which played a well-known role in the Roman world. This has not yet been adequately studied in the case of the medieval West.[108]

The Chinese case, then, is an interesting one, inviting a closer analysis of the ritual, an analysis that would take account of "sites—movements of the principals—reciprocal value of gestures, words, and objects—function of the onlookers." Nevertheless, for reasons previously indicated, it is by turning toward Africa, as we shall now do, that we may hope to glean the finest fruits of comparative study.

I am going to draw from two comprehensive works, Jacques Maquet's *Pouvoir et société en Afrique* (Paris, 1970) and the collection of articles assembled by M. Fortes and E. E. Evans-Pritchard, *African Political Systems* (London, 1940), as well as a number of articles.[109]

As a good many African specialists have pointed out, the institutions studied in these works concern in general the region of the Great Lakes and, more broadly, central and eastern black Africa. I will not consider the question of whether this has more to do with the novel features of these societies (and the kinship of their structures) or with the fact that, for one reason or another, students of Africa have focused their attention on this region.

Except for Maquet's work and works used by him, and J. J. Tawney's article on a feudal custom among the Waha, all the studies are concerned with "royal" ceremonial. This is not the place to discuss whether the term "king" should apply to the persons of rank considered by these studies. It is true, nevertheless, that there are clear and profound differences between the ceremonials represented in these works and the ritual of vassalage. Hardly anything other than the transmission of certain symbolic objects can be said to be similar in the two cases. In the African ceremonies, however, the objects in question are *emblems of power* and the forces involved are clearly *political,* which is not the case with entry into vassalage. There is a crowd representing the populace, along with a few high-ranking individuals with special roles, such as members of the royal family, priests, and dignitaries, but there is only one hero, the "king." The function of the rites is to assure *continuity* and to perpetuate or foster fertility and prosperity. More generally, as Meyer Fortes points out—borrowing an expression from Marcel Mauss's celebrated *Essai sur le don* (1925), in a remark that is also valid for royal rituals in the medieval West, which we have excluded from our investigation—these ceremonies concern "total institutions," which incorporate "politics and law, rank and kinship, religious and philosophical values and concepts, the economics of display and hospitality, the aesthetics and symbolism of institutional representation, and last but not least the social psychology of popular participation."[110]

Does this mean there is nothing in these studies useful for our purposes?

I am going to single out two ideas put forward by eminent African experts concerning royal "investiture" ceremonies.

The first relates to what Audrey I. Richards calls "social mnemonics" in the case of the Bemba in northern Rhodesia.[111] In all these ceremonies, it is important to take careful note of what is aimed at the social memory, what is intended to insure perpetuation of the symbolic commitment. I believe that A. I. Richards's remark on the investiture of the supreme chiefs of the Bemba is valid also for the ritual of entry into vassalage in the medieval West: "More important as charters of political office are the relics themselves and the ceremonial by which they are handled."[112] Of course, the relics used in the medieval West were different in kind and function from those used in African royal ceremonials. In the former case, they were only tokens of the commitments made and oaths sworn, while in the latter, they "validated the exercise of authority and were a means of access to the supernatural powers on which that authority depended." In both cases, however, the witnesses to the ceremony and the symbolic objects used in it and preserved afterward carried more weight than written texts. In the justification of many rights, it was certainly of great importance in the medieval West that a charter be drawn up and preserved (although the charter collections assembled by their beneficiaries were neither as systematic nor as numerous as one might infer from the very useful cartularies created by nineteenth- and twentieth-century scholars). Nevertheless, such fundamental institutions as vassalage and monarchy depended for their perpetuation more on the continuity of rites, transmission of symbolic objects, and collective memory than on written texts of investitures *per chartram* or charters of entry into vassalage, which played a quite secondary role.

Furthermore, I believe that at least part of what Meyer Fortes has written about "installation ceremonies" is applicable to the ritual of entry into vassalage and investiture. He is persuaded that only anthropological research can reveal "the mutuality in the connexion between occupied office and the society in which it is encapsulated."[113] He points out that in installation ceremonies "the community must directly participate both through its representatives and as a congregation."[114] Here, of course, this requirement derives from the fact that a total institution is involved. I wonder, though, if a detailed examination of the ritual of vassalage would not show that the role of spectators went beyond that of mere witnesses, and that the ceremony's symbolism needs to be expanded beyond its two principal characters, the lord and the vassal.

Still, the comparative data collected in African societies are limited and disappointing, to judge from my information, at least. Perhaps this particular trail is more or less a dead end. But I think the confusion thus far between royal rites and rites of vassalage has blocked the comparative path. The fault often lies with historians, who have started anthropologists down the wrong paths.[115]

I am afraid, however, that the tendency of African specialists to turn toward political anthropology, while it has the merit of reacting against the excesses of a timeless and static anthropology, opens them to the risk of getting bogged down in the misleading explanations implicit in certain recent problematics involving the concept of power; as a result, they neglect the study of the fundamental social and economic phenomena, the kinship structures to which they refer, and the singular symbolic systems connected with them.[116]

Still, when African specialists have studied institutions and rites related to those of medieval Western feudalism, both differences and similarities have appeared.

Going beyond the analyses of the *ubuhake* in Ruanda, which I have already used, Jacques Maquet makes the interesting observation that "an essential aspect of the relation of dependence is that protector and dependent choose each other because of their individual qualities ... With the exception of the marriage tie, the other networks all subject each actor to the tutelage of all the other actors ... It sometimes happens, moreover, that a dependency relation becomes hereditary ... Even in that case, a vestige of choice remains: both heirs must reaffirm the continuance of the bond which united their predecessors. This initial choice bestows an individual quality on the ensuing relationship, which stimulates confidence and even friendship."[117]

I will not enlarge upon the references to the matrimonial tie and friendship, which, though interesting, are more metaphoric than scientific. Instead, I will concentrate on the reciprocity of desire which has been noted in vassalage. In addition to the words expressing this choice or desire (cf., in Galbert of Bruges, "the count demanded [of the future vassal] if he wished without reserve to become his man, and the latter answered: 'I wish it.'"), one needs to investigate whether this voluntary aspect of reciprocal personal choice is reflected in the ritual.

Finally, the *ugabire* studied by J. J. Tawney as a "feudal custom" of the Waha is more comparable, I think, to the *precarium*, since it is a way for a man of small means to place himself under the protection of a wealthier man by asking if he is willing to exchange livestock for services. The livestock, of course, takes the place of the land or tenure which was generally the object of the precarium.[118] Tawney does not say whether the agreement to a *ugabire* contract gives rise to a ceremony which includes a ritual.

The author does, however, give some interesting further details concerning the relationship between the *Mgabire* who has obtained the *ugabire* and his superior, as well as the symbolic manifestations of this relationship:

> The relationship of Mgabire and patron is a subtle one; it is necessary for the Mgabire to salute him on certain occasions, partly, it seems, because there is a feeling that the patron is superior in rank and partly to make sure that the Mgabire demonstrates the continuance of the bond before the world. The slight feeling of a difference in rank is not one that arouses any resentment; on the contrary it appears to be bound up with the affection existing at the back of the relationship, and a Mgabire acquires a reflected glory from his patron's "*heshima*"; the Mgabire greets his patron as "Datajuba," which means "Father-Master," but he is the only person who can so address him—if others wish to refer to a Mgabire's patron they call him "Shebuja."[119]

Thus we see inequality compensated by reciprocal and partly emotional bonds contracted in the presence of outside witnesses, as well as the use of a vocabulary of the "kinship" type. Despite the great differences, then, we find ourselves, socially speaking, on common ground with the feudal contract of vassalage.[120]

Thus, although comparative study does provide some useful similarities and does call for further inquiry into the conditions under which a society creates its institutions, as well as the symbolic procedures which make them work, its main value, in my view, is that it emphasizes the novelty and specificity of the system of vassalage in the medieval West.

D. The Role of Christianity

As one might expect, Christianity appears in virtually every phase of the ritual of vassalage. In the first place, even if neither of the two participants is a cleric, the ceremony can take place in a church, one of the preferred locations—along with the lord's *aula*—for the entry into vassalage. It is even fairly frequently specified that the ceremony take place in the most sacred part of the church, *super altare*.

The *oath,* an essential part of fealty, was usually taken on a religious object, even one particularly sacred, such as the Bible or relics.

As can be seen in the list taken from Du Cange's article *Investitura,* the symbolic object of investiture was sometimes an ecclesiastical or religious object (staff and ring, chalice, bishop's crook, candelabra, keys to the church, abbatial cross, prioral hat, communion—an act could replace the object, just as the *osculum* could, cakes of incense, missal, monastery rule, psalm book, etc.). It is true that Du Cange has relied heavily on investitures involving clerics, in many cases ecclesiastical investitures, and, as I have pointed out, their connections to rites of vassalage in the proper sense are still questionable. Even in the ecclesiastical case, however, although the participants in the ceremony were laymen, the symbolic object was kept in a church.

On the other hand, even if clerics were parties to the contract and involved in the sanctioning ceremony, the symbolic object could perfectly well be profane. I will cite one case which offers certain interesting details. Frédéric Joüon des Longrais has devoted an excellent study to the charters of the priory of Hatfield Regis, in Essex, a dependency of the celebrated Benedictine abbey Saint-Melaine of Rennes, in Brittany.[121] In 1135, a Chamberlain of England, Aubrey de Vere, enfeoffed to this priory two parts of the tithes from the domain of Reginald Son of Peter at Ugley. He did so using a broken knife as a symbol, and the knife, with a black horn handle 8.2 centimeters long and a broken blade 3.1 centimeters long, attached by a braid of harp strings to the left side of the document registering the act, which had a hole pierced through it, was still preserved in the library of Trinity College, Cambridge, when Joüon des Longrais wrote his study (and is no doubt still there today). The document is traditionally known, moreover, as the "deed with the black hafted knife." In it we find mentioned an invaluable detail. The transfer as fief of these tithes by Aubrey de Vere to the monks of Hatfield Regis was done - "for the soul of his predecessors and successors."[122] Thus it is possible for the religious character of a contract of vassalage to reside in the lord's intentions.

There is nothing surprising in all this. Since medieval Western society was Christian, and medieval Christianity was rich in rites and symbols, we should expect to find the mark of the dominant ideology on the ritual of one of its fundamental institutions, the occasion of a public ceremony.

Here we find several important functions of the medieval Church: its tendency to monopolize sacred spaces (churches), its efforts to supply the only absolute guarantees for oaths sworn on the Bible and relics (strengthening the role of Scripture and the cult of the saints), its preeminent position as interpreter and guardian of the collective memory, and its zealous promotion of the glory of God, hence of the Church, and of individual and collective salvation as the justifications for the most important social activities, beginning with those of major economic consequence. The Hatfield Regis document is one indication of the great movement by which the feudal aristocracy was brought to root itself solidly, in the twelfth century, in a *longue durée* of familial existence; prayers for the dead (*pro animabus antecessorum et successorum*) would lead to the invention of a purgatory that facilitated the creation of a web linking the living and the dead.

Still, the ritual was neither Christian nor even truly Christianized. It had nothing in common with the dubbing ceremony—totally Christianized—which would emerge around the middle of the twelfth century. No preparation of a religious nature was required, no fast or vigil such as the future knight had to make, no celebration of a Christian office, no rites with Old Testament resonances, bringing into play the typological symbolism so widespread in the twelfth century. It is true that the ecclesiastical world was involved in the institution of vassalage in three ways: in a temporal sense, it was a part of the system (there were ecclesiastical lords and vassals); there was contamination between temporal and ecclesiastical "investitures"; and the system was largely consistent with its ideology (hierarchy, reciprocity). Yet the ecclesiastics did not succeed in doing with the ritual of vassalage what they nearly succeeded in doing with the ceremony of knighthood, magnificently reflected on the artistic and ideological level by Chrétien de Troyes: forging an intimate union between *knighthood* and *clergy*. If there was a confusion in the system between religious and secular forms, it was on the level not of the *osculum* but rather of the faith (*fides* or *fidelitas*?)

If I am correct in thinking that an institution can be clarified through ethnographic study of its ritual, there is nothing specifically Christian in the ritual of vassalage. I hope I have shown this in the case of the *osculum;* there should be no mistake about the role of the hand, either, in particular in the *immixtio manuum* of homage. The extensive polysemy of the hand must not lead to a confusion of institutions or symbolisms.

We see how such confusions may become established in the article entitled "Homage" contributed by Dom H. Leclercq in 1925 to Dom Cabrol's *Dictionnaire d'archéologie chrétienne et de liturgie*. The author compares rites of homage with those of entry into religion. He gives the example of an act of the abbey of Farfa in 801: "and once more, Perculf delivered himself *into the joined hands* of the lord abbot Mauroald in order to live in the monastery under the holy rule."[123] He points out that, according to the rule of Saint Benedict, a child offered to a monastery by its parents is shown at the altar, its hand wrapped in the altar cloth, and adds that the gesture "is equivalent to a homage between the hands of God." This equivalence is very dangerous! The rite of oblation of the child is much earlier than the institution of vassalage, which it has nothing to do with. What we ought to see in the Farfa document is an example of the old custom of *commendatio manibus* or *in manus,* which, as Dom Leclercq himself says, had come "to be employed in any sort of patronage or relationship of protection."

By way of contrast it should be noted that in what Dom Leclercq acknowledges to be the oldest text to mention the *immixtio manuum,* the Marculf formula of the seventh century,[124] when the king describes the new antrustion as "coming here in our palace, with his weapon, and having sworn, in sight of all, *in our hand,* fidelity," he is referring not to the *commendatio manibus* but rather to an oath sworn "between the hands of the king."

In the ritual of vassalage, by contrast with what takes place in dubbing, Christianity merely provides the setting and accessories—important as they may be—but neither substance nor symbolism. The ritual of vassalage is essentially profane rather than pagan, for though the system did borrow certain elements from pre-Christian practices, these again, in my view, were only isolated details, objects, or gestures.[125]

Two additional questions will suffice to conclude our rapid survey of this final problem.

We have seen in the examples cited that in black Africa and to an even greater degree in China, the religious, sacred character of the ritual is more marked than in Europe. Is this due to the fact that in most cases these were royal rites or rites in which the king took part? This was also the case in the medieval West. Or is it true that these civilizations and societies are or were more highly sacralized than was the medieval West?

Finally, we know that one of the indications of the religious character of dubbing was the fact that it usually took place—in the twelfth and thirteenth centuries in any case—on the occasion of an important Christian festival, Pentecost. Here we plainly see the continuity with paganism, for which this date was of great importance in the rituals marking the beginning of the warm season, and it is undoubtedly important to note what pains the medieval Christian Church took to obliterate all traces of pagan origin in the dubbing ceremony. This was unnecessary in the ritual of vassalage. Moreover, it was practically impossible for ceremonies of entry into vassalage and investiture to take place at a fixed date, assuming that there may have been precedents or calendar references. The travels of the lords, the date of the death of lord or vassal occasioning renewal of the contract and rites, the vagaries of the "politics of vassalage" in the feudal class all justify the fact that such dates as we possess for vassalage and investiture ceremonies vary considerably. Are there no favored dates? As we try to interpret its symbolism, it would be useful to ascertain that the ritual of vassalage is not concealing any calendar reference.

Conclusion: Faithful Servants, Hence Vassals

Having reached the end of this preliminary outline of an attempt which still includes many hypotheses, I offer two general observations by way of conclusion.

First, my interpretation of the feudal ritual, which gives a leading role to the personal bond, does not in any way reduce feudalism to a mere phenomenon of mentality.[126]

The novelty of feudalism in the medieval West was in fact its association of investiture of a fief with a personal commitment, and we may, in distinguishing motivations from causes, also distinguish superstructures from infrastructures, even though the methodological reflections of certain anthropologists inspired by Marxism[127] tend toward the idea that every society functions through the agency of structures in which a portion of the superstructure acts also as infrastructure.

In the case of feudal investiture, there would be no bond of vassalage if investiture of the fief were not rooted in homage and faith. The symbolic system shows that we are dealing with a unified whole. It is not "faithful servants *or* vassals," it is "faithful servants *and* vassals."

My second and final observation is that, even if we take account of the fact that the symbolic scientific thought of medieval Christians was a way of deciphering the deeper reality underlying appearances, this symbolic interpretation cannot satisfy us.

A symbolic system, to borrow the concept recently put forward by Dan Sperber in his essay "Le symbolisme en général" (1974), signifies nothing. It is not a reflection or a translation. It is a body of words, gestures, and objects, which, structured in a way that must remain essentially intangible, makes the whole something more than the mere sum or combination of its parts, something that brings the whole into the sphere of the sacred, a certain species of the sacred. In this respect as in many others (e.g., "political Augustinism"), medieval thought schematized and impoverished the most far-reaching and profound aspects of Augustine's conception. The symbolism of feudal investiture seems to me to belong to the sphere of the familial-sacred.

I will conclude with a comparison which, I hasten to say, does not express the essence of feudal investiture but is a simple way to present more clearly my tentative hypothesis concerning its interpretation. Just as Christians became members of the Christian family through baptism, or, in other words, joined the faithful and hence became Christians, so vassals became members of the lord's family through investiture, that is, they joined his *faithful servants and hence became vassals.*

NOTES, BIBLIOGRAPHIES,
AND APPENDIXES

The documentation for each essay—whether in the form of notes, selected bibliographies, appendixes, or a combination of these elements—will be found grouped together under the respective essay titles.

ABBREVIATIONS

Annales E.S.C.	*Annales: Economies. Sociétés. Civilisations*
CSEL	*Corpus scriptorum ecclesiasticorum latinorum*
DACL	*Dictionnaire d'archéologie chrétienne et de liturgie*
MGH, AA	*Monumenta Germaniae Historica, Auctores antiquissimi*
MGH, Script. rer. Lang.	*Monumenta Germaniae Historica, Scriptores rerum Langobardicarum*
MGH, Script. rer. Mer. (*MGH, SRM*)	*Monumenta Germaniae Historica, Scriptores rerum Merowingicarum*
Ottob. lat.	*Ottoboniani latini*
PG	J.-P. Migne, *Patrologiae cursus completus, series graeca*, 162 vols. (Paris, 1857–66)
PL	J.-P. Migne, *Patrologiae cursus completus, series latina*, 221 vols. (Paris, 1844–64)

THE SEVERAL MIDDLE AGES OF JULES MICHELET

1. "And there then took place a strange dialogue between the time of the old, stood back on its feet, and me, its resuscitator." Michelet is speaking here of the Middle Ages in the important, hitherto unpublished text put out by Paul Viallaneix, "Michelet," *L'Arc*, no. 52 (1973), p. 9.

MERCHANT'S TIME AND CHURCH'S TIME IN THE MIDDLE AGES

1. Cf. esp. Henri Pirenne, *Histoire économique de l'Occident médiéval* (posthumous collection, 1951), p. 169.

2. Ms. Flor. Bibl. Laurent. S. Croce Plut. VII, sin 8, f°. 351. Cf. Guillaume d'Auxerre

(1160–1229), *Summa aurea,* III, 21, f° 225v: "The usurer acts in contravention to universal natural law, because he sells time, which is the common possession of all creatures. Augustine says that every creature is obliged to give of itself; the sun is obliged to give of itself in order to shine; in the same way, the earth is obliged to give all that it can produce, as is the water. But nothing gives of itself in a way more in conformity with nature than time; like it or not, every thing has time. Since, therefore, the usurer sells what necessarily belongs to all creatures, he injures all creatures in general, even stones. Thus even if men remain silent in the face of usurers, the stones would cry out if they could; and this is one reason why the Church prosecutes usury. This is why it was especially against the usurers that God said: 'When I take back possession of time, when time is in my hands so that no usurer can sell it, then I will judge in accord with justice.'" Cited by John T. Noonan, Jr., *The Scholastic Analysis of Usury* (1957), pp. 43–44. He points out that Guillaume d'Auxerre was the first to use this argument, which was repeated by Innocent IV (*Apparatus super libros decretalium*, V, 39, 48; V, 19, 6). At the end of the thirteenth century, the author of the *Tabula exemplorum* (ed. J. T. Welter [1926], p. 139) argues: "Since usurers sell nothing other than the hope of money, that is, time, they are selling the day and the night. But the day is the time of light and the night the time of rest; therefore, they are selling eternal light and rest." Cf. also Duns Scotus, *In IV libros sententiarum* (Op. Oxon) IV, 15, 2, 17.

3. Invaluable data are found in Giovanni di Antonio da Uzzano, *La pratica della mercatura*, ed. G. F. Pagnini Della Ventura, vol. 4 of *Della decima . . .* (1766), and in *El libro di mercatantie e usanze de' paesi*, ed. F. Borlandi (1936). For example, we find: "In Genoa, silver is dear in September, January, and April because of the sailing of the ships . . . in Rome or wherever the pope is located, the price of silver depends on the number of vacant benefices and on the pope's travels, which causes the price of silver to rise wherever he is . . . in Valence, it is dear in July and August because of the wheat and rice . . . , in Montpellier, there are three fairs which cause the price of silver there to be very high." Cited by Jacques Le Goff, *Marchands et banquiers du Moyen Age* (1956), p. 30. For speculation on the rate of circulation of information, cf. P. Sardella, *Nouvelles et spéculations à Venise au début du XVIᵉ siecle* (1949).

4. Cf. G. Post, K. Giocarinis, R. Kay, "The medieval heritage of a Humanistic Ideal: 'Scientia donum Dei est, unde vendi non potest,'" *Traditio* 2 (1955), 196–234; and Jacques Le Goff, *Les intellectuels au moyen age* (1957), pp. 104 ff.

5. Oscar Cullmann, *Temps et histoire dans le christianisme primitif* (1947), p. 35. Gerhard Delling, *Das Zeitverständnis des Neuen Testaments* (1940), cited in Cullmann, p. 35, note 2.

6. Cullmann, p. 32.

7. Ibid., p. 93.

8. Ibid., p. 98.

9. Ibid., p. 111.

10. Ibid., p. 152.

11. On millenarianism, see Ray C. Petry, *Christian Eschatology and Social Thought: A Historical Essay on the Social Implications of Some Selected Aspects in Christian Eschatology to A.D. 1500* (1956), which is entirely theoretical. It is still possible to consult E. Waldstein, *Die eschatologische Ideengruppe: Antichrist, Weltsabbat, Weltende und Weltgeschichte* (1896), and even Tommaso Malvenda, *De Antichristo* (Rome, 1604; 3d ed., 1647). Gordon Leff has opposed the historian's problems ("In search of the Millennium," in *Past and Present* [1958], pp. 89–95) to the abstract work of Norman Cohn, *The Pursuit of the Millennium* (1957). There are divergent views on the relations between medieval heresies and social classes. The social aspects are minimized by Father Ilarino da Milano, "Le eresie popolari del secolo XI nell' Europa occidentale," *Studi greg. raccolti da G. B. Borina* 2 (1947), 43–101 and A. Borst, *Die Katharer* (1953). In the

opposite direction there are: G. Volpe, *Movimenti religiosi e sette ereticali nella società medievale italiana* (1922), and the Marxist interpretations of N. Sidorova, "The popular heretical movements in France in the eleventh and twelfth centuries" (in Russian) in *Srednie Veka* (The Middle Ages, 1953), and E. Werner, *Die gesellschaftlichen Grundlagen der Klosterreform im 11. Jahrhundert* (1955). A survey by R. Morghen is to be found in *Medivo Cristiano* (1951), pp. 212 ff., and in the *Relazioni* of the tenth International Congress of Historical Sciences (Rome, 1955), vol. 3, pp. 333ff. There is a suggestive essay by Chrales P. Bru, "Sociologie du catharisme occitan," in *Spiritualité de l'hérésie: le Catharisme*, ed. R. Nelli (1953).

12. Georges Poulet, *Etudes sur le temps humain* (1949).

13. Marc Bloch, in *Annales d'histoire économique et sociale*, 1936, p. 582.

14. Henri I. Marrou, *L'Ambivalence du temps de l'histoire chez saint Augustin* (1950). On time in Saint Augustine, see, in the collection *Augustinus Magister*, Congrès international augustinien, Paris, 21–24 September 1954, 3 vols. (1955), the following articles: J. Chaiz-Ruy, "La Cité de Dieu et la structure du temps chez saint Augustin," pp. 923–31; R. Gillet, O.S.B., "Temps et exemplarisme chez saint Augustin," pp. 933–41; J. Hubaux, "Saint Augustin et la crise cyclique," pp. 943–50.

15. E. Bernheim, *Mittelalterliche Zeitanschauung in ihrem Einfluss auf Politik und Geschichtsschreibung* (1918); H. X. Arquillière, *L'Augustinisme politique* (1934).

16. Cf. P. Rousset, "La conception de l'histoire à l'époque féodale," in *Mélanges Halphen*, pp. 623–33: "The notion of duration and of precision did not exist for men of the feudal era" (p. 629); "the taste for the past and the need to mark off epochs was accompanied by a desire to ignore time" (p. 630); "the same sentiment flared up at the origin of the Crusades; the knights wanted to eliminate time and space and to attack Christ's executioners" (p. 631). The author echoes Marc Bloch, who uncovered in the feudal era "a broad indifference to time" (*La Société feodale* 1, p. 119 [Bloch's work has been translated as *Feudal Society*, Chicago and London, 1961.—Trans.]). On Otto of Freising, cf. H. M. Klinkenberg, "Der Sinn der Chronik Ottos von Freising," in *Aus Mittelalter und Neuzeit: Gerhard Kullen zum 70. Geburtstag dargebracht* (1957), pp. 63–76.

17. M.-D. Chenu, "Conscience de l'histoire et théologie," *Archives d'Histoire doctrinale et littéraire du Moyen Age*, 1954, pp. 107–33; reprinted in *La Théologie au XIIe siècle* (1957), pp. 62–89. See also Etienne Gilson, *L'Esprit de la philosophie médiévale*, 2d ed. (1948), chap. 19, "Le Moyen Age et l'histoire," pp. 365–82. On two "historians" of the twelfth century, cf. R. Daly, "Peter Comestor, Master of Histories," *Speculum*, 1957, pp. 62–72; and H. Wolter, *Ordericus Vitalis: Ein Beitrag zur Kluniazensischen Geschichtsschreibung* (1955).

18. M.-D. Chenu, *Archives*, pp. 210–20, "L'Ancien Testament dans la théologie médiévale." B. Smalley's work *The Study of the Bible in the Middle Ages* is fundamental. The symbolic aspect of Christian thought in the twelfth century has been treated by M. M. Davy in *Essai sur la Sybolique romane* (1955), which stresses only the most traditional aspect of twelfth-century theology.

19. M.-D. Chenu, *La Théologie au XIIe siècle*, pp. 66–67.

20. Ibid., p. 76.

21. Cf. Etienne Gilson, *Les Idées et les lettres*, pp. 183 ff., and P. Renucci, *L'Aventure de l'humanisme européen au Moyen Age*, pp. 138 ff. The Franco-Italian *translatio studii*.

22. M.-D. Chenu, *La Théologie au XIIe siècle*, pp. 79–80.

23. Ibid., p. 86.

24. Cf. H. Liebeschutz, *Medieval Humanism in the Life and Writings of John of Salisbury* (1950).

25. For a general view of the medieval merchant, see Y. Renouard, *Les Hommes d'affaires italiens du Moyen Age* (1949); A. Sapori, *Le Marchand italien au Moyen Age* (1952); Jacques Le Goff, *Marchands et banquiers du Moyen Age* (1956).

26. On monetary problems in the Middle Ages, see Marc Bloch, *Esquisse d'une histoire monétaire de l'Europe* (posthumous, 1954); C. M. Cipolla, *Money, Prices, and Civilization in the Mediterranean World, 5th to 16th Centuries* (1956); T. Zerbi, *Moneta effetiva e moneta di conto nelle fonti contabili di storia economica* (1955); R. S. Lopez, *Settecento anni fa: Il ritorno all'oro nell'Occidente duecentesco* (1955).

27. Cf. J. Meuvret, "Manuels et traités à l'usage des négociants aux premières époques de l'age moderne," *Etudes d'Histoire moderne et contemporaine* 5 (1953).

28. Cf. Raymond de Roover, *L'Evolution de la lettre de change* (1953).

29. Cf. R. H. Bautier, "Les foires de Champagne: Recherches sur une évolution historique," *Recueils de la Société Jean Bodin: La Foire* (1953), pp. 97–147.

30. Published by J. Rouyer, *Aperçu historique sur deux cloches du beffroi d'Aire: La bancloque et le vigneron* (P.J.I.), pp. 253–54; G. Espinas and H. Pirenne, *Recueil de documents relatifs à l'histoire de l'industrie drapière en Flandre* I (1906), 5–6.

31. Georges Friedmann, "Frederic Winslow Taylor: l'optimisme d'un ingénieur," *Annales d'Histoire économique et sociale*, 1935, pp. 584–602.

32. On the measurement of time and clocks, there are interesting ideas to be found, but often requiring further study with more precise data, in Lewis Mumford, *Technics and Civilization* (1934), pp. 22 ff.; an excellent sketch is found in Renouard, pp. 190–92. It should be pointed out, in any case, that decisive progress in this area was to come only after the beginning of the sixteenth century. A. P. Usher nevertheless is exaggerating in the opposite direction when he states: "The history of clocks prior to the 16th century is largely a record of essentially empirical achievements," in *A History of Mechanical Inventions*, 2d ed. (1954), p. 304. Cf. A. C. Crombie, *Augustine to Galileo: The History of Science, A.D. 400–1650*, 2d ed. (1957), pp. 150–51, 183, 186–87. From a vast literature, we will single out F. A. B. Ward, *Time Measurement* (1937), for its documentation, and the popularization of F. Le Lionnais, *Le Temps*, for pleasure of reading. The quote from Jean de Garlande is taken from his *Dictonarius*, Geraud ed., p. 590.

It is well known that psychologists have stressed that the child acquires his spatial and temporal notions concomitantly. See Jean Piaget, *Le Développement de la notion de temps chez l'enfant* (1946), pp. 181–203; P. Fraisse, *Psychologie du temps* (1957), pp. 277–99; P. Malrieu, "Aspects sociaux de la construction du temps chez l'enfant," *Journal de Psychologie*, 1956, pp. 315–32.

33. Pierre Francastel, *Peinture et Société: Naissance et destruction d'un espace plastique; De la Renaissance au Cubisme* (1951).

34. On the relations between theatrical representations and Uccello's painting, cf. P. Francastel, "Un mystère parisien illustré par Uccello: Le miracle de l'hostie d'Urbino," *Revue archéologique*, 1952, pp. 180–91.

35. For examples, see especially J. Lestocquoy, *Les Villes de Flandre et d'Italie sous le gouvernement des patriciens (XIe–XVe s.)* (1952), pp. 204 ff.: "Les patriciens et l'Evangile."

36. We are aware of the fact that recent detailed studies are leading to considerable modification and correction of the classic theses of Max Weber, *Die protestantische Ethik und der Geist des Kapitalismus* (1920), and of R. H. Tawney, *Religion and the Rise of Capitalism* (1926).

37. Maurice Halbwachs, "La mémoire collective et le temps," *Cahiers internationaux de sociologie*, 1947, pp. 3–31.

38. Robert Mandrou has pointed out (*Annales*, 1960, p. 172) what the requirements of the historian are and has recalled some old suggestions of Marc Bloch, in connection with recent works of philosophers relatively unconcerned with concrete history.

39. Poulet, p. vi, echoing Duns Scotus, *Questiones quodlibetales*, q. 12.

40. Besides general works on the history of philosophy and the sciences, the reader may consult, on the role of the Arabs, A. Mieli, *Panorama general de historia de la ciencia*, vol. 2, *El mundo islamico y el occidente medieval cristiano* (1946); and F. Van

Steenberghen, *Aristotle in the West* (1956). On one particular point: E. Wiedemann, *Über die Uhren im Bereich der islamischen Kultur* (1915).

41. M.-D. Chenu, *La Théologie au XIIe siècle*, chaps. 12 and 13, "L'entrée de la théologie grecque et oriéntale," pp. 274–322.

42. Cullmann, p. 36; cf. L. Laberthonnière, *Le Réalisme chrétien et l'idéalisme grec* (1904); and J. Guitton, *Le Temps et l'éternité chez Plotin et chez saint Augustin* (1933).

43. Etienne Gilson, *L'Esprit de la philosophie mediévale*, 2d ed. (1948), p. 66. See the whole beginning portion of chapter 4, "Les êtres et leur contingence," pp. 63 ff.

44. Cf. G. Le Bras, art. "Usure," in *Dictionnaire de théologie catholique* 2, part 2 (1950), cols. 2336–72; B. N. Nelson, *The Idea of Usury: From Tribal Brotherhood to Universal Otherhood* (1949); and Noonan.

45. Joannes Andreae (1270–1348), professor of canon law at Bologna, in his treatise *De regulis juris*, art. "Peccatum," 12 (cited by Noonan, p. 66), states that the argument according to which time cannot be sold is "frivolous," for many contracts include a period of time without implying a sale of time. The mechanism of commercial transactions was therefore known to the doctors after this date, and understood by them in a properly technical sense.

46. M. de Gandillac, *Valeur du temps dans la pédagogie spirituelle de Jean Tauler* (1955).

47. Gordon Leff, "The 14th Century and the decline of Scholasticism," *Past and Present*, no. 9 (April 1956), pp. 30–41. Id. *Bradwardine and the Pelagians* (1957).

48. Alberto Tenenti, *La Vie et la mort à travers l'art du XVe siècle* (1952); and *Il senso della more e l'amore della vita nel Rinascimento* (1957), chap. 2, "Il senso della durata," pp. 48–79.

49. Abbot Combes, ed., *Conclusiones de Jean de Ripa*, critical text with introduction and notes (1956).

50. The most recent bibliography is to be found in Crombie, pp. 414–16. See also the works of M. Clagett, A. Koyré, A. Maier, and C. Michalsky. In addition, the studies of G. Beaujouan and his sketch in *Histoire générale des sciences*, vol. 1, *La Science antique et médiévale*, ed. R. Taton (1957). On the origins of this current, see H. Shapiro, "Motion, Time, and Place according to William Ockham," *Franciscan Studies*, 1956.

51. S. Pines, *Beiträge zur islamischen Atomenlehre* (1936), and "Les précurseurs musulmans de la théorie de l'impetus," *Archeion*, 1938.

LABOR TIME IN THE "CRISIS" OF THE FOURTEENTH CENTURY

These pages are the elaboration of a paper presented to the Société Thomiste at a colloquium, "Time in the Experience of Medieval Man." I want to take this opportunity to thank R. P. Hubert, who authorized their publication here [in the 1977 Gallimard edition.—Trans.], as well as all those who made invaluable remarks during the discussion, especially the Reverend Father de Cotenson, and Messrs. Bautier, Beaujouan, Dufeil, Glenisson, and Lefèvre. On the transition from medieval time to modern time, cf. the recent studies of S. Stelling-Michaud, "Quelques aspects du problème du temps au Moyen Age," *Etudes suisses d'histoire générale* 17 (1959); Jacques Le Goff, "Merchant's Time and Church's Time in the Middle Ages," above, pp. 29–42; P. Wolff, "Le temps et sa mesure au Moyen Age," *Le Moyen Age*, 1962.

1. *Paradiso*, cantos 10 and 14.

2. Cf. however E. M. Casalini, O.S.M., "Condizioni economiche a Firenze negli anni 1286–89," *Studi Storici O.S.M.*, 1960.

3. On Dante's *reactionary* character, cf. esp. H. Baron, "A sociological Interpretation of the early Renaissance in Florence," *South Atlantic Quarterly* 38 (1939), 432.

4. Cf. *Divina Commedia*, ed. Tommaso Casini, 5th ed. (1907), p. 682.

5. Gustav Bilfinger, *Die mittelalterlichen Horen und die modernen Stunden: Ein Beitrag zur Kulturgeschichte* (1892), p. 142.

6. On the relation between Church time and peasant's time, see the fantastic

etymology of John of Garland (above, p. 36).

7. Gunnar Mickwitz, "Die Kartellfunktionen der Zünfte und ihre Bedeutung bei der Entstehung des Zunftwesens," *Societas Scientiarum Fennica: Commentationes Humanorum Litterarum* 8, no. 3 (1936), 88–90.

8. The English word *noon* reflects this.

9. Cf. Casalini, in *Studi Storici O.S.M.*, 1960.

10. Cf. D. Knoop and G. P. Jones, *The Mediæval Mason* (1949), p. 117.

11. I do not believe that there was an absolute depression in the fourteenth century. Cf. E. A. Kosminsky, "Peut-on considérer le XIVᵉ et le XVᵉ siècle comme l'époque de la décadence de l'économie européenne?" *Studi in onore di Armando Sapori* I (1957).

12. G. Espinas and H. Pirenne, *Recueil de documents relatifs à l'histoire de l'industrie drapière en Flandre* 1 (1906), 200.

13. R. de Lespinasse, *Les Métiers et corporations de Paris* (1886), part 1, p. 1.

14. Bilfinger, pp. 163–64.

15. Espinas and Pirenne 2, 411–12.

16. A. Thierry, *Recueil des monuments inédits de l'histoire du tiers etat* (1850), pp. 456–57.

17. Espinas and Pirenne 2, 230–33.

18. Ibid. 1, 6.

19. I am thinking here only of the role of the textile industry in the progress made in certain specialized techniques of medieval economic organization. In my view, certain historians go too far in making textiles the motor of medieval economic growth. The takeoff of the medieval economy occurred in two basic, rather than advanced, sectors: land and construction.

20. G. Fagniez, *Etudes sur l'industrie et la classe industrielle à Paris au XIIIᵉ et au XIVᵉ siècle* (1877), p, 84.

21. On measures and social history, cf. the exemplary article by Witold Kula, "La métrologie historique et la lutte des classes: l'exemple de la Pologne au XVIIIᵉ siècle," *Studi in onore di Amintore Fanfani* (1962), vol. 5.

22. Espinas and Pirenne 2, 471.

23. Ibid. 3, 395.

24. Ibid. 2, 596.

25. *Ordonnances des Rois de France . . .* 4, 209.

26. On the revolutionary role of this group, cf. esp. Ernest Labrousse, *La Crise de l'économie française à la fin de l'Ancien Régime et au début de la Révolution* 1 (1943), 592 ff.

27. Cf. E. Maugis, "La journée de 8 heures et les vignerons de Sens et d'Auxerre devant le Parlement en 1383–1393," *Revue historique* 145 (1924); I. M. Delafosse, "Notes d'histoire sociale: Les vignerons d'Auxerrois (XIVᵉ–XVᵉ siècle),"*Annales de Bourgogne*, 1948.

28. Cf. the references to acts of the parlements cited by B. Geremek, *Le salariat dans l'artisanat parisien aux XIIIᵉ–XVᵉ siècles: Etude sur le marché de la main-d'œuvre au Moyen-Age* (Paris, 1968).

29. Lespinasse, p. 52.

30. The decree of the Parlement of Paris for Auxerre of 26 July 1393 states: " . . . suum opus relinquentes, quidam eorum ad proprias vineas excollendas, alii vero ad tabernas ac ludos palme vel alibi accedunt, residuis horis diei ad laborem magis propiciis et habilioribus omnino (*or* ottiose) pervagando" (cited by Maugis, p. 217).

31. In addition to the preceding text, cf. this passage from the ordinance of Charles VI for Sens, in July 1383: they "abandon their work and leave between midday and None or thereabout, a particularly long while before the sun has set, and go to work on their vines or at other jobs, and there they labor and do as much or more work than they did the whole day for those who paid them their daily wages; and what is more, by working by the day, they take care of and spare themselves, without doing their

duty, so that they may be stronger and less exhausted for work in the places they go after quitting their jobs" (ibid., p. 210).

32. Bilfinger, pp. 163–64. The names of the bells must not, however, be interpreted in too narrowly economic a sense. Thus J. Rouyer, in his study *Aperçu historique sur deux cloches du beffroi d'Aire: La bancloque et le vigneron*, suggests that the second of these two names must indicate a reference to a hypothetical grape culture in the Aire region. But actually this was merely the bell which replaced the *crieur de vin*, whose shout sometimes marked the end of the working day: it was thus for the fullers in Paris in the thirteenth century, who "quit work on the night of Ascension when the crier brought wine" and, on the eve of certain festivals, "as soon as the first *crieur de vin* comes" (*Le Livre des Métiers d'Etienne Boileau*, ed. R. de Lespinasse and F. Bonnardot, pp. 108–9).

33. With all its symbolic consequences, the destruction or banishment of the communal bell could be punishment for a rebellious city, as the razing of a house or destruction of a fortified castle could be for an individual or nobleman. This is what Philippe d'Alsace is said to have done as early as 1179 at Hesdin: "Comes Flandrensis Philippus Sancti Quintini et de Parona castra graviter afflixit, eorumque cives obsidione, et persequutione diu multumque humiliavit: Hesdiniensibus reipublicae dignitatem abstulit; campanam communiae apud Ariam transmisit, et quosdam pro interfectione cujusdam de turri praecipitari jussit" (*Chronicon Andrensis Monasterii* apud D'Achery, *Spicilegium* II, 817).

34. With fiscal advances came the premises of a statistical mentality in the fourteenth century. Giovanni Villani has, of course, been singled out in this regard.

35. Cf. L. F. Salzman, *Building in England down to 1540* (1952), pp. 61–62.

36. *Sancti Benedicti Regula Monachorum*, ed. Dom Philibert Schmitz (1946), chap. 43, "De his qui ad opus Del vel ad mensam tarde occurunt," pp. 64–66.

37. There seem to be two major zones: northern and central Italy and a region which H. Ammann defines as the area of the *Tuchindustrie Nordwesteuropas* (cf. *Hansische Geschichtsblätter* 72 [1954]).

38. There is, of course, an enormous bibliography on the introduction of the clock. Cf. A. P. Usher, *A History of Mechanical Inventions*, 2d ed. (1954). On the famous clock of the Bourges cathedral, see the particularly interesting work of E. Poulle, *Un constructeur d'instruments astronomiques au XVᵉ siècle: Jean Fusoris* (1963).

39. Cf. R. Mandrou, *Introduction à la France Moderne* (1961), pp. 95–98.

40. Time would be unified, of course, only in the nineteenth century with the industrial revolution, the transportation revolution (schedules and timetables on the railroads imposed a unified hour), and the establishment of time zones. There followed rapidly the age of the minute and then of the second, the age of chronometers. One of the first literary indications of the unified time was Jules Verne's *Around the World in Eighty Days* (1873).

41. Cf. J. Vielliard, "Horloges et horlogers catalans à la fin du Moyen Age," *Bulletin hispanique* LXIII (1961). In connection with these repairs, the author points out the existence of specialist clockmakers, which shows that already the clock was in use over a fairly wide area.

42. Cf. the legends surrounding the constructors of clocks, who were fabulous personages sometimes suspected of having made a pact with the devil. This was the degree to which their knowledge appeared mysterious. Cf., e.g., the legend of the clockmaker of Prague.

43. On the beginnings of a calculating mentality and practice, see the suggestive article of U. Tucci, "Alle origini dello spirito capitalistico a Venezia: La previsione economica," *Studi in onore di Amintore Fanfani* 3 (1962).

44. From the end of the fourteenth century on, the clock is nearly always present in miniatures representing princes in their palaces, particularly the dukes of Burgundy.

Cf. A. Chapuis, *De Horologiis in Arte* (1954).

45. Cited by A. Maier, "Die Subjektivierung der Zeit in der scholastischen Philosophie," *Philosophia Naturalis* 1 (1951), 387, 391. On the psychological level, genuine subjectivization would come only with the personal watch—a moment of prime importance in the development of individual awareness of time.

46. A good point of departure is the study by M. de Gandillac, *Valeur du temps dans la pédagogie spirituelle de Jean Tauler* (1955).

47. Concerning the meaning of death in the late Middle Ages, an aspect of the upheaval in the consciousness of time, see the new, fruitful studies by A. Tenenti, *La Vie et la mort à travers l'art du XVe siècle* (1952), and *Il senso della morte e l'amore della vite nel Rinascimento* (1957).

48. The important texts are in the *Gaufridi declamationes ex S. Bernardi sermonibus* (PL 184, 465) and in the sermons of Guerri d'Igny (PL 185, 90).

49. Domenico Calva, *Disciplina degli Spirituali,* ,ed. G. Bottari (1838), chaps. 19 and 20.

50. Ibid., p. 132.

51. Yves Lefèvre, *L'Elucidarium et les Lucidaires* (1954), p. 279, n. 1. As early as the end of the thirteenth century, Philippe de Novare outlined a daily schedule very close to this one. Cf. E. Faral, *La Vie quotidienne au temps de Saint Louis* (1938), pp. 23–24.

52. "Pari racione dicebat, immortalem Deum praecepturum, atque ita, ut homines quot tempora vixissent, ipse Deus computaret quantum in dormiendo spatii, quantum in capiendo cibo ex necessitate posuissent, diligenter consideraturus annos, menses, dies, horas, atque momenta brevia... Ob hanc igitur causam, quod sibi datum erat, ad vivendum tempus ita dispensabat, ut ex eo nihil umquam perdidisse videretur (*Vita Jannotii Manetti a Naldo Naldio florentino scripta*, Muratori, 20:582). The importance of this text was recognized by H. Baron, p. 438.

53. Cf. Baron, p. 437.

54. Leon Battista Alberti, *I libri della famiglia*, ed. Cecil Grayson, in *Opera volgari* 1 (1960), 168–69.

55. Ibid., p. 177.

56. Cf. Chapuis, *De Horologiis;* and H. Michel, "L'horloge de Sapience et l'histoire de l'horlogerie," *Physis* 2 (1960).

A NOTE ON TRIPARTITE SOCIETY, MONARCHICAL IDEOLOGY, AND ECONOMIC RENEWAL IN NINTH- TO TWELFTH-CENTURY CHRISTENDOM

1. This, of course, is the point of view put forward by Georges Dumézil in many works. Cf. H. Fugier, "Quarante ans de recherche sur l'idéologie indo-européene: La méthode de M. Georges Dumézil," *Revue d'histoire et de philosophie religieuses*, 1965, pp. 358–74. P. Boyancé, "Les origines de la religion romaine: Théories et recherches récentes," *L'Information littéraire* 7 (1955), 100–107, "doubts that the tripartite schema was present in the mind of the Latins, since they never describe it explicitly." In the ninth to eleventh centuries, we do find explicit expressions of the schema and clear and precise formulations (see later in this chapter). We get the impression, furthermore, of two different types of mental structure juxtaposed, rather than an impression of confused thought evolving into clear thought. Should we speak of two types of coherent and parallel thought, "primitive" or "savage" on the one hand, "historical" on the other?

2. This was recently asserted by Vasilji I. Abaev, "Le cheval de Troie. Parallèles caucasiens," *Annales E.S.C.*, 1963, pp. 1041–70. D. Třeštík has rightly called attention to the importance of the passage in Genesis (9:18–27) in the treatment of the theme of the tripartite society in medieval literature (*Československý Časopis Historický*, 1964, p.

453). Noah's curse on his son Ham in favor of his brother Shem and Japheth ("Maledictus Chanaan, servus servorum erit fratribus suis"), was used by medieval authors to define the relations between the two superior orders and the third, subordinate order. The exploitation of this text seems to have come relatively late, however, and will not be treated here.

3. *King Alfred's Old-English Version of Boethius' "De Consolatione Philosophiae,"* ed. W. J. Sedgefield (Oxford, 1899–1900). Alfred's text says that the king must have "gebedmen & fyrdmen & weorcmen," "men for prayer, men for war, and men for work." Cf. the suggestive article by Jean Batany, "Des 'Trois Fonctions' aux 'Trois Etats'?" in *Annales E.S.C.*, 1963, pp. 933–38; and F. Graus, *Československý Časopis Historický*, 1959, pp. 205–31.

4. On Alfred, besides the fundamental work of F. M. Stenton, *Anglo-Saxon England* (Oxford, 1945), and B. A. Lees's book with the significant title *Alfred the Great: The Truthteller, Maker of England* (New York, 1919), the reader may consult the more recent studies of Eleanor Duckett, *Alfred the Great: The King and His England* (1957), and P. J. Helm, *Alfred the Great: A Re-assessment* (1963).

5. A convincing case for this dating has been made by J.-F. Lemarignier in *Le gouvernement royal aux premiers temps capétiens (987–1108)* (Paris, 1965), p. 79, n. 53. The text with a (French) translation may be found in G. A. Huckel, *Les Poèmes satiriques d'Adalbéron*, Bibliothèque de la Faculté des Lettres de l'Université de Paris, 13 (1901). A French translation also appears in E. Pognon, *L'An Mille* (Paris, 1947).

6. Here is the text: "Sed his posthabitis, primo de virorum ordine, id est de laicis, dicendum est, quo alii sunt agricolae, alii agonistae: et agricolae quidem insudant agriculturae et diversis artibus in opere rustico, unde sustentatur totius Ecclesiae multitudo; agonistae vero, contenti stipendiis militiae, non se collidunt in utero matris suae, verum onmi sagacitate expugnant adversarios sanctae Dei Ecclesiae. Sequitur clericorum ordo." (*PL* 139, 464). On Abbo, see P. E. Schramm, *Der König von Frankreich: Das Wesen der Monarchie vom 9. zum 16. Jahrhundert*, 2d ed. (Darmstadt, 1960), vol. 1; and the posthumous edition, with updated notes, of the old thesis of the Ecole des Chartes by A. Vidier, *L'Historiographie à Saint-Benoît-sur-Loire et les Miracles de saint Benoît* (Paris, 1965).

On the Abbo text, for an anthropological point of view, see the enlightening remarks of Claude Lévi-Strauss in *Anthropologie structurale* (Paris, 1958), translated by C. Jacobson and B. G. Schoepf as *Structural Anthropology* (New York: Basic Books, 1963), chap. 8, "Do Dual Organizations Exist?" which explains the third circle of concentric village organization as that of land clearing, the conquest of the soil, the field of labor.

7. Abbo was defending monastic privileges against Bishop Arnoul of Orleans. By contrast, Adalbero, in a violent attack on Cluny, was deploring the hold that monks had on the government of the kingdom.

8. On the role of Fleury (Saint-Benoît-sur-Loire) in the formation of the monarchical ideal in France for the benefit of the Capetians (along with Saint-Denis, which would take over the role for itself, quite effectively, beginning in the twelfth century), see, in addition to Vidier, *L'Historiographie*, R. H. Bautier's introduction to Helgaud of Fleury, *Vie de Robert le Pieux (Epitoma Vitae Regis Roberti Pii)* (Paris, 1965). The publication of the Fleury texts, announced by R. H. Bautier, under the aegis of the Institut de Recherche et d'Histoire des Textes du Centre National de la Recherche Scientifique should make possible more detailed studies of this subject. Cf. also the important article of J.-F. Lemarignier, *Autour de la royauté française du IXe au XIIIe siècle*, Bibliothèque de l'Ecole des Chartes, 113 (1956), 5–36.

9. *Monumenta Poloniae Historica*, n.s. II, ed. K. Maleczyński (Krakow, 1952), 8. In his remarkable works (*Podstawy gospodarcze formowania sie państw slowiańskich* [Warsaw, 1953]; "Economic Problems of the Early Feudal Polish State," *Acta Poloniae His-*

torica 3 (1960), 7–32; and "Dynastia Piastów we wczesnym średniowieczu," in *Poczatki Państwa Polskiego*, ed. K. Tymieniecki, 1 [Poznan, 1962]), H. Lowmiański has stressed this classification and given its socioeconomic significance. "Gallus's definition, *milites bellicosi, rustici aboriosi*, contains a reflection, unintentional as regards the chronicler, of the objective fact of division of the community into consumers and producers" (p. 11).

10. Cf. K. Maleczyński's introduction to the edition cited in the preceding note; M. Plezia, *Kronika Galla na tle historiografii XII wieku* (Krakow, 1947); J. Adamus, *O monarchii Gallowej* (Warsaw, 1952); T. Grudzinski, "Ze studiow nad kronika Galla," in *Zapiski Historyczne* (1957); J. Bardach, *Historia państwa i prawa Polski* (Warsaw, 1965) 1, 125–27. B. Kürbisówna, "Wieź najstarszego dziejopisarstwa polskiego z państwem", in *Poczatki Państwa Polskiego* (Poznan, 1962), vol. 2, and J. Karwasińska, *Państwo polskie w przekazach hagiograficznych*, ibid., pp. 233–44. D. Borawska's hypotheses (*Przeglad Historyczny*, 1964) on the Venetian sources of the chronicle of Gallus Anonymus, if verified, do not seem to be such as to require modification of our interpretation.

11. It would be pushing the interpretation rather far to say that Adalbero adopted the term *oratores* out of a desire to remind his Cluniac adversaries that their exclusive duty was to the *opus Dei*, in view of his accusation that they were too much involved in the affairs of the day.

12. We have no intention here of going into the problem of the thaumaturgic king or the saint-king (see, on this subject, the articles by R. Folz, "Zur Frage der heiligen Könige: Heiligkeit und Nachleben in der Geschichte des burgundischen Königtums," 14 [1958], and "Tradition hagiographique et culte de saint Dagobert, roi des Francs," in *Le Moyen Age*, jubilee vol., 1963, pp. 17–35, and the article in *Annales E.S.C.*, 1966, by K. Górski on the saint-king in northern and eastern medieval Europe). On monarchical ideology in the Middle Ages, the basic work is the collection, *Das Königtum: Seine geistigen und rechtlichen Grundlagen*, Vorträge und Forschungen, ed. T. Mayer, 3, 1956. On the ecclesiastical character of kingship according to Abbo of Fleury, in the tradition of the Council of Paris of 829 and the *De institutione regia* of Jonas of Orleans, see Lemarignier, pp. 25–27.

13. Cf. preceding note. On the unification of the clerical order and the place of the monks in that order in the eleventh and twelfth centuries, in relation to the economic development, see the interesting remarks of G. Constable, *Monastic Tithes* (1964), pp. 147 ff.

14. On this new nobility, cf. esp. the surveys of Léopold Genicot ("La noblesse au Moyen Age dans l'ancienne Francie" in *Annales E.S.C.*, 1961, and "La noblesse au Moyen Age dans l'ancienne Francie: Continuité, rupture ou evolution?" *Comparative Studies in Society and History*, 1962); G. Duby ("Une enquête à poursuivre: La noblesse dans la France médiévale," *Revue historique*, 1961); and O. Forst de Battaglia ("La noblesse européenne au Moyen Age," *Comparative Studies in Society and History*, 1962). A colloquium on the theme "Royalty and Nobility in the Tenth and Eleventh Centuries," organized by the German Historical Institute of Paris, was held in April 1966 at Bamberg.

15. There is scarcely anything to note other than the interesting articles by M. David, "Les laboratores jusqu'au renouveau économique des XIe–XIIe siècles," in *Etudes d'historie du droit privé offertes à Pierre Petot* (1959), pp. 107–19, and "Les 'laboratores' du renouveau économique, du XIIe à la fin du XIVe siècle," *Revue historique de droit français et étranger*, 1959, pp. 174–95, 295–325.

16. The situation was perhaps different in Italy, at least in Northern Italy, because of the survival of ancient traditions and the precocity of the urban revival. It would be especially useful in this regard to investigate Ratherius of Verona.

17. Cf., e.g., G. Duby, *La Société aux XIe et XIIe siècles dans la région mâconnaise*

(Paris, 1953), although, for him, this evolution was not completed in the Mâconnais until the early twelfth century (pp. 245–61), while the origin of the uniformity of the peasant class in the ecclesiastical literature of the early eleventh century is said to stem from the ignorance and contempt of the writers, such as Raoul Glaber (p. 130–31).

18. This is the case with Adalbero of Laon, who uses it to come to the defense of the serfs, with the obvious ulterior motive of denigrating the monks, who are masters of great numbers of serfs, in particular, the Cluniacs.

19. The clearest text is that of a canon from a Norwegian national synod of 1164, "Monarchi vel clerici communem vitam professi de laboribus et propriis nutrimentis suis episcopis vel quibuslibet personis decimas reddere minime compellentur," which in the British Museum MS Harley 3405 appears with a gloss above the word "laboribus": "id est novalibus." This text is cited by J. F. Niermeyer, "En marge du nouveau Ducange," in Le Moyen Age (1957), where the reader may find some well-chosen examples, with fine commentaries, of labor in the sense of "results of agricultural labor or, rather, of recently cleared land." The author rightly points out that in Carolingian capitularies labor designates the "fruit of any acquisitive activity as opposed to inherited patrimony" (e.g., in the Capitulatio de partibus Saxoniae, probably from 785: "ut omnes decimam partem substantiae et laboris suis ecclesiis et sacerdotibus donent," of which Hauch has given a good interpretation in Kirchengeschichte Deutschlands 2 [1912], 398, by translating substantia by Grundbesitz and labor by alles Erwerb) and laborare, "to acquire by clearing land" (e.g., 'villas quas ipsi laboraverunt' in the Capitulary of 812 for the Spaniards, which may have been at the bottom of a whole series of similar usages in the población charters of the Reconquista). We find the same vocabulary in a series of records of gifts to the Abbey of Fulda (8th–10th c.). The reader may also find it profitable to consult G. Keel, Laborare und Operari: Verwendungs- und Bedeutungsgeschichte zweier Verben für 'arbeiten' im Lateinischen und Galloromanischen (Saint Gall, n.d. [1942]). On the novalia and the meaning of labor, see also Constable, Monastic Tithes, pp. 236, 258, 280, 296–97.

20. For all this, see Georges Duby's basic work, L'Economie rurale et la vie des campagnes dans l'Occident médiéval (Paris, 1962), translated by C. Postan as Rural Economy and Country Life in the Medieval West (Columbia, S.C., 1968). On the progress of agriculture during the Carolingian age and its repercussions in the institutional and cultural area, see the fine article by H. Stern, "Poésies et représentations carolingiennes et byzantines des mois," Revue archéologique, 1955.

21. This definition is found in a 926 act in the cartulary of Saint-Vincent de Mâcon, ed. C. Ragut (Mâcon, 1864), 501. It was noticed by A. Déléage, La Vie rurale en Bourgogne jusq'au début du XIe siècle (Mâcon, 1942) 1, 249 n. 2; Duby, La Société, p. 130, n. 1; and David, Etudes d'histoire, p. 108. This term has, of course, persisted in old French (laboureur) to denote a well-off peasant, owning work animals and tools, as distinct from manouvrier or brassier with only his own hands and arms for work. On the uses of laboureur in this sense at the end of the Middle Ages, cf. esp. R. Boutruche, La Crise d'une société: Seigneurs et paysans du Bordelais pendant la guerre de Cent Ans (Strasbourg, 1947; new ed. Paris, 1963), passim, esp. pp. 95–96. This distinction and meaning are already found in the cartulary of Saint-Vincent de Mâcon, 476, in a text from the period 1031–60: "illi . . . qui cum bobus laborant et pauperiores vero qui manibus laborant vel cum fossoribus suis vivant," also cited by Duby, La Société, p. 130 n. 1. On the whole problem of the laboratores, I hope the reader will allow me merely to open a question here, which I shall take later in a more detailed and searching manner.

22. Cf. B. Töpfer, Volk und Kirche zur Zeit der Gottesfriedenbewegung in Frankreich (1951); Recueils de la Société Jean Bodin, XIV; La Paix (1962); and G. Duby's study, I laici e la pace di Dio, in the setting of the III Settimana Internazionale di Studi Medioevali (Passo della Mendola, 1965) on "I Laici nella Societa reliosa dei secoli XI e XII" (Milan, 1968). Traditionally, royalty assured prosperity by means of arms. Cf. Georges

Dumézil, "Remarques sur les armes des dieux de troisième fonction chez divers peuples indo-europeens," *SMSR* 28 (1957). The Carolingian stage is again important here. We detect its echo in the popular lamentations on the death of Robert the Pious (1031) recorded by his biographer-hagiographer Helgaud: "In cujus morte, heu! pro dolor! ingeminatis vocibus adclamatum est: 'Rotberto imperante et regente, securi viximus neminem timuimus'" (R. H. Bautier, [see n. 8 above] p. 136). In the eleventh century, however, royal protection was not hailed for bringing a sacralized and somehow metaphysical prosperity but rather for specific institutions which required workers, works, beasts of burden, and tools under royal guidance. It is not at all surprising that representatives of this economic elite should appear in the king's own entourage (cf. J.-F. Lemarignier, in *Le Gouvernement royal*, p. 135: Philippe I "welcomed into his entourage not only bourgeois... but particularly, and with increasing frequency, certain quite obscure characters who defy identification and appear only once: clerics or monks; or else laymen: farmers of some importance, so that their presence matters, and particularly village mayors."

23. Cf. Georges Dumézil's *Jupiter, Mars, Quirinus,* and, on certain aspects of the third function in Greek antiquity, the remarkable study by Jean-Pierre Vernant, "Prométhée et la fonction technique," *Journal de psychologie,* 1952, pp. 419–29 (republished in *Mythe et pensée chez les Grecs,* [Paris, 1965], pp. 185–95). Among the Scythians, for example, it is known that there was a triad of objects corresponding to the three functions: the cup, the axe, the plow and harness. It is tempting to compare this symbolism with the medieval legends which, among the Slavs, connect the plow with the founding heroes of the dynasties of the Piasts in Poland and the Przemyslides in Bohemia. It is also interesting to see the economic function appear in the monarchical hagiographical propaganda in France in our time. The most remarkable text is found in the *Vita Dagoberti* in which the king, at the behest of the peasants, tosses the seeds with his own hand, from which *frugum abundantia* is born (*MGH, SRM* 2, 515). F. Graus, *Volk, Herrscher und Heiliger im Reich der Merowinger* (Prague, 1965), p. 403, dates this text from the end of the tenth century at the earliest, and Folz, whose interesting commentary may be read in *Le Moyen Age,* p. 27, from the last third of the eleventh century (ibid. p. 29). This dating corroborates our thesis. On this legendary aspect of kingship, one should not forget James Frazer's classic, *The Golden Bough,* I, *The Magic Art and the Evolution of Kings* (London, 1911), and his *Lectures on the Early History of Kingship* (London, 1905). If we lay stress on these aspects, which belong to the domain of ideology on which this study is focused, we are not forgetting that it is important, as it was in actuality in the past, to relate them to economic context of the phenomena considered. For example, it should not be forgotten that the monastery of Fleury was located at the southern end of the Paris-Orleans road, where the Capetians in the eleventh and twelfth centuries had increased the amount of cleared land and the number of new centers of habitation, and which Marc Bloch has called the "axis of the monarchy" (*Les Caractères originaux de l'histoire rurale française* [Paris, 1952], p. 16 and plate 2).

24. The Carolingian imprint is again strong here. Heinrich Fichtenau (in *Das karolingische Imperium*) rightly points to these words of a Carolingian poet: "One alone reigns in heaven, he who hurls the thunderbolts. It is natural that one alone should reign after him on earth, one alone who should be an example for all men." In spite of the essentially liturgical character of the monarchical ideology in the Carolingian era, it is perhaps possible to observe a form of the third function in the epithet *Summus agricola* bestowed upon the emperor by the *Libri Carolini*.

25. The nightmare, reported by the chronicler John of Worcester, was illustrated by very explicit miniatures in the Oxford MS., Corpus Christi College, 157, ff. 382–83. A reproduction may be found in Jacques Le Goff, *La Civilisation de l'Occident médiéval* (Paris, 1964), pp. 117–18.

LICIT AND ILLICIT TRADES IN THE MEDIEVAL WEST

1. This is what we will attempt to do in a work now in preparation: *Les images du travail dans l'Occident médiéval*.

2. The systematic elaboration of these cases starting with the Decretum of Gratian, hence from the middle of the twelfth century, represents an important stage in the history of the contemptible professions, to which we shall return below.

3. On activities forbidden to clerics, see Naz, *Dictionnaire de Droit Canonique* 3 (1942), article on "clerc," § xiv–xvii, cols. 853–61; and M. Berry, "Les professions dans le Décret de Gratien" (thesis, Faculté de Droit de Paris, 1956).

4. The expression *inhonesta mercimonia* is from the statutes of the synod of Arras (c. 1275), which was used for the title of the article of J. Lestocquoy, "Inhonesta mercimonia," *Mélanges Halphen*, 1951, pp. 411–15. *Artes indecorae* is found in Naz (see note 3 above). *Vilia officia* is also found in the statutes of Arras. The statutes of the synod of Liège, from the same period, speak of *negotia turpia et officia inhonesta*.

5. This derived from the passage in Saint Paul forbidding all secular professions to clerics: "Nemo militans Deo implicat se negotiis sæcularibus" (2 Tim. 2:4), among other things.

6. The presence of soldiers on this list may be surprising: was not medieval Western society as "military" as it was "clerical"? We shall have more to say about medieval antimilitarism below.

7. On merchants, cf. Jacques Le Goff, *Marchands et banquiers du Moyen Age* (Paris, 1956).

8. Along with executioners, these professions figure in the statutes of the synod of Arras from around 1275 (cf. Dom Gosse, *Histoire d'Arrouaise* [1783]), and E. Fournier in *Semaine religieuse d'Arras* (1910), pp. 1149–53.

9. These figure secondarily in the statutes of the diocese of Tournai of 1361 (cf. E. de Moreau, *Histoire de l'Eglise en Belgique* 3 [1945], 588) which forbids clerics from exercising the trades of innkeeper, butcher, mountebank, weaver.

10. These are found in the statutes of the synod of Liège from the second half of the thirteenth century (cf. Moreau, ibid., p. 343, and J. Lejeune, *Liège et son pays*, p. 277) which also mentions jongleurs, innkeepers, executioners, pimps, usurers, crossbowmen, champions, coiners(?), cooks, cup-bearers, and fishermen.

11. A list of servile works forbidden on Sundays may be found in the *Admonitio generalis*, published by Charlemagne in 789 (art. 81, ap. Boretius, Capitul. I, p. 61).

It should be noted that these interdictions were valid only for Christians. From this point of view, the Jewish usurer had long been accepted in medieval western society. Popes and cardinals, in particular, had often turned to Jewish physicians. In this respect, the history of the professions, of course, offers a special chapter in the history of medieval anti-semitism. See B. Blumenkranz, *Juifs et Chrétiens dans le monde occidental, 430–1096* (1960), and L. Poliakov, *Histoire de l'antisémitisme*, 2 vols. (1955–61).

12. Cited by De Poerck, *La Draperie médiévale en Flandre et en Artois* (1951) 1, 316–17.

13. Adalbero of Laon, Poem to King Robert in E. Pognon, *L'An Mille* (1947), p. 225.

14. Aquinas, *Sententia libri politicorum* I, *lectio* 9.

15. Primitive mentalities are not exempt from contradictions. One of the most noteworthy of these was the one which made coiners powerful and respected men in the early Middle Ages. Cf. R. Lopez, "An Aristocracy of Money in the Early Middle Ages," *Speculum*, 1953. A thirteenth-century manuscript (Ottob. lat. 518) lists five professions "which are difficult to engage in without sinning." In addition to the military profession, the four others are essentially related to the handling of money: accounting (*cura rei familiaris*), commerce (*mercatio*), the trade of the attorney (*procuratio*), and that of the administrator (*administratio*).

16. Plutarch recalls Plato's contempt for the mechanical arts (*Markellos*, XIV, 5–6). Cicero expresses his, particularly in the *De Oficiis*, 1142. Among the texts of the Fathers

of the Latin Church, who intervene between the antique mentality and the medieval mentality, Saint Augustine's *De opere monachorum* XIII, PL 40, 559–60, should be noted.

17. According to John of Garland, cited by De Poerck.

18. Albertus Magnus' opinion regarding the militia and the condemnation of ablebodied beggars is found in several confessors' manuals, esp. the *Summa* of John of Freiburg.

19. The interdiction placed on the regular clergy by Pope Alexander III (council of Turin, 19 May 1163), forbidding them to leave their convents "ad physicam legesve mundanas legendas" is in Mansi, *Sacrorum conciliorum nova et amplissima collectio* 21, 1179. The constitution "Super speculam" of Honorius III, which forbade the University of Paris to teach civil law, may be found ibid. 22, 373.

20. This important point of Christian theology (usually implicit) relating to work has recently been stressed by L. Daloz, *Le travail selon saint Jean Chrysostome* (1959).

21. This appears clearly in several confessors' manuals, notably in Thomas of Chobham, who cites Aristotle on this point.

22. Cf. G. Le Bras, Article on "Usure," in *Dictionnaire de théologie catholique*, fasc. 144–45 (1948), and John T. Noonan, Jr., *The Scholastic Analysis of Usury* (1957).

23. Cf. E. Schönbach, "Studien zur Geschichte des altdeutschen Predigt." *Sitzungen und Berichte der philologisch-historischen Klasse der kaiserlichen Akademie der Wissenschaften* 154 (1907), 44.

24. This phrase from an unpublished confessors' manual (Ottob. lat. 518) may be found, for example, in the *Summa* of John of Freiburg.

25. Cf. G. Post et al., *Traditio*, 1955.

26. This problem was treated superficially in the classic works by Jubinal, *Jongleurs et trouvères,* and by Faral, *Les Jongleurs en France au Moyen Age.* From the standpoint of the rehabilitation of the jongleur, the theme of the Jongleur of Notre Dame and the surnames taken by Saint Francis of Assisi and the Franciscans, "jongleur of Christ" and "jongleurs of God," should be recalled (cf. P. Asupicius Van Corstanje, "Franciscus de Christusspeler," in *Saint-Franciscus* 58 [1956]). It should be noted, furthermore, that, although the condemnation of the jongleur-contortionist was similar in certain respects to Saint Bernard's condemnation of certain tendencies of Romanesque sculpture, it nevertheless passed from Romanesque into Gothic art (especially in the windows).

27. This anecdote is found in the *Summa* of Thomas of Chobham.

28. Cf. Le Goff, *Marchands et banquiers*, pp. 77–81.

29. For example, in the thirteenth century, Robert Kildwarby, taking his inspiration from Gundissalinus and Al-Farabi, made a distinction between a trivium and a quadrivium of mechanical arts, imitating the liberal arts. The first included agriculture, food, and medicine; the second, construction, weaponry, architecture, and commerce (*De ortu sive divisione scientiarum*). This comparison between the liberal and mechanical arts had earlier appeared, in the twelfth century, in the *Didascalicon* (book 2, chaps. 20–23) of Hugh of Saint-Victor, and had certain analogies in antiquity.

30. John of Salisbury, *Polycraticus*, book 6, chap. 20.

31. "De animae exsilio et patria," PL CLXXII, 1241 ff. On all aspects of this important turning point in the history of ideas and mentalities, see M.-D. Chenu, *La Théologie au XII*e *siècle* (1957).

32. "Ut etiam ad comprimendos vicinos materia non careant, inferioris conditionis iuvenes vel quoslibet contemptibilium etiam mechanicarum artium opifices, quos ceterae gentes ab honestioribus et liberioribus studiis tamquam pestem propellunt, militiae cingulum vel dignitatum gradus assumere non dedignantur" (Gesta Friderici I Imperatoris, *Scriptores rerum germanicarum* II [1912], 13, p. 116).

33. See Montaigne, *Journal du voyage en Italie.*

34. Cf. La Rigne de Villeneuve, *Essai sur les théories de la dérogeance de la noblesse,* and the works of G. Zeller, in *Annales E.S.C.,* 1946, and *Cahiers internationaux de sociologie,* 1959.

35. "Di questa sconfitta (Courtrai, 1302) abassò molto l'honore, lo stato, e la fama dell'antica nobiltà e prodezza dé Franceschi, essendo il fiore della cavalleria del mondo sconfitta e abassata da'lore fedeli, e dalla più vile gente, che fosse al mondo, tesserandoli, e folloni, e d'altre vili arti e mestieri, e non mai usi di guerra che per dispetto, e loro viltade, da tutte le nationi del mondo erano chiamati conigli pieni di burro" (Muratori, *Scriptores rerum italicarum* XIII, 388); " . . . alli artefici minuti di Brugia, come sono tesserandoli, e folloni di drappi, beccai, calzolari" (ibid., 382). "Alla fine si levo in Guanto uno di vile nazione e mestiere, che facea e vendea il melichino, cioè cervogia fatta con mele, ch'havea nome Giacopo Dartivello" (ibid., 816).

36. Cf. E. Perroy, "Les Chambon, bouchers de Montbrison" (circa 1220–1314), *Annales du Midi* 67 (1955).

37. This idea was most recently expressed in the Introduction to H. Luthy's *La Banque protestante en France,* 2 vols. (Paris, 1959–61).

LABOR, TECHNIQUES, AND CRAFTSMEN IN THE VALUE SYSTEMS OF THE EARLY MIDDLE AGES

Selected Bibliography

A. Sapori, "Il pensiero sul lavoro attraverso ai secoli," *Rivista del diritto commerciale e del diritto generale delle obbligazioni,* 1946, 267–89, 367–79, 467–80.

A. Tilgher, *Homo Faber. Storia del concetto di lavoro nella civiltà occidentale,* 3d ed. (Rome, 1944).

L. Mumford, *Technics and Civilization* (New York, 1934).

A. Aymard, "Hiérarchie du travail et autarchie individuelle dans la Grèce archaïque," *Revue d'Histoire de la Philosophie et d'Histoire générale de la civilisation,* 1943, 124–46.

Id., "L'idée de travail dans la Grèce archaïque," *Journal de Psychologie,* 1948, 29–45.

V. Tranquilli, "Il concetto di lavoro in Aristotele," *La Rivista trimestrale* 1 (1962), 27–62.

J. P. Vernant, "Le Travail et la Pensée technique," in *Mythe et Pensée chez les Grecs* (Paris, 1965), 183–248.

J. M. André, *L'Otium dans la vie morale et intellectuelle romaine des origines à l'époque augustéenne* (Paris, 1966).

B. Bilinski, "Elogio della mano e la concezione ciceroniana della società," in *Atti del 1° congresso internazionale di studi ciceroniani* (Rome, 1961).

N. Charbonnel, "La condition des ouvriers dans les ateliers impériaux aux ive et ve siècles," in *Aspects de l'Empire romain* (Paris, P.U.F., 1964), 61–93.

S. Mazzarino, "Aspetti sociali del quarto secolo," in *Ricerche di storia tardo romana* (Rome, 1951).

L. Robert, "Noms de métier dans des documents byzantins," in *Mélanges A. Orlandos* (Athens, 1964), 1, 324–47.

E. Troeltsch, *The Social Teaching of the Christian Churches* (New York, 1956).

W. Bienert, *Die Arbeit nach der Lehre der Bibel* (Stuttgart, 1954).

A. T. Geoghegan, *The Attitude towards Labor in Early Christianity and Ancient Culture* (Washington, 1945).

F. Gryglewicz, "La valeur morale du travail manuel dans la terminologie grecque de la Bible," *Biblica* 37, (1956), 314–37.

H. Holzapfel, *Die sittliche Wertung der körperlichen Arbeit im christlichen Altertum* (Würzburg, 1941).

E. B. Allo, *Le Travail d'après saint Paul* (Paris, 1914).

L. Daloz, *Le Travail selon saint Jean Chrysostome* (Paris, 1959).

J. Daniélou, *Les Symboles chrétiens primitifs* (Paris, 1961).

M. D. Chenu, *Pour une théologie du travail* (Paris, 1955).

La Vie Spirituelle Ascétique et Mystique, Numéro spécial, t. 52, n° 3, (1er septembre 1937).

Histoire générale du travail, ed. L. H. Parias. II. *L'âge de l'artisanat (Ve–XVIIIe siècle)*, Livre premier par Ph. Wolff (Paris, 1962), 13–85.

G. Keel, *Laborare und operari. Verwendungs- und Bedeutungsgeshchichte zweier Verben für "arbeiten" im Lateinischen und Galloromanischen* (Berne, 1942).

J. Neubner, *Die Heiligen Handwerker in der Darstellung der Acta Sanctorum*, Münsterische Beiträge zur Theologie, cahier 4, 1929.

E. Coornaert, "Les ghildes médiévales (ve–xive s.)," *Revue historique*, 1948.

E. Delaruelle, "Le travail dans les règles monastiques occidentales du ive au ixe siècle," *Journal de Psychologie*, 1948 (avec une intervention de Marc Bloch).

H. Dedler, "Vom Sinn der Arbeit nach der Regel des heiligen Benedikt," in *Benedictus, der Vater des Abendlandes, 547–1947*, Weihegabe der Erzabtei St. Ottilien zum 1400ten Todesjahr, ed. H. S. Brechter (Munich, 1947), 103–18.

A. de Vogüé, "Travail et alimentation dans le Règles de saint Benoît et du Maître," *Revue bénédictine* 74 (1964), 242–51.

J. O. Bodmer, *Der Krieger der Merowingerzeit und seine Welt* (Zurich, 1957).

E. Salin, *La Civilisation mérovingienne d'après les sépultures, les textes et le laboratoire*, 4 vols. (Paris, 1949–1959).

A. Solmi, *Le Corporazioni romane nelle città dell'Italia superiore nell'alto medioevo* (Padua, 1929).

G. Monti, *Le Corporazioni nell'evo antico e nell'alto medioevo* (Bari, 1934).

P. S. Leicht, *Corporazioni romane e arti medievali* (Turin, 1937).

C. Munier, *Les Statuta Ecclesiae Antiqua* (Paris, 1960).

M. L. W. Laistner, "The Influence during the Middle Ages of the Treatise De Vita Contemplativa and Its Surviving Manuscripts," in *The Intellectual Heritage of the Early Middle Ages* (Ithaca, 1957), 40–56.

R. S. Lopez, "An Aristocracy of Money in the Early Middle Ages," *Speculum* 28 (1953), 1–43.

Lynn White Jr., *Medieval Technology and Social Change* (Oxford, 1962).

J. Imbert, "Le repos dominical dans la législation franque," in *Album J. Balon* (Namur, 1968), 29–44.

La bonifica benedettina (Rome, n.d. [1965]).

V. Fumagalli, "Storia agraria e luoghi comuni," *Studi medievali*, 1968, 949–65.

V. Simoncelli, *Il principio del lavoro come elemento di sviluppo di alcuni istituti giuridici* (1888), repr. in *Scritti giuridici*, I (Rome, 1938).

R. Grand, "Le contrat de complant depuis les origines jusqu'à nos jours," *Nouvelle Revue historique de Droit français et étranger*, 1916.

F. Maroi, *Il lavoro come base della riforma dei contratti agrari*, Scritti giuridici II (Milan, 1956).

P. Grossi, "Problematica strutturale dei contratti agrari nella esperienza giuridica dell'alto medioevo italiano," in *Agricoltura e mondo rurale in Occidente nell'alto medioevo*, Settimane di studio XIII, (Spoleto, 1966), 487–539.

J. C. Webster, *The Labors of the Months in Antique and Mediaeval Art to the end of the XIIth century* (Princeton, 1938).

H. Stern, "Poésies et représentations carolingiennes et byzantines des mois," *Revue archéologique*, 6e série, 45–46, 1955.

K. Th. von Inama-Sternegg, "Rheinisches Landleben im 9. Jahrhundert. Wandaberts Gedicht über die 12 Monate," *Westdeutsche Zeitschrift für Geschichte und Kunst* 1 (1882).

J. Le Goff, "Note sur société tripartie, idéologie monarchique et renouveau économique dans la Chrétienté du ixe au xiie siècle," in *L'Europe aux IXe–XIe siècles*, ed. T. Manteuffel and A. Gieysztor (Warsaw, 1968), 63–72.

R. S. Lopez, "Still another Renaissance?" *American Historical Review* 57 (1951–52), 1 ff.

Miniature sacre e profane dell'anno 1023 illustranti l'enciclopedia medioevale di Rabano Mauro, ed. A. M. Amelli (Montecassino, 1896).

C. Stephenson, "In Praise of Mediaeval Tinkers," *Journal of Economic History* 8 (1948), 26–42.

M. David, "Les *Laboratores* jusqu'au renouveau économique des xie–xiie siècles," in *Études d'Histoire du Droit privé offertes à P. Petot* (Paris, 1959), 107–20.

C. Violante, *La Società milanese nell'Età precomunale* (Bari, 1953).

Other Works Consulted

A. Grabar, "Le thème religieux des fresques de la synagogue de Doura-Oropos," *Revue de l'Histoire des Religions* 123 (1941).

W. Seston, "L'Église et le baptistère de Doura-Europos," *Annales de l'École des Hautes Études de Gand* 1 (1937).

D. Savramis, "*Ora et labora* bei Basilios dem Groszen," *Mittellateinisches Jahrbuch* 2 (1965) (Festschrift für K. Langosch).

H. Dörrie, "Spätantike Symbolik und Allegorie," *Frühmittelalterliche Studien* 3 (1969).

W. Rordorf, *Der Sonntag. Geschichte des Ruhe- und Gottesdienstages im ältesten Christentum* (Zurich, 1961).

K. Bücher, *Arbeit und Rythmus,* 6th ed. (Leipzig, 1924).

E. Castelli (ed.), *Tecnica e Casistica* (Convegno del Centro Internazionale di Studi Umanistici e dell'Istituto di Studi Filosofici) (Rome, 1964): E. Benz, *I fondamenti cristiani della tecnica occidentale* (pp. 241–63) and M. de Gandillac, *Place et significa-tion de la technique dans le monde médiéval* (pp. 265–75).

G. Boas, *Primitivism and Related Ideas in the Middle Ages* (Baltimore, 1948).

J. Leclercq, "*Otia monastica.*" *Études sur le vocabulaire de la vie contemplative au Moyen Age* (Rome, 1963).

K. Weber, "Kulturgeschichtliche Probleme der Merowingerzeit im Spiegel des frühmittelalterlichen Heiligenleben," *Mitteilungen und Studien zur Geschichte des Benedikterordens und seiner Zweige* 48 (1930).

F. Graus, *Volk, Herrscher und Heiliger im Reich der Merowinger. Studien zur Hagiographie der Merowingerzeit* (Prague, 1965).

F. Prinz, *Frühes Mönchtum im Frankenreich. Kultur und Gesellschaft in Gallien, den Rheinlanden und Bayern am Beispiel der monastischen Entwicklung (4. bis 8. Jahrhundert)* (Munich, 1965).

J. Werner, "Waage und Geld in der Merowingerzeit," *Sitzungsberichte der Bayerischen Akademie der Wissenschaften,* Phil.-Hist. Kl., 1954, I.

J. Werner, *Die archäologischen Zeugnisse der Goten in Südrussland, Ungarn, Italien und Spanien,* summarized in Settimane di Spoleto, III (*I Goti in Occidente,* 1955) (Spoleto, 1956), p. 128.

J. Werner, *Fernhandel und Naturalwirtschaft im östlichen Merowingerreich nach archäologischen und numismatischen Zeugnissen,* in Settimane di Spoleto, VIII (*Moneta e scambi nell'alto medioevo,* 1960) (Spoleto, 1961).

A. H. Krappe, "Zur Wielandsage," *Archiv für das Studien der neueren Sprache und Literatur* 158 (1930).

K. Hauck, "Vorbericht über das Kästchen von Auzon," in *Frühmittelalterlichen Studien* 2 (1968).

H. R. Ellis Davidson, "The Smith and the Goddess. Two Figures on the Frank Casket from Auzon," *Frühmittelalterlichen Studien* 3 (1969).

H. R. Ellis Davidson, "Wieland the Smith," *Folklore* 69 (1958).

P. Buddenborg, "Zur Tagesordnung in der Benediktinerregel," *Benediktinische Monatschrift* 18 (1936).

G. Fasoli, *Aspetti di vita economica e sociale nell'Italia del secolo VII,* in Settimane di

Spoleto, V (*Caratteri del secolo VII in Occidente,* 1957) (Spoleto, 1958).

F. L. Ganshof, *Quelques aspects principaux de la vie économique dans la monarchie franque au VIIe siècle,* ibid.

F. Vercauteren, *La vie urbaine entre Meuse et Loire du VIe au IXe siècle,* Settimane di Spoleto VI (*La città nell'alto medioevo,* 1958) (Spoleto, 1959).

R. Latouche, *Les Origines de l'économie occidentale* (Paris, 1956).

U. Monneret de Villard, "L'organizzazione industriale nell'Italia longobarda," *Archivio Storico Lombardo,* ser. 4, XLVI (1919).

F. L. Ganshof, "Manorial organization in the Low Countries in the 7th, 8th and 9th centuries," in *Transactions of the Royal Historical Societies,* 4th ser., XXXI (1949).

A. Verhulst, "Karolingische Agrarpolitik. Das Capitulare de Villis und die Hungersnöte von 792/93 und 805/06," *Zeitschrift für Agrargeschichte und Agrarsoziologie,* 13/2 (1965) (excerpted in *Studi Historica Gandensia* 38 [1965]).

A. Verhulst and J. Semmler, "Les statuts d'Adalhard de Corbie de l'an 822," *Le Moyen Age* 68 (1962).

Sources
The texts used and cited are according to current editions. I have used:

a) for Salic law, K. A. Eckhardt, *Die Gesetze des Merowingerreiches. 481–714* (Weimar, 1935).

b) for monastic customs, *Corpus Consuetudinorum monasticarum,* ed. Dom C. Morgand, I, *Initia consuetudinis benedictinae. Consuetudines saeculi octavi et noni,* ed. K. Hallinger (Siegburg, 1963).

c) for the acts of Fulda, E. E. Stengel, *Urkundenbuch des Klosters Fulda,* I, *Die Zeit der Äbte Sturmi und Baugnef (744–802)* (Marburg, 1958).

d) for the capitulary *De villis,* the famous *Explication* by Benjamin Guérard (Paris, 1853).

e) Lawrence Stone, *Sculpture in Britain. The Middle Ages* (The Pelican History of Art) (1955), pp. 10–11, and pl. 2 for the cross of Ruthwell.

Addenda
For this revision of my text I have profited from two works that were not known to me before the original lecture: P. M. Arcari, *Idee e sentimenti politici dell'Alto Medioevo* (Pubbl. della Facoltà di Giurisprudenza dell'Università di Cagliari, ser. II, vol. I) (Milan, 1968); and P. Sternagel, *Die Artes Mechanicae im Mittelalter. Begriffs- und Bedeutungsgeschichte bis zum Ende des 13. Jahrhunderts* (Münchener Historische Studien. Abt. Mittelalterliche Geschichte II) (1966), which my friend, Professor Rolf Sprandel, had the kindness to bring to my attention in Spoleto.

I did not, however, have time to consult the important work by Renée Doehaerd, *Le Haut Moyen Age Occidental. Économies et sociétés* (Paris, 1971).

PEASANTS AND THE RURAL WORLD IN THE LITERATURE OF THE EARLY MIDDLE AGES

1. E. K. Rand, *The Founders of the Middle Ages* (Cambridge, 1928).

2. *MGH, AA* I; and M. Pellegrino, *Salviano di Marsiglia, studio critico,* 2 vols. (Rome, 1939–40).

3. Caesarius, *Sermones,* ed. G. Morin, in *Caesarii opera omnia* 1 (1937; 2d ed. 1953). *Corpus Christianorum, Series Latina* CIII.

4. *Opera omnia,* ed. C. W. Barlow, Papers and Monographs of the American Academy in Rome 12 (1950).

5. *MGH, SRM* 1-2.

6. *Dialogi,* ed. U. Moricca, *Fonti per la Storia d'Italia* 57 (1924).

7. "Carmina," in *MGH, AA* 4-1.

8. Cf. A. Dupont, "Problèmes et méthodes d'une histoire de la psychologie collective," *Annales, E.S.C.,* 1961; and A. Besançon, "Histoire et psychanalyse," ibid., 1964.

9. J. Marouzeau, *Lexique de la terminologie linguistique*, 2d ed. (1943).

10. Cf. W. E. Heitland, *Agricola* (Cambridge, 1921).

11. Ernst R. Curtius, *European Literature and the Latin Middle Ages* (1953).

12. Serverus Endelechius, *Bibliotheca maxima Sanctorum Patrum*, VI, 376.

13. On Theodulf and his fortune, see Gröber, *Grundriss der romanischen Philologie* (1906) 2, 755 and 1067; G. L. Hamilton, *Modern Philology* 7 (1909), 169; P. von Winterfield, *Deutsche Dichter des lateinischen Mittelalters* (1922), pp. 480 ff.

14. Cf. P. Grossi, "L'agricoltura e il mondo rurale nell'alto medioevo, *Settimane di studio del Centro italiano di studi sull' alto medioevo* 13 (Spoleto, 1971).

15. From the middle of the eighth century, manuscripts attest the success of the *De vita contemplativa* by Pomerius, who was the teacher of Caesarius of Arles. Cf. M. L. W. Laistner, "The influence during the Middle Ages of the Treatise 'De vita Contemplativa' and Its Surviving Manuscripts," *Miscellanea Giovanni Mercati* 2 (1946), 344–58. This treatise gives a good representation of the mentality of the spiritual guides of the western world in the late fifth century.

16. Caesarius, *sermo* 45, p. 201.

17. Cf. C. Sanchez-Albornoz, *Settimane . . .* 13 (1971).

18. Cf. M. Pellegrino, *Salviano di Marsiglia*, pp. 102 and 172–73, and G. Sternberg, "Das Christentum des 5. Jahrhunderts im Spiegel der Schriften des Salvianus von Massilia," *Theologische Studien und Kritiken* 82 (1909).

19. Pellegrino, p. 167.

20. The whole story of the scene and Gregory the Great's letter may be found in Gregory of Tours, *Historia Francorum* X, I.

21. Here is the Pseudo-Cypriot's list: "sapiens sine operibus, senex sine religione, adolescens sine obedientia, dives sine elemosyna, femina sine pudicitia, dominus sine virtute, christianus contentiosus, pauper superbus, rex iniquus, episcopus neglegens, plebs sine disciplina, populus sine lege." See Hellmann, *Pseudo-Cyprianus de XII abusivis saeculi*, Texte und Untersuchungen zur altchristlichen Literatur 34, 1.

22. J. P. Bodmer, *Der Krieger der Merowingerzeit und seine Welt* (1957), p. 137.

23. C. M. Figueras, *De impedimentis admissionis in religionem usque ad Decretum Gratiani*, *Scripta et Documenta* 9 (Montserrat, 1957).

24. G. Penco, *La composizione sociale delle communità monastiche nei primi secoli*, Studia monastica, 4 (1962).

25. F. Graus, *Volk, Herrscher und Heiliger im Reich der Merowinger: Studien zur Hagiographie der Merowingerzeit* (Prague, 1965).

26. Cf. J.-F. Lemarignier, *Settimane . . .* 13.

27. Michel Roblin, "Paganisme et rusticité," *Annales, E.S.C.*, 1953, p. 183.

28. Sulpicius Severus, *Epistola ad Desiderium de Vita B. Martini*, chaps. 13 and 14; Fortunatus, *Vita S. Martini*, MGH, AA 4-1, pp. 300, 321, 325, 326.

29. Cf. P. Poese, *Superstitiones Arelatenses e Cesario collectae* (Marburg, 1909). W. Boudriot, *Die altgermanische Religion in der amtlichen kirchlichen Literatur vom 5. bis 11. Jahrhundert*, Untersuchungen zur allgemeinen Religionsgeschichte, no. 2 (Bonn, 1928). S. McKenna, *Paganism and Pagan Survivals in Spain up to the Fall of the Visigothic Kingdom* (Washington, D.C.: Catholic University of America, 1938).

30. Luis Chaves, *Costumes e tradicões vigentes no seculo VI e na actualidade*, Bracara Augusta 8 (1957).

31. This is Graus's opinion, op. cit., pp. 197 ff.

32. Cf. A. Varagnac, *Civilisation traditionelle et genres de vie* (1948).

33. Cf. K. J. Hollyman, *Le développement du vocabulaire féodal en France pendant le haut Moyen Age (Étude semantique)* (1957), which cites, p. 164 n. 54, "frightening descriptions of the villeins," from H. Sée, *Les Classes rurales et le régime domanial en France au Moyen Age* (1901), p. 554, and J. Calmette, *La Société féodale*, 6th ed. (1947), pp. 166–67. He compares the descriptions of the villeins with those of pagans in the gests. Cf. J.

Falk, *Etude sociale sur les chansons de geste* (1899); S. L. Galpin, "Cortois and vilain" (diss., New Haven, 1905). Cf. the expression of the "humanist" poet from around 1100 cited by Curtius, p. 142 n. 1: "Rustici, qui pecudes possunt appellari."

34. Cf. the interesting remarks of K. J. Hollyman, p. 72: "the opposition *dominus-servus* is fundamental in Latin vocabulary, and the religious uses are based on it; they do not alter, but rather enrich it by adding yet another special application."

35. Caesarius, *sermo* 44, p. 199, and *sermo* 47, p. 215.

36. "Denique quicumque (filii) leprosi sunt, non de sapientibus hominibus, qui et in aliis diebus et in festivitatibus castitatem custodiunt, sed maxime de rusticis, qui se continere non sapiunt, nasci solent," *sermo* 44, p. 199.

37. On the meaning of *pauper* in the early Middle Ages, see K. Bosl, *Potens und Pauper: Festschrift für Otto Bruner* (1963), pp. 60–80 (reproduced in *Frühformen der Gesellschaft im mittelalterlichen Europa*, 1964), and Graus, pp. 136–37.

38. Migne, *PL* 40, 310–47.

39. Gregory of Tours, *Liber in gloria confessorum*, *MGH, SRM* 1-2, 766.

40. Ibid., p. 533.

41. Ibid., p. 558.

42. *MGH, SRM* III, 623.

43. *Dialogi* II, 31.

44. J. Höffner, *Bauer und Kirche im deutschen Mittelalter* (Paderborn, 1939).

45. *Sermo* 25, p. 107. On the indifference of Merovingian hagiography to social conditions, see F. Graus, "Die Gewalt bei den Anfängen des Feudalismus und die 'Gefangenbefreiungen' der merowingischen Hagiographie," *Jahrbuch für Wirtschaftsgeschichte* 1 (1961).

46. On the Bagaudes, cf. Salvianus, in Pelegrino ed.

47. *MGH, SRM* V, 15.

48. J. N. Biraben and J. Le Goff. "La peste dans le Haut Moyen Age." *Annales E.S.C.*, 1969, pp. 1484–1508.

49. This folkloric detail may be compared with the episode of the heretical peasant Leutard in Champagne in the early eleventh century, according to Raoul Glaber, *Historiae* II, 11.

50. *Historia Francorum* X, 25. Cf. another pseudoprophet, Desiderius, ibid. IX, 6–7.

51. Cf. Erich Auerbach, *Literary Language and Its Public in Late Latin Antiquity*, translated by Ralph Mannheim (London, 1965). C. Mohrmann, "Latin vulgaire, latin des chrétiens, latin médiéval," *Revue des Etudes Latines*, 1952, and *Settimane di studio del Centro italiano di studi sull' alto medioevo* 9 (Spoleto, 1961).

52. Isidore of Seville, *Differentiae*, *PL* 83, 59: "inter rusticitatem et rusticationem. Rusticitas morum est, rusticatio operis."

53. *Vitae patrum* IX, I, *MGH, SRM* 1-2, 702. Cf. Sidonius Apollinaris' contempt for the *rustici: Epistolae*, 1,6.

54. Hollyman, pp. 72–78. The author observes, ibid., p. 145: "In the literary vocabulary, no virtue was designated by a peasant name." On the relations between social classes and language in the Middle Ages, cf. G. Gougenheim, "Langue populaire et langue savante en ancien français" in *Mélanges 1945, V: Etudes linguistiques, Publications de la Faculté des Lettres de Strasbourg*, f. 108 (1947). Hollyman has also observed that "the use of the terminology of the rural classes for the pejorative vocabulary is not particular to old French." (p. 169). Cf. L. R. Palmer, *An Introduction to Modern Linguistics* (1936), p. 102. F. Martini's work *Das Bauerntum im deutschen Schrifttum von den Anfängen bis zum 16. Jahrhundert* (1944), does not go farther back than the eleventh century.

Academic Expenses at Padua in the Fifteenth Century

Appendix I: Cost of Examinations at the University of Padua in 1427 (*Codex vaticanus latinus* 11503, f° 8, pl. I)

Ihesus Christus.
Expense que fiunt in privato examine in studio paduano
    in primis

pro xii doctoribus collegii	duc. xii.
Item pro rectore studii	duc. ii.
Item pro vicario domini episcopi	duc. i.
Item pro priore collegii	duc. i.
Item pro cancellario domini episcopi	duc. iii.
Item pro tribus promotoribus	duc. iii.
Item pro utraque universitate	libr. vii.
Item pro collegio doctorum	libr. i.
Item pro bidello generali	libr. i.
Item pro notario collegii	libr. i.
Item pro notario universitatis	libr. i.
Item pro bidellis specialibus	libr. iii.
Item pro campania et disco	libr. i.
Item pro bancalibus	solid. xii.
Item pro quinque libris confeccionum	libr. iii et solid. x.
Item pro octo fialis et triginta ciatis	solid. xiiii.
Item pro quinque fialis malvaxie	libr. ii et solid. xii.
Item pro quatuor fialis vini montani	solid. xvi.
Item pro pifaris et tubis	duc. i.

Expense que fiunt in conventu publico seu in doctoratu
    in primis
      pro quolibet promotore brachia xiiii de panno, vel duc. xii.
Item pro bidello generali brachia viii de panno et duc. i.
Item pro quolibet bidello speciali promotorum suorum brachia
viii panni.

Item pro xii doctoribus collegii	duc. vi.
Item pro priore collegii	duc. 1/2
Item pro collegio doctorum	libr. i.
Item pro notario collegii	libr. i.
Item pro bancalibus	libr. i.
Item pro quinque paribus cirotecarum cum serico	libr. xii et 1/2.
Item pro quinque duodenis cirotecarum caprieti	libr. xxv.
Item pro septem duodenis cirotecarum mutonis	libr. xvii.
Item pro sex anulis auri	libr. xii.
Item pro septem biretis	libr. v et solid. v.
Item [pro] bancis cathedra et campana	libr. ii et solid. xvi.
Item [pro] privilegio	duc. i.
[Item pro] una carta, cera et serico	solid. xiii.
[Item pro tu]bis et pifaris	duc. i et 1/2.

He sunt expense taxate per statutum studii paduani tam in examine quam in conventu ibidem faciendis.

Appendix II: Expenses Made for Furnishings of the College of Jurists at Padua in 1454 (pl. II) (Archives of the University of Padua, *Statuti del collegio dei legisti,* 1382)

In Christi nomine.

Racio expense facte per me Franciscum de Alvarotis priorem almi collegii doctorum utriusque iuris padue pro banchis vi altis de novo factis pro sessione doctorum et pro reparacione vi banchorum antiquorum et cathedre magistralis de anno 1454 de mense Julii.

Primo die mercurei x Julii pro lignis octo de teullis emptis in aqua in racione l. 2 s. 16 pro quolibet ligno capit	l.	32 s.	8
Item pro lignis octo de remis emptis in aqua in racione s. 4 pro ligno capit	l.	9 s.	12
Item pro trabibus sex magnis emptis in aqua in racione l. 1 pro quolibet trabe	l.	6 s.	0
Item pro conductura a porta Sancti Johannis per aquam et pro extrahendo de aqua	l.	3	
Item pro uno carizio a sancta croce s. 16, et pro fachinis qui exoneraverunt bancas de mea careta super qua feci conduci bancas ad ecclesiam l. 1, et pro conductura carete pro aliquibus vicibus l. 1, capit	l.	2 s.	16
Item die mercurei ultimo Julii pro 36 cidellis cum suis cavillis et pro factura earum in racione s. 2 pro qualibet cidella cum sua cavilla capit	l.	3 s.	12
Item pro ligno de nogaria pro cidelis[53] et pro disgrossando cidellas et pro ligno cavillarum l. 3 s. 12 capit	l.	7 s.	4
Item pro medio linteamine veteri ad incollandum fixuras cathedre magistralis	l.	2	
Item pro tribus magistris qui laboraverunt diebus 10 pro l. 1 pro quolibet in die et ulterius feci sibi expensas	l.	30	
Item pro clavis 1400 adn (?) in raciones s. 9 pro cento capit l. 5 s. 9 et pro clavis 500 a mezano in racione s. 18 pro cento l. 4 s. 10 in s.	l.	9 s.	10
Item pro pictura cathedre pro duobus diebus quibus laboraverunt duo pittores et pro incollatura telle super fixuris cathedre et pro coloribus duc. 1 capit	l.	6	
Summa	l.	109 s.	5

De qua summa et expensa l. 109 s. 5 secundum statuta et consuetudines observatas mediatas tangit collegio [n]ostro iuristarum et alterius medietatis unus quartus tangit collegio artistarum et medicorum, alius quartus collegio theologorum qua teologi *(sic)* non utuntur, et sic extractis l. 6 pro pictura catedre tangit collegio theologorum l. 25 s. 16 et collegio medicorum pro suo quarto l. 27 s. 5 d. 8, et legistis pro medietate l. 56 s. 4.

Infra scripta est expensa facta per me Franciscum de Alvarotis priorem antedictum almi collegii Padue pro banchis xv pro sessione scolarium sumptibus propriis quas dono predicto collegio.

Primo pro piaguis xvi grossis a torculo emptis ab apoteca in racione s. 22 pro quolibet capit	l.	17 s.	12
Item pro tavolis squadratis vii et piaguis v acceptis ab apoteca M. Felipi pro s. 12 pro qualibet pro gantellis bancharum	l.	7 s.	4
Item pro clavis 300 a mezano pro s. 18 pro cento et pro clavis 500 aden° (?) pro s. 9 pro cento capit	l.	4 s.	19
Item pro manufactura trium magistrorum duobus diebus	l.	6	
Item pro duobus scrinis	l.	0 s.	10
Summa	l.	36 s.	5

Expensa facta pro bancha, alta tabula tripedibus altis et scabello sub pedibus pro sessione doctorandorum et promotorum quam similiter dono predicto collegio ego Franciscus de Alvarotis supradictus.

Primo pro piaguis duobus grossis a torculo acceptis ab apoteca pro

s. 24 pro quolibet	l.	2 s.	8
Item pro galtellis piaguum 1. Item pro tabula piaguum 1.	l.	1	
Item pro piaguis tribus pro scabello sub pedibus	l.	1 s.	10
Item pro una ascia pro pedibus tripedium	l.	0 s.	12
Item pro clavis aden° (?) et amezano et duplonis	l.	0 s.	10
Item pro ligno tripedium et manufactura predictorum	l.	2	
Summa......	l.	8	

Supradicta expensa bancarum et cetera capit l. 44
quam dono collegio.

Notes

1. This very ancient custom represented a considerable expense. In the thirteenth century, the English kings sent presents of game or wine to certain young doctors for this banquet. For example, we have the following letter of Henry III in 1256: "Mandatum est custodi foreste regis de Wiechewode quod in cadem foresta faciat habere Henrico de Wengh', juniori, studenti Oxonie, IIII^{or} damos contra festum magistri Henrici de Sandwic', qui in proximo incipiet in theologia apud Oxoniam . . . de dono nostro (*Calendar of Close Rolls, Henry III*, 1254–1256, p. 308). More than a mark of honor, this was a veritable subsidy which made a place for high personages or official bodies in the politics of university patronage. Besides the banquet, some were bent on showing their munificence by such diversions as tournaments, balls, etc. In Spain, some universities went so far as to ask new masters to stage a bullfight (cf. Rashdall, *The Universities of Europe in the Middle Ages*, ed. Powicke-Emden [1936] 1, 230). What is the meaning of these customs? One might think of the sumptuary obligations of the Greek and Roman magistracies; although there is no historical continuity, one might measure the social rise of "professors" from antiquity to the Middle Ages. Even more striking is the comparison with the *potaciones* or carousing sessions of the first guilds and corporations. In both cases, although there need not have been conscious imitation, the essential rite is the same, a communion by means of which a social body became aware of its fundamental solidarity. On the links between *potus* and "gift" as a ritual manifestation in Germanic groups, cf. the observations of Marcel Mauss in his article: "Gift, Gift," *Mélanges Adler*, 1924, p. 246. In any case, a sociohistorical study of the "university estate" will have to take account of these anthropological data.

2. The transition from a moral obligation to a statutory obligation relative to these gifts took place as early as the inception of academic regulation. At Oxford, for example, between 1250 and 1260, we find a new master wealthy enough to take on the fees of certain of his less well-off colleagues: "Omnibus autem istis etiam quibusdam artistis in omnibus tam in robis quam aliis honorifice predictus magister R. exibuit necessaria" (N. R. Ker and W. A. Pantin, "Letters of a Scottish Student at Paris and Oxford c. 1250," in *Formularies which bear on the history of Oxford* 2 [1940]). Sometime prior to 1350, the fees were fixed at the equivalent of the *communa* of a beginner (*Statuta antiqua Universitatis Oxoniensis*, ed. Strickland Gibson [1931], p. 58). In Paris, in spite of the 1213 prohibition, renewed in 1215 and 1231, against requiring "pecuniam . . . nec aliquam aliam rem loco pecunie aliquo modo pro licentia danda" (*Chartularium Universitatis Parisiensis*, ed. Denifle and Chalelain, 1 [1889], 75, 79, 138), the artists' statutes of the English nation of 1252 indicate that the *examinatores* are to make the candidates pay in advance: "pecuniam ad opus Universitatis et nacionis" (ibid. 1, 229).

3. The description of this manuscript may be found in a volume of the catalogue

prepared by the Abbot J. Ruschaert, Scriptor at the Vatican Library, who called it to our attention, and whom I would like to take this opportunity to thank in the warmest possible terms. The title is *Prosdocimi de Comitibus Patavini et Bartholomaci de Zabarellis lectura in libri II decretalium titulos XX–XXX.* The first of these courses is found on f°. 9–41 v° and 42 v°–428 v°, and the second on 418 v°–442. F° 1–8 contain the table of contests and various texts, including ours in f° 7. As we shall see, the author of the manuscript and its date of composition are given on f° 447.

4. A description for the case of Bologna may be found in Rashdall 1, 224–28. Padua was similar.

5. The description of this ceremony may be found in the notarized deeds executed at Bologna in the fourteenth century and published in volume 4 of the *Chartularium Studii Bononiensis,* ed. L. Frati (1919), esp. p. 81.

6. A study of these coffers, and of the use of funds deposited in them (originating from taxes, fines, and gifts), as well as their possible role in assisting or financing masters and students, has yet to be made. It is important for understanding the medieval university. Some pieces of documentation exist, at least at Oxford and Cambridge (cf. Rashdall 3, 35–36; *Statuta antiqua* passim, see index under *Chests*; D. F. Jacob, "English university clerks in the later Middle Ages: the problem of maintenance," *Bulletin of the John Rylands Library* 29, no. 2 [1946], 21–24).

7. Our text alludes to the maintenance costs of the benches for the assistants (*pro bancalibus, pro bancis*), of the chair of which the new doctor symbolically took possession (*pro cathedra*), of the bell that was rung (*pro campana*), the desk where the notary sat (*pro disco*), as well as to the payments for paper for the diploma received by the novice, wax for the seal affixed to it (*pro carta, cera et scrico*), and, finally, musicians who played trumpets and fifes during the ceremony (*pro tubis et pifaris*).

8. The bishop, who granted the *licentia docendi,* closely watched the university (cf. Rashdall 2, 15). His vicar and chancellor received money from the university at the time of the examination. The ecclesiastical authorities are not mentioned in connection with the *conventus,* however, which was a basically corporate ceremony.

9. The notaries and beadles cited in our text were important personages in the academic world, and shared in its privileges. In Paris, in 1259, the masters in arts complained that the sums disbursed to them caused a deficit in the academic budget (*Chartularium Universitatis Parisiensis* 1, 376–77).

10. Cf. Gaines Post, "Masters' Salaries and Student-Fees in Mediaeval Universities," *Speculum* 7 (1932), 181–98. This interesting article calls for completion, broadening, and deepening. We indicate below some of the directions we believe this research ought to take.

11. Cf., e.g., Cicero, *De officiis* I, 42. See L. Grasberger's interesting remarks in *Erziehung und Unterricht im klassischen Altertum* (1875) 2, 176–80; and those of H. I, Marrou, *Histoire de l'éducation dans l'antiquité,* 2d ed. (1950), p. 362.

12. When Saint Augustine quit his profession, he said: "Renuntiavi . . . ut scholasticis suis Mediolanenses venditorem verborum alium providerent"(*Confessiones* IX, v, 13). We have the familiar sentence of Saint Bernard: "Et sunt item qui scire volunt ut scientiam suam vendant, verbi causa pro pecunia, pro honoribus; et turpis quaestus est" (*Sermo* 36 in *Canticum,* n. 3). But Saint Augustine was thinking of pagan verbiage and Saint Bernard was open neither to the material conditions nor to the intellectual methods of urban instruction, as indicated by his attitude toward Abelard. Yet Honorius Augustodunensis, who was attentive to the problems of the work, also wrote: "Talis igitur quaerendus est, qui doceat: qui neque causa laudis, nec spe temporalis emolumenti, sed solo amore sapientie doceat (Migne, *PL* 177, 99).

13. Post (see n. 10 above) did not make systematic use of the canonical texts and penitentials which shed light on the debate over new conditions of instruction beginning in the thirteenth century, as well as on the solutions arrived at. Nearly all the

confessors' summaries from the thirteenth and fourteenth centuries ask the question: "Utrum magister possit collectam imponere vel exigere?" The two objections are that it is a duty of the estate and a spiritual good, whence the risk of simony: "symoniam committeret quia venderet obsequium spirituale quod ex officio suo tenetur facere" (*Summa Pisanella*, ms. *Padova Bibliotheca Universitaria, 608*, u. v° *magister*); the same text is in an anonymous *Summa* (*Codex Vaticanus Ottoboniani latini 758* c. v° *magister*: this is Henricius de Segusio's (*Hostiensis*) classic formulation. From the end of the thirteenth century, the problem arose only in connection with exemptions, as the invaluable *Confessionale* of John of Freiburg proves. Here the question has become: "si exegit collectam seu salarium ab hiis a quibus non debuit ut a pauperibus et ceteris prohibitis." For the rest, salary was allowed as payment, not for the master's knowledge, but for his labor: "potest accipere collectam pro laboribus suis (*Ottob. lat. 758*). This was the solution indicated by Saint Thomas of Aquinas and Raymond of Pennafort for lawyers and physicians. Here, we touch on an important point: the recognition of the liberal profession, the intellectual worker. The masters refer to it constantly; for example, our doctors of Padua in 1382: "Irracionabile credimus laborantem sui laboris honorificenciam non habere. Ideo statuimus quod doctor qui scolari presentato de mandato prioris sermonem pro collegio fecerit responsalem libras tres confectionum et fialas quatuor vini aut unum ducatum a scolare pro sui laboris honore percipiat" (*Statuti del Collegio dei Legisti*, ed. A. Gloria, *Atti del reale Istituto Veneto*, s. VI, VII-I [hereafter cited as Gloria], 393).

14. Even as they asked for the salary of laborers, the masters themselves laid claim to the homage due to their prestige. A manuscript cited by Charles Homer Haskins, *Studies in Mediaeval Culture* (Oxford, 1929), p. 55, says: "Nec magistri ad utilitatem audiunt, legunt, nec disputant, sec ut vocentur Rabbi." See Johan Huizinga's interesting remarks in *The Waning of the Middle Ages* on "the tendency to give to the title of doctor the same rights as to that of knight." A semantic study of the word *magister* (at one pole a leader of work, a foreman [*contremaître* in French], such as the *magister officinae*, or shop foreman; at the other, a dignitary in a social hierarchy, a "chief" with mysterious power) would help to show how the medieval academic "estate" was caught between two conflicting scales of social values, one ancient and "feudal," the other "modern."

15. Cf. n. 13 above.

16. The first important lay initiative in the area of university instruction was the foundation of the University of Naples by Frederick II in 1224 (cf. Charles Homer Haskins, *Studies in the History of Mediaeval Science*, 2d ed., p. 250).

17. A study of the social origin of the students, the intellectual equipment of the academics, the efforts (how successful?) of certain (how many?) to escape the ecclesiastical estate for more lucrative secular careers would make it possible, in at least one area, to make the somewhat theoretical views of G. de Lagarde more precise; cf. *La Naissance de l'esprit laïque au déclin du Moyen Age* 1 (Saint-Paul-Trois-Châteaux, 1934).

18. Here, again, most of the work remains to be done. On the novelty of the coexistence at Oxford in the thirteenth century of a community of "producers" (the "bourgeois" and a community of "consumers" (the academics) of almost equal size, cf. A. B. Emden, *An Oxford Hall in Mediaeval Times*, pp. 7–8; and H. E. Salter, *Munimenta Civitatis Oxonic*, pp. xv–xvi.

19. Here is the text, found in A. Gloria, *Statuti del Comune di Padova dal secolo XII all'anno 1285*, and Denifle, *Die Entstehung der Universitäten des Mittelalters* 1, 805: "Tractatores studii possint constituere salarium doctoribus legum usque ad summam tricentarum librarum et non ultra, magistris decretorum et decretalium librarum ducentarum et non ultra. Et dicti tractatores possint providere de utilitate communi super dictis salariis."

20. Unfortunately, we were unable to consult G. Luzzatto, "Il costo della vita a Venezia nel Trecento," in *Atenco Veneto* (1934).

21. A. Gloria, *Atti del reale Istituto Veneto,* s. VI, vol. VII, p. 1.

22. We would like to take this opportunity to thank the Rector of the university and his assistant, the archivist, who were kind enough to assist us in our work.

23. Gloria, *Atti del reale Istituto Veneto,* p. 395.

24. *Statuti del collegio dei legisti* 1382, Archives of the University of Padua (hereafter cited as *Statuti*), f° 31 v°: "Quoniam multociens evenit quod in examinibus privatis pauci doctores ultra doctores numerarios intervenerunt, ut examina plurium doctorum concursu venerentur statuimus et ordinamus quod collectio que fieri consuevit in examine completo convertatur ad pecunias inter supernumerarios presentes qui tamen non fuerint promotores equaliter dividendas, iuribus tamen familie reverendisimi domini episcopi reservatis."

25. *Statuti,* f° 29.

26. A sociological study of the faculty of arts in the thirteenth century would no doubt add a good deal to our understanding of the doctrinal battles of this era (cf., e.g., part of Rutebeuf's poetic work). We regret not yet having been able to acquaint ourselves with the recent work of A. L. Gabriel.

27. In the preceding period, the masters must have been more generous, because the text reproves the "nimia liberalitas collegarum nostrorum." It is also alleged that the desire is to avoid fraud by students falsely claiming poverty: "importunitas scolarium falso paupertatem allegantium."

28. In Gloria, *Atti del reale Istituto Veneto,* p. 361.

29. The text is directed at any "doctor canonici vel civilis paduanus originatus civis ac padue doctoratus qui doctoris de collegio nostro sit vel fuerit filius sive nepos ex filio etiam non doctore vel sit pronepos vel ulterior descendens per lineam masculinam" (*Statuti,* f° 15 v°).

30. "Lege civili sancitum esse cognoscentes ut juris doctorum filii pre ceteris in honoribus ex peritia juris consequendis honorentur, ordinamus ut natus doctoris nostri collegii ex legittimo matrimonio sive genitore diem functo sive in humanis agente etiam si desierit esse de nostro collegio liberaliter in examine privato et publico per doctores nostri collegii promoveatur. Ita quod nec a suis promotoribus nec ab aliquo doctore collegii possit occasione dictorum examinum vel alterius eorum compelli ad solvendum stipendium ad quod ex hujusmodi causa secundum formam nostrorum statutorum promovendi noscuntur obligati. Et ne contingat aliquos ex doctoribus in talibus examinibus deesse volumus ut contra eos qui cessante justo impedimento defuerint procedatur secundum formam alterius statuti quod incipit" (*Statuti,* ff°s 18 v°–19 r°).

31. "Quum omnis labor optat premium" (and not *salarium,* as the masters of the preceding eras had requested) "et prima caritas incipit a se ipso et ne nimia liberalitas in vitium prodigalitatis a jure reprobatum convertatur statuiumus et statuendo decernimus, addimus et delaramus quod statutum situm sub rubrica quod filii doctorum nostri collegii in examine privato et publico gratis promoveantur quod incipit "priore domino Petro de Zachis" intelligatur et locum habeat in filiis dumtaxat doctorum nostri collegii qui fuerint aut sint cives origine propria aut paterna aut saltem origine propria vel paterna civitatis Padue vel districtus. Nec tamen declaratio non intellegatur nec habeat locum in domino Hendrico de Alano qui per collegium nostrum habitus est et omnino habetur pro originali cive" (*Statuti,* f° 20 v°).

32. "Cum orte sint alique dubitationes super certis emolumentis ex hoc sacratissimo collegio percipiendis ut omnes tollantur dubietates et scandala per consequens evitentur et ut omnis dilectio et caritas fraternalis inter collegas remaneat semper ferventissima, statuimus quod nullus doctor forensis legens in hoc felici studio qui de

cetero intrabit hoc venerandum collegium possit habere emolumentum ducati qui datur duodecim numerariis vel supernumerariis aliquo numerariorum deficiente, non obstante aliquo statuto vel consuetudine in contrarium loquente" (*Statuti*, f° 28).

33. C. Zonta and G. Brotto, *Acta graduum academicorum gymnasii Patavini*, 612. These biographical details are taken from F. Marletta, *Archivio Storico per la Sicilia* (1936–37), p. 178.

34. M. Catalano-Tirrito, "L'istruzione pubblica in Sicilia nel Rinascimento," in *Archivio storico per la Sicilia orientale* 7, 430, no. 66.

35. Pirro, *Sicilia Sacra* 1, 632.

36. Catalano, *Storia dell'università di Catania*, p. 33.

37. Cf. V. Casagrandi, "Scuole superiori private di jus civile in Sicilia avanti la fondazione dello Studium generale di Catania," in *Rassegna Universitaria Catanese* (Catania, 1903) V, fasc. I–II, pp. 46–53; L. Genuardi, "I giuristi siciliani dei secoli XIV e XV anteriormenti all'apertura dello studio di Catania," in *Studi storici e giuridici dedicati ed offerti a Federico Ciccaglione* (1909); Catalano-Tirrito, p. 418.

38. In favor of Bologna, Sabbadini, p. 8. In favor of Padua, N. Rodolico, "Siciliani nello studio di Bologna nel medio evo," *Archivio storico Siciliano* XX (1895), and Marletta, p. 150.

39. Cf. Rashdall 2, 19–20.

40. On these scholarships, cf. Catalano-Tirrito, pp. 427–37, where a list of 113 Sicilian scholarship recipients between 1328 and 1529 may be found.

41. After the student received his doctorate, he was generally asked either to defend the rights and privileges of his fatherland or to assume a public office in it. Cf. Catalano-Tirrito, p. 428.

42. Although, according to the official bull, the new university was organized "ad instar Studii Bononiensis," Marletta (p. 151) observes, "lo studio catanese infatti, nei primi anni della la sua esistenza, bien può considerarsi una sezione staccata di quello padovano."

43. It may be found at the beginning of our manuscript from the University of Padua Archives and appears in Gloria, p. 358, n. 1.

44. "Sacratissimis constitucionibus canonicis ac legalibus cautum esse cognoscentes ut variato cursu monete condicio ejus quod est debitum non propter ea varietur decernimus ut solidi triginta duo qui quondam statuti fuerunt et sic hactenus persoluti pro singulo duodecim doctorum antiquorum nostri collegii qui publico conventui sive in canonibus sive in legibus adessent intelligantur esse et sint prout etiam venetorum boni auri et justi ponderis sic quoque deinceps tantum monete que ducati medietatem constituat secundum cursum qui tempore solucionis esse reperietur sine ulla detractione persolvatur (*Statuti*, f° 16 v°).

45. This academic evolution may be fitted into the economic and social current of western Europe in the fourteenth century. Faced with rising prices, the response was stubbornness and wage controls on the part of administrative authorities and employers, who admitted no connection between the cost of living and remunerations, leading to the establishment of a sliding scale (cf. G. Espinas, *La Vie urbaine de Douai au Moyen Age* 2, 947 ff; G. Des Marez, *L'Organisation du travail à Bruxelles au XVᵉ siècle*, pp. 252 ff; H. Van Werveke, *Annales de la Société d'émulation de Bruges* 73 (1931), 1–15; H. Laurent *Annales d'histoire économique et sociale* 5 (1933), 159). On the other hand, there were frequently successful efforts on the part of beneficiaries of rents, rates, and dividends to adjust their value to the cost of living, either by valuations in kind or by conversion of payments evaluated in money of account into real terms (cf. Van Werveke, who observes this tendency in Flanders, particularly beginning in 1389–90, and Laurent). Thus the academics are seen to join the social groups living on feudal, seigneurial—or capitalist—incomes. It is important to follow this evolution beyond

the economic and social sphere, into the intellectual and ideological area. The Renaissance humanist comes into being in a totally different milieu from that of the medieval academic.

46. Cf. Carlo Cipolla, *Studi di storia della moneta*, I: *I movimenti dei cambi in Italia dal secolo XIII al XV*, Publications of the University of Pavia, 29 (1948). The author thinks, in particular, that he can show that 1395 marks the beginning of a phase of monetary crisis.

47. Cf. Perini, *Monete di Verona* (pp. 29–30), who asserts that Padua's abandonment of the Veronese monetary system coincided with the Venetian conquest. In certain sectors, at least, the change came earlier.

48. Cf. Rashdall 2, 21.

49. In Gloria, pp. 397 and 399.

50. *Statuti*, f° 32.

51. Cf. the invaluable indications collected by F. Fossati, "Lavori e lavoratori a Milano nel 1438," *Archivio storico lombardo*, s. VI, a. LV, fasc. III–IV (1928), 225–58, 496–525.

52. We have been unable to find the term designating a type of nail, ignorance of which prevented our reading a word in our manuscript: adn, aden° (?).

53. *Pro cidelis* (sic): between the lines.

TRADES AND PROFESSIONS AS REPRESENTED IN MEDIEVAL CONFESSORS' MANUALS

1. On the education of laymen in the Middle Ages, we single out only Pirenne's classic article on the education of the merchant, P. Riché's examination of this problem in the time of Saint Bernard in *Mélanges Saint Bernard*, 1953, and in the period between the ninth and the twelfth centuries (*Cahiers de civilisation médiévale*, 1962), and H. Grundmann, "Literatus-illiteratus," *Archiv für Kulturgeschichte*, 1958.

2. For reservations to the hypothesis advanced by N. Sidorova concerning the birth of a lay culture in the ninth and twelfth centuries, see vols. 5 and 6 of *Cahiers d'histoire mondiale* (1959 and 1960), and the article by M. de Gandillac, "Sur quelques interprétations récentes d'Abélard," *Cahiers de civilisation médiévale*, 1961.

3. From a vast literature, we cite the works of Aloïs Thomas on the mystical press, "Die Darstellung Christi in der Kelter," (1936) and "Christus in der Kelter," in *Reallexikon zur deutschen Kunstgeschichte* (1953), and J. Daniélou's *Les Symboles chrétiens primitifs* (1961).

4. On the contribution of hagiographic and iconographic sources to the history of technology, cf. esp. B. Gille, "Les développements technologiques en Europe de 1100 à 1400," in *Cahiers d'histoire mondiale*, 1956.

5. There is quite a history of miracles connected with technical and economic development: miracles of land clearing (Saint Benedict and the iron tool which fell into the water, the falling tree from which the blessed hermit Gaucher d'Aureuil saved his comrade), miracles of construction (miraculous cures or resurrections from work accidents).

6. On attitudes of heretics toward labor, cf. esp., the treatise by Cosmas the Priest on the Bogarmiles, edited and translated by Puech and Vaillant, and the works by P. Dondaine and Miss Thouzellier on the Waldensian-Catharist polemic.

7. Worthy of note are Father Chenu's essay *Pour une théologie du travail* (1955); and L. Daloz, *Le Travail selon saint Jean Chrysostome* (1959).

8. Esp. in *Annales, E.S.C.*, 1959.

9. H. Dedler's subtle article, "Vom Sinn der Arbeit nach der Regel des Heiligen Benedikt," in *Benedictus, der Vater des Abendlandes* (1947), still interprets Saint Benedict's own conception too much in terms of the history of the Benedictine order, in my view.

10. Here, there is no question about the important role played—from the beginning—by Benedictines in the areas both of manual labor and of intellectual labor. In practice, somewhat contrary to Saint Benedict's idea, they were exemplary. It is well known, of course, that after the seventeenth century, people spoke of "working like a Benedictine."

11. Cf. J. W. Baldwin, *The Mediaeval Theories of the Just Price* (1959).

12. Cf. G. Mickwitz, *Die Kartellfunktionen der Zünfte und ihre Bedeutung bei der Entstehung des Zunftwesens* (1936).

13. As G. Le Bras has admirably pointed out.

14. Cf. "Licit and Illicit Trades in the Medieval West," above.

15. On the presence of confessors' manuals in the libraries of merchants, cf. esp. P. Wolff, *Commerces et marchands de Toulouse* (c. 1350–c. 1450) (1954).

16. On the spiritual climate of the twelfth century, cf. Father Chenu's illuminating book *La Théologie au douzième siècle* (1957).

17. Cf. G. Le Bras, art. "Pénitentiels," in *Dictionnaire de théologie catholique;* C. Vogel, *La Discipline pénitentielle en Gaule* (1952).

18. Cf. M. W. Bloomfield, *The Seven Deadly Sins* (1952).

19. Cf. J. W. Baldwin, "The intellectual preparation for the canon of 1215 against ordeal," *Speculum* 36 (1961).

20. Cf. P. Anciaux, *La Théologie du sacrement de pénitence au XIIᵉ siècle* (1949).

21. For Prémontré, cf. P. Petit, *La Spiritualité des Prémontrés* (1950).

22. On the importance of the evidence of the *Liber de diversis ordinibus,* cf. M.-D. Chenu, *La Théologie au douzième siècle,* pp. 227 ff. It should be noted that the missing book 4 was to have been entirely devoted to the problems of manual labor.

23. Cf. G. Lefranc, *Du travail maudit au travail souverain?* Rencontres internationales de Genève (1959).

24. Among other significant instances from the first years of the twelfth century, the canonization of Saint Homebon, merchant of Cremona, connected with the Umiliati.

25. *Polycraticus* VI, c. 20.

26. Cf. M.-D. Chenu, *La Théologie au douzième siècle,* p. 239.

27. *De animae exsilio et patria,* in *PL* 172, 1241. A sonorous echo of his century in its traditionalism as well as its innovations, Honorius expressed some ancient views on professional categories in the *Elucidarium.*

28. On the "dissolution du régime des sept arts," cf. G. Paré, A. Brunet, and P. Tremblay, *La Renaissance du XIIᵉ siècle: Les Ecoles et l'Enseignement* (1933), pp. 97 ff.

29. On the origins of the confessors' manuals, see the works of P. Michaud-Quantin.

30. On the diffusion of a whole literature *de officiis,* see G. B. Fowler, "Engelbert of Admont's *Tractatus de officiis et abusionibus eorum,*" in *Essays in Medieval Life and Thought Presented in Honor of A. P. Evans* (1955).

31. We cite from the Ms. Padova, Bibl, Antoniana, scaff. XVII cod. 367. This text, according to two manuscripts of the B.N. Paris, was used by B. Comte for an unpublished thesis defended before the Faculty of Letters of Paris in 1953.

32. On the treatment of these excluded categories, see M. Foucault, *L'Histoire de la folie à l'âge classique* (1961).

33. Cf. Jacques Le Goff, *Marchands et banquiers du Moyen Age,* 2d ed. (1962).

34. Cf. Jacques Le Goff, *Les Intellectuels au Moyen Age* (1957).

35. Cf. G. Post, K. Giocarinis, R. Kay, "The medieval heritage of a Humanistic Ideal: Scientia donum Dei est, unde vendi non potest," *Traditio,* 1955.

36. Cf. "Merchants' Time and Church's Time in the Middle Ages," above.

37. To take one example from many texts, the *Summa pisanella* (cited from Ms BN Paris Res. D 1193, f.L) answers the question "utrum negotiando liceat aliquid carius vendere quam emptum sit," following Saint Thomas, *II a II e* q. LXXVII: "lucrum

expetat non quasi finem sed quasi stipendium sui laboris et sic potest quis carius vendere quam emit."

How Did the Medieval University Conceive of Itself?

1. For an overall view of these problems, see: Jacques Le Goff, *Les Intellectuels au Moyen Age* (1957); H. Grundmann, *Vom Ursprung der Universität im Mittelalter*, Berichte über die Verhandlungen der Sächsischen Akademie der Wissenschaften zu Leipzig, 103 no. 2 (1957); and the report by S. Stelling-Michaud to the Eleventh International Congress of Historical Sciences, Stockholm, 1960.

2. On this metamorphosis and emergence, we think the best guides are G. Paré, A. Brunet, and P. Tremblay, *La Renaissance du XIIe siècle: Les Ecoles et l'enseignement* (1953); and P. Delhaye, "L'Organisation scolaire au XIIe siècle," *Traditio* 5 (1947).

3. It would be impossible here to give even a preliminary bibliography on Abelard. We will single out the classic, magisterial work of E. Gilson, *Héloïse et Abélard*, 2d ed. (1948). Among the works we have found particularly suggestive, A. Borst, "Abälard und Bernhard," *Historische Zeitschrift* 186, no. 3 (December 1958); and M. Patronnier de Gandillac, "Sur quelques interprétations récentes d'Abélard," *Cahiers de civilisation médiévale*, 1961, pp. 293–301. Here, we have used the excellent edition of J. Monfrin, *Bibliothèque des textes philosophiques* (1962).

4. "Patrem autem habebam litteris aliquantulum imbutum antequam militari cingulo insigniretur; unde postmodum tanto litteras amore complexus est, ut quoscumque filios haberet, litteris antequam armis instrui disponeret," Monfrin ed., p. 63, 13–17. On lay culture in this period, cf. P. Riché, in *Mélanges Saint Bernard*, 1953, and *Cahiers de civilisation médiévale*, 1962; and H. Grundmann's informative study "Literatus-Illiteratus: Der Wandel einer Bildungsnorme von Altertum zum Mittelalter," *Archiv für Kulturgeschichte* 40 (1958), 1–65.

5. Monfrin ed., pp. 63–64, 24–28.

6. Ibid., pp. 64, 37.

7. Ibid., pp. 64, 46.

8. Ibid., pp. 64, 58.

9. In his article "Héloïse et Abélard," *Revue des sciences humaines*, 1958, P. Zumthor thought he recognized in the relationship between Abelard and Heloise a typical "courtly" love. Even if it is possible to find a certain style of expression comparable with that of courtly love, it seems to us that the Abelard-Heloise couple belongs on quite a different, if not opposite, plane, is set in a quite different atmosphere. It would require a digression from our subject to explain here why we believe that this was the first "modern" couple in the West. We will simply point out that Jean de Meung, who would take this couple as a paragon in the second part of the *Roman de la rose*, wrote what was precisely an "anti-courtly" novel, as G. Paré has skilfully demonstrated, *Les Idées et les lettres au XIIIe siècle: Le Roman de la rose* (1947).

10. The fact is given even greater weight by his placing in the mouth of his adversaries the remark "quod scilicet proposito monachi valde sit contrarium secularium librorum studio detineri" (Monfrin ed., pp. 82, 683–85). The opposition is more direct between "monachi" and "philosophi" (ibid., pp. 77, 506 ff), to which we shall return.

11. Ibid., pp. 99, 1283–89.

12. Ibid., pp. 97, 1201.

13. In connection with William of Champaux, ibid., pp. 67, 133.

14. Ibid., pp. 94, 1092–93.

15. Ibid., pp. 94, 1109–13.

16. Ibid., pp. 81, 645.

17. Recall the well-known formula: "Scientia donum Dei est, ergo vendi non potest," which is the subject of a useful article—wanting, however, in economic and

social background—by G. Post, K. Giocarinis, and R. Kay, "The Medieval Heritage of a Humanistic Ideal," *Traditio* 2 (1955).

18. In connection with work on the confessional manuals, we propose to study the metamorphosis of psychological and spiritual life which is revealed, in particular, by the substitution of a social morality (of estates) for an individual morality (that of the deadly sins).

19. Monfrin ed., pp. 78, 533–35.

20. Ibid., pp. 75, 428, 431.

21. Ibid., pp. 71, 266–67.

22. Ibid., pp. 69, 208–10.

23. Ibid., pp. 82–83, 690–701, underscored *a contrario* pp. 84, 757–59.

24. Although we are quite far from belittling the necessity of situating the term in its underlying terrain, the inconsequence of Ernst Robert Curtius's remarks is disappointing: *European Literature and the Latin Middle Ages*, trans. W. R. Trask (New York, 1953), chap. 11, "Poetry and Philosophy," pp. 214–27.

25. On Philip of Harvengt, cf. Dom U. Berlière, in *Revue Bénédictine*, 1892; and A. Erens, in *Dictionnaire de théologie catholique* 12-1, 1407–11.

26. *Ep. XVIII ad Richerum*, in *PL* 203, 158.

27. *De Institutione clericorum* III, xxxv, in *PL* 203, 710.

28. Ibid., 706.

29. Ibid., 31.

30. Ibid., 33.

31. *Ep. XVIII ad Richerum*, in *PL* 203, 701. "Sicut autem isti a labore discendi nociva revocantur prosperitate, sic multi, ut aiunt, praepediuntur paupertate. Videntes enim sibi non ad votum suppetere pecuniariae subsidia facultatis, imparati sufferre aliquantulae molestias paupertatis, malunt apud suos indocti remanere quam discendi gratia apud exteros indigere."

33. "non tam audiri appetens quam audire," *PL* 203, 157.

34. Ibid., 31.

35. Ibid., 159.

36. *De institutione Clericorum*, in *PL* 203, 706. "Possunt enim (clerici) et curas ecclesiasticas licenter obtinere, et labori manuum aliquoties indulgere, si tamen ad haec eos non vitium levitatis illexerit, sed vel charitas vel necessitas quasi violenter impulerit. Apostolus quippe et sollicitudinem gerebat Ecclesiarum, quia eum charitas perurgebat, et laborabat manibus quando necessitas incumbebat. Denique cum Timotheum instrueret, non ab eo laborem relegavit penitus, sed eum potius ordinavit, ut osenderet non esse alienum a clerico aliquoties laborare, si tamen id loco suo noverit collacare. Debet enim studium praeponere scripturarum, et ei diligentius inhaerere, laborem vero manuum, non delectabiliter sed tolerabiliter sustinere, ut ad illud eum praecipue alliciat delectatio spiritalis, ad hunc quasi invitum compellat necessitas temporalis."

37. *PL* 203, 159.

38. P. Delhaye: "Saint Bernard de Clairvaux et Philippe de Harvengt," *Bulletin de la Société historique et archéologique de Langres* 12 (1953).

39. *De conversione ad clericos sermo*, in *PL* 182, 834–56.

40. *Ep. ad Heroaldum*, in *PL* 203, 31.

41. There is a vast literature on this conflict. The most important works are cited in the survey, in a traditional spirit, of D. Douie, "The Conflict between the Seculars and the Mendicants at the University of Paris in the 13th Century," in Aquinas Society of London, *Aquinas Paper no. 23* (1954).

42. *Exposition quatuor magistrorum super regulam fratrum minorum* (1241–42), ed. L. Oliger (1950).

43. K. Esser, "Zu der *Epistola de tribus questionibus* des hl. Bonaventura," *Franziskanische Studien* 17 (1940), 149–59, has shown that Saint Bonaventura took the majority of his commentary from the Joachimite Hugh of Digne (*Expositio Regulae* published in *Firmamenta trium ordinum beatissimi patris nostri Francisci* [Paris, 1512], pars IV). On Saint Francis's attitude toward manual labor, Bonaventura goes further than Hugues de Digne, giving one detail which is found nowhere else in the thirteenth century Franciscan literature: "Ipse autem (Franciscus) de labore manuum parvam vim faciebat nisi propter otium declinandum, quia, cum ipse fuerit Regulae observator perfectissimus, non credo quod unquam lucratus fuerit de labore manuum duodecim denarios vel eorum valorem" (loc. cit. 153). Cf. contra *Testamentum:* "Et ego manibus meis laborabam, et volo laborare. Et omnes alii fratres firmiter volo, quod laborent de laboritio, quod pertinet ad honestatem" (H. Boehmer, "Analekten zur Geschichte des Franciscus von Assisi," *Sammlung ausgewählter Kirchen- und Dogmengeschichtlicher Quellensschriften* 4 [1930], 37).

44. Contra impugnantes Dei cultum et religionem, I, IV ad 9: "Quando enim aliquis per laborem manuum non retrahitur ab aliquo utiliori opere, melius est manibus laborare, ut exinde possit sibi sufficere, et aliis ministrare ... Quando autem per laborem manuum aliquis ab utiliori opere impeditur, tunc melius est a labore manuum abstinere ... sicut patet per exemplum Apostoli, qui ab opere cessabat, quando praedicanci opportunitatem habebat. Facilius autem impedirentur moderni praedicatores a praedicatione per laborem manuum quam Apostoli, qui ex inspiratione scientiam praedicandi habebant; cum oporteat praedicatores moderni temporis ex continuo studio ad praedicandos paratos esse."

45. Ed. F. Stegmuller, "Neugefundene Quaestionen, *Recherches de théologie ancienne et médiévale* 3 (1931), 172–77.

46. Boethius of Dacia, *De Summo Bono sive de vita philosophie,* ed. Grabmann, in *Archives d'histoire doctrinale et littéraire du moyen-âge* 6 (1931), 297–307.

47. R.-A. Gauthier, *Magnanimité: L'Idéal de la grandeur dans la philosophie païenne et dans la théologie chrétienne* (1951).

48. See especially the text cited by R.-A. Gauthier, p. 468, n. 2, and attributed by him to Jacques de Douai: "Sicut tamen alias dixi, status philosophi perfectior est statu principis ... "

49. Stegmuller, p. 172.

50. Ibid., p. 175.

51. H. Denifle and A. E. Chatelain, *Chartularium Universitatis Parisiensis* 1, 545.

52. Ibid., p. 549.

53. Ibid., p. 551.

54. Ibid., p. 552.

55. Ibid., p. 555.

56. Gauthier, p. 469, note.

57. Cf. proposition 153 of 1277: "Quod nichil plus scitur propter scire theologiam." Denifle and Chatelain 1, 552.

58. Ibid., p. 548.

59. R.-A. Gauthier, "Trois commentaires 'averroïstes' sur l'Ethique à Nicomaque," *Archives d'histoire doctrinale et littéraire du moyen-âge* 16 (1948), 224–29.

60. On Gerson, the importance of the work of Msgr. Combes and the article by Msgr. Glorieux, "La vie et les œuvres de Gerson," ibid. 25/26 (1950–51), 149–92, is known. Louis Mourin, *Jean Gerson, prédicateur français* (1952), is useful. I was unable to consult G. H. M. Posthumus Meyjes, *Jean Gerson, zijn kerkpolitek en ecclesiologie* (1963).

61. *Vivat Rex* (1951 ed.) f° II r° and 45 v°.

62. Ibid., f° 2 r°.

63. Ibid., f° 3 r°.

64. Ibid., f° 7 v°.

65. Ibid., f° 4 v°.

66. "Recommendatio licentiandorum in Decretis," in Gerson, *Opera* (Paris, 1606) 2, 828–38. "Dominus ita vobis opus habet... et hoc ad regimen suae familiae grandis quietum et tranquillum... Ea enim demum vera pax erit, ea gubernatio idonea ea servitus placens Domino, si manet unicuique debitus ordo. Ordo autem quid aliud est nisi parium dispariumque rerum sua unicuique tribuens collatio. Hunc ordinem docere habetis" (ibid., p. 829).

67. "On parle d'aucuns pais gouvernez par tyrans, qui travaillent en plumant leurs subiects: mais le demeurant est seur et bien gardé, tellement qu'il n'est homme qui osast ravir un seul poussin, ou geline sur la hart." ("Some people speak of countries ruled by tyrants, who pluck their subjects bare for an occupation: but what is left over is safe and secure, for there is not a soul who would so much as filch a chick or a roosting hen.") *Vivat Rex*, f° 33 v°.

68. "Recommendatio," *Opera* 2, 832.

69. "De onere et difficultate officii cancellariatus et causis cur eo se abdicare voluerit Gersonius." *Opera* (1606) 2, 825–28.

70. "Sequamur tritum iter commodius plane et ab errorum scandalorumque discrimine remotius" (ut, posthabitis recentioribus, antiquiores legant), *Opera* (1606) 1, 558.

71. The University of Paris is characterized as "daughter of the King" in *Vivat Rex*, ff°s 2 r°, 4 v°, etc.

72. *Vivat Rex*, f° 9 r°.

THE UNIVERSITIES AND THE PUBLIC AUTHORITIES IN THE MIDDLE AGES AND THE RENAISSANCE

Selected Bibliography

I *General studies*

H. Grundmann, "Vom Ursprung der Universität im Mittelalter," *Berichte über die Verhandl. der Sächs. Akad. der Wiss. zu Leipzig. Phil. hist. Kl.*, 103–2, 1957.

P. Kibre, "Scholarly Privileges in the Middle Ages. The Rights, Privileges, and Immunities, of Scholars and Universities at Bologna, Padua, Paris and Oxford, *Mediaeval Acad. of America*, publ. no. 72 (London, 1961).

A. Kluge, *Die Universitätsselbstverwaltung. Ihre geschichtliche und gegenwärtige Rechtsform* (Frankfurt am Main, 1958).

R. Meister, "Beiträge zur Gründungsgeschichte der mittelalterlichen Universitäten," *Anz. der phil. hist. Kl. der Österr. Akad. der Wiss.*, 1957.

H. Rashdall, *Universities of Europe in the Middle Ages*, new ed. by F. M. Powicke and A. B. Emden, 3 vols. (Oxford, 1936).

S. Stelling-Michaud, "L'histoire des universités au Moyen Age et à la Renaissance au cours des vingt-cinq dernières années," *XIᵉ Congrès international des Sciences historiques*, Stockholm, 1960; Rapports, t. I.

II *Works published before 1960*

V. Beltran de Heredia, "Los origines de la Universidad de Salamanca," *La Ciencia tomista* 81 (1954).

F. Benary, *Zur Geschichte der Stadt und der Universität Erfurt am Ausgang des Mittelalters* (Gotha, 1919).

F. von Bezold, "Die ältesten deutschen Universitäten in ihrem Verhältnis zum Staat," *Historische Zeitschrift* 80 (1898) (repr. in *Aus Mittelalter und Renaissance*, 1918).

E. Bonjour, "Zur Gründungsgeschichte der Universität Basel," *Basler Zeitschrift für Geschichte und Altertumskunde* 54 (1955) (repr. in *Die Schweiz und Europa*, Basle, 1958).

G. Cencetti, "Sulle origini dello Studio di Bologna," *Rivista Storica Italiana*, VI-5 (1940).

G. Cencetti, "Il foro degli scolari negli Studi medievali italiani," *Atti e Memorie della R. Deputaz. di Storia Patria per l'Emilia e la Romagna* V (1939–40).

M. M. Davy, "La situation juridique de l'université de Paris au xiiie siècle," *Revue d'Histoire de l'Église de France* 17 (1931).

G. Ermini, "Il concetto di *studium generale*," *Archivio giuridico*, ser. 5, 7 (1942).

L. Van der Essen, "Les *nations* estudiantines à l'Université de Louvain," *Bulletin de la Commission royale d'Histoire* 88 (1924).

F. Eulenburg, "Die Frequenz der deutschen Universitäten von ihrer Gründung bis zur Gegenwart," *Abh. der phil. hist. Kl. der Sächs. Gesell. der Wiss.*, 24-2 (1904).

A. L. Gabriel, "La protection des étudiants à l'Université de Paris au xiiie siècle," *Revue de l'Université d'Ottawa*, 1950.

A. Gaudenzi, "La costituzione di Federico II che interdice lo Studio Bolognese," *Archivio Storico Italiano*, ser. 5, XLII (1908).

R.-A. Gauthier, *Magnanimité, L'Idéal de la grandeur dans la philosophie païenne et dans la théologie chrétienne* (1951).

H. Grundmann, "Sacerdotium—Regnum—Studium. Zur Wertung der Wissenschaft im 13. Jahrhundert," *Archiv für Kulturgeschichte* 34 (1951).

H. Grundmann, "Freiheit als religiöses, politisches und persönliches Postulat im Mittelalter," *Historische Zeitschrift* 183 (1957).

K. Hampe, "Zur Gründungsgeschichte der Universität Neapel," *Sitz. Ber. Heidelberg, phil. hist. Kl.*, 1923, 10 (1924).

H. Heimpel, *Hochschule. Wissenschaft, Wirtschaft, in Kapitulation vor der Geschichte?* (1956).

E. F. Jacob, "English University Clerks in the Later Middle Ages: The Problem of Maintenance," *Bulletin of the John Rylands Library* 29 (1945–46).

G. Kaufmann, "Die Universitätsprivilegien der Kaiser," in *Deutsche Zeitschrift für Geschichtswissenschaft* 1 (1889).

H. Keussen, "Die Stadt Köln als Patronin ihrer Hochschule," *Westdeutsche Zeitschrift* 9 (1890).

P. Kibre, "The Nations in the Mediaeval Universities," *Mediaeval Acad. of America*, publ. n° 49 (1948).

S. Kuttner, *Papst Honorius III und das Studium des Zivilrechts. Festschrift für Martin Wolff* (1952).

M. Meyhöfer, "Die kaiserlichen Stiftsprivilegien für Universitäten," *Archiv für Urkundenforschung* 4 (1912).

A. Nitschke, "Die Reden des Logotheten Bartholomäus von Capua," *Quellen und Forschungen aus italienischen Archiven und Bibliotheken* 35 (1955).

A. Palmieri, "Lo studio bolognese nella politica del secolo XII," *R. Deputaz. di storia patria per le prov. di Romagna*, ser. 4, XIII (1932).

J. Paquet, "Salaires et prébendes des professeurs de l'université de Louvain au xve siècle," *Studia, Universitatis "Lovanium"* 2 (1958).

F. Pegues, "Royal Support of Students in the XIIIth Century," *Speculum* 31 (1956).

G. Post, "Masters's Salaries and Student-Fees in the Mediaeval Universities," *Speculum* 7 (1932).

G. Post, "Parisian Masters as a Corporation (1200–1246)," *Speculum* 9 (1934).

G. Rossi, "*Universitates scolarium* e Commune. Sec. XII–XIV," *Studi e Memorie St. Univ. Bol.; NS I* (1956).

L. Simeoni, "Bologna e la politica di Enrico V," *Atti e Memorie della Deputaz. di storia patria per l'Emilia e la Romagna* 2 (1936–37).

———. "Un nuovo documento su Irnerio," *ibid.* 4 (1938–39).

———. "La lotta dell'investiture a Bologna e la sua azione sulla città e sullo studio," *Memorie della R. Accad. delle sc. dell'Ist. di Bologna, cl. mor.* ser. IV, 3 (1941).

L. Sighinolfi, "Gli statuti del Comune di Bologna e i privilegi degli scolari forestieri,"

R. *Deputaz. di storia patria per le prov. di Romagna*, sér. 4, XXIII (1932–33).

F. Stein, *Die akademische Gerichtsbarkeit in Deutschland* (1891).

S. Stelling-Michaud, "L'université de Bologne et la pénétration des droits romain et canonique en Suisse aux xiiie et xive siècles," *Travaux d'Humanisme et Renaissance* 17 (Geneva, 1955).

P. Torelli, "Comune ed Università," *Studi e Memorie St. Univ. Bol.* 16 (1943).

W. Ullmann, "The Medieval Interpretation of Frederick I's Authentica *Habita*," *L'Europa e il diritto romano. Studi in memoria di P. Koschaker* I (Milan, 1953).

W. Ullmann, "Honorius III and the Prohibition of Legal Studies," *Juridical Review* 60 (1948).

G. de Vergottini, *Aspetti del primi secoli della storia dell'Università di Bologna* (1954).

G. de Vergottini, "Lo Studio di Bologna, l'Impero, il Papato," *Studi e Memorie St. Univ. Bol.* NS I (1956).

M. Waxin, *Le Statut de l'étudiant étranger dans son développement historique* (Paris, 1939).

A. von Wretschko, *Universitätsprivilegien der Kaiser aus der Zeit von 1412–1456*, Festschrift Otto Gierke (1911).

See also the studies on the financing of various German universities cited by S. Stelling-Michaud in his Stockholm report, p. 137, n. 185.

III   Works published after 1960 (including some which, published shortly before 1960, could not be used by S. Stelling-Michaud in his report to the Stockholm conference) but before 1965 (when this study was presented to the Vienna conference)

H. R. Abe, "Die soziale Gliederung der Erfurter Studentenschaft im Mittelalter. 1392–1521," I, *Beiträge zur Geschichte der Universität Erfurt* VIII (1961).

Actes du Colloque de la Commission internationale d'Histoire des Universités à l'occasion du jubilé de l'Université Jagellonne, 1364–1964 (Krakow, May 1964): "La conception des universités à l'époque de la Renaissance."

Actes du Congrès sur l'ancienne université d'Orléans, 6–7 May 1961 (Orléans, 1962).

"Aus der Geschichte der Universität Heidelberg und ihrer Fakultäten hrsg. v. G. Ninz," *Ruperto-Carola* (1961) XIII, Sonderband (Heidelberg, 1961).

G. Baumgärtel, "Die Gutachter und Urteilstätigkeit der Erlanger Juristenfakultät in dem ersten Jahrhundert ihres Bestehens," *Erlanger Forschungen*, ser. A, XIV (Erlangen, 1962).

A. Blaschka, "Von Prag bis Leipzig. Zum Wandel des Städtelobs," *Wissenschaftliche Zeitschrift der Universität Halle. Gesellschafts-Sprachwiss.* ser. 7, 1959.

A. C. Chibnall, *Richard de Badew and the University of Cambridge* (Cambridge, 1963).

F. Claeys Bouuaert, "A propos de l'intervention de l'Université de Louvain dans la publication des décrets du Cōncile de Trente," *Revue d'Histoire ecclésiastique* LV (1960).

M. H. Curtis, *Oxford and Cambridge in Transition. 1558–1662* (Oxford, 1959).

M. H. Curtis, "The Alienated Intellectuals of Early Stuart England," *Past and Present*, no. 23 (1962).

Das 500-jährige Jubiläum der Universität Greifswald 1956, ed. G. Erdmann et al. (Greifswald, 1961).

J. Dauvillier, "La notion de chaire professorale dans les universités depuis le Moyen Age jusqu'à nos jours," *Annales de la Faculté de Droit de Toulouse*, 1959.

J. Dauvillier, "Origine et histoire des costumes universitaires français," *ibid.* 1958.

"Dekret Kutnohorsky a jeho misto v dêjinach" (The decretum of Kutna Hora and its place in history), *Acta Universitatis Carolinae. Philosophica et Historica* 2 (Prague, 1959).

Dzieje Uniwersytetu Jagiellonskiego w latach 1364–1764 (History of the University of Jagellona, 1364–1764) ed. K. Lepszy (Krakow, 1964).

A. B. Emden, "The Remuneration of the Medieval Proctors of the University of Oxford," *Oxoniensia* XXVI–XXVII (1961–62).

J. H. Hexter, "The Education of the Aristocracy in the Renaissance," in *Reappraisals in History* (London, 1961).

I. Hlavacek, "Jeden dokument k vztahu university a prazskych měst v druhé polovoně 14. stoleti" (A document on the relations between the university and the towns of Prague in the second half of the 14th century), *Acta Universitatis Carolinae. Historia Universitatis Carolinae Pragensis* II (1961).

J. Kejr, "Sporné otazky v badani o Dekretu kutnohorskem" (Controversial questions in the research on the Decretum of Kutna Hora), *ibid.*, III-I (1963).

G. Kisch, "Die Anfänge der Juristischen Fakultät der Universität Basel, 1459–1529," *Studien zur Geschichte der Wissenschaften in Basel* XV (Basle, 1962).

G. Koprio, "Basel und die eidgenössische Universität," *Basler Beiträge zur Geschichtswissenschaft* LXXXVII (Basle, 1963).

B. Kürbisowna, "Proba zalozenia uniwersytetu w Chelmnie w r. 1386" (The question of the founding of the University of Chelmno in 1386), *Opuscula Casimiro Tymieniecki septuagenario dedicata* (Poznan, 1959).

J. Le Goff, "Quelle conscience l'université médiévale a-t-elle eue d'elle-même?" *Miscellanea Mediaevalia. Veröffentlichungen des Thomas-Instituts an der Universität Köln. 3: Beiträge zum Berufsbewßtsein des mittelalterlichen Menschen* (1964).

P. Ourliac, "Sociologie du concile de Bâle," *Revue d'Histoire ecclésiastique* LVI (1961).

J. Paquet, "Bourgeois et universitaires à la fin du Moyen Age. A propos du cas de Louvain," in *Le Moyen Age* (1961).

J. A. Robson, *Wyclif and the Oxford Schools* (Cambridge, 1961).

J. Simon, "The Social Origins of Cambridge Students, 1603–1640," *Past and Present*, no. 26 (1963).

C. E. Smith, *The University of Toulouse in the Middle Ages. Its Origins and Growth to 1500* (Milwaukee, 1958).

S. Stelling-Michaud, "Le transport international des manuscrits juridiques bolonais entre 1265 et 1320," in *Mélanges Antony Babel* (Geneva, 1963).

L. Stone, "The Educational Revolution in England, 1560–1640,"*Past and Present*, no. 28 (1964).

A. Wyczanski, "Rola Uniwersytetu Jagiellonskiego w pierwszej polowie xvi wieku" (The role of the University of Jagellona in the first half of the 16th century) *Kwartalnik Historyczny* LXXI (1964).

D. Zanetti, "A l'Université de Pavie au xvᵉ siècle: les salaires des professeurs," *Annales, E.S.C.*, 1962.

P. Michaud-Quantin, "Le droit universitaire dans le conflit parisien de 1252–1257," *Studia Gratiana* VIII (1962).

F. J. Pegues, *The Lawyers of the Last Capetians* (Princeton, 1962).

N. A. Sidorova, "Les problèmes fondamentaux de l'histoire des Universités au Moyen Age dans l'optique de l'historiographie bourgeoise contemporaine (en russe), *Srednia Veka* 23 (1963).

M. de Boüard, "Quelques données nouvelles sur la création de l'Université de Caen (1432–1436)," *Le Moyen Age* LXIX (1963).

CLERICAL CULTURE AND FOLKLORE TRADITIONS IN MEROVINGIAN CIVILIZATION
1. Cf. bibliography (below, p. 329), no. 25.
2. Cf. bibliography, no. 33.
3. Ibid., p. 350.
4. "The Social Background of the Struggle between Paganism and Christianity," in Momigliano (bibliography, no. 47).
5. *Comm. in Ep. Gal.* II.

6. *Dialogi* I, 27.

7. "The counts and *saiones* sent on missions to the Roman officials had to know a few Latin phrases, of the sort that eventually any officer or even soldier comes to know in an occupied country" (P. Riché [bibliography, no. 37], p. 101). "There is no doubt that Barbarian aristocrats were very quickly Romanized. But it is clear that this was only a minority and that the mass of the Barbarians kept their own customs" (ibid., p. 102).

8. This was different from what happened at the beginnings of Roman culture. In that case, the rural basis continued to impregnate a culture which was in the process of urbanization and constant expansion (cf., e.g., W. E. Heitland, *Agricola* [Cambridge, 1921]; and the remarks of J. Marouzeau on Latin, "the language of peasants," in *Lexique de terminologie linguistique,* 2d ed. [1943]). Here, the peasant, eliminated from the cultural universe and kept apart from it (see Jacques Le Goff, "Peasants and the Rural World in the Literature of the Early Middle Ages," this volume, p. 87) threatened the culture in such a way as to oblige the clerics to act in the opposite direction, from the top down, to lessen their risks.

9. Jones, n. 6.

10. Cf. Marrou's classic work (bibliography, no. 30) and, for the Greek basis of Greco-Roman culture: W. Jaeger, *Paideia: The Ideals of Greek Culture* 1–3 (Oxford, 1936–45).

11. On the problematics of acculturation, see the survey of A. Dupront, "De l'acculturation," in *Comité international des sciences historiques,* XIIᵉ Congrès international des sciences historiques (Vienna, 1965). Rapports, 1, *Grands thèmes* (1965), pp. 7–36. Translated into Italian, with additions, in, *L'acculturazione: Per un nuovo rapporto tra ricerca storica e scienze umane* (Turin, 1966). The problems of internal acculturation stemming from the coexistence of distinct levels and cultural complexes within a single ethnic area are a particularly important aspect of acculturation.

12. For example, the major portion of the ethnographic knowledge bequeathed by Greco-Latin culture to the medieval West was to come from Solinus' mediocre compilation in the third century (ed. Mommsen, 2d ed. [Berlin, 1895]).

13. Cf. W. H. Stahl, "To a Better Understanding of Martianus Capella," *Speculum* 40 (1965).

14. It was from Macrobius that the clerics of the Middle Ages took, for example, the typology of dreams—so important in a civilization in which the oneiric universe occupied such a large place; cf. L. Deubner, *De Incubatione* (Giessen, 1899).

15. The *Vita Samsonis* has been subjected to a severe critique by its editor, R. Fawtier (Paris, 1912). Even if the additions and emendations in the text which has come down to us are noteworthy, however, the historians of Irish monasticism tend to regard the "liberal" culture of the Irish abbeys (Saint Iltud and Saint Cadoc are in the same boat as Saint Samson) as a reality and not a Carolingian fiction (cf. Riché, p. 357; and O. Loyer [bibliography, no. 26], pp. 49–51).

16. Although archaeology has revealed a warrior culture (see E. Salin [bibliography]), the military aristocracy of the early Middle Ages remained distant from written culture, awaiting its rise in the Carolingian and pre-Carolingian era (cf. n. 25 below), at which time, moreover, it was caught up in clerical culture before finally breaking through in the Romanesque era with the gests (cf. J.-P. Bodmer [bibliography, no. 6]).

17. By folkloric culture, I particularly mean the deep stratum of traditional culture (or civilization) (in the sense of A. Varagnac [bibliography, no. 48]) which underlies every historical society and crops up or is close to cropping up in the chaotic period between antiquity and the Middle Ages. What makes identification and analysis of this cultural stratum particularly delicate is that it is riddled with historical contributions disparate in age and kind. Here, it will scarcely be possible to distinguish this deep-lying

stratum from the level of Greco-Roman "high" culture which colored it so strongly. These, if you will, were the two paganisms of the era: one of traditional beliefs enduring over the very long period; the other of the official Greco-Roman religion, more susceptible of development. Christian authors of late antiquity and the early Middle Ages fail to distinguish them properly and seem, moreover (as shown, e.g., by an analysis of the *De correctione rusticorum* by Martin of Braga; cf. L. Chaves and S. McKenna [bibliography, nos. 13 and 27] and text in C. Wɪ Barlow, "Martin de Braga," *Opera omnia* [1950]), more concerned with fighting official paganism than the old superstitions, which they find difficult to tell apart. To a certain extent, their attitude encouraged the emergence of these ancestral beliefs more or less purged of their Roman veneer and not yet Christianized. Even Saint Augustine does not always make the distinction, although he still carefully distinguishes *urbanitas* from *rusticitas* as to the social aspects of mentalities, beliefs, and behaviors (cf., e.g., his discriminating attitude in this respect concerning funerary practices in the *De cura pro mortuis gerenda*, PL XL—CSEL 41—Bibliothèque augustinienne 2; and more generally the *De catechizandis rudibus*, PL XL, Bibliothèque augustinienne 1, 1). Thus the celebrated passage from *De civitate Dei* XV, 23, on the *Silvanos et Faunos quos vulgo incubos vocant*, the birth certificate of the demonic incubi of the Middle Ages, as Ernest Jones saw clearly in his pioneering essay on the psychoanalysis of medieval collective obsessions, in *On the Nightmare*, 2d. ed. (London, 1949), p. 83.

In practice, I consider as folkloric elements the themes from Merovingian literature which relate to a motif in Stith Thompson, *Motif-Index of Folk-literature*, 6 vols. (Copenhagen, 1955–58).

On the historicity of folklore, cf. a brilliant article which, despite its title, is quite general in scope, by G. Cocchiara, "Paganitas: Sopravivenze folkloriche del paganesimo siciliano," *Atti del I° congresso internazionale di studi sulla Sicilia antica*, Studi pubblicati dall'Istituto di storia antica dell'Università di Palermo, 10–11 (1964–65), 401–16.

18. It is known that the Rogation days date from the fifth or sixth century. According to tradition, they were instituted by Saint Mamertus, bishop of Vienne (d. 474), in a context of calamities and rapidly spread across Christendom, as Saint Avitus (d. 518) testifies in *Homilia de rogationibus* (PL 59, 289–94). It is not certain that they were intentionally and directly substituted for the antique *Ambarvalia*: cf. article "Rogations" in *Dictionnaire d'archéologie chretienne et de liturgie* XIV-2 (1948), cols. 2459–61, H. Leclercq). On the other hand, it is certain that they included folkloric elements. But it is difficult to know whether these elements colored the liturgy of the Rogations immediately, as early as the era we are considering, or whether they were introduced or, in any event, developed at a later date. Concerning, for example, the processional dragons, our evidence dates only from the twelfth and thirteenth centuries where theoretical texts are concerned (the liturgists Jean Beleth and Guillaume Durand) and from the fourteenth and fifteenth centuries for concrete individual mentions. I have studied the problem of these processional dragons from the Merovingian era on in an essay entitled "Ecclesiastical Culture and Folklore in the Middle Ages" (this volume, p. 159). On the folkloric characteristics of the Rogations, cf. the admirable pages of Arnold van Gennep with the significant title "Fêtes liturgiques folklorisées," *Manuel de folklore français contemporain* I/4-2 (1949), 1637 ff.

19. Their origin is urban and their nature basically liturgical, as is shown by the letter of institution sent by the pope to the Romans after his elevation to the pontificate at the time of the epidemic of Black Plague in 590—a letter which Gregory of Tours included in the *Historia Francorum* because a deacon from Tours, then in Rome to acquire relics, had brought it back to him (*Historia Francorum* X, 1). But their inclusion in the liturgical calendar as *liturgiae majores* alongside the *liturgiae minores* of the Rogations no doubt laid them open to a popular degradation.

20. The dragon of folklore—symbol of ambivalent natural forces which can turn either to our advantage or to our detriment (cf. E. Salin [bibliography, no. 45] 4, 207–8)—existed throughout the Middle Ages, alongside the Christian dragon, the latter being identified with the devil and signifying evil exclusively. In the late sixth century, when Fortunatus wrote the *Vita Marcelli* (cf. Bruno Krusch, *MGH, Scriptores rerum merovingiarum* IV-2, 49–54), the theme of the victorious saint who defeats the dragon remains midway between the two conceptions, in the lineage of the antique interpretation, which, having granted the heros a victory over the dragon, hesitated between domesticating and killing the monster. On the folkloric aspects of this theme, cf. Stith Thompson, Motif A 531: "Culture hero (demigod) overcomes monsters." I have tried to treat this problem in the article cited in n. 8 above; "L'ambivalence des animaux rêves" has been pointed out by Jean Györy, *Cahiers de civilisation médiévale* 1964, p. 200). For a psychoanalytic interpretation of this ambivalence, cf. Jones, p. 85.

21. Constantius of Lyons, *Vie de saint Germain d'Auxerre*, ed. R. Borius (Paris, 1965), pp. 138–43; Pliny the Younger, *Letters* VII, 27.

22. It is important to make a distinction here. The thesis of P. Saintyves, which is stated in the suggestive title of his book with a "modernist" imprint, *Les Saints successeurs des dieux* (bibliography), which appeared in 1907, is false insofar as the antique ancestors of the saints were not gods but demigods and heros and insofar as the Church wanted to make the saints not the successors but the replacements of the heroes, situated in another system of values. On the other hand, G. Cocchiara's thesis, which asserts that the Church triumphed in this area, takes no account of the fact that the vast majority of Christians in the Middle Ages and later behaved in the same way toward saints as their ancestors had toward heroes, demigods, and even gods. Contrary to what Cocchiara thinks, the frequent rough treatment, common in medieval communities, of a saint (or his statue) guilty of not having answered the prayers of his faithful is attributable to a persistent "primitive" mentality and not to some sort of affectionate mutation of piety. What remains is that the distinction between the role of God and that of the saints (pure intercessors) in miracles offers a safety valve to individual and collective psychology which safeguards to a certain extent the devotion to God.

23. It is no doubt simplifying the mental and intellectual role of Christianity to insist on its contribution to the progress of rationalization in these areas. In the medium run of the history of collective mentalities, it seems to have more to do with a mystical, "oriental" reaction against a certain Greco-Roman "rationalism" to which, moreover, the critical sensibility prepared the way for Judeo-Christianity, and medieval Christians were aware of a certain continuity in bringing Vergil and Seneca to the verge of Christianity. Still, in the area of mental and intellectual structures, I believe that Christianity represented a new phase of rational thought—as Pierre Duhem maintained in connection with science, where, according to him, by desanctifying nature, Christianity had enabled scientific thought to achieve crucial progress. In this respect, the opposition of folklore to Christianity (more basic, I think, than amalgams and symbioses) represents the resistance of the irrational, or rather of another mental system, another logic, that of "la pensée sauvage."

24. Constantius of Lyons, pp. 142–43. Sheltered by villagers, Saint Germain gives in to their pleas and restores the voice to mute cocks by giving them blessed bread. The biographer clearly does not understand the importance and significance of this miracle, which he excuses himself for mentioning. "Ita virtus diuina etiam in rebus minimis maxima praeeminebat." These *res minimae*, often spoken of in early medieval hagiographies, are miracles of a folkloric type which entered clerical literature by the back door. In the case cited here, we see a combination of several folkloric themes embodied in the miracle of the village sorcerer who repairs the magical order of nature. Cf. Stith Thompson, Motif A 2426, "Nature and meaning of animal cries" (esp.

A 2426.2.18, "Origin and meaning of cock's cry"); A 2489, "Animal periodic habits (esp. A 2489.1, "Why cock wakes man in morning"; A 2489.1.1, "Why cock crows to greet sunrise"); D 1793, "Magic results from eating or drinking"; D 2146, "Magic control of day and night"; J 2272.1, "Chanticleer believes that his crowing makes the sun rise."

25. The clerical aristocratic culture flourished in the Carolingian era with the stranglehold of the Church over secular values and, reciprocally, of the lay aristocracy over religious values. If, in the era which concerns us here, the fifth and sixth centuries, the aristocracy colonized the Church socially, it did so only by abandoning its lay culture, not as technical equipment, but as a system of values. Among others, the example of Cesarius of Arles is significant (*Vita Caesarii* I, 8–9, ed. G. Morin, in *S. Caesarii opera omnia* 2 [1937]). Weakened by his ascetic practices at Lérins, Caesarius was sent to Arles to an aristocratic family which puts him in charge of "quidam Pomerius nomine, scientia rhetor, Afer genere, quem ibi singularem et clarum grammaticae artis doctrina reddebat . . . ut saecularis scientiae disciplinis monasterialis in eo simplicitas poliretur." Author of the *De vita contemplativa*, which would enjoy a great vogue in the Middle Ages, Pomerius, moreover, was a Christian who had nothing of the "rationalist" about him. But once he had acquired the intellectual technique, Cesarius turned away from this profane science, as suggested to him by a dream in which he saw a dragon devour his shoulder, supported on a book on which he had fallen asleep. At the other extreme of our period (seventh and eighth centuries), we see the aristocratic ideal (we will not here enter into the arguments about the existence of a "nobility" in this period) invade hagiographic literature to the point of imposing on it an aristocratic type of saint; cf. F. Graus (bibliography, no. 22); and F. Prinz (bibliography, no. 36), esp. pp. 489, 501–7, "Die Selbstheiligung des frankischen Adels in der Hagiographie, 8; Heiligenvita-Adel-Eigenkloster, 9; Ein neues hagiographisches Leitbild"; and the works cited ibid., pp. 493–94, nn. 126 and 127, to which we should add K. Bosl, "Der 'Adelsheilige,' Idealtypus und Wirklichkeit, Gesellschaft und Kultur in Merowingerzeiten: Bayern des 7 und 8. Jahrhunderts," in *Speculum historiale: Geschichte im Spiegel von Gedichtsschreibung und Gedichtsdeutung*, ed. C. Bauer (1965), pp. 167–87.

26. After the fashion of Erich Köhler, I interpret the renascence of profane literature in the eleventh and twelfth centuries as the product of the small and medium aristocracy of the *milites*, who desired to create for themselves a culture relatively independent of the clerical culture with which the Carolingian lay *proceres* had put up quite well (cf. E. E. Köhler, *Trobadorlyrik und höfischer Roman* [Berlin, 1962]; id., "Observations historiques et sociologiques sur la poésie des troubadours," *Cahiers de civilisation médiévale*, 1964, pp. 27–51). I also believe, with D. D. R. Ower, "The secular inspiration of the 'Chanson de Roland'" (*Speculum* 37 [1962]), that the mentality and morality of the original Roland were completely secular, "feudal." And I think that this new feudal, lay culture borrowed extensively from the underlying folkloric culture because the latter was the only substitute culture that the lords could establish alongside—if not in opposition to—clerical culture. Marc Bloch, moreover, had sensed the importance of the deep folkloric character of the gests ("The plot of the *Chanson de Roland* has more to do with folklore than history—hatred between stepson and stepfather, envy, betrayal." *La Société féodale* 1, 148. Cf. ibid., p. 133). Of course, clerical culture would easily and quickly conclude a compromise with this seigneurial culture, a Christianization of a lay and folkloric base. Between Geoffrey of Monmouth, for example, and Robert of Boron, there is barely time to observe a wild Merlin, a non-Christian prophet, a madman alien to Catholic reason, a wild man fleeing the Christian world, offspring of a Myrdclin in whom the semi-aristocratic culture of the Celtic bards had put some of the traits of the village sorcerer. In contrast with the Merovingian era, however, the Gothic-Romanesque age was unable to entirely repress this

folkloric culture. It had to compromise and allow folklore to become implanted prior to the new growth of the fifteenth and sixteenth centuries. The eminently folkloric theme laden with aspirations coming from the collective depths, that of Never-Never Land, appeared in thirteenth-century literature before making a decisive breakthrough in the sixteenth century (cf. Cocchiara, *Il paese di Cuccagna*, 1954). In this respect, the twelfth and thirteenth centuries were indeed the first stage of the Renaissance.

Selected Bibliography

1. J.-F. Alonso, *La cura pastoral en la España romanovisigoda* (Rome, 1955).
2. E. Auerbach, *Literatursprache und Publikum in der lateinischen Spätantike und im Mittelalter* (Berne, 1958).
3. H. G. Beck, *The Pastoral Care of Souls in South-East France during the Sixth Century* (Rome, 1950).
4. C. A. Bernoulli, *Die Heiligen der Merowinger* (Tübingen, 1900).
5. H. Beumann, *Gregor von Tours und der "sermo rusticus."* Spiegel der Geschichte, Festgabe Max Braubach (Münster, 1964), pp. 69–98.
6. J.-P. Bodmer, *Der Krieger der Merowingerzeit und seine Welt* (1957).
7. R. Boese, *Superstitiones Arelatenses e Caesario collectae* (Marburg, 1909).
8. I. Bonini, "Lo stile nei sermoni di Caesario di Arles," *Aevum*, 1962.
9. M. Bonnet, *Le Latin de Grégoire de Tours* (Paris, 1890).
10. R. Borius, *Constance de Lyon: Vie de saint Germain d'Auxerre* (Paris, 1965).
11. W. Boudriot, *Die altgermanische Religion in der amtlichen kirchlichen Literatur vom 5. bis 11. Jahrhundert* (Bonn, 1928).
12. S. Cavallin, *Literarhistorische und textkritische Studien zur "Vita S. Caesari Arelatensis,"* (Lund, 1934).
13. L. Chaves, "Costumes e tradicoes vigentes no seculo VI e na actualidade," *Bracara Augusta* VIII (1957).
14. P. Courcelle, *Les Lettres grecques en Occident de Macrobe à Cassiodore* (Paris, 1943).
15. *Id., Histoire littéraire des grandes invasions germaniques* (Paris, 1948).
16. E.-R. Curtius, *European Literature and the Latin Middle Ages,* trans. Willard R. Trask (New York, 1953).
17. H. Delehaye, *Les Légendes hagiographiques* (Brussels, 1905).
18. *Id., "Sanctus." Essai sur le culte des saints dans l'Antiquité* (Brussels, 1954).
19. A. Dufourcq, *La Christianisation des foules. Étude sur la fin du paganisme populaire et sur les origines du culte des saints,* 4th ed. (Paris, 1907).
20. *Études mérovingiennes,* Actes des journées de Poitiers, 1–3 mai 1952 (Paris, 1953).
21. J. Fontaine, *Isidore de Séville et la culture classique dans l'Espagne wisigothique* (Paris, 1959).
22. F. Graus, *Volk, Herrscher und Heiliger im Reich der Merowinger,* (Prague, 1965).
23. H. Grundmann, "*Litteratus-illiteratus.* Der Wandlung einer Bildungsnorm vom Altertum zum Mittelalter," *Archiv für Kulturgeschichte* 40 (1958).
24. C. G. Loomis, *White Magic. An Introduction to the Folklore of Christian Legends* (Cambridge, Mass., 1948).
25. F. Lot, "A quelle époque a-t-on cessé de parler latin?" *Archivum Latinitatis Medii Aevi, Bulletin Du Cange,* 1931.
26. O. Loyer, *Les Chrétientés celtiques* (Paris, 1965).
27. S. McKenna, *Paganism and Pagan survivals in Spain up to the Fall of the Visigothic Kingdom* (Washington, 1938).
28. A. Marignan, *Études sur la civilisation mérovingienne. I. La Société mérovingienne. II. Le Culte des saints sous les Mérovingiens* (Paris, 1899).
29. H.-I. Marrou, *Saint Augustin et la fin de la culture antique,* 2e éd., (Paris, 1937) and *Retractatio* (1959).
30. *Id., Histoire de l'éducation dans l'Antiquité,* 5e éd. (Paris, 1960).

31. *Id., Nouvelle Histoire de l'Eglise. I. Des origines à Grégoire le Grand* (avec J. Daniélou) (Paris, 1963).
32. L. Musset, *Les Invasions. I. Les Vagues germaniques* (Paris, 1965). *II. Le Second Assaut contre l'Europe chrétienne* (Paris, 1966).
33. Dag Norberg, "A quelle époque a-t-on cessé de parler latin en Gaule?" *Annales, E.S.C.*, 1966.
34. G. Penco, "La composizione sociale delle communità monastiche nei primi secoli," *Studia Monastica* IV (1962).
35. H. Pirenne, "De l'état de l'instruction des laïcs à l'époque mérovingienne," *Revue belge de Philologie et d'Histoire*, 1934.
36. F. Prinz, *Frühes Mönchtum im Frankenreich. Kultur und Gesellschaft in Gallien, den Rheinlanden und Bayern am Beispiel der monastischen Entwicklung, IV bis VIII Jahrhundert* (Munich-Vienna, 1965).
37. P. Riché, *Éducation et Culture dans l'Occident barbare* (Paris, 1962).
38. M. Roblin, "Paganisme et rusticité," *Annales, E.S.C.*, 1953.
39. *Id.*, "Le culte de saint Martin dans la région de Senlis," *Journal des Savants*, 1965.
40. J.-L. Romero, *Sociedad y cultura en la temprana Edad Media* (Montevideo, 1959).
41. *Saint Germain d'Auxerre et son temps* (Auxerre, 1960).
42. "Saint Martin et son temps. Mémorial du XVIᵉ Centenaire des débuts du monachisme en Gaule," *Studia Anselmiana* XLVI (Rome, 1961).
43. P. Saintyves, *Les Saints successeurs des dieux* (Paris, 1907).
44. *Id., En marge de la Légende Dorée. Songes, miracles et survivances. Essai sur la formation de quelques thèmes hagiographiques* (Paris, 1930).
45. E. Salin, *La Civilisation mérovingienne d'après les sépultures, les textes et le laboratoire* (Paris, 4 vols., 1949–59).
46. *Settimane di studio del Centro Italiano di Studi sull'alto Medioevo* (1954 sqq.), esp. IX. *Il passaggio dell'Antichità al Medioevo in Occidente* (1962).
47. *The Conflict between Paganism and Christianity in the IVth century*, ed. A. Momigliano (Oxford, 1963).
48. A. Varagnac, *Civilisation traditionnelle et genres de vie* (Paris, 1948).
49. G. Vogel, *La Discipline pénitentielle en Gaule des origines à la fin du XIIᵉ siècle* (Paris, 1952).
50. *Id., Introduction aux sources de l'histoire du culte chrétien au Moyen Age* (Spoleto, 1965).
51. J. Zellinger, *Augustin und die Volksfrömmigkeit. Blicke in den frühchristlichen Alltag* (Munich, 1933).

ECCLESIASTICAL CULTURE AND FOLKLORE IN THE MIDDLE AGES

1. On the aristocratic origins of saints in Merovingian hagiography, see the excellent remarks of F. Graus, *Volk, Herrscher, und Heiliger im Reich der Merowinger* (Prague, 1965), pp. 362 ff. On the monastic milieu, cf. F. Prinz, *Frühes Mönchtum im Frankenreich* (Munich and Vienna, 1965), pp. 46 ff: "Lerinum als 'Fluchtlingskloster' der nordgallischen Aristokratie."
2. On Fortunatus, cf. W. Wattenbach and W. Levison, *Deutschlands Geschichtsquellen im Mittelalter: Vorzeit und Karolinger*, 1 (Weimar, 1952), 96 ff.
3. The *Vita S. Marcelli* by Fortunatus was published by Bruno Krusch in *MGH, Script. Rer. Mer.* IV/2 (1885²), 49–54. At the end of this essay, we have included the tenth and final chapter of the *Vita* according to this edition. On Saint Marcellus of Paris, cf. *Acta Sanctorum*, Nov., I (1887), 259–67 (G. van Hoof), in which may be found the text of Fortunatus' *Vita* reproducing that of Migne, *PL* 88, 541–50; and *Vies des Saints et des Bienheureux selon l'ordre du calendrier avec l'historique des fêtes*, by the Benedictines of Paris, vol. 10, November (Paris, 1954), 45–49. These two articles contain nothing about the processional dragon.
4. *Gloria Confessorum c. 87*, in *MGH, Script. Rer. Mer.* I/2, p. 804.

5. Concerning Saint Marcellus of Chalon-sur-Saône and his cult in the Parisian region (this cult is supposed to have been encouraged in the sixth century by king Gontran; in the ninth century, Saint Marcellus of Chalon was the patron of the largest parish in the domain of Saint-Denis), cf. M. Roblin, *Le Terroir de Paris aux époques gallo-romaine et franque* (Paris, 1951), p. 165.

6. Two theses from the Ecole des Chartres were devoted to the *bourg* Saint-Marcel of Paris: J. Ruinaut, *Essai historique sur les origines et l'organisation de l'église de Saint-Marcel de Paris, 5th c.–1597* (1910) ("Positions des thèses... de l'Ecole des Chartes," 1910, pp. 179–84); and, on the bourg itself, M. L. Concasty, *Le Bourg Saint-Marcel à Paris, des origines au XVIe siècle* (1937) (ibid., 1937, pp. 26 ff.). On the church and cemetery of Saint-Marcel, cf. "Les églises suburbaines de Paris du IVe au Xe s." by M. Vieillard-Troïekouroff, D. Fossard, E. Chatel, C. Lamy-Lassalle, in *Paris et Ile-de-France*, Mémoires publiés par la Fédération des Sociétés historiques et archéologiques de Paris et de l'Ile-de-France, 11 (1960), pp. 122 ff.

7. On the history of the cult of Saint Marcellus of Paris, cf. P. Perdrizet, *Le Calendrier parisien à la fin du Moyen Age d'après le bréviaire et les livres d'heures* (Paris, 1933), under the heading "Marcel."

8. When Saint Louis requested all the relics of Paris to come and welcome the crown of thorns into the city in 1248, when it came from Saint-Denis where it had been awaiting the consecration of the Sainte-Chapelle, the relics of Saint Marcellus and Saint Genevieve did not come. Cf. Don Michel Félibien, *Histoire de la ville de Paris*, edited, expanded, and brought up to date by Dom G. A. Lobineau (Paris, 1725) 50, I, 295. On Saint Louis and the relics of Saint Genevieve, cf. Carolus-Barre, "Saint Louis et la translation des corps saints," in *Etudes d'histoire du droit canonique dédiées à Gabriel Le Bras* 2 (Paris, 1965), 1110–12.

9. It was here, for example, that the council of the province of Sens was held in 1346. Cf. e.g. Berty, *Les Trois Ilots de la Cité* (1860), p. 29.

10. Le Nain de Tillemont, *Histoire de Saint Louis* (1693) 10, 415.

11. It will not be possible to treat the polyvalent symbolism of the dragon in anything approaching an exhaustive manner here, nor will we attempt to cite the vast literature devoted to this subject. Mircea Eliade, especially, stresses the "polysymbolism of the dragon and serpent" (*Traité d'histoire des religions*, new ed. [Paris, 1964], p. 179). Interesting observations are to be found in two articles concerning dragon symbolism: L. Mackensen, in *Handwörterbuch des deutschen Aberglaubens* 2 (1929–39), cols. 364–405; and R. Merkelbach, in *Reallexicon für Antike und Christentum* 4 (1959), cols. 226–50. The latter states, concerning the dragon of Saint Marcellus, that "nicht ganz klar ist die Legende vom Drachensieg des heiligen Marcellus" and summarizes Fortunatus' text without giving an interpretation. We shall return to Mackensen's article (see n. 139 below).

12. On the medieval symbolism of lust-serpent and the depiction of the woman devoured by a serpent, cf. esp. Emile Mâle, *L'Art religieux du XIIe siècle en France* (Paris, 1953⁶) [translated by Dora Nussey as *The Gothic Image* (New York, 1958)], "La Femme aux serpents," pp. 374–76 (which neglects the whole archaic background of a theme connected with the myth of the Mother-Goddess); and V. H. Debidour, *Le Bestiaire sculpté en France* (Paris, 1961), pp. 48, 309, 317, 320, and figs. 438 and 440. The variants serpent-dragon (the medieval bestiary, when concerned with the tempter in Genesis, adds the griffin to this list) are very old; in the Greek tradition, the pair *drakon-ophis* is found, and, in the Hebrew *tannîn-nâhâsh*. In the Middle Ages there was even an explanation for the loss of wings and paws which transformed the dragon-griffin into a serpent, using a text from Genesis 2:14 ("Et ait Dominus Deus ad serpentem: quia fecisti hoc, maledictus es inter omnia animantia et bestias terrae; super pectus tuum gradieris"). Cf. F. Wild, *Drachen im Beowulf und andere Drachen* (Vienna, 1962).

13. On this episode, cf. W. Levison, *Konstantinische Schenkung und Silvester-Legende,*

Stude e Testi, 38 (Rome, 1924), pp. 155–247; reprinted in *Aus rheinischer und frankischer Frühzeit* (Dusseldorf, 1948), pp. 390–465; and G. de Tervarent, *Les Enigmes de l'art du Moyen Age*, 2d series, *Art flamand* (Paris, 1941), 6, "Le pape au dragon," pp. 49–50.

14. On these exotic creatures in churches, cf. Perdrizet, under "Marcel," and Mâle, pp. 325–26. (No document, to my knowledge, permits the assertion that medieval churches were "veritable museums of natural history"—this phenomenon seems to me to have come later.) Mâle cites J. Berger de Xivrey, *Traditions tératologiques* (1836), p. 484. But the griffin's claw suspended in the vault of the Sainte-Chappelle is not found in Bartholomew the Englishman nor in the translation made by Jean de Corbichon for Charles V. This was an addition to the manuscript transcribed by Berger de Xivrey, written in 1512.

15. "Lettre adressée à M. Alexandre Lenoir au sujet de son Mémoire sur le dragon de Metz appelé Graouilli," from *Magasin encyclopédique* 1 (1812).

16. In *Revue encyclopédique* 30, nos. 88 and 89 (1826).

17. Paris, 1829; Paris, 1842², preceded by the speech of François Arago at the tomb of Eusèbe Salverte, 30 October 1839; Paris, 1856³, with an introduction by Emile Littré.

18. L. Dumont, *La Tarasque: Essai de description d'un fait local d'un point de vue ethnographique* (Paris, 1951), pp. 213 ff.

19. This may have been the case with the crocodile of Nîmes, which was said to have been brought from Egypt by Roman legionnaires. But this explanation, from L. J. B. Feraud, *Superstitions et survivances étudiées au point de vue de leur origine et de leurs transformations* (Paris, 1896), is subject to caution; for the author was a *rationalist*, a descendant of Salverte.

20. On "depth psychology," cf. the exploratory propositions of A. Dupront, "Problèmes et méthodes d'une histoire de la psychologie collective," *Annales, E.S.C.*, 1961. On the historicity of folklore, cf. G. Cocchiara, "Paganitas: Sopravivenze folkloriche del paganesimo siciliano," *Atti del 1° congresso internazionale di studi sulla Sicilia antica*, Studi pubblicati dall'Istituto di storia antica dell'Università di Palermo, 10–11 (1964–65), 401–16.

21. The importance of these physical details has been shown particularly well by Dumont (in the rite, pp. 51–63; in the legend, pp. 155–63; in the interpretation, pp. 207–8).

22. The best work on Merovingian hagiography is that of F. Graus (cf. n. 1 above), where an ample bibliography may be found.

23. Cf. F. Spadafora, *Dizionario Biblico* (Rome, 1955), under "Dragone."

24. On the "two Geneses" and the "two serpents" which may be traced through certain contradictions or discrepancies in the biblical text, cf. James G. Frazer, *Folk-lore in the Old Testament*, abridged ed. (London, 1923), pp. 15 ff.

25. Among the characteristic signs which make it comparable with the dragon of Saint Marcellus, note the following: (1) the habitat in moist places ("in locis humentibus," Job 40:16; in the twelfth century, on a miniature from the *Hortus deliciarum* of Herrad of Landsberg, wavy marks indicate that the dragon is in the ocean; cf. M. M. Davy, *Essai sur la symbolique romane* [Paris, 1955], p. 167). (2) The tail (Behemoth: "stringit caudam suam quasi cedrum," Job 40:12). (3) The neck (and more generally, the head of Leviathan: "in collo ejus morabitur fortitudo," Job 41:13). On dragons, and especially Daniel's dragon, in the biblical Apocrypha, Graus, p. 231, and Merkelbach, col. 247.

26. E.g., Ps. 73:13; 90:13; 148:7.

27. Rev. 12:3. On the medieval commentaries on the Apocalypse, see the incomparable repertoire of F. Stegmuller, *Repertorium biblicum medii aevi*. M. R. Sanfacon, professor at the Université Laval in Quebec, and Msgr. G. Vézin are preparing works on the iconography of the Apocalypse. The dragons of the Apocalypse had many uses, moral, aesthetic, and political.

28. There is little to be gleaned in the article "dragon" (H. Leclercq) in the *Dictionnaire d'archéologie chrétienne et de liturgie* IV/2 (1921), cols. 1537–40, which is derivative of older works which were valuable in their time but useful for following the progress of the historiography of the question. According to Dom Jérôme Lauret, e.g., in *Sylva allegoriarum totius sacrae Scripturae* (Venice, 1575), "for the Fathers of the Church, the dragon was a species of serpent of large dimensions, living in the water, pestilential and horrible; dragons usually signify Satan and his companions; Lucifer is called great dragon." In Marangoni's work *Delle cose gentilesche e profane trasportate ad uso e ad ornamento delle chiese* (Rome, 1744), the link was established between pagan and Christian dragons on the one hand, and archaeological and iconographic texts and documents on the other. The early methods of the history of religion and anthropology may be found in A. Longpérier, "Sur les dragons de l'antiquité, leur véritable forme, et sur les animaux fabuleux des légendes," *Comptes rendus de la 2e session du Congrès international d'anthropologie et d'archéologie préhistorique*, 1867, pp. 285–86, and in M. Meyer, "Ueber die Verwandtschaft heidnischer und christlicher Drachentödter," *Verhandlungen der XL Versammlung deutscher Philologie* (Leipzig, 1890), pp. 336 ff. This article has the additional merit of calling attention to the text of Gregory the Great (*Dialogi* II, c. XXV): "De monacho qui, ingrato eo de monasterio discedends, draconem contra se in itinere invenit" which shows the ancient usage of the dragon in the Benedictine disciplinary symbolism and the political use of dragon symbolism in the Carolingian era, beginning with a text from the *Vita* of Saint Eucherius (*MGH, Script. Rer. Mer.* VII, 51), in the context of the ecclesiastical campaign to discredit Charles Martel, despoiler of churches: in 858, Louis the German heard the opinion of the bishops of the provinces of Reims and Rouen that his great-great-grandfather Charles Martel was surely damned because Saint Eucherius of Orleans saw him one day right in the middle of hell, and a dragon had escaped from his tomb—a theme bearing a striking relationship with the dragon of the *Vita S. Marcelli* (cf. A. de Bastard, "Rapport sur une crosse du XII⁰ siècle," *Bulletin du Comité de la langue, de l'histoire et des arts de la France* (1860) 4, 450 and 683 n. 206).

29. Saint Augustine, *Enarratio in Psalmos* 103:27, PL 36/37, 1381–83.

30. This is a terrestrial dragon.

31. Saint Augustine, *Enarratio in Psalmos* 103:9, PL 36/37, 1943.

32. Cassiodorus, *Complexiones in Apocalypsim*, PL 70, 1411; and *Expositiones in Psalterium*, ibid., 531, (commentary on Ps. 73:13).

33. Primasius, *Commentarium in Apocalypsim*, PL LXVIII, 873–75.

34. Bede, *Hexameron*, PL 91, 53. *Commentarii in Pentateuchum*, PL 210–11; *Explanatio Apocalypsis*, PL 93, 166–67.

35. Isidore, *Etymologiae*, XII, iv, 4, PL 82, 442.

36. "Qui saepe a speluncis abstractus fertur in aerem, concitaturque propter eum aer . . . Vim autem non in dentibus, sed in caude habet, et verbere potius quam rictu nocet" (ibid.).

37. Isidore, *Differentiae* I, 9, (PL 83, 16): "in mari angues, in terra serpentes, in templo dracones." Isidore in fact reproduces Servius' commentary on Vergil, *Aenead* 2, 204.

38. Isidore, *Etymologiae* XII, iv, 42, PL 82, 455.

39. "In quarum hortis fingunt fabulae draconem pervigilem aurea mala servantem" (*Etym.* XIV, vi, 10, PL 82, 14).

40. "Draconum signa ab Apolline morte Pythonis serpentis inchoata sunt. Dehinc a Graecis et Romanis in bello gestari coeperunt" (*Etym.* XVIII, iii, 3, PL 82, 643).

41. "Annus quasi annulus . . . Sic enim et apud Aegyptis indicabatur ante inventas litteras, picto dracone caudam suam mordente, quia in se recurrit" (*Etym.* V, xxxvi, 2, PL 82, 222). On the "rolled up" dragon in the art of the Steppes and Merovingian art, cf. E. Salin, *La Civilisation mérovingienne d'après les sépultures, les textes et le laboratoire* 4

(Paris, 1959), 241–44, in which the author, following J. Grimm, gives the rather improbable and in any case derivative interpretation of the dragon as guardian of a treasure. Cf. Mircea Eliade, *Le Mythe de L'Eternel Retour: Archétype et répétition* (Paris, 1949). Translated by William R. Trask as *The Myth of the Eternal Return* (Princeton, 1954).

42. "Per idem tempus Donatus, Epiri episcopus, virtutibus insignis est habitus. Qui draconem ingentem, expuens in ore ejus peremit, quem octo juga boum ad locum incendii vix trahere potuerunt, ne aerem putredo ejus corrumperet" (*Chroniscon* 107, *PL* 83, 1051). In a different, more diabolical context, we find a dragon in the *Vita* of Saint Caesarius of Arles (ed. G. Morin [Maredsous, 1942] 2, 299–300); after Caesarius has left the monastery of Lérins for reasons of health, and has gone to Arles to devote himself to profane science, he falls asleep one night over his book and sees a dragon devouring his arm.

43. Cf. the works cited by the *Dictionnaire d'Archéologie* and mentioned in n. 28. It is unfortunate that the work of C. G. Loomis, *White Magic: An Introduction to the Folklore of Christian Legend* (Cambridge, Mass., 1948), is difficult to use because of its confusion and lack of chronological distinctions. Father Delehaye, whose works on hagiography remain fundamental in spite of their frequently outmoded problematics, did not approach this theme systematically. According to Graus, p. 231, n. 203, a general study of the theme of the dragon and of the combat with it has recently been undertaken by V. Schirmunski (cf. *Vergleichende Epenforschung* I[1], Deutsche Akademie der Wissenschaften zu Berlin, Veröffentlichungen des Instituts fur Deutsche Volskunde, 24 (Berlin, 1961), pp. 23 ff, which I have been unable to consult).

44. *PG* 26, 849. On the influence of the Life of Saint Anthony by Athanasius on Western hagiography in the early Middle Ages, cf. S. Cavallin, *Literarhistorische und textkritische Studien zur Vita S. Caesarii Arelatensis* (Lund. 1934).

45. This is the case studied by W. Levison, cited n. 13.

46. Cf. A. Graf, *Roma nella memoria e nell'immaginazione del medio evo* (Turin, 1923), pp. 177 and 442.

47. Cf. C. Cahier, *Caractéristiques des saints dans l'art populaire* (1867), p. 316, and Tervarent (see n. 13 above), p. 50. It is curious that Sylvester and Marcellus were both granted another miracle of the same type and similar to that of the fight with the dragon: they were said to have tamed a wild escaped bull (cf. for Sylvester, *The Golden Legend*, and for Marcellus, J. A. Dulaure, *Histoire physique, civile, et morale de Paris* (1837[5]) 1, 200 ff). Is this mere coincidence, a common memory of the struggle against the cult of Mithra, or a broader symbolism linked to the archaic symbolism of the bull?

48. Cf. R. M. Grant, *Miracle and Natural Law in Graeco-Roman and Early Christian thought* (Amsterdam, 1952), and R. Bloch, *Les Prodiges dans l'Antiquité classique* (Paris, 1963).

49. Gregory of Tours, *Historia Francorum* X, 1.

50. Cf. E. Kuster, "Die Schlange in der griechischen Kunst und Religion," *Religiongeschichtliche Versuche und Vorarbeiten* 13, no. 2 (1913).

51. Cf. L. Deubner, *De incubatione* (Giessen, 1899); M. Hamilton, *Incubation for the cure of Disease in pagan temples and Christian Churches* (London, 1906); P. Saintyves, *En marge de la légende dorée: Songes, miracles, et survivances* (Paris, 1930), pp. 27–33.

52. Suetonius, *Divi Augusti Vita* 94.

53. K. Herquet, "Der Kern der rhodischen Drachensage," *Wochenblatt des Johanniterordens Balley* (Brandenburg) 10, (1869), 151 ff.; R. Herzog, *Kos, Ergebnisse der deutschen Ausgrabungen und Forschungen,* 1 *Asklepieion* (Berlin, 1952).

54. For psychoanalytic interpretations of incubation, cf. in the orthodox Freudian tradition, Ernest Jones, *On the Nightmare* (1949[2]), pp. 92–97 (and on the medieval *incubi*, ibid., passim); by a disciple of Jung, C. A. Meier, *Antike Inkubation und moderne Psychotherapie*, Studien aus dem C. G. Jung-Institut, 1 (Zurich, 1949). For the

psychoanalytic and anthropological interpretation of the symbolism of the dragon and dragon slayers, I have been unable to consult the works of G. Roheim, "Dragons and Dragon Killers," *Ethnographia* (Budapest) 22, 1911; "The Dragon and the Hero," *American Imago* 1 (1940). In *Psychoanalysis and Anthropology* (New York, 1950), Géza Roheim follows Freud and Jones in defining the symbol as "the outward representative of a latent repressed content" (a definition which, if used, might revolutionize the study of medieval symbolism), treats the sexual symbolism of the serpent in antiquity (pp. 18–23), and suggests that of the dragon (cf. the statement of an Australian aborigine: "your penis is like a *muruntu* = dragon," ibid., p. 119).

55. Cf. Fontenrose, *Python: A study of Delphic Myth and its origins* (1959).

56. G. Elliot Smith, *The Evolution of the Dragon* (Manchester, 1919). Mircea Eliade, who has greatly stressed the connection of serpents and dragons with water, and dragons as "emblems of water" (Traité, pp. 179–82), does not cite this work.

57. Jurgis Baltrusaitis, *Le Moyen Age fantastique: Antiquités et exotismes dans l'art gothique* (Paris, 1955), chap. 5, "Ailes de chauve-souris et Démons chinois," pp. 151 ff. "The same evolution may be observed in the dragon, one of the incarnations of the devil. In Romanesque art, it is a serpent without wings or feet or a bird with a lizard's tail. In Gothic art, it has membrane-like wings. In this new form, one of the first representations may be seen in the Psalter of Edmond de Laci (d. 1258, Belvoir Castle)" (p. 153). Though bat wings may have influenced this evolution, the Romanesque dragon could perfectly well have wings and feet, as indicated by the one on the south wall of the Baptistry of Saint-Jean in Poitiers, which dates from around 1120 (P. Deschamps and M. Thibout, *La Peinture murale en France: Le Haut Moyen Age et l'époque romane* [Paris, 1951], p. 94). On Chinese and Asiatic dragons, particularly Hindu, cf. Eliade, *Traité*, pp. 180–82, and the bibliography, pp. 186–87, to which may be added, among others, H. C. Du Bose, *The Dragon: Image and Demon* (London, 1886); J. C. Ferguson, *Chinese Mythology* (Boston, 1928); R. Benz, *Der orientalische Schlangendrache* (1930); F. S. Daniels, "Snake and Dragon Lore of Japan," *Folklore* 71 (1960), 145–64. Cf. n. 133 below.

58. For example, the tempter may be seen in the form of a winged griffin on the bronze doors of the cathedral of Hildesheim (1015). Cf. H. Leisinger, *Bronzi Romanici: Porte di Chiese nell'Europa medioevale* (Milan, 1956), pl. 19. On the symbolism of the griffin, cf. K. Rathe, "Der Richter auf dem Fabeltier," in *Festschrift für Julius von Schlosser* (1927), pp. 187–208, and F. Wild, *Gryps-Greif-Gryphon (Griffin): Eine sprach-, kultur-, und stoffgeschichtliche Studie* (Vienna, 1963).

59. Forrer, "A propos d'un bijou à dragon émaillé trouvé à la Meinau," *Cahiers d'archéologie et d'histoire d'Alsace*, 1930, pp. 250 ff.

60. Salin, *La Civilisation mérovingienne* 4, 241.

61. Ibid., pp. 207–8.

62. Cf. A. Lenoir, "Mythologie celtique: Du dragon de Metz appelé Graouilli...," *Mémoires de l'Academie celtique* 2 (1808), 1–20; J. F. Cerquand, "Taranis et Thor," *Revue celtique* 6 (1883–86), 417–56; G. Henderson, *Celtic Dragon Myth* (Edinburgh, 1911).

63. Cf. J. J. Falsett, "Irische Heilige und Tiere in mittelalterlichen lateinischen Legenden," diss., Bonn, 1960; Graus, p. 231, n. 203, gives the example of a saint fighting with a dragon in Irish hagiography taken from episodes of the *Vita S. Abbani*, c. 15, 16, 18, 24 (in C. Plummer, *Vitae Sanctorum Hiberniae* 1 (Oxford, 1910), 12, 13, 15, 18 ff).

64. Cf. A. J. Reinach, "Divinités gauloises au serpent," *Revue archéologique*, 1911; P. M. Duval, *Les Dieux de la Gaule* (Paris, 1957), p. 51.

65. Cf. P. M. Duval, "Le dieu Smertrios et ses avatars gallo-romains," *Etudes celtiques* 6, no. 2 (1953–54).

66. On the dragon and the combat against it in universal folklore, cf. the abundant references in Stith Thompson, *Motif-Index of Folk Literature* (Copenhagen, 1955–58) 1,

348–55. These motives appear under reference B.11; but the dragon and similar motifs may also be found under other references, such as A.531, D.418.1.2 (Transformation: snake to dragon), H.1174.

67. Cf. Jacques Le Goff, "Clerical Culture and Folklore Traditions in Merovingian Civilization," reprinted above.

68. It cannot, however, be ruled out that Fortunatus may have been influenced by the assimilation which could have been made, according to R. Merkelbach (*Reallexicon*, col. 240), between the martyr and the fight with the dragon. We could then be faced with one of those attempts by early medieval hagiographers to keep the mythology of martyrology for the benefit of saints who were no longer martyrs. This interpretation, which as far as we know has never been proposed, seems to us complicated and risky.

69. Cf. G. Penco, "Il simbolismo animalesco nella letteratura monastica," *Studia monastica*, 1964, pp. 7–38; and "L'amicizia con gli animali," *Vita monastica* 17 (1963), 3–10. The dragon, considered a real animal, took part in that mysticism of interior creation for which W. von den Steinen has marvelously explained the role of the symbolic animal: "Altchristliche-mittelalterliche Tiersymbolik," *Symbolum* 4 (1964).

70. M. L. Concasty has demonstrated the importance of the floods of the Bièvre (*Positions*, 1937, p. 28).

71. M. Roblin, *Le terroir*, p. 114.

72. Cf. the Tarasque between forest and river ("a nemore in flumine"), L. Dumont, pp. 156–57.

73. On the economic role of the saints and bishops of the early Middle Ages, there are numerous indications in hagiography. One of the earliest examples, in the significant context of the valley of the middle Danube in the fifth century, may be found in the *Vita S. Severini* of Eugippius (*MGH, Auct. ant.* 1 [1877], 1–30).

Was dynastic propaganda Fortunatus' intention? This has been held in connection with the life of Saint Radegonde. Cf. D. Laporte, "Le royaume de Paris, dans l'œuvre hagiographique de Fortunat," in *Etudes mérovingiennes* (Paris, 1953), pp. 169 ff.

74. Concerning the legendary dragon and the establishment of Krakow, at the foot of the Wavel hills and on the banks of the Vistula, cf. art. "Krak" in *Slownik Folkloru Poskiego* (Dictionary of Polish Folklore), ed. J. Krzyzanowski (Warsaw, 1965), pp. 185–86.

75. *Vita s. Hilarii, MGH, Script. Rer. Mer.*, IV/2, p. 5.

76. The dragon of the Apocalypse, moreover, sustains a similar fate: "et misit eum in abyssum, et clausit, et signavit super illum, ut non seducat amplius gentes" (XX, 3).

77. "Apparet quantum est melio Adam secundus antiquo. Ille serpenti paruit, iste servos habet, qui possunt serpentibus imperare. Ille per bestiam de sede paradysi proiectus est, iste de suis cubilibus serpentem exclusit."

78. *PL* 76, 680.

79. Rabanus Maurus, *De universo* VIII, 3; *PL* 3, 229–30.

80. "Mystice draco aut diabolum significat aut ministros ejus vel etiam persecutores Ecclesiae, homines nefandos, cujus mysterium in pluribus locis Scripturae invenitur" (ibid., 230). On this exegetical method, cf. H. de Lubac, *Exégèse médiévale, les quatre sens de l'Ecriture* (Paris, 1959–64).

81. Little on the dragon is to be found in the still basic work by E. Mâle, *L'Art religieux*. The work of F. d'Ayzac, "Iconographie du dragon," *Revue de l'art chrétien* 8 (1864), 75–95, 169–94, 333–61 (cf. on the tail of the dragon pp. 183–89) has aged. L. Réau, *Iconographie de l'art chrétien* 1 (Paris, 1955). "Le symbolisme animal: dragon," pp. 115–16, is hasty and confused. V. H. Debidour, *Le Bestiaire sculpté en France* (Paris, 1961), passim (cf. Index, dragon), is hasty but contains some judicious observations and fine illustrations.

82. There is moreover no dragon in the Latin *Physiologus* from the fourth or fifth

century, whose influence would be great in the late Middle Ages, particularly from the thirteenth to the fifteenth centuries. Cf. *Physiologus latinus*, ed. F. Carmoody (1939), p. 97.

83. Cf. Mâle, pp. 384–85. Odo of Cluny, *PL* 133, 489. Bruno of Asti, *PL* 164, 685. Honorius Augustodunensis, *Speculum Ecclesiae*, *PL* 172, 937. It is interesting to note that there is no dragon in Honorius' encyclopedia, the *Imago Mundi*.

84. On the iconography of the dragon in the book of Revelation, see Réau, *Iconographie* 3/2 (1957), 708–12.

85. Cf. Debidour, pp. 129–33. On the Cistercian environment and the game of Romanesque forms in the initials of manuscripts, cf. O. Pächt, "The pre-Carolingian roots of early romanesque art," in *Studies in Western Art*, 1, *Romanesque and Gothic Art*, Acts of the Tenth International Congress of the History of Art (Princeton, 1963), p. 71 and pl. XIX, 6.

86. On the dragons depicted on baptismal fonts (symbolism of water and the aquatic dragon), cf. J. T. Perry, "Dragons and monsters beneath baptismal fonts," *Reliquary*, s. 3, II (1905), 189–95; G. Le Blanc Smith, "Some Dragonesque Forms on, and beneath, Fonts," ibid. 13 (1907), 217–27.

87. Cf. C. Heitz, *Recherches sur les rapports entre architecture et liturgie à l'époque carolingienne* (Paris, 1963).

88. Illus. in Debidour, p. 347. From the vast bibliography on Saint George and the dragon, a theme far from having given up all its secrets, see Aufhauser, "Das Drachenwunder des hl. Georg," in *Byzantinisches Archiv*. 5 (1911), 52–69.

89. Cf. Debidour, illus. p. 98.

90. Cf. plate from the catalogue of the exposition *Cathédrales* (Paris: Musée du Louvre, 1962). Note that the personage in question was the founder of a feudal dynasty, and a pioneer land clearer.

91. Cf. R. Mentz, *Die Träume in den altfranzösischen Karls- und Artusepen* (Marburg, 1888); K. Heisig, "Die Geschichtsmetaphysik des Rolandliedes und ihre Vorgeschichte," *Zeitschrift für romanische Philologie* 55 (1935), 1–87. K. J. Steinmeyer, *Untersuchungen zur allegorischen Bedeutung der Träume im altfranzösischen Rolandlied* (1963) (and a review of it by J. Györy in *Cahiers de civilisation médiévale*, 1964, pp. 197–200).

92. "Ambivalence des animaux rêvés" (J. Györy, p. 200). Cf. J. Györy, "Le cosmos, un songe," in *Annales Universitatis Budapestinensis, Sectio philologica* 4 (1963), 87–110.

93. On the dragon in medieval dreams, from a psychoanalytical point of view, cf. E. Jones, *On the Nightmare*, pp. 170, 306.

94. Cf. *DACL*. For the representations of dragons on currency, cf. R. Merkelbach, *Reallexicon*, pp. 243–45.

95. Cf. F. Stenton, *The Bayeux Tapestry* (London, 1957).

96. In connection with the banner-dragon, one may be surprised to read in G. Gougenheim, *Les Mots français dans l'histoire et dans la vie* 2 (Paris, 1966), 141–42: "No indication makes it possible to determine exactly what this dragon was nor what relationship it had with the fantastic animal denoted *dragon* (from the Latin *draco*). It is a pure product of the imagination to suppose that an image of this fantastic animal was painted or embroidered on the banner." A simple glance at the tapestry of Bayeux (cf. note 95 above) refutes these assertions.

97. Cf. J. S. P. Tatlock, "Geoffrey and King Arthur in Normannicus Draco," *Modern Philology* 31 (1933–34), 1–18, 113–25.

98. Cf. A. H. Krappe, "The fighting snakes in the Historia Britonum of Nennius," *Revue celtique* 43 (1926). A miniature from a late thirteenth-century manuscript (Paris, BN, Ms. fr. 95) shows Merlin carrying the standard-dragon in a battle. This miniature is reproduced in *Arthurian Literature in the Middle Ages*, ed. R. S. Loomis (Oxford, 1959), pl. 7, p. 320. Cf. R. Bromwich, *Trioedd Ynys Prydein: The Welsh Triads* (1961), pp. 93–95.

99. In connection with the Robert of Boron's Merlin: "The two dragons lying under the foundations of the tower that Vertigier wants to build are never precisely described, and their combat does not arouse horror or anguish. Above all, they have ceased to be monsters from another age, escaped from some bestiary of another world, with an ambiguous meaning that could be pondered endlessly. Through the voice of Merlin, Robert puts an end to all the equivocations and explains the symbol, which loses its poetic value." "L'Art du récit dans le Merlin de Robert de Boron, le Didot Perceval et le Parlevaus," *Romance Philology* 17 (1963–64), 579–80.

100. Cf. F. L. Utley, "Arthurian Romance and International Folklore Method," *Romance Philology* 17 (1963–64), in which the author indicates that Alan Loxterman and Miriam Kovitz are studying the relations between Type 300 (dragon-slayer) and Type 303 (the two brothers) with the story of Tristan.

101. Cf. M. Aubert's classic monograph *La Cathédrale Notre Dame de Paris, notice historique et archéologique* (1909, new ed. 1945), and for the illustrations, P. du Colombier, *Notre-Dame de Paris* (Paris, 1966).

102. Cf. Aubert, p. 117–18. The statue of Saint Marcellus currently in place is a copy from the nineteenth century. The deteriorated original belongs to the Cluny Museum and is presently kept in the north tower of the cathedral. I would like to take this opportunity to thank Mr. F. Salet, curator of the Cluny, for the information he was kind enough to provide. On the history of the sculptures in the Saint Anne portal, cf. *Cathédrales* (n. 90 above), p. 31.

103. Cf. W. Sauerländer, "Die kunstgeschichtliche Stellung der Westportale von Notre-Dame in Paris," *Marburger Jahrbuch fur Kunstwissenschaft* 17 (1959). A. Katzenellenbogen, *Sculptural Programs of Chartres Cathedral: Christ-Mary-Ecclesia* (Baltimore, 1959), and "Iconographic Novelties and Transformations in the Sculpture of French Church Façades, ca. 1160–1190," in *Studies in Western Art*, pp. 108–18.

104. Curiously called the "vampire of the cemetery" by Emile Mâle (p. 315).

105. Mâle, who clearly saw the role of the dragon in the *Golden Legend*, was mistaken in making a clerical initiative responsible for the origin of the theme ("originally, the story of the dragon was a pious metaphor thought up by the clerics," p. 291, n. 3).

106. Mâle, pp. 384–86.

107. On the processional dragons in France, cf. A. van Gennep, *Manuel de Folklore Français contemporain* 3 (Paris, 1937), 423–24 (with bibliography). An abridged list, with references, of processional dragons and saints who tame or vanquish dragons in France may be found in R. Devigne, *Le Légendaire des provinces françaises à travers notre folklore* (Paris, 1950), p. 152.

108. *Quart Livre,* chap. 59.

109. Cf. n. 18 above.

110. Cf. L. J. B. Berenger-Feraud, *Traditions et reminiscences populaires de la Provence* (Paris, 1886). E. H. Duprat, "Histoire des légendes saintes de Provence," *Mémoires de l'Institut historique de Provence* 17–20 (1940–46).

111. Cf. A. van Gennep, *Manuel* 1-4/2 (1949), 1644–45. In Troyes, "the dragon was carried triumphantly, decorated with flowers, ribbons and pompons; it seemed to be leading the crowd, which threw biscuits into its gaping jaws." (C. Lalore, "Le dragon—vulgairement dit Chair-Salée—de saint Loup évêque de Troyes. Etude iconographique," *Annuaire administratif, statistique et commercial du département de l'Aube* 51 [1877], 150). In Metz "in times past, the image of Graouilli, carried in the Rogation festivals in the city, would stop in front of the doors of bakers and pastry makers, who would throw breads and cakes into its mouth" (R. de Westphalen, *Petit Dictionnaire des traditions populaires messines* [Metz, 1934], col. 318).

112. Cf. J. Maehly, *Die Schlange im Mythus und Cultus der classischen Völker* [Basel, 1867], p. 13.

113. J. G. Frazer, *The Golden Bough* (London, 1915). Balder the Beautiful, vol. 2, pp.

31 ff, cited and apparently followed by A. Varagnac, *Civilisation traditionelle et genres de vie* (Paris, 1914), p. 105.

114. St. Avitus, *Homilia de rogationibus*, in *PL* 59, cols. 289–94. Cf. article "Rogations" in *DACL* XIV/2 (1948), cols. 2459–61 (H. Leclerq).

115. The text of the *Vita Barbati* concerning the Lombards (*MGH, Script. Rer. Lang.*, p. 557) and that relative to the council of Auxerre (*Concilia Galliae* II, ed. C. de Clerq, "Corpus christianorum," S. Latina 148A [1963]) may be found in E. Salin, 4, 48 and 494. The text of Saint Caesarius is in sermon 130, ed. G. Morin, "Corpus Christianorum," S. Latina 103 (1953).

116. On the representation of folklore by ecclesiastical culture in the early Middle Ages, cf. Graus and Le Goff.

117. A. van Gennep, *Le Folklore de la Flandre et du Hainaut français (département du Nord)* 1 (Paris, 1935), 154 ff.

118. For this information, noted by V. Gay in his *Glossaire archéologique* 1 (1887), 569, I am indebted to Françoise Piponnier, to whom I express my gratitude. According to the same sources, a processional dragon is found in the *Inventaire de Saint-Père de Chartres* in 1399.

119. Réau, *Iconographie* III/2 (1958), 874.

120. *Histoire civile, physique, et morale de Paris* (Paris, 1821-25), with many reeditions in the nineteenth century, some of them annotated. I would like to take this opportunity to express my warmest thanks to Father Baudoin de Gaiffier and Anne Terroine, who were good enough to share with me their incomparable knowledge of Parisian hagiography and history in connection with Saint Marcellus' processional dragon.

121. Dulaure (1823²) 2, 228, n. 1.

122. Several old editions of Guillaume Durand's *Rationale* are extant; it is worthy of a modern critical edition. I used the Lyons edition of 1565. Processional dragons are treated in chapter 102, "De rogationibus." According to L. Falletti, (*Dictionnaire de droit canonique,* ed. R. Naz, vol. 5 [Paris, 1953], cols. 1055–57), the *Rationale* was "the earliest work published by Durand as bishop of Mende" (col. 1033). It would therefore date from around 1290.

123. Jean Beleth, *Rationale divinorum officiorum, PL* 202, 130. As presumptive evidence in favor of the thesis, one may note that there has been no continuity in animal disguises or mannequins since the early Middle Ages, but that the processional dragons must have appeared around the middle of the twelfth century. One may also note that Rupert of Deutz (d. 1129) in his liturgical treatise *De divinis oficiis*, lib. IX, cap. V, "de rogationibus," *PL* 170, 248–50, makes no allusion to processional dragons and mentions only the crosses and the banners ("cruces atque vexilla praeferuntur"), and alludes to the "labarum."

124. James of Vitry, *Sermones* (Venice, 1518), p. 762.

125. This symbolism was frequently not understood by twelfth-century clerics. E.g., *Glossa ordinaria* (*PL* 114, 732) which, commenting on Rev. 12:4, "Et cauda," explains: "id est deceptione, quibus celant vitia, ut cauda celantur turpia." Similarly, Alan of Lille (*Distinctiones dictionum theologicarum, PL* 210, 775–76, article "draco") interprets *cauda* as *extrema ejus persuasio*. This article contributes little to dragon symbolism but does show the state of the question among scholastic clerics in the late twelfth century. Alan distinguishes the proper meaning (i.e., that the dragon is a real animal) and five symbolic meanings: "malitia," "diabolus," "gentilis populus," "Antichristus," and, in the plural, "gentes malitiosae" and, more especially, "superbi Judaei." This is where the dragon and antisemitism meet. But the theme seems not to have been exploited. It is true that the basilicus, rather a rare symbol of the Jewish people in the Middle Ages, is quite close to the dragon as the "king of the serpents" (cf. B. Blumenkranz, *Le Juif médiéval au miroir de l'art chrétien* [Paris, 1966], p. 64). At most, we see on a miniature of the *Liber Floridus* (early twelfth century) the mouth of the infernal

Leviathan alongside the symbolic Synagogue (Blumenkranz, fig. 121, p. 107).

126. Once again we have an ancient feature repeated uncomprehendingly by liturgy: that of the "backward-looking monster" (cf. Salin, 4, 209–22). On the third day, Guillaume Durand notes that the dragon went "quasi retro aspiciens."

127. Text of the Pseudo-Marcella and references in Dumont, p. 150. Pseudo-Marcella in Mombritus, *Sanctuarium seu vitae sanctorum . . .*, new ed. (1910) 2, 128–29. Vincent of Beauvais, *Speculum Historiae* 10, 99. Jacobus da Varagine, *Legenda aurea*, ed. Graesse (1846), pp. 444–45.

128. Dumont, p. 161.

129. Ibid., p. 226.

130. Ibid., p. 199.

131. On carnival masks, cf. O. Karf, "Über Tiermasken," in *Wörter und Sachen* 5 (1913); *Deutsche Fastnachtspeile aus dem 15ten Jahrhundert*, ed. A. von Keller (Tübingen, 1853–58); A. Spamer, *Deutsche Fastnachtsbräuche* (Jena, 1936).

132. Dumont, p. 227.

133. M. Battard, *Beffrois, Halles, Hôtels de ville dans le nord de la France et la Belgique* (Arras, 1948), p. 36. On the dragons which are guardians of treasures, cf. H. R. Ellis, "The Hill of the Dragon: Anglo-Saxon Burial Mounds in Literature and Archaeology," *Folklore* 61, 169–85.

134. Cf. F. Wild, *Drachen im Beowulf und andere Drachen mit einem Anhang: Drachenfeldzeichen, Drachenwappen und St. Georg.*, Osterreichische Akad. der Wiss. Phil.-hist. Kl. Sitzungsber, 238, 5 Abh. (Vienna, 1962).

135. Westphalen, *Petit Dictionnaire*, col. 317. The text of Rupert of Deutz cited in n. 123 gives this text a certain theoretical basis, however. Should one see a historical relationship between Saint Clement of Metz and his Graouilly on the one hand, and Saint Marcellus of Paris and his dragon on the other? According to tradition, the suburban church of Saint-Marcel was constructed on the site of a chapel originally dedicated to Saint Clement. In "Les églises suburbaines" (see n. 6 above), it is stated that the cult of Saint Clement appeared in Saint-Marcel only in the twelfth century, i.e., during the period which we believe to be critical for the processional dragons (a seal of Saint-Marcel affixed to an act of 1202 bears the images of Saint Clement and Saint Marcellus). But it could be Saint Clement, pope, rather than Saint Clement of Metz.

136. A. van Gennep, *Manuel* I–IV/2, pp. 1624 ff., "Fêtes liturgiques folklorisées (et specialement les Rogations)." On "folklorization" of the cult of the saints, cf. M. Zender, *Räume und Schichten mittelalterlicher Heiligenverehrung in ihrer Bedeutung für die Volkskunde: Die Heiligen des mittleren Maaslandes und des Rheinlandes in Kultgeschichte und Kultverbreitung* (Düsseldorf, 1959).

137. Cf. Erich Köhler, *Trobadorlyrik und höfischer Roman* (Berlin, 1962). And from the same author, "Observations historiques et sociologiques sur la poésie des troubadours," *Cahiers de civilisation médiévale*, 1964, pp. 27–51.

138. Lalore, *Le Dragon (vulgairement dit Chair-Salée)*, p. 150. The almost hundred-year-old study by Abbot Lalore testifies to an exceptional perspicacity and open-mindedness. Having noted the medieval liturgical sources, the images of dragons on money and banners, the author saw that there were two dragons in one, the one tamed by Saint Lupus and the one carried in the procession. He looked for Chinese ancestors for the guardian dragons and found a good citation from a Chinese source showing that the dragon was the image of benevolent spirits and protectors of man for the Chinese, an emblem of superior intelligence: "I do not know how the dragon is carried through the winds and clouds and raised as high as the sky. I have seen Lao-Tse, and he resembles the dragon." (Windischmann, *Mémoires concernant les Chinois*, p. 394).

139. Conversely, Mackenson, as shown by Dumont, p. 221, was incapable (*Handwörterbuch*, art. "Drachen") of recognizing the specificity of popular practices reduced

to substitutes for legends of scholarly origin.

140. Varagnac, p. 105.

141. Dumont, pp. 219–20.

The Medieval West and the Indian Ocean

In addition to the sources cited below, I have particularly relied on the remarkable and well-illustrated article of Rudolf Wittkower, "Marvels of the East: A Study in the History of Monsters," *Journal of the Warburg and Courtauld Institutes* 5 (1942), 159–97, which also treats the Renaissance, even though this study focuses primarily on iconography and at times offers different interpretations from my own. Since the paper on which this article is based was first read (Venice, September 1962), a dissertation by H. Gregor, *Das Indienbild des Abendlandes (bis zum Ende des 13. Jahrhunderts)*, Wiener Dissertationen aus dem Gebiete der Geschichte, (Vienna, 1964), has appeared. In the introduction (p. 5), the author defines his subject as follows: "Indien ist schon für die Antike auf Grund seiner fernen Lage mehr ein Objekt der Phantasie als der realen Beobachtung gewesen... Der schreibende Mönch, der gelehrte Abt, sie waren in ihrem Wissen uber diesen Teil der Erde auf das angewiesen, was die antiken Autoren erzählten. Und von diesen oft kuriosen Berichten angeregt, wurde in ihrer Vorstellung Indien zum Wunderland schlechthin, in dem dank seiner Grösse, seines Reichtums und des fruchtbaren Klimas alles möglich war, was sich auf dieser Welt denken lässt". I would add that, by means of the miniature and sculpture, as well as scientific, didactic, romantic, and homiletic literature, the image of India penetrated medieval western society quite broadly and was not limited to an educated audience. It therefore furnishes evidence of the collective psychology and sensibility.

1. Medieval cartography is the object of a vast literature. We pay homage to the pioneer work of the Polish historian Joachim Lelewel, *La Géographie du Moyen Age*, 5 vols. (Brussels, 1853–57) and an atlas (1849), and cite the following useful works: K. Miller, *Mappae Mundi: 1895–1898;* F. Pulle, "La cartografia antica dell'India," *Studi italiani di filologia indo-iranica* 4–5 (1901–5). J. K. Wright, *The geographical lore of the Time of the Crusades* (New York, 1925); R. Uhden, "Zur Herkunft und Systematik der mittelalterlichen Weltkarte," *Geographische Zeitschrift* 37 (1931), 321–40; A. Kammerer, *La mer Rouge, l'Abyssinie et l'Arabie depuis l'Antiquité*, vol. 2, *Les guerres du poivre: Les Portugais dans l'océan Indien et la mer Rouge au XVIe siècle*, Histoire de la cartographie orientale (Cairo, 1935); G. H. T. Kimble, *Geography in the Middle Ages* (London, 1938); J. O. Thomson, *History of Ancient Geography* (Cambridge, 1948); L. Bagrow, *Die Geschichte der Kartographie* (Berlin, 1951). According to Kimble (p. 145), the only treatise on geography prior to the great discoveries which seems even vaguely aware of voyages in the Indian Ocean is the *Tractatus optimus super totam astrologiam* by Bernard of Verdun (cf. 1300). On the Catalonian mappemonde from the Biblioteca Estense, cf. Kammerer, p. 348.

2. Kammerer, p. 350.

3. Ibid., pp. 362, 354 ff., 369–70, 387–89.

4. Cf. F. Kunstmann, *Die Kenntnis Indiens im 15. Jahrhundert* (Munich, 1863).

5. Cf. Kimble, pp. 211 ff. The Pierre d'Ailly text is in chapter 19 of the *Imago Mundi* edited by E. Buron (Paris, 1930). Here is the text of Pius II, cited by Kimble, p. 213: "Plinius nepotis testimonio utitur qui Metello Celeri Gallie pro consuli donatos a rege Sueuorum Indos astruit qui ex India commercii causa navigantes tempestatibus essent in Germaniam arrepti. Nos apud Ottonem (Otto of Freising) legimus sub imperatoribus teutonicis Indicam navim et negociatores Indos in germanico littore fuisse deprehensos quos ventis agitatos ingratis ab orientali plaga venisse constabat. Quod accidere minime potuisset si ut perisque visum est septentrionale pelagus innavigabile concretumque esset a columnis herculeis Mauritanie atque Hispanie et Galliarum circuitus totusque ferme Occidens hodie navigatur. Orientem nobis in-

cognitum cum religionum atque impiorum diversitas tum barbaries immensa reddidit. Veteres tamen navigatum et Oceano qui extremas amplectitur terras a suis littoribus nomina indiderunt... Straboni multi consentiunt. Ptolemeus plurimum adversatur qui omne illud mare quod Indicum appellatur cum suis sinibus Arabico, Persico, Gangetico et qui proprio vocabulo magni nomen habet undique terra concludi arbitratus est."

6. Cf. Kammerer, pp. 353–54, and F. von Wieser, *Die Weltkarte des Antonin de Virga.*

7. Kammerer, pp. 354 ff.

8. Jurgis Baltrusaitis, *Reveils et prodiges: Le Gothique fantastique* (Paris, 1960), p. 250.

9. Cf. R. Hennig, *Terrae Incognitae*, 2d ed., 4 vols. (Leyden, 1944–56); A. P. Newton, *Travel and Travellers of the Middle Ages* (London, 1926); M. Mollat, "Le Moyen Age," in *Histoire universelle des explorations*, ed. L. H. Parias, vol. 1 (Paris, 1955); J. P. Roux, *Les Explorateurs au Moyen Age* (Paris, 1961); R. S. Lopez, "Nuove luci sugli Italiani in Estremo Oriente prima di Colombo," in *Studi Colombiani* 3 (Genoa, 1952), and "L'extrême frontière du commerce de l'Europe médiévale," *Le Moyen Age* 69 (1963).

10. Cf. Wittkower, p. 195, n. 1, which mentions the medieval statues of New College, Oxford, in which the students' reading of the *mirabilia mundi* is discussed. Cf. also Roux, pp. 138 ff, in a chapter improperly entitled "Des yeux ouverts sur l'inconnu."

11. Cf. L. Olschki, *L'Asia di Marco Polo* (Florence, 1957). On the Venetians' distrust of the Indian Ocean boats, cf. p. 17, and on the change of the character of Marco Polo's narrative, pp. 31–32.

12. Concerning the amazing resemblance between the fabulous India of the manuscripts of Kazwin (in particular, the *Cod. Arab.* 464 of Munich from 1280), cf. Wittkower, p. 175. On what Western scholars borrowed from Arab works that were more astrological and magical than scientific, cf. R. Lemay, "Dans l'Espagne du XIIe siècle: les traductions de l'arabe au latin," *Annales, E.S.C.*, 1963, pp. 639–65.

13. Strabo, II, 1, 9.

14. Aulus-Gellius, *Noctes Atticae* IX, 4.

15. Cf. E. L. Stevenson, *Geography of Claudius Ptolemy* (New York, 1932).

16. On the text of Saint Augustine, *De civitate Dei* XVI, 8: "An ex propagine Adam vel filiorum Noe quaedam genera hominum monstrosa prodiderint," cf. Wittkower, pp. 167–68. Albertus Magnus (*De animalibus* XXVI, 21) states, in connection with the gold-seeking ants of India, "sed hoc non satis est probatum per experimentum."

17. Pliny states (*Historia naturalis* VII, ii, 21) "praecipue India Aethiopumque tractus miraculis scatent."

18. The *Collectanea rerum memorabilium* of Solinus were published by Mommsen (2d ed. Berlin, 1895).

19. Martianus Capella's geography may be found in the sixth book of *De nuptiis Philologiae et Mercurii*, devoted to geometry.

20. Published by H. Omont, "Lettre à l'Empereur Adrian sur les merveilles de l'Asie," in *Bibliothèque de l'Ecole des Chartes* 24 (1913), 507 ff, based on the *Ms. Paris B.N. Nouv. acq. lat.* 1065, ff^{os}. 92 v°–95, from the ninth century.

21. The first two treatises, *Mirabilia* and *Epistola Premonis regis ad Traianum Imperatorem*, have been published by M. R. James, *Marvels of the East: A Full Reproduction of the Three Known Copies* (Oxford, 1929). The third, *De monstris et belluis*, was published by M. Haupt in *Opuscula* 2 (1876), 221 ff.

22. These texts have been published by F. Pfister, *Kleine Texte zum Alexanderroman*, Sammlung vulgär-lateinischer Texte, 4 (1910). W. W. Boer has put out a new critical edition of the *Epistola Alexandri ad Aristotelem* (The Hague, 1953).

23. All sources concerning Prester John have been collected by F. Zarncke in *Abhandlungen der phil.-hist. Klasse d. kgl. sachs. Gesell. d. Wiss.* 7 and 8 (1876–79). Cf. Henning, no. 13, III, chap. 115; L. Thorndike, *A History of Magic and Experimental*

Science (London, 1923) 2, 236 ff. C.-V. Langlois, *La Vie en France au Moyen Age* III, *La connaissance de la nature et du monde* (Paris, 1927), pp. 44–70. L. Olschki sees in the Letter of Prester John a text concerning a political utopia. "Der Brief des Presbyters Johannes," *Historische Zeitschrift* 144 (1931), 1–14, and *Storia letteraria delle scoperte geografiche* (1937), pp. 194 ff. I have been unable to consult Slessarev Vsevolod, *Priester John* (University of Minnesota, Minneapolis, 1959).

24. From the abundant literature on the medieval Alexander, I single out three recent, fundamental books: A. Abel, *Le Roman d'Alexandre, légendaire médiéval* (Brussels, 1955); G. Cary, *The Medieval Alexander* (Cambridge, 1956), and D. J. A. Ross, *Alexander historiatus: A Guide to Medieval Illustrated Alexander Literature*, Warburg Institute Surveys, 1 (London, 1963).

25. J. W. McCrindle, *Ancient India as Described by Ktesias the Knidian* (Westminster, 1882).

26. E. A. Schwanbeck, *Megasthenis Indica* (Bonn, 1846).

27. Isidore of Seville, *Etymologiae*, ed. W. M. Lindsay (London, 1911), chaps. 11, 12, 14, 16, 17. Cf. J. Fontaine, *Isidore de Seville et la culture classique dans l'Espagne wisigothique*, 2 vols. (Paris, 1959).

28. Rabanus Maurus, *De universo* or *De rerum naturis*, 8, 12, 4, 17, 19. Migne *PL* 111. Amelli, *Miniature sacre e profane dell'anno 1023 illustranti l'Enciclopedia medioevale di Rabano Mauro* (Montecassino, 1896). A. Goldschmidt, "Frühmittelalterliche illustrierte Enzyklopadien," *Vorträge der Bibliothek Warburg*, 1923–24. Lynn White Jr., "Technology and Invention in the Middle Ages" *Speculum* 15 (1940).

29. Migne, *PL* 172, I, 11–13.

30. *Historia Orientalis*, chaps. 86–92.

31. Cf. Wittkower, p. 169, n. 5.

32. Cf. James, n. 25, pp. 41 ff.

33. Cf. Wittkower, p. 170, n. 1. The Indian marvels are discussed in the *De proprietatibus rerum* in chaps. 12, 15, 16–18.

34. Cf. Wittkower, p. 170, nn. 8 and 9.

35. Cf. ibid., n. 2. On Dante, cf. De Gubernatis, "Dante e l'India," *Giornale della Società Asiatica Italiana* 3 (1889).

36. The Indian passages may be found in book 31, chaps. 124–31 (in particular, following Solinus and Isidore), in the *Speculum naturale;* and, in the *Speculum historiale*, a chapter "De India et ejus mirabilibus" (1, 64) and a long passage (4, 53–60), "De mirabilibus quae vidit Alexander in India," taken from the *Epistola Alexandri ad Aristotelem.*

37. Cf. A. Bovenschen, *Die Quelle für die Reisebeschreibung des Johann von Mandeville* (Berlin, 1888). *Mandevilles Reise in mittelniederdeutscher Übersetzungen*, ed. S. Martinsson (Lund, 1918). In John of Mandeville, we hear the echo of the adventures of Sinbad the Sailor, partly drawn from the same sources (esp. Pliny and Solinus). On the theme of the explorers of the Indian Ocean in medieval Moslem literature, cf. the edition by Eusebe Renaudot, *Anciennes relations des Indes et de la Chine de deux voyageurs mahométans* (Paris, 1718), and C. R. Beazley, *The Dawn of Modern Geography* (London, 1897) 1, 235–38, 438–50.

38. Cf. Grässe, *Gesta Romanorum* (Leipzig, 1905), and H. Oesterley, *Gesta Romanorum* (Berlin, 1872), pp. 574 ff. On the Indian *exempla* in medieval moral literature, cf. J. Klapper, *Exempla*, Sammlung mittellateinischer Texte, 2 (Heidelberg, 1911).

39. Pierre d'Ailly, *Imago Mundi*, ed. E. Buron (Paris, 1930), "De mirabilibus Indiae," pp. 264 ff.

40. On the iconography of the *mirabilia*, besides Wittkower's article, see two admirable works by J Baltrusaitis, *Le Moyen Age fantastique: Antiquités et exotismes dans l'art gothique* (Paris, 1955), and *Reveils et prodiges: Le Moyen Age fantastique* (Paris, 1960). It is still possible to read E. Mâle, *L'Art religieux du XIIe siècle en France*, 6th ed. (Paris,

1953): "La géographie du XIIᵉ siècle. La tradition antique. Les fables de Ctésias, de Megasthène, de Pline, de Solin sur les monstres. La colonne de Souvigny, tableau des merveilles du monde. Le tympan de Vézelay et les différents peuples du monde évangélisés par les apôtres," p. 321 ff. On the tympanum at Vezelay, see A. Katzenellenbogen, "The Central Tympanum at Vezelay," *Art Bulletin*, 1944, and F. Salet, *La Madeleine de Vézelay* (Melun, 1948).

41. On the iconographic and stylistic filiations in the miniatures of the *mirabilia Indiae* of the early Middle Ages, especially the Byzantine influences, cf. Wittkower, pp. 172–74.

42. Cf. ibid., p. 117.

43. Cf. the texts cited by Wittkower, p. 168, nn. 2 and 4. "Portenta esse ait Varro quae contra naturam nata videntur; sed non sunt contra naturam, quia divina voluntate fiunt." (Isidore of Seville, *Etymologiae* XI, iii, 1), and "Portentum ergo fit non contra naturam, sed contra quam est nota natura. Portenta autem, et ostenta, monstra, atque prodigia, ideo nuncupantur, quod portendere, atque ostendere, mostrare, atque praedicere aliqua futura videntur" (ibid., 2). A folio from the *Cod. 411* of Bruges is reproduced in Wittkower, fig. 44ª, p. 178.

44. See esp. the works of J. Baltrusaitis, cited n. 40.

45. On the three Indias, cf. e.g., Gervase of Tilbury, *Otia Imperialia*, ed. F. Liebrecht (Hannover, 1856) 1, p. 911, and H. Yule, *Cathay and the Way Thither* (London, 1914) 2, pp. 27 ff, and J. K. Wright, *The Geographical Lore . . .* , pp. 307 ff.

46. Cf. Wittkower, p. 197, and Jean de Plan Carpin, *Histoire des Mongols*, ed. J. Becquet and L. Hambis (Paris, 1965), n. 57, pp. 153–54.

47. Adam of Bremen, *Gesta Hammaburgensis ecclesiae*, book 4 passim, esp. chaps. 12, 15, 19, 25 (*MGH, SS* 7, and B. Schmeidler, *MGH, SS*, R. G. ed 2, 1917). Adam transplants the monstrous races of India to Scandinavia. Cf. K. Miller, *Mappae mundi* 4, 18.

48. Marco Polo, *La Description du Monde* (with the reproduction of miniatures from Ms. fr. 2810, Paris, BN entitled *Le Livre des Merveilles*), ed. L. Hambis (Paris, 1955), p. 292.

49. Rabanus Maurus, *De universo*, Migne *PL* 111, chap. 5, "De insulis": "Insulae dictae, quod in sale sint, id est in mari positae, quae in plurimis locis sacrae Scripturae aut ecclesias Christi significant aut specialiter quoslibet sanctos viros, qui truduntur fluctibus persecutionum, sed non destruuntur, quia a Deo proteguntur."

50. Marco Polo, p. 276.

51. Ibid., p. 253. Here is how the isles of gold and silver appear in Pierre d'Ailly's *Imago Mundi* (chap. 41, "De aliis insulis Oceani famosis"): "Crise et Argire insule in Indico Oceano site sunt adeo fecunde copia metallorum ut plerique eas auream superficiem et argenteam habere dixerunt unde et vocabulum sortite sunt."

52. *De Imagine Mundi*, Migne, *PL* 172, chaps. 11–13, cols. 123–25. The sentence cited is the beginning of chap. 12.

53. "Ut sunt ii qui aversas habent plantas, et octonos simul sedecim in pedibus digitos, et alii, qui habent canina capita, et ungues aduncos, quibus est vestis pellis pecudum, et vox latratus canum. Ibi etiam quaedam matres semel pariunt, canosque partus edunt, qui in senectude nigrescunt, et longa nostrae aetatis tempora excedunt. Sunt aliae, quae quinquennes pariunt: sed partus octavum annum non excedunt. Ibi sunt et monoculi, et Arimaspi et Cyclopes. Sunt et Scinopodae qui uno tantum fulti pede auram cursu vincunt, et in terram positi umbram sibi planta pedis erecti faciunt. Sunt alii absque capite, quibus sunt oculi in humeris, pro naso et ore duo foramina in pectore, setas habent ut bestiae. Sunt alii juxta fontem Gangis fluvii, qui solo odore cujusdam pomi vivunt, qui si longius eunt, pomum secum ferunt; moriuntur enim si pravum odorem trahunt" (ibid., chap. 12).

54. Let alone giant serpents that could swim the Indian Ocean, we are told that "Ibi est bestia ceucocroca, cujus corpus asini, clunes cervi, pectus et crura leonis,

pedes equi, ingens cornu bisulcum, vastus oris hiatus usque ad aures. In loco dentium os solidum, vox pene hominis . . . Ibi quoque Mantichora bestia, facie homo, triplex in dentibus ordo, corpore leo, cauda scorpio, oculis glauca, colore sanguinea, vox sibilus serpentum, fugiens discrimina volat, velecior cursu quam avis volatu, humanas carnes habens in usu. . . . " (ibid., chap. 13).

55. "On this island are the most marvelous and most wicked people in the world. They eat raw flesh and all manner of filth and are guilty of the worst cruelties. For there father eats son and son father, the husband eats his wife and the wife her husband" (*Les voyages en Asie au XIVe siècle du bienheureux frère Odoric de Pordenone, religieux de saint François. Recueil de voyages et de documents pour servir à l'histoire de la géographie depuis le XIIIe jusqu'à la fin du XVIe siècle* 10, ed. Henri Cordier [Paris, 1891], chap. 19, p. 237, "De l'isle de Dondiin").

56. "On this island (Necuveran, i.e., Nicobar), they have neither king nor lord but are like wild animals. And I tell you that they go completely naked, both men and women, and cover themselves with nothing at all. They have carnal relations like dogs in the street, wherever they may be, completely shamelessly, and respect no one; the father does not respect his daughter, nor the son his mother, and everyone does as he pleases and is able. They are a lawless people." Marco Polo, p. 248). This theme is combined with that of innocence, the golden age, and the "pious" brahmins, which I shall speak of below. E.g., "We go naked," say the ciugni, a special category of brahmins of Malabar, "because we want nothing from this world, because we came into this world without clothing and naked; and if we are not ashamed to show our member, it is because we commit no sin with it" (ibid. p. 269).

57. "It is the honest truth that this king has five hundred wives, and I mean brides, because, I tell you, as soon as he sees a beautiful lady or maid, he wants her for himself and takes her for his wife. And in this kingdom, there are some very beautiful women. And what is more, they make themselves up beautifully on their faces and their whole bodies" (ibid., p. 254). And further, e.g., "These little virgins, as long as they stay little virgins, have such firm flesh that you cannot squeeze it or pinch it anywhere. For a small coin, they'll let a man pinch them as much as he wants . . . On account of this firmness, their breasts do not hang down at all, but stand straight out in front. There are plenty of girls like that throughout the kingdom" (ibid., p. 261).

58. On Gog and Magog, cf. A. R. Annderson, *Alexander's Gate, and Magog and the Inclosed Nations* (Cambridge, Mass., 1932). On the antipodes, cf. G. Boffito, "La leggenda degli antipodi" in *Miscellanea di Studi storici in onore di Arturo Graf* (Bergamo, 1903), pp. 583–601, and J. Baltrusailis, *Cosmographie chrétienne dans l'art du Moyen Age* (Paris, 1939).

59. E. Tisserant, *Eastern Christianity in India* (London, 1957); U. Monneret de Villard, "Le leggende orientali sui Magi evangelistici," *Studi e Testi* 163 (1952); J. Dahlmann, *Die Thomaslegende* (Freiburg-in-Brisgau, 1912); L. W. Brown, *The Indian Christians of St. Thomas* (Cambridge, 1956). The passage from Gregory of Tours may be found in the *Liber in gloria martyrum* 31–32 (*MGH, SRM,* 1). On the pilgrimage of Heinrich von Moringen to India around 1200, cf. Caesarius of Heisterbach, *Dialogus miraculorum,* dist. VIII, cap. LIX, and R. Henning, *Terrae Incognitae* (Leyden, 1936–39) 2, 380 ff. On the embassy of Sigelmus, cf. William of Malmesbury, *De gestis regum anglorum libri quinque,* coll. Rerum britannicarum medii aevi scriptores, 90, ed. W. Stubbs, 1 (London, 1887), 130, and Henning, 2, 204–7.

60. On the Earthly Paradise, cf. L. I. Ringbom's basic work *Paradisus Terrestris: Myt, Bild och Verklighet* (with a summary in English and abundant illustrations).

61. Cf. R. Bernheimer, *Wild Men in the Middle Ages: A study in Art, Sentiment, and Demonology* (Cambridge, Mass., 1952). The brahmins were the inspiration of an abundant literature, both in the Middle Ages (since the *De moribus Brachmanorum* by Pseudo-Ambrosius: in Migne *PL* 17) and in modern historiography. Cf. H. Becker, *Die*

Brahmanen in der Alexandersage (Konigsberg, 1889); F. Pfister, "Das Nachleben der Überlieferung von Alexander und den Brahmanen," *Hermes* 76 (1941); G. Boas, *Essays on Primitivism and Related Ideas in the Middle Ages* (Baltimore, 1948), and H. Gregor, *Das Indienbild...*, pp. 36–43. Petrarch wrote "Illud importunae superbiae est quod se peccatum non habere confirmant... Placet ille contemptus mundi, qui iusto maior esse non potest, placet solitudo, placet libertas qua nulli gentium tanta est; placet silentium, placet otium, placet quies, placet intenta cogitatio, placet integritas atque securitas, modo temeritas absit; placet animorum aequalitas, unaque semper frons et nulli rei timor aut cupiditas, placet sylvestris habitatio fontisque vicinitas, quem ut in eo libro scriptum est quasi uber terrae matris incorruptum atque integrum in os mulgere consueverant." It is important to link this myth of the Indian Earthly Paradise to the numerous marvels which recur traditionally among the *mirabilia Indiae:* the fountain of youth in which Prester John bathed six times, by virtue of which he was already more than five hundred years old; the trees whose leaves were always green; theriaca, a panacea for all ailments; the immortal phoenix; the unspotted unicorn, etc. It was in India that the Middle Ages located the sun tree and the moon tree, talking trees that pronounced oracles and played an important role in alchemy (they are indicated on the table of Peutinger, the cards of Ebstofer and of Hereford; cf. C. G. Jung, *Psychologie und Alchimie*, 2d ed. (Zurich, 1952), pp. 105 and 321). To these marvelous trees, Solinus added the table of the sun, the Ethiopian magi sitting around it, their plates constantly refilled by miraculous means—a myth that was a precursor of Never-Never Land, in which it is easy to see the obsession with food of a world haunted by hunger. Finally it should be noted that, in contrast with the myth of a primitive, forested India prior to the corruptions of civilization, we also find a myth of a populous and suburbanized India (five thousand large cities and nine thousand nations according to Solinus, 52, 4).

62. Cf. Wittkower, p. 177. With Emile Mâle (p. 330), we should observe that the monstrous races of India represented on the tympana of Vézelay and other churches represented the physical and moral degradation of humanity after the original sin, as a twelfth-century poet explains (*Histoire littéraire de la France* 10, 8).

63. Cf. Sigmund Freud, "Mythologische Parallele zu einer plastichen Zwangs-vorstellung, *Internationale Zeitschrift für ärztliche Psychoanalyse* 4 (1916–17) (cited by Wittkower, p. 197, n. 7). In literary dreams in the medieval West, of course, the monsters, especially the dragons and griffins that abound in India, represent the dreamer's enemy. Can we ask whether the army of ferocious and fantastic beasts that attack the Frankish troops in Charlemagne's nightmare (*Chanson de Roland*, lines 2525–54) and that are supposed to be the soldiers of the "Emir of Babylon," is not really the fantastic world of India sweeping down on Christendom? Cf. R. Mentz, *Die träume in altfranzösischen Karls- und Artus-Epen* (Marburg, 1887), pp. 39 and 64–65; K. J. Steinmeyer, *Untersuchungen zur allegorischen Bedeutung der Träume im altfranzösischen Rolandslied* (Munich, 1963), and J. Györy's note in *Cahiers de Civilisation médiévale* 7 (1964), 197–200. To the theme of the cosmos in medieval literature ("Le cosmos, un songe," *Annales Universitatis Budapestinensis, Sectio philologica* 4 [1963]) Györy has applied a method which I think is close to the one I am applying here to the geographical and ethnographic myth of India.

64. H. Hosten, "The Mouthless Indians," *Journal and Proceedings of the Asiatic Society of Bengal* 8 (1912).

65. Niccolò Conti, who traded in India, China, and the Sunda Isles from 1419 to 1444, had to become a Moslem in order to carry on his business. When he returned to Europe, he asked the pope to grant him absolution, and as penitence the pope required him to write an account of his travels. Cf. M. Longhena, *Viaggi in Persia, India e Giava di Niccolò de' Conti* (Milan, 1929), p. 179; Poggio Bracciolini, *Historia de varietate fortunae*, lib. IV; Henning, *Terrae Incognitae* 4, 29 ff., and Wittkower, p. 163, n. 5.

66. "Homodubii qui usque ad umbilicum hominis speciem habent, reliquo corpore onagro similes, cruribus ut aves . . ." (legend on a manuscript of the *Mirabilia Indiae*, London, British Museum, Tiberius B V, f° 82 v°, from around the year 1000; cf. R. Wittkower, loc. cit., p. 173, n. 1).

DREAMS IN THE CULTURE AND COLLECTIVE PSYCHOLOGY OF THE MEDIEVAL WEST

1. Cf. A. Besançon, "Vers une histoire psychanalytique," I and II, *Annales E.S.C.*, 1969, nos. 3 and 4, pp. 594–616 and 1011–33.

2. Dom Paul Antin, in "Autour du songe de Saint Jérôme," *Revue des Etudes latines* 41 (1963), 350–77, has presented a remarkable body of information but has kept to a medical interpretation without interest, like the majority of "scientistic" explanations.

3. K.-J. Steinmeyer, *Untersuchungen zur allegorischen Bedeutung der Träume im altfranzösischen Rolandslied* (Munich, 1963), is useful but does not go to the bottom of things. A good bibliography, from which we will single out, for literary thematics, R. Mentz, *Die Träume in den altfranzösischen Karls- und Artusepen* (Marburg, 1888), and, from a comparative and ethnological point of view, A. H. Krappe, "The Dreams of Charlemagne in the Chanson de Roland," *PMLA 36* (1921), 124–41.

4. Although Jung's concepts and vocabulary, for example, might attract the historian by their apparent relevance to his curiosities, we have thought it wise for a good many reasons to use Freud's work as our psychoanalytic reference, in as faithful an interpretation as possible. We found help in such tools as the *Vocabulaire de la psychanalyse* by J. Laplanche and J.-B. Pontalis (Paris, 1967), and the volumes of *The Hampstead Clinic Psychoanalytic Library*, particularly volume 2, *Basic Psychoanalytic Concepts on the Theory of Dreams*, ed. H. Nagera (London, 1969). Recall that in connection with the *Traumdeutung*, Freud was interested in historical studies, particularly P. Diepgen, *Traum und Traumdeutung als medizinisch-wissenschaftliches Problem im Mittelalter* (Berlin, 1912), which he cites beginning with the 4th edition of the *Traumdeutung* (1914). On the dream, social structures, and psychoanalysis, one may wish to consult two studies that appeared in *Le Rêve et les sociétés humaines*, ed. R. Caillois and G. E. von Grunebaum (Paris, 1967): A. Millan, "Le rêve et le caractère social," pp. 306–14, closely dependent on the psychoanalytic theories of Erich Fromm, and Toufy Fahd, "Le rêve dans la société islamique du Moyen Age," pp. 335–65, which is very suggestive. More broadly, see Roger Bastide, "Sociologie du rêve," ibid., pp. 177–88.

5. "The Chronicle of John of Worcester (1118–40)," ed. I. R. H. Weaver, *Anecdota Oxuniensia* 13 (1908), 32–33. The chronicler sets Henry's dream in 1130. In it, the king is successively threatened by the *laboratores*, the *bellatores*, and the *oratores*. The manuscript of the chronicle is decorated with miniatures depicting the triple dream. They are reproduced in Jacques Le Goff, *La Civilisation de l'Occident médiéval* (Paris, 1964), ill. 117–18. Cf. "A Note on Tripartite Society, Monarchical Ideology, and Economic Renewal in Ninth- to Twelfth-Century Christendom," above, pp. 53–57. On the tradition of royal dreams in eastern societies, cf. *Les Songes et leur interprétation*, coll. "Sources orientales," 2 (Paris, 1959), Index, under "Roi." Of course, Charlemagne's dreams should be analyzed as royal dreams.

6. Macrobius, *Commentarium in Somnium Scipionis* I, 3, ed. J. Willis, vol. 2 (Leipzig, 1963). Cf. W. H. Stahl, Macrobius, *Commentary on the Dream of Scipio*, translated with introduction and notes by . . . (1952), and P. Courcelle, author of several important works on Macrobius, in particular, "La postérité chrétienne du songe de Scipion," in *Revue des Etudes latines* 36 (1958), 205–34.

7. Gregory the Great, *Moralia in Job* I, viii (*PL* 75, 827–28) and *Dialogi* IV, 48 (*PL* 77, 409).

8. Isidore of Seville, *Sententiae* III, cap. VI: *De tentamentis somniorum* (*PL* 83, 668–71) and Appendix IX, *Sententiarum liber* IV, cap. XIII: *Quae sint genera somnibrum* (ibid., 1163).

9. Saint Jerome, *Ep.*, 22, 30 (ad Eustochium), ed. Hilberg, *CSEL* 54 (1910), 189–91, and Labourt, coll. "Bude," vol. 1 (1949), 144–46.

10. Sulpicius Severus, Life of Saint Martin, 3, 3–5, 5, 3, 7, 6, ep. 2, 1–6, and cf. Index, under "Rêves," in the edition with a remarkable commentary by Jacques Fontaine, 3 vols. Sources chrtiennes, nos. 133–134–135 (Paris, 1967–69).

11. Gregory of Tours, *De miraculis sancti Juliani,* c. IX: *De Fedamia paralytica.* Gregory of Tours, *De virtutibus sancti Martini,* c. LVI: *De muliere quae contractis in palma digitis venit.* It should be noted that the dream of Herman of Valencia cited below (end of twelfth century) is, in a degenerate form, a dream of incubation. One of Jung's disciples has studied incubation from a psychoanalytic standpoint. C. A. Meier, *Antike Inkubation und modern Psychotherapie* (1949). He has also contributed "Le rêve et l'incubation dans l'ancienne Grèce" to the previously cited work, *Le Rêve et les sociétés humaines,* pp. 290–304.

12. John of Salisbury, *Polycraticus* II, 15–16, ed. Webb (1909), pp. 88–96: "De speciebus somniorum, et causis, figuris et significationibus et Generalia quaedam de significationibus, tam somniorum, quam aliorum figuralium."

13. *Hildegardis Causae et Curae,* ed. P. Kaiser (Leipzig, 1903): *De Somniis,* pp. 82–3, *De nocturna oppressione et De somniis,* pp. 142–43.

14. *Liber De Spiritu et Anima (Pseudo-Augustinus),* c. XXV *PL* 40, 798). The reliance of *Pseudo-Augustinus* on Macrobius has been shown by L. Deubner, *De incubatione* (1900).

15. *Ci commence la senefiance de songes,* ed. Walter Suchier: "Altfranzösische Traumbücher," *Zeitschrift für französische Sprache und Literatur* 67 (1957), 154–56. Cf. Lynn Thordike, *A History of Magic and Experimental Science* 2 (London, 1923), chap. 50, "Ancient and Medieval Dream-Books," pp. 290–302.

16. It should be noted that Latin has no word for nightmare (Macrobius has no Latin equivalent for the Greek *ephialtes,* which he lumps with popular beliefs). This does appear in the vulgar languages during the Middle Ages. Cf. the fine historical psychoanalytic study by Ernest Jones, *On the Nightmare,* 2d ed. (1949).

17. *The Chronicle of John of Worcester,* pp. 41–42.

18. The *Roman de Sapience* by Herman of Valenciennes, unpublished portion of Ms. B. N. fr. 20039, lines 399–466. I owe this text to the kindness of J. R. Smeets of the University of Leyden.

19. M. Mauss, "Les techniques du corps," *Journal de Psychologie,* 1935, pp. 271–93, reprinted in *Sociologie et Anthropologie* (Paris, 1950).

20. Cf. the special number *"Histoire biologique et société"* of *Annales E.S.C.,* no. 6, November–December 1969.

21. Cf. esp. the contributions of G. Devereux, "Rêves pathogènes dans les sociétés non occidentales," in *Le Rêve et les sociétés humaines,* pp. 189–204; D. Eggan, "Le rêve chez les Indiens hopis," ibid., pp. 213–56; A. Irving Hallowell, "Le rôle des rêves dans la culture ojibwa," ibid., pp. 257–81. Geza Roheim, himself the author of "Psychoanalysis of Primitive Cultural Types," in *International Journal of Psycho-Analysis* 13 (1932), 1–224, has severely criticized the work of J. S. Lincoln, *The Dream in Primitive Cultures* (London, 1935). In the very suggestive collection mentioned previously, *Le Rêve et les sociétés humaines,* G. von Grunebaum has given an interesting definition of the characteristics of civilizations that he calls "medieval" or "premodern" (pp. 8–9), thus helping to situate them in relation to "primitive" civilizations. The prestige associated with comparative study, which is necessary and enlightening, should not obscure the importance of the differences.

22. On Artemidoros, C. Blum, *Studies in the Dream-Book of Artemidorus* (1936), and from a psychoanalytic point of view, W. Kurth's invaluable study "Das Traumbuch des Artemidoros im Lichte der Freudschen Traumlehre," *Psyche,* 4 Jg, 10 H (1951), 488–512.

23. We are referring to the famous passage (*Aeneid* VI, 893–98) dealing with the two gates of sleep, one of which, the horn gate, lets true shades pass, while the other, the ivory gate, lets false visions by:

> Sunt geminae somni portae: quarum altera fertur
> cornea, qua veris facilis datur existus umbris,
> altera candenti perfecta nitens elephanto,
> sed falsa ad caelum mittunt insomnia manes.
> His tibi tum natum Anchises unaque Sibyllam
> prosequitur dictis portaque emittit eburna.

These gates have obviously lent their name to the last book of G. Roheim, *The Gates of the Dream* (1953). Concerning this passage, the scholarly exegesis of E. L. Highbarger, *The Gates of Dreams: An Archaeological Examination of Aeneid VI, 893–899*, The Johns Hopkins University Studies in Archaeology, no. 30 (1940), expends a good deal of ingenuity and learning in the vain search for a geographical localization of the Vergilian oneiric universe. See also H. R. Steiner, *Der Traum in der Aeneis*, Diss. (Berne, 1952). On the meaning of *insomnia* in this text, see R. J. Getty, "Insomnia in the Lexica," *American Journal of Philology* 54 (1933), 1–28.

24. The Middle Ages made no clear distinction between dream and vision. The essential division was between sleep and wakefulness. Everything seen by a sleeping person belongs to the sphere of the dream. As so often happens, the researcher lacks a serious semantic study in this case. Cf. however the interesting and perceptive article by F. Schalk, "Somnium und verwandte Wörter im Romanischen," published in *Exempla romanischer Wortgeschichte* (Frankfurt am Main, 1966), pp. 295–337. To be of real use, the philological inquiry must be carried on in all the languages of medieval Christendom. One dreams of a work dealing with medieval societies comparable to the magisterial book by E. Benveniste, *Le Vocabulaire des institutions indo-européennes*, 2 vols. (Paris, 1969), which, moreover, is invaluable to the medievalist.

25. A typology and list of dreams from the Old Testament in E. L. Ehrlich, *Der Traum im Alten Testament* (1953). N. Vaschidé and H. Piéron, "La valeur du rêve prophétique dans la conception biblique," *Revue des traditions populaires* 16 (1901), 345–60, think that the Old Testament's reticence with regard to dreams comes particularly from the hostility between the Jewish prophets and the Chaldean soothsayers. Cf. A. Caquot, "Les songes et leur interprétation selon Canan et Israël," in *Les Songes et leur interprétation*, pp. 99–124.

26. A (brief) list of the dreams in the New Testament in A. Wikenhauer, "Die Traumgeschichte des Neuen Testaments in religionsgeschichtlicher Sicht," in *Pisciculi: Studien zur Religion und kultur des Altertums, Festschrift Franz Joseph Dolger* (Münster, 1939), pp. 320–33. The five dreams of the Gospels (all in Matthew concern the childhood of Christ and Saint Joseph) and the four in the Acts of the Apostles (all concern Saint Paul) refer to an oriental and a Hellenic model, respectively.

27. Cf. e.g., E. Ettlinger, "Precognitive Dreams in Celtic Legend and Folklore," *Transactions of the Folk-Lore Society* 59 (1948), 43. On divination, cf. the excellent collection of studies, *La Divination*, ed. A. Caquot and M. Lebovici, 2 vols. (Paris, 1968), from which the medieval West is, alas! absent.

28. On dreams in Saint Augustine, I am indebted to the kindness of J. Fontaine for having been able to consult the excellent study by Martine Dulaey, "Le Rêve dans la vie et la pensée de saint Augustin" (D.E.S. mimeographed, Paris, 1967), which makes use of F. X. Newman, "Somnium: Medieval Theories of Dreaming and the Form of Vision Poetry" (Ph.D. diss., Princeton University, 1963), which I have not yet been able to look at.

29. Cf. P. Saintyves, *En marge de la Légende Dorée* (1930): incubation in western Christian churches in the Middle Ages, and more particularly in the sanctuaries of the

Virgin. See also article on Incubation by H. Leclercq in *Dictionnaire d'archéologie chrétienne et de liturgie* VII-I (1926), coll. 511–17.

30. Albertus Magnus, *De somno et vigilia* (*Opera* V [Lyons, 1651], 64–109). Arnaud de Villeneuve, "Expositiones visionum, quae fiunt in somnis, ad utilitatem medicorum non modicam" (*Opera omnia* [Basel, 1585], pp. 623–40). Lynn Thorndike, *A History of Magic and Experimental Science* (New York, 1934) 3, 300–302, attributes this treatise to a certain master Guillaume d'Aragon on the basis of Ms. Paris B.N. lat. 7486.

31. Garde la moie mort n'i soit pas oubliee,
De latin en romanz soit toute transpose.
(Roman de Sapience, Ms. Paris, B.N. fr. 20039, lines 457–58.)

32. John of Salisbury, *Policraticus* II, 15–16. One may wish to compare this with the narrower, more scholastic conception, still rather similar, of the Ms. Bamberg Q VI 30, from the first half of the twelfth century, cited by M. Grabmann, *Geschichte der scholastischen Methode* (1911; repr. 1957) 2, 39, according to which the dream is one of the three ways for the soul to know *occulta Dei*.

MELUSINA: MOTHER AND PIONEER

1. Walter Map, *De nugis curialium*, ed. M. R. James (Oxford, 1914).

2. The only complete (but very imperfect) edition is in G. W. Leibniz, *Scriptores rerum Brunsvicensium* 1 (Hannover, 1709), 751, 784. F. Liebrecht has published the "marvelous" passages of the *Otia Imperialia*, with very interesting folkloric commentaries, with the subtitle *Ein Beitrag zur deutschen Mythologie und Sagenforschung* (Hannover, 1856). J. R. Caldwell was preparing a critical edition of the *Otia Imperialia* (cf. articles in *Scriptorium* 11 (1957) and 16 (1962), and in *Medieval Studies* 24 (1962). On Gervase of Tilbury: R. Bousquet, "Gervais de Tilbury inconnu," *Revue historique* 191 (1941), 1–22, and H. G. Richardson, "Gervase of Tilbury," *History* 46 (1961), 102–14.

3. This episode (*Otia Imperialia* III, 57, ed. Liebrecht, p. 26) is repeated by Jean d'Arras and placed in the Orient. One of Melusina's sisters, Melior, is exiled to the Castle of the Espervier in Greater Armenia by her mother Presine (ed. L. Stouff, p. 13).

4. This episode (*Otia Imperialia* I, 15, ed. Liebrecht, p. 4) has been compared with the story of Melusina but generally not with the story of Henno, even though they comprise a unified whole. In certain manuscripts of Jean d'Arras, Raymond of the *Otia Imperialia* is called Roger (p. 4). Is this a contamination Rocher-Roger or from another tradition? Cf. A. Duchesne's thesis referred to in note 11 below. In any event, it should be noted that Raymond already had a name when Melusina still had not.

5. Walter tells Edric's story twice. The second, shorter version does not mention Edric by name and follows immediately after the story of Henno (*De nugis curialium* IV, 10, ed. M. R. James, p. 176).

6. "Ad domum in hora nemoris magnam delatus est, quales Anglici in singulis singulas habebant diocesibus bibitorias, *ghildhus* Anglice dictas." This curious text seems to have escaped the notice of the historians of the guilds.

7. L. Stouff has compared this text with one of Jean d'Arras (p. 79) in which the city of Saintes is called Linges. E. Renardet, *Légendes, contes et traditions du Pays Lingon* (Paris, 1970), p. 260, mentions Melusina without giving a genuinely Lingonian version. Similarly, Marcelle Richard, in *Mythologie du Pays de Langres* (Paris, 1970), notes no specifically local elements, but she does make interesting observations about the serpent-dragon transformations, the chthonic and aquatic backgrounds, and the ambivalence of the dragon-serpent, which may not be maleficent but may rather symbolize, in the words of P.-M. Duval, "the reproductive fertility and prosperity of the earth." We have given an identical interpretation in "Ecclesiastical Culture and Folklore in the Middle Ages: Saint Marcellus of Paris and the Dragon," this volume, pp. 159–88.

8. "In Lingonensi provincia quidam nobilis in sylvarum abditis reperit mulieicm speciosam preciosis vestibus amictam, quam adamavit et duxit. Illa plurimum balneis delectabatur in quibus visa est aliquando a quadam puella in serpentis se specie volutare. Incusata viro et deprehensa in balneo, numquam deinceps in comparitura disparuit et adhuc durat ejus projenies" (Vincent of Beauvais, *Speculum naturale* II, 127, cited by L. Hoffrichter, p. 67).

9. A previously unnoticed comparison confirms the links among these stories, it seems to me. Edric's son Alnold, who wants to regain his health, is told to make a pilgrimage to Rome to ask for a cure from the apostles Peter and Paul. Angry, he answers that he will go first to Hereford to plead with Saint Ethelbert, king and martyr, of whom he is a "parishoner." (*De nugis curialium*, ed. M. W. James, p. 77).

10. Along with Melusina and in the same category, Walter Map, Gervase of Tilbury, and Jean d'Arras mention other fairies (demonic succubi) that are not serpents. Christianity had caused an upheaval in the typology. Although we point this out, we will confine ourselves to the "restricted" question. Cf. the fairy of Argouges noted by E. Le Roy Ladurie in his bibliographic note. The reader will have noticed other episodic echoes and transfers. "Large-toothed Henno" and "Geoffroy with the large tooth," the castle of Espervier in Dauphiné and that of Epervier in Armenia, etc.

11. Jean d'Arras must have known the *Otia Imperialia* through the fourteenth-century translation made by Jehan du Vignay, who was also the translator of the *Speculum naturale* of Vincent of Beauvais. These "sources" were available to Jean d'Arras in the library of Jean de Berry. A. Duchesne has devoted a thesis of the Ecole des Chartes (1971) to medieval French translations of the *Otia Imperialia*.

12. The study of popular culture or phenomena, or of works impregnated with popular culture, brings the historian into contact with a disconcerting "historical time." Slow rhythms, flashbacks, losses, and resurgences are not easily reconciled with the unilinear time in which he is at most accustomed to detecting "accelerations" or "retardations." This is yet another reason to rejoice that the broadening of the historical horizon to include folklore will result in calling this inadequate notion of time into question.

13. On Neapolitan and Vergilian *mirabilia*, see D. Comparetti, *Vergilio nel Medio Evo*, 2d ed. (1896), in English transl. republ. in 1966. J. W. Spargo, *Virgil the Necromancer* (Cambridge, Mass., 1934).

14. Cf. note 7 above.

15. M. R. James, Preface to the edition of *De nugis curialium* of Walter Map, p. xxii.

16. It should be noted that the existence of a nonwritten high culture (bards connected with "aristocratic" circles?) complicates the problem of Celtic and Germanic cultures, etc. The distinction between oral tradition and popular tradition is a matter of elementary prudence.

17. *Otia Imperialia*, ed. Liebrecht, p. 4.

18. It should be recalled that an important French review of folklore, established by Henri Gaidoz and Eugène Rolland, which brought out eleven volumes irregularly distributed over the period 1877 to 1912, was named *Mélusine* (a collection of mythology, popular literature, traditions, and customs).

19. Arnold van Gennep, *Manuel de folklore français contemporain* 4 (1938), 651–52. Van Gennep places the following "header" above the entries: "The origins of this quite typical folkloric theme are not known; Jehan d'Arras surely drew on popular material; despite its literarization, the theme has remained popular in certain regions, as may be seen in the monograph by Leo Desaivre, to which I am adding folkloric supplements classified in chronological order, without taking the works of medievalists into account, which would be beyond the limitations imposed on this Manual."

20. Antti Aarne and Stith Thompson, *The Types of the Folktale: A Classification and Bibliography*, 2d revision, FFC no. 184 (Helsinki, 1964). Faced with this monument, one is torn between admiration and gratitude on the one hand, and doubts as to the principles of classification on the other. Marie-Louise Tenèze, with the authority and courtesy which are hers, has expressed her reservations concerning that other monument, the *Motif-Index of Folk-Literature* by Stith Thompson, 6 vols. (Copenhagen, 1955–58) (M.-L. Tenèze, "Introduction à l'étude de la littérature orale: Le conte," *Annales, E.S.C.*, 1969, p. 1116, and "Du conte merveilleux comme genre," in *Approches de nos traditions orales*, ed. G. P. Maisonneuve and Larose, [Paris, 1970], p. 40). We believe that these reservations may be extended to *Types of the Folktale*.

21. In particular, we refer the reader to the remarkable study by M.-L. Tenèze cited in the preceding note.

22. From the abundant literature concerning the problem of the genres of "popular" literature, we single out H. Bausinger, *Formen der "Volkpoesie"* (Berlin, 1968), particularly vol. 3: (1) *Erzählformen*; (2) *Märchen*; (3) *Sage*; (4) *Legende*, pp. 154 ff. German authors refer to the Melusin*sage*.

23. J. and W. Grimm, *Die deutschen Sagen*, Preface to vol. 1 (Darmstadt, 1956), p. 7, cited by Bausinger, p. 170.

24. Cf. Hoffrichter, p. 68.

25. K. Heisig, "Über den Ursprung der Melusinensage," *Fabula* 3 (1959), 170–81. P. 178: "Aix liegt etwa 30 km nordlich von Marseille; man wird daher kaum fehlgeben, wenn man annimmt, dass Kaufleute aus Marseille die älteste Fassung des Märchens aus Zypern in ihre Heimat mitgebracht haben werden!".

26. Almost all the studies treat the etymology of Melusina. See particularly Henri Godin, "Mélusine et la philologie," in *Revue du Bas-Poitou*, and P. Martin-Civat, *Le Très Simple Secret de Mélusine* (Poitiers, 1969).

27. Cf. Hoffrichter and Desaivre, pp. 257 ff.

28. *Slownik Folkloru Polskiego*, ed. J. Krzyzanowski, under heading "Meluzyna," pp. 226–27.

29. *Zeitschrift für vergleichende Sprachforschung*, ed. Kuhn, 18 (1869).

30. Cf. Tenèze, "Du conte merveilleux comme genre," pp. 12–13, 16–17.

31. Vladimir Propp, *Morphology of the Folktale*, Eng. trans. (Indiana University Research Center in Anthropology, Folklore, and Linguistics), pp. 24–26.

32. Concerning all of this, in addition to the work of Claude Lévi-Strauss (particularly the series *Mythologiques*) and the collective work under the direction of E. F. Leach cited in the bibliography, see *Communications*, special number, "L'Analyse structurale du récit," no. 8 (1966), and Tenèze, esp. " . . . vers la structure 'logique' du genre" (pp. 20 ff.).

33. On the hero, cf. esp. Tenèze, p. 15, n. 7.

34. On this evolution, Jan de Vries, *Betrachtungen zum Märchen besonders in seinem Verhältnis zu Heldensage und Mythos*, FFC no. 154 (Helsinki, 1954). Cf. "Les contes populaires," *Diogène*, no. 22 (1958), 3–19. One could cite almost the whole of George Dumézil's work in this respect. We will single out the most recent work, *Du mythe au roman: La saga de Hadingus et autres essais* (Paris, 1970).

35. "Audivimus demones incubos et succubos, et concubitus eorum periculosos; heredes autem eorum aut sobolem felici fine beatam in antiquis historiis aut raro aut nunquam legimus, ut Alnoldi qui totam hereditatem suam Christo pro sanitate sua retribuit, et in eius obsequiis residuum vite peregrinus expendit" (Walter Map, conclusion of the story of Edric the Savage, *De nugis curialium* XI, 12, ed. James, p. 771). The same explanation is found in Gervase of Tilbury (*Otia Imperialia* I, 15, before the story of Raymond of Château-Rousset), which compares the case of serpent-women with that of werewolves. Similarly Jean d'Arras, who refers to Gervase of Tilbury. Jean d'Arras's originality was to stress the identification of these demonic succubi with

fairies (the importance in his work and mind of popular sources), and, moreover, his indication of the three taboos: "They made (their husbands) swear in some cases that they would never look at them naked, in others that on Saturdays they would never inquire what had become of them, in others that if they had children, the husbands would never look at them in their beds" (ed. Stouff, p. 4). He adds a good explanation of the mechanism of prosperity associated with the pact: "And as long as they kept their word, they enjoyed great happiness and prosperity. And as soon as they faltered, they lost these things and all their happiness fell away little by little." Earlier, Geoffrey of Monmouth, in the *Historia Regum Britanniae*, had spoken of love between humans and demons (incubi and succubi) in connection with the birth of Merlin (here the pair is reversed: mortal + demonic incubus).

36. In a youthful work, in connection with Urvashti, Georges Dumézil treated Melusinian themes by mentioning the totemic hypotheses of Frazer and, more particularly, by reference to J. Kohler's study and Slavic, especially Polish, works: "The nymph Urvashti is the head of a clan widespread in folklore: that of supernatural women who marry a mortal under a certain condition and disappear forever on the day the pact is violated, sometimes leaving the unfortunate spouse the consolation of a son, the first of a heroic line. In Europe, this theme from folklore is quite widespread, and the romances of Melusina have given it both literary consecration and new vitality: it flourishes from the *lemuziny* to the banks of the Vistula. But the Negroes and Redskins tell similar stories, and Sir James G. Frazer has advanced the hypothesis that these tales are the remains of a totemic mythology; indeed, among the Ojibways and on the Gold Coast, the form of these tales is closely linked to the organization of the society into totemic clans, and even in our European folklore, the half-human, half-animal nature of the heroine (if not the hero) has persisted . . . For our purposes, however, so obscure and remote an origin is unimportant; what matters to us, on the other hand, is the traits by which the story of the Pururavas and Urvashti is distinguished from the typical Melusinian tale" (*Le Problème des Centaures* [Paris, 1929], pp. 143–44).

37. Stated esp. in "Observations historiques et sociologiques sur la poésie des troubadours," *Cahiers de Civilisation médiévale* 7 (1964), reprinted in *Esprit und arkadische Freiheit: Aufsätze aus der Welt der Romania* (Frankfurt, 1966).

38. Cf. Claude Lévi-Strauss's comment: "Totemism is firstly the projection outside our own universe, as though by a kind of exorcism, of mental attitudes incompatible with the exigency of a discontinuity between man and nature which Christian thought has held to be essential" (*Totemism*, Eng. trans. [Beacon Press, 1963], p. 3). On the anti-humanism which vigorously opposed Romanesque and Gothic Christian humanism (continuity between man and the animal and vegetable kingdoms), cf. the iconographic information and stylistic analyses of Jurgis Baltrusaitis, *Le Moyen Age fantastique* (Paris, 1955), and *Réveils et Prodiges: Le gothique fantastique* (Paris, 1960). The touchstone, the great challenge to the idea of man made *ad imaginem Dei*, was the werewolf. Cf. Montague Summers, *The Werewolf* (London, 1933). Also disconcerting were the cases of the ape and the wild man. Cf. H. W. Janson, *Apes and Ape Lore in the Middle Ages and the Renaissance* (London, 1952), and Richard Bernheimer, *Wild Men in the Middle Ages: A Study in Art, Sentiment and Demonology* (Cambridge, Mass., 1952). F. Tinland, *L'Homme sauvage* (Paris, 1968).

39. Georges Dumézil, *Mythe et Epopée* 1 (Paris, 1968), 10.

40. Jan de Vries, *Les Contes populaires*, p. 13; cf. Tenèze on the *Wunschdichtung*, compensatory literature according to Max Luthi, "Du conte merveilleux," pp. 26–29.

41. Since the old, classic study by Alfred Maury, *Les Fées du Moyen Age* (Paris, 1843; new ed. 1896), medieval fairies have not greatly interested historians and appear in the works of folklorists only in connection with particular points. Cf. however, C. S. Lewis, *The Discarded Image: An Introduction to Medieval and Renaissance Literature*

(Cambridge, 1964), chap. 6, "The Longaevi," pp. 122–38. Lewis had noted, particularly in Walter Map, the reference to the souls of the dead; but his whole book seems to us vitiated by his conception of the Middle Ages as a "bookish" era (cf. esp. p. 11), which we believe false because blinkered by the traditionalist view of medieval studies and by the use of the myth of the "man of the Middle Ages" (e.g., p. 10: "Medieval man was not a dreamer nor a wanderer; he was an organiser, a codifier, a builder of systems, etc." *Filii mortue*, says Walter Map of the children of a pseudo-Melusina mentioned just before Henno's fairy (*De nugis curialium* IV, 8, ed. James, p. 174). J. Kohler had observed: "Es ist der Sagenstoff, der sich um die Orpheussage schlingt," p. 31. For his part, A. Maury pointed out that Melusina in Jean d'Arras "emits mournful cries each time death claims a Lusignan."

42. I would like particularly to thank Mr. Claude Gaignebet, who obtained for me the issues of the *Bulletin de la Société de Mythologie française* in which the articles concerning Melusina appeared, and Mr. Jean-Michel Guilcher, who called my attention to the miniatures in the Ms. Fr. 12575 of the B.N. (the oldest manuscript of Couldrette's *Roman de Mélusine*, from the fifteenth century).

THE SYMBOLIC RITUAL OF VASSALAGE

Appendix I(A): Symbolic objects of the system of vassalage, according to Du Cange
(art. *Investitura*)

1) Per cespitem (piece of turf)
2) Per herbam et terram
3) Per ramum et cespitem
4) Cum rano et guasone (vel wasone)
5) Per guazonem, andelaginem et ramos de arboribus
6) Per baculum
7) Per baculum et annulum
8) Per fustem
9) Cum ligno
10) Per cultellum
11) Per cultellum plicatum (incurvatum)
12) Per amphoram (full of sea water, Charta of Otto III)
13) Per annulum
14) Per beretam et beretum
15) Per berillum (14th–15th-century texts)
16) Per bibliothecam (Biblia)
17) Per calicem
18) Per cambutam (crook) episcopi (for abbot's investiture)
19) Per candelabrum
20) Canum venationum apprehensione
21) Per capillos capitis
22) Per chartam super altare
23) Per chirothecam (glove)
24) Per claves ecclesiae
25) Per clocas ecclesiae
26) Per coclear de turibulo (censer spoon)
27) Per colonnam
28) Per coronam
29) Per cornu (drinking horn)
30) Per corrigiam (belt)
31) Cum crocia abbatis
32) Per capellum prioris

33) Per cupam auream
34) Per cultrum, vel cultellum
35) Per communionem
36) Per denarios
37) Per digitum vel digito
38) Per dextrum pollicem
39) Per elemosynariam, hoc est marsupium
40) Per ferulam pastoralem
41) Per floccilum capillorum
42) Per folium
43) Per folium nucis
44) Per forfices (scissors)
45) Per fossilem chartae inhaerentem (fusciola, ribbon)
46) Per funes seu chordas campanarum
47) Per furcam lignean
48) Per gantum
49) Per gladium
50) Per grana incensi
51) Per haspam (hinge pin?)
52) Per hastam
53) Per herbam et terram
54) Per juncum
55) Per lapillum (boundary stone)
57) Per librum
58) Per librum manualem
59) Per librum missalem
60) Per librum collectarium (collect book)
61) Per librum evangeliorum et calicem
62) Cum libro regulae et cum regula
63) Per lignum
64) Per linteum (shirt)
65) Per lini portiunculam
66) Per malleolum (young plant, young vine)
67) Per manicam (glove)
68) Per mappulam (handkerchief)
69) Cum marmore
70) Per particulam marmoris
71) Per marsupium de pallio (cloth or silk purse)
72) Per martyrologium
73) Per unam mitram
74) Per nodum (the knot of a Sicilian chevalric order, 1352)
75) Per notulas (charts)
76) Per osculum
77) Per ostium domus
78) Per palam (altar cloth?)
79) Per pallium seu pallam
80) Per panem et librum
81) Per pannum sericum
82) Cum penna et calamario (inkwell)
83) Per pergamenum
84) Cum duobus phylacteris
85) Per pileum (Phrygian cap)
86) Per pisces

87) Per pollicem
88) Per psalterium
89) Per ramum filgerii (fern)
90) Per regulam
91) Per sceptrum
92) Per scyphum (cup)
93) Per spatae capulum (hilt?)
94) Per tellurem
95) Per textum evangelii
96) Cum veru (sharpened stake, pointed iron hafted at the end of a long stick)
97) Per vexillum
98) Per virgam vel virgulam
to which *manu* and *per manum* should be added, making 100 in all.

N.B.—I have already offered a critique of the typology which underlies this remarkable and suggestive list, but I would like to mention a couple of additional points. For reasons connected both with the nature of his sources and with his conception of medieval society, Du Cange took many of his examples from ecclesiastical investitures. In spite of the clear and significant contaminations, it is our opinion that these should be distinguished from the rites of vassalage as such, just as royal rites of coronation are. Similarly, it seems to me that he is too fascinated by the *baculus* and symbols of command. Although Von Amira does not make this distinction either, his justly celebrated article makes clear that the symbolism of the stick is found also in quite different societies and rites. Here, ethnohistorical analysis makes it possible to distinguish what learned studies in history and law have been too prone to confuse. Set in a broad comparative context, the novelty of Western medieval vassalage is brought out even more clearly.

Appendix I(B): Symbolic objects in contracts, according to M. Thévenin, *Textes relatifs aux institutions . . . mérovingiennes et carolingiennes* (1887), pp. 263–64.
Juridical symbols used in contracts, legal procedure, etc.
1) Andelangum (gauntlet). 42, 76, 117, 124
2) Anaticula. 30—Axadoria. 124
3) Arbusta. 98
4) Atramentarium. 50, 52, 136
5) Baculum. 135
6) Brachium in collum, et per comam capitis. 38
7) Claves. 37
8) Cibum et potum. 84
9) Cultellus. 50, 52, 105, 136, 143
10) Corrigia ad collum. 110—Cordas ad collum. 155
11) Denarius. Penny and denarius, 42. Quatuor denarii super caput. 151, 155, 157, 161, 162, 171
12) Finger: incurvatis digitis, 148, 159
13) Ensis. 48
14) Festuca. 16 (see page 18, note 2, 29, 42, 52, 73, 103, 105, 107, 108, 124, 136, 143, 148. Jactare et calcare (the straw), 137, 141
15) Fuste buxea. 116
16) Herba. 29, 30, 100 ter (et cespitem), 124
17) Sod.—*See also* Wasonem
18) Launegild. 48. Camisia 6. Facetergis (handkerchief). 61
19) Ligamen serici. 170
20) Medella. 70
21) Osculum. 177

22) Ostium. 30, 124
23) Ramum arboris. 52, 136, 143
24) Radicem. 121
25) Secmento. 170
26) Terra. 29, 30, 98, 124. Clod of earth, 79
27) Vinea. 98. Vineas faciebat et ad radicem fodicabat et operas faciebat per potestatem, 121
28) Virgula. 173
29) Wantonem. 48, 52, 136, 143
30) Wasonem terrae. 52, 105, 136, 143
31) Wadium. Settlement of pledges. *See* Security by pledges.

Appendix I(C): Schema of feudo-vassal symbolism

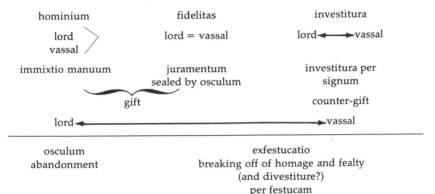

Appendix II: Concerning the *festuca*

In the wake of my lecture at Spoleto and the ensuing discussion, I received an interesting letter from Mr. Alessandro Vitale-Brovarone of the Istituto di Filosofia Moderna de la Facoltà di Magistero of the University of Turin. This may be found reproduced in the *Settimane* XXIII, 775–77.

Notes

1. Walter Ullmann, *The Carolingian Renaissance and the Idea of Kingship*, The Birkbeck Lectures 1968–69 (London, 1969).

2. I would like to thank Gerard Genette for having been kind enough to send me the French translation of the interesting article by Johan Chydenius, "La théorie du symbolisme médiéval" (published in English in *Societas scientiarum fenmica*, 1960) before its appearance in *Poétique*, no. 23 (1975), 322–41.

It would be possible to complete this study by reference to any one of several indices, particularly that of Migne's *Patrologiae latina*, which is incomplete and in need of checking, but here, as so often, fertile in leads. In particular, one might consult the second volume of the index, cols. 123–274, for references to the article *De allegoriis* under the heading *De Scripturis*, which has, among other things, definitions of *allegoria* ("eum aliud dicitur et aliud significatur," according to Saint Jerome), *figura seu typus* ("antiphrasis cum per contrarium verba dicuntur," according to Saint Augustine, who gives, among other examples, "transgressio Adae typus justitiae Salvatoris et baptisma typus mortis Christi," with indications of a semantic field including *praefigurare, praesignare, designare, interpretari, exprimere*, etc.), *parabolae* ("similitudines rerum quae comparantur rebus de quibus agitur," according to

Rufinus), etc. In ibid., cols. 919–28, in connection with *symbolum*, Migne can do no more than reflect the poverty of the use of the word in medieval Latin. Apart from its meaning in Greek (with the equivalent in classic Latin, *indicatio* and *collatio*), the only meaning indicated is *regula fidei*. To this absence of *symbolum* from medieval Latin with its Greek and modern senses, it is possible to find exceptions which confirm the rule, among the rare Latin theologians with a smattering of Greek, e.g. John Scotus Erigena.

3. Cited by Du Cange, *Glossarium ad scriptores mediae et infimae latinitas* (1733 ed.) 3, col. 1533, art. *Investitura*. We should emphasize that Du Cange takes *investitura* in the broad sense, including not only ecclesiastical "investitures" but also a variety of donations which give rise to symbolic rituals.

4. Emile Chénon, "Le rôle juridique de l'*osculum* dans l'ancien droit français," *Mémoires de la Société des Antiquaires de France*, ser. 8, vol. 6 (1919–23), 133, no. 2, citing the cartulary of Obazine from René Fage, *La Propriété rurale en Bas-Limousin pendant le Moyen Age* (Paris, 1917), p. 260.

5. Guillaume Durand, *Speculum juris* II, lib. IV, 3, sec. 2, no. 8, cited by Chénon, p. 139, no. 2.

6. Lambert d'Ardres, *Historia comitum Ghisnensium* in *MGH, Scriptores* 16, 596.

7. F. L. Ganshof, *Qu'est-ce que la féodalité?* Translated as *Feudalism* (see bibliography, p. 367 below, sec. B).

8. Galbert de Bruges, *Histoire du meurtre de Charles le Bon*, ed. H. Pirenne (Paris, 1891), p. 89. This work has been translated by J. B. Ross as *Murder of Charles the Good* (New York, 1967). The English edition of Ganshof, *Feudalism*, contains a translation of the relevant portions of Galbert's account (p. 71) along with the Latin. A slightly different translation of the account of the homage may be found in *Murder of Charles the Good*, pp. 206–7.

9. Ermold the Black, *In honorem Hludowicii*, Classiques de l'histoire de France, ed. and transl. E. Faral (1932), lines 2484–85, in Boutruche, p. 366.

10. *Formulae Marculfi* I, 18, in *MGH, Formulae Merowingici et Karolini aevi*, ed. Zeumer, part 1 (1882), p. 55, with (French) translation in Boutruche, pp. 364–35.

11. *Annales Regni Francorum*, ed. F. Kurze (1895), p. 14, in *MGH, Scriptores Rerum Germanicorum in usum scholarum* 6, cited and translated (into French) in Boutruche, p. 365.

12. It would be useful to have as complete and as exact as possible an inventory of the expressions used. On the basis of the examples given by Ganshof, *Feudalism*, pp. 73–78. I think it is possible for our purposes, i.e., to understand the reciprocity of the gesture, to make an initial classification which would distinguish the expressions which stress the vassal's initiative ("manus alicui dare," "in manus alicuius venire," "regis manibus sese militeturum committit" concerning William Long Sword, Second Count of Normandy, who became vassal of Charles the Simple in 927) from those which give precedence to the lord's acceptance ("aliquem per manus accipere") and those which primarily express the juxtaposition of the two gestures and the mutual commitments ("omnes qui priori imperatori servierant . . . regi manus complicant . . .") according to Thietmar of Merseburg in connection with homages done to Henry II on the eastern borders of Germany in 1002, or else the expression "alicuius manibus iunctis fore feodalem hominum" from an English charter of the time of William the Conqueror, studied by D. C. Douglas, "A Charter of Enfeoffment under William the Conqueror," *English Historical Review* 42 (1927), 427.

13. In addition to the work of P. Ourliac and J. de Malafosse (see bibliography, p. 367, sec. B), for ancient Roman law I have used primarily the great work by Edoardo Volterra, *Istituzioni di diritto privato romano* (Rome, 1961).

14. C. Sanchez Albornoz, *En torno a los origenes del feudalismo* (Mendoza, 1942).

15. H. Grassotti, *Las Instituciones feudo-vassaláticas en León y Castilla*, 2 vols.

(Spoleto, 1969), esp. vol. 1, *El vassalaje*, chap. 2, "Besamanos," pp. 141–62.

16. To judge from the examples given by Hilda Grassotti, it may be that a certain royal model, probably of oriental origin reinforced by Moslem practices, played a special role in Spain. More than the problem of oriental and Moslem influences, what we find interesting in this hypothesis is the problem of the relation between rites of vassalage and royal rites, on which we shall have more to say later. H. Grassotti points out the many examples of hand kissing in the *Poema del Cid*, noted by Menendez Pidal, for example: "Por estos vos besa las manos,. commo vassalo a señor," but also "Besamos vos las manos commo a Rey y a señor." In Moslem Spain what is stressed (again, reciprocity of the gesture) is the signal favor being accorded by the Caliph when he gives his hand to be kissed. When Jean de Gorze, ambassador of Otto I, is received by 'Abd-al-Rahman III in 956, the latter gives his hand to be kissed "quasi numen quoddam nullis aut raris accessibile." Similarly, when Ordono IV is received by al-Hakam II at Medina-al-Zahra, of which Claudio Sanchez Albornoz has given a very realist account following al-Maqquari, probably using medieval sources.

17. Cf. note 3 above.

18. *Livre de jostice et de plet* XII, 22, sec. 1, ed. Rapetti (Paris, 1850), p. 254, cited by Chénon, p. 138.

19. In a 1322 charter, Hugh, bishop-elect of Carpentras, receives the homage of a minor child and his governess. He takes the hands of both the child and its governess between his for the homage and faith, but he gives the *osculum* only to the child, "remisso ejusdem dominae tutricis osculo propter honestatem." Cited by Du Cange, *Glossarium*, art. *Osculum*, and Chénon, pp. 145–46, and p. 146, n. 1.

20. Chénon, p. 149.

21. *Casus S. Galli*, c. 16, ed. von Arx, *MGH, SS* 2, 141, in Boutruche, p. 367.

22. Cf. note 11 above.

23. Teulet, *Layettes du Trésor des chartes* 1, no. 39, cited in Chénon, p. 141, n. 1.

24. Ramos y Loscertales, "La sucesion del Rey Alfonso VI," in *Anuario de Historia del Derecho español* 13, 67–69, cited in Grassotti, p. 169.

25. Du Cange, *Glossarium* 3, art. *Investitura*, cols. 1520–38. I am unstinting in my praise for this remarkable article, a fine example of the erudition of the era in which it was written. At the same time, of course, it is open to criticism. As I pointed out above, in note 3, one particular difficulty is that *investitura* is taken in too broad a sense. But even if there are many symbolic objects used in ecclesiastical "investitures" or just plain gifts, I have used Du Cange's references because, for this part of the feudal ceremonial of vassalage, the ritual and its symbolism seem identical to me.

26. This list may be found in Appendix I A above. Of course, regardless of the extent of Du Cange's erudition, his list should be completed by as broad as possible a collection of data, which should be analyzed statistically, though the result would be only approximate and subject to caveat.

For example, Benjamin Guérard, in his introduction to the *Cartulaire de l'abbaye de Saint-Père de Chartres* 1, (Paris, 1840), has briefly studied (pp. ccxxiv–ccxxvi) "symbols of investiture." We find the knife, the stick, the incense spoon, the *virga* or *virgula* (or the *ramusculus*). Generally, the wood of the *virga* or *ramusculus* is specified (e.g., *virgula de husso*: small sprig of holly; *savinae ramusculo*, sprig of juniper). In the article cited below (see bibliography, sec. C), Von Amira accords a great importance from an ethnohistorical point of view to the wood of the symbolic stick. We also find the gesture of *breakage* to which we shall return in note 28 (e.g. "quam virgam . . . in testimonium fregit"). The symbols of investiture as such are juxtaposed with symbols of *gift* and *witness*.

I will enlarge below on what I think is interesting about another list, in appendix I(B) above, of juridical symbols from the Merovingian and Carolingian eras, gathered by M. Thévenin in his edition of texts (see bibliography, sec. A).

359

27. Of course, this remark takes none of the value away from the problem of the influence of Roman juridical models on medieval law (I will discuss this below in connection with the *festuca*, with special reference to the previously cited book by Volterra, cf. note 13). Furthermore, it is in no way applicable to the remarkable work of P. Ourliac and J. de Malafosse, *Droit romain et Ancien Droit*, vol. 1, *Les obligations* (Paris, 1957), one of the rare books to treat the early medieval origins of the *festucatio* with learning and intelligence.

28. The French literature on the subject is very brief. One may cite A. Laforet, "Le bâton (le bâton, signe d'autorité, la crosse épiscopale et abbatiale. Le bâton cantoral, le sceptre et la main de justice)," in *Mémoires de l'Académie des Sciences Belles-Lettres et Arts de Marseille* 21 (1872–74), 207 ff, and 22 (1874–76), 193 ff. For Ernst von Moeller, the breaking of the stick was the most important in a class of ceremonials concerned more with officers, judges and outlaws than with vassals. He gives a simplistic interpretation: the breaking is the symbol of the rupture of a bond. On the contrary, it was the reunion of two pieces which first *had to be broken* from a single whole that created the bond between two persons, if we follow the line of the etymology of the Greek term. Von Amira has given a pertinent critique of Von Moeller's interpretation, which Marc Bloch has renewed. Because the point is important for the subject of ethnohistorical method, it bears repeating that the scope of comparative study must be broadened, though not so far as to introduce confusion. Bloch puts it excellently: "The breaking of the stick . . . resembles the breaking of the straw, considered as a rite of renunciation of homage, in no more than an external and fortuitous manner" ("Les formes," p. 209).

29. See bibliography, sec. C. From the comparative point of view, which I will make explicit below, I regret having been unable to consult the work of M. Gluckman, *Rituals of Rebellion in South East Africa* (Manchester, 1954).

30. Chénon, pp. 130–32. Chénon also notes that the *osculum* can replace the symbolic object in the ritual, which might be worthy of further study (ibid., pp. 132–34).

31. Cf. note 12 above.

32. Ibid.

33. Cf. note 9 above.

34. Cf. note 21 above.

35. Cf. note 8 above.

36. J. Maquet, *Pouvoir et Société en Afrique* (Paris, 1970), chap. 8, "Dépendre de son seigneur," pp. 191–215.

37. Ibid., p. 192.

38. Ibid., p. 193.

39. Cf. note 8 above.

40. Chénon, p. 149.

41. Cf. note 5 above.

42. Cf. C. Gaignebet, *Le Carnaval* (Paris, 1974), chap. 7, "La circulation des souffles," pp. 117–30.

43. Information received in the seminar of R. Guideri and Cl. Karnoouh, whom I would like to thank for having been good enough to discuss this research.

44. There is unfortunately little to be gleaned from N. J. Perella's *The Kiss sacred and profane: An Interpretive History of Kiss Symbolism and Related Religious Erotic Themes* (University of California Press, 1969), which, in spite of its good intentions, has not profited from ethnographic literature and turns out to be just another book on courtly love.

45. Cf. note 8 above.

46. Cf. note 11 above.

47. Cf. note 9 above.

48. Maquet, p. 197. The author points out, pp. 200–202, that institutions similar to

the *ubuhake* may be found in the region of the African Great Lakes, e.g. in Ankole, Burundi, and the chiefdoms of the Buha.

49. M. Bloch, *La Société féodale,* critical ed. (Paris, 1968), p. 320. English translation: *Feudal Society,* trans. L. A. Manyon (Chicago and London,, 1961), p. 228.

50. Maquet, p. 196.

51. Cf. note 28 above.

52. Cf. the work by Volterra cited in note 13 above, esp. pp. 205–7.

53. E. Chénon, "Recherches historiques sur quelques rites nuptiaux," *Nouvelle Revue historique de droit français et étranger,* 1912.

54. Cf. article *Baiser* in Dom Cabrol, *Dictionnaire d'archéologie chrétienne et de liturgie* II/1 (1910). Tertullian's text may be found in *De velamine virginum, PL* 1, cols. 904–5.

55. Volterra, p. 206.

It should be noted that the aim of the other form of oath in Roman private law, the *sacramentum in personam,* was to acquire the *manus iniectio.* In my view, however, no parallelism or continuity of significance should be looked for between the *festuca* and the *manus* of Roman law and those of the ritual of vassalage. Societies normally make a distinction between law pertaining to persons and law pertaining to things; with Volterra, we reiterate that *manus* in Roman imperial law no longer has any but an abstract sense, and it is the symbolism more than the symbol that matters. Only concrete historical study can make it possible—often with much difficulty, it is true—to distinguish the part played by continuity from that played by change. The case of the *festuca* requires attention, because the word and the object are not "obvious."

56. P. Ourliac and J. de Malafosse (see bibliography, sec. B), pp. 372–73. I would like to thank Mr. Alain Guerreau, who called my attention to these texts and attempted the difficult job of translating them.

In their remarkable study, Ourliac and Malafosse make several important observations which have points in common with some of the ideas stated in this lecture.

a) On medieval symbolism (pp. 58–59): "The striking feature of Salic law was the symbolism characteristic of all primitive law. A good is transferred by transmission of the *festuca* or *wadium* (security), which was apparently an object of little value (cf. Du Cange, art. *Wadia*); and anything could become a symbol: a clod of grass, a vine stem, a branch, a knife, silk knots, locks of hair; appropriate sign language and words are added; sometimes the object was attached to the act: an act of 777 (*Neues Archiv* 32, 169) still has the branch used in the transfer attached to the parchment. The clerics would tend to replace the profane objects with certain cult accessories: the missal, but also the ring and the staff."

b) On the polysemy of symbols (cf. below). Thus the *festuca* should not be taken out of context but in an institutional and symbolic complex which we think comparable to the feudal ritual of vassalage (p. 59): "Such symbols were well suited to contracts which involved the transfer of the good, sale or division; but the *festuca* was used in many other contracts: as power of attorney (*Marculf* I, 21, 27–29); promise to appear before a tribunal, bail. Other symbols would appear, such as the joining of the hands in homage or the gift of the ring in marriage. The preparation (and delivery) of a charter was soon to appear only as one of these symbols. One may think that in the South of France, the influence of Germanic symbols was more limited; there, earnest money was given to mark the conclusion of an agreement. This is still practiced for the marriage contract. In any case, the flourishing of symbols is characteristic of the progress of the law and marks the pace of its advance."

c) On the symbolic complex—gestures, objects, words (p. 59): "Symbolism is allied with formalism: gestures and speech are regulated by custom. The acts generally mention that the witness 'see and understand'; contracts were frequently concluded before the mallus and, in the Carolingian era, on the occasion of the pleadings of the missi."

d) Finally, the idea of "counter-prestation" or "symbolic counter-gift," which is found in *affatomie* in connection with the role of the *festuca*, and the practice of reciprocity (p. 69): "A prestation always presupposed a counter-prestation; a gift was not valid without a symbolic counter-gift, which gave it the appearance of an exchange. In this connection, one may single out a Lombard institution, the launegild: the donor gave the object to the donee, a ring, for example, the word's very etymology attesting to its character of being compensation for services rendered. The symbol of the *festuca* or *wadium* might be explicable in the same way: it would represent the counterpart of what was furnished by the creditor."

57. *Pactus Legis Salicae,* ed. K. A. Eckhardt in *MGH, Legum Sectio* I, 4/1 (Hanover, 1962).

58. See bibliography, sec. C.

59. Du Cange, *Glossarium* 3, cols. 412–13.

60. Bloch, "Les formes," p. 197.

61. Bloch, moreover, finds troubling a text from the *Coutumes du Beauvaisis* by Beaumanoir (from the end of the thirteenth century, it is true, and seminormative in character), and he tries to limit its significance. Ibid., p. 197, n. 4.

62. This is Georges Duby's outlook in his course at the Collège de France. The study of family structures and kinship relations occupies an important place in the recent important theses of P. Toubert, *Les Structures du Latium médiéval: Le Latium méridional et la Sabine du IXe à la fin du XIVe siècle,* 2 vols. (Rome, 1973), and P. Bonnassie, *La Catalogne du milieu du Xe à la fin du XIe siècle,* 2 vols. (Toulouse, 1975–76).

63. Bloch, *La Société féodale,* pp. 183–86; Eng. trans., p. 124.

64. Cf. note 19 above.

65. Cf. note 24 above. Boutruche, without giving references, unfortunately, notes that where a woman was concerned, "a kiss on the right hand" sufficed (Boutruche 2, 154–58).

66. Cf. the works of Erich Köhler on the protest aspect of courtly love, esp. "Les troubadours et la jalousie," in *Mélanges Jean Frappier* (Geneva, 1970) 1, 543–99.

67. G. Duby, *La Société aux XIe et XIIe siècles dans la région mâconnaise,* new ed. (Paris, 1971), p. 116, n. 35.

68. Cited by Chénon, p. 144, from the edition of the *Roman de la Rose* by Francisque Michel, p. 63.

69. C.-E. Perrin, *Recherches sur la seigneurie rurale en Lorraine d'après les plus anciens censiers, IXe–XIIe s.* (Paris, 1935), pp. 437–38.

70. Cf. note 20 above.

71. Robert Boutruche has clearly seen the significance of the kiss: "Significant gesture! It was a sign of peace, friendship, and 'mutual fidelity.' It brought the 'man of mouth and hands' closer to his superior" (2, 154). He adds "The kiss was not indispensable, however. 'Classic' in France and the lands of the Norman conquest after the year 1000, and later in the Latin states of the East, it made little headway in the kingdom of Italy. It was rare in Germany before the thirteenth century, probably because there was a more marked social distance between lord and vassal and a greater concern for hierarchy." I have no desire to replace the rigidity and abstraction of certain theories of scholars, jurists rather than historians, with an overly "systematic" ethnographic model. Boutruche has rightly emphasized the diversity connected with different historical traditions in different locales. Nevertheless, it seems to me that rather than being a question of influences, the progress of the *osculum* in medieval Germany reflects the form taken by the system in a space in which the social and political structures (connected with the imperial system) had hitherto retarded its implantation.

72. *MGH, Capitularia regum francorum* I, 104, (p. 215) C.3.

73. G. Fasoli, *Introduzione allo studio del Feudalismo Italiano* (Bologna, 1959), p. 121.

74. Texts cited and translated (into French) by Boutruche, pp. 364–66.

75. *Annales regni Francorum,* ed. Kurze, p. 14, cited in Boutruche, p. 365.

76. *Casus S. Galli,* c. 16, ed. von Arx in *MGH, SS* 2, 141, cited and translated by Boutruche, p. 367.

77. Cf. esp. G. Duby, *L'An Mil* (Paris, 1967).

78. With the inspiration of the brilliant works of Georges Dumézil, I have touched on the problem of tripartite society in the Middle Ages in "A Note on Tripartite Society, Monarchical Ideology, and Economic Renewal in Ninth- to Twelfth-Century Christendom," this volume, pp. 53–57. G. Duby has given a more probing treatment of these problems in a course at the Collège de France and is preparing a work on the subject.

79. Bloch, "Les Formes," p. 421.

80. Without embarking on an analysis of the problem, I have carefully researched and indicated in this essay such evidence as is available of perception of the symbolic system of vassalage by men of the Middle Ages, at least by the clerics who described it, because I regard a society's consciousness of itself, or lack of it, as very important.

81. Chénon, pp. 130 ff. "In the second place, the *osculum* was used for renouncing contested rights; it was then a symbol of abandonment (*guerpitio*)."

82. Chénon has fallen, I think, into the error of looking for a single symbolic meaning in a given symbol instead of respecting the polysemy of the symbol when he writes: "Regardless of the form of the rite and the meaning of the symbol, whether confirmation, abandonment, transfer of goods, it is possible to reduce it to a single idea: the idea that the situation created by the contract which is followed by the *osculum* will be respected ... This is the idea that emerges from the words *osculum pacis et fidei* which are encountered so frequently in the charters." ("L'osculum en matière de fiançailles: Recherches historiques sur quelques rites nuptiaux," extract from the *Nouvelle Revue historique de Droit français et étranger,* Paris, 1912, p. 136).

83. Du Cange, art. *Investitura,* col. 1520.

84. Thévenin, pp. 263–64.

85. Elze, *Simboli e simbologia,* Settimane di Studio del Centro italiano di studi sull'alto medioevo XXIII (Spoleto, 1976).

86. J.-F. Lemarignier, *Recherches sur l'hommage en marche et les frontières féodales* (Lille, 1945).

87. Boutruche, p. 368. Galbert writes: "Non. aprilis, feria tertia Aqua sapientiae, in crepusculo noctis, rex simul cum noviter electo consule Willelmo, Flandriarum marchione, Bruggas in subburbium nostrum venit... Octavo idus aprilis, feria quarta, convenerunt rex et comes cum suis et nostris militibus, civibus et Flandrensibus multis in agrum consuetum in quo scrinia et reliquiae sanctorum collatae sunt... Ac deinceps per totum reliquum dies tempus hominia fecerunt consuli illi qui feodati fuerant prius a Karolo comite piisimo..." (ed. Pirenne, pp. 86–89). The ceremony took place in *agro consueto* in order to respect custom, to accommodate the crowd, and, as was peculiar to Flanders, to involve the burgesses. The relics were brought to sanctify the site.

88. It should be noted that the vassal also had to make a journey when he came out of vassalage. In Galbert of Bruges's account of the *exfestucatio* of Ivan of Alost, studied by Marc Bloch, the notary of Bruges observes: "Illi milites... *sese et plures alios transmiserunt* consuli Willelmo in Ipra, et exfestucaverunt fidem et hominia."

89. For example, the charter of 1123 cited above, note 3, conserved in the cartulary of Saint-Nicolas d'Angers. "De hoc dono revistivit Quirmarhocus et duo filii ejus Gradelonem monachum S. Nicolai cum uno libro in *ecclesia S. Petri super alture S. Petri.*" In a charter of Robert, Duke of Burgundy, from 1043: "Hune oblationis chartam, quam ego ipse legali concessione per festucam, per cultellum, per wantonem, per wasonem *super altare,* posui, ..." (Du Cange, art. *Investitura,* col. 1525).

90. E.g. "Hanc concessionem fecit Dominus Bertrandus *in aula sua*, et pro intersigno confirmationis hujus eleemosynae, tradidit quendam baculum, quem manu tenebat, Armando priori Aureae Vallis" (Charter of Bertrand de Moncontour, cited by Du Cange, art. *Investitura*, col. 1525). In 1143, the gift of several small manors by the Viscountess of Turenne to the monastery of Obazine took place in the great hall of the castle of Turenne "Hoc donum factus fuit in aula Turenensi" (Chénon, "L'osculum en matière de fiançailles," p. 133, n. 2).

91. For example, in a charter of Marmoutier (Du Cange, art. *Investitura*, col. 1530): "Quod donum ... posuit super altare dominicum per octo denarios, in *praesentia multorum*." Sometimes the spectators are explicitly acknowledged in their function as witnesses and guarantors of the collective memory: e.g., in this charter from the monastery of Marmoutier cited by Du Cange, col. 1536: "Testes habuimus legitimos, qui omni lege probare fuerunt parati, quod Hildegardis ad opus emerit, et per pisces ex ejus piscaria investituram de derit in vito sua monachis Majoris Monasterii."

92. C. Walter, *L'Iconographie des conciles dans la tradition byzantine* (Paris, 1970).

93. In a charter of Marmoutier, it is the abbot of the monastery who is named as the principal (and sufficient) witness: "Quodam fuste, qui apud nos nomine ejus inscriptus servatur in testimonium, *praesente Abbate Alberto*, fecit guerpitionem" (Du Cange, art. *Investitura*, col. 1521).

94. Maquet, p. 195.

95. The records give hardly any indication other than the genuflection of the vassal in the phase of homage: e.g., in an act of Rabastens of 18 January 1244 cited by Chénon, "L'osculum en matière de fiançailles," p. 142, n. 3: "et inde vobis homagium facio, *flexis genuis* ...," which is the only detail given by Guillaume Durand in *Speculum juris*, part 21, IV, 3, 2, n. 8: "Nam is qui facit homagium, *stans flexis genuis* ..." *Stans* appears to indicate that the lord is seated, as one might expect.

96. Chénon, "L'osculum en matière de fiançailles," pp. 132–33. "Finally, a more curious and also rarer phenomenon, the *osculum* could also serve in making a transfer of goods; in this case, it replaced the symbolic object which was not at hand." Was this really the case?

97. Du Cange gives several examples of conservation of the symbolic objects of investiture, e.g., in connection with a gift "Facto inde dono per zonam argenteam, ab altari in armario S. Petri repositam ..." (art. *Investitura*, col. 1521). He cites Wendelin in his Glossary: "Hujusmodi cespites cum sua festuca multis in Eclessiis servantur hactemus, visunturque Nivellae et alibi." He says that he himself has seen in the archives of Saint-Denis, thanks to Mabillon, several charters with symbolic objects (cf. below, note 122): "complures chartas, in quarum imis (limbis intextae erant festucae, vel certe pusilla ligni fragmenta" (ibid., col. 1522).

98. Du Cange, in regard to the broken *festuca*, recalls the Roman *stipulatio* and cites Isidore of Seville (*Origines* III): "Veteres enim quando sibi aliquid promittebant, stipulam tenentes frangebant, quam iterum jungentes sponsiones suas agnoscebant" (*Glossarium*, art. *Festuca*, col. 411). I am not sure that the breaking of the straw (or knife) was intended to provide two pieces, one for each principal to keep.

99. Ganshof, *Feudalism*, pp. 106–69.

100. F. Joüon des Longrais, *L'Est et l'Ouest: Institutions du Japon et de l'Occident comparées* (six studies in juridical sociology) (Tokyo, 1958). Other works in Western languages treating Japanese "feudalism" may be found in Boutruche 1, 463–64.

Both Marc Bloch and Robert Boutruche, in particular, placed too great and too exclusive an emphasis on the Japanese case, I think, in their comparative efforts.

101. I wish to thank Marc Augé for furnishing useful references to works of African specialists.

102. H. Maspero, "Le régime féodal dans la Chine antique," in *Recueils de la Société Jean Bodin*, vol. 1, *Les liens de vassalité et les immunités* (1935, 1936, 2d ed., Brussels,

1958), pp. 89–127. The collection of Li-chi is treated on page 91.

103. Ibid., pp. 94–95. [I have rendered French *officier de bouche*—a dignitary in charge of transmitting imperial orders—simply as "officer."—Trans.]

104. D. Bodde, "Feudalism in China," in *Feudalism in History*, ed. R. Coulborn (Princeton, 1956), pp. 49–92. The author cites a work in Chinese by Ch'i Ssu-ho, "Investiture ceremony of the Chou period," in *Yenching, Journal of Chinese Studies*, no. 32 (June, 1947), pp. 197–226, which I was clearly unable to consult.

105. Bodde, p. 56.

106. Ibid., p. 61.

107. Ibid., p. 51.

108. Cf. the interesting note presented by T. Wasowicz to the "settimana" where this paper was first read (Settimane di studio del Centro italiano di studi sull'alto Medievo, XXIII).

109. Beattie (J.H.M.), "Rituals of Nyoro Kingship," in *Africa—Journal de l'Institut international africain* 29, no. 2 (1959), 134–45; E. M. Chilver, "Feudalism in the Interlacustrine Kingdoms," in *East African Chiefs*, ed. A. Richards (London, 1960); M. Fortes, "Of Installation Ceremonies," in *Proceedings of the Royal Anthropological Institute of Great Britain and Ireland for 1967* (1968), pp. 5–20; F. Lukyn Williams, "The Inauguration of the Omugabe of Ankole to Office," *Uganda Journal* 4 (1937), 300–312; K. Oberg, "Le Royaume des Ankole d'Ouganda," in *African Political Systems*, ed. Fortes and Evans-Pritchard; A. P. Richards, "Social Mechanisms for the Transfer of Political Rights in Some African Tribes," *Journal of the Royal Anthropological Institute...*, 1960, pp. 175–90; R. A. Snoxall, "The Coronation Ritual and Customs of Buganda," *Uganda Journal* 4 (1937), 277–88; J. J. Tawney, "Ugabire: A Feudal Custom amongst the Waha," *Tanganyika Notes and Records*, no. 17 (1944), pp. 6–9. K. W., "The Procedure in Accession to the Throne of a Nominated King in the Kingdom of Bynyoro-Kitara," *Uganda Journal* 4 (1937), 289–99.

Since my concern was not feudalism, I did not use the justly classic book of J. F. Nadel, *A Black Byzantium* (London, 1942); nor the early works of J. Maquet, *Systèmes des relations sociales dans le Ruanda ancien* (Tervuren, 1954), and a hypothesis for the study of African feudalisms in *Cahiers d'Etudes africaines* 2 (1961), 292–314; nor the works of J. Lombard on a society "of feudal type," the Banba of North Dahomey; nor the contribution of I. I. Potekhin, "On Feudalism of the Ashani," to the Fifteenth International Congress of Orientalists, Moscow, 1960. I share the view expressed in the fine article by Jack Goody, "Feudalism in Africa?" *Journal of African History*, 1963, pp. 1–18, particularly where he writes: (1) "I could see no great profit (and possibly some loss) in treating the presence of clientship or fiefs as constituting a feudality... There seems even less to be gained from the view which sees African societies as feudalities on the basis of political or economic criteria." (2) "To suggest that there appears little to be gained by thinking of African societies in terms of the concept of "Feudalism" implies neither a rejection of comparative work that European medievalists can make to the study of African institutions... *While the reverse is perhaps even more true* (emphasis mine—J. Le G.), Africanists certainly have something to learn from the studies of medieval historians." Still, though I agree that it is best to speak in comparative terms not of "feudalism" but of particular institutions analyzed with comparative methods, it seems to me that as far as my subject here is concerned, viz., the symbolic ritual of the feudal system of vassalage, the points of comparison with African material are rare, since most of the rituals studied by Africanists are royal. Nevertheless, I would again like to underscore, along with Jack Goody, that if one thinks a priori that "institutions defy comparison because of their uniqueness" (ibid. p. 2), then one is condemning research in the human sciences, including history, to a singular impoverishment.

110. Fortes, "Of installation ceremonies," p. 7.

111. A. I. Richards, p. 183.

112. Ibid.

113. Fortes, "Of installation ceremonies," p. 7.

114. Ibid., p. 8.

115. Fortes, for example, in commenting on the coronation of Queen Elizabeth II of England, compares the homage which follows the ceremony with "the homage of the 'magnates with the feudal kiss'.' which "served to dramatise her sovereign supremacy." Fortes is led to this comparison by the work of P. E. Schramm—which, incidentally, has opened many fruitful avenues for medievalists. Cf. *A History of the English Coronation* (Oxford, 1937), p. 147.

116. The suggestive essay of G. Balandier, *Anthropologie politique* (Paris, 1967), fails to take this risk fully into account.

117. Maquet, p. 194.

118. Tawney, cf. note 109 above.

119. Tawney, p. 7.

120. K. Oberg, in his article "Le Royaume des Ankole d'Ouganda" (cf. note 109 above), gives interesting details concerning the breaking-off of a relationship which he calls one of "clientèle" [patron-client relationship], the *okoutoiz ha.* "An owner of livestock *mouhina* appeared before the *Mongabe* or king and swore to follow him to war. In order to keep this bond active, he commits himself to give a certain number of head of livestock to the *Mongabe* periodically. Furthermore, the refusal of the client to offer his homage, *omoutoizha*, could break the patron-client relationship. This way of putting an end to the relationship was perfectly legitimate. Only when a large number of Bahima acted together in this way in order to defy the king more effectively was the act considered one of rebellion. Even in this case, if the rebels reverted to doing homage, they were pardoned." Unfortunately, the author does not describe the rites to which these diverse practices associated with a single institution must have given rise.

121. F. Joüon des Longrais, "Les Moines de l'abbaye Saint-Melaine de Rennes en Angleterre: Les chartes du prieuré d'Hatfield Regis," in *Mémoires et Documents publiés par la société de l'Ecole des Chartes*, vol. 12, a collection of works presented to M. Clovis Brunel (Paris, 1955), pp. 31–54.

122. Here is the brief text of this act (ibid., p. 52): "Per istum cultellum feoffavit Albericus de Veer primus ecclesiam de Hatfeld Regis monachorum de duabus partibus decimarum de dominico Domini Reginaldi filii Petri in Uggeleya die Assumpcionis beate Maris Virginis, pro animabus antecessorum et successorum suorum. Anno . . ." I would like to thank M. Berlioz, who sent me photos of several symbol objects (they seem to be rare) still preserved today.

123. Giorgi de Beltrani, *Regesto di Farfa* 2, 37, no. 165.

124. Cf. note 10 above.

125. That investiture with the aid of a symbolic object was a rite foreign to Christianity is demonstrated, in my view, by the following charter of 993 concerning Belgium, cited by Du Cange (col. 1523): "Mox post haec subsequenti die, ut firmius et stabilius esset, infra terminum praedicti comitatus, in villa quoque Thiele nuncupata, eisdem praenominatis testibus et aliis nonnullis astantibus, sine alicujus retractatione *cum ramo et cespite jure rituque populari*, idem sancitum est, rationabiliterque sancitum." Here, popular is quasi-synonymous with pagan.

126. G. Duby, "La Féodalité? Une mentalité médiévale," *Annales E.S.C.*, 1958, pp. 765–71, reprinted in *Hommes et structures du Moyen Age* (Paris, The Hague, 1973), pp. 103–10. Reacting with good reason against excessively juridical conceptions of feudalism, and promoting a pioneering history of mentalities, Georges Duby has shown in the rest of his work that he does not mean to reduce feudalism to a phenomenon of mentality.

127. I am thinking in particular of Marc Augé and Maurice Godelier in France. Cf., e.g., C. Lévi-Strauss, M. Augé, and M. Godelier, "Anthropologie, Histoire, Idéologie," L'Homme 90, nos. 3–4 (July-December, 1975) 177–88.

Selected Bibliography

A. Documents

Du Cange, Charles du Fresne, Glossarium mediae et infimae latinitatis (1678), Articles Festuca et Investitura.

Thévenin, M., Textes relatifs aux institutions . . . mérovingiennes et carolingiennes (1887), esp. list of symbols, pp. 263–64. Lex Salica, XLVI; Lex Ripuaria, XLVIII; d. Rotharii, 157, 158, 170, 172; d. Liutprandi, 65.

B. General studies of vassalage

Boutruche, R., Seigneurie et féodalité, 2 vols. (Paris, 1968, 1970).

Fasoli, G., Introduzione allo studio del feudalesimo italiano in Storia medievale e moderna (Bologna, 1959).

Ganshof, F. L., Qu'est-ce que la féodalité? 3d ed. (Brussels, 1957). Translated by Griersen as Feudalism (New York, 1964).

Grassotti, M., Las instituciones feudo-vasalláticas en León y Castilla, vol. 1 Cap. Seg. Entrada en Vasallaje, pp. 107 sqq.

Mor, G., L'età feudale, II (Milan, 1952).

Ourliac, P. et De Malafosse, J., Droit romain et Ancien Droit, I, Les Obligations (Paris, 1957).

Mitteis, H., Lehnrecht und Staatsgewalt (Weimar, 1933).

C. Specialized studies

Amira, K. von, "Der Stab in der germanischen Rechtsymbolik," Abhandlungen der Kg. Bayerischen Akademie der Wissenschaften, Philologische und historische Klasse, 35 (Munich, 1909).

Bloch, M., "Les formes de la rupture de l'hommage dans l'ancien droit féodal," Nouvelle Revue historique de droit français et étranger, 1912. Reprinted in Mélanges historiques I (Paris, 1963), 189–209.

Chénon, E., "Recherches historiques sur quelques rites nuptiaux," Nouvelle Revue historique de droit français et étranger, 1912.

———, "Le rôle juridique de l'Osculum dans l'ancien droit français," Mémoires de la Société des Antiquaires de France, 8 ser. 6 (1919–23).

Moeller, E. von, "Die Rechtssitte des Stabsbrechens," Zeitschrift der Savigny-Stiftung für Rechtsgeschichte, G.A. XXI (1900).

D. Comparative studies

1. Feudalism in history

Coulborn, R., ed. Feudalism in History (Princeton, 1956), esp. D. Bodde, "Feudalism in China," pp. 49–92.

2. African feudalism

Fortes, M., "Of installation ceremonies," in Proceedings of the Royal Anthropological Institute . . . , 1967 (1968), 5–20.

———and Evans-Pritchard, E. E., eds. Systèmes politiques africains, French trans., Paris, 1964.

Maquet, J., Pouvoir et société en Afrique (Paris, 1970).

———, Systèmes des relations sociales dans le Ruanda ancien (Tervuren, 1954).

———, "Une hypothèse pour l'étude des féodalités africaines," Cahiers d'Études africaines II (1961), 292–314.

INDEX

Aarne, Antti, 212
Abbo of Fleury, 54
Abel, Wilhelm, 233
Abelard, Peter: and confession, 113; *Historia calamitatum*, 122, 123; on intentions, 39; social origins of, 123; use of military vocabulary by, 124. *See also* Michelet, on Abelard
Academic expenses, 101–6, 309–11
Academics, 141–44; attitudes toward labor of, 70; formation of closed caste of, 104, 147; legal status of, 136; peculiarity of, as social group, 136; prestige of, 141, 148; pride (*superbia*) of, 125; privileges of, 139, 142, 143; self-consciousness of, 124; views of, 122–34, passim. *See also* Humanism
Acculturation, 235, 265; bibliography, 325 n. 11
Adalbero of Laon, 53, 54; condemnation of certain trades by, 60; and tripartite schema, 267
Adamites. *See* Heresy
Adam (of Bremen), 196
Aeneas, 203
Afdeling Agrarische Geschiednis, 233
Affatomie, 260; and vassalage, 266. *See also* Salic law
Africa. *See* Feudalism, in Africa
Age classes, 230
Ages of man, 33, 226
Agricola, 225
Agricolae, 56, 89. *See also* Peasants
Agriculture: Roman treatises on, 89; in Carolingian era, 83

Ailly, Pierre d', 190, 194
Alan of Lille, 119, 196
Albertus Magnus (Albert the Great): on military profession, 61; and dreams, 204; skepticism of, 192
Albigensians, 19, 20
Albornoz, Claudia Sanchez, 242
Alcuin, 34
Alexander (legendary medieval hero), 193, 198–99
Alexander the Great, 193
Alexander III (pope), 63, 65; letter to Prester John from, 196
Alfonso the Battler, 244, 261
Alfonso the Magnanimous, 105
Alfred the Great (king of England) 53–54, 86; and Sigelmus, 198
Allodial property, 254
Ambarvalia (Gallo-Roman festival), 180
Ambrose (saint), 156, 168
Amira, Karl von, 246, 256, 258
Anchises, 226
Annales: Economies, Sociétés, Civilisations, 233
Annales regni Francorum, 241, 273
Anselm (saint), 113
Anthony (saint), 168; dreams of, 203
Anthropology: and history, 225–36; and Marxism, 286; political, 281. *See also* Augustine; Culture; Ethnology; Folklore; Structuralism
Antichrists, 96, 198
Antipodes, 198, 345 n. 58
Antisemitism, 301 n. 11
Antrustion, 241, 265

Index